Rethinking Globalization
Teaching for Justice in an Unjust World

Edited by
Bill Bigelow and Bob Peterson

ress

Rethinking Globalization: Teaching for Justice in an Unjust World
Edited by Bill Bigelow and Bob Peterson

Rethinking Schools, Ltd. is a nonprofit educational publisher of books, booklets, and a
    quarterly journal on school reform, with a focus on issues of equity and social justice.
    To request additional copies of this book or a catalog of other publications, or to
    subscribe to the *Rethinking Schools* journal, contact:

Rethinking Schools
1001 East Keefe Avenue
Milwaukee, Wisconsin 53212 USA
800-669-4192
www.rethinkingschools.org

Rethinking Globalization: Teaching for Justice in an Unjust World
© 2002, Rethinking Schools, Ltd.

Book design and layout by C.C. Krohne.

Production Editor: Leon Lynn.

Editorial Assistance: Stacie Williams, Roxanne Ciatti, Malaka Sanders.

Graphics: Paul Duquesnoy.

Additional Layout: Jill Rosenmerkel.

Proofreaders: Joanna Dupuis, Jennifer Morales.

Special thanks to the Joyce Foundation for its generous support of this project.

Special thanks also to Donnelly/Colt Progressive Resources.

Front cover illustration based on a photo courtesy of NASA. Back cover photo by Michel Spingler
    for Associated Press.

Title page photo by Jennifer Cheek Pantaléon.

ISBN 0-942961-28-5

A constant source of encouragement and inspiration came from the Portland Area Rethinking Schools globalization workgroup. Frequent participants since 1997, when we began this book, include: John Ambrosio, Renée Bald, George Bishop, Andrew Brown, Sandra Childs, Tim Dittmer, Molly Dwyer, Pedro Ferbel, Sylvia McGauley, Hyung Nam, Zach Post, Greg Smith, Julie Treick, Amanda Weber-Welch, and Josh Weiner. Other advisers in Portland included Norm Diamond, Erin Bailey, Jeff Edmundson, Sorca O'Connor, Katie Wood, Tim King, Rob van Nood, and Tom McKenna. Lesson ideas throughout the book benefited from the teaching genius of Linda Christensen.

Bill Bigelow offers special thanks to his 1999-2000 first and third period Global Studies classes at Franklin High School in Portland, Oregon. They were brilliant, funny, compassionate, and hardworking — they influenced this book in countless ways.

Bob Peterson thanks the fifth-grade students he has taught at La Escuela Fratney in Milwaukee, Wisconsin. He also acknowledges the support of Fratney's deeply committed staff, whose vision of social justice teaching and bilingualism continues to be an inspiration for his own teaching.

In a variety of ways, Barbara Miner, Floralba Vivas, David Levine, Mary Jane Karp, Deborah Menkart, Millie Thayer, Jennifer Morales, Joanna Dupuis, and Howard Machtinger made valuable contributions to the book. Thanks to C.C. Krohne for the book's design and layout, to Jill Rosenmerkel for additional layout assistance, and to Paul Duquesnoy for his superb rendering of illustrations.

Rethinking Globalization, as all Rethinking Schools books, was supported by the broader Rethinking Schools community, especially editors Linda Christensen, Beverly Cross, Kelley Dawson, Brenda Harvey, Stan Karp, Larry Miller, Kathy Swope, Rita Tenorio, and Stephanie Walters; editorial associates David Levine and Dale Weiss; and office staff Barbara Miner, Mike Trokan, Susan Bates, Linda Fausel, Stacie Williams, Renee Rodgers, Roxanne Ciatti, and Malaka Sanders.

Finally, thanks to Rethinking Schools Press director Leon Lynn, who spent countless hours on every aspect of this book.

ABOUT THE EDITORS

Bill Bigelow teaches social studies at Franklin High School in Portland, Oregon, and is an editor of Rethinking Schools. He is author of *Strangers in Their Own Country: A Curriculum on South Africa*, *The Line Between Us: Teaching About the Border and Mexican Immigration*, and (with Norm Diamond) *The Power in Our Hands: A Curriculum on the History of Work and Workers in the United States*. With Bob Peterson he edited *Rethinking Columbus: The Next 500 Years*. He can be reached at bbpdx@aol.com.

Bob Peterson teaches fifth grade at La Escuela Fratney, a two-way bilingual public school in Milwaukee, Wisconsin. He is a founding editor of Rethinking Schools, and is a frequent writer and speaker. He co-edited (with Bill Bigelow) *Rethinking Columbus: The Next 500 Years*, (with Michael Charney) *Transforming Teacher Unions: Fighting for Better Schools and Social Justice*, and (with Eric Gutstein) *Rethinking Mathematics: Teaching Social Justice by the Numbers*. In 1995 he was selected as Wisconsin Elementary Teacher of the Year. He can be reached at repmilw@aol.com.

RETHINKING GLOBALIZATION
Table of Contents

INTRODUCTION

Questions from a Worker Who Reads

BY BERTOLT BRECHT

Who built the seven towers of Thebes?

The books are filled with names of kings.

Was it kings who hauled the craggy blocks of stone?

And Babylon, so many times destroyed,

Who built the city up each time? In which of Lima's houses,

That city glittering with gold, lived those who built it?

In the evening when the Chinese wall was finished

Where did the masons go? Imperial Rome

Is full of arcs of triumph. Who reared them up? Over whom

Did the Caesars triumph? Byzantium lives in song,

Were all her dwellings palaces? and even in Atlantis of the legend

The night the sea rushed in,

The drowning men still bellowed for their slaves.

Young Alexander plundered India.

He alone?

Caesar beat the Gauls.

Was there not even a cook in his army?

Philip of Spain wept as his fleet

Was sunk and destroyed. Were there no other tears?

Frederick the Great triumphed in the Seven Years War. Who

Triumphed with him?

Each page a victory,

At whose expense the victory ball?

Every ten years a great man,

Who paid the piper?

So many particulars.

So many questions.

From **Selected Poems** by Bertolt Brecht and H.R. Hays
(New York: Harcourt Brace Jovanovich, Inc., 1947).

Page 1 image: A Honduran boy falls asleep at his workbench while making softballs. Photo courtesy of UNICEF.

Women and children near a chemical plant in Bombay, India.

INTRODUCTION

Why We Wrote This Book

We began this book with the intention of focusing on sweatshops and child labor around the world. Like many others, we'd been outraged by stories of beatings at Nike factories in Vietnam, by images of children as young as six years old toiling over brand-name soccer balls in Pakistan, and by revelations that major clothes manufacturers pay workers pennies an hour in places like Haiti and Honduras while they charge top dollar at home.

But the more we focused on the larger "why?" questions, the harder it was to contain our teaching in simple "sweatshop" and "child labor" categories. It was impossible to separate our teaching about wretched conditions for workers around the world from all the factors that produced the desperation that forces people to seek work in those conditions. These factors include:

- The history of colonial domination of much of the world that took self-sufficient economies and horribly distorted them.
- The debt crisis, and how it has been manipulated by Western-led institutions like the World Bank and the International Monetary Fund, which bully poor countries with "structural adjustment programs."
- The free trade, "neo-liberal" emphasis of recent trade agreements like NAFTA, and now the World Trade Organization, that encourage poor countries to export their way to economic health and to specialize in the "commodity" of cheap labor.
- Military interventions in places as far apart as Vietnam, Guatemala, and the Congo which have discouraged alternative routes to development.

The more we taught about issues of globalization, the more we found ourselves telling our students: "Everything is connected. You can't really understand what's going on in one part of the world without looking at how it's related to everything else."

For example, in the Huaorani Indian struggle in eastern Ecuador (depicted in the role play, "Oil, Rainforests, and Indigenous Cultures," p. 268), the debt crisis forces the government to aggressively seek sources of cash — like oil — to make interest payments to international

> This book is an argument for the necessity of holding, in our minds and in our classrooms, the big global picture. Every effort to make a difference needs to be grounded in that broader analysis.

banks. Transnational oil companies take advantage of widespread poverty to pay starvation wages to workers in terribly unsafe conditions. And like a bull in a china shop, they maraud through fragile rainforest ecosystems. In the quest for profits, oil companies treat people and the environment simply as resources to exploit. But not only are rainforests being ravaged, the indigenous cultures that depend on those rainforests are also in danger of being wiped out.

If oil companies successfully sucked all the oil out of the Huaorani's territory in Ecuador — perhaps as much as $2 billion worth — it would power cars in the United States for only 13 days. Thus, the more we taught about issues in the Third World, the more it brought us home — home to an epidemic of consumption that links us to the poverty of others around the world, and links us to the growing ecological crisis that threatens the very existence of life on earth.

And casting a large shadow on the crisis in Ecuador and so many other poor countries is the legacy of U.S. military interventions — especially in this hemisphere — that have aborted alternative models of democracy and development. Globalization is not merely an economic phenomenon; it is accompanied by a big stick that

> The more we taught about issues of globalization, the more we found ourselves telling our students: "Everything is connected. You can't really understand what's going on in one part of the world without looking at how it's related to everything else."

has been wielded time and again, most often by the United States, to protect wealth and privilege.

This interconnectedness of issues was brought home powerfully in late 1999 with the mass demonstrations against the World Trade Organization in Seattle, summed up by the celebrated placard, "Turtles and Teamsters: Together at Last." What was so remarkable about the events in Seattle was that for the first time massive protests targeted not simply one single issue, but an entire constellation of grievances. The presence of U.S. steelworkers, Korean farmers, South African miners, French environmentalists, and Canadian teachers marching side by side underscored this new political awareness.

As we teach and organize around these matters, it's vital that we emphasize the centrality of race. The development of European colonialism was sheathed in theories of white supremacy which sought to justify the slaughter of indigenous peoples, the theft of their lands, and the enslavement of millions of Africans. Today's system of global inequality builds from these enormous crimes and is similarly legitimated, albeit more subtly, by notions of white supremacy. Vast imbalances of wealth and power still correlate heavily with skin color. Centuries of racism have

Nicolas Lampert and Susan Simensky Bietila

normalized this inequality and have blinded too many people to its contemporary manifestations.

"THEIR" LIVES AND "OURS"

Much of today's media coverage of globalization draws lines between "us" and "them." "We" don't have things like child labor and sweatshops. But of course we do. Indeed most knowledgeable observers believe that we have more sweatshops in this country than ever before — especially if we include the "sweatshops in the fields" for farm workers. So as we considered the big, interconnected picture in crafting this book, we tried to focus also on conditions at home. We especially didn't want this to be a curriculum of pity. We hoped that students would consider that whether one works in a "sweatshop" or not, our lives here are directly affected by the global "race to the bottom" that pits workers around the world against one another. People here do have a moral imperative to help people everywhere. But we also have a personal stake in challenging the poor conditions around the globe that exert a downward pull on conditions here.

Early in this book's development, one teacher made this point a little differently. She advised us not to focus solely on exploitation "over there." "It's not just happening in the Third World," she said. "My kids are getting cheated out of hours at McDonald's; they're forced to

"IS THIS BOOK BIASED?"

Historian Howard Zinn once wrote, "In a world where justice is maldistributed there is no such thing as a neutral or representative recapitulation of the facts." We agree. Every curriculum begins from certain convictions about the world, even if they may not be conscious. Neutrality is neither possible nor desirable. Teaching — regardless of grade level or discipline — always takes place against the backdrop of certain global realities.

And as articles in this book amply document, today's realities are grim: Vast inequalities of wealth yawn wider and wider, the earth is being consumed and polluted at a ferocious pace, and commercial values are supplanting humane ones. It seems that all aspects of life now wear "For Sale" signs and are subject to privatization. With the patenting of the genetic codes of plants and even human beings, we can be excused for feeling that we have entered a world of bizarre *Twilight Zone* reruns. As *Rethinking Schools* editors observed in an editorial for our 15th anniversary issue: "The wish-dreams of the privatizers are exemplified well in a recent MasterCard commercial that depicts an auctioneer offering his latest sale items: the letter 'B,' the color red, gravity. The ad delights in a future where every last aspect of life is commodified."

In a world where the very idea of "public" is being threatened, for educators to feign neutrality is irresponsible. The pedagogical aim in this social context needs to be truth rather than "balance" — if by balance we mean giving equal credence to claims that we know to be false and that, in any event, enjoy wide dispersal in the dominant culture. The teacher who takes pride in never revealing his or her "opinions" to students models for them moral apathy.

Nonetheless, we would never urge that teachers shelter their students from views that they find repugnant. Indeed, the way to develop critical global literacy is only through direct engagement with diverse ideas. Nor is it ever appropriate for teachers to hand students worked-out opinions without equipping students to develop their own analyses of important issues. Simply because we have not given "equal time" in this book to proponents of corporate-driven globalization does not mean that we believe that students should be denied access to pro-globalization perspectives.

We see a distinct difference between a biased curriculum and a partisan one. Teaching is biased when it ignores multiple perspectives and does not allow interrogation of its own assumptions and propositions. Partisan teaching, on the other hand, invites diversity of opinion but does not lose sight of the aim of the curriculum: to alert students to global injustice, to seek explanations, and to encourage activism. This is the kind of teaching we hope *Rethinking Globalization* will encourage.

— *The editors*

> **In a world where the very idea of "public" is being threatened, for educators to feign neutrality is irresponsible.**

RETHINKING OUR LANGUAGE

Words are metaphorical, and may generate misleading images. When we say that the United States is a "developed" nation, the word paints pictures of a social or economic process that is somehow complete; it suggests a society that has fulfilled its *natural* destiny, that is as it was meant to be. Likewise, the use of terms like "developing" or "underdeveloped" to describe a country or culture, implies only a deficit status. It defines other peoples by what they are not, and establishes a Western-type industrial society as the model toward which all societies are heading — or at least ought to be heading.

The "developing" or "underdeveloped" tags miss the ways in which other countries, other cultures, are already developed. So-called developing nations have thousands of years of traditional knowledge stored in their cultural patterns. For example, in another Rethinking Schools book, *Rethinking Columbus*, Philip Tajitsu Nash and Emilienne Ireland describe a typical elder of the Wauja people of the Amazon rainforest, who

> has memorized hundreds of sacred songs and stories; plays several musical instruments; and knows the habits and habitats of hundreds of forest animals, birds, and insects, as well as the medicinal uses of local plants. He can guide his sons in building a two-story tall house using only axes, machetes, and materials from the forest. He is an expert agronomist. He speaks several languages fluently; knows precisely how he is related to several hundred of his closest kin; and has acquired sufficient wisdom to share his home peacefully with in-laws, cousins, children, and grandchildren. Female elders are comparably learned and accomplished.

The integrity of traditional cultures may be missed when we define development as increases in gross national product. Listen, for example, to the arrogance in the comments of the head of Nike corporate education when he told a reporter, "I think we're doing a great job quite frankly, to help evolve some of these cultures." He said that Vietnam's culture was "just emerging," thanks in part to Nike investment. He made these claims about a culture that was well-established centuries before the United States existed. Even to call other countries "poor," which we do in this book from time to time, hides the ways they may be rich in traditional knowledge and relationships.

More often in this book we use the term Third World to characterize the countries not part of the industrialized First World (the United States, Europe, etc.) or the industrialized Second World (the former Soviet bloc countries). It's an older term, one that gained wide usage after the 1955 conference of Afro-Asian countries in Bandung, Indonesia, and is still favored by many advocates for global justice — for example, the Third World Network (www.twnside.org.sg) — along with the newer expression Global South. Both terms acknowledge broad commonalities among countries, but don't carry the connotation that those countries are being held to the standard of thing-rich industrial societies, as is true with "developing" or "underdeveloped" labels.

The term we include in this book's title may itself be misleading. "Globalization" can imply that we are all mutually influencing one another, growing together, becoming a "global village," in the words of that unfortunate cliché. It can miss the profound imbalances in who determines and benefits from a "globalized" world. And it's a grand-sounding title that suggests that we've entered a new epoch of human history. More accurately, we're witnessing the quickening spread of the profit system as more and more areas of the globe are drawn into its orbit. Life throughout the world is becoming increasingly commodified. The scope of this development may be new, but the process is not. Thus when we use the term "globalization" in the book, we are referring to this profit-driven process, rather than to the potential of global networking for a better world, although some use expressions like "grassroots globalization" or "globalization from below" to imagine a more humane and ecologically sane connectedness.

The point is simply that language is political and metaphorical. Every time we speak to our students, our language offers them images that may communicate more than we intend. Thus part of "rethinking globalization" is rethinking the language we use to talk about the world.

— *The editors*

work late, and managers disrespect them." Despite important differences, the same essential market forces at play in Mexico or Indonesia influence life here as well — and often in much grimmer ways than are to be found, say, at McDonald's. Globalization has so disrupted communities around the world that people's desperation has left them easy targets for countless abuses. The traffic in women and children as virtual sex slaves is one of the more tragic examples. Immigrants around the world, including in the United States, labor in some of the worst conditions imaginable; and people die every day attempting to cross the U.S.-Mexican border.

One of our students recently took to heart our constant "everything is connected" refrain: "If everything is connected," she said, "then you can't change anything without changing everything. But you can't change everything, so that means that you can't change anything."

Hers was a profound but troubling observation. In our teaching and in this book, we want to indicate that people's efforts to fight for decent lives make an enormous difference. Throughout the book we highlight historical and contemporary struggles to address the diverse but interconnected problems detailed here. The world is a better place for these efforts, and they are vital sources of hope for the future.

But our student's insight also needs to be considered. She's wrong that we can't change anything. But she's right that we have to change everything, if by "everything" we mean the interlocking ideas and practices that make private interests paramount, and undermine the common good. This book is an argument for the necessity of holding in our minds and in our classrooms the big global picture. The world is a web of relationships. To be truly effective, every effort to make a difference needs to be grounded in that broader analysis. Likewise, every effort to teach about the world also needs to be informed by the bigger picture.

When we put "globalization" in the title of this book, we realized that we were promising readers, literally, the world. We did our best. But there are enormous areas that we may have touched upon but did not adequately cover here: the global AIDS crisis and public health issues, in general; many of the ways that globalization particularly impacts women and children; the vast and ongoing global migrations; the war against drugs and the military intervention in Colombia; the threat posed by global warming; the privatization of water; global

housing shortages; issues of reparations for the slave trade and colonialism. Nor did we address as fully as we would have liked movements for global justice and questions about the social and economic systems needed to address the ills that profit-driven globalization creates.

As we neared publication, the world was stunned by the horrific events of September 11, 2001. On one level, these events brought into focus other limitations of this volume. We don't directly address the issues of religious fundamentalism or terrorism. Nor do we feature articles that examine how globalization is playing out in the Muslim world — and how this might be related to the development of violent networks like al-Qaeda.

However, the events of September 11th are the clearest argument imaginable for the the kind of inquiry that we propose in this book: A deep global literacy must come to be seen as a basic

Protesters in sea turtle costumes at the meeting of the World Trade Organization in Seattle in 1999.

HOW TO USE THIS BOOK

Rethinking Globalization includes background readings, lesson plans, teaching articles, role plays and simulations, student handouts, interviews, poems, cartoons, annotated resource lists, and teaching ideas. It is curricular without being a curriculum, in that it is not designed as a day-by-day guide to teaching about globalization.

The book opens with several articles that introduce some of the broad themes that weave throughout the book. We then offer background on the colonial roots of global wealth and power inequalities, although we don't necessarily recommend a chronological approach to teaching about globalization. Sometimes it works best to pick a dramatic issue like child labor, global sweatshops, or the clash between "development" and indigenous cultures, and then later pull back to examine historical roots to current problems.

Some articles and activities are aimed at upper elementary students; others are aimed at students who are high school-aged and older. Many of the readings and activities included here work well in teacher inservice, college-level courses and other adult education contexts. We did not segregate the book into sections for different grade levels. This is because many, if not most, of the activities and readings aimed at elementary students could be adapted for use with high school-aged and older students, and vice versa.

Readings that we've designed to accompany a specific teaching activity — and which are intended to be duplicated — are labeled "Handout," but many other readings could also be copied and used with students.

Each chapter begins with an introduction to outline the issues covered in that section, and ends with a description of further teaching ideas.

The book closes with a short "Final Words" chapter, including lesson ideas for how students can use the Organization and Website Resources.

All the Resources and many additional readings and activities are posted on our website at www.rethinkingschools.org/rg, and will be regularly updated.

—The editors

skill in every school. It is more urgent than ever that students take a profoundly critical look at the direction the world is headed. How is the reach of the global market impacting cultures everywhere? What are the consequences of the vast and growing inequalities of wealth and power? Is this the best we can do? What alternatives can we imagine? Addressing questions like these is not simply important from an academic standpoint. It is literally an issue of survival.

We hope this book will join the conversation about how we can meaningfully teach for global justice. And we encourage you to contribute to this conversation, perhaps by signing up for the Rethinking Schools critical teaching listserv (instructions at www.rethinkingschools.org/rg).

As we think about nurturing student success, let's remind ourselves that yes, we teach to secure the future of individual students, but that future is intimately linked to the future of other people around the world — and of the earth itself. ∎

—Bill Bigelow and Bob Peterson

A busy street in Port-au-Prince, Haiti.

Globalization: A View from Below

BY JEAN-BERTRAND ARISTIDE

Our planet is entering the new century with fully 1.3 billion people living on less than one dollar a day. Three billion people, or half the population of the world, live on less than two dollars a day. Yet this same planet is experiencing unprecedented economic growth. The statistics that describe the accumulation of wealth in the world are mind-boggling. From where we sit, the most staggering statistics of all are those that reflect the polarization of this wealth. In 1960 the richest 20% of the world's population had 70% of the world's wealth, today they have 86% of the wealth. In 1960 the poorest 20% of the world's population had just 2.3% of the wealth of the world. Today this has shrunk to just barely 1%.

Imagine that the five fingers of your hand represent the world's population. The hand has $100 to share. Today the thumb, representing the richest 20% of the world's population, has $86 for itself. The little finger has just $1. The thumb is accumulating wealth with breathtaking speed

and never looking back. The little finger is sinking deeper into economic misery. The distance between them grows larger every day.

Behind the crisis of dollars there is a human crisis: among the poor, immeasurable human suffering; among the others, the powerful, the policymakers, a poverty of spirit which has made a religion of the market and its invisible hand. A crisis of imagination so profound that the only measure of value is profit, the only measure of human progress is economic growth.

We have not reached the consensus that to eat is a basic human right. This is an ethical crisis. This is a crisis of faith.

Global capitalism becomes a machine devouring our planet. The little finger, the men

> In 1960 the poorest 20% of the world's population had just 2.3% of the wealth of the world. Today this has shrunk to just barely 1%.

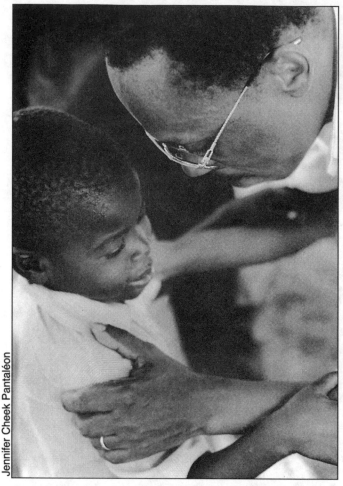

Jean-Bertrand Aristide comforts an orphan at Lafanmi Selavi, a center for street children he founded in 1986.

and women of the poorest 20%, are reduced to cogs in this machine, the bottom rung in global production, valued only as cheap labor, otherwise altogether disposable. The machine cannot and does not measure their suffering. The machine also does not measure the suffering of our planet. Every second an area the size of a soccer field is deforested. This fact alone should be mobilizing men and women to protect their most basic interest — oxygen. But the machine overwhelms us. The distance between the thumb and the little finger stretches to the breaking point.

GLOBALIZATION: A CHOICE BETWEEN DEATH AND DEATH

A morgue worker is preparing to dispose of a dozen corpses. One living soul lifts himself off of the table, shakes his head and declares, "I am not dead!" To which the morgue worker answers, "Yes you are. The doctors say that you are dead, so lie down."

In today's global marketplace trillions of dollars are traded each day via a vast network of computers. In this market no one talks, no one touches. Only numbers count.

And yet today this faceless economy is already five times larger than the real, or productive, economy.

We know other marketplaces. On a plain high in the mountains of Haiti, one day a week thousands of people still gather. This is the marketplace of my childhood in the mountains above Port Salut. The sights and the smells and the noise and the color overwhelm you. Everyone comes. If you don't come you will miss everything. The donkeys tied and waiting in the woods number in the thousands. Goods are displayed in every direction: onions, leeks, corn, beans, yams, cabbage, cassava, and avocados, mangoes and every tropical fruit, chickens, pigs, goats, and batteries, and tennis shoes, too. People trade goods and news. This is the center; social, political, and economic life roll together. A woman teases and coaxes her client: "*Cherie,* the onions are sweet and waiting just for you." The client laughs and teases back until they make a deal. They share trade, and laughter, gossip, politics, and medical and child-rearing tips. A market exchange, and a human exchange.

We are not against trade, we are not against free trade, but our fear is that the global market intends to annihilate our markets. We will be pushed to the cities, to eat food grown on factory farms in distant countries, food whose price depends on the daily numbers game of the first market. "This is more efficient," the economists say. "Your market, your way of life, is not efficient," they say. But we ask, "What is left when you reduce trade to numbers, when you erase all that is human?"

Globalization, the integration of world markets, has promised to "lift all boats," rich and poor, to bring a global culture of entertainment and consumer goods to everyone — the promise of material happiness. And indeed, since 1980 most Third World countries have embraced globalization. They have opened their economies to the world, lowered tariffs, embraced free trade, and allowed goods and services from the industrialized world to flow in. It seems the world is brought closer together. In fact the gap between the thumb and the little finger has never been larger.

What happens to poor countries when they embrace free trade? In Haiti in 1986 we imported just 7,000 tons of rice, the main staple food of the country. The vast majority was grown in Haiti. In the late 1980s Haiti complied with free trade policies advocated by the international lending agencies and lifted tariffs on rice imports. Cheaper rice immediately flooded in from the United States, where the rice industry is subsidized. In fact the liberalization of Haiti's market coincided with the 1985 Farm Bill in the United States which increased subsidies to the rice industry, so that 40% of U.S. rice growers' profits came from the government by 1987. Haiti's peasant farmers could not possibly compete. By 1996 Haiti was importing 196,000 tons of foreign rice at the cost of $100 million a year. Haitian rice production became negligible. Once the dependence on foreign rice was complete, import prices began to rise, leaving Haiti's population, particularly the urban poor, completely at the whim of rising world grain prices. And the prices continue to rise.

What lessons do we learn? For poor countries free trade is not so free, or so fair. Haiti, under intense pressure from the international lending institutions stopped protecting its domestic agriculture while subsidies to the U.S. rice industry increased. A hungry nation became hungrier.

In a globalized economy, foreign investment is trumpeted as the key to alleviating poverty. But in fact, the top beneficiary of foreign investment from 1985-95 was the United States, with $477 billion. Britain ran a distant second at $199 billion, and Mexico, the only Third World country in the top 10, received only $44 billion in investment. When the majority of this money fled the country overnight during Mexico's financial meltdown in 1995, we learned that foreign investment is not really investment. It is more like speculation. And in my country, Haiti, it's very hard to find investment statistics.

We are still moving from misery toward poverty with dignity.

Many in the First World imagine the amount of money spent on aid to developing countries is massive. In fact, it amounts to only .03% of GNP of the industrialized nations. In 1995, the director of the U.S. aid agency defended his agency by testifying to his congress that 84¢ of every dollar of aid goes back into the U.S. economy in goods and services purchased. For every dollar the United States puts into the World Bank, an estimated $2 actually goes into the U.S. economy in goods and services. Meanwhile in 1995, severely indebted low-income countries paid $1 billion more in debt and interest to the International Monetary Fund (IMF) than they received from it. For the 46 countries of Sub-Saharan Africa, foreign debt service was four times their combined governmental health and education budgets in 1996. So, we find that aid does not aid.

The little finger knows that she is sinking deeper into misery each day, but all the while the thumb is telling her that profits are increasing, economies are growing and he is pouring millions of dollars of aid into her country. Whose profit? Whose economy? What aid? The logic of global capitalism is not logical for her. We call this economic schizophrenia.

The history of the eradication of the Haitian Creole pig population in the 1980s is a classic parable of globalization. Haiti's small, black, Creole pigs were at the heart of the peasant economy. An extremely hearty breed, well adapted to Haiti's climate and conditions, they ate readily available waste products, and could survive for

> We have not reached the consensus that to eat is a basic human right.

Two boys at Lafanmi Selavi waiting for soccer practice.

Jennifer Cheek Pantaléon

Jennifer Cheek Pantaléon

Girls playing jump-rope at Lafanmi Selavi.

pens. Haitian peasants quickly dubbed them as *"prince à quatre pieds,"* (four footed princes). Adding insult to injury, the meat did not taste as good. Needless to say, the repopulation program was a complete failure. One observer of the process estimated that in monetary terms, Haitian peasants lost $600 million. There was a 30% drop in enrollment in rural schools, there was a dramatic decline in the protein consumption in rural Haiti, a devastating decapitalization of the peasant economy, and an incalculable negative impact on Haiti's soil and agricultural productivity. The Haitian peasantry has not recovered to this day.

Most of rural Haiti is still isolated from global markets, so for many peasants the extermination of the Creole pigs was their first experience of globalization. The experience looms large in the collective memory. Today, when the peasants are told that "economic reform" and privatization will benefit them they are understandably wary. The state-owned enterprises are sick, we are told, and they must be privatized. The peasants shake their heads and remember the Creole pigs.

The 1997 sale of the state-owned flour mill confirmed their skepticism. The mill sold for a mere $9 million, while estimates place potential yearly profits at $20-30 million a year. The mill was bought by a group of investors linked to one of Haiti's largest banks. One outcome seems certain: This sale will further concentrate wealth — in a country where 1% of the population already holds 45% of the wealth of the country.

If we have lingering doubts about where poor countries fall in this "new" economic order, listen to the World Bank. In September 1996, *The London Guardian* newspaper cited a draft World Bank strategy paper that predicted that the majority of Haitian peasants — who make up 70% of Haiti's population — are unlikely to survive bank-advocated free market measures. The Bank concluded: "The small volume of production and the environmental resource constraints will leave the rural population with only two possibilities: to work in the industrial or service sector, or to emigrate." At present the industrial sector employs only about 20,000 Haitians. There are already approximately 2.5 million people living in Port-au-Prince, 70% of them are

three days without food. Eighty to 85% of rural households raised pigs; they played a key role in maintaining the fertility of the soil and constituted the primary savings bank of the peasant population. Traditionally a pig was sold to pay for emergencies and special occasions (funerals, marriages, baptisms, illnesses and, critically, to pay school fees and buy books for the children when school opened each year in October).

In 1982 international agencies assured Haiti's peasants their pigs were sick and had to be killed (so that the illness would not spread to countries to the North.) Promises were made that better pigs would replace the sick pigs. With an efficiency not since seen among development projects, all of the Creole pigs were killed over a period of 13 months.

Two years later the new, better pigs came from Iowa. They were so much better that they required clean drinking water (unavailable to 80% of the Haitian population), imported feed (costing $90 a year when the per capita income was about $130), and special roofed pig-

> **We must lift ourselves up off the morgue table and tell the experts we are not yet dead.**

Junior Thelusma takes in some shade at the Ministry of Agriculture in Tabarre outside Port-au-Prince, where the children of Lafanmi Selavi tend their own fields of beans, bananas, and mangoes.

officially unemployed and living in perhaps the most desperate conditions in the Western Hemisphere. Given the tragic history of Haiti's boat people, emigration, the second possibility, can hardly be considered a real option.

The choices that globalization offers the poor remind me of a story. Anatole, one of the boys who had lived with us at Lafanmi Selavi*, was working at the national port. One day a very powerful businessman offered him money to sabotage the main unloading forklift at the port. Anatole said to the man, "Well, then I am already dead." The man, surprised by the response, asked, "Why?" Anatole answered: "Because if I sneak in here at night and do what you ask they will shoot me, and if I don't, you will kill me." The dilemma is, I believe, the classic dilemma of the poor: a choice between death and death.

Either we enter a global economic system, in which we know we cannot survive, or we refuse, and face death by slow starvation. With choices like these the urgency of finding a third way is clear. We must find some room to maneuver, some open space simply to survive. We must lift ourselves up off the morgue table and tell the experts we are not yet dead. ∎

Lafanmi Selavi is the center for street children in Port-au-Prince founded by Aristide in 1986.

Jean-Bertrand Aristide is a lifelong human rights activist who was elected president of Haiti in 1990. This article is adapted from his book Eyes of the Heart: Seeking a Path for the Poor in the Age of Globalization (*Common Courage Press, 2000*).

(For teaching ideas, see page 56.)

Globalization Myths

The mainstream media, corporations and government officials acknowledge that globalization has "winners and losers," but with one voice they proclaim that the benefits are much greater than any negatives. In the book The Field Guide to the Global Economy *(The New Press, 2000), Sarah Anderson, John Cavanagh, and Thea Lee examine a number of the major claims that they found in materials produced for middle school, high school, and college students. The following is based on findings described in greater detail in their book on pages 39-63.*

MYTH #1:
Increased Trade Equals More Jobs for Americans at Higher Wages.

U.S. government and corporate officials claim that jobs in the export sector pay more than jobs on average. Hence, they argue, increasing exports should be encouraged.

There are several problems with this reasoning. In today's factories, companies can boost productivity and increase exports without hiring more employees. Caterpillar, for example, had record exports worth $5.5 billion from its plants in 1996, even though the firm had cut its U.S. workforce by about one-quarter during the previous three years. Meanwhile, Caterpillar used its global power to withstand a long fight with its U.S. unions.

Do new export-related jobs make up for job losses from imports? U.S. trade involves firms exporting goods and services to other countries ($931 billion worth in 1998) as well as importing from the rest of the world ($1,100 billion in 1998). Both exports and imports have been growing rapidly as corporations shift goods and parts among their factories around the world. "Free trade" advocates boast about jobs created by growing U.S. exports, but ignore the jobs lost to increased imports. If consumers switch from buying a U.S.-made product to one made somewhere else, this *does* result in lost U.S. jobs and poorer quality jobs.

And even though it is true that export jobs pay better than the average job, so do jobs in industries that face intense import competition. This is because both export and import jobs are usually in manufacturing, while the average job is in the lower-paying service sector.

But what about all those new American jobs created? The big question is, "What kind of jobs?" The Economic Policy Institute has found that nearly 30% of Americans have "nonstandard" jobs, which includes all those that are not permanent, full-time jobs. On average, these jobholders earn less, are less likely to receive health insurance and pensions, and face greater insecurity than full-time workers in standard jobs, even when they have the same level of education and experience. The majority of nonstandard jobs are held by women and people of color.

And globalization leads to insecurity in more and more jobs. Americans who manage to maintain jobs in manufacturing must contend with employers who may threaten to shut down a plant and move production to a lower wage area.

MYTH #2:
Governments Protect the Environment More as Global Trade Creates Economic Growth.

Globalization pollutes. The rapid industrialization in China, Indonesia, Mexico, and elsewhere has vastly increased pollution around the world. Some companies deliberately choose production locations where enforcement of environmental rules is lax. Further, the World Bank and International Monetary Fund pressure countries to pay off loans through increased exports. This often means cutting down forests for timber exports, plantation expansion, depleting fishing stocks, or expanding open-pit mines.

Defenders of globalization argue that economic growth will give poor governments the resources to clean up the environment. But it doesn't work that way. Look at China, for example. Since 1980, China has had the world's highest economic growth rate, but it has quickly become one of the world's most polluted countries. At least 5 of the 10 cities with the world's worst air pollution are in China.

Globalization also threatens the environment in so-called developed countries. Corporations make threats to move out of countries like the United States to Mexico if new environmental

> "Free trade" advocates boast about jobs created by growing U.S. exports, but ignore the jobs lost to increased imports.

regulations are passed. Also, environmental regulations have been overturned by the World Trade Organization and others as "unfair barriers to trade." (See p. 95.)

The very idea of globalization — dramatically expanding trade between nations — is hostile to the environment. Every mile that goods travel from one nation to another is fueled with polluting fossil fuels.

MYTH #3:
Foreign Investment Automatically Raises Living Standards.

How do poor countries attract investment? By offering low taxes, repressing workers, and not enforcing regulations. Without strong protections for workers and citizens, there is no guarantee that foreign investment will benefit the average person in any country.

In Mexico, direct foreign investment jumped from less than $3 billion per year in the 1980s to $11 billion in 1998. Some Mexicans did benefit. But real wages in Mexico are less today than in the 1980s. Between 1987 and 1998, the real worth of the minimum wage declined by 72%. And there are fewer jobs in Mexico than there were before. Likewise, in Nigeria, oil has produced billions of dollars of revenue, but per capita income has fallen.

MYTH #4:
Free Trade Benefits Consumers.

This is perhaps the most widely made claim. No question: From Manila to Mexico City, globalization has expanded the variety of goods available.

But who benefits? Just because corporations pay less to produce goods in Haiti or Indonesia does not necessarily mean that those savings are passed along to consumers. This may happen in industries where many small firms compete. But in sectors where a handful of huge global corporations dominate the market, like in automobiles, international trade does not necessarily

result in lower prices.

For example, in 1994 General Motors built a new factory in Silao, Mexico to produce Suburbans for the U.S. market. GM paid $18.96 per hour for labor in the United States but only $1.54 per hour in Mexico. And yet the price of Suburbans continued to go up. Suburbans produced in Mexico didn't cost less than Suburbans produced in the United States. GM's dramatic savings from lower wages did not benefit consumers.

> **Who benefits?**
> Just because corporations pay less to produce goods in Haiti or Indonesia does not necessarily mean that those savings are passed along to consumers.

(Cartoon text:)
AMERICAN CEOs MAKE OVER 200 TIMES AVERAGE WORKERS' WAGES!

THAT'S BECAUSE WE HAVE TO BE GLOBALLY COMPETITIVE

BUT IT'S MUCH HIGHER THAN ANY OTHER INDUSTRIAL NATION

SEE— WE'RE WINNING!

WASSERMAN © '97 BOSTON GLOBE DIST. BY L.A. TIMES SYND.

MYTH #5:
Globalization "Lifts All Boats."

The World Bank argues that speeded-up globalization has coincided with greater world equality, pointing out that so-called developing countries as a whole are growing faster than the major industrial nations. But "growth" does not automatically help people. During this period of rapid growth, the gap between rich and poor within most nations has widened. This is true in countries as diverse as China, Chile, Poland, the Philippines, Tanzania, and Ecuador. Growing inequality is also occurring in industrialized countries like the United States, Great Britain, Japan, and Germany. And the gap between the world's richest and poorest people has never been greater. In 1999, the wealth held by the world's 475 billionaires was greater than the combined income of the poorest half of *all the people in the world*.

> "Growth" does not automatically help people. During this period of rapid growth, the gap between rich and poor within most nations has widened.

MYTH #6:
What Benefits Corporations Benefits Us All.

Corporations claim that when they are more competi- tive and profitable, everyone in our society benefits. But increasingly, corporations pay fewer taxes and provide fewer jobs, although they have become more and more powerful. Since 1960, the share of federal tax revenues paid by corporations has dropped by more than half, from 23.2% to 11.4%.

The top 10 U.S. manufacturing corporations employ far fewer people today than they did 30 years ago, despite much higher revenues. Since 1968, their worldwide employment has dropped 33%, while their sales have increased 94%.

Bottom line: When companies make more money it does not necessarily "trickle down."

MYTH #7:
Sweatshops Are Not Necessarily a Bad Thing; That's How the United States Developed, After All.

Some economists claim that the low wages and harsh conditions of overseas "sweatshops" are essential as poor countries take steps toward prosperity. Sweatshop defenders claim that this is how the United States became prosperous.

However, what led to improved conditions in the United States was not the sweatshops themselves, but the struggles *against* sweatshops and for decent working conditions and wages. The United States has a long history of labor organizing and struggle. History does not teach us that, on their own accord, corporations will improve conditions as they make greater profits. Change happens when people work for it.

MYTH #8:
Immigrants Are a Drain on the U.S. Economy.

Often the same people who champion the rights of U.S. corporations to operate freely in other countries also scapegoat immigrants in the United States for draining social programs, stealing jobs, and dragging down wages. The National Academy of Sciences calculates that each immigrant and his or her descendants will provide $80,000 more in tax revenues over their lifetimes than they will use in services. The

Urban Institute calculated that all immigrants who arrived in the United States between 1970 and 1992 paid between $25 and $30 billion more in taxes than they used in welfare and social services during this period.

By and large, through increased purchasing power, immigrants don't just fill jobs, they create them. The National Academy of Sciences concludes that there are no negative effects on American workers, with one exception: the very low-skilled, with less than a high school education, who earn an estimated 5% less because of increased competition. But as the UNITE apparel union points out: "The best way to help America's low wage workers is to stick to the basics: improved wages, improved health care, and reform of our labor laws so that all workers — immigrant and native born — can freely join unions and protect their rights."

MYTH #9:
Globalization Will Spread Freedom and Democracy by Increasing Trade Between Nations.

This simply is not true. In most cases, increased trade does not go hand in hand with greater freedom. In a recent human rights report the U.S. State Department revealed that many countries with export growth rates well above the world average during the 1990s were anything but free societies. In order to protect "friendly investment climates," governments often repress workers and suppress freedom of expression. This is especially true because, as mentioned, free trade policies increase the

> In 1999, the wealth held by the world's 475 billionaires was greater than the combined income of the poorest half of all the people in the world.

inequality between rich and poor. For example, the State Department reported that Thailand, with one of the highest growth rates between 1990 and 1995, also was the site of death squad killings, torture, restrictions on freedom of speech and religion, and a significant amount of child labor.

MYTH #10:
U.S. Workers Don't Need to Worry About Globalization Because We're So Much More Productive.

According to one argument, people in the United States shouldn't be concerned about firms moving jobs to low-wage countries because U.S. workers can out-compete anyone. This overlooks the fact that corporations already are achieving comparable levels of productivity in countries where workers are denied rights and production costs are cheaper. For example, by 1997, 26.5% of China's exports to the United States were not just cheap consumer goods, but were comprised of machinery, including electrical goods, as well as industrial equipment. ■

> In most cases, increased trade does not go hand in hand with greater freedom. In a recent human rights report the U.S. State Department revealed that many countries with export growth rates well above the world average during the 1990s were anything but free societies. In order to protect "friendly investment climates," governments often repress workers and suppress freedom of expression. This is especially true because, as mentioned, free trade policies increase the inequality between rich and poor.

Students in Milwaukee, Wisconsin protest the North American Free Trade Agreement.

Planting Seeds of Solidarity
Weaving World Justice Issues into the Elementary Classroom

BY BOB PETERSON

My fifth-grade students love stories. Almost every day after lunch I light a candle, turn off the lights, and read or tell a story. If something interferes with story time, I receive a chorus of complaints.

One of the stories I use to start my students' study of globalization issues is from my own teenage experience when I lived in Cairo, Egypt in the mid-1960s. I tell them that I lived in Cairo among pyramids and sphinxes, close to the world's longest river, the Nile. I attended a middle school with kids from all over the world, in an old palace of former King Farouk of Egypt. Because my family was from the United States and my father had a good job as a soil scientist,

we lived comfortably in a suburban home south of Cairo.

I had many adventures — riding horses and camels by the Great Pyramids of Cheops, visiting Tutankhamen's tomb in the Valley of the Kings, swimming in the Red Sea — but one incident stands out in my memory.

One sunny afternoon my family got into our blue 1965 Ford station wagon and drove 20 kilometers south of Cairo to climb a lesser known pyramid called the Red Pyramid. My mother had packed a lunch in our cooler, including some cans of imported diet soda for my diabetic brother, Don.

We picnicked in an isolated spot in the desert

a ways from the Red Pyramid. By the time we finished, a small group of children had gathered around our car and they called out in Arabic, "Baksheesh! Baksheesh!" They wanted a tip — money. Their little hands poked through the open car windows, begging.

We did not give money to the kids — U.S. tourists were "not encouraged" to do so — but we did "give" them something. As we were leaving we threw out the window my brother's two empty aluminum cans. "They want them for a toy," my father said as we drove away. The children screamed with joy. I looked out the back window as we slowly drove toward the pyramid. The children were piled on top of the cans, fighting to be owner of their newfound playthings.

We hiked to the top of the pyramid's peak, but my thoughts remained focused on the children fighting over what I had thrown away. Why was I destined to be the one in the car tossing junk to poor kids, instead of the one who was begging for a penny or an empty can?

Why?

Using simple stories to raise profound questions is among the oldest and best of teaching techniques. It is also an essential strategy in my teaching about globalization issues.

> **Why was I destined to be the one in the car tossing junk to poor kids, instead of the one who was begging for a penny or an empty can?**

I view teaching about globalization and world justice issues much as I view issues of multicultural education. They need to be both woven throughout the curriculum and highlighted in specific lessons. This approach is necessary in part to find the time to teach about the issues, given all that elementary teachers are expected to cover. But also I find that an integrated approach helps motivate students, and teaches them that these are central issues that cannot be dealt with in one or two activities. As a result, my lessons in math, science, social studies, writing, reading, current events — even discipline discussions — all have a world justice and multicultural theme woven throughout.

The story from my year in Egypt provokes thoughtful comments and questions among students. They express surprise that some children have so little and they wonder what life is like for children around the world. "I can't believe kids actually wanted just an old can," I recall a student saying. A response from another student stressed our commonality: "I believe it. Every kid wants to play!"

PROBLEM-POSING APPROACH

Throughout my classroom discussions on globalization, I pose more questions, not so much in search of a specific answer, but for all of us to think about: How are our lives different from theirs? How are they similar? What do people in the United States have to learn from people in other countries? Why does chance allow for some to live a life of relative luxury while others don't know where their next meal is coming from? And what might we do about such things?

There's no doubt that global problems are complex. However, even with elementary children there is no reason to unnecessarily simplify things. Questioning or problem-posing is an effective means to keep discussions both interesting and complicated.

Early in the year, I use Tracy Chapman's song *Why?* to pose questions. Chapman asks, for example: "Why do the babies starve when there's enough food to feed the world?" I give my students a copy of the lyrics (as I do with dozens of songs and poems we use in the classroom) to keep in a special three-ring binder, so that they might refer to them throughout the year.

Needless to say, we don't answer Chapman's "Why?" We note it, sometimes adding it to the spiral notebook hanging on the wall entitled "Questions We Have." I ask students what answers to Chapman's questions might be, and we note them as well. Ideas usually include a range of possibilities: lack of food, no jobs, too many people, war, drugs, and lazy people. I tell my students that this is but one example of the important questions we will ponder in fifth grade.

In the beginning weeks, I also share a few basic statistics from UNICEF, including the fact that about 30,000 children die daily from malnutrition and preventable illness. I ask my class, "How many schools with the same student population as ours would it take to equal the number of children who die each day?" This helps make the large number meaningful, and usually surprises the students at the depth of the problem. I also share that approximately 130 million children do not attend elementary school, 1.1 billion people have no access to safe drinking water, and 3 billion lack adequate sanitation facilities.

I tell students that we are going to try to not just feel sorry or sympathy for those people, but to develop "solidarity." I have a student look up the word "solidarity" in the dictionary and they find that it means "unity, based on a community of interests." We discuss what unity means and I ask, "What do you have in common with the kids who we're talking about?"

"We all need to eat," a student might respond. "We have to breathe!" So it goes, with kids usually identifying basic needs. I ask: "What are the basic needs of all humans, particularly children?" Working sometimes in small groups and sometimes as the entire class, students come up with food, shelter, clothes, water, schools, doctors, and toys. We discuss whether items are a basic need or a "desire." For example, some classes have decided that while toys may not be a basic need for children, playing is. Out of such a discussion comes more questions, such as: "What would it feel like if your basic needs were not met?" "How many kids don't have their basic needs met?" "Is anyone doing something to help kids who don't have their basic needs met?" I encourage students to look up "children's rights" and "human rights" in our school library and on the Internet. One book that kids find is *A Children's Chorus* published by UNICEF (see Resources, p. 378). This beautifully illustrated book goes through the ten principles contained in the 1959 United Nations Declaration of the Rights of a Child.

As a follow-up activity to Chapman's song and the rights of children discussion, I occasionally have children in small groups choose different rights out of a hat and improvise short skits to show the class what those rights are. Again, the question I pose is: "Why? Why do some kids have these and others don't? How can we express solidarity with those kids, instead of just feeling sorry?"

> **Helping students recognize there is a commonality to such problems helps lay the groundwork for developing attitudes of solidarity that go beyond mere charity.**

OVERCOMING THE 'US VS. THEM' DICHOTOMY

One challenge is to make sure that from the very start, such immense problems are not seen as "foreign," only occurring among "others." Thus I like to start my in-depth study of world justice issues at home. Some of my students bring to class certain stereotypes about the rest of the world, especially stereotypes they have gotten from TV and the media. Starting with problems in this country acts to counter stereotypes of "poor" Africa, Asia, and Latin America. It also centers the children in something that is familiar to many of them: poverty and homelessness in the United States.

One of my first reading/language arts units is on homelessness in the United States. I begin by displaying on my overhead projector a photo of a snowy scene in front of the White House. Before showing the caption I ask students to make observations. They ultimately are surprised that what they guessed were snow-covered rocks or garbage are actually sleeping homeless people. (The photo is reproduced on p. 32 of *Rethinking Our Classrooms, Volume 1.*) As with other photos I use, we make observations, talk about how we feel, connect it to what we already know, ask why the situation exists, and think about what might be done.

EVICTION STORIES

After this introduction, we take a few days to read Sharon Bell Mathis' *Sidewalk Story*, which tells of a family being evicted from its apartment and the role of a nine-year-old neighbor girl in fighting the eviction. Throughout my entire curriculum I try to highlight times when individuals and groups saw their interests tied to the interests of others, and acted on those convictions. We also read Langston Hughes' "Ballad of the Landlord" and Lucille Clifton's poem "Eviction," and write some of our own poems.

I share news stories that talk of the continuing poverty in the United States and the intense poverty in some places overseas. I find it beneficial to begin with discussion of U.S. poverty because it is close to home and virtually all my students have stories to tell about homeless people who are relatives, or whom they encounter in their neighborhoods or when they travel.

During these discussions, I occasionally find that some of my own students or members of their families are homeless. Because the stories and poetry I use portray homelessness as main-

AN EXPANDING FREE MARKET EXTENDS ALL BELLIES

ly a social problem — not something to be ashamed of, my homeless students are usually willing to describe their situation. Their classmates listen with respectful curiosity.

One year a student explained that during summer his house burned down and that he was living in a motel room with several other family members. Once he shared the story, his classmates were more sensitive to some of his moods and needs. One student assisted him in co-writing a dialogue poem between a small home (the motel room) and a big home (the apartment where his family finally relocated). "We are both homes," the poem started, and then the "little house" says, "Lots of kids have to sleep in the same bed and room," while the big house responds, "Every kid has their own room in me." The little house goes on to say, "Friends can't visit because I'm too small," while the big house responds, "Lots of friends can visit me because we have lots of space."

After children gain some basic background about conditions in the United States, I feel more comfortable exploring poverty and injustice in other countries. Helping students recognize there is a commonality to such problems helps lay the groundwork for developing attitudes of solidarity that go beyond mere charity. In other

words, I want students to recognize patterns in world problems and how those patterns are connected to problems in our own communities and country. Then students are more likely to begin to understand that working for global justice also involves changing "our" world as well, and that when we help to change conditions for "others" we are helping to change them for ourselves.

I try to help my students develop a feeling of solidarity through understanding the often expressed notion that "no person is an island," or, as Dr. Martin Luther King, Jr. put it so eloquently: "Injustice anywhere is a threat to justice everywhere." This is no simple task in a culture that glorifies individual consumption as a vehicle to personal satisfaction. My students are little different than many U.S. youths — 65% of whom have TVs in their bedrooms and who watch on average nearly 25 hours of TV a week and more than 20,000 television commercials a year. The materialism and narrow individualism promoted in the ads are obstacles to students beginning to think about their interests in more social, collective terms. One message students will never hear from a commercial is: "Think about the people who make the things you buy. What conditions do they work under, what are

Three students cram into a desk designed for two at an elementary school in Baghdad, Iraq, which constantly struggles to provide enough desks, books, and school supplies for all its students.

they paid, how could you help improve their lives?"

In one activity, I place a shopping bag in front of the class and ask the students to guess what's inside. As their guesses get more accurate I take out a T-shirt, a McDonald's Happy Meal toy, and a Nike shoe. I then ask how far these items have traveled. Initial responses are, "from McDonald's" or "from the store." As I question students, it becomes clear to them that the items were made somewhere else — somewhere much farther away.

I have a student come up and read where each item is from; we then locate the country on the world map. We talk about where other things are from as we examine backpacks, shoes, and clothing. For homework, students do a "Where Are My Things From?" activity (see p. 140), in which they list at least 10 household items, the brand name, and where they are made. The next day students share lists and label and color maps indicating the origins of their common things.

SWEATSHOP CONDITIONS

To probe the reality behind the Made in Honduras or Made in Indonesia labels, I show the video *When Children Do the Work* (see "Videos With a Global Conscience," p. 365), which graphically portrays the harsh conditions of sweatshops and how some children are robbed of their childhood. The first segment of the video is an excerpt from the National Labor Committee's *Zoned for Slavery* video which describes sweatshop conditions in garment factories in El Salvador and Honduras. The video's narrator explains that a Gap shirt made in El Salvador sells in the United States for $20, but the workers receive just 12¢. "Who gets the other $19.88?" the narrator demands. I later use these and other statistics for story problems in math.

The second segment of the video examines child workers in Pakistan. A carpet factory manager explains that he has 40 looms worked by 100 children and that "we chain them three or four hours a day to teach it not to run away." Yes, the manager says "it" when referring to children. He adds that the children also sleep chained to their looms. My students are repelled by scenes of such oppression, but inspired by the story of Iqbal Masih, a child worker who became an activist with the Bonded Labor Liberation Front and who was killed under suspicious circumstances (see p. 206).

The final segment shows the Women's Network of the United Food and Commercial Workers union leafleting a Wal-Mart store, protesting the sale of products made by eight- to twelve-year-olds in Bangladesh. The workers explain why such practices are both morally wrong and an attack on working people in this country. I remind my students of newspaper articles we've read about area companies moving to places of cheap labor, putting area workers out of work. This reinforces my emphasis on building a sense of solidarity with others around the world who are fighting economic oppression.

To further deepen children's understanding of their interconnectedness to conditions around the world, I use Bernice Reagon's song *Are My Hands Clean?* It tells the story of a blouse created from the labor and resources of El Salvador, Venezuela, Trinidad, Haiti, South Carolina, and New Jersey. The children trace the route of the blouse and its raw materials on a map, and contrast the wages of the workers described in the song.

When I first used this song I assumed that children would easily get the message of connectedness and potential responsibility the title implies. No such luck. After playing the song I ask, "What does 'Are my hands clean?' really mean?" I receive a range of responses including "The workers' hands get dirty in those sweatshops;" "All those chemicals in the shirts must dirty our hands;" "Because it's been everywhere we should wash the shirts before we wear them or our hands will get dirty;" and "Maybe we're responsible for how those people have to work so hard because we buy the clothing." I tell students that the expression "to wash one's hands of something" means to take no responsibility and I ask, "What would it mean to make our hands clean?"

I have also found using poems that make comparisons and show contrast to be helpful. They reinforce similarities between people and yet highlight conflicts and inequalities that need to be explored. I use a dialogue poem as one model (see *Rethinking Our Classrooms, Volume 1*, p. 42, and see p. 152 in this volume) in which two characters talk to each other. Sometimes I use photos of child workers or sweatshop laborers to spark the poetry writing. In pairs students examine the pictures and then write a dialogue poem — between a boss and a worker, between a child worker and child student, between a poor child and a rich child. I also use a specific poem,

Masks, which was written by Cameron Robinson, a former Portland high school student (see p. 135). Robinson's poem starts off: "Michael Jordan flies through the air/ on shoes of unpaid labor," and ends, "The world is full of masks,/ the hard part is seeing beneath them." We read the poem out loud and talk about what "mask" signifies. "We don't think about what we buy sometimes," one student says. "Some people don't know either," added another. "Some don't care what happens." "We don't realize our clothes have been so many other places and have traveled farther than us!" "We should help those people working in sweatshops."

> **The materialism and narrow individualism promoted in the ads are obstacles to students beginning to think about their interests in more social, collective terms.**

Later the students share their poems, show them to fourth grade students, and post them on a "Stop Child Labor and Sweatshops" bulletin board. Here's a portion of one dialogue poem:

Child Worker	Child Student
I work 10 hours a day.	I go to school or play all day.
I carry things on my head.	I carry a book bag on my back.
I get paid 19¢ an hour.	I get $5 every Sunday for allowance.

THE ROOTS OF INEQUALITY

It's relatively easy to get elementary children to recognize some manifestations of injustice around the world — poverty, hunger, child labor, and sweatshops. What's much more difficult is to get them to understand some of the causes.

I believe that only through understanding something about colonialism will people grasp why the world is divided as it is. On this broad issue of globalization teachers needn't be locked into a strict chronology. I try to grab the interest of the students, first by exploring aspects of today's world, and then ask the question: "How did this get to be like this?"

I use Columbus' encounter with Native Americans as the jumping off point for demonstrating the transfer of wealth from one part of the world to another and the destruction of sustainable Native cultures. Using materials and resources contained in the Rethinking Schools

book *Rethinking Columbus*, I have children examine the impact of Columbus' arrival on the Native population. Through stories, poetry, songs, and a role play trial of Columbus, students begin to see the relationship of exploitation that has existed between rich countries and their colonies. In the role play, some students take on the role of Taínos who were among the first to greet Columbus, and talk about how their lands were taken, forests cut down, people killed, and language "taken out of our mouths," all for the sake of making a few people in a European colonial system rich.

Later, as we study the impact of the American Revolution, we look at particular British policies that economically hurt the 13 colonies, with students dramatizing the conflicts between British tax collectors and American colonists. As we study the trans-Atlantic slave trade we read about the devastating effects slavery had on west Africa and the resistance to slavery in the Americas. For example, I use the chapter book *The Captive*, by Joyce Hansen, a fictionalized account of the capture and eventual escape to freedom of Prince Olaudah Equiano (Gustavus Vass) of western Africa.

Obviously, limited study in an elementary classroom is going to touch on only some of the factors that have contributed to the distorted development of much of Asia, Africa, and Latin America. But these broader historical studies provide some background to students about the origin of current global inequalities.

BROADER ECONOMIC ISSUES

I do various activities with students to place child labor and sweatshops in the context of broader economic issues. As part of math class, I have students graph and demonstrate the disparities of wealth between continents (see p. 68). In one activity, I have each of my 25 students represent 240 million people and then spread out to assigned continents on the global map that is painted on our school's playground. I then distribute 25 "treats" (usually cookies) according to the distribution of the world's wealth; the continents of Europe and North America get nearly two-thirds of the wealth, or 17 of the 25 cookies. At times this leads to considerable dissent and even cookie robbery, but also to an emotional learning experience that begins to reveal aspects of the great disparities in the distribution of wealth around the world.

Afterwards, I have students write and reflect on this activity. They invariably express disbelief and outrage. As one student put it: "How come

Asia has so many people and so few cookies, I mean resources?" Often the students representing North America and Europe refuse to share their treats, which other students see as the highest form of selfishness. I then ask, "What would it mean in the real world for North America and Europe to share?"

I also want to show children that even within a country, wealth is not evenly divided. To do so, I use the "Ten Chairs of Inequality" simulation from the group United for a Fair Economy (see p. 115). In this exercise, the U.S. population is divided into tenths and represented by 10 students. The wealth in the United States is represented by 10 chairs in the front of the classroom. We start off with each of the 10 students sitting on one chair — how the country would be if wealth were evenly distributed. I then explain that, according to U.S. government statistics, a mere 10% of the population (represented by one person) occupied seven chairs as of 1998.

This activity elicits considerable conversation. I draw connections to earlier activities on the world distribution of resources, sweatshops, and child labor. This helps students realize that the key isn't just disparities in wealth between different countries, but disparities within countries as well, in particular the United States. By recognizing that great divisions of wealth exist both within our country and throughout the world, students begin to see that problems can have common roots, thus further nourishing the seeds of solidarity. They can begin to see that the problem is not so much a division of wealth and power between countries as it is a division of wealth and power between social classes. The wealthy of, say, Brazil, have more economic interests in common with the wealthy of the United States than they do with the majority of people in their own country.

The second way I deepen the world distribution of wealth activity is to have students read clippings from mainstream and alternative media about global issues. I duplicate appropriate articles for us to read together and for students to keep in their 3-ring binders. These include articles on factories moving from Milwaukee to Mexico in search of cheaper labor, such as Johnson Controls; about religious activists protesting sweatshop-produced clothing; and on demonstrations against the World

> If we are not careful, we can easily paint such a bleak picture of the world's problems that all appears hopeless.

Trade Organization. A business page newspaper article as simple as "Shoe Factory to Move 250 Jobs to Mexico" can be very enlightening in the context of the broader study of some of these issues. Students are quick to pick up the direct effect such a runaway factory has on the lives of people in our local community. "They're moving there to make a sweatshop, just like in the video we saw!" exclaims one student. "And people here are going to lose their jobs." Seeds of solidarity continue to germinate.

My students draw on their own families' experiences as well. Sometimes when we talk about sweatshops the students describe conditions of some of the places that their family members work. One year when workers from a nearby factory were on strike, a group of my students went out with a teacher assistant and interviewed the striking workers (the company spokesperson refused to meet with them). In the conversation that followed, one of my students announced to the class that what the workers were currently earning was more than her mother received at a different job. "Maybe my mom needs to organize a union too," she concluded.

NUANCING EVERYTHING

Things always seem more simple than they really are. Even something as seemingly clear-cut as child labor is not what it may first appear to be. I was reminded of this recently when I discussed writing dialogue poems with my class and gave child labor as one possible topic. Someone suggested writing a dialogue poem between a child worker and a child student, when ten-year-old Terrance raised a concern. He said that he worked every day after school at the local candy store but that it wasn't child labor.

"How long do you work each day?" I asked.

"Three hours and I get paid $5 an hour."

"That's fifteen dollars a day!" a student called out, evoking a chorus of "ahas" from the rest.

"I know," said Terrance with a wide grin. "Today is pay day!"

Momentarily at a loss for words, I asked my class if they thought this was a case of child labor. "No!" was the adamant answer. I played devil's advocate and argued that it must be. "Terrance is ten years old and by law is a child."

"He gets paid good!" was one response.

At that point another girl in the class

announced that she worked too, but she didn't get paid at all, but it was still not child labor. "I work for my family," she explained. "What I do is for all of us and I like doing it."

The conversation continued covering considerable territory ranging from discussion of weekly allowance to the barbarities of child labor in certain parts of the world. I couldn't get them to budge on considering Terrance a child laborer. So I challenged them to define child labor. Together they came up with this:

> Child labor is when children are forced to work because they don't have any choice. Sometimes children get beaten. Most times they don't get paid much money. Sometimes kids get hurt with the materials or tools they are using. Sometimes kids work for so long they fall asleep.

I still wasn't satisfied. I challenged them to distinguish between that and when they work. They added to their definition:

> Sometimes we work but we don't say it's child labor because we are not forced, we don't get beaten, we're paid pretty good wages, we don't work for long hours, we can go to school even though we work, our parents also work and we are helping our family.

While I wasn't completely satisfied with how the students defined child labor, I realized by the end of the conversation that their grasp of problems with children working and sweatshops in general was pretty good. (See "Rethinking Child Labor," p. 194.)

AVENUES FOR ACTION

A big dilemma for any teacher who encourages students to examine injustice is that it can tend to engender hopelessness and cynicism. If we are not careful, we can easily paint such a bleak picture of the world's problems that all appears hopeless. I have encountered that more than once in my classroom.

"What can we do?" is a common question students ask soon into our study. "We can't do anything!" is almost as common a retort.

I acknowledge the sense of frustration, but I then throw the question back to students: "What do you think we can do?"

Responses vary. Many suggest writing letters to the president. Others suggest boycotting certain companies or holding a generic "protest." Still others suggest writing to the newspaper. By far the most typical response is to suggest that we all give money or hold a food or clothing drive. (Having worked at schools with high rates of poverty, it never ceases to amaze me how generous even the poorest children can be.) Our student council of third through fifth graders sponsors a UNICEF fund drive during Halloween. It's a start and students are generally enthusiastic.

I try to add a critical concern to this type of fundraising. On the one hand, I think the work of

"The third world war has already started. It is a silent war. Not, for that reason, any less sinister. This war is tearing down Brazil, Latin America, and practically all the Third World. Instead of soldiers dying, there are children. It is a war over the Third World debt, one which has as its main weapon, interest, a weapon more deadly than the atom bomb, more shattering than a laser beam."

—Luis Inacio Lula da Silva,
Head of Brazil's Workers' Party

UNICEF is helpful. On the other hand, I encourage students to recognize the scope of the problem, and the limitations of doing only this kind of people-to-people aid. The total amount raised throughout the country by UNICEF in one year, for example, ($90 million) is minuscule compared to the task at hand. Perhaps more importantly, the fundraising strategy suggests to students that additional money would solve problems which arise more from deep inequalities of power than they do from a simple absence of funds.

Still, it can be an enlightening exercise to compare various budgets. For example, the U.S. spends about $300 billion on its military budget, while the 1999 U.N. Human Development Report estimates that the additional cost of achieving and maintaining universal access to basic education for all, basic health care for all, reproductive health care for all women, adequate food for all, and clean water and safe sewers for all is roughly $40 billion a year. But, as mentioned, underlying these numbers is the issue of power relations, something that UNICEF strategy doesn't deal with. These deeper global issues — such as the fact that rich nations and organizations such as the International Monetary Fund force poor countries to cut back social programs and promote export crop/free trade zone strategies — need to be addressed as well, even in a fifth-grade classroom.

Interestingly, during some of the discussions of what can be done about these problems, some children are fearful. "If we work against child labor we might get killed like Iqbal Masih," a student recently said. I explain that Iqbal was in a situation much different than we are: He was a child worker organizing other child workers in Pakistan and had become a significant threat to the carpet factory owners (see p. 206). This understanding shows that students can grasp the seriousness of the struggle. One of my stu-

A student puts the finishing touches on a social studies project.

dents was so moved by the story of Iqbal Masih that she wrote: "Iqbal Masih risks his life.... I would do the same thing because I want freedom and if it's my life then I would give my life for the world."

I like to use the example of Craig Kielburger from Canada. (See p. 325) At age 12 he was so moved by a newspaper article about Iqbal Masih's death that he took direct action. First he did research to find out what was really going on — which eventually led him to Pakistan to personally investigate child labor. He confronted the Canadian Prime Minister, who happened to be visiting Pakistan at the same time. Later Craig and his friends set up an organization called Free The Children (www.freethechildren.org). Upon hearing this story, my students quickly point out that their parents couldn't afford a trip to Pakistan. But I ask: "How else might we act in solidarity with people around the world in ways that might not require so many resources?"

Children suggest writing letters; buying things made in places that don't use sweatshops; educating young children about the issue through our writings, petitions, and poetry; and setting up their own organizations.

One year students were so interested in pursuing these issues that they asked to set up what became the "No Child Labor Club," which ultimately included third, fourth, and fifth graders. The club did additional research, made posters, circulated a petition, and eventually participated in a local march sponsored by labor organizations against NAFTA and sweatshops. A couple of my students spoke at the rally, which started at our school and marched to a nearby factory that had moved its operations to Mexico. Even though my students focused almost exclusively on the issue of child labor, they were among the most warmly received speakers.

Keshia Hernandez, a fifth-grade student at the time, told the crowd of about 150 people that she hated child labor. "I will spread my feelings around the world," she promised. "Kids should stand up and be courageous like Joan of Arc." She described what was bad with child labor and concluded: "Iqbal Masih was one of the millions of kids that was in child labor, but he was strong and brave. He fought for justice for kids to get out of bondage. But the rug merchants in Pakistan found Iqbal and killed him. Let's remember Iqbal Masih and stop child labor."

Keshia had heard the story about my experience in Egypt with the empty soda cans. How much of it she remembered, I don't know. We can never answer the existential question of why some children are born to lives of privation while others are born to comfort. However, elementary students can and should begin to wrestle with questions like "What causes such inequality and unfairness in the world?" and "What can we do to make it a more just place?" Through such questioning, I hope the seeds of solidarity will take hold and begin to flourish. ∎

Bob Peterson (repmilw@aol.com) teaches fifth grade at La Escuela Fratney in Milwaukee, Wisconsin and is a Rethinking Schools editor.

"Charity consoles but does not question. 'When I give food to the poor, they call me a saint,' said Brazilian bishop Helder Camara. 'And when I ask why they have no food, they call me a communist.'

Unlike solidarity, which is horizontal and takes place between equals, charity is top-down, humiliating those who receive it and never challenging the implicit power relations. In the best of cases, there will be justice someday, high in heaven. Here on earth, charity doesn't worry injustice, it just tries to hide it."

—Eduardo Galeano,
Upside Down: A Primer for the Looking-Glass World, New York: Metropolitan Books, 2000. pp. 311-312.

Rethinking Development

Economic "Development" Doesn't Alleviate Poverty, It Creates It

BY TEDDY GOLDSMITH

Economic development, in spite of its devastating effects on societies and the environment, remains the overriding goal of international agencies, national governments, and the transnational corporations that are of course its main promoters and beneficiaries.

This is justified on the grounds that only development, and of course the global free trade that fuels it today, can eradicate poverty. Hardly anyone in a position of authority today seems willing to question this thesis, even though it is backed by neither any empirical nor any serious theoretical evidence.

Consider for a start that since shortly after World War II, when world trade and economic development really got under way, the former has increased by 19 times and the latter by no less than six times — an unprecedented performance. If these processes really provide the answer to world poverty, then it should by now have been reduced to little more than a faint memory of our barbaric and underdeveloped past.

However, the opposite is true. In Indonesia poverty increased by 50% between 1997 and 2001. In South Korea it doubled during that same period; in Russia, it rose from 2.9% to 32.7% between 1966 and 1998 alone.

Much the same thing has happened throughout South America, as well as the Caribbean. Poverty has also increased in the rich industrial world, where 37 million people are now unemployed, and 100 million are homeless. To reasonable people, these facts should be enough to discredit the dogma that development eradicates poverty. But for the promoters of development, it merely indicates that development has not proceeded fast enough.

We have been trained to believe that all preindustrial people who lived in non-money economies were poor — but that is not true.

Early travelers always noted how healthy and well fed were the traditional people whom they visited.

Thus Mungo Park, in his *Travels in Africa*, tells us that the Gambia River abounds with fish and that nature "with a liberal hand" has bestowed on the inhabitants of the area "the blessings of fertility and abundance." Poncet and Brevedent, two 18th-century French travelers, noted that the Gezira area of the Sudan, now occupied by eroded cotton fields, was once covered in forests and "fruitful and well-cultivated plains," and that it was called God's Country (*Belad-Allah*) "by reason of its great plenty."

Sir George Grey, who was Governor General of New Zealand in the early part of the 19th century, spent time among tribal peoples and insisted that he always found the greatest abundance in their huts.

However, today's poverty is as nothing compared to what it will be, as development enters its final stage in a global economy that is controlled by uncompromising transnational corporations.

Consider, for instance, that in accordance with WTO regulations (see Chapter 3, p.

WHY DO YOU ENCOURAGE US DEVELOPING COUNTRIES TO EXPORT FOOD WHILE WE, THE POOR STARVE?

EFFICIENCY!! JUST THINK OF THE WORLD AS A GIANT GLOBAL SUPERMARKET! THE FOREIGN...

MULTINATIONALS ARE PRODUCERS OF THE GOODS, THE FOREIGN COUNTRIES ITS CONSUMERS!!

BUT WHAT ABOUT WE THE POOR HERE, WHAT ARE WE IN THE GLOBAL SUPER MARKET?

YOU KNOW THE PEOPLE WHO CARRY GROCERIES FROM THE STORE TO THE PEOPLES CARS?...

Christian

61), markets throughout the world are being systematically opened up to highly subsidized U.S. food products. It has already begun in India with devastating results.

There are somewhere between 2 and 3 billion small farmers in India, China, Indonesia, Thailand, and other parts of South and Southeast Asia, where the average farm size is only a few acres. Few are likely to survive the opening up of their markets — few, too, of the artisans, small shopkeepers, and street vendors who depend entirely on the farming community. Most will be forced to seek refuge in the slums of the nearest conurbations and, without land on which to grow their food, without jobs, and without any unemployment benefits, they will be reduced to a state of destitution.

Plus, in accordance with the WTO's General Agreement on Trade in Services (GATS), just about all government services would be included. This means that services would now all be taken over by unaccountable corporations who would charge the maximum price that they could get away with — creating an unprecedented number of poor people who would thus be deprived access to the basic requirements of life.

But the overriding contribution of economic development to the growth of world poverty must be the generation of ever greater amounts of the greenhouse gases that cause global warming. Indeed, if we do not rapidly put this process into reverse, much of our planet will soon be largely uninhabitable with ever worsening heat waves, floods, droughts, storms, and half-starved refugees across the surface of our planet. To combat global warming means putting many development processes into reverse, and this is irreconcilable with everything we have been taught to believe in. ■

Teddy Goldsmith is founder of The Ecologist *magazine, from which this article was excerpted (Vol. 31, #6, July/August 2001).*

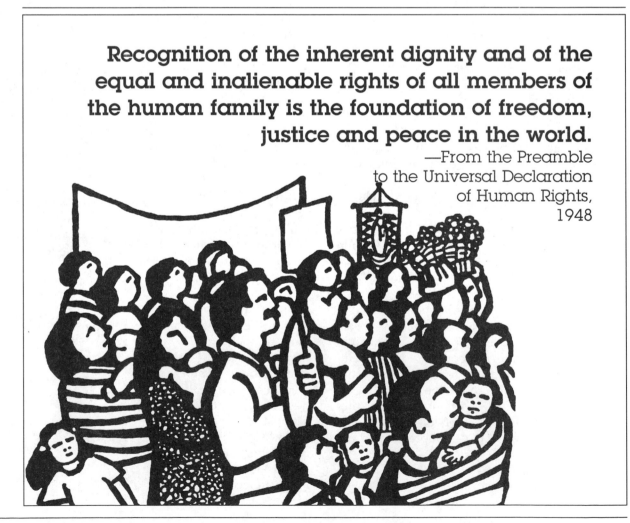

Recognition of the inherent dignity and of the equal and inalienable rights of all members of the human family is the foundation of freedom, justice and peace in the world.

—From the Preamble to the Universal Declaration of Human Rights, 1948

CHAPTER TWO
Legacy of Inequality: Colonial Roots

Contribution to Our Museum

BY MARGE PIERCY

I cannot worship ancestors.
All the tall ruffled ghosts
kept servants who pressed those linen shirts,
who murmur still in the carved and fitted stone
the life that was stolen from them.

In each cut diamond is hardened the anguish
carbonized of choking miners.
Each ruby bleeds the buried cries
of women who bloated with hunger after they harvested.
Each opal secretes the milky grief
of babies bombed sedately by computer
or spitted on bayonets in the Indian wars.

The gentry dance at the Diamond Ball at the Plaza
charitably, on behalf of Third World education.
In the gutter the dead leaves scuttle,
the hungry rustle on the wind blowing
up from Bolivia, which the oil men own.

Always in the tidy fiefdoms of history taught
Louis on the guillotine is weighed in chapters
while fifty thousand peasants who starved
are penned in a textual note.
My folks were serfs, miners, factory women.
Their bent shoulders never bore the brocades in those cases.
They did not embroider the gossip at Versailles.
They were not invited to hunt with the czarina.
How can I love Mount Vernon
with its green alleys and its river perspective
and its slave quarters?
When the ghosts of Susan B. Anthony and Mother Jones,
of Harriet Tubman and Tecumseh and August Spies
dance on our small smokes as we picnic on the lawn,
we will preserve the slave quarters tenderly
because there are no more ghettos, no wage-slaves
and no soft domestic slavery bounded by rape.

The past leads to us if we force it to.
Otherwise it contains us
in its asylum with no gates.
We make history or it
makes us.

From Living in the Open, *by Marge Piercy. New York: Knopf, 1976.*

Page 31 image: Dwellers of a shanty town in Buenos Aires, Argentina live in the shadows of luxury office buildings. Photo by Associated Press

Members of Hong Kong's Legislative Council pose in front of Government House, the colonial governor's residence, in 1897. Whites held at least some seats on the council until 1995.

INTRODUCTION

Legacy of Inequality: Colonial Roots

As we look at today's world, we can make the mistake of thinking that the global division of poor countries and rich countries, powerful and powerless, has always been with us. To begin to grasp the causes of this inequality, we need to travel back at least as far as Columbus, to the origins of European colonialism. As Marge Piercy writes in her poem, "Contribution to Our Museum" (see opposite), "The past leads to us if we force it to." History matters.

We open this chapter with quotes from eyewitness observers who describe the Brazil of the early 1500s as "a lush land" of strong, well-fed people existing "on a succulent diet of exotic fruits, herbs, game, and an infinity of fish" — a land that must be "near the terrestrial paradise." Not quite 500 years later, eyewitnesses describe the same territory as polluted and malnourished — "one of the poorest areas in the world."

Why this change? Sandwiched in between these contrasting social portraits is a story of invasion and colonialism — one that differs depending on the society, but which, from Kenya to India to Brazil, shares certain features.

This chapter includes readings and activities to acquaint students with some of the dynamics of European colonialism. Part of rethinking globalization entails searching for continuities that connect past to present. What connections can students find, for example, between the cash crop demands of European colonialists and the "structural adjustment" demands of the International Monetary Fund and the World Bank? Students may find that, in important respects, globalization is a new name for an old game. ■

— *The editors*

COLONIALISM: BEFORE AND AFTER

BEFORE COLONIALISM AND "DEVELOPMENT" IN BRAZIL, from diaries and letters of Europeans there for the first time:

"The lush land belongs to all, just like the sun and water. The people live in a golden age and do not surround themselves with ditches, walls, or hedges."

Pietro Martire d'Anghiera, 1500

"The people are stronger and better fed than we are. They are well cared for and very clean and in this way they seem to me rather like birds. Their bodies are so plump and so beautiful that they could not be more so."

Pero Vaz Caminha in a letter to Portuguese King Manoel I, 1500

"They exist on a succulent diet of exotic fruits, herbs, game and an infinity of fish: crabs, oysters, lobsters, crayfish, and many other things which the sea produces. This is a delightful land with brightly colored birds, evergreen trees that yield the sweetest aromatic perfumes, and an infinite variety of fruit. I fancied myself to be near the terrestrial paradise."

Amerigo Vespucci in a letter to Prince de Medici, 1503

AFTER COLONIALISM AND "DEVELOPMENT" IN BRAZIL, adapted from the early 1990s research of Nancy Scheper-Hughes:

Today the Northeast region of Brazil is one of the poorest areas in the world. Scenes of hunger, disease, and child death are commonplace. Two-thirds of all rural children suffer stunted growth from inadequate food. Hunger has made the people lean, nervous, and desperate. The Brazilian press refers to the region as "The Valley of Death." The country's rivers are "spoiled, brackish, salty, putrid and contaminated by pollutants." Their fish are gone. Children search through piles of garbage for food. Every four minutes two children less than a year old die in Brazil from starvation and disease.

What happened? How did Brazil change from a "terrestrial paradise" to the "valley of death"?

From Stephanie Kempf, Finding Solutions to Hunger. *New York: World Hunger Year, 1997.*

COLONIALISM: The Building Blocks

1 Grabbing the Cash
— looting Asia

The colonies of Asia—India, Malaya (now Malaysia), the Dutch East Indies (now Indonesia), Ceylon (now Sri Lanka), the Philippines—were rich in natural resources. But the money from their crops and mines and forests wasn't spent in developing industries for the countries themselves. The money sailed off to Europe.

What do you mean?

Well, for instance, from 1850 to 1872, the Dutch East Indies (now Indonesia) contributed one-third of the total budget of Holland. The Dutch were able to reduce their national debt, and this money also paid for the building of the Dutch state railways.

Think about it:
If Asian money had been used to develop Asia rather than Europe, what differences might there be today?

2 The Raw Deal
— exporting crops to Europe

So what was so bad about growing a few crops to send to Europe? The people got paid, didn't they?

Well, for one thing, if you had just enough land for your family, and suddenly you were told that you had to grow crops to send to Europe, you'd probably find yourself getting pretty hungry! Plus the prices were set very low, and most of the money went to pay the heavy European taxes. So there wasn't enough money to buy food.
But that's not all. The Europeans organized their colonies so that each one grew just two or three different crops. India grew jute, cotton and tea. Ceylon grew tea. Malaya grew rubber.

Think about it:
Having only one or two export crops might cause problems later on.
What might those be?

3 The Craft Crash
— de-skilling Asia

The division of labour idea also affected the craftspeople and manufacturers of Asia. European countries went to great lenths to ensure that Asians would produce raw materials (to be sold at low prices to the mother country), and buy manufactured products (at high prices) from the mother country. Yet in Asia there were many expert weavers, potters, leatherworkers and other craftspeople. The colonialists discouraged these businesses through taxation, and made sure that the new machinery available in Europe wasn't brought to Asia.

DUTCH CLOTH FOR SALE

OUT OF BUSINESS

Think about it:
How might this attack on Asian craftspeople affect Asia's development?

Adapted from the booklet *Colonialism in Asia, a Critical Look*, by Susan Gage and Don McNair. For details and a complete citation see Resources, page 375.

4 Drawing the Line
— *problems of addition and division*

Often, when the colonialists created a colony, people with little in common were chucked together, or those with a lot in common had a line drawn between them. Indonesia, for instance, is a collection of all the different people — some of them Asian, some Melanesian — whose countries were taken over by the Dutch in the region.

To make things worse, many of the colonizers came up with a great idea for running colonies.

Divide and rule! If we encourage distrust between the different groups, they won't rise up and throw us Europeans out!

In the Dutch East Indies (Indonesia), for example, the Ambonese people were used as soldiers to suppress the other Indonesian people. When Indonesia became independent, the Ambonese were so hated by the rest of the country that most of them went to Holland as refugees.

Think about it:
What problems might the artificial colonial boundaries cause later?

Nearly all our major problems today have grown up during British rule and as a direct result of British policy. . . .
—Jawaharlal Nehru, later India's first prime minister, written from prison where he was serving his 9th term for protesting British rule, 1944

5 Holding up Hierachies

The European colonizers had another problem:

There are so few of us, and so many of them! How are we going to keep all these Asians under control?

OUR RESOURCEFUL COLONIAL ADMINSTRATOR DISCOVERS THE ANSWER!

My dear chap, we'll help you stay in power as long as you keep all these peasants under control.

"Ah, now I can do what I want, and the English will support me!"

Think about it:
The colonialists used military might to keep in power leaders who were not chosen by the people. What problems might this cause after these countries became independent?

6 West is Best

In education, culture, agriculture, development, and economics, the colonialists pushed thier own idea about the world:

WEST IS BEST!

". . . colonialism tended not only to deprive a society of its freedom and its wealth, but of its very character, leaving its people intellectually and morally disoriented . . . "
— *D.K. Fieldhouse,* **Colonialism** *1870-1945*

Think about it:
In schools and universities, in literature and newspapers, and in countless other ways, Europeans insisted that Europe was the model of goodness.
How might this "cultural colonialism" affect Asia even today?

Burning Books and Destroying Peoples

How the World Became Divided Between "Rich" and "Poor" Countries

BY BOB PETERSON

Imagine going on a trip to a new place, one that you and your friends have never been to before. When you get there it seems strange: different types of plants and animals, and fruits that you've never tasted, but which are delicious. The people you meet appear friendly, but dress differently and speak a language you don't understand. In the middle of their large city you find a building that holds thousands of books — proof that these people have a history of writing and education.

Needless to say, you can't read their books. So what do you do?

You burn all of their books, every single one that you can find.

While this story might sound ridiculous, that is exactly what happened when the Spanish colonialists met the Mayan people in what is now Central America.

In 1562 Fray Diego de Landa ordered that all Mayan books be collected and burned. Landa wrote, "We found a large number of books and they contained nothing in which there was not to be seen superstition and lies of the devil, so we burned them all, which they [the Mayas] regretted to an amazing degree and which caused them much affliction." Not only the Mayas but also the Totonac, Mixtec, and other Indians of "high culture" had books. They were all burned. (See "1562: Conquistadores Destroy Native Libraries," p. 43)

The mass book burnings deprived all of us of the Mayan people's written history, and most of their written knowledge about mathematics and astronomy, two areas of science which they studied a great deal. Only three books remain, by mistake, and they are now in museums.

This is but one consequence of what colonialism meant for those who were colonized — the destruction of important parts of their cultures and the loss of their histories.

PORTUGAL ATTACKS AFRICA

Colonialism is a system of control by a country over an area or people outside its borders. Modern colonialism started in the late 1400s, when those in power in a few European countries decided that they might become richer and more powerful by trading goods with people in other parts of the world. The rich people of Portugal, in an attempt to expand their country's trade with India and China, sent sailors on boats south along the Atlantic coast of Africa and then north into the Indian Ocean. The Portuguese traders found cities and peoples with a high level of education and culture. However, there was a problem: While the people of east Africa and India had lots of items like spices, porcelain, and ivory that the Portuguese wanted, the Portuguese didn't have much that the Africans and Asians wanted

Haitian revolutionary Toussaint L'Ouverture.

besides metal pots and pans — and guns (which the Portuguese weren't eager to supply to others).

The Portuguese solved this problem on future voyages. They took well-armed ships and soldiers and forced the Africans and Asians to "trade" with them. A Portuguese ship would arrive on the east coast of Africa armed with cannons, guns, and soldiers. The soldiers would get off and circle the port city. The Africans who resisted the soldiers were murdered. The soldiers broke into houses and palaces, stealing all that was valuable. The Africans fled in panic, unable to resist the better-equipped European soldiers. The Portuguese filled their ships with gold, ivory, and other valuables. They then bombarded the cities with their cannons and burned them to the ground. In just a few years the splendid commercial cities along the coast were in ruins. The Portuguese also attacked Islamic merchant ships that had been trading between east Africa and Asia — bombarding the ships and taking the goods. The Portuguese eventually controlled almost all the ocean-based trading between Europe, Africa, and Asia. They set up trading enclaves and forts along the coast which acted as collection points for the gold, ivory, and slaves brought from the interior. This wealth flowed into Europe.

SPAIN ATTACKS THE AMERICAS

This was only the beginning. In the Americas, the Spanish became the main colonizers. They claimed lands that were inhabited by tens of millions of Native peoples and forced those people into virtual slavery. Spaniards took vast quantities of gold and silver from the Americas, which enriched small numbers of people in Europe. According to the Mexican indigenous leader Cuaicaipuro Cuautémoc, official receipts from Europe show that between 1503 and 1660, 185,000 kilos of gold and 16,000,000 kilos of silver were shipped from America (see p. 93). The Native people resisted and were almost wiped out by the superior weapons of the Europeans, as well as the diseases carried by the colonists. England, France, and Holland sent their own ships around the world in order to claim land and peoples as their own.

The Europeans wanted colonies for several reasons. They wanted raw materials from these places — not only gold and silver but spices, cotton, cocoa, palm oil, timber, and rubber. They also wanted the Native peoples to work for them for hardly any pay at all, so that the products the Native people made could be taken by the Europeans. In the West Indies the main product was sugar; other areas produced tea, coffee, cocoa, timber, tobacco, and cotton.

AFRICANS STOLEN

The European colonizers had problems finding people to work their mines and plantations in the Americas. In part this was because so many Native peoples in the Americas died as a result of the initial arrival of the Europeans. Also, those who survived did not want to work as slaves. They resisted and oftentimes were able to escape, because they knew the land better than the Europeans.

The European colonists tried to "solve" this problem by stealing millions of people from Africa. They brought them in chains, stacked in holds of ships like sacks of flour, without enough food or water. The 3,000-mile voyage across the Atlantic, which typically took five or six weeks, was grueling and deadly. Millions died in what became know as the Middle Passage.

Slavery devastated western Africa. Millions of people, particularly youths and young adults, were taken away or died resisting. Some Africans helped the European slave traders, increasing conflict between Africans themselves. Western Africa became so engulfed in the slave trade that little attention or resources were put toward improving farming or people's lives.

Haitian poet René Depestre described this in his poem "Black Ore" which reads in part:

When all of a sudden the stream of Indian sweat was dried up by the sun

When the gold-fever drained out the final drop of Indian blood in the marketplace

And every last Indian vanished from around the mines

It was time to look to Africa's river of muscle

For a changing of the guard of misery

And so began the rush to that rich and limitless

Storehouse of black flesh

And so began the breathless dash

To the noonday splendor of the black-skinned body

Then all the earth rang out with the clatter of the picks

Digging deep in the thick black ore.

RESISTANCE TO OPPRESSION

The history of colonialism is full of stories of the horrible treatment of those who were colonized. It is also full of stories of resistance, when people fought back against the Europeans. For example, it took the Spaniards years of war to wipe out Native resistance in Peru, doing so only after suppressing a major revolt involving more than 100,000 people led by Tupac Amaru II in 1781-82. The Araucanian Indians of Chile weren't defeated until the late 1890s, after hundreds of years of battle. Native American armed resistance in what is now the United States continued up through the late 1890s with the Massacre of Wounded Knee. Colonialists met similar resistance throughout Asia and Africa.

But the results were more or less the same throughout the world. Resistance was crushed by the more militarily advanced European armies and navies. As a result, some Native peoples of Africa, Asia, and the Americas were completely wiped out. The wealth of those continents was sent back to Europe, which in turn made Europe all the more able to continue its domination of the world.

Associated Press

The Duchess of Kent addresses Parliament House in Ghana in 1957, shortly after Ghana ceased being a British colony.

TYPES OF COLONIALISM

Not all colonialism was the same. Some colonies were established by the migration of settlers from the colonizing country, as in the British colonies in North America, Australia, and New Zealand. Some colonies were founded by religious groups fleeing persecution, such as the Pilgrims who settled in what is now Massachusetts. Other colonies were organized by groups of merchants or businessmen, such as the British, Dutch, and French East India Companies.

In North America most colonialism was of the settler variety, and the Europeans who moved to North America in the 13 colonies soon found themselves in disagreement with the "mother" country of England. The resulting American Revolution of 1776 led to a temporary decline in the power of England. In a very different kind of revolution, the slaves of Haiti, led by Toussaint L'Ouverture, rebelled and kicked out the French in 1804; the Mexicans, led by Miguel Hidalgo, and much of Latin America, led by Simón Bolivar, kicked out the Spaniards by 1825. Spain continued to hold Cuba and the Philippines until 1898, but otherwise retired from its role as a colonial power. England and other European nations, meanwhile, entered a new colonial era in the 19th century, looking to get rich off of other parts of the world.

SECOND COLONIAL PERIOD

The riches produced by colonialism helped stimulate the Industrial Revolution of the 19th century. This tremendous increase in the use of machines greatly strengthened the military power of European countries, allowing them to extend their rule over areas of Asia and Africa. In parts of Asia and Africa where before there had been only European commercial posts, European nations sent troops along with commercial agents, government officials, and Christian missionaries. The Europeans forced these areas to become markets for their industrial products and suppliers of raw materials.

By mid-century the British controlled all of India, which was ruled by a British viceroy; the Dutch assumed similar control over Indonesia, then known as the Netherlands East Indies; and the French seized Indochina. The entire continent of Africa, except for Ethiopia and Liberia, was divided up among the European powers after the Conference of Berlin in 1885. The British had almost all of eastern and southern Africa as well as large portions in the west; the French took over the areas north and south of the Sahara Desert; Germany took territories on the Atlantic coast and on the Indian Ocean; Portugal extended its coastal enclaves of Angola and Mozambique toward the interior; and Belgium obtained the Congo. One colonialist referred to the continent that was being so greedily sliced up as "this magnificent African cake." One young sea captain, later a famous author, Joseph Conrad, found a situation which he called "the vilest scramble for loot that ever disfigured the history of human conscience."

Historian W. E. B. DuBois describes the pillage of Central Africa because of the profiteers set on supplying the world with ivory for billiard balls and piano keys:

> Thousands of miles of fertile country were turned into wilderness and ruin, Hundreds of thousands of elephants were slain and thousands of human beings. It has been estimated that not more than one in five of the captives bearing ivory ever reached the ocean. Starved and weakened by disease and the strain of marching, they line the long paths with their dead.

Ivory was exported by the ton. As early as 1788, London was importing more than 100 tons of ivory a year. This continued for a century: 514 tons were imported in 1884. This meant the death of 75,000 elephants a year and, as DuBois noted, thousands of people. Henry M. Stanley wrote in 1891: "Every tusk, piece, and scrap.... had been steeped and dyed in blood. Every

"A single shelf of a good European library was worth the whole native literature of India.... Neither as a language of the law, nor as a language of religion has the Sanskrit any particular claim to our engagement.... We must do our best to form a class of persons, Indian in blood and color but English in taste, in opinions, in morals and in intellect."

Lord Macaulay, introducing the India Education Act in the British Parliament

pound weight has cost the life of a man, woman or child, for every five pounds a hut has been burned, for every two tusks a whole village has been destroyed.... It is simply incredible that because ivory is required... populations, tribes, and nations should be utterly destroyed."

FORCED LABOR AND CASH CROPS

The European colonialists forced Africans to produce cash crops no matter how low the prices were. They did this mainly by taxing people. Africans could get money to pay taxes only if they grew the "cash" crops the Europeans wanted. In some cases colonial powers went to even greater extremes. According to Guyanese writer Walter Rodney, French officials banned the Mandaja people (now part of Congo Brassaville) from hunting, so they would engage solely in cotton cultivation.

Often the British and French colonial governments would use forced labor to get work done at no cost to the Europeans. They demanded that Africans "give" their labor to colonial officials for a certain number of days. According to Rodney "a great deal of this forced labor went into the construction of roads, railways, and ports to provide the infrastructure for private capitalist investment and to facilitate the export of cash crops."

> One colonialist referred to the continent that was being so greedily sliced up as "this magnificent African cake."

Rodney describes the impact of these policies on Africans:

> Taking only one example from the British colony of Sierra Leone, one finds that the railway which started at the end of the 19th century required forced labor from thousands of peasants driven from their villages. The hard work and appalling conditions led to the death of a large number of those engaged in the work on the railway.

The French accomplished the same using different tactics. They forced Africans to join the French army and then used them as unpaid laborers. Rodney estimates that in one railroad project lasting 12 years, 25% of the workers died annually from starvation and disease — thousands of Africans.

Among the most barbaric of all the colonial powers were the Belgians under King Leopold II. According to historian Adam Hochschild, writing in *King Leopold's Ghost*, an estimated 5 to 8 million people were killed in the Belgian colonialists' attempt to force the people of the Congo to supply rubber for Europe's needs.

Just as in earlier periods of colonialism, the European powers wanted the colonies only to provide raw materials, low-paid workers, and open markets so that European products could be bought. The English, for example, took fine cotton from India and Egypt but banned the Indians and Egyptians from processing the cotton into finished clothing. Instead Indians and Egyptians had to buy imported (and more expensive) clothing made in England. Thus Indian artisans who made fine textiles were forced out of business, and India became poorer.

In this way the economies of many countries of Asia, Africa, and Latin America were stunted. Instead of "developing," they were actually "underdeveloped" by Europeans. Prohibited by European powers from continuing their own cultures based largely on farming, and also prohibited from developing manufacturing, the colonies came to depend heavily on a few crops or minerals, the prices of which went up and down in world markets. These policies led to African economies becoming "monocultures," relying on one agricultural crop or mineral for most of their foreign currency and trade. For example, Gold Coast grew mainly cocoa and Senegal and Gambia grew groundnuts (peanuts).

RESISTANCE CONTINUES

Africans and Asians continued to fight against European domination and were met with barbaric repression. In 1898, for example, British troops massacred 20,000 Sudanese at Obudrman, near Khartoum. The "Boxer Rebellion" in 1900 by the Chinese against European colonizers was another such example. The Chinese were particularly angered because the British were trying to get their people addicted to opium, a harmful drug, so that they could profit and control a vast part of Asia. The British successfully used military force against the Chinese so that opium could be unloaded in Chinese ports. This led to widespread opium addiction in parts of China.

The United States eventually became a colonial power itself. The U.S. military fought its own "colonial" wars early in the nation's history — dozens of wars with the Native peoples throughout the 1700s and 1800s. From 1846 through 1848, the United States fought a war with Mexico, which resulted in the U.S. seizure of one third of Mexico. The United States annexed Hawai'i in 1898, and a short time later defeated Spain in a war, acquiring Puerto Rico, the Philippines, and Guam, as colonies, and control over Cuba. The subsequent U.S. war against Filipino independence fighters was especially horrific. The United States had become a colonial power in its own right.

It wasn't until after World War II (1939-1945) that the countries of Asia and Africa were able to force a weakened Europe into beginning to grant them independence. In some cases it came with huge struggles, such as that of the Indian people, led by Mahatma Gandhi and the Indian National Congress against the British, or that of the Vietnamese people, led by Ho Chi Minh and the Viet Minh against the French.

Even though almost all countries of Africa, Asia, and Latin America are now formally independent and have their own representatives at the United Nations, many of the economic and political relationships that were established during colonialism continue. Because of colonialism, many countries of the Third World still rely on one or two main crops. Most have never fully developed an industrial base. In addition, many of these countries owe lots of money to wealthy nations — that is, they are in debt (see p. 75) and cannot afford to spend money on things their own people need.

When people in more wealthy nations think about helping other people who are hungry and in poverty, it's important to recognize how they got that way. The fact that Spanish colonialists, for example, took tons of gold and silver from the Americas is connected to today's widespread hunger in South America.

Walter Rodney explains this connection when he writes about a well-established European-based organization that sees itself helping Third World people. This organization "called upon the people of Europe to save starving African and Asian children from kwashiorkor [a deadly, protein-deficiency disease] and such ills.... [but] never bothered their consciences by telling them that capitalism and colonialism created the starvation, suffering, and misery of the child in the first place." ■

Bob Peterson (repmilw@aol.com) teaches fifth grade at La Escuela Fratney in Milwaukee, Wisconsin and is a Rethinking Schools editor.

1562: *Conquistadores* Destroy Native Libraries

Fray Diego de Landa throws into the flames, one after the other, the books of the Mayas.

The inquisitor curses Satan, and the fire crackles and devours. Around the incinerator, heretics howl with their heads down. Hung by the feet, flayed with whips, Indians are doused with boiling wax as the fire flares up and the books snap, as if complaining.

Tonight, eight centuries of Mayan literature turn to ashes. On these long sheets of bark paper, signs and images spoke: They told of work done and days spent, of the dreams and the wars of a people born before Christ. With hog-bristle brushes, the knowers of things had painted these illuminated, illuminating books so that the grandchildren's grandchildren should not be blind, should know how to see themselves and see the history of their folk, so they should know the movements of the stars, the frequency of eclipses and the prophecies of the gods and so they could call for rains and good corn harvests.

In the center, the inquisitor burns the books. Around the huge bonfire, he chastises the readers. Meanwhile, the authors, artist-priests dead years or centuries ago, drink chocolate in the fresh shade of the first tree of the world. They are at peace, because they died knowing that memory cannot be burned. Will not what they painted be sung and danced through the times of the times?

When its little paper houses are burned, memory finds refuge in mouths that sing the glories of men and of gods, songs that stay on from people to people and in bodies that dance to the sound of hollow trunks, tortoise shells, and reed flutes.

From Eduardo Galeano, Memory of Fire: Genesis. New York: Pantheon, 1985, p. 137.

"We must find new lands from which we can easily obtain raw materials and at the same time exploit the cheap slave labour that is available from the natives of the colonies. The colonies would also provide a dumping ground for the surplus goods produced in our factories."

—Cecil Rhodes, British colonialist, southern Africa

European colonialism in Africa exploited people as well as resources.

The Coming of the Pink Cheeks

BY CHIEF KABONGO AS TOLD TO RICHARD ST. BARBE BAKER

Before European colonialism, most Africans made their living from the soil. More importantly, traditional Africans considered land to be a sacred part of nature and a part of the tribe. Land was not a commodity that could be bought and sold; it was a gift from God that belonged to everybody, like the air.

After many generations — and sometimes after many centuries — a tribe became identified with a particular area. The land was their "property," belonging not only to the living members but also to the ancestors who had worked the land and to the unborn children who would work the land in the future.

When Europeans came and "bought" land, many misunderstandings developed, for the Africans never meant to "sell" what in their eyes couldn't be sold.

In the following selection, Chief Kabongo, of the Kikuyu tribe of Kenya, describes what happened to his people when the Europeans took control of Kikuyu land. In his lifetime — from the 1870s to the 1950s — Chief Kabongo saw the sharp changes that took

place after the coming of the whites, whom he called the "Pink Cheeks." (Adapted from Leon Clark (Ed.) Through African Eyes, Vol. 1. *New York: CITE Books, 1991.)*

For some years my eldest son had been going to a school kept by some Pink Cheeks only two hours' journey away. These were not the White Fathers, to whom my brother had gone, but were quite different. They wore clothes like the Pink Cheeks who farmed, and many of them were women. They had a medicine house where there were many ill people; there were good medicine-men and good things were done and sick people were made well. Every day my son would go before the sun was high and would come back before the sun set. Then he would eat and fall asleep, too tired to sit around the fire and be told the stories and history of our people and their laws and conduct.

It was in these days that a Pink Cheek man came one day to our Council. He came from far, from where many of these people lived in houses made of stone and where they held their own Council.

He sat in our midst and he told us of the king of the Pink Cheeks, who was a great king and lived in a land over the seas.

"This great king is now your king, " he said. "And this land is all his land, though he has said that you may live on it as you are his people and he is as your father and you are as his sons."

This was strange news. For this land was ours. We had bought our land with cattle in the presence of the Elders and had taken the oath and it was our own. We had no king, we elected our Councils and they made our laws. A strange king could not be our king and our land was our own. We had had no battle, no one had fought us to take away our land as, in the past, had sometimes been. This land we had had from our fathers and our fathers' fathers, who had bought it. How then could it belong to this king?

With patience, our leading Elder tried to tell this to the Pink Cheek and he listened. But at the end he said: "This we know. But in spite of this, what I have told you is a fact. You have now a king — a good and great king who loves his people, and you are among his people. In the town called Nairobi is a council or government that acts for the king. And his laws are your laws ...."

For many moons this thing was much talked of by us. Then, when no more Pink Cheeks came and things went on as they had always been, we spoke no more.

Sometimes we heard of strange happenings, or even saw them ourselves, but for the most part life was still as it had always been. The Iron Snake [railroad], which I had never seen, had come and had carried men on it, not of our people; then a big path was made through the country half a day from our land. It was wide enough for three elephants to walk abreast. And stones were laid on it and beaten flat, so that grain could have been threshed there.

As the years passed and more and more strange things happened, it seems to me that this path or road was a symbol of all change. It was along this road now that came news from other parts; and along it came the new box-on-wheels that made men travel many days' journey in one day and that brought things for the market that the women wanted to have, clothes or beads to wear and pots for cooking. Along this road the young men went when they left to work with the Pink Cheeks and along it too they went when that day came that they traveled to fight in the war over the sea that the Pink Cheeks made against each other.*

It was along this road that many did not come back and some came with no legs, or who could not see. Two of my sons went and only one came back, and he brought only one hand and many strange new ideas and tales. Along the road, too,

World War I.

> **As the years passed and more and more strange things happened, it seems to me that this path or road was a symbol of all change.**

went the trees that men cut down when they made more and more farms. Without trees to give shade the ground was hot and dry and food grew not well.

By the time that my father, Kimani, died and his spirit joined those of our ancestors, our own land was poor too. For even though many of our family had gone away to work for the Pink Cheeks, our numbers had increased and there was now no room for the land to rest and it was tired. The food it grew was poor and there was not enough grown on it for all to eat. Those of our family who worked for the Pink Cheeks sent us food and coins that we could buy food with, for else we could not live.

Little by little, too, the rains fell less. When I was a boy I remember the rains came in plenty twice every year, the little rains and the big rains, and on the hottest days there would be heavy dews, for the trees kept the land cool.

Now it was different; now the little rains had gone and the big rains had become little rains. The big rivers had become little ones and dried up in the hottest time, and I saw this was not good.

Now that my father, Kimani, was dead, I had been chosen Muramati of our *mbari*. I was also now a ceremonial Elder, a member of the Sacrificial Council.

It seemed to me that Ngai was tired of us. He sent so little rain. We must ask him to look upon us again and must sacrifice a ewe to please him.

I spoke of this one evening, and the Elders said it was good to make sacrifice, for the time of rain had long passed. So the day was fixed and I was chosen to be the leader.

Little Kabongo, my eldest grandson, who bore my name according to our custom, sat with us; he spoke then as do the young age group today before their elders, but which when we were young we did not.

"This is good," he said. "For three weeks the Pastor at the Mission School has prayed for rain."

"Which will send rain, do you think, the God of the Pink Cheeks or Ngai?" asked a small boy.

"Neither," announced a young man, son of one of my brothers, who was a schoolteacher. "I have read in books that it is the trees that make the rains come. Now that the trees are cut down there is no rain. In the Sacred Grove on the hills

there is rain."

The small boy was listening, full of wonder.

"And who makes the trees grow? Surely that is God," said my grandson.

"For the Pastor says that God made everything, that God is greater than Ngai."

Such discussions among the young were frequent, and to hear them made me sad. For this new learning seemed to pull this way and that way so that no one knew what was right.

But all this talk did not make more food nor bring us rain.

As there was now so little land and we were so many, the boys as they became men would go away, some to work on farms for the Pink Cheeks, some to a new kind of school-farm for men, where they learned the new customs and also some curious ways; for these grown men were made to play games like little boys, running after balls which they threw. This they did instead of good work.

Munene, one of my younger brothers, had been one of these. He had been away a long time, and when he came back he wore clothes like a Pink Cheek and he came with one of them, in a box-on-wheels, which is called motor-car, along the new road.

The Pink Cheek called a Council together and when all, both Elders and the young men, were assembled and sat round, he spoke. He spoke of Munene; he told us of his learning and of his knowledge of the customs of the Pink Cheeks and of his cleverness at organizing.

"Because of this," he said, "and because he is a wise man, the Government, the Council of Muthungu that meets in Nairobi, have honored him and, in honoring him, are honoring you all."

He paused and looked around at us. Beside him Munene stood smiling.

"He has been appointed Chief of this district and he will be your mouth and our mouth. He will tell us the things that you want to say and he will tell you the things that we want to say to you. He has learned our language and our laws and he will help you to understand and keep them."

We Elders looked at each other. Was this the end of everything that we had known and worked for? What magic had this son of my father made that he who was not yet an Elder should be made leader over us all who were so

> We Elders looked at each other. Was this the end of everything that we had known and worked for?

much older and wiser in the ways of our people? It was as if a thunderbolt had fallen among us.

RULE OF THE PINK CHEEKS

The Pink Cheek went on.

"Your new Chief will collect the tax on huts, and choose the places for the new schools that you will build everywhere, so that your children may be taught to read and write. He will raise the money for that from you all. I have spoken."

When the Pink Cheek had gone there was much talk. We asked Munene to tell us how this had come about and why he was set above the Elders in this way.

"It is because they do not understand our laws and Councils, he told us. "Because I speak their language and because when I went away in their wars I had many medals."

The medals we knew about, for we had seen them. Many had them.

We spoke then of the tax on huts. It was heavy, for some men had many huts. Those men who had gone to work on the farms of the Pink Cheeks sent us money, but this we needed to buy food. More men, therefore, must go.

Munene gave us some good advice. He told that men were wanted in Nairobi to build the new houses made of stone, both for the Pink Cheeks to live in and where they sat to make business and trading. Our men could go there and earn coins and then they could come back when they had plenty.

This was good, for in this way we would pay our tax and no man would be taken by the Pink Cheeks for not paying. So our young men went away down the new road, we were left to grow what food we could, and all was as usual.

It was while these men were still away to make money for our hut tax that 10 of our people came back from the farms where they worked. They were not needed, they said, there was no work for them there. With many others, they had been sent back without money and without food, because there were bad people who troubled the land.

This was the beginning. Along the new road had come big boxes-on-wheels that they called lorries [trucks], in which they had carted logs from the forest. Now these came filled with people. Many had no homes, for their land had gone to the Pink Cheeks. Some had no homes because their land had gone to be mined for gold. We could not let them starve, so we took them on our land.

It was the end of the dry season and there was little food left in the storehouses. Our *mbari* had now grown big, and all these newcomers on our land must eat too. Altogether there were 1,200 people on the 200 acres of land [that had been in our family since my grandfather's father.] There was not enough room to grow all the food.

In the dry season many goats and cattle had died for want of water. The harvest had been thin and there was little left, and there was no money to buy food; the last had gone for our hut tax. I

Cambridge University Library

Ivory traders at Zanzibar in the 1880s, before poaching became illegal.

heard the crying of children and I saw the women weaken in their work. The old men would sit near their huts, too feeble to walk.

Wangari, whose once-strong breasts hung like empty bags and whose eyes were deep in her head, came to me where I sat by my hut.

"Kabongo, son of Kimani," she said, sitting close, "we women are tired; there is no food and the children are hungry; the young men have no stomachs and the old men are withering as dry leaves. You yourself are weak or before this you would have taken counsel with the Elders. Speak now, for our people wait to hear your word."

I was roused. What she said was true. This was no time to sit and wait. We must hold Council.

The Council met again under the Mugomo tree. There were few, for the new laws of the Pink Cheeks had forbidden big meetings. I looked round at my friends and was sad. Their faces were anxious and their skin was loose on their bones. Even Muonji, who always used to joke, had no smile. For each one had been hungry for many days, and each one told the same story. Everywhere there was a shortage of food, for there was no land and all the time people were being sent back from distant parts. There was uneasiness and some of our tribesmen were troubling our people too much because they wanted to drive the Pink Cheeks out of our country. This the Elders told in Council and were uneasy, for we wanted no war with the Pink Cheeks; we only wanted land to grow food.

"We must ask the Council of the Pink Cheeks to lend us some of the land we had lent to them," said one who came from a place where there was land held by the government for future farms and not yet in use.

All agreed that this would be good and for Munene, who as Chief was our spokesman, we made a message to give to the governor. What we told to Munene he made marks with and, when we had finished, he spoke it to us again and it was good.

Munene took our message and he took also a gift of honey and eggs and went away down the long road and left us to wait.

We waited many days, with hope. It was a whole moon before Munene came back. He came to us slowly and sadly, and we knew from his ways that the news was bad.

"They will not give the land," he said. "They say they have no more land for us."

And he told us many things that were not good; he told us of rebellions of some of our people, bad men who took our laws and ceremonies and degraded them; of the Pink Cheek warriors and of some he called Police who did unjust things to our people, who took good men and loyal to the Queen away from their work, and after much useless talk, sent them too to live on this land where there is no food.

So I am sitting before my hut and I wait. For soon the time will come for me to creep away into the forest to die. Day by day my people grow thinner and weaker and the children are hungry; and who am I, an old man, to eat the food that would come to them?

> These good things of the days when we were happy and strong have been taken, and now we have many laws and many clothes and men dispute among themselves and have no love.

As I sit I ponder often on the ancient prophesy of Mogo wa Kebiro. Has the Pink Cheek brought good to my people? Are the new ways he has shown us better than our own ways?

Something has taken away the meaning of our lives; it has taken the full days, the good work in the sunshine, the dancing and the song; it has taken away laughter and the joy of living; the kinship and the love within a family; above all, it has taken from us the wise way of our living in which our lives from birth to death were dedicated to Ngai, supreme of all, and which, with our system of age groups and our Councils, insured for all our people a life of responsibility and goodness. Something has taken away our belief in our Ngai and in the goodness of men. And there is not enough land on which to feed.

These good things of the days when we were happy and strong have been taken, and now we have many laws and many clothes and men dispute among themselves and have no love. There is discontent and argument and violence and hate, and a vying with each other for power, and men seem to care more for disputes about ideas than for the fullness of life where all work and live for all.

The young men are learning new ways, the children make marks which they call writing, but they forget their own language and customs, they know not the laws of their people, and they do not pray to Ngai. They ride fast in motorcars, they work fire-sticks that kill, they make music from a box. But they have no land and no food and they have lost laughter. ■

Song of Lawino: A Lament

BY OKOT P'BITEK, UGANDA

Husband, now you despise me
Now you treat me with spite
And say I have inherited the stupidity of my aunt;
Son of the Chief,
Now you compare me
With the rubbish in the rubbish pit,
You say you no longer want me
Because I am like the things left behind
In the deserted homestead.
You insult me
You laugh at me
You say I do not know the letter A
Because I have not been to school
And I have not been baptized
You compare me with a little dog
A puppy.
…
My husband pours scorn
On Black people,
He behaves like a hen
That eats its own eggs,
A hen that should be imprisoned under a basket.
…
He says Black people are primitive
And their ways are utterly harmful,
Their dances are mortal sins
They are ignorant, poor and diseased!
Ocol says he is a modern man,
A progressive and civilized man,
He says he has read extensively and widely
And he can no longer live with a thing like me
Who cannot distinguish between good and bad,
He says I am just a village woman,
I am of the old type,
And no longer attractive.
He says I am blocking his progress.
My head, he says,
Is as big as that of an elephant
But it is only bones,

There is no brain in it,
He says I am only wasting his time.
…
Listen Ocol, my old friend,
The ways of your ancestors are good,
Their customs are solid,
And not hollow.
They are not thin, not easily breakable.
They cannot be blown away
By the winds
Because their roots reach deep into the soil.
I do not understand
The ways of foreigners
But I do not despise their customs.
Why should you despise yours?
…
When the drums are throbbing
And the black youths
Have raised much dust
you dance with vigor and health,
You dance naughtily with pride,
you dance with spirit,
You compete, you insult, you provoke,
You challenge all!
It is true, Ocol,
I cannot dance the ballroom dance.
Being held so tightly
I feel ashamed,
Being held so tightly in public
I cannot do it,
It looks shameful to me!
They come to the dance dead drunk,
They drink white man's drinks
As well as waragi.
They close their eyes,
And they do not sing as they dance,
They dance silently like wizards.
If someone tries
To force me to dance this dance

I feel like hanging myself
Feet first!

It is true
I cannot do my hair
As white women do.
Listen,
I am a true Acholi,
I am not a half caste,
I am not a slave girl.
Ask me what beauty is
To the Acholi
And I will tell you;
I will show it to you
If you give me a chance!
My mother taught me
Acholi hair fashions;
Which fit the kind
Of hair of the Acholi,
And the occasion.
Listen,
Ostrich plumes differ
From chicken feathers,
A monkey's tail
Is different from that of the giraffe.
…

A white woman's hair
Is soft like silk;
It is light
And brownish, like
That of the brown monkey,
And is very different from mine.
A black woman's hair
Is thick and curly.
…

[Some black women] cook their hair
With hot iron
And pull it hard
So that it may grow long.

Then they rope the hair on wooden pens
like a billy goat
Brought for the sacrifice
Struggling to free itself.
They fry their hair
In boiling oil
As if it were locusts,
And the hair sizzles,
It cries aloud in sharp pain
As it is pulled and stretched.
And the vigorous and healthy hair,
Curly, springy and thick,
That glistens in the sunshine
Is left listless and dead
Like the elephant grass
Scorched brown by the fierce
February sun.
It lies lifeless
Like the sad and dying banana leaves
On a hot and windless afternoon.
I am proud of the hair with which I was born
And as no white woman
Wishes to do her hair like mine,
Because she is proud
Of the hair with which she was born,
I have no wish
To look like a white woman.

My husband says he rejects me because I do not appreci-
ate
White men's foods,
And that I do not know
How to hold
The spoon and fork.
He is angry with me
Because I do not know
How to cook
As white women do.
…

He complains endlessly.
He says
Had I been to school
I would have learnt
How to use
White men's cooking stoves.
I confess
I do not deny!
I do not know
How to cook like a white woman.
I really hate
The charcoal stove!
Your hand is always
Charcoal-dirty
And anything you touch
Is blackened;
And your fingernails
Resemble those of the poison woman.
It is difficult to start.
You wait for the winds
To blow
But whenever you are in a hurry
The winds go off to visit
Their mothers-in-law.
...
I am terribly afraid
Of the electric stove,
And I do not like using it
Because you stand up when you cook.
Who ever cooked standing up?
The white man's stoves
Are good for cooking
White men's food:
For cooking the tasteless,
Bloodless meat of cows
That were killed many years ago
And left in the ice
To rot!
For frying an egg
Which when ready
Is slimy like mucus,
For boiling hairy chicken

In saltless water.
You think you are chewing paper!
And the bones of the leg
Contain only clotted blood
And when you bite
The tip of the bones of the leg
It makes no cracking sound,
It tastes like earth!
The white man's stoves
Are for boiling cabbages
And for baking the light spongy thing
They call bread.
They are for warming up
Tinned beef, tinned fish,
Tinned frogs, tinned snakes,
Tinned peas, tinned beans.
They are for preparing foods for the toothless
For infants and invalids,
It is for making tea or coffee!
I do not know how to cook
Like white women;
I do not enjoy white men's foods;
And how they eat —
How could I know?
And why should I know it?
...
Ocol has brought home
A large clock.
It goes tock-tock-tock-tock
And it rings a bell.
He winds it first
And then it goes!
But I have never touched it,
I am afraid of winding it!
I wonder what causes
The noise inside it!
And what makes it go!
I do not know
How to tell the time
Because I cannot read
The figures.
And Ocol has strange ways

Of saying what the time is.
In the morning
When the sun is sweet to bask in
He says
"It is Eight o'clock!"
When the cock crows
For the first time
He says
"It is Five!"
My head gets puzzled,
Things look upside-down
As if I have been
Turning round and round
And I am dizzy.
If my husband insists
What exact time
He should have morning tea
And breakfast,
When exactly to have coffee
Lunchtime, teatime,
And supper time — I must first look at the sun,
The cock must crow
To remind me.
Time has become
My husband's master,
It is my husband's husband.
My husband runs from place to place
Like a small boy,
He rushes without dignity.
And when visitors have arrived
My husband's face darkens,
He never asks you in,
And for greeting
He says
"What can I do for you?"
I do not know
How to keep the white man's time.
My mother taught me
The way of the Acholi

And nobody should
Shout at me
Because I know
The customs of our people!
When the baby cries
Let him suck milk
From the breast.
There is no fixed time
For breast feeding.
Listen, My husband,
In the wisdom of the Acholi
Time is not stupidly split up
Into seconds and minutes
It does not flow
Like beer in a pot
That is sucked
Until it is finished.
It does not resemble
A loaf of millet bread
Surrounded by hungry youths
From a hunt.
It does not get finished
Like vegetables in the dish.
My husband says
My head is numb and empty
Because, he says,
I cannot tell
When our children were born.
I know that Okang,
My first-born,
Was born at the beginning
Of the Dry Season.
A person's age
Is shown by what he or she does
It depends on what he or she is,
And on what kind of person
He or she is.

Excerpted from Okot p'Bitek, Song of Lawino: An African Lament. *Cleveland, OH: The World Publishing Co., 1969 (first published by East African Publishing House, 1966).*

A Small Place

BY JAMAICA KINCAID

In the book A Small Place, *Antigua writer Jamaica Kincaid attacks the lingering effects of colonialism. The Caribbean island of Antigua was "discovered" by Columbus in 1493 and became a British colony in the 17th century. It gained "independence" in 1967.*

Have you ever wondered to yourself why it is that all people like me seem to have learned from you is how to imprison and murder each other, how to govern badly, and how to take the wealth of our country and place it in Swiss bank accounts? Have you ever wondered why it is that all we seem to have learned from you is how to corrupt our societies and how to be tyrants?

You will have to accept that this is mostly your fault.

Let me just show you how you looked to us. You came. You took things that were not yours, and you did not even, for appearances' sake, ask first. You could have said, "May I have this, please?" and even though it would have been clear to everybody that a yes or no from us would have been of no consequence you might have looked so much better. Believe me, it would have gone a long way. I would have had to admit that at least you were polite.

You murdered people. You imprisoned people. You robbed people. You opened your own banks and you put our money in them. The accounts were in your name. The banks were in your name. There must have been some good people among you, but they stayed home. And that is the point. That is why they are good. They stayed home.

But still, when you think about it, you must be a little sad. The people like me, finally, after years and years of agitation, made deeply moving and eloquent speeches against the wrongness of your domination over us, and then finally, after the mutilated bodies of you, your wife, and your children were found in your beautiful and spacious bungalow at the edge of your rubber plantation — found by one of your many house servants (none of it was ever yours; it was never, ever yours) — you say to me, "Well, I wash my hands of all of you, I am leaving now," and you leave, and from afar you watch as we do to ourselves the very things you used to do to us.

And you might feel that there was more to you than that, you might feel that you had understood the meaning of the Age of Enlightenment (though, as far as I can see, it had done you very little good); you loved knowledge, and wherever you went you made sure to build a school, a library (yes, and in both of these places you distorted or erased my history and glorified your own).

But then again, perhaps as you observe the debacle in which I now exist, the utter ruin that I say is my life, perhaps you are remembering that you had always felt people like me cannot run things, people like me will never grasp the idea of Gross National Product, people like me will never be able to take command of the thing the most simpleminded among you can master, people like me will never understand the notion of rule by law, people like me cannot really think in abstractions, people like me cannot be objective, we make everything so personal. You will forget your part in the whole setup, that bureaucracy is one of your inventions, that Gross National Product is one of your inventions, and all the laws that you know mysteriously favour you.

Do you know why people like me are shy about being capitalists? Well, it's because we, for as long as we have known you, *were* capital, like bales of cotton and sacks of sugar, and you were the commanding, cruel capitalists, and the memory of this is so strong, the experience so recent, that we can't quite bring ourselves to embrace this idea that you think so much of.

As for what we were like before we met you, I no longer care. No periods of time over which my ancestors held sway, no documentation of complex civilisations, is any comfort to me. ■

Jamaica Kincaid was born in St. John's, Antigua. She is author of At the Bottom of the River *and* Annie John. *This reading is excerpted from* A Small Place. *New York: Penguin, 1988, pp. 34-37.)*

Gandhi Is Fasting

BY LANGSTON HUGHES

Mighty Britain, tremble!
Let your empire's standard sway
Let it break entirely —
My Gandhi fasts today.

You may think it foolish —
That there's no truth in what I say —
That all of Asia's watching
As Gandhi fasts today.

All of Asia's watching.
And I am watching, too,
For I am also jim crowed —
As India is jim crowed by you.

You know quite well, Great Britain,
That it is not right
To starve and beat and oppress
Those who are not white.

Of course, we do it too.
Here in the U.S.A.
May Gandhi's prayers help us, as well,
As he fasts today.

From The Collected Poems of Langston Hughes, *edited by
Arnold Rampersad, New York: Vintage Classics, 1994, p. 578.
The poem was originally published in 1943. At the time Hughes wrote
this poem, Mahatma Gandhi had been imprisoned by the British in India
along with about 20,000 other advocates for independence. Gandhi was a
leader of the Congress Party, which had advocated for Indian independence
since its formation in 1885. Gandhi led strikes of workers, boycotts of
British products, and mass protests.*

Introduction and Legacy of Inequality: Colonial Roots

"GLOBALIZATION: A VIEW FROM BELOW"
Reading by Jean-Bertrand Aristide
(p. 9, in the Introduction)

Have students hold out one of their hands and use their fingers to illustrate global inequality, as Aristide suggests in the reading. Student volunteers might go to the front of the class to represent the "hand of wealth." (See Polly Kellogg's article, "Ten Chairs of Inequality" (p. 115) for more ideas on graphically demonstrating economic inequality.)

In the reading, Jean-Bertrand Aristide employs several metaphors to get us to picture global reality: hands, the machine, the market, a morgue table. Encourage students to brainstorm additional metaphors that express important insights about globalization and to complete metaphorical drawings.

Discuss: Why couldn't Haitian rice farmers compete with U.S. rice farmers? Is destruction of Third World agriculture and industries an inevitable consequence of free trade? Why or why not? Elsewhere in Aristide's book, *Eyes of the Heart* — from which this reading is drawn — he describes a "third way" for poor countries like Haiti. What might that third way look like?

"COLONIALISM: BEFORE AND AFTER "
Opening quotes (p. 34)

Ask students to use the information in other readings in this chapter, as well as in Michael Parenti's "Myths of Underdevelopment" (p. 64) to propose answers to the ending questions, "What happened? How did Brazil change from a 'terrestrial paradise' to the 'valley of death'?"

"COLONIALISM: THE BUILDING BLOCKS"
Adapted from Susan Gage (p. 35)

Divide students into six groups. Each group should design a poster explaining or demonstrating their particular colonial "building block," including their answer(s) to the "Think About It" question. Obviously, these will be sketchy, but students can understand a great deal about the lingering effects of colonialism simply by reflecting on some of its basic features. In a similar assignment on African colonialism, one group of students drew a poster featuring masked thieves emptying the shelves of a building labeled "African Goods," and carrying the loot down the street to a lavishly-stocked store labeled "Major European Cities." A poster in the window reads, "Tour Our Beautiful Paris," with a portrait of the Eiffel Tower. Have each group restate its "Think About It" question and present its poster to the rest of the class.

We recommend that in conjunction with using the "Colonialism: The Building Blocks" you have students read "The Coming of the Pink Cheeks," which fleshes out some of the broad points made in "Building Blocks."

"BURNING BOOKS AND DESTROYING PEOPLES"
Article by Bob Peterson (p. 38)

If your students have strong reading skills, have them read the entire article or the first part of it, silently or in pairs. Then discuss and read it with a whole group, using questions and activities listed below. In classes where students' reading skills are weaker, read the article out loud. Since the article is relatively long and packed with important concepts, it's helpful to read it in two or three sittings. Some ideas:

Vocabulary list. As you read the article out loud keep a running list of key vocabulary words on chart paper to refer to throughout your colonialism study.

Dramatization. Have a few students dramatize a few mini-stories in the article: For example, Spaniards discovering and destroying Mayan libraries; Portuguese being told they have little of interest to trade with the Africans and the military response of the Portuguese.

Discussion Questions.

- Why do you think the Spanish colonialists burned the books of the Mayans? What effect do you think that had on Mayan peoples?

- What might have occurred had the Spanish viewed Mayans as equals and tried to learn to read their language and respect their culture? (Note: When the Romans conquered the Greeks, they incorporated and learned from them and didn't burn all their writings.)

- What role did racism play in the European conquest of the Americas?

- How did the different types of colonialism affect Native peoples and the environment?

- How did colonialism in Africa and Asia distort the development of those societies?

- Why do you think the United States changed from being a colony to be a colonizing power?

- How do you think some people in the United States have justified taking over other people's societies? How do such practices match the United States' commitment to "life, liberty and the pursuit of happiness"?

Writing activity. Have students write a dialogue poem between various protagonists: Mayan scribe and Spanish colonialist; Portuguese trader and African artisan; American patriot and British official; Haitian slave and French settler.

Complementary resource: *The Middle Passage* by Tom Feelings (New York: Dial Books, 1995). A powerful collection of black and white drawings that depict the Middle Passage, the brutality of slavery, and strength of resistance. Make overhead transparencies of the drawings and use these on an overhead projector to give visual images to this part of colonial history.

"THE COMING OF THE PINK CHEEKS"

Reading by Chief Kabongo (p. 45)

Ask students to discuss or write:
- List the ways that the Pink Cheeks transformed Kikuyu culture.

- Why didn't the Kikuyu simply attack and drive out the Pink Cheeks?

- How was the new road a "symbol of all the changes," as Chief Kabongo says?

- How does "the coming of the Pink Cheeks" affect the Kikuyu's relationship with Ngai (God)?

- According to the reading, what do the Pink Cheeks want? What are they after?

- On page 49, Kabongo says that "Something has taken away the meaning of our lives." What is that "something"?

- The final lines of the reading describe how life has changed for the new generation of Kikuyu: "They ride fast in motorcars, they work fire-sticks that kill, they make music from a box. But they have no land and no food and they have lost laughter." Does the experience of the Kikuyu have any significance for us today?

Other possible activities:
- Ask students to write a letter to Kabongo from his deceased father, Kimani, or from another ancestor, reflecting on what has happened to the Kikuyu.

- Wangari comes to Kabongo in his hut and scolds him: "[W]e women are tired; there is no food and the children are hungry; the young men have no stomachs and the old men are withering as dry leaves. You your self are weak or before this you would have taken counsel with the Elders. Speak now, for our people wait to hear your word." Ask students to write the speech that Kabongo could give.

- As with the assignment suggestion for Jamaica Kincaid's "A Small Place" (p. 58), have students do a text-rendering of the reading.

- Brainstorm ideas with students for a dialogue (two-voice) poem. Some possible pairings include: Kabongo and a white colonialist; the Africans' Ngai and and the Europeans' God; Wangari and Kabongo, etc.

- See other readings in the valuable book *Through African Eyes* (edited by Leon Clark) for more resources on the effects of colonialism on Africa.

"SONG OF LAWINO"
Poem by Okot p'Bitek (p. 50)

Give the following writing assignment to students:

(Note: The entire assignment is on the Rethinking Schools website at www.rethinkingschools.org/rg)

Imagine that you are Lawino, Ocol's wife in the poem "Song of Lawino." Remember your rejection of the "modern" ways of the white Europeans. Remember your bitterness at the scorn your husband heaps on you because you have kept your traditional ways and refuse to become like the Europeans.

You have been hired by a newspaper that is trying to help African people resist European influences. The newspaper editors consider these influences to be "cultural imperialism" — one nation trying to impose its culture on the people of another nation. They want you to write a kind of African "Dear Abby" column, to promote traditional values. As Lawino, respond to the letters below. Write at least a paragraph response to each letter. (Such a column is not entirely fanciful. "Tell Me, Josephine" began in *The Central African Mail*, a weekly Zambian newspaper, in 1960. Although the advice was ostensibly provided by a woman — Josephine — most of the letters printed in the paper were from men, because more men than women could write, and perhaps because women were less likely to express themselves in a public forum such as a newspaper column.)

Here is one letter of the five included on the website:

Dear Lawino,

My husband has changed a lot recently. Our village has always been a good place to live. People are kind to each other, help each other out with housework and in our gardens. When there is work to be done on someone's house, we all pitch in. It feels good to be working all together. We are one people, not just a collection of individuals.

But my husband says this is old fashioned. "Look out for yourself," he says. "You can't depend on others — and don't give handouts to people who can't help themselves."

These are ideas my husband gets while working for the Europeans in the cities.

Lawino, I want to respect my husband, but he is criticizing everything I believe in. What would you do if you were in my position?

Signed,

Village woman

"A SMALL PLACE"
Reading by Jamaica Kincaid (p. 54)

The following lesson idea is taken from an unpublished curriculum on the International Monetary Fund by Portland, Oregon teacher Jeff Edmundson, used here by permission.

While there are many ways to work with powerful literature, this lesson plan suggests you use a "text-rendering:" letting students pick phrases to read aloud, and "tearing apart" the text so as to see its power. When it works well, the class creates a kind of choral poem.

1. Point out to students that the reading is written from the point of view of a Third World person speaking to a First World person. A woman from the Caribbean island of Antigua speaks to the British in particular, but to all colonizing powers in general. Read the selection aloud.

2. Try a "text rendering:" Ask students to go back over the reading (it may help to read it aloud a second time) and underline about five words or short phrases that struck them for some reason.

When everyone is ready, give the following instructions: We're going to do an exercise to dig a little further into the writing. When we start, we'll take turns speaking out one of the phrases we underlined. You don't need to go around the room and "wait your turn" — simply speak out when it seems right. You can speak different phrases each time, or repeat the same one. You can say the same thing someone else said. There's no right or wrong way. But it's important that no one say anything else while we're doing this.

It's important for the teacher to participate, too. End the process when it seems to have reached an appropriate ending place. Discuss by first asking what they heard and learned from the phrases that were spoken out. Very often, students report seeing a whole new aspect to the reading. Usually, some phrases will have been spoken frequently. What is it about those phrases? Why did they speak to so many? Use this discussion to explore further the points Kincaid makes.

Other discussion questions:
- What is Kincaid angry about?
- Is her anger justified?
- How does she say that people of her country were changed by colonialism? by neo-colonialism (i.e., control by powerful

Western countries without actual outright ownership)? Why does she think it would be better to have come from people who lived in trees than to be "what I became after I met you"?

- "People like me cannot be objective, we make everything so personal," Kincaid says ironically. What is she saying about objectivity? Do you agree?

Possibilities for writing:

- Have students line-out, in poem form, the phrases they underlined in the text-rendering. Ask them to write about the "poem" they have created.

- Use one or more of the phrases you underlined, as well as ideas and images from previous lessons, to write your own poem about neo-colonialism.

- Write a reply to Kincaid's essay from a white British person. This could be either a defense of colonialism or a letter of support explaining what you will do to try to make sure that the wrongs are not continued.

- Imagine you are a tourist visiting Antigua. Having read Kincaid's piece, what are you thinking as you meet Antiguans?

- How should people from rich countries behave when they visit Third World countries?

ADDITIONAL RESOURCES

In class, we've used a number of short stories and excerpts from autobiographies to personalize colonialism for our students, and especially to get them to see various ways that colonized people resisted. Some of these include:

- **"The Old Chief Mshlanga"** by Doris Lessing, about a white girl's growing awareness of the brutality of colonialism and the dignity of the colonized. (Included in Hazel Rolchman (Ed.), *Somehow Tenderness Survives: Stories of Southern Africa*, New York: Harper, 1990.)

- **"By Any Other Name"** by Santha Rama Rau. Set in colonial India, the story describes an incident involving two Indian sisters in a school with mostly British children, and how the girls refuse to be humiliated for being Indian. (Included in *World Literature*. New York: Holt, Rinehart and Winston, 1993.)

- **"Ibrahimo Becomes a Christian"** as told to Colin Turnbull. A Congolese boy is torn between traditional beliefs and practices and those of Christian missionaries. (In Leon Clark (Ed.), *Through African Eyes: The Colonial Experience*. New York: Holt, Rinehart and Winston, 1971.)

- **"Houseboy"** by Ferdinand Oyono. The story of a young African man who goes to work for a white government official in colonial Cameroon. (Also in *Through African Eyes: The Colonial Experience*.)

- **"Lessons in Black and White."** Set in Southwest Africa (Namibia) colonized by the Germans until World War I and afterwards by the white South African government, this describes the growing political awareness of a young man, who in later chapters will join the SWAPO guerrilla movement. (From John Ya-Otto's autobiography, *Battlefront Namibia*, Westport, CT: Lawrence Hill and Co., 1981; also included in Bill Bigelow, *Strangers in Their Own Country: A Curriculum Guide on South Africa*, Trenton, NJ: Africa World Press, 1985.)

- **"Crackling Day"** by Peter Abrahams. The story of a young South African boy's confrontation with a group of white boys and the poignant aftermath. (An excerpt from Abrahams' autobiography, *Tell Freedom*, also found in *Somehow Tenderness Survives*.)

Some questions that students might discuss or write about:

- What were some of the subtle ways that people resisted colonialism?

- In some of the stories, how do people overcome obstacles and change for the better?

- How did colonialism change people? How did it affect their feelings about themselves? How did it affect their relationships?

- Why did colonialism and racism go hand in hand?

- What things kept colonialism from changing?

- What were the contradictions — the "cracks" — within colonialism that made it unstable?

- How do people's social class and gender influence their experiences in the stories (as well as race and nationality)?

- What are the similarities between colonialism and our own society? In what ways are we "colonized" today? Who or what does the colonizing?

"COLONIALISM: THEIR LIVES AND OURS"
A concluding writing assignment

One way to conclude a unit on colonialism is to attempt to draw the issues back to our students' lives. Most students will be unable to adequately grasp what colonialism meant to the lives of the colonized, but assignments like this might help nurture empathy. The following personal narrative might be assigned to students. Afterwards, give them the opportunity to read their writing to one another in a read-around format. (See "How To Do Read-Arounds," p. 186 in *Rethinking Our Classrooms, Volume 1*, Milwaukee, WI: Rethinking Schools, 1994):

Colonialism: Their Lives and Ours

At its core, colonialism was a system where one group of people controlled and exploited other people. Colonized people had their lives totally rearranged by powerful others who benefited from that rearrangement. Colonized people's food, customs, language, and occupations — their entire cultures — were influenced by representatives from the colonizing country. Even when they resisted colonization in countless ways, colonialism must have deeply influenced how people felt about their own power (or lack of it) in the world. It profoundly influenced their relationships with one another.

We can never know how people in other lands, at other times, felt. But we can draw on our own experiences and feelings to put ourselves in the positions of other people.

Below are some possible writing topics to help stimulate our "empathetic imaginations."

- Write about a time when you felt used or exploited by an individual or group.
- Write about a time when you witnessed or experienced a real unfairness.
- Write about a time when your mind was "colonized" — when some person or group exerted way too much influence on you, and when that influence benefited them, but not you.

Complete this as a story, not as an essay. Try to paint pictures with words for your reader. Use lots of dialogue. (It's OK to invent dialogue, if you can't remember exactly word for word what you or others said.)

CHAPTER THREE
The Global Economy:
Colonialism Without Colonies

"Invading New Markets" by Andy Singer

INTRODUCTION

Colonialism Without Colonies

The patterns of colonial domination that we examined in Chapter 2 help explain today's inequality of wealth and power. In this chapter, through simulations, stories, and background readings, we aim to help students appreciate some of the effects of these historical global relationships, and to learn more about the economic system and institutions that maintain those relationships.

Thanks to organizing by social justice and environmental movements, the International Monetary Fund (IMF), the World Bank, and the World Trade Organization (WTO) have become familiar to millions of people. The policies of these global institutions ripple through the lives of everyone in the world — but not with the same consequences. In readings like "Stories of Debt and Hope" (see p. 83), students can appreciate the daily struggle of people in poor countries simply to survive. But they can also recognize the resilience and creativity of these people in the face of exploitative economic conditions.

This chapter offers "big picture" readings and activities that help show students some of the key underlying social and economic forces that shape their world. Many of the most important things to know about the world are not particular places, people, or even organizations, but processes and relationships. They're invisible — nowhere and everywhere, all at once. The context-setting activities and accompanying readings in this chapter seek to bring these dynamics to life in the classroom — to make the invisible visible.

The chapter closes with a brief examination of the U.S. military's role in perpetuating the Third World's subordinate position in the global economy. While it is usually bankers and businessmen who manage the global economy, unequal economic relationships have been established and upheld by military force ever since the launching of colonialism. To "restore order" throughout the 20th century, U.S. military forces intervened regularly in other nations. Often left unexamined was the question: Whose order were they restoring? ∎

— *The editors*

> **The policies of these global institutions ripple through the lives of everyone in the world — but not with the same consequences.**

Children pick coffee beans in Chirqui, the westernmost province of Panama.

Myths of Underdevelopment

BY MICHAEL PARENTI

The impoverished lands of Asia, Africa, and Latin America are known to us as the "Third World," to distinguish them from the "First World" of industrialized Europe and North America and the now largely defunct "Second World" of communist states. Third World poverty, called "underdevelopment," is treated by most Western observers as an original historic condition. We are asked to believe that it always existed, that poor countries are poor because their lands have always been infertile or their people unproductive.

In fact, the lands of Asia, Africa, and Latin America have long produced great treasures of foods, minerals, and other natural resources. That is why Europeans went through so much trouble to steal and plunder them. One does not go to poor places for self-enrichment. The Third World is rich. Only its people are poor — and it is because of the pillage they have endured.

The process of expropriating the natural resources of the Third World began centuries ago and continues to this day. First, the colonizers extracted gold, silver, furs, silks, and spices;

then flax, hemp, timber, molasses, sugar, rum, rubber, tobacco, calico, cocoa, coffee, cotton, copper, coal, palm oil, tin, iron, ivory, ebony; and later on oil, zinc, manganese, mercury, platinum, cobalt, bauxite, aluminum, and uranium. Not to be overlooked is the most hellish of all expropriations: the abduction of millions of human beings into slave labor.

Through the centuries of colonization, many self-serving imperialist theories have been spun. I was taught in school that people in tropical lands are slothful and do not work as hard as we denizens of the temperate zone. In fact, the inhabitants of warm climates have performed remarkably productive feats, building magnificent civilizations well before Europe emerged from the Dark Ages. And today they often work long, hard hours for meager sums. Yet the early stereotype of the "lazy native" is still with us. In every capitalist society, the poor, both domestic and overseas, regularly are blamed for their own condition.

We hear that Third World peoples are culturally retarded in their attitudes, customs, and technical abilities. It is a convenient notion embraced by those who want to depict Western investments as a rescue operation designed to help backward peoples help themselves. This myth of "cultural backwardness" goes back to ancient times, used by conquerors to justify the enslavement of indigenous people. It was used by European colonizers over the last five centuries for the same purpose.

What cultural supremacy could be claimed by the Europeans of yore? From the 15th to 19th centuries, Europe was "ahead" in such things as the number of hangings, murders, and other violent crimes; instances of venereal disease, smallpox, typhoid, tuberculosis, plagues, and other bodily affliction; social inequality and poverty (both urban and rural); mistreatment of women and children; and frequency of famine, slavery, prostitution, piracy, religious massacre, and inquisitional torture. Those who believe the West has been the most advanced civilization should keep such "achievements" in mind.

More seriously, we might note that Europe enjoyed a telling advantage in navigation and armaments. Muskets and cannons, Gatling guns and gunboats, and today missiles, helicopter gunships, and fighter bombers have been the deciding factors when West meets East and North meets South. Superior firepower, not superior culture, has brought the Europeans and Euro-North Americans to positions of supremacy that today are still maintained by force, though not by force alone.

It was said that colonized peoples were biologically backward and less evolved than their colonizers. Their "savagery" and "lower" level of cultural evolution were emblematic of their inferior genetic evolution. But were they culturally inferior? In many parts of what is now considered the Third World, people developed impressive skills in architecture, horticulture, crafts, hunting, fishing, midwifery, medicine, and other such things. Their social customs were often far more gracious and humane and less autocratic and repressive than anything found in Europe at that time. Of course we must not romanticize these indigenous societies, some of which had a number of cruel and unusual practices of their own. But generally, their people enjoyed healthier, happier lives, with more leisure time, than did most of Europe's inhabitants.

Other theories enjoy wide currency. We hear that Third World poverty is due to overpopulation, too many people having too many children

to feed. Actually, over the last several centuries, many Third World lands have been less densely populated than certain parts of Europe. India has fewer people per acre — but more poverty — than Holland, Wales, England, Japan, Italy, and a few other industrial countries. Furthermore, it is the industrialized nations of the First World, not the poor ones of the Third, that devour some 80% of the world's resources and pose the greatest threat to the planet's ecology.

This is not to deny that overpopulation is a real problem for the planet's ecosphere. Limiting population growth in all nations would help the global environment but it would not solve the problems of the poor — because overpopulation in itself is not the cause of poverty but one of its effects. The poor tend to have large families because children are a source of family labor and income and a support during old age.

ARTIFICIALLY CONVERTED TO POVERTY

What is called "underdevelopment" is a set of social relations that has been forcefully imposed on countries. With the advent of the Western colonizers, the peoples of the Third World were actually set back in their development, sometimes for centuries. British imperialism in India provides an instructive example. In 1810, India was exporting more textiles to England than England was exporting to India. By 1830, the trade flow was reversed. The British had put up prohibitive tariff barriers to shut out Indian finished goods and were dumping their commodities in India, a practice backed by British gunboats and military force. Within a matter of years, the great textile centers of Dacca and Madras were turned into ghost towns. The Indians were sent back to the land to raise the cotton used in British textile factories. In effect, India was reduced to being a cow milked by British financiers.

By 1850, India's debt had grown to £53 million. From 1850 to 1900, its per-capita income dropped by almost two-thirds. The value of the raw materials and commodities the Indians were obliged to send to Britain during most of the 19th century amounted yearly to more than the total income of the 60 million Indian agricultur-

> In every capitalist society, the poor, both domestic and overseas, regularly are blamed for their own condition.

al and industrial workers. The massive poverty we associate with India was not that country's original historical condition. British imperialism did two things: first, it ended India's development, then it forcibly underdeveloped that country.

Similar bleeding processes occurred throughout the Third World. The enormous wealth extracted should remind us that there originally were few really poor nations. Countries like Brazil, Indonesia, Chile, Bolivia, Zaire, Mexico, Malaysia, and the Philippines were — and in some cases still are — rich in resources. Some lands have been so thoroughly plundered as to be desolate in all respects. However, most of the Third World is not "underdeveloped" but overexploited. Western colonization and investments have created a lower rather than a higher living standard.

> Most of the Third World is not "underdeveloped" but overexploited.

The Mayan Indians in Guatemala had a more nutritious and varied diet and better conditions of health in the early 16th century before the Europeans arrived than they have today. They had more craftspeople, architects, artisans, and horticulturists than today. What is called underdevelopment is a product of imperialism's superexploitation. Underdevelopment is itself a development.

Imperialism has created what I have termed "maldevelopment:" modern office buildings and luxury hotels in the capital city instead of housing for the poor, cosmetic surgery clinics for the affluent instead of hospitals for workers, cash export crops for agribusiness instead of food for local markets, highways that go from the mines and *latifundios* to the refineries and ports instead of roads in back country for those who might hope to see a doctor or a teacher.

Wealth is transferred from Third World peoples to the economic elites of Europe and North America (and more recently Japan) by direct plunder, by the expropriation of natural resources, the imposition of ruinous taxes and land rents, the payment of poverty wages, and the forced importation of finished goods at highly inflated prices. The colonized country is denied the freedom of trade and the opportunity to develop its own natural resources, markets, and industrial capacity. Self-sustenance and self-employment give way to wage labor. The number of wage workers in the Third World is accelerating dramatically.

Hundreds of millions of Third World people now live in destitution in remote villages and congested urban slums, suffering hunger, disease, and illiteracy, often because the land they once tilled is now controlled by agribusiness firms that use it for mining or for commercial export crops such as coffee, sugar, and beef, instead of beans, rice, and corn for home consumption.

In India, 55 million children are pressed into the work force. Tens of thousands labor in glass factories in temperatures as high as 100 degrees. In one plant, four-year-olds toil from 5 o'clock in the morning until the dead of night, inhaling fumes and contracting emphysema, tuberculosis, and other respiratory diseases. In the Philippines and Malaysia, corporations have lobbied to drop age restrictions for labor recruitment. The pursuit of profit becomes a pursuit of evil.

DEVELOPMENT THEORY

When we say a country is "underdeveloped," we are implying that it is backward and retarded in some way, that its people have shown little capacity to achieve and evolve. The negative connotations of "underdeveloped" have caused the United Nations, *The Wall Street Journal*, and parties of various political persuasions to refer to Third World countries as "developing" nations, a term somewhat less insulting than "underdeveloped" but equally misleading. I prefer to use "Third World" because "developing" seems to be just a euphemistic way of saying "underdeveloped but belatedly starting to do something about it." It still implies that poverty was an original historic condition and not something imposed by imperialists. It also falsely suggests that these countries *are* developing when actually economic conditions are usually worsening.

The dominant theory of the last half century, enunciated repeatedly by writers like Barbara Ward and W. W. Rostow and afforded wide currency, maintains that it is up to the rich nations of the North to help uplift the "backward" nations of the South, bringing them technology and proper work habits. This is an updated version of "the white man's burden," a favorite imperialist fantasy.

According to the development scenario, with the introduction of Western investments, workers in the poor nations will find more productive employment in the modern sector at higher wages. As capital accumulates, business will reinvest its profits, thus creating still more products, jobs, buying power, and markets.

Factory workers in the Nicaraguan free-trade zone of Las Mercedes ride home on trucks and buses.

Eventually a more prosperous economy evolves.

This "development theory" or "modernization theory," as it is sometimes called, bears little relation to reality. What has emerged in the Third World is an intensely exploitive form of dependent capitalism. Economic conditions have worsened drastically with the growth of transnational corporate investment. The problem is not poor lands or unproductive populations but foreign exploitation and class inequality. Investors go into a country not to uplift it but to enrich themselves.

People in these countries do not need to be taught how to farm. They need the land and the implements to farm. They do not need to be taught how to fish. They need the boats and the nets and access to shore frontage, bays, and oceans. They need industrial plants to cease dumping toxic effusions into the waters. They do not need to be convinced that they should use hygienic standards. They do not need a Peace Corps volunteer to tell them to boil their water, especially when they cannot afford fuel or have no access to firewood. They need the conditions

> **The problem is not poor lands or unproductive populations but foreign exploitation and class inequality.**

that will allow them to have clean drinking water and clean clothes and homes. They do not need advice about balanced diets from North Americans. They usually know what foods best serve their nutritional requirements. They need to be given back their land and labor so that they might work for themselves and grow food for their own consumption.

The legacy of imperial domination is not only misery and strife, but an economic structure dominated by a network of international corporations which themselves are beholden to parent companies based in North America, Europe, and Japan.

In sum, what we have is a world economy that has little to do with the economic needs of the world's people. ∎

Michael Parenti received his Ph.D. from Yale University in 1962, and is a prolific writer on issues of political power and foreign policy. This reading is excerpted from his book Against Empire, *San Francisco: City Lights Books, 1995.*

Introduction to Inequality Activities

Students' awareness of global problems of poverty and hunger can be increased in a variety of ways. Statistics, videos, and photos all have impact, but by themselves may be limited. Statistics may overwhelm students, heart-wrenching photos may draw sympathy, but neither necessarily gets students to really understand our planet's vast inequalities.

I have used the following activities to help students experience classroom doses of inequality. Such simulations often elicit emotional responses and broad-ranging discussions of what is fair and just. The simulations begin to bring home to students the enormous inequities that exist within the world. In addition, I use the "Ten Chairs of Inequality" simulation (p. 115) to help students recognize social class inequalities within countries, including the United States.

Like role plays, simulations can evoke emotional responses from students that deepen their involvement in the activity and strengthen what they take from it. In the midst of an angry realization that "That's not fair!" I ask the student to try to imagine how much more unfair it appears to people suffering, for example, life-threatening diseases because of the inequalities.

When we study colonialism, my students occasionally ask why we dwell so much on the past: "It's all history!" they proclaim. I tell them that only by knowing more about the past can we begin to understand what's going on today in the world. These simulations attempt to help students make the connection between a colonial past and a post-colonial, but still unequal, present.

Two notes of caution. As with any simulation (or role play) these should be understood to be just that — simulations. We can in no way reenact the violence of poverty and hunger that kills tens of thousands of children daily. We are providing a mere glimpse. The second point is particular to these simulations: They seek to describe rather than to explain current power and wealth arrangements. They can, however, be powerful tools in motivating students to want to study and figure out the answer to the essential question: Why?

— Bob Peterson

WORLD POPULATION AND WEALTH

Continent	Population (in millions) 2000	% of world Population	# in class of 25	Wealth (GNP in billions of dollars)	% of world GNP	# of treats out of 25
Africa	794	13.1 %	3	495.4	1.8 %	0.5
Asia	3,672	60.6 %	15	7,172.6	25.5 %	6
Oceania	31	0.5 %	0	442.4	1.6 %	0
Europe	727	12.0 %	3	9,606.3	34.2 %	9
USA & Canada	314	5.2 %	1	8,933.6	31.8 %	8
Latin America	519	8.6 %	2	1,430.7	5.1 %	1
World Total	6,057	100 %	24*	28,081	100 %	24.5

Sources: World population figures are from the United Nations Population Division: http://www.un.org/esa/population.

For purposes of this chart, one-third of Russia's GNP was attributed to Asia and two-thirds to Europe. Latin America includes Mexico, the Caribbean Islands and South America. The data were broken down this way to highlight the great disparity in wealth between Mexico and the United States and Canada, all of which are considered part of North America.

*Because of rounding, there are only a total of 24 students needed to represent the world's population.

GNP figures are from the World Bank, quoted in the Universal Almanac, 1994. GNP is defined as the total national output of goods and services. Percentage of world wealth is an estimate based on total GNP. (Not shown in the graph.)

Poverty and World Resources

BY SUSAN HERSH AND BOB PETERSON

An important part of a person's understanding of global issues is the recognition of the dramatic inequalities between nations and social classes within countries.

The purpose of this activity is to graphically demonstrate the vast differences in wealth between different areas of the world. It combines math, geography, writing, and social studies.

We remind students of some of the things we learned about colonialism — such as how great quantities of silver and gold were stolen from the Americas and taken to Europe. We also explain that current relations between countries and international organizations such as the World Trade Organization also affect how wealthy countries are. We make sure that students know the following terms: resources, GNP, wealth, distribution, income, power, and colonialism.

MATERIALS

- 11" x 17" blank world maps for each student, or pair of students, to write on
- 50 chips (25 of one color, and 25 of another) for each map
- 25 slips of paper with "I was born in [name of continent, based on chart]"
- 25 chocolate chip cookies
- playground map, or signs with names of continents and yarn to distinguish boundaries
- transparency of resource table on page 68
- six "negotiator" signs with yarn to hang around students' necks
- writing paper
- additional cookies for students who don't get any during the simulation (optional)

SUGGESTED PROCEDURE

- Give each student or pair of students a world map. Have them identify the continents and other places you may have been studying.
- Ask students how many people they think are in the world (about 6 billion in early 2002). After students have guessed, show them an almanac with the current estimate. Ask: If we represent all the people in the world with 25 chips, how many people is each chip worth?

(For six billion people, each chip represents approximately 240 million people.)

- Give 25 chips to each student/group and have them distribute them by continent where they think people live. Discuss student estimates and then tell them the accurate figures. Have them rearrange their chips to reflect the facts. Ask students what the differing stacks of chips tell them about the world's population.

- Explain that you are now going to give them another 25 chips of a different color and that they represent all the wealth produced in the world (the monetary worth of all the goods and services produced every year — from health care to automobiles). Tell them to put the chips on the continents to indicate their estimate of who gets this wealth. (Each chip represents 1/25 of the world's total amount of goods and services produced.)

- Discuss student estimates and record them on the chalkboard. Have students reflect on the size of the two different stacks of chips, population and resources. Collect the chips.

- Tell students you are going to demonstrate how population and wealth are distributed by continent. Have each student pick a slip of paper from a container. (The "I was born...." slips.) They may not trade continents. (As you distribute the slips, listen for stereotypical reactions to the continents — these will be useful in the follow-up discussion and will indicate possibilities for future lessons.)

- Have students go to an area in the room that you have designated to represent that continent. (Playground maps work great for this.) After students are in their areas, remind them that they each represent about 240 million people and that you are going to distribute the world's riches. Have each continent/group designate one person to be a "traveling negotiator" and distribute a "traveling negotiator" sign to those people.

- Explain that once the bag of resources is passed out to a representative from each continent, each group needs to sit in a circle and discuss their situation. They are to talk about how many resources they have compared to people on other continents, and discuss ways they should negotiate to increase their resources. They may plead and/or promise. Tell the students there will be a cross-continent negotiation session, then a time for the traveling negotiators to return to their home base to discuss their negotiations with the rest of their group, and finally a time for any trading or donating of resources to take place. (Note: Every continent, except North America, will have at least one "stay at home negotiator" and one traveling negotiator. The North American person can stay put or travel throughout the world.)

- Use a popular treat — rice crispy bars or chocolate chip cookies — and distribute them according to the percentages given in the chart. Announce the number of treats you are giving to each continent as you do so. Provide a paper bag for each continent to keep the treats in as you dramatically place each of the resources into the bag. Remind students they are not to eat the treats until after the negotiation session.

- Announce that the negotiation session is to begin. Only traveling negotiators may move to a different continent. When they come, they should sit in a circle with the "stay-at-home negotiators" and discuss the distribution of wealth and what should be done about it.

- After about 5 or 10 minutes, tell all traveling negotiators to return to their home continents. Each group should discuss the negotiations. After a few minutes, announce that the trading session may begin and if a continent wishes to trade or donate resources, they may. After that, instruct the people holding the resource bags to distribute the resources to people in their group.

- Give each continental group tag board and markers. Tell them to make some signs that describe what they think of the way the resources were distributed.

- Bring students back together for a whole-class discussion. Have each group share their posters and perspectives. Show students the information from the chart via a transparency or handout. Connect their emotions and feelings of fairness to the information on the chart. (At this time a teacher can give out additional treats to those students who did not get any, if one desires.)

Some questions worth posing if the students don't ask them themselves:

- How did the distribution of wealth get to be so unequal?
- What does the inequality of wealth mean in terms of the kinds of lives people lead?
- Who do you think decides how wealth is distributed?
- Should wealth be distributed equally?
- Do you think that, within a particular continent or nation, wealth is distributed fairly?
- How does the unequal distribution of wealth affect the power that groups of people hold?
- Within our community, is wealth distributed fairly?
- What can be done about the unequal way wealth is distributed?
- Who can we talk with to find out more information about these matters?

If you did any of the activities from the chapter on colonialism, ask students what role they think colonialism played in creating this inequality.

- After the discussion, have students write an essay about their feelings, what they learned, what questions they continue to have, and what they might want to do about world poverty.

- A few days after this simulation, "Ten Chairs of Inequality" (p. 115) is a useful activity to help students understand that in individual countries wealth is also unequally distributed.

- Students can do follow-up research on related topics, such as: the role colonialism played in the wealth disparity; how current policies of U.S. corporations and the U.S. government affect people in poorer nations; the role of groups such as the WTO and the IMF; and what different organizations and politicians are doing about world poverty. (See "Organizations and Websites for Global Justice" in the Resources section.) ∎

Susan Hersh developed this lesson while teaching fifth graders at La Escuela Fratney in Milwaukee, Wisconsin. She currently teaches seventh grade social studies at Preuss School in San Diego, California. Bob Peterson (repmilw@aol.com) teaches fifth grade at La Escuela Fratney and is a Rethinking Schools editor. A version of this article first appeared in Rethinking Our Classrooms, Volume 1 *(Milwaukee, WI: Rethinking Schools, 1994). For sample student handouts visit our website: www.rethinkingschools.org/rg.*

Building Miniature Houses — Simulating Inequality

BY BOB PETERSON

This hands-on lesson can be used in a variety of theme-based units at any grade level. Sometimes I use it in my fifth-grade class after we have discussed unequal distribution of resources in the world and the United States using the math/cookie activity described on p. 69 and the "Ten Chairs of Inequality" activity described on p. 115. Other times I use it in the context of discussing people's basic needs and various declaration of rights — the U.N. Declaration of Human Rights, for example, and the Declaration of the Rights of the Child.

First I have students suggest what the basic needs of human beings are. They generally mention food, water, medicine, clothes, shelter, etc. I ask if they think everyone has the same chance to get these necessities. "No — some people are rich!" and "Some have lots more than others," are common responses. I ask, "What do you mean, some people have more than others?" Inevitably students talk about money, better jobs, more "things" like cars and houses. I explain that such "things" are sometimes called "resources." I explain that what they said about some people having more and some having less is true not only between countries but within countries (and if appropriate I refer back to previous activities or readings). I tell them that today's activity will serve as a spark for more discussion about inequality of resources and wealth.

By the time I conduct this activity, the students in my classroom have experience working in groups and know that they are to stay in their own group and work cooperatively.

MATERIALS

Art materials for each group as described below. (They can vary according to what is available; the main point is that they should be unequal.)

STEP 1

Divide students into small groups of four and tell them the objective of the lesson: to build a small building — a miniature house with the materials that each group has. Tell them they may fold, cut, tear and use any materials that they are given, but may not use any other materials. Remind them to work cooperatively and that they will have a set amount of time to build a house that will be judged on durability (strength), practicality (does it have a door?), and aesthetics (how pretty it looks). Even though I sometimes have small groups in my class work in the coat room or out in the hallway, for this exercise I have all groups work in the classroom so that they can observe the unequal distribution of resources.

Small groups 1 and 2:
Two 10" x 12" sheets of tag board and 3 pencils for each group.

Small groups 3 and 4:
Four 10" x 12" sheets of tag board, 2 large sheets of construction paper, 4 pencils, and one marker for each group.

Small groups 5:
Four 10" x 12" sheets of tag board, 3 large sheets of construction paper, 4 pencils, a pair of scissors, a ruler, and four markers.

Small group 6:
Six 10" x 12" sheets of tag board, 4 large sheets of construction paper, 4 pencils, two scissors, two rulers, eight markers, scotch tape, a glue stick, four brass fasteners, a hole puncher, and yarn.

(Other materials can be added or subtracted depending on the availability of material such as: 4" x 6" filing cards, toothpicks, wire, glitter, craft sticks, etc.)

STEP 2:

After the students have worked together for 10 or 15 minutes, announce that they have 10 minutes left before you select the "best" one. If students object to the unfair distribution of resources, tell them the class will discuss that later.

STEP 3:

At the end of the work time, the class gathers and listens to a representative of each group present their constructions. I display each building on a bookcase or table in front of the room.

STEP 4:

Hold a class discussion asking some of the following questions:

- How did it feel to be in a group that had lots of (or some, or few) materials?
- Was there anything else besides the amount of supplies that had an effect on your group's ability to build something?
- Did the amount of materials affect the size of the house? Would it affect the comfort of the people living in the house?
- Did any small group try to do something about the inequality? If so, what? Was this effective?
- What would have been a fair way to distribute the materials?
- Would it have been fair to give prizes or hold a contest, given that not everyone had the same access to materials to begin with? Why or why not? Is it fair to judge people by how many resources they have?
- This was only a simulation of inequality. Where in our community or world can you see the results of people having different amounts of wealth and resources? Are these people or groups still judged by the same rules or standards? Is that fair?
- What can students do in real life to help change such unequal situations?
- Why do you think there are unequal resources for building houses in the real world?
- Display the quotation from Anatole France's *La Lys Rouge* about the "law" (see below), read it together as a class, and ask, "How does this quotation relate to the activity that we just did?"

Note that it is important to make sure that differences in resources are not just portrayed as a Northern/Southern dichotomy. These kinds of inequalities characterize our own community and country. Without that understanding, younger children in particular tend to think that lack of resources is caused mainly by geography and climate rather than by a maldistribution of power and wealth.

STEP 5:

Have students reflect individually on the activity. Younger children can draw a picture and older students can write and/or draw. I sometimes pose these questions:

- Given what you experienced in the activity, what do you think about people who argue that there should be a fairer distribution of wealth and resources in our community and world?
- Based on what we've studied thus far, why do you think there is such inequality in wealth and resources in the world?

Students can share their reflections with partners, in small groups, or with the whole class.

Bob Peterson (repmilw@aol.com) teaches fifth grade at La Escuela Fratney and is a Rethinking Schools editor. The above lesson was adapted from Susan Fountain's lesson, "The Toy Contest," from her book, Education for Development: A Teacher's Resource for Global Learning, *Portsmouth, NH: Heinemann, 1995, pp. 187-189. A useful book to help children visualize differences in material well-being between "average" citizens in various countries is the book* Material World: A Global Family Portrait *by Peter Menzel. San Francisco: Sierra Club Books, 1995.*

> **"The law, in its majestic equality, forbids the rich as well as the poor to sleep under bridges, to beg in the streets, and to steal bread."**
>
> —Anatole France,
> *La Lys Rouge*, 1894

'The world is just'

"The World Is Just" Cartoon

BY BOB PETERSON

Students tend to have a sense of what is "fair." Most root for the underdog. Students compare their own treatment with the treatment of others — and when dealt with more shoddily than their peers, will be the first to explain why what happened to them is not fair.

These two simple cartoons can be used as triggers to help students recognize that opinions on justice and injustice are related to one's social position. The cartoons can also help students realize that certain groups may benefit from injustices done to another. Furthermore, the second cartoon offers a graphic representation of the "oppressed" organizing to fight injustice.

Teachers can use these cartoons in a variety of whole class, small group, or individual settings. One approach is suggested below:

1) Display a copy of "The World is Just" cartoon using an overhead projector. Ask the students, "What do you see?" and write down their observations. Then tell the students that they

will work in small groups and discuss the following questions:

- What is the message of this cartoon?
- What does this simple cartoon say about the idea of "power" and "justice"?

Provide copies of the cartoon to each group. Have group representatives share a summary of each group's discussion with the whole class.

2) Next, tell students that they will write a conversation — or a "dialogue" or "trialogue" poem (see p. 186) — between the two or three groups of people in society whom the fish might represent. Ask students, "Which fish has the most power, and how might each fish's sense of justice change depending on how much power it has?" After a brief discussion say, "Now think of human society. Who has power and who doesn't? Please give specific examples." I list the students' thoughts so that they'll have lots of ideas to choose from when it's time

for them to write. In my class students have suggested super rich, middle class, and the "power people"; Harriet Tubman and her owner; three different-aged brothers; a white person, a Mexican, and an African American; a child laborer, an adult worker, and a boss. Students can work individually or in pairs to write their poems.

3) After students share their poems, pose some of these questions:

- What did the poems — the interpretations of the cartoon — have in common?
- What other situations in our community or in the world might have something to do with the cartoon?
- In the animal kingdom, it is common for a bigger or more ferocious animal to "eat" a smaller animal? Is this also true with human society? Does it have to be? Can we organize society so it is more "just"?
- What can be done to change unjust situations?
- How does a cartoon like this oversimplify real situations? Is that oversimplification OK or is it a problem?

Other options:

- The exercise can be repeated using the "Organize" cartoon (left).
- Without showing the "Organize" cartoon, the teacher can ask students to transform the first cartoon into a comic strip showing how things might lead to greater justice and equality.
- Have students present their "real life" versions of either cartoon as short impromptu skits, and then discuss them with the class.

Bob Peterson (repmilw@aol.com) teaches fifth grade at La Escuela Fratney and is a Rethinking Schools editor. This activity was adapted from Susan Fountain's lesson, "The World is Just," from her book, Education for Development: A Teacher's Resource for Global Learning. *Portsmouth, NH: Heinemann, 1995, pp. 187-189.*

Plantu

Debt and Disaster:
Notes on Teaching the Third World Debt Crisis

BY BILL BIGELOW

If you borrow money you ought to pay it back. That's the piece of common sense that confounds many Americans when thinking about international debt: Too bad some countries are so poor, but if they weren't going to be able to pay their debts they should have thought of that before borrowing billions of dollars.

With this in mind during a recent school year, I began my unit on the International Monetary Fund, the World Bank, and the effects of the debt crisis by appointing a "class leader." In plain view of other students, I then gave this "leader" — let's call him Erik — five one-dollar bills and told him that technically it was a loan, but that he would never need to worry about paying it back. I followed this loan by offering Erik a hall pass, with the message: "The bearer of this hall pass has permission to use the vending machine to purchase candy during class time" — which is ordinarily a violation of school rules. I read it aloud so everyone in class understood the privilege I'd granted Erik. Next, I urged Erik-the-leader to go forth and buy candy to his heart's content — or at least until his (my) five dollars ran out.

When he left, I ordered the rest of the class to get out some money and pay me back, because I had lent their leader five dollars and that was a lot of money. And because he was the class leader, he had borrowed the money (and spent it) on behalf of all of them. Like it or not, they all

were now in debt.

Not surprisingly, most students objected. Some of their comments: "We never asked for any loans;" "Erik's going to eat the candy, he's not going to give us any;" "Erik's not our leader, we didn't elect him;" and some a bit stronger and ruder.

This would be a ludicrous exercise if it didn't simulate so accurately what happened in the real world beginning in the 1970s when banks began to lavish loans on Third World governments, many of them led by tyrants. (See "Debt: The New Colonialism" on p. 78.) Elites enriched themselves on the banks' money, but it is now the countries' poor who must pay it back, and suffer under draconian "structural adjustment policies" imposed by the International Monetary Fund. (See p. 82.)

My idea for this simulation came from an interview with Noam Chomsky conducted by María Luisa Mendonça, and published in the July/August 1999 issue of NACLA's *Report on the Americas*. Chomsky used the example of Brazil's enormous debt:

> Who borrowed it? Not the peasants, not the working people. In fact the large majority of the population of Brazil didn't have anything to do with the debt, but they're being asked to pay it. That's like you being asked to pay if I spent my money somewhere else and couldn't

pay it back. To the extent that there is a debt — if you believe in capitalist principles — the debt ought to be paid by the people who borrowed it. In this case they are military dictators, some landowners, and the super-rich.

Our opening gimme-back-my-money exercise framed the unit that came after. Of course, no simulation can begin to capture the horrific toll exacted by the IMF from indebted countries: huge cuts in spending on health care, education and other social services; the loss of subsidies on basic necessities; privatization of state enterprises; currency devaluations that attack the living standards of the poor and working people; carte blanche invitations to corporations to drill for oil, clearcut forests, displace small farmers for massive tourist resorts and export-crop plantations; and more.

The readings and activities in the following pages introduce students to the human and ecological costs of the debt crisis. See "Videos With a Global Conscience," p. 356, for short reviews of several films that are useful for teaching about Third World debt. These include *Banking on Life and Debt; The Debt Crisis: An Un-natural Disaster; Cancel the Debt, Now! The Jubilee 2000 Campaign; Where Are the Beans?; Deadly Embrace: Nicaragua, The World Bank, and the International Monetary Fund;* and *Life and Debt.*

USING THE READINGS IN THIS SECTION

"Debt: The New Colonialism" (p. 78)

This is a brief history of the Third World debt crisis and some of the consequences of IMF- and World Bank-imposed "structural adjustment programs." Read it aloud or allow students to read it in small groups. Possible questions:

- As you read, list how the Debt Crisis is and is not like colonialism. Afterward, talk about the title of the article. Is debt the "new colonialism"?

> "I have always believed that the more important the issue, the fewer people should be involved in the decision."
>
> —Robert McNamara, former U.S. Secretary of Defense and President of the World Bank, 1995

- Who or what is to blame for the debt crisis?
- If you did the money-lending activity with students (described above), relate the information in the article to the class simulation. How is it similar? How is it different?
- "Crisis" is a word that implies that something bad is happening. Are there any groups for whom the crisis is *good* — who benefit from such huge amounts of Third World debt?
- How do you think an IMF or World Bank official would respond to the quote from Dominga de Velasques on p. 79? Why should Dominga and people like her be responsible for paying back the debts accumulated by their government?
- On p. 80, U.S. official R. T. MacNamara warns what could happen to Third World countries if they try to challenge their debts. How should people in poor countries respond to the enormous debt, and to threats like MacNamara's?
- What can people in this country do to help people in poor countries respond to the debt crisis and "structural adjustment programs"?

See the valuable lesson, "Don't Get SAPped! Women and Structural Adjustment Programs," in the curriculum *Women's Education in the Global Economy* by Miriam Ching Louie with Linda Burnham, p. 47; available from www.teaching forchange.org. The lesson asks students to reflect on how specific structural adjustment programs affect women's lives, and draws students' attention to the unequal burden the IMF/World Bank-mandated policies impose on women and children.

"Stories of Debt and Hope" (p. 83)

Have students read about the lives of people from Mexico and Venezuela in "Stories of Debt and Hope." Ask them to write on the following questions:

- How do the conditions described in each story connect to at least one of the six structural adjustment programs (or policies) pushed on poor countries by the IMF and World Bank (described in the reading on p. 82)?
- List other features besides structural adjustment programs that make these people's lives difficult.
- What social changes would improve these individuals' lives?
- What glimpses of hope do you see from

these readings?

- What advice would you give the person in each reading? Think not only about individual solutions, but also ones that would require getting together with other people. Instead of making this a written assignment, you might ask students to circle-up and to read each selection aloud. Afterward, students must discuss these people's lives and agree on at least two actions that they think each of the individuals in the readings should take. Remind them that these could be collective actions as well as individual.

You might ask students to choose one of the individuals described in the reading and write a short story on his or her life.

Finally, students may be interested in watching the video, *Maquila: A Tale of Two Mexicos*, that focuses on Ciudad Juarez. (See "Videos With a Global Conscience," p. 362.)

"The Kalinga Women Against the Chico Dam" (p. 89)

It's important that students are exposed to the enormous amount of organized opposition to World Bank- and International Monetary Fund-imposed or supported projects. This account may remind students of land expropriations carried out under colonial rule. Ask students:

- Do the events in this account remind you of anything else you are familiar with or that we have studied?

- List the resistance tactics that the women used.

- If you had known about this struggle when it was occurring, what could you have done that might have supported the women?

- Why do you think it was women who took the lead in this struggle?

You might watch the video *A Narmada Diary*, which recounts another struggle against a dam in India. Available from First Run Icarus Films, 32 Court St., 21st Floor, Brooklyn, NY 11201; 718-488-8900; www.frif.com. Also look at writer Arundhati Roy's eloquent critique of dams and development, "The Greater Common Good," at www.narmada.org/gcg/gcg.html. It's a long but wonderful essay that could be excerpted for use with students. ■

Bill Bigelow (bbpdx@aol.com) teaches at Franklin High School in Portland, Oregon and is a Rethinking Schools editor.

Who Are the World Bank and the IMF?

As World War II raged across Europe and Asia, the leaders of England and the United States realized that, in order to ensure a liberal, capitalist world economy after the war, they would need multilateral institutions that could enforce rules favoring the free movement of capital internationally. In July 1944 the two governments convened a conference at Bretton Woods, New Hampshire.

The International Monetary Fund (IMF) was established to smooth world commerce by reducing foreign exchange restrictions. It also created a reserve of funds to be tapped by countries experiencing temporary balance-of-payments problems, so they could continue trading without interruption. This pump-priming of the world market, it was believed, would benefit all trading countries, especially the biggest traders, the United States and Britain.

Also founded at Bretton Woods was the International Bank for Reconstruction and Development (World Bank). The World Bank was given the task of making post-war development loans for infrastructure projects (such as roads and utilities) which, because they were unprofitable, were not likely to be initiated by private capital. The Bank also was mandated to promote private foreign investment by means of guarantees or participation in loans and other investments made by private investors.

The unwritten goal of the World Bank and the IMF — one that has been enforced with a vengeance — has been to integrate countries into the capitalist world economy. Despite all the rhetoric about development and the alleviation of poverty, the central function of these multilateral lending institutions has been to draw the rulers and governments of weaker states more tightly into a world economy dominated by large, transnational corporations.

— *Kevin Danaher*

excerpted from 50 Years is Enough: The Case Against the World Bank and the International Monetary Fund, *edited by Kevin Danaher. Boston: South End Press, 1994.*

Associated Press/Luis Romero

Two small children play amid grave markers in the town of Old Cuscatlan, El Salvador, where poverty forces many families to make their homes in public cemeteries.

Debt: The New Colonialism

BY JEAN SOMERS

According to the World Bank, Third World debt stands at the astronomical level of $2.5 trillion. Poor countries pay Northern governments, banks, and financial institutions $31.3 billion every month, or $1 billion each day, in debt repayments. This represents a huge outflow of desperately needed resources from poor countries. They are, in fact, paying their debts with the health, welfare, and even, in extreme cases, the lives of their people.

GETTING INTO DEBT

The immediate roots of the crisis can be found in the quadrupling of oil prices in 1973. This generated billions of surplus dollars for the oil producing countries, much of which they deposited in Western banks. These became known as petrodollars. The banks were anxious to lend these dollars so they would earn interest. Northern governments encouraged them to lend money to so-called developing countries. Governments of wealthier countries wanted to avoid a serious recession in the industrialized

world by ensuring that the countries of the South were able to continue to import from the North. The International Monetary Fund (IMF) supported this.

Poor countries themselves were desperate for loans — to cover their increased oil costs and also for development. The needs of the banks and those of poor countries appeared neatly matched. Interest rates were low, money was plentiful. Banks were so anxious to lend that they poured out loans without taking normal banking precautions, such as checking the viability of the projects for which they were lending. According to Angel Gurria, head of Mexico's Office of Public Credit: "The banks were hot to get in. All the banks in the U.S. and

This reading is excerpted and adapted from "Debt: The New Colonialism" by Jean Somers, in 75/25: Development in an Increasingly Unequal World, *edited by Colm Regan, Birmingham, UK: The Development Education Centre, 1996. Jean Somers (ddc@connect.ie) is coordinator of the Debt and Development Coalition in Ireland.*

Europe and Japan stepped forward. They showed no foresight. They didn't do any credit analysis. It was wild." The banks were particularly interested in large-scale projects because they wanted to shift big sums of money. They operated on the principle: "We're lending to governments and governments can't go bankrupt," so they felt their loans were safe.

HOW WAS THE MONEY SPENT?

First, poor countries used the money they borrowed to pay for the increased costs of energy following the oil price rises — and this accounted for a quarter of the debt they accumulated. Large amounts of money were spent unproductively or disappeared through corruption. This was partly due to the undemocratic nature of most of the borrowing governments: Most Latin American countries, where the bulk of the loans went, were run by military dictatorships during the 1970s.

Poor countries also had only one major model of "development": modernization along the lines of the United States and Europe. Because of this, much of the money that Southern governments received went to large-scale projects like building roads, airports, and dams. The idea was to promote rapid industrialization, which left agriculture — the source of income for the majority of people in many countries — seriously neglected.

Large scale projects: The banks preferred these because they wanted to shift large sums of money as quickly as possible. Military governments also preferred giant projects, many of which had devastating effects on the environment. Big projects were seen as prestigious and could easily be accompanied by corruption. In the Philippines, the Bataan nuclear power plant planned in 1976 was built in the middle of the Pacific earthquake zone, at the foot of a volcano. It cost $2.1 billion and according to *The New York Times*, President Ferdinand Marcos received $80 million in commission from the company contracted to build the plant.

Capital flight: Some of the loans never even made it into the borrowing country's economy. Massive sums were siphoned off and returned to bank accounts in the United States. The prominent researcher and author Susan George estimates that wealthy elites in Third World countries sent $55 billion to U.S. banks in capital flight between 1977 and 1983.

Military spending: Given that many borrowing countries were run by military dictators, it

> Unaccountable military dictators were supported by loans from equally unaccountable bankers.

isn't surprising that military spending rocketed between 1972 and 1981 from $2.5 billion to $29 billion.

WHO WAS RESPONSIBLE?

Unaccountable military dictators were supported by loans from equally unaccountable bankers. Northern governments and the IMF also carry a share of the blame, as their main concern was to protect the industrialized world against recession.

However, it is the people of Third World countries who must now shoulder the debt burden. Dominga de Velasques, speaks on behalf of Amas de Casa (housewives) of La Paz, Bolivia:

> And we, the housewives, ask ourselves: What have we done to incur this foreign debt? Is it possible that our children have eaten too much? Is it possible that they have studied in the best colleges? Have our wages become too great? Together we say: No, no, we have not eaten too much. No, we have not dressed any better. We do not have better medical assistance. Then to whom have the benefits gone? Why are we the ones who have to pay for this debt?

An insider's view comes from Jorge Sol, former IMF director for Central America: "The Third World elites who borrowed the money came from the same class as those who lent it and those who managed it at the IMF. They went to the same schools, belonged to the same clubs. They all profited from the debt."

THE BUBBLE BURSTS

A number of developments toward the end of the 1970s brought the lending and spending spree to a halt. The cost of repaying loans from the banks shot up as interest rates rose sharply, a result of a rise in U.S. interest rates. Prices that Third World countries received for commodities — goods like cocoa, coffee, cotton, bananas, copper, etc. — also fell dramatically. Poor countries depend on export of products like these to earn the foreign exchange needed to repay their debts. Debts owed to foreign banks or govern-

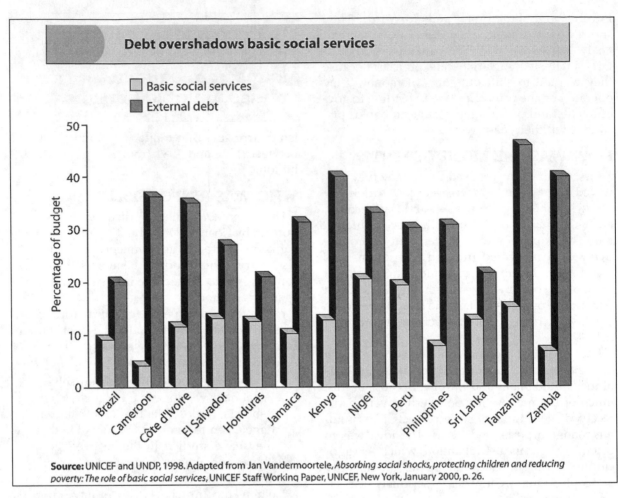

Debt overshadows basic social services

Basic social services
External debt

Percentage of budget (y-axis: 0, 10, 20, 30, 40, 50)

Countries (x-axis): Brazil, Cameroon, Côte d'Ivoire, El Salvador, Honduras, Jamaica, Kenya, Niger, Peru, Philippines, Sri Lanka, Tanzania, Zambia

Source: UNICEF and UNDP, 1998. Adapted from Jan Vandermoortele, *Absorbing social shocks, protecting children and reducing poverty: The role of basic social services*, UNICEF Staff Working Paper, UNICEF, New York, January 2000, p. 26.

ments must be paid in "hard currencies" like dollars, British pounds, or yen. Indebted countries now faced a situation where the cost of their loans had rocketed, while their ability to repay had declined. On top of this, oil prices rose steeply once more.

DIVIDE AND RULE

Fearing the collapse of their banks, Northern governments moved swiftly to contain the crisis. If poor countries defaulted on their loans, this could undermine confidence in major banks. Thus the priority of Northern governments was to protect the banks from the consequences of their own irresponsibility. They looked at the crisis as a problem of individual poor countries that had simply borrowed too much — not a result of the behavior of wealthy Northern countries.

Governments of wealthy countries wanted to prevent Third World countries from uniting in a debtors' cartel — a union of poor countries — which could speak from a position of strength and might be able, for example, to set limits on how much they would repay. Representatives

from wealthy countries made threats to the poorer, debtor countries. In a speech to the U.S. Chamber of Commerce in October 1983, R. T. MacNamara, then Deputy Secretary of the U.S. Treasury, warned:

> The foreign assets of a country that repudiated [refused to pay] its debt would be attacked by creditors throughout the world; its exports seized by creditors at each dock where they landed; its national airlines unable to operate; and its sources of desperately needed capital goods and spare parts virtually eliminated. In many countries, even food imports would be curtailed. Hardly a pleasant scenario.

Newly elected President Alan Garcia in Peru announced in his inaugural speech in 1985 that he would limit debt payments to 10% of export earnings. The IMF retaliated by declaring Peru ineligible for all loans. Peru was boycotted by all lenders, all commercial banks, and the World Bank. With the country starved of resources, living conditions in Peru became worse.

POLICING THE DEBT CRISIS: ENTER THE IMF AND THE WORLD BANK

The IMF and the World Bank play a dual role in the debt crisis:

As major creditors. While the debt crisis began as a problem between banks and Third World countries, the biggest burden for the poorest countries is now "multilateral debt" — in other words, debt owed to agencies representing multiple countries, like the IMF and the World Bank. These bodies made loans to enable countries to continue to service their debts. By the second half of the 1990s, half of the debt repayments of the poorest countries was going to international financial bodies, especially the IMF and World Bank. The IMF and World Bank were particularly harsh creditors as their debt could neither be postponed nor canceled. Action from debt campaigners around the world forced the World Bank and IMF to agree to cancel some debt. They introduced the Heavily Indebted Poor Countries Initiative (HIPC) in 1996 which involves all creditors in canceling some debt. Forty-one countries are potentially eligible under this initiative. However, the majority of the 22 countries which have received debt deals under HIPC are still paying more on debt than on their people's health.

As managers of the debt repayment process. Member nations gave the IMF the role of "reforming" poor countries' economies so they could repay their debts from their own foreign exchange earnings. This was done by imposing "structural adjustment programs" (SAPs) on indebted countries. While "adjustment" is a word that makes us think of minor changes, the SAPs force huge changes in how the Southern economies relate to the Northern economies. Debt provided an opportunity for the North to tighten its stranglehold on the South.

SAPs vary slightly from country to country, but typical policies include currency devaluation; the removal of tariffs; cutting social spending, for example on health, education, and food subsidies; selling off public enterprises (like water or electrical utilities) to corporations; cutting wages; limiting credit; and increasing interest rates on loans. The goal is to get countries to export more, spend less, and "open up" their economies to foreign investors.

CUTS IN GOVERNMENT SPENDING

Throughout the Third World, public spending cuts have been savage. Health and education have been heavily affected; there have been

- In 2000, the African country of Mali spent $88 million servicing its debt. This is significantly higher than the government spent on health programs for its people — in a country where one in four children dies before turning five years old.
  Source: U.N. Human Development Report, 2000

- Due to the HIV/AIDS crisis, life expectancy in Zambia is expected to drop from 43 to 33 years, a level last experienced in Europe in medieval times. Over half a million children are out of school. Yet debt service payments by the Zambian government are greater than it spends on health and education combined.
  Source: U.N. Human Development Report, 2000

- The Nigerian government spends $1.5 billion servicing its debt. This is 30% of the country's total export earnings, three times more than the government gives to education and nine times more than it spends on healthcare.
  Source: Jubilee 2000-UK, 2001

widespread layoffs of public employees and the removal of food subsidies. These cuts mostly affect poor people. As a UNICEF report observes: "Hundreds of thousands of the developing world's children have given their lives to pay their countries' debts, and many millions more are still paying the interest with their malnourished minds and bodies."

The removal of food subsidies is often the first adjustment shock for ordinary people. In Tanzania the price of cornmeal, the main staple food, shot up 450% when the subsidy was removed. The removal of food subsidies hurts poor people most. The household diet changes, less is eaten per meal, and fewer meals per day are eaten. Malnutrition, mostly in children, rises, with irreversible future consequences.

Because IMF- and World Bank-ordered SAPs force countries to emphasize exports to earn the dollars needed to repay debts, the most fertile land is often used to grow cash crops for export. Crops like tobacco, cotton, soya, and sugar cane are given priority; these crops get the best land, access to the most credit and technical support. Beans, cassava, and other food crops are not given support. This bias favors large commercial farms and increases inequality as wealthy landowners become wealthier and small holders are forced off their land and become landless laborers or swell the numbers of people flocking to slums in the cities. ■

"Structural Adjustment Policies"

Innocent Name, Deadly Consequences

When the International Monetary Fund (IMF) and the World Bank lend money to poor countries, those loans come with strings attached. The IMF and World Bank demand that the countries that receive money enact "structural adjustment policies" — SAPs. There are at least six different kinds of SAPs, all of which hurt poor people:

1. Massive Public Sector Layoffs

Bank and Fund policies in poor countries can be summed up in four words: "Spend less, export more." As governments attempt to cut expenditures, thousands of government employees lose their jobs. (The IMF and World Bank also promote "privatizing" state-owned enterprises: water, telephone, electricity, etc. Workers are often laid off, wages are slashed, and prices rise when this occurs.)

2. Spending Cuts in Basic Social Services

In addition to public sector layoffs, governments have been pressured to cut basic social services. As education, health care, and other social program budgets are cut, not only are jobs lost directly, but the future health and well-being of the country is undermined.

3. Crippling Wage Freezes and Labor Suppression

The Bank and Fund also push countries to slow or stop increases in wages, both to attract foreign investment and to lower consumer demand. In some countries, lending programs have also pushed governments to weaken the rights of public sector unions. However, the Bank and Fund do not demand dramatic cuts in funding for the military, which is often used to put down worker demonstrations or strikes.

4. Devaluation of Local Currencies

One of the main reasons why workers face rising prices in countries implementing SAPs is that the Bank and Fund press these countries to devalue their currencies. Devaluations have the effect of making a country's exports cheaper and its imports more expensive — so prices for many goods rise. But wages don't keep pace with price increases.

5. Promotion of Export-Oriented Production

The Bank and Fund urge countries to shift more land away from basic food crops to export-oriented products such as shrimp, broccoli, cut flowers, and coffee. This is very ecologically damaging. Shrimp farms, for example, can ruin the water table; cash crops often require a greater use of pesticides, herbicides, and chemical fertilizers that harm the environment. As food prices rise, the poor cannot afford to feed their families, and malnutrition increases. What's more, millions of peasants and indigenous people have been kicked off their land in order to make room for the new crops. The World Bank has also been a big promoter of "free trade zones" where young women often work in exploitative sweatshop conditions to produce light manufactured goods for export to Wal-Mart, Sears, Kmart and other stores.

6. Abolition of Price Controls on Basic Foodstuffs

Traditionally, poor country governments subsidize the price of basic goods like bread and cooking oil. The IMF and World Bank demand that these subsidies be cut, which threatens the nutrition and even the lives of poor people. In several countries, the removal of food subsidies has led to bloody riots. ■

IF YOU POOR NATIONS WANT MORE LOANS, HERE'S WHAT WE WANT TO SEE—

GREATER BALANCE OF TRADE EQUILIBRIUM, APPROPRIATE CURRENCY ADJUSTMENTS...

AND AN END TO SUBSIDIZED CONSUMPTION

WHAT DOES ALL THAT MEAN?

EAT LESS

Excerpted and adapted from "Behind the Cloak of Benevolence: World Bank and IMF Policies Hurt Workers at Home and Abroad," by John Cavanagh, Sarah Anderson and Jill Pike in Corporations Are Gonna Get Your Mama, *Kevin Danaher (Ed.), Monroe, ME: Common Courage Press, 1996.*

Stories of Debt and Hope

The following stories were collected in Mexico and Venezuela by Maryknoll Catholic missionaries. They were originally presented at Maryknoll's Justice and Peace Conference "The Human Face of Globalization" at Queretero, Mexico, in October 1997. Used here by permission. Note that the descriptions of life in Venezuela are prior to the election of the populist government of Hugo Chavez.

MARIA — FROM VENEZUELA

As told to Mary Jo Commerford, a Maryknoll lay missioner working in Barquisimeto, Venezuela.

My name is Maria. I am 34 years old and I live in a small village called Pavia outside of the big city of Barquisimeto in Venezuela. I am the mother of three young girls. My husband and I struggled in our marriage for many years. Little of the money he earned came home to help me with the girls. He would not even buy them shoes when they needed them. Also, if I left the house for any reason he would be crazy with jealousy and accuse me of awful things. Once I went out to visit a friend and he came running after me, waving a stick and screaming for me to get home. My family was afraid he would hurt us. Finally my daughter told me how scared she

was and I knew I had to leave him — but now I have to raise the girls by myself. I live with my mother and there are 11 of us in a small *ranchito*.

It has been especially hard the last few years. Our money is watered down and doesn't buy anything anymore. Three years ago the "b" (bolivar) was worth 170 to the dollar. Now it goes for 550 to the dollar. For us that means things have gone sky high in prices. It used to be that I could buy a bag of corn flour to make *arepas* for 100 b's, today it costs over 350 b's. Each time I go to the store the price has gone way up — how can they do that? I used to give my children milk each day but the price has gone up 5 times so we don't buy it anymore — often they drink watered-down coffee.

I am grateful that I have a job, but it doesn't make ends meet. I take care of children in a day-

A woman and her child in their makeshift home under a bridge in Caracas, Venezuela.

care center. I work five days a week. I cook, care, teach, and bathe young children all day long. You should see us some days. If it is my turn to bathe the children we have 80 little ones running around naked because they are wanting to play in the water. I have to line each one up and wash their hair and check it for bugs. My hands get very wrinkled by the end of the day.

The government runs this day care program. It is one of the programs that they say are supposed to help the poor. The trouble is they often go months without paying us. And the pay is not enough to care for a family. We make 31,000 bolivars a month [about $60 — the minimum cost of feeding a family is $150 a month. Three years ago that many bolivars would have been worth $180 but with the devaluation of the bolivar it has lost its purchasing power.] On this I have to raise three children! This does not cover their uniforms, books, medical needs, food, and clothes. I get up at 5 a.m. and wake my young children and walk across town each morning to begin work. When I am done for the day I am so tired I can hardly think. At night and on the weekends I do sewing for more money.

At the day care I work with many good women — we are all young mothers who are trying to feed our families. We cannot afford to quit because at least at the day care our children get fed breakfast and lunch. Once, all of us caretakers got together and went to the Ministry of the Family [the state agency that runs these day-care centers] and told them we have to have a raise — we cannot live on these wages. They told us that if we don't like our jobs, we can quit. They told us there is no use in organizing around the government — we should be glad to have these jobs. And to think, these are the programs our president brags about when he tells the world that the Venezuelan government is helping the poor!

I dream at night of having a house of my own. I do not like it that when my brother drinks and brings his girlfriends home, my youngest daughters must see this. It is hard to live with so many people under one roof. If my children are sick at night and cry, I am afraid their tears will wake up my mother and father and they will tell me that we cannot live here. If only I had a home of my own!

> "I used to give my children milk each day but the price has gone up 5 times so we don't buy it anymore — often they drink watered-down coffee."

FELICIANO — OAXACA, MEXICO

As told to Sister Joan Malherek, a Maryknoll Sister working in Oaxaca, Mexico.

My name is Feliciano and I grew up in a rural village. Like many people in my community we were not able to study very much. I went to school for only a little more than a year. But later, my wife and I moved to the big city of Oaxaca [pronounced Wah-HA-kah]. I got work doing construction. I worked very hard and am one of the lucky ones. I became a Master of Construction. I oversaw workers. I supervised them when they built small buildings and private family homes. It was a lot of responsibility to make sure everybody was working hard and seeing that things were built well. It gave me a lot of pleasure to see a building go up from start to finish.

When we first started out in Oaxaca we lived in a tin shack in a housing subdivision. By 1994 we had built a small house of brick and we were happy to have a home and a future for our three children.

But the real turning point for us was the devaluation of our currency, the peso, in December of 1994. Within days, a peso became worth a half-peso on the international market. Construction came to a standstill and many works were suspended. For six months I was without work. The costs of construction tripled. Prices fluctuated greatly from one day to the next. In the early part of 1995, there was 85% less construction than in the previous year. Those who had worked received lower salaries than they had previously.

Before, I was hired to supervise an entire job. Now I work by the day. This past year the price of materials has been stable — competition among those who sell materials has made this so. Salaries have not increased but the cost of living has continued to rise monthly over these past three years.

Today [in 1997] there is an increase in construction in Oaxaca, but most of it is in the hands of large businesses. They bring their own architects and supervisors and many of the workers are from outside Oaxaca. They buy their materials from factories or basic sources, so the local middlemen are bypassed. Only those who work for the government or for a big business can afford to buy the houses that are being built.

A mother and children wait for a truck ride home from the marketplace in Matagalpa, Nicaragua.

Michael Trokan

Education costs continually climb higher. School uniforms cost double what they cost three years ago. All food, electricity, water, bus fares, and other living expenses constantly go up. Even the corn we can afford to buy now is imported from Argentina and Brazil! It is of the quality that is fed to the animals and does not taste like locally produced corn.

These policies are destroying our economy and our hopes for improvement in the future.

EINAR — VENEZUELA

As told to Lisa Rodriguez, Maryknoll lay missioner working in Barquisimeto, Venezuela.

I live in a hillside *barrio* called Loma de Leon in Barquisimeto, Venezuela with my wife and four children. I am a *campesino* (farmer) from the *llanos* (plains), but I have lived in the city for 15 years. I am very proud to be a *campesino*.

There are three great loves in my life: my family, my chickens, and Venezuela. My oldest daughter is in the second grade and she gets very good marks. My second daughter is in kindergarten and she already knows how to read. She has fire in her eyes like her great-grandmother who rode a horse and carried a gun and fought against the dictator Perez Jimenez. She asks me hard questions and I think that someday my daughter will also be a leader and fight for a Venezuela where there is dignity.

I work painting *bombonas* (gas tanks) through a subcontract for the company Servigas. There are six steps to painting each *bombona:* sanding, cleaning, asphalt, base paint, synthetic paint and stenciling. I am not an official employee of the company and so I receive no benefits.

Even though we use lead paint there are no masks. Sometimes my head hurts so bad I can hardly breathe and I want to run away, but then I think of my children and I stay.

I work hard, I make 17,000 bolivars ($34) a week. We spend about 14,000 b's for food each week, and the rest goes to bus fare. Every morning we eat corn flour *arepas* and coffee, at midday we eat black beans and spaghetti and *arepas* again at night.

I look at my children and I know they are malnourished even though their bellies are filled with *arepas*. I can see it in their eyes. My one hope is that because they are often able to eat on our chicken's eggs that this will give them special strength.

I have many roosters because I love their spirit and their colors. I love to watch them and care for them, and through them I feel connected to the earth.

When one of my children gets sick or needs a pair of shoes, we must skip a few meals that week. This month the electric bill went from 67 bolivars to 560 even though our only electrical appliance is one light bulb. I got up at 4 a.m. the next day to go to the radio station and denounce this raise in prices. It is hard for me to keep quiet when I see something wrong, and this has often gotten me in trouble.

In August, my wife left me because of this. She took all the money that we had from a few construction jobs I did on the weekends to buy cinder blocks. We were going to build a few rooms so that we could move out of the tin *ranchito*. She left a note saying: "I am going because of your politics." But I cannot stop, I love Venezuela too much, and I cannot sit still when I see what is happening.

Right now I am helping a group of neighbors to get land to build their *ranchos*. We took over some land up in the mountain and the National Guard came and kicked us out with tear gas and took some of us to jail. But we went back and we are still there. Venezuela is such a rich land — how can people not have a right to a few meters of rocky hillside so that they can live? But sometimes my wife doesn't understand why I spend my time helping others in this way, since we already have our own land. She says that I should use this time instead to find a second job.

Even though I was so angry that she had taken the children and the money for our house, I went to ask her to come back. The two girls were enrolled in school there and we have already paid the registration and we couldn't afford to pay it twice. So I asked her to come back so the children can study. Last week school started and they returned.

I know that she is also angry because she is pregnant again. With our last baby we couldn't afford the 500 b's to have her tubes tied. Now it will cost even more. She feels very tired with this pregnancy and she hasn't been in prenatal care. It used to be free, but now you have to pay. I am glad my family is back, because at least we can face the even harder moments to come.

> **"This month the electric bill went from 67 bolivars to 560 even though our only electrical appliance is one light bulb."**

LEDIS — VENEZUELA

As told to Lisa Rodriguez, a Maryknoll lay missioner working in Barquisimeto, Venezuela.

I am 25 years old and I live in *barrio* Jose Felix Ribas. I was born in *barrio* El Cementerio. When my father saw my brother and me washing tombstones for money he knew that this wasn't the future he wanted for us, so he moved us to Barquisimeto. I am always grateful for that move, because Barquisimeto is in the state of Lara which is the music capital of Venezuela, and music is my life.

My father is a very good musician and when I was very young he would sit me on his lap and put the *cuatro* (four string guitar) in front of me. He would play the chords and I would strum. The rhythms of Venezuela vibrated in my body before I could talk.

In Barquisimeto, I used to sit outside in the hot afternoons and turn a bucket into my drum. A Catholic sister lived on the next street and she used to walk by and see me. She invited me to play for the Christmas services. She gave me my first real drum and I started playing each Sunday, even though I was embarrassed to tell my brother and friends where I was going.

I met Lisa (a Catholic lay missioner) in 1991. She asked me to teach her to play the *cuatro* and I did. Afterwards we began to sing together for church, and then we started a music group in the *barrio*. We called it *"Canto y Compromiso"* (Song and Commitment) because we wanted our music to be a way of reaching out to others.

We started teaching other children and youth, and soon we had over 150 children playing the drums and the *cuatro* in our *barrios*. There were so many of them that we had to split into four groups and take shifts in the Christmas services, or otherwise we would take up all the seats in the chapel.

Today in Venezuela many youth forget who they are. They want to wear authentic U.S. baseball hats and in Caracas they even kill one another for a pair of Michael Jordan shoes. And now there is cable TV and McDonald's and English-language rap music on the radio that we don't even understand.

A lot of kids who play with us now, and who teach other kids to play, used to feel like they had no worth because they couldn't afford a

Workers drawn to factory jobs in Ciudad Juarez, Mexico often live in houses they build themselves. In *colonias* like this one, there are usually no sewers or running water, and paved streets are rare.

Florida Marlins hat or pair of Michael Jordan shoes. But when they play the drums and take the hands of the children into theirs, to show them the rhythms, they begin to feel a different strength, a different pride.

The power of the drums reminds us who we are — sons and daughters of African slaves and native Indians. Here in Lara we feel the most passion when we play and dance *tamunangue*. It has seven songs that have been played and danced the same way for over 400 years. In it the drums are deep and haunting and sensual. It helps us to remember, to know, and to celebrate who we are, to feel the power of who we can become.

ARMANDO AND CATA — MEXICO

As told to Katie Hudak, a Maryknoll lay missioner working in Ciudad Juarez, Mexico (on the U.S. border.)

Armando: *Me gusta presentar mi esposa Cata.* I would like to introduce my wife Cata. She is much younger than I am — I am an old man of 48 and she is just 37 years old. Besides being a wife and mother to our four children, she is a lay leader in our community. She speaks very clearly and can tell you what is really happening to people's family and working lives here in Mexico.

Cata: *Hola, mucho gusto a conocerles:* Hello, nice to meet you. We are so happy to finally finish making a house of our own. When we first arrived in Ciudad Juarez we had to live in an abandoned school bus — imagine that with four young children! The best we could do for housing so far is make a "house" out of cardboard and wooden pallets. We hope someday to be able to make a better house.

We moved from the southern part of the state of Chihuahua. We lived in a small agricultural community. But people can no longer live there because there is very poor credit availability. The banks were once owned by the government but now that they are in private hands they will not give the credit out to small businesses or farmers. Another reason that everyone is leaving their land is that there was a big change in the Mexican constitution allowing family/community land of the traditional *ejido* system to be sold [and bought by wealthy land owners. The *ejidos* were parcels of community land, that were strictly not to be sold.] With the loss of land and the lack of any possibility for making a living, many people from the interior have come to Ciudad Juarez looking for a better life.

Armando: I come from the state of Mexico and it might seem odd to you, but I haven't seen my family in 15 years. I am so busy with my work. I work as a security guard and am often gone all night long. I only have two Sundays off a month. Can you believe that my wife Cata has never met her mother-in-law in person! All of this is due to the work I have to do in Ciudad Juarez.

Cata: It is like this with many families who come to Juarez looking for work in the *maquilas*. [*Maquiladoras, maquilas* for short, are factories set up in Mexico and other poorer countries by large corporations to take advantage of cheap labor and weak environmental regulations.] People work 12-15 hour days, never seeing their families and often earn as little as $20 a week. This isn't enough money for even the basic necessities, let alone medical care or educational needs. Unless several members of the family work, it is very difficult to survive.

Armando: This is our problem. You see our oldest daughter, Paty, is in her last year of middle school. We are so proud of her. Very few of her friends have been able to do that. But the school costs are many. We have to pay for registration, uniforms, books, transportation and schools — that alone can cost over 1,000 pesos ($120)! And can you believe this is from a government that says that education is constitutionally guaranteed to be free?

Cata: Yes, this is our concern. I have chosen to stay home with the children. They are at an important age (ages 7-14). There are so many problems in the *colonia* [neighborhood] due to working mothers who have to leave their children on their own. When the parents go to work, they are left roaming the streets with no one to watch over them. They skip classes and get into trouble with gangs and drugs — they sniff a terrible drug called *agua celeste* to get high. I do not want this for my children.

Armando: Many families have it even worse than we do. They look for work in the *maquilas*. When they find that they can barely survive, they begin to look for other ways to add to their income. I have seen single mothers turn to prostitution. Some people can look across into the U.S. on a daily bus ride downtown and see so many images of things that look so good that they cannot have here.

Cata: I worry so much about my children. I do not want them to be influenced by all they see around them. On the other hand, if I do not go to work soon, I will have to choose which of my four children continues their education and which ones must go to work to help the family. This is a horrible decision that no mother should have to make. ■

Joel Salcido

Workers, almost all of them women, leaving a foreign-owned *maquiladora* in Ciudad Juarez, Mexico at shift change.

The Kalinga Women Against the Chico Dam

BY LETICIA BULA-AT

The men first came to my village [in the Philippines] when I was 19 years old — that was in 1967. The men spoke with our elders. They said that they were sent by the government to survey our land. Our people became wary. We did not exactly know about this plan by the government. We were never consulted, just like when the authorities surveyed our land the first time. My elders remember that it was during the American colonial period. First the white men came for a visit carrying some kind of gadgets through which they peeped and wrote some things on paper. Then after a few years, some men came back and said that all of the people in my village were required to apply for the titles for the land on where we lived. The men said that without this, we could not own our land. Our people did not understand this — what paper title? What piece of paper to show ownership? Wasn't it enough that this land was where all the generations of our people had lived and died?

Then they said that we would have to pay taxes to the government for the land! This was our land, why should we pay? These ideas were totally alien to us.

Now here was another survey. Yes, that is exactly the word that the Americans used — survey! Our people asked, "What is the government up to now?" A high government official from our province in Kalinga came and said that we must not oppose the survey. It would be beneficial to many and that he had already seen the area where we were going to be resettled.

Resettled? We got more confused. We started to ask more questions. Our people started to hold meetings and consultations with other villages being surveyed. Our people tried to investigate. Then we found out! All along, the government had been planning to build four big dams along our Chico River!

And it was not only our village that was going to be affected, but many other villages. It would cross over two provinces. We did not know what a dam was then — but we had heard stories from the men in my village who had worked in the construction of a dam in the 1950s in a southern province in the Cordillera, peopled by Ibalois.

They said that they would build big and high walls in our rivers. The dam would be big

Ibaloi women protest the San Roque Dam project in the Philippines in 1999.

A supervisor gestures toward a construction site at the San Roque Dam project in 1999.

enough to submerge our villages, the forests, the land where our ancestors were buried! This was what had happened to the village of our Ibalois brothers and sisters who had been displaced because of the construction of a dam. They were promised land where they could be resettled and the government had said that they would be paid. But these promises were never fulfilled.

MALARIA-INFESTED

It was only the time when they planned to build the dam along the Chico river that the government offered and gave them a resettlement site — but in an area far away from their original village, where there was no clear source of water, where the land was not arable and in an area that was malaria-infested on an island so far away from home. Many of the people got sick. They left the area to live with their relatives. Others went to live in the cities but were considered as squatters.

At another time, they were offered a resettlement area in the nearby lowlands. Again this was not arable and worse, it was the ancestral

home of another group of indigenous people. Some went to Casecnan — the ancestral land of another tribe which is presently being threatened by displacement because of another World Bank-funded dam project of the government.

The government went on with the survey of the land where the dam was to be constructed, while our people went on with the meetings and consultations with other villages to discuss and plan how we were to oppose the construction of the dam. At first we sent petitions and delegations to the president to express our opposition. The president did not respond. Instead in the mid-1970s, more men came — this time, they were in fatigue uniforms and carried guns.

They had with them big construction equipment and materials. They had come to start the construction of the dam. They started first to set up big tents. When we learned about this, some women in the village stopped working and went to the site to confront the men. They asked the men not to continue with what they were doing. The men did not listen to them so the women dismantled the tents themselves. This was the start of a long period of active resistance by the people against the International Monetary Fund/World Bank-funded Chico River Dam Development Project of the government where women played key and important roles.

Our people and the people from other villages forged peace pacts through our traditional systems and united to oppose the dam project. We kept vigil at night and barricaded the site — men, women, and children were all involved. We took turns in cooking, planting, keeping a vigil, and watching over the barricades. Almost everyone in the affected villages was mobilized. Each day, callers were assigned to provide the signal whenever government men brought in construction equipment and materials or if they made a move to start to build. And if we heard the loud cry which was the signal, all of us stopped what we had been doing and went to the site and stopped any move to construct the dam.

At one time, when they attempted to set up their tents again, the loud cry came and we all rushed to the site. We dismantled and took the tents and other equipment with us and brought them to the barracks in the town center. We had to march for miles. We started walking late in the afternoon. We shouted slogans against the construction of the dam as we marched along. We arrived at the barracks early the next day. This we did as an act of protest.

But after several days, the soldiers brought the equipment back.

At another time, during the height of the struggle, women tried to prevent the entry of a truck that was bringing in more construction materials. We lay down on the road so that the trucks would not be able to pass. When they tried to bring the materials down from the truck, others tried to physically struggle with the men. The men were becoming more aggressive and many among us were getting hurt. We cried but at the same time we fought back and kicked them.

All the women who were there did what they could to prevent any move by the men to construct the dam or set up their tents. In desperation, one woman removed her clothes while others followed. One lactating mother had to squeeze out milk from her breast to prevent a soldier from getting near her. But the men had guns, so they were able to take many of my elders, sisters, and brothers to the barracks where they were detained. After a few days, our leaders were brought to a detention center in Manila.

DEMAND FOR RELEASE

Demanding for their release was what occupied us for the next few months. Many more people were mobilized not only from our villages but from other villages as well. We were able to gather support from our sisters and brothers from the other sectors of society and gain support from the national and international levels. They struggled alongside us and they also demanded the release of the villagers who were detained.

However, this was also the time that the men were able to set up concrete structures at the site that would serve as their camp and at the same time as a site for the delivery of equipment and materials that would be used for the construction of the dam.

Because of the widening support and pressure, the government was forced to release our people after six months of detention. When they came back to our villages, we sustained and continued our opposition to the construction of the dam. Many of our villagers, including some of our women, joined in the armed resistance.

Finally, in 1987, 20 years after they started the survey, the government officially shelved the Chico River Dam Development Project. Our people rejoiced and held celebrations. This was an historic event because we learned that it was the first time that an IMF/World Bank-funded project had been successfully stopped by the militant opposition of the people.

A few years ago, we again learned that the government was planning to implement another

> "To attract companies like yours, we have felled mountains, razed jungles, filled swamps, moved rivers, relocated towns, and in their place built power plants, dams, roads ... all to make it easier for you to do business here."
>
> —Philippine government ad that ran in *Fortune* magazine in the early 1970s

International Rivers Network

Protesters against the San Roque Dam project at Baguio City, Luzon, Philippines in 1999.

so-called development project. But this time the project was not going to be limited to our villages, but was going to extend throughout the entire Cordillera. This time they were planning to build not 4 but 17 dams. Our government has a vision of making our country a newly industrializing country. It claims that these dams are necessary to generate power and electricity for the needs of the big companies that would be set up.

The government has also recently passed a mining law that allows mining companies to further exploit our lands. We know that the companies being allowed by our government to mine our lands are owned by foreign big business. They are to be permitted to mine the land from 50 to 75 years to a maximum area of 81,000 hectares.

The government is also planning to convert our rice fields and terraces for the production of cash crops such as cut flowers and mango trees. The government claims that this would be good for us as it would bring about development to our country.

But we know that it is not us, poor people, who will benefit from these programs. Not us in our village, not the majority of the people in my country who are poor. Formerly, the Marcos government used to say, "we must sacrifice for the sake of the majority." But it was not even the majority who benefited, but foreign big companies.

The generations of our people have nurtured, protected, and defended our lands for many centuries now. Our people resisted hundreds of years of colonial rule and struggled against vested interests who considered our lands only as resource bases. Today, we continue to fight and struggle against these oppressors. We will not allow our lands to be taken away from us. We will not allow our resources to be further exploited. For us, land is life, it is sacred. This land is where our ancestors are buried. This land is what kept generations of our people alive and this is where we are going to die. ∎

* * *

Indigenous peoples' struggles against dams in the Philippines continue. In March of 2001, 40 Filipino organizations signed a declaration demanding a stop to all dam construction and a moratorium on the construction of new dams. For existing dams, they called for full compensation and provision of sustainable sources of livelihood for dam-affected communities, and the immediate environmental rehabilitation of damaged ecosystems. A new proposed dam, the San Roque, located in the Cordillera region of Luzon island in the Philippines, would be the tallest dam in Asia, if built. It is being opposed by the Cordillera Peoples' Alliance. Contact the International Rivers Network at www.irn.org to learn more. — *The editors*

Leticia Bula-at is an activist with the Cordillera Women's Education and Resource Centre in the Philippines. A version of this article was first published in Third World Resurgence.

The Marshalltezuma Plan

BY CUAICAIPURO CUAUTÉMOC

In 1519 Hernando Cortés and the Spaniards defeated Motecuhzoma (sometimes spelled Montezuma), the Aztec ruler. This began the transfer of tremendous wealth from Central America to Europe. In 1947, the U.S. government initiated the "Marshall Plan," consisting of massive loans and grants to reconstruct Western Europe after World War II. Put them together, as Cuaicaipuro Cuautémoc does in the following article, and the result is the Marshalltezuma Plan.

I am a descendant of those who colonized America 40,000 years ago and I've got a bone to pick with those Europeans who claim to have "discovered" us 500 years ago.

Why is it that your banks and moneylenders ask me to pay for debts which I never authorized to be sold to me in the first place? You tell me that all debts must be paid with interest, even if it means selling human beings and sometimes even whole countries without their consent.

But I also have payments to claim. And I, too, can claim interest. The evidence is in the archives where paper after paper, receipt after receipt, signature after signature, show that from 1503 to 1660, 185,000 kilos of gold and 16 million kilos of silver were shipped from America.

Plunder? I wouldn't say so. Because that would mean that our Christian brothers were violating their seventh commandment.

Genocide? May Tanatzin have mercy on me for thinking that the Europeans, like Cain, kill and then deny their brother's blood!

Pillage? That would mean giving credit to slanderers like Bartolomé de las Casas, who equated the discovery of the Indies with its destruction, or to extremists such as Dr. Arturo Petri who thinks that the growth of capitalism and of the current European civilization was due to that early flood of precious metals from the Americas!

But I would rather consider those thousands of kilos of gold and silver as the first of several friendly loans granted by Native Americans for Europe's development. If these were not considered loans, it would mean that they were war crimes, which would require their immediate return and also compensation for damages. I prefer to believe in

> **I would rather consider those thousands of kilos of gold and silver as the first of several friendly loans granted by Native Americans for Europe's development.**

the least offensive of the hypotheses. Such fabulous capital exports were nothing short of a Marshalltezuma Plan to guarantee the reconstruction of a barbarian Europe, ruined by deplorable wars against the Muslim foe.

For this reason we must ask ourselves: What have you, our European brothers, done in a rational, responsible, or at least productive way with the resources so generously advanced by the International Indo-American Fund?

The answer is, unfortunately, nothing. Strategically, you squandered it on wars, invincible armies, Third Reichs, and other forms of mutual extermination, only to end up being occupied by the Yankee troops of NATO. Like Panama, but without a canal.

Financially, you were incapable — even after a moratorium of 500 years — of either paying back capital with interest or of becoming independent from raw materials and cheap energy imported from the Third World.

This pitiful picture corroborates U.S. economist Milton Friedman's assertion that a subsidized economy can never function properly. And it compels us to claim — for your own good — the repayment of capital and interest which we have so generously delayed reclaiming for all these centuries.

Nonetheless, we want to make clear that we will refrain from charging our European brothers the despicable floating rates of 20% or even 30% that they charge Third World countries. We shall only demand the return of all precious metals advanced, plus a modest fixed interest rate of 10% per year accumulated over 500 years. On this basis, we want to inform our discoverers that they owe us, as a first payment against the debt, only 185,000 kilos of gold and 16 million kilos of silver. And to this sum, of course, we must add the European invention of compound interest.

What huge piles of gold and silver! How much human blood would weigh the same? To say that in half a millennium Europe has not been able to produce sufficient wealth to pay back this modest interest is to admit the total failure of capitalism. ∎

Cuaicaipuro Cuautémoc is a Mexican indigenous leader. This article was first printed in translation in the journal, Resurgence, #184, *and was reprinted in* The New Internationalist, *May 1999.*

Cancel the Debt

Social justice and religious organizations around the world have called for a cancellation of the poorest countries' debts. These groups recognize that governments of impoverished countries are making interest payments on debt with money that should go instead to provide for people's basic needs and to protect the environment.

Jubilee USA Network is one of the main organizations coordinating international efforts to cancel the debt. It draws its inspiration from the book of Leviticus, which describes a Year of Jubilee every 50 years where, according to Jubilee USA Network, "social inequalities are rectified: Slaves are freed, land is returned to original owners, and debts are canceled."

Jubilee USA Network's platform calls for:

- Definitive cancellation of the crushing international debt, in situations where countries burdened with high levels of human need and environmental distress are unable to meet the basic needs of their people or achieve a level of sustainable development that ensures a decent quality of life.

- Definitive debt cancellation that benefits ordinary people and facilitates their participation in the process of determining the scope, timing, and conditions of debt relief, as well as the future direction and priorities of their national and local economies.

- Definitive debt cancellation that is not conditioned on policy reforms that perpetuate or deepen poverty or environmental degradation.

- Acknowledgment of responsibility by both lenders and borrowers, and action to recover resources that were diverted to corrupt regimes, institutions, and individuals.

- Establishment of a transparent and participatory process to develop mechanisms to monitor international monetary flows and prevent recurring destructive cycles of indebtedness.

To get involved, contact Jubilee USA Network, 222 East Capitol St., Washington, D.C. 20003-1036; (202) 783-3566; www.j2000usa.org.

Rethinking "Free Trade" and the World Trade Organization

BY BILL BIGELOW

We've been taught that anything with the word "free" in front of it must be good: free speech, free enterprise, free press. Thus encouraging students to think critically about "free trade" means asking them to suspend their positive associations not only with the word "free," but also with a word that conjures similar images of equality, mutual benefit, and fairness: "trade." And yet any curricular inquiry that aims to take an honest look at globalization needs to pry beneath some of the sweet-sounding terms that are tossed about so casually by pundits and politicians. Terms like "free trade" — or as we discussed earlier in this chapter, "structural adjustment."

In late November and early December of 1999, the little-known World Trade Organization (WTO) suddenly became a household name. Tens of thousands of protesters converged on Seattle to draw attention to the version of globalization and free trade represented by the WTO. Conscientious teachers across the world scrambled to find resources that might help their students make sense of the demonstrations and the issues being raised so dramatically.

Supporters of the World Trade Organization argued that nations need a rule-governed system of trade, that without it there would be economic chaos, promoting trade wars that can rapidly turn into shooting wars. They claimed that trade is the engine of global prosperity and that all boats will be lifted as trade becomes freer and more abundant. The leadership of both Democrats and Republicans held these positions. Prominent columnists, like *The New York Times*' Thomas Friedman, slammed the Seattle WTO protesters as "a Noah's ark of flat-earth advocates, protectionist trade unions and yuppies looking for their 1960s fix."

Critics of the WTO argued that the organization is profoundly undemocratic — with unelected trade bureaucrats making decisions about everything from nations' environmental policies to the kind of chemicals that may or may not be allowed in food, to whether or not sweatshop labor may be permitted around the world. They maintained that WTO rules seek to zealously protect the rights of corporations, but offer no such protection for labor and human rights or for the environment — that the only boats lifted by free trade and globalization are the yachts of the wealthy. Environmentalists argued that the very aims of the WTO, to greatly expand global trade, are hostile to the environment and portend greater ecological destruction.

In the following pages we offer some resources that we've developed, or that we've found helpful to sort through the claims and counterclaims. Included are ideas for using these materials, as well as some additional thoughts on engaging students in these key issues. ■

Bill Bigelow (bbpdx@aol.com) teaches at Franklin High School in Portland, Oregon and is a Rethinking Schools editor.

"DILEMMAS OF GLOBAL TRADE"
Situations for students to reflect on (pp. 98-99)

Because students can sort out the implications of "free trade" only with examples, one way to begin to explore these issues is by looking at some specific cases — both real and hypothetical. Review one or two of the "Dilemmas of Global Trade" with students, simply to make sure that they are clear what's being asked of them, and then divide the class into small groups to work with these. Afterward, lead a whole-class discussion.

Try to get students to clarify the *principles* that underlie their opinions. What different definitions of "freedom" might be at work? For example, in question #1, Gerber's freedom to use its chubby baby trademark anywhere and everywhere is set against the freedom of mothers to raise healthy children and the freedom of a government to take measures to protect its citizens. However students answer each question, ask them, "Who might have a different definition of freedom?"

One point to underscore here — and it's a vital one in the globalization debate — is the fundamentally different views of the meaning of a commodity. In one view, a commodity is simply a product, a potential item of global trade, which must be judged solely in terms of price and quality. The other view insists that commodities should be regarded as bundles of social and ecological relationships — that it is crucial how something is produced, under what conditions, by whom, with what effects on the environment, with what effects on the society where it is both produced and marketed. All these questions cannot be swept aside by glib assertions of the right to "free trade."

After discussing students' answers to the questions, ask them to make a list of the principles that they believe should govern trade between different nations.

Note that more information on the problems can be found in "The WTO in Action: Case Studies" (www.rethinkingschools.org/rg), and also in the chapter "Just Food?," p. 221.

"TEN BENEFITS OF THE WTO SYSTEM"
"THE WTO: POWERFUL, SECRETIVE, BAD FOR HUMANITY, BAD FOR THE EARTH"
"TEN ARGUMENTS AGAINST THE WORLD TRADE ORGANIZATION"
"THE WTO IN ACTION: CASE STUDIES"
Readings for students (pp. 100-107)

Some discussion or writing questions for use with "Ten Benefits of the WTO":

- In your own words, summarize the benefits of the WTO, according to the WTO.

- In point #2, the WTO uses the word "constructively" three times to describe how its system allows disputes to be resolved. What exactly is meant by this term? What is being "constructed"?

- Point #3 contrasts a system based on rules with one based on power. Can systems be based on both? Think about rules that you have to follow: Are any of these based on some people having more power than others?

- In point #4, the WTO claims that its system leads to lower prices for all goods. Can you think of any groups that might be hurt by lower prices? (Students might consider poor farmers around the world, whose countries are flooded by cheap corn and rice, for example. In general, cheap commodity prices will depress earnings of small farmers and wages of farm workers. Encourage students to think about the perspectives that are missed when they are asked to view the world solely as consumers.)

- The WTO makes a number of claims about how "consumers" will benefit from its system. What claims does it make for how its system will benefit workers? Farmers? (This is a bit of a trick question: the WTO does not claim any benefits for these groups. The only group it specifically names is "consumers.") In general, make an effort to prompt students to think about groups and issues *not* discussed in the "Ten Benefits."

- According to the "Ten Benefits of the WTO," how does the WTO trading system help protect the environment? (This is another trick question, as the WTO never mentions the environment in the reading.)

- What are the ecological implications of point #5? If the WTO aims to give all the consumers in the world "more choice," with goods that have traveled great distances, how would that affect the earth?

- Point #9 claims that the WTO system shields governments from "narrow interests." Who are these "narrow interests"? Look at the case studies (see our website at www.rethinkingschools.org/rg) to discover some of the groups that have been denied influence by WTO rules.

- In point #10, the WTO suggests that one result of the WTO is that it makes it difficult for a government "to reverse" its course. Think of some circumstances where this inability to reverse course could be a problem.

- Use "Ten Arguments Against the World Trade Organization" to raise questions about or critique "Ten Benefits of the WTO System."

- After reading "Ten Benefits of the WTO System," read the International Forum on Globalization's descriptions of some of the specific cases resolved by the WTO (see www.rethinkingschools.org/rg). Do these cases support or contradict the claims made by the WTO? Give examples.

- Look back to the "Globalization Myths" in the Introduction (p. 14). Use them to raise questions about the "WTO benefits."

Class Debate:

Tell students that the class will debate: "Be it resolved that the WTO is more beneficial than harmful to humanity and the environment." Inform them that they won't know which side they will debate until just before you begin. Divide the class into workgroups and have them

Dock workers in San Francisco protest against the World Trade Organization on November 30, 1999. An anti-WTO strike by the International Longshore and Warehouse Union snarled cargo movement all along the West Coast that day.

use the readings — and any other materials they can find in their research — to prepare debating points for each side. (Helpful websites for research include: www.wto.org [site of the World Trade Organization], www.ifg.org [site of the International Forum on Globalization], and www.twnside.org.sg, [site of the Third World Network, based in Penang, Malaysia.])

Project:

Ask students to choose one of the points raised in either of the two "10 point" readings, or in one of the cases in "The WTO in Action: Case Studies" (www.rethinkingschools.org/rg). Ask them to research this issue and teach what they learn to the class. They might perform this as a skit, design and lead a class activity, write and read a children's book, or simply make a presentation and lead a discussion.

Essay:

Have students develop a thesis on the WTO and write an essay supporting that thesis. You might begin by suggesting one or two thesis statements and brainstorming others with students.

Dilemmas of Global Trade: Problem Solving

Read each of the situations below. Answer the "yes" or "no" question that concludes each situation and explain the reasoning behind your opinion.

1.

For many years, advertising has encouraged women in poor countries to buy infant formula. Many poor women do not have access to clean water or they can't read the instructions on the can (because it's not in their language or because they can't read at all). Many can't afford to buy sufficient quantities of the formula, so they end up "stretching" it by diluting it. Babies become malnourished and often die.

The government of Guatemala passed a law that the packaging of food products for infants could not feature pictures of healthy babies because this could discourage women from breast-feeding. This law is based on guidelines issued by the World Health Organization and UNICEF.

Gerber's says that this is an "unfair trade practice" because it means that they can't use their trademark in Guatemala. They say this violates principles of free trade. Gerber's was supported by the U.S. State Department.

Do you agree with Gerber's position?

2.

Most people agree that the government of Burma (known also as Myanmar) is repressive. The U.S. State Department issued a report saying that Burmese "soldiers have committed serious human rights abuses, including extra judicial killing and rape." Human rights organizations have documented the widespread use of forced labor. In order to protest human rights abuses there, the government of Massachusetts passed a law saying that it will not purchase major goods or services from any company that has investments in Burma.

The European Union and Japan complained that this was a violation of free trade because what is important about a good is the product itself, not how it was produced or who produced it. The National Foreign Trade Council, representing 580 U.S. companies — 346 of which do business with Burma — agreed. They said that Massachusetts has no right to pick and choose whom it will buy from based on anything other than the price and the quality of goods to be provided — period.

Do you agree with the position of the National Foreign Trade Council?

3.

Much of the shrimp sold in the United States is caught with nets that capture and kill endangered sea turtles. There is a simple way to avoid killing the turtles, if the nets are fitted with TEDs (turtle extruder devices). The United States has banned shrimp products from countries that do not use TEDs.

On behalf of fishing interests in their countries, the governments of India, Malaysia, Pakistan, and Thailand have complained, saying that this banning is an unfair trade practice. The only thing that should matter is the quality of the shrimp, not how it was or was not caught, they say.

Do you agree with the position taken by these governments?

4.

Small farmers all over the world grow just enough food for their families and a little extra to be sold in the market for cash to buy medicines, education, and household goods, or for savings. Farms in industrial countries like the United States use machinery and pesticides to produce food much more cheaply than can be produced on small farms in Third World countries. Some people in poor countries want to put tariffs on imports of cheap food from the United States and Europe, or to maintain the ones they have.

The U.S. and European governments argue that this supports inefficient farming practices, and leads to more expensive food for their people.

Also, they say it is an attack on the freedom of producers to sell their goods to anyone at any time.

Do you agree with the U.S. and European governments?

5.

Suppose that students at our school decide to push the school board to enact a policy that forbids schools from purchasing athletic equipment or clothing made in countries that do not enforce a minimum living wage and do not enforce restrictions against child labor. Let's say students do not want to buy T-shirts, hats, or other clothing, or kick soccer balls, made in sweatshops.

The school board agrees to adopt the policy urged by the students. But immediately the governments of Indonesia, Pakistan, Nicaragua, El Salvador and others protest that this is an unfair interference in their internal affairs and a violation of free trade. They argue that no government agency in the United States has the right to discriminate against particular countries on the basis of policies those countries did or did not enact. According to these countries, it is a clear instance of an unfair trade practice. They point out that you don't see Indonesia refusing to buy paper products from the United States because they are clear-cutting their forests.

Do you agree with the governments of Indonesia, Pakistan, et al.?

6.

Recently, African nations proposed a trade "rule" that would outlaw the patenting of any life forms. This would include plants, genetic material, seeds, etc. — whether found in nature, "naturally" bred, or genetically engineered. The African nations (and many others, including indigenous organizations) argue that it is immoral to patent life. They also say that patenting life is theft, because food or medicinal uses of many plants were developed over thousands of years by indigenous people.

Corporations and many scientists argue that genetic research is the new frontier. Perhaps new organisms will be able to clean oil spills. Perhaps we can produce food that is much more nutritious and resists spoilage. If governments don't grant patents for all inventions, including those involving life, then there will be little incentive to invent because the invention would become common property as soon as it was developed. They insist that patents are necessary for human progress and for the protection of the environment, and any restrictions are a violation of free trade.

Do you agree with these corporations?

7.

Some consumer groups, scientists, and others believe that genetically engineered crops might be harmful. They think that not enough research has been done to prove them safe, and they point out that pollen from genetically engineered corn has been shown to harm monarch butterflies. At the least, they want any food that has been genetically modified to be labeled as such, and are working for government regulations to that effect. They point out that as it stands now, no one in the United States has the slightest idea about whether or not they are eating genetically modified food — that we are all a bunch of guinea pigs who have not given our consent to be experimented on.

Others say: Nonsense. There is no hard scientific proof that genetically engineered food hurts anyone. Just the opposite: Genetically engineered food offers countless benefits, from enhanced vitamins to better flavor. Further, they argue, if companies were forced by the government — any government — to begin labeling genetically engineered food, then it would imply that non-genetically engineered food was superior. And that is discrimination. And discrimination violates principles of free trade.

Do you agree with these food companies?

"Ten Benefits of the WTO System"

The following is condensed from a reading on the website of the World Trade Organization, www.wto.org.

The WTO's paramount objective is to help trade flow smoothly, freely, fairly, and predictably. It does this by:

- Administering trade agreements.
- Acting as a forum for trade negotiations.
- Settling trade disputes.
- Reviewing national trade policies.
- Assisting developing countries in trade policy issues through technical assistance and training programs.
- Cooperating with other international organizations.

1. The system helps to keep the peace.

How does this work? Crudely put, sales people are usually reluctant to fight their customers — usually. In other words, if trade flows smoothly and both sides enjoy a healthy commercial relationship, political conflict is less likely.

What's more, smoothly flowing trade also helps people all over the world become better off. People who are more prosperous and contented are also less likely to fight.

The short-sighted protectionist view is that defending particular sectors against imports is beneficial. But that view ignores how other countries are going to respond. The longer term reality is that one protectionist step by one country can easily lead to retaliation from other countries, a loss of confidence in freer trade, and a slide into serious economic trouble for all — including the sectors that were originally protected. Everyone loses.

Confidence is the key to avoiding that kind of no-win scenario. When governments are confident that others will not raise trade barriers, they will not be tempted to do the same. They will also be in a much better frame of mind to cooperate with each other.

The WTO trading system plays a vital role in creating and reinforcing that confidence. Particularly important are negotiations that lead to agreement by consensus, and a focus on abiding by the rules.

2. The system allows disputes to be handled constructively.

As trade expands in volume, in the numbers of products traded, and in the numbers of countries and companies trading, there are more opportunities for trade disputes to arise. The WTO system helps resolve these disputes peacefully and constructively.

When member nations bring disputes to the WTO, the WTO's procedure focuses their attention on the rules. Once a ruling has been made, countries concentrate on trying to comply with the rules, and perhaps later renegotiating the rules — not on declaring war on each other.

Nearly 200 disputes have been brought to the WTO since it was set up in 1995. Without a means of tackling these constructively and harmoniously, some could have led to more serious political conflict.

3. A system based on rules rather than power makes life easier for all.

The WTO cannot claim to make all countries equal. But it does reduce some inequalities, giving smaller countries more voice, and at the same time freeing the major powers from the complexity of having to negotiate trade agreements with each of their numerous trading partners.

Decisions in the WTO are made by consensus. The WTO agreements were negotiated by all members, were approved by consensus and were ratified in all members' parliaments.

The agreements apply to everyone. Rich and poor countries alike can be challenged if they violate an agreement, and they have an equal right to challenge others in the WTO's dispute settlement procedures.

The result for smaller countries is some increased bargaining power. Without the WTO's system, the more powerful countries would be freer to impose their will on their smaller trading partners. Smaller countries would have to deal with each of the major economic powers individually, and would be much less able to resist unwanted pressure.

The fact that there is a single set of rules applying to all members greatly simplifies the entire trade regime.

4. Freer trade cuts the cost of living.

We are all consumers. The prices we pay for our food and clothing, our necessities and luxuries, and everything else in between, are affected by trade policies.

Protectionism is expensive: It raises prices. The WTO's global system lowers trade barriers through negotiation and applies the principle of non-discrimination. The result is reduced costs of production (because imports used in production are cheaper) and reduced prices of finished goods and services, and ultimately a lower cost of living.

The system now entrusted to the WTO has been in place for over 50 years. In that time there have been eight major rounds of trade negotiations. Trade barriers around the world are lower than they have ever been in modern trading history. They continue to fall, and we are all benefiting.

5. The WTO system gives consumers more choice, and a broader range of qualities to choose from.

Think of all the things we can now have because we can import them: fruits and vegetables out of season, foods, clothing and other products that used to be considered exotic, cut flowers from any part of the world, all sorts of household goods, books, music, movies, and so on.

Think also of the things people in other countries can have because they buy exports from us and elsewhere.

Look around and consider all the things that would disappear if all our imports were taken away from us. Imports allow us more choice — both more goods and services to choose from, and a wider range of qualities. Even the quality of locally produced goods can improve because of the competition from imports.

6. Trade raises incomes.

Lowering trade barriers allows trade to increase, which adds to incomes — national incomes and personal incomes. But some adjustment is necessary.

The fact that there is additional income means that resources are available for governments to redistribute. The WTO's own estimates for the impact of the 1994 Uruguay Round trade deal were between $109 billion and $510 billion

Residents of Shanghai, China pass a Pepsi billboard.

added to world income (depending on the assumptions of the calculations and allowing for margins of error).

Trade clearly boosts incomes. Trade also poses challenges as domestic producers face competition from imports. But the fact that there is additional income means that resources are available for governments to redistribute the benefits from those who gain the most — for example to help companies and workers adapt by becoming more productive and competitive in what they were already doing, or by switching to new activities.

7. Trade stimulates economic growth, and that can be good news for employment.

It is also true that some jobs are lost even when

trade is expanding. Some countries are better at making the adjustment than others. This is partly because some countries have more effective adjustment policies. Those without effective policies are missing an opportunity.

The E.U. Commission calculates that the creation of its Single Market means that there are somewhere in the range of 300,000–900,000 more jobs than there would be without the Single Market.

Often, job prospects are better in companies involved in trade.

In the United States, 12 million people owe their jobs to exports; 2 million of those jobs were created between 1993 and 1997. And those jobs tend to be better-paid with better security. Between 1987 and 1992, employment growth in companies involved in exporting was around 18% higher than in other comparable companies.

8. The basic principles make the system economically more efficient, and they cut costs.

Trade allows a division of labor between countries. It allows resources to be used more appropriately and effectively for production.

Also, when governments charge the same duty rates on imports from all countries, and use the same regulations for all products, no matter where they come from, whether imported or locally produced, life for companies is much simpler.

Non-discrimination is just one of the key principles of WTO's trading system. Others include: transparency (clear information about policies, rules, and other regulations); increased certainty about trading conditions (commitments to lower trade barriers and to increase other countries' access to one's markets are legally binding); simplification and standardization of customs procedure, etc.

9. The WTO system shields governments from narrow interests.

Governments are better-placed to defend themselves against lobbying from narrow interest groups by focusing on trade-offs that are made in the interests of everyone in the economy.

Superficially, restricting imports looks like an effective way of supporting an economic sector. But if you protect your clothing industry, everyone else has to pay for more expensive clothes, which puts pressure on wages in all sectors, for example.

Protectionism can also escalate as other countries retaliate by raising their own trade barriers. That's exactly what happened in the 1920s and '30s with disastrous effects. Even the sectors that were demanding protection ended up losing.

If, during a WTO trade negotiation, one pressure group lobbies its government to be considered as a special case in need of protection, the government can reject the protectionist pressure by arguing that it needs a broad-ranging agreement that will benefit all sectors of the economy.

10. The system encourages good government.

Under WTO rules, once a commitment has been made to liberalize a sector of trade, it is difficult to reverse. The rules also discourage a range of unwise policies.

For businesses, that means greater certainty and greater clarity about trading conditions.

For governments, it can often mean good discipline. ■

> "Protectionism is expensive: it raises prices. The WTO's global system lowers trade barriers through negotiation and applies the principle of non-discrimination. The result is reduced costs of production (because imports used in production are cheaper) and reduced prices of finished goods and services, and ultimately a lower cost of living.
>
> "The system now entrusted to the WTO has been in place for over 50 years. In that time there have been eight major rounds of trade negotiations. Trade barriers around the world are lower than they have ever been in modern trading history. They continue to fall, and we are all benefiting."

Seattle police in riot gear during protests against the World Trade Organization in November 1999.

The WTO:
Powerful, Secretive, Bad for
Humanity, Bad for the Earth

This article is condensed from the International Forum on Globalization's publication Invisible Government — The World Trade Organization: Global Government For The New Millennium? *by Jerry Mander and Debi Barker. For more information see Resources, p. 370.*

The World Trade Organization (WTO) is the primary rule-making regime of the globalization process. In only a few years of existence the WTO has become one of the most powerful and secretive international bodies on earth. The main principle of the WTO is that global commercial interests are more important than all others. Obstacles to the smooth operation and rapid expansion of global corporate activity are therefore routinely suppressed — even if those "obsta-

cles" are national, provincial, state, and community laws and standards that are made on behalf of labor rights, environmental protection, human rights, consumer rights, local culture, social justice, national sovereignty, and democracy.

The WTO was formed in 1995 by an agreement among 125 countries (expanded to 144, as of early 2002) and was given powers far greater than had ever before been granted to an international body, including the three primary characteristics of governments: executive, legislative, and judicial authority.

Operating from Geneva, Switzerland, the WTO has now incorporated within itself more than 20 separate international agreements. The WTO has full executive authority over all these accords.

VIOLENCE AT THE FREE TRADE AREA OF THE AMERICAS SUMMIT

Kirk

The WTO can strike down laws, programs, and policies of its member nations and compel them to establish new laws that conform to WTO rules. This authority extends to provinces, states, counties, and cities.

The WTO's judicial powers are expressed through its Dispute Settlement Body (DSB). This is comprised of panels of corporate and trade lawyers and officials who preside, in secret hearings, as final judges and arbiters of disputes among members.

Unlike other international bodies, including the United Nations, the WTO has also been granted far-reaching enforcement powers. It has the ability to demand compliance from its members, and to coerce and force compliance where necessary by means of a variety of disciplines, penalties, and trade sanctions, which can be so economically severe that even the largest nations must yield. ■

"Intellectual property rights are important to indigenous peoples all over the world. Our knowledge, our medicine, our art, our internal democracy, are very rich. When the scientists come they steal our rights and our knowledge without recognizing that they are ours. Everybody knows about the *Uña de gato*, a medicine of the indigenous people from Peru that's been stolen. A lot of songs and stories have been stolen. A U.S. anthropologist patented quinoa — a high-protein grain that is the patrimony of the Quechua and Aymara people of Bolivia and Peru — and he has the rights to its sale. In the Amazon, the Yanomami people have a certain type of poison that they throw into the water to kill the fish, made from a special plant. And now there is a corporation that's saying that they discovered it and that they want to patent it.

"The WTO thinks of everything in terms of trade and commercializing things. For us it isn't somebody's private property; it's the spiritual patrimony of our community."

—Taira Stanley and Ibe
Movimiento de la Juventud Kuna
Panama

Ten Arguments Against the World Trade Organization

Adapted from the website of Global Exchange, www.globalexchange.org. Another version of this article can be found in Globalize This! The Battle Against the World Trade Organization and Corporate Rule, *edited by Kevin Danaher and Roger Burbach. See Resources, p. 370.*

1. THE WTO ONLY SERVES THE INTERESTS OF MULTINATIONAL CORPORATIONS.

The WTO is not a democratic institution, and yet its policies impact all aspects of society and the planet. The WTO rules are written by and for corporations with inside access to the negotiations. For example, the United States Trade Representative relies on its 17 "Industry Sector Advisory Committees" to provide input into trade negotiations. Citizen input by consumer, environmental, human rights, and labor organizations is consistently ignored. Even requests for information are denied, and the proceedings are held in secret.

2. THE WTO IS A STACKED, SECRETIVE COURT.

The WTO's dispute panels, which rule on whether domestic laws are "barriers to trade" and should therefore be abolished, consist of three trade bureaucrats who are not screened for conflicts of interest. For example, in the tuna/dolphin case that Mexico filed against the United States — which forced the United States to repeal its law that barred tuna from being caught by mile-long nets that kill hundreds of thousands of dolphins each year — one of the judges was from a corporate front group that lobbied on behalf of the Mexican government for NAFTA.

3. THE WTO TRAMPLES OVER LABOR AND HUMAN RIGHTS.

The WTO has refused to address the impact of free trade on labor rights, despite the fact that countries that actively enforce labor rights are disadvantaged by competition from countries that consistently violate international labor conventions. Many "developing" countries, such as Mexico, contend that labor standards constitute a "barrier to free trade" for countries whose competitive advantage in the global economy is cheap labor. Potential solutions to labor and human rights abuses are blocked by the WTO, which has ruled, for example, that it is illegal for a government to ban a product based on the way it is produced (e.g., with child labor), and that governments cannot take into account the

AIDS orphans at a children's center in Mombasa, Kenya. Several African nations have accused drug companies of charging too much for anti-AIDS drugs, thus limiting their availability.

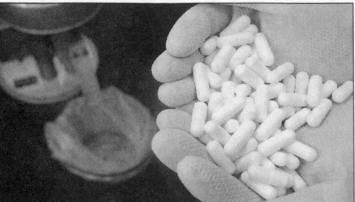

Capsules of the anti-AIDS drug Indinavir.

"Lives Before Profit"

This was a common protest sign in the demonstrations in South Africa and other parts of the world in the spring of 2001. People demanded that drug companies make available generic versions of anti-AIDS drugs at low cost. The movement against the AIDS epidemic is growing, but so is the disease. Consider these facts:

- In 2001 there were over 36 million people living with AIDS/HIV.

- 1.3 million children under 15 years of age have AIDS, the overwhelming majority were born to mothers with HIV.

- Sub-Sahara Africa which has only 10% of the world's population has 70% of the world's HIV/AIDS-infected people, 80% of AIDS deaths, and 90% of AIDS orphans.

- More than 2 million adults die each year of AIDS, creating millions of orphans.

- As of 2000 more than 10 million children under 15 had lost their mother or both parents to AIDS.

- Between 1990 and 1997 the number of people infected with HIV/AIDS more than doubled, from less than 15 million to more than 33 million.

One reason that people are so angry at the drug companies is that the companies make so much money off this epidemic. For example, according to Oxfam, an international aid organization, the anti-AIDS drug stavudine anti-retroviral costs $6.10 per daily dose in Uganda, where it is marketed by Bristol-Myers Squibb, but just 55¢ in Brazil where it is produced generically. Brazil and India are among the few countries in the world that started local anti-AIDS drug production before World Trade Organization (WTO) rules on intellectual property rights were applied.

More than 880 million people lack access to health services, and 2.6 billion people lack access to basic sanitation.

"So many of our brothers, sisters and children have died, and I could be the next one to die," Ms. Mabele, leader of the organization Positive Women, told a *New York Times* reporter in South Africa. "Why do they put profits over our lives? Life is such a beautiful thing."

behavior of companies that do business with vicious dictatorships such as Burma (Myanmar).

4. THE WTO IS DESTROYING THE ENVIRONMENT.

The WTO is being used by corporations to dismantle hard-won environmental protections, which they call barriers to trade. In 1993 the very first WTO panel ruled that a regulation of the U.S. Clean Air Act, which required both domestic and foreign producers alike to produce cleaner gasoline, was illegal. In 1998, the WTO declared illegal a provision of the Endangered Species Act that requires shrimp sold in the United States to be caught with an inexpensive device that allows endangered sea turtles to escape. The WTO wants to eliminate tariffs on wood products, which would increase the demand for timber and escalate deforestation.

5. THE WTO IS KILLING PEOPLE.

The WTO's fierce defense of "intellectual property rights" — patents, copyrights and trademarks — comes at the expense of health and human lives. The organization's support for pharmaceutical companies against governments seeking to protect their people's health has had serious implications for places like sub-Saharan Africa, where 80% of the world's new AIDS cases are found. The U.S. government, on behalf of U.S. drug companies, is trying to block poor countries' access to less expensive, generic, life-saving drugs. For example, the South African government has been threatened with a WTO challenge over proposed national health laws that would encourage the use of generic drugs, ban the practice of manufacturers offering economic incentives to doctors who prescribe their products, and institute "parallel importing," which allows companies to import drugs from other countries where the drugs are cheaper.

6. THE U.S. ADOPTION OF THE WTO WAS UNDEMOCRATIC.

The WTO was established out of the Uruguay Round of the General Agreement on Tariffs and Trade (GATT) negotiations. On December 1, 1994, Congress approved GATT under a "fast track" arrangement during a lame-duck session of Congress. "Fast track" limits public debate by not allowing amendments. The approval of the WTO required entire sections of U.S. laws to be rewritten to conform with the WTO rules, similar to the way that treaties often redefine how the United States will interact with other countries. Had the agreement been voted on as a treaty, requiring a two-thirds majority in the Senate, it would have been defeated.

7. THE WTO UNDERMINES LOCAL DEVELOPMENT AND PENALIZES POOR COUNTRIES.

The WTO's "Most Favored Nation" provisions require all of the WTO member countries to treat each other equally and to treat all corporations from these countries equally, regardless of their track record. Local policies aimed at rewarding companies that hire local residents, use domestic materials, or adopt environmentally sound practices are essentially illegal under the WTO. Under the WTO rules, "developing" countries are prohibited from following the same polices that so-called developed countries once pursued, such as protecting young domestic industries until they can be internationally competitive.

8. THE WTO IS INCREASING INEQUALITY.

Free trade is not working for the majority of the world. During the most recent period of rapid growth in global trade and investment — 1960 to 1998 — inequality worsened both internationally and within countries. The U.N. Development Program reports that the richest 20% of the world's population consumes 86% of the world's resources, while the poorest 80% consumes just 14%. WTO rules have hastened these trends by opening up countries to foreign investment and thereby making it easier for production to go where the labor is cheapest and most easily exploited, and where environmental costs are low. This pulls down wages and environmental standards in "developed" countries that have to compete globally.

HOW CAN I BE CROWDING YOU?! YOU'RE ALL SO FAR AWAY!!

KIRK ©2001

9. THE WTO UNDERMINES NATIONAL SOVEREIGNTY.

By creating a supranational court system that has the power to economically penalize countries to force them to comply with its rulings, the WTO has essentially replaced national governments with an unelected, unaccountable, corporate-backed government. After the European Union (E.U.) banned beef raised with artificial growth hormones, the WTO ruled that this public health law is a barrier to trade and should be abolished. The E.U. has to rollback its ban or pay stiff penalties. Under the WTO, governments can no longer act in the public interest.

10. THE TIDE IS TURNING AGAINST FREE TRADE AND THE WTO.

There is a growing international backlash against the WTO and the process of corporate globalization over which it presides. Movement-building by coalitions such as People's Global Action, the Direct Action Network, the Citizen's Trade Campaign, the Fifty Years Is Enough Network, and the Alliance for Sustainable Jobs & the Environment are growing fast, as public support for a corporate-managed global economy dwindles. ■

For case studies of how WTO decisions have affected local businesses and economies, visit our website: www.rethinkingschools.org/rg

Transnational Capital Auction: A Game of Survival

BY BILL BIGELOW

Students are familiar with transnational corporations — Disney, Nike, Sony, Pepsi, Toyota. Corporations are entities with recognizable slogans and logos; they have public faces. Articles in the popular media describe the fortunes of this or that transnational corporation, the behavior of this or that CEO.

But transnational "capital" has no face. It has no jingles, no slogans, no logos. Capital is real, but invisible.

I wrote this simulation game, The Transnational Capital Auction, because I wanted students to grasp some aspects of capital as a force in today's world — to help them see capital as a kind of living being that has certain needs and inclinations. The game is a metaphor for the auction that capital holds to determine who in the world will make the most attractive bid for its "services." Students engage this dynamic from the standpoint of Third World elites, and simulate a phenomenon that has been called the "race to the bottom," whereby these elites compete against one another to attract capital. The game's "punch line" is an examination of the social and ecological consequences of the auction.

Note: If any of what follows starts to feel complicated, don't worry. The game has been used by lots of teachers, with excellent success. It's more simple than it may appear — and it works. (See my article, "The Human Lives Behind the Labels," p. 128, for a description of the activities that I've used before and after the game.)

MATERIALS NEEDED:

1. Several desirable candy bars — at least six.
2. Copies of the student handout, "Transnational Capital Auction: Instructions" — one for each student in the class.
3. Copies of the "Transnational Capital Auction Credit Sheet" — a minimum of seven, enough so that each country group can have at least one.
4. A minimum of 35 copies of the "Bids to Capital" slips so that each group has one per round (seven groups, five auction rounds.)

SUGGESTED PROCEDURE:

1. Before the activity, create the auction scoring guide on the board or on an overhead transparency. It should look something like *Figure A below.*

FIGURE A

Auction Results

	Round 1		Round 2		Round 3		Round 4		Round 5	
	Friendly to Capital Credits	Game Points	Friendly to Capital Credits	Game Points	Friendly to Capital Credits	Game Points	Friendly to Capital Credits	Game Points	Friendly to Capital Credits	Game Points
Country #1										
Country #2										
Country #3										
Country #4										
Country #5										
Country #6										
Country #7										

2. If you have at least 21 students in your class, divide them into seven groups. Ask the groups to form around the classroom, as far away from one another as possible.

3. Distribute copies of "Transnational Capital Auction: Instructions," "Transnational Capital Auction Credit Sheet," and the "Bids to Capital" slips. Read aloud with students "Transnational Capital Auction: Instructions." It should be obvious, but emphasize the distinction between Friendly-to-Capital credits and game points.

   Answer any questions students might have. Review the "Transnational Capital Auction Credit Sheet." Point out that a group earns more credits the friendlier it is to capital. Show them the candy bars and announce that the three groups with the most game points will win all the candy bars.

4. Begin the first round: Tell students to make their bids in each of the categories and to total up their Friendly-to-Capital credits on the "Bids to Capital" slips. Note that this is really the hardest round because students don't have any way of knowing what the other groups are bidding.

   I play "Capital" in the game, and wander the classroom as the small groups decide on their bids, urging them to lower the minimum wage, taxes on corporate profits, and the like. "Come on, show that you really want me!"

5. After each group has submitted its bid, write these up on the board or overhead. Award the first game points based on the results — again, 100 game points for the third highest number of Friendly-to-Capital credits, 50 for the second highest and 25 for the first. (This is explained in the Instructions handout.) After this first round has been played, and the points are posted, I scoff at the losers and urge them to get with the program and start making some bids that will attract Capital.

   From this point on, for better or worse, the competition to "win," or for candy bars, takes over, and students continue to "race to the bottom" of conditions for their respective countries. Sometimes they even realize what they're doing as they decide on their bids. "This is like 'The Price is Right,' oppression style," I overheard one of my students say one year.

6. After each round of bids, continue to post the Friendly-to-Capital credit scores and award

game points for that round. Keep a running total of each country team's game points. As Capital, I continue to urge students lower and lower: "Team five, you think I'm going to come to your country if your tax rate is 30%? Come on, next round let's get that way down."

7. For the fifth and final round, ask each student to write down their group's last bid, separate from the "Bid to Capital" slips — not just the number of credits, but the actual minimum wage, the child labor laws, etc. For their homework writing assignment, each student needs to know the specific social and environmental conditions created by the auction in their pretend country.

   Award candy bars to the "winners." Distribute the homework assignment, "Transnational Capital Auction Follow-up," on p. 114.

8. The next day, we discuss the homework questions. Some additional questions to raise:

• What does it mean to have no environmental laws in a country? What might Capital do?

• What would be the social effects of such low wages? (You might list these on the board or overhead.) How would families be able to survive? How could a family supplement its income? You might point out that even if a country did have child labor laws, the low wages for adults would put pressure on a family to send its children to work. If students don't point it out, you might also note the relationship between the "race to the bottom" and increased immigration. Of course, there are other factors leading to immigration, such as the dramatic rise in cash crop agriculture which throws peasants off the land (see, for example, the video *The Global Banquet*), but it's vital that students begin to see the interconnectedness of global issues.

• Ask students to look at the El Salvador ads from 1990 and 1991 (p. 110). How are these ads examples of the "race to the bottom"? Whom is the ad trying to appeal to?

• With homework question #2, I want students to begin to think critically about some of the ideas that are presented as obvious and absolute in much of the media: *Is* corporate investment always a good thing? You might make two columns on the board or overhead and ask students to list possible benefits of investment and some of the harmful effects of investment and how it is attracted.

Encourage students to ground their answers in the their own experiences with the Transnational Capital Auction, as my student Sam did in the following part of his answer to question #2: "Poor countries may need investment, but it is not necessarily a good thing when transnational companies invest capital there. I come to this conclusion by the simple attraction of Capital. Capital is attracted to a place that has less restrictions, on everything. In order to make our country more 'Capital friendly' we were willing to sell out the lives of individuals more and more, step by step. The worse the conditions got, the more Capital was interested."

- Why did you keep driving down conditions in your country? Why didn't you get together and refuse to bid each other down?

- Who benefits and who doesn't benefit from the "race to the bottom" we simulated in class? How could people in various countries get together to stop attacks on their social

and environmental conditions?

- What could we do in this country to respond to the global "race to the bottom"?

9. One option would be to give students an opportunity to play the Transnational Capital Auction all over again, except this time they could represent labor and environmental activists instead of a country's elite.

It's important that, if possible, students not be left with the sense that the downward leveling they experience in the auction is inexorable. There are things that people can do, and are doing — many of which are highlighted in this book. You might also watch the video, *Global Village or Global Pillage* (see Resources p. 357). Students need to see "big pictures" in order to understand seemingly disconnected events in countries around the world. But it's vital that they not feel defeated by this awareness. ∎

Bill Bigelow (bbpdx@aol.com) teaches at Franklin High School in Portland, Oregon and is a Rethinking Schools editor.

A real-world example of the race to the bottom: These two ads appeared a few months apart in trade magazines catering to clothing manufacturers. Note that the text is almost identical, except that the hourly wage has dropped significantly in the second ad.

TRANSNATIONAL CAPITAL AUCTION

YOUR ROLE:

You are leaders of a poor country. Each of your countries was either colonized by European countries or dominated by them economically and militarily. You need to attract foreign investment (capital) from transnational corporations for many different reasons. Of course, not all of your people are poor. Many, including a number of *you*, are quite wealthy. But your wealth depends largely on making deals with corporations that come to your country. You get various kickbacks, bribes, jobs for members of your families, etc. Some of this is legal, some not. But in order to stay in power you also need to provide jobs for your people, and the owners of capital (companies like Nike, Disney, Coca-Cola, Levi Strauss, etc.) are the ones who provide thousands of jobs in their factories. The more jobs you can bring into your country, the more legitimacy you have in the eyes of your people. *And,* your government collects taxes from these companies, which help keep your government working, and also help you pay back loans to the International Monetary Fund and other foreign-owned banks. The bottom line is this: You badly need these companies to invest capital in your country.

But here's the problem: You must compete with other poor countries that also need capital. Corporations are not stupid, and so they let you know that if you want their investment, you must compete with other countries by:

- keeping workers' wages low.
- having few laws to regulate conditions of work (overtime, breaks, health and safety conditions, age of workers), or not enforcing the laws that *are* on the books.
- having weak environmental laws.
- making sure that workers can't organize unions; having low taxes on corporate profits, etc.

Basically, companies hold an auction for their investments. The countries who offer the companies the most "freedom" are the ones who get the investment.

THE GAME:

The goal is to win the game by ending up with the most game points after five auction rounds.

Each country team's goal is to "win" by attracting capital. The team that bids the third highest number of "Friendly-to-Capital" credits in a round is awarded 100 game points; the team with the 2nd highest number of Capital credits is awarded 50 game points; and the team with the highest number of Capital credits is awarded 25 game points. The other teams get no points for the round. The auction is "silent" — you don't know until the end of each round who has bid what.

Again, Capital will go where the people are "friendliest" to it. However, the "friendlier" you are to Capital, the angrier it may make your own people. For example, Capital wants workers to work for very little and to not worry about environmental laws. But that could start demonstrations or even rebellions, which would not be good for Capital or for you as leaders of your country. That's why the team bidding the highest number of Capital credits does not get the highest number of game points. Last rule: Your team may be the highest (Capital credit) bidder *twice* and not be penalized. But for each time you are highest bidder more than twice, you lose ten game points — 10 the first time, 20 the second, etc. This is a "rebellion penalty." Good luck.

HANDOUT
TRANSNATIONAL CAPITAL AUCTION CREDIT SHEET

MINIMUM WAGE/HR.

$5.00 ....zero "Friendly-to-Capital" credits	$2.50 ....46 credits	$.55 ....76 credits
$4.75 ....10 credits	$2.25 ....49 credits	$.45 ....79 credits
$4.50 ....15 credits	$2.00 ....52 credits	$.35 ....82 credits
$4.25 ....20 credits	$1.75 ....55 credits	$.30 ....85 credits
$4.00 ....25 credits	$1.50 ....58 credits	$.25 ....88 credits
$3.75 ....30 credits	$1.25 ....61 credits	$.20 ....91 credits
$3.50 ....33 credits	$1.00 ....64 credits	$.15 ....94 credits
$3.25 ....37 credits	$.85 ....67 credits	$.10 ....97 credits
$3.00 ....40 credits	$.75 ....70 credits	$.05 ....100 credits
$2.75 ....43 credits	$.65 ....73 credits	

CHILD LABOR

Child labor below 16 is illegal/enforced.............................zero credits
Child labor below 16 is illegal/weakly enforced ....15 credits
Child labor below 16 is illegal/not enforced ....30 credits
Child labor below 14 is illegal/enforced.............................50 credits
Child labor below 14 is illegal/weakly enforced ....70 credits
Child labor below 14 is illegal/not enforced ....85 credits
No child labor laws...100 credits

WORKER ORGANIZING

Unions fully legal/allowed to organize.. zero credits
Unions fully legal/some restrictions on right to strike ....15 credits
Only government approved unions legal/some restrictions ....30 credits
Only government organized unions allowed ....45 credits
Unions banned/no right to strike...60 credits
Unions banned/no right to strike/military stationed in factories ....85 credits
Unions banned/no right to strike/military stationed in factories/
suspected Union organizers jailed/military used against strikes ....100 credits

TAXATION RATE ON CORPORATE PROFITS

75% ....zero credits		35% ....40 credits	
70% ....5 credits		30% ....50 credits	
65% ....10 credits		25% ....60 credits	
60% ....15 credits		20% ....70 credits	
55% ....20 credits		15% ....75 credits	
50% ....25 credits		10% ....80 credits	
45% ....30 credits		5% ....90 credits	
40% ....35 credits		no taxes.............100 credits	

ENVIRONMENTAL LAWS

Strict environmental laws/enforced ....zero credits
Strict environmental laws/weakly enforced ....15 credits
Strict environmental laws/not often enforced ....30 credits
Some environmental laws/enforced......................................50 credits
Some environmental laws/weakly enforced.......................70 credits
Some environmental laws/not often enforced....................85 credits
Almost no environmental laws..100 credits

BIDS TO CAPITAL

Country # _____ Round # _____

Minimum wage credits   _____

Child labor credits   _____

Worker organizing credits   _____

Taxation rate credits   _____

Environmental laws credits   _____

TOTAL CREDITS THIS ROUND: _____

- -

BIDS TO CAPITAL

Country # _____ Round # _____

Minimum wage credits   _____

Child labor credits   _____

Worker organizing credits   _____

Taxation rate credits   _____

Environmental laws credits   _____

TOTAL CREDITS THIS ROUND: _____

- -

BIDS TO CAPITAL

Country # _____ Round # _____

Minimum wage credits   _____

Child labor credits   _____

Worker organizing credits   _____

Taxation rate credits   _____

Environmental laws credits   _____

TOTAL CREDITS THIS ROUND: _____

HANDOUT

TRANSNATIONAL CAPITAL AUCTION FOLLOW-UP

COMPLETE THESE ON A SEPARATE SHEET OF PAPER.

1. Look over your auction "bids" for the fifth and final round of the Transnational Capital Auction — on minimum wage, child labor, worker organizing, taxation rates, and environmental laws. If Capital were to accept your "bid" and come to your country, what would be the real human and environmental consequences there? Answer this question in detail.

2. Based on your experience with the auction, agree and/or disagree with the following statement, and back up your answer with evidence: Poor countries need investment, so it's a good thing when transnational companies invest there.

3. The global process that we simulated in class is sometimes called "downward leveling" or the "race to the bottom." What, if anything, could people in poor countries do to stop this race to the bottom?

4. One company used to manufacture all its products in the United States, paying wages that averaged (with benefits) around $16 an hour. The investment director for this company now travels every month to places like Indonesia, El Salvador, and Nicaragua looking for sites to produce his company's products. He says that he would prefer to keep all production in the United States. Based on this simulation and what you know, why do you think this person's company feels *forced* to send production to countries that have a lot of "Friendly-to-Capital" points?

5. What impact does the race to the bottom have on workers in this country? In what ways might it affect *your* lives? In answering the question, you might think about the three quotes, below.

"It is not that foreigners are stealing our jobs, it is that we are all facing one another's competition."
William Baumol,
Princeton University economist

"Downward leveling is like a cancer that is destroying its host organism — the earth and its people."
Jeremy Brecher & Tim Costello,
Global Village or Global Pillage

"Globalization has depressed the wage growth of low-wage workers [in the United States]. It's been a reason for the increasing wage gap between high-wage and low-wage workers."
Laura Tyson, former Chairperson,
U.S. Council of Economic Advisers

Ten Chairs of Inequality

BY POLLY KELLOGG

*Countries are not families. They are stratified based on race, class, gender, nationality, and language. Not only is inequality **between** nations becoming more pronounced, so too is inequality **within** nations increasing. The United States is no exception. The processes that get labeled as "globalization" affect North Americans as well as those in the Third World. In this article, Polly Kellogg describes how she engages her students in reflecting on these dynamics.*

Inequalities of wealth are becoming more extreme in the United States. While billionaires double their wealth every three to five years, we have by far the highest poverty rate in the industrialized world. No industrialized country has a more skewed distribution of wealth. Students need information about this concentration of wealth — and the power that accompanies it — in order to become critical thinkers and aware citizens.

A Boston-based group, United for a Fair Economy, has developed a simulation activity to dramatize the increasingly unequal distribution of wealth. I describe here how my college human relations classes respond to the exercise. It can easily be adapted for younger students.

To begin the simulation, I ask 10 students to volunteer to line up at the front of the room, seated in their chairs and facing the rest of the class. I explain that each chair represents 10% of the wealth in the United States and each occupant represents 10% of the population; thus when each chair is occupied by one student, the wealth is evenly distributed. I explain that wealth is what you own: your stereo, the part of your house and car that are paid off, savings like stocks and bonds, vacation homes, any companies you own, your yachts, villas on the Riviera, private jet airplanes, etc. Then I ask students to estimate how much wealth each family would have if the wealth were equally distributed.

> **Students need information about this concentration of wealth — and the power that accompanies it — in order to become critical thinkers and aware citizens.**

Students usually guess about $50,000 and are surprised to hear that the answer is $250,000.

I ask them what it would feel like if every family could have a $100,000 home, a $10,000 car paid for and $140,000 in savings. Some make comments like, "It'd be wonderful. I wouldn't have to work two jobs and take out a loan to go to college." But many can't imagine such a society. Others express concern that the incentive to work would be taken away: "It sounds like socialism."

I tell those worried about socialism, that they have nothing to fear. We have nowhere near an equal distribution of wealth in this country. The poorest 20% of the population is in debt, and the next 30% averages only $5,000 in wealth (primarily in home equity).

I ask students at either end of the lineup which one of them wants to represent the richest 10% and experience being rich. Some students volunteer happily and others express distaste at the idea. When asked about their motives, they say, "I'll never be rich, so I'd like to see what it feels like," or "I don't want to oppress other people, and rich people exploit their workers." Sometimes a student, often female, will say, "I don't like to be above other people."

I invite the class to speculate how many chairs belong to the richest student, whom I will call Sue. In 1998, the richest 10% owned 71% of the wealth — thus Sue controls about seven chairs. I tell the six students sitting nearest to Sue to give up their chairs to her and move to the poorer end of the lineup. I provoke them by telling them that the standing students can sit on the laps of the three students seated at the end, and I invite Sue to sit in the middle of her seven chairs, to stretch out, relax, or even lie down across the chairs.

I then announce that Sue's arm represents the wealthiest 1% of families and that her arm's share of the wealth went up from two chairs (22% of the wealth) to four chairs (38%) during the years from 1979 to 1998. I solicitously help Sue find a comfortable position with one arm stretched over four chairs. To engage Sue in clowning and playing up her role, I offer her food or drink.

I ask the other nine students crowded around three chairs what life is like at their end of the line. "We're pissed and tired of working all the time," is a typical comment. Another is, "I want a revolution." I ask students if, in real life, they or people they know are crowded into the bottom one or two chairs, and what that's like. Working-class students tell stories of financial stress they have experienced, such as, "My mother had to work at two jobs to support us." "My family was really poor when my dad was laid off. We lived on macaroni and cheese." Often one student, usually a white male, says he has hopes that he can work hard and join Sue.

Students' knowledge of how inequality is rationalized erupts when I ask, "What do those in power tell us to justify this dramatic inequality?" Typical student answers are: "They work harder than we do." "They create jobs." "The U.S. stands for equality and justice for all." "It's our fault if we don't make it." If students do not mention scapegoating, I bring it up. I may select one student to represent the poorest 10% and ask, "Wouldn't there be more money for the rest of you if he or she weren't ripping off the system for welfare?" I also ask, "Who does Sue want you to blame for your tough economic conditions?" Answers range from welfare moms and immigrants to gays and lesbians, and bad schools.

When I ask the nine students grouped around the three chairs why they don't get organized to force a redistribution of the wealth, they offer a variety of answers. "We're too busy working to organize." "We are told we can't change things." "We don't get along with each other." "They'd call out the army to stop us."

At some point I ask the class to describe the "super rich" — the 1%, Sue's arm. College students share examples from their experiences. A junior high coach described a local billionaire who offered to write the coach's school a check of any amount in order to get his child on the baseball team. Another student worked as a waiter in an elite club where "you had to be elected to be able to have lunch there." The club was all white and only recently began allowing women on the premises; some of the older men refused to let her serve them because they resented her presence. Another student described doing carpentry in a mansion of the

> I ask the other nine students crowded around three chairs what life is like at their end of the line. "We're pissed and tired of working all the time," is a typical comment.

DuPonts, "The faucet in the kid's bathroom cost $3,000."

The athletes and entertainers whose salaries are hyped in the media and newly rich entrepreneurs like Donald Trump and Bill Gates are always mentioned. I point out that these are the upwardly mobile people, who moved from the three chairs up to Sue's chair. How often does this happen? Why do we hear so much about them? I want students to understand that the exaggerated publicity about these rags-to-riches icons perpetuates the myth that anyone who tries can make it.

Most texts and teachers stop after they have taught about the unequal distribution of wealth, but that is only a piece of the picture. We need to go on to ask why wealth is so unequally distributed. Where does wealth come from? Why does our system concentrate wealth in the hands of so few? And what can ordinary people do to effect change? The simulation creates a foundation for these later lessons. ■

Polly Kellogg is an assistant professor in the Human Relations and Multicultural Education Department at St. Cloud State University, St. Cloud, Minnesota. More teaching resources are available from United for a Fair Economy. See Resources, p. 388.

> **"The moral perversity of economic liberalism is perhaps most evident in what it views as economic success in a world in which more than a billion people live in absolute deprivation, go to bed hungry each night, and live without the minimum of adequate shelter and clothing.**
>
> **The publications that most aggressively advocate the economic liberalist ideology — such as *Fortune*, *Business Week*, *Forbes*, *The Wall Street Journal*, and *The Economist* — rarely, if ever, praise an economy for its progress toward eliminating absolute deprivation.**
>
> **Rather, they measure an economy's performance by the number of millionaires and billionaires it produces; they evaluate the competence of managers by the cool dispassion with which they fire tens of thousands of employees; they gauge the success of individuals by how many millions of dollars they acquire in a year; and they judge companies as successful according to the global reach of their power and their monopolistic domination of the markets in which they operate."**
>
> —David Korten,
> *When Corporations Rule the World*, 1995

"The Marines Have Landed"
U.S. Military Interventions and Globalization

BY BOB PETERSON

In the wake of the terrorist bombings of September. 11, 2001, a wave of horror and patriotism swept the United States. Virtually everyone agreed that those who practice terrorism against innocent civilians should be brought to justice. What's more difficult for Americans to realize, however, is that the interests of our own security, and the pursuit of a more just world, are best served by a critical look at U.S. foreign policy, a policy that has engendered resentment in much of the world.

Woody Guthrie used to sing that "some will rob you with a six-gun, others with a fountain pen." There are a number of global "fountain pen" organizations, such as the World Trade Organization and the World Bank. But the six-gun was the colonizers' preferred means to divide the world between rich and poor nations. And the six-gun has been — and still is — used to enforce global inequality, and to crush alternative paths of economic development.

The British used military force in India and

throughout Africa, the Spanish throughout the Americas, the French in Algeria and Indochina, the Portuguese in Angola and Mozambique, and the Dutch in the East Indies. Throughout human history, empires and nations have used military force to get their way. In fact, school history textbooks tend to focus on, and even romanticize, the military feats of various periods.

Usually left out of such books is a critical examination of how the United States has used — and continues to use — military intervention to control other lands and peoples for the economic interests of its dominant classes. As president, George Washington ordered his army to burn and destroy Native American villages in New York. Since that time virtually every U.S. president has ordered the U.S. military to intervene in at least one foreign country or territory. It is a sad, usually neglected story.

The U.S. interventions that make it into school textbooks are usually described from the perspective of the U.S. policymakers who ordered the interventions. In 1846, for example, the United States invaded Mexico and after the ensuing war, forced Mexico to "sell" nearly half its territory to the United States. Textbook maps ratify this conquest with sanitary terms like "Mexican Cession." There was significant opposition to that war in the United States — from pacifists like Henry Thoreau to the Irish-American soldiers who, disgusted with the brutal treatment of the Mexicans by the U.S. army, mutinied and joined the Mexican side as the San Patricio Brigade. That part of the story goes untold in most textbooks.

In the 1898 Spanish-American War, the United States acquired Cuba, Puerto Rico, Guam, and the Philippines through armed force, wresting control from the former colonial power of Spain. Many people in those countries, however, wanted to be independent — to form their own governments without Spanish or U.S. control. In the Philippines such sentiment was particularly strong. It took 75,000 U.S. soldiers fighting for three horrific years to defeat the Filipinos in their war for independence. Senator Henry Cabot Lodge explained why the United States wanted the Philippines: "We must on no account let the islands go: The American flag is up and it must

> **The U.S. interventions that make it into school textbooks are usually described from the perspective of the U.S. policymakers who ordered the interventions.**

stay, it will keep us open to the markets of China." Labor leader Samuel Gompers called it "an unjust war" and Mark Twain wrote passionately against it.

The Spanish-American War marked a turning point for U.S. foreign policy. The United States became recognized as a world power and acted as such. Big business and government colluded to use the military to make the world safe for U.S. commerce. President Wilson explained, "Our industries have expanded to such a point that they will burst their jackets if they cannot find a free outlet to the markets of the world."

The U.S. military occupied countries like Haiti and Nicaragua for decades. In 1911, for example, Nicaragua failed to pay its debts to U.S. companies. President Taft sent in the Marines. A few years later, President Wilson sent Marines to the Dominican Republic and Haiti. U.S. troops stayed in Haiti for 19 years and killed an estimated 78,000 people. President Wilson noted that "the U.S. was involved in a struggle to command the economic fortunes of the world." In 1914 he ordered troops to seize the Mexican port city of Veracruz while Mexican patriots like Pancho Villa were fighting to help the landless and the poor.

A few years later, the United States joined forces with 14 other nations to invade the newly established Soviet Union after the 1917 revolution. Despite the sad evolution of the Soviet Union into a dictatorship, many working people around the world did look to the revolution as a form of social democracy that would bring increased equality. The United States and other European powers didn't want non-capitalist alternative forms of government to be successful, as they were afraid working people in their own countries and elsewhere around the world would get similar ideas. (This was not so farfetched, as 1917 was a year of huge electoral gains for the Socialist Party throughout the United States.) U.S. Secretary of State Robert Lansing defended the intervention, saying that the Russian revolutionaries sought "to make the ignorant and incapable mass of humanity dominant in the earth" and that they were appealing "to a particular class and not to all classes of society, a class which does not have property but hopes to obtain a share by process of government rather than by individual enterprise. This is of course a direct threat at existing social order in all countries."

But it was after World War II, with the decline in power of the old British and French colonial powers, that United States interventionist activity increased most dramatically. Richard Barnet of the Institute of Policy Studies estimates that since WWII, the United States intervened abroad on the average of once every six months — either overtly with military troops or covertly with the Central Intelligence Agency — to overthrow or prop up a government in the Third World. The list of the most notorious span the globe: Iran, in 1953; Guatemala, in 1954; Lebanon, in 1958; Cuba, in 1961; Guyana, in 1962; Brazil, in 1964; The Dominican Republic, in 1965; Vietnam, 1960-1975; Laos, 1971-1973; Cambodia, 1969-1975; Chile, in 1973; Nicaragua, 1981-1990; El Salvador, 1982-1990; Grenada, in 1983. And these are just the tip of an interventionist iceberg.

Certainly the most important U.S. interven-

> **U.S. troops stayed in Haiti for 19 years and killed an estimated 78,000 people. President Wilson noted that "the U.S. was involved in a struggle to command the economic fortunes of the world."**

tion in the last half century was in Vietnam. The United States began its involvement by siding with the French (who had colonized Vietnam in the mid-19th century) and those Vietnamese who had collaborated with the Japanese during World War II. These forces opposed Ho Chi Minh (the most prominent leader advocating Vietnamese independence) and his followers even though the Vietnamese had worked closely with the Allied war effort. Ho Chi Minh, who headed the Indochinese Communist Party and later the nationalist Viet Minh, had written numerous letters to President Truman and the State Department asking for America's help in winning Vietnamese independence from the French and finding a peaceful solution for his country. Ho Chi Minh modeled the new Vietnamese declaration of independence on the U.S. declaration, beginning it with "All men are created equal. They are endowed by their Creator with certain inalienable rights...." But this counted for little in Washington. All of Ho's efforts were ignored. By 1954, the United States was paying for more than 75% of the French effort to reconquer Vietnam.

Years later, President Eisenhower admitted that "had elections been held as of the time of the fighting, possibly 80% of the population would have voted for the Communist Ho Chi Minh." But U.S. policymakers discounted the popular sentiment for independence and were frightened by the radical social justice programs of the Vietnamese Communists. The United States sent military advisors in 1960 and then upwards of a half mil-

lion troops to oppose Vietnamese independence. It dropped more tons of bombs on Vietnam than all the tonnage dropped by the Allies during the entire Second World War. It also used massive amounts of chemical defoliants and anti-personnel bombs — small explosive devices designed to kill and maim people but not to harm property. Twenty-three years later, and after as many as 3 million deaths, the United States withdrew its military forces from Vietnam.

Why would the United States waste so many lives, wreak havoc on the environment, and squander so much money? Simply put, Vietnam was the threat of a good example. In the words of British economist Joan Robinson, the U.S. war against Vietnam was "a campaign against development." As Robinson points out, the United States has used force "to try to suppress every popular movement that aims to overthrow ancient or modern tyranny and begin to find a way to overcome poverty and establish national self-respect." Thus the "Vietnam War" was about more than just Vietnam. It was as much aimed at other social movements around the world that might seek to free their countries from the global capitalist system that relegates poor countries to being suppliers of raw materials and cheap labor.

In earlier European colonial domination, racism justified brutality and prevented the invaders from imagining viable, independent societies managed by people of color. This was the case also in Vietnam. Here's the former Commander of U.S. Forces in Vietnam, General William Westmoreland, explaining why it's OK to kill so many Vietnamese: "Well, the Oriental doesn't put the same high price on life as does the Westerner. Life is plentiful; life is cheap in the Orient. And as the philosophy of the Orient expresses it, life is not important."

AN EXPANDED ARSENAL

Under the guise of defending the "free world," U.S. foreign policy has consisted of a double standard: hostility toward dictatorial Soviet bloc countries, but friendship and millions of aid dollars to repressive right-wing regimes such as Franco's Spain, apartheid South Africa, the Shah's Iran, and the brutal military rulers of Brazil.

Sometimes U.S. interventions are out in the open — christened with high-sounding speeches and patriotic drumming. Sometimes they are covert — with CIA agents or military intelligence intervening in another nation's affairs

> It's hard to see how the democratic ideals represented in our Declaration of Independence are not contradicted by such a Big Stick foreign policy.

through espionage, financial support of reactionary groups, and covert military operations like sabotage, assassination of leaders, and providing arms to rebel forces.

These methods proved particularly effective in Iran in 1953, just when many Middle Eastern countries were beginning to recognize the potential of their oil reserves. In 1953 Iranian Prime Minister Mossadegh was overthrown in a joint U.S./British operation. Mossadegh had been elected to his position by a large majority of parliament, but he had made the mistake of spearheading the movement to nationalize a British-owned oil company, the sole oil company operating in Iran. The U.S./British-supported coup restored the Shah of Iran to absolute power and began a period of 25 years of repression and torture. The oil industry was restored to foreign ownership, although the post-coup division was 40% each for British and U.S. corporations and 20% for corporations from other countries.

The United States also poured millions of dollars into undermining and overthrowing the socialist democracy of Salvador Allende in Chile in the 1970s.

Another famous — although less successful — covert attempt that has been well documented is the CIA's efforts to kill Cuban President Fidel Castro. The CIA did everything from hiring snipers, to putting an explosive in Castro's cigar, to poisoning his drinks. These initiatives were launched even though it is against U.S. law for a government agency to attempt to kill the leader of another government.

For some U.S. citizens, it's hard to see how the democratic ideals represented in our Declaration of Independence are not contradicted by such a Big Stick foreign policy.

But there are clear patterns that can be discerned from studying the history of U.S. interventions. When pressed, U.S. policymakers claim the issue is "freedom." But U.S. interventions have installed or propped up too many tyrants, from Diem in Vietnam to Somoza in Nicaragua, for this to ring true.

At issue is a different kind of freedom: the "freedom" of multinational corporations to locate in whatever country they choose, extract raw materials cheaply, hire workers at low wages, and sell their products, regardless of consequences on domestic industries.

And, as Joan Robinson noted, it is also about making sure that no society has a chance to organize itself around principles of human need rather than private profit. For years Cuba had better health care, housing, and education for its people than all other Latin American countries; this threatened the notion that societies could "develop" only through private ownership. If a small country like Cuba could dramatically reduce poverty, despite a U.S.-orchestrated campaign of economic and political isolation, what might a larger and wealthier country like Brazil or Argentina be able to do?

As we "rethink globalization," we are tempted to see global inequality, poverty, and environmental destruction as primarily caused by economic factors: IMF structural adjustment programs; WTO-mandated restrictions on the production and sale of life-saving drugs; the spread of free market principles; the octopus-like reach of advertising; and the sweatshop exploitation of Third World workers by transnational corporations.

But military intervention has paved the way for economic penetration. Like the neighborhood bully who has regularly beaten up his weaker peers, after awhile he can ease up: Everyone knows what he's capable of doing to enforce his will. The United States is a bully, and Third World nations and social movements understand what they risk should they defy its mandates.

Bullies or not, we still need to focus on making the "neighborhood" — the world — more just. For people of good will in this country the question is: What should we do when a third of the world's population lives in poverty, when according to UNICEF nearly 33,000 children die each day of malnutrition-related diseases?

Something is wrong with how the world's resources are distributed. Something is wrong with the structure of the global economy. What can we do to help solve these problems, not make them worse? How can we help create the political climate in our own country so that social movements around the world can pursue alternative paths of development without being attacked? Given the long history of military interventions, people who live in the United States must urgently confront these questions. ∎

Arguments Against the Bombing

LISA SUHAIR MAJAJ

consider the infinite fragility of an infant's

skull

how the bones lie soft and open

only time knitting them shut

consider a delicate porcelain bowl

how it crushes under a single blow

— in one moment whole years disappear

consider that beneath the din of explosions

no song can be heard

no cry

consider your own sky on fire

your name erased

your children's lives "a price worth paying"

consider the faces you do not see

the eyes you refuse to meet

"collateral damage"

how in those words

the world cracks open

First published in Al Jadid, *Winter 1998.*
Lisa Suhair Majaj is a widely published Palestinian-American poet and author.

Bob Peterson (repmilw@aol.com) is a fifth grade teacher at La Escuela Fratney in Milwaukee, Wisconsin and is a Rethinking Schools editor.

THE GLOBAL ECONOMY: COLONIALISM WITHOUT COLONIES

Numerous teaching ideas are included elsewhere in this chapter. See "Poverty and World Resources," p. 69; "Building Miniature Houses: Simulating Inequality," p. 71; "Transnational Capital Auction," p. 108; and "Ten Chairs of Inequality," p. 115. "Debt and Disaster," p. 75, includes many teaching ideas on the readings on the World Bank/International Monetary Fund and the debt crisis and "Rethinking 'Free Trade' and the WTO" (p. 95) offers numerous teaching ideas on the World Trade Organization articles included in this chapter.

"MYTHS OF UNDERDEVELOPMENT"
Article by Michael Parenti (p. 64)

Before reading, brainstorm with students all the possible explanations they can think of for why so many countries in Asia, Africa, and Latin America are poor. As students read, ask them to think about which of these theories are supported or refuted by Parenti. For example, Parenti discusses myths that overpopulation, cultural backwardness, and hot climate cause Third World poverty.

Parenti says that most of the Third World is not underdeveloped but overexploited. What does he mean?

Analyze the word "underdevelopment." In what ways is it a helpful concept? In what ways is it misleading? How about the term "developing"? (See "Rethinking Our Language," p. 6.)

Parenti describes one "development scenario": The North brings the South investment, technology, and proper work habits, which lead to employment, reinvestment, and eventual prosperity. According to Parenti, what's wrong with this picture? If this is not the route to prosperity, then what is?

Have students write on the following question: "A friend says to you, 'I have a theory. I think that the reason that the Third World is so poor is because it's really hot there and so people aren't able to work as hard. They end up just sitting around while people in places like Europe and America are hard at work producing wealth.' In writing, offer your friend another way to look at poverty in the Third World. If you like, write this as a dialogue."

"'THE MARINES HAVE LANDED': U.S. MILITARY INTERVENTIONS AND GLOBALIZATION"
Article by Bob Peterson (p. 118)

This is an article that could be read by skilled readers or could provide a framework to teach about the history of U.S. military interventions around the world.

Some issues to consider:
- What claims has the United States government made about why it has used military force outside of its own borders?
- How do these claims compare with the results of U.S. intervention?
- What kind of relationships between nations has the United States sought to achieve through use of military might? Who benefited from U.S. intervention?
- Who did not benefit from U.S. intervention?
- What resistance has the U.S. government encountered, both at home and abroad, to its use of the military?
- How do textbooks explain the use of the U.S. military in other people's countries? Which interventions are included? Which are omitted? Whose voices are heard in the accounts?

Divide students into small groups and have each research one of the interventions mentioned in this article — e.g., the invasion of Mexico in 1846 (see "Students as Textbook Detectives," in *Rethinking Our Classrooms, Volume 1*, p. 158.); the wars against Cuba and the Philippines, begun in 1898; occupations of Haiti, Nicaragua, and the Dominican Republic in the early 20th century; etc. Ask students to consider some of the above questions as they research a particular intervention. Have each group write a dialogue poem between different "players." For example, the group researching the U.S. war with Mexico in 1846-48 might pair the perspectives of a U.S. antiwar protester in Boston with President Polk; a U.S. soldier with a Mexican soldier; a U.S. soldier and a U.S. officer, etc.

For a more complete listing of military interventions by the United States, visit our website at www.rethinkingschools.org/rg.

According to the article, "there are clear patterns that can be discerned from studying the history of U.S. interventions." Have representatives of each small group circulate throughout the classroom on a "pattern hunt," trying to see what commonalities they can find from intervention to intervention.

Ask students to compare the behavior of organizations like the International Monetary Fund and the World Trade Organization with U.S. military interventions. For example, how are structural adjustment programs similar to and/or different from the outcomes of U.S. military interventions in the countries with which students are familiar? What is the relationship between military interventions and globalization?

"ARGUMENTS AGAINST THE BOMBING"
Poem by Lisa Suhair Majaj, p. 122

For more background on the effects of sanctions and bombing against Iraq, see the website of Citizens Concerned for the People of Iraq & Interfaith Network of Concern for the People of Iraq, www.scn.org/ccpi/.

Ask students to choose other aspects of global injustice from which to write "Arguments Against..." poems. Note how Majaj uses the repetition "Consider..." in opening most of the stanzas of the poem. Students might model their poems after this technique.

"The 3,000 participants at the [2002] World Economic Forum, which drifted through the hallways of the Waldorf Astoria, dropped $100 million on New York hotels, ballrooms, and restaurants, according to the New York City tourism board. That comes out to $33,333.33 per person. In five days in New York, each participant of the World Economic Forum spent on average what the average American makes in a year, four times what the average Mexican makes in a year, 14 times what the average person in India makes in a year, 22 times what the average person makes in Bangladesh, and 74 times what the average person makes in a year in Sierra Leone, according to United Nations figures."

—"The Elite's Pure Greed," by Derrick Z. Jackson,
The Boston Globe, 2/8/2002

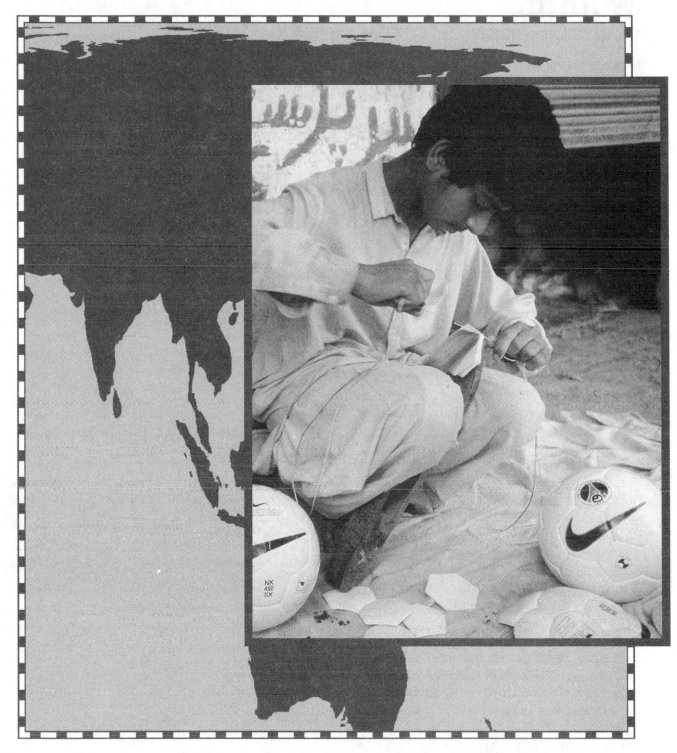

CHAPTER FOUR
Global Sweatshops

Woman

BY ANDREA TOWNSEND

In this world a woman is not a woman
She is hands
She is a short breath of stale air
She is lungs raked by flyaway fibers
And a raw nose and eyes dripping from glue fumes

A woman is not a woman in a world like this
She is numbers on clothing, 50% cotton, 50% polyester....
A word in someone else's language

A woman cannot be a woman
It's against regulations
Only when the late night supervisors overstep their boundaries
Then she is a woman for a moment, in his eyes
Beneath his rough hands,
Never under her own

These hands bleed,
So that people can love their children in the "American" way
Curl them up with a plush toy in a warm home
While her children curl up with the night

A woman is not a woman
She is hours of labor
Hours of sitting,
Her back bent like a willow in a windstorm

In every second, minute, hour, day — she becomes the whir of machinery
Years go by and she is a sound,
A breath,
A thrumming pattern
A needle charging across fabric, a suspended heartbeat

Then, all at once and slowly,
a whisper rises through the stale air, the dim light,
Cuts through the ceaseless mechanical droning
And a hand slows its perpetual motion,
Stretches slowly across the space between the machine and the woman

Down the rows of workbenches,
one by one, these hands close over one another
Become clenched fists
Remind themselves that they are not just hands,
They are women

Andrea Townsend was an 11th grade student at Franklin High School in Portland, Oregon when she wrote this poem.

Page 125 image: A Pakistani child stitches together a soccer ball using only basic hand tools. Photo by Corbis.

Ben Emerson drew this cartoon when he was a student at Metropolitan Learning Center in Portland, Oregon.

INTRODUCTION

Global Sweatshops

In 1922, one of the leading U.S. advertising copywriters, Helen Woodward, gave other copywriters some advice. "If you are advertising any product," she said, "never see the factory in which it was made.... Don't watch the people at work.... Because, you see, when you know the truth about anything, the real inner truth — it is very hard to write the surface fluff which sells it."

Of course, these days it's increasingly difficult for advertising copywriters to visit their clients' factories — that is, if they were so inclined. Because, more and more, goods are produced in faraway places like Honduras, Bangladesh, Indonesia, or China, or secreted away in sweatshops in our own urban centers.

In this era of globalization, part of the "real inner truth" is this: All of us are intimately connected to the lives of working people — many of whom labor in global sweatshops. Every time we put on a pair of shoes, turn on the TV, ride in a car, kick a soccer ball, use a computer, or eat a piece of fruit, we enter into invisible relationships with workers and cultures around the world. And these relationships pose a choice for us and our students: We can confront the world as narrowly self-interested consumers, or we can begin to reflect on the ethical and political nature of the hidden connections embedded in our daily lives. Choosing the latter route requires us also to consider our responsibilities to other individuals and other cultures: Once we gain knowledge, what do we do with it?

In this chapter, we invite students to reflect on these issues. And in articles and activities, we share with students how others around the country — and around the world — are trying to work for justice for sweatshop workers.

A caveat: The term "sweatshop" can, ironically, distance our students from other workers. "They" work in sweatshops; "we" don't. We hope that educators use the resources in this chapter to help students reflect on the similarities between "normal" working conditions and "sweatshop" working conditions. What is normal may also be exploitative, insecure, alienating labor. Looking at similarities, as well as differences, may give students a window into their own work lives, and conditions that need changing here. ∎

— *The editors*

> We can confront the world as narrowly self-interested consumers, or we can begin to reflect on the ethical and political nature of the hidden connections embedded in our daily lives.

Associated Press/Richard Vogel

A Nike factory on the outskirts of Ho Chi Minh City, Vietnam.

The Lives Behind the Labels
Teaching About the Global Sweatshop and the Race to the Bottom

BY BILL BIGELOW

I began the lesson with a beat-up soccer ball. The ball sat balanced in a plastic container on a stool in the middle of the circle of student desks. "I'd like you to write a description of this soccer ball," I told my high school Global Studies class. "Feel free to get up and look at it. There is no right or wrong. Just describe the ball however you'd like."

Looks of puzzlement and annoyance greeted me. "It's just a soccer ball," someone said.

Students must have wondered what this had to do with Global Studies. "I'm not asking for an essay," I said, "just a paragraph or two."

As I'd anticipated, their accounts were straightforward — accurate if uninspired. Few students accepted the offer to examine the ball up close. A soccer ball is a soccer ball. They sat and wrote. Afterwards, a few students read their descriptions aloud. Brian's is typical:

> The ball is a sphere which has white hexagons and black pentagons. The black pentagons contain red stars, sloppily outlined in silver.... One of the hexagons contains a green rabbit wearing a soccer uniform with "Euro 88" written parallel to the rabbit's body. This hexagon seems to be cracking. Another hexagon has the number 32 in green, standing for the number of patches that the ball contains.

But something was missing. There was a deeper social reality associated with this ball — a reality that advertising and the consumption-oriented rhythms of U.S. daily life discouraged students from considering.

"Made in Pakistan" was stenciled in small print on the ball, but very few students thought that significant enough to include in their descriptions. However, these three tiny words offered the most important clue to the human lives hidden in "just a soccer ball" — a clue to the invisible Pakistanis whose hands crafted the ball sitting in the middle of the classroom.

I distributed and read aloud Bertolt Brecht's poem "A Worker Reads History"(see p. 2) as a tool to pry behind the soccer-ball-as-thing:

Who built the seven gates of Thebes?
The books are filled with names of kings.
Was it kings who hauled the craggy blocks of
stone?...
In the evening when the Chinese wall was finished
Where did the masons go? Imperial Rome
Is full of arcs of triumph. Who reared them up?...

Young Alexander conquered India.
He alone?
Caesar beat the Gauls.
Was there not even a cook in his army?...

Each page a victory.
At whose expense the victory ball?
Every ten years a great man,
Who paid the piper?...

"Keeping Brecht's questions in mind," I said, after reading the poem, "I want you to re-see this soccer ball. If you like, you can write from the point of view of the ball, you can ask the ball questions, but I want you to look at it deeply. What did we miss the first time around? It's not 'just a soccer ball.'" With not much more than these words for guidance — although students had some familiarity with working conditions in poor countries — they drew a line beneath their original descriptions and began again.

Versions one and two were night and day. With Brecht's prompting, Pakistan as the country of origin became more important. Tim wrote in part: "Who built this soccer ball? The ball answers with Pakistan. There are no real names, just labels. Where did the real people go after it was made?" Nicole also posed questions: "If this ball could talk, what kinds of things would it be able to tell you? It would tell you about the lives of the people who made it in Pakistan.... But if it could talk, would you listen?" Maisha played with its colors and the "32" stamped on the ball: "Who painted the entrapped black, the brilliant bloody red, and the shimmering silver? Was it made for the existence of a family of 32?" And

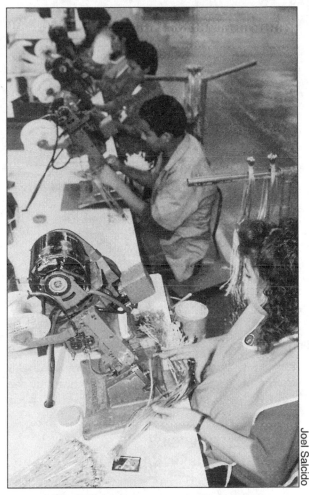

Joel Salcido

Assembly line workers at one of hundreds of *maquiladoras* in Ciudad Juarez, Mexico.

Sarah imagined herself as the soccer ball worker:

I sew together these shapes of leather. I stab my finger with my needle. I feel a small pain, but nothing much, because my fingers are so calloused. Everyday I sew these soccer balls together for 5¢, but I've never once had a chance to play soccer with my friends. I sew and sew all day long to have these balls shipped to another place where they represent fun. Here, they represent the hard work of everyday life.

When students began to consider the human lives behind the ball-as-object, their writing also came alive.

Geoffrey, an aspiring actor, singer, and writer, wrote his as a conversation between himself and the ball:

"So who was he?" I asked.

"A young boy, Wacim, I think," it seemed to reply.

I got up to take a closer look. Even though the soccer ball looked old and its hexagons and other geometric patterns were cracked, the sturdy and intricate stitching still held together.

"What that child must've gone through," I said.

"His father was killed and his mother was working. Wacim died so young.... It's just too hard. I can't contain these memories any longer." The soccer ball let out a cry and leaked his air out and lay there, crumpled on the stool. Like his master, lying on the floor, uncared for, and somehow overlooked and forgotten.

Students had begun to imagine the humanity inside the ball; their pieces were vivid and curious. The importance of making visible the invisible, of looking behind the masks presented by everyday consumer goods, became a central theme in my first-time effort to teach about the "global sweatshop" and child labor in poor countries.

TEACHING ABOUT THE GLOBAL SWEATSHOP

The paired soccer ball writing assignment was a spur-of-the-moment classroom introduction to

Sydney Schanberg's June 1996 *Life* magazine article, "Six Cents an Hour." Schanberg, best known for his *New York Times* investigations of Cambodia's "killing fields," had traveled to Pakistan and posed as a soccer ball exporter. There, he was offered children for $150 to $180 who would labor for him as virtual slaves. As Schanberg reports, in Pakistan, children as young as six are "sold and resold like furniture, branded, beaten, blinded as punishment for wanting to go home, rendered speechless by the trauma of their enslavement." For pennies an hour, these children work in dank sheds stitching soccer balls with the familiar Nike swoosh and logos of other transnational athletic equipment companies.

Nike spokesperson Donna Gibbs, defended her company's failure to eliminate child labor in the manufacture of soccer balls: "It's an ages-old practice," she was quoted as saying in Schanberg's article, "and the process of change is going to take time." But as Max White, an activist with the "Justice. Do It NIKE!" coalition, said when he visited my global studies class: "Nike knew exactly what it was doing when it went to Pakistan. That's why they located there. They went because they knew child labor was an 'ages-old practice.'"

My initial impulse had been to teach a unit on child labor. I thought that my students would empathize with young people around the globe, whose play and education had been forcibly replaced with the drudgery of repetitive work — and that the unit would engage them in thinking about inequities in the global division of labor. Perhaps it might provoke them to take action on behalf of child workers in poor countries.

But I was also concerned that we shouldn't reduce the growing inequalities between rich and poor countries to the issue of child labor. Child labor could be entirely eliminated and that wouldn't affect the miserably low wages paid to adult workers, the repression of trade unions and democratic movements, the increasing environmental degradation, and the resulting Third World squalor sanitized by terms like "globalization" and "free trade." Child labor is one spoke on the wheel of global capitalism, and I wanted to present students with a

Strawberries and Farm Workers

In my U.S. History class, I adapt the soccer ball exercise when we study farm worker issues. I bring in a basket of beautiful ripe strawberries, sit it on a stool in the center of the classroom and ask students to describe what they see. We follow this with the Brecht poem, "A Worker Reads History," (p. 2) and "re-viewing" of the strawberries (as described with the soccer ball in this article), and then watch ¡Aumento Ya!, a video about the 1995 strike of Oregon strawberry pickers, organized by the farm worker union, Pineros y Campesinos Unidos del Noroeste — PCUN. (See "Videos With a Global Conscience," p. 365.) Other teachers have used athletic shoes, apples, and even broccoli to alert students to the human lives behind the things we too often take for granted. Also see the story, "Cebolleros," p. 250.

— Bill Bigelow

broader framework to reflect on its here-and-now dynamics. What I share here is a sketch of my unit's first draft — an invitation to reflect on how best to engage students in these issues.

THE TRANSNATIONAL CAPITAL AUCTION

It seemed to me that the central metaphor for economic globalization was the auction: governments beckoning transnational corporations to come hither — in competition with one another — by establishing attractive investment climates (e.g., by maintaining low-wage/weak union havens and not pressing environmental concerns.) So I wrote what I called "The Transnational Capital Auction: A Game of Survival" (see p. 108.) I divided students into seven different "countries," each of which would compete with the others to accumulate "Friendly-to-Capital points" — the more points earned, the more likely Capital would locate in that country. In five silent auction rounds, each group would submit bids for minimum wage, child labor laws, environmental regulations, conditions for worker organizing, and corporate tax rates. For example, a corporate tax rate of 75% won no points for the round, but a zero tax rate won 100 points. (There were penalty points for "racing to the bottom" too quickly, risking popular rebellion, and thus "instability" in the corporate lexicon.)

I played Capital and egged them on: "Come on, group three, you think I'm going to locate in your country with a ridiculous minimum wage like $5 an hour? I might as well locate in the United States. Next round, let's not see any more sorry bids like that one." A bit crass, but so is the real-world downward spiral simulated in the activity.

At the game's conclusion, every country's bids hovered near the bottom: no corporate taxes, no child labor laws, no environmental regulations, pennies-an-hour minimum wage rates, union organizers jailed, and the military used to crush strikes. As I'd anticipated, students had breathed life into the expressions "downward leveling" and "race to the bottom." In the frenzied competition of the auction, they'd created some pretty nasty conditions, because the game rewarded those who lost sight of the human and environmental consequences of their actions. I asked them to step back from the activity and to write on the kind of place their country would become should transnational Capital decide to accept their bids and locate there. I also wanted

them to reflect on the glib premise that underlies so much contemporary economic discussion: that foreign investment in poor countries is automatically a good thing. And finally I hoped that they would consider the impact that the race to the bottom has on their lives, especially their future work prospects. (That week's *Oregonian* carried articles about the Pendleton Co.'s decision to pull much of its production from Oregon and relocate to Mexico.) I gave them several quotes to reflect on as they responded:

> "It is not that foreigners are stealing our jobs, it is that we are all facing one another's competition."
> —William Baumol,
> Princeton University economist

> "Downward leveling is like a cancer that is destroying its host organism — the earth and its people."
> —Jeremy Brecher and Tim Costello, authors of *Global Village or Global Pillage*

> "Globalization has depressed the wage growth of low-wage workers [in the United States]. It's been a reason for the increasing wage gap between high-wage and low-wage workers."
> —Laura Tyson, former Chairperson, U.S. Council of Economic Advisers

Many global issues courses are structured as "area studies," with units focusing on South America, sub-Saharan Africa, or the Middle East. There are obvious advantages to this region-by-region progression, but I worried that if I organized my curriculum this way, students might miss how countries oceans apart, such as Indonesia and Haiti, are affected by the same economic processes. I wanted students to see globalization as, well, global — that there were myriad and far-flung runners in the race to the bottom.

This auction among poor countries to attract Capital was the essential context my students needed in order to recognize patterns in such seemingly diverse phenomena as child labor and increased immigration to the world's so-called developed nations. However, I worried that the simulation might be too convincing, corporate power depicted as too overwhelming. The auction metaphor was accurate but inexorable: Students could conclude that if transnational Capital is as effective an "auctioneer" as I was in the simulation, the situation for poor countries must be hopeless.

In the follow-up writing assignment, I asked what, if anything, people in these countries could do to stop the race to the bottom, the "downward leveling." By and large, students' responses weren't as bleak as I feared. Kara wrote: "Maybe if all the countries come together and raise the standard of living or become 'Capital unfriendly,' then Capital would have no choice but to take what they receive. Although it wouldn't be easy, it would be dramatically better." Adrian suggested that "people could go on an area-wide strike against downward leveling and stand firm to let Capital know that they won't go for it." And Matt wrote simply, "Revolt, strike." Tessa proposed that people here could "boycott products made in countries or by companies that exploit workers."

But others were less hopeful. Lisa wrote: "I can't see where there is much the people in poor countries can do to stop this 'race to the bottom.' If the people refuse to work under those conditions the companies will go elsewhere. The people have so little and could starve if they didn't accept the conditions they have to work under." Sara wrote, "I don't think a country can get themselves out of this because companies aren't generous enough to help them because they wouldn't get anything out of it."

What I should have done is obvious to me now. After discussing their thoughts on the auction, I should have regrouped students and started the auction all over again. Having considered various alternative responses to the downward spiral of economic and environmental conditions, students could have practiced organizing with each other instead of competing against each other, could have tested the potential for solidarity across borders. At the least, re-playing the auction would have suggested that people in Third World countries aren't purely victims; there are possible routes for action, albeit enormously difficult ones.

T-SHIRTS, BARBIE DOLLS, AND BASEBALLS

We followed the auction with a "global clothes hunt." I asked students to: "Find at least ten items of clothing or toys at home. These can be anything: T-shirts, pants, skirts, dress shirts, shoes, Barbie dolls, baseballs, soccer balls, etc.," and to list each item and country of manufacture — see "Clothes, Toys, and the World," p. 140.) In addition, I wanted them to attach geographic locations to the place names, some of which many students had never heard of (for example, Sri Lanka, Macau, El Salvador, and Bangladesh). So in class they made collages of drawings or magazine clippings of the objects they'd found, and with the assistance of an atlas, drew lines on a world map connecting these images with the countries where the items were produced.

We posted their collage/maps around the classroom, and I asked students to wander around looking at these to search for patterns for which kinds of goods were produced in which kind of countries. Some students noticed that electronic toys tended to be produced in Taiwan and Korea; that more expensive shoes, like Doc Martens, were manufactured in Great Britain or Italy; athletic shoes were made mostly in Indonesia or China. On their "finding patterns" write-up, just about everyone commented that China was the country that appeared most frequently on people's lists. A few kids noted that most of the people in the manufacturing countries were not white.

As Sandee wrote, "The more expensive products seem to be manufactured in countries with a higher number of white people. Cheaper products are often from places with other races than white." People in countries with concentrations of people of color "tend to be poorer so they work for less." We'd spent the early part of the year studying European colonialism, and some students noticed that many of the manufacturing countries were former colonies. I wanted students to see that every time they put on clothes or kick a soccer ball they are making a connection, if hidden, with people around the world — especially in Third World countries — and that these connections are rooted in historic patterns of global inequality.

From here on, I saturated students with articles and videos that explored the working conditions and life choices confronting workers in poor countries. Some of the resources I found most helpful included: *Mickey Mouse Goes to Haiti*, a video critiquing the Walt Disney Co.'s exploitation of workers in Haiti's garment industry (workers there, mostly women, made 28¢ an hour; Disney claimed it couldn't afford the 58¢ an hour workers said they could live on); a CBS *48 Hours* exposé of conditions for women workers in Nike factories in Vietnam, reported by Roberta Baskin; several Bob Herbert "In America" *New York Times* columns; a *Washington Post* article, "Boot Camp at the Shoe Factory:

Where Taiwanese Bosses Drill Chinese Workers to Make Sneakers for American Joggers," by Anita Chan; *Tomorrow We Will Finish*, a UNICEF-produced video about the anguish and solidarity of girls forced into the rug-weaving industry in Nepal and India; and an invaluable collection of articles called a "Production Primer," collected by "Justice. Do It NIKE!," a coalition of Oregon labor, peace, and justice groups. (See Resources, p. 351, for an annotated list of materials on teaching about globalization.)

I indicated above that the advantage of this curricular globe-trotting was that students could see that issues of transnational corporate investment, child labor, worker exploitation, poverty, and the like are not isolated in one particular geographic region. The disadvantage was that students didn't get much appreciation for the peculiar conditions in each country we touched on. And I'm afraid that after awhile, people in different societies began to appear as generic global victims. This was not entirely the fault of my decision to bounce from country to country, but was also a reflection of the narrow victim orientation of many of the materials available.

I was somewhat unaware of the limits of these resources until I previewed a 25-minute video produced by Global Exchange, *Indonesia: Islands on Fire*. One segment features Sadisah, an Indonesian ex-Nike worker, who with dignity and defiance describes conditions for workers there and what she wants done about them. I found her presence, albeit brief, a stark contrast to most of the videos I'd shown in class that feature white commentators with Third World workers presented as objects of sympathy. Although students generated excellent writing during the unit, much of it tended to miss the humor and determination suggested in the *Islands on Fire* segment and concentrated on workers' victimization. (See "Videos With a Global Conscience," p. 356, for reviews of global sweatshop videos.)

CRITIQUE WITHOUT CARICATURE

Two concerns flirted uncomfortably throughout the unit. On the one hand, I had no desire to feign neutrality — to hide my conviction that people here need to care about, and to act in solidarity with, workers around the world in their struggles for better lives. To pretend that I was a mere dispenser of information would be dishonest, but worse, it would imply that being a spectator is an ethical response to injustice. It would model a stance of moral apathy. I wanted students to know these issues are important to me, that I care enough to do something about them.

On the other hand, I never want my social concerns to suffocate student inquiry or to prevent students from thoughtfully considering opposing views. I wanted to present the posi-

The Stitching Shed

BY THO DONG

Day by day

Sit in the stitching shed.

Stitch by stitch.

Hope I could do faster,

Do faster to earn money,

Do faster so my brother

won't cry because of hunger,

Do faster so my family can

survive.

Stitch by stitch.

One by one.

I want to cry out,

But can't do that.

Family still there.

I want to give up.

But can't do that.

My family needs food!

Can't do it faster.

My hands hurt.

I hear the voices through the winds.

They tell me to let go of the pain.

Oh, god! I am too young to give up.

The hope eases my pain.

Hope tomorrow will be better.

Tho Dong was an 11th-grade student at Franklin High School in Portland, Oregon when she wrote this poem.

Students and community activists at an anti-Nike rally in New York City in 1999.

tions of transnational corporations critically, but without caricature.

Here, too, it might have been useful to focus on one country in order for students to evaluate corporate claims — e.g., "Nike's production can help build thriving economies in developing nations." I'd considered writing a role play about foreign investment in Indonesia with roles for Nike management as well as Korean and Taiwanese subcontractors. (Nike itself owns none of its own production facilities in poor countries.) This would have provoked a classroom debate on corporate statements, where students could have assessed how terms like "thriving economies" may have different meanings for different social groups.

Instead, I tried in vain to get a spokesperson from Nike, in nearby Beaverton, to address the class; I hoped that at least the company might send me a video allowing students to glean the corporate perspective. No luck. They sent me a PR packet of Phil Knight speeches, and their "Code of Conduct," but stopped returning my phone calls requesting a speaker. I copied the Nike materials for students, and they read with special care the Nike Code of Conduct (see p. 153) and did a "loophole search" — discovering, among other things, that Nike promises to abide by local minimum wage laws, but never promis-

es to pay a living wage; they promise to obey "local environmental regulations" without acknowledging how inadequate these often are. Having raced themselves to the bottom in the transnational capital auction, students were especially alert to the frequent appearance of the term "local government regulations" in the Nike materials. Each mention might as well have carried a sticker reading "WEASEL WORDS."

I reminded students of our soccer ball exercise, how we'd missed the humanity in the object until we read Bertolt Brecht's poem. I asked them to write a "work poem" that captured some aspect of the human lives connected to the products we use everyday. They could draw on any situation, product, individual, or relationship we'd encountered in the unit. As prompts, I gave them other work poems that my students had produced over the years. Students brainstormed ways they might complete the assignment: from the point of view of one of the objects produced, or that of one of the workers; a dialogue poem from the point of view of worker and owner, or worker and consumer (see "Two Women" in *Rethinking Our Classrooms, Volume 1*, p. 112; and "Two Young Women," p. 152); a letter to one of the products, or to one of the owners (like Oregon-based Phil Knight, CEO of Nike).

Cameron Robinson's poem, below, expressed the essence of what I was driving at with the assignment:

Masks

Michael Jordan soars
through the air,
on shoes of unpaid labor.

A boy kicks a soccer ball,
the bloody hands are forgotten.

An excited girl combs
the hair of her Barbie,
an overworked girl makes it.

A child receives a teddy bear,
"Made in China" has no meaning.

The words "hand made"
are printed,
whose hands were used
to make them?

A six year old in America starts his first day of school,
A six year old in Pakistan starts his first day of work.

They want us to see the ball,
not to see the millions
of ball stitchers.

The world is full of many masks,
the hard part
is seeing beneath them.

As we read our pieces aloud (I wrote one too), I asked students to record lines or images that they found particularly striking and to note themes that recurred. They also gave positive feedback to one another after each person read. Sandee wrote: "I liked the line in Maisha's paper that said, 'My life left me the day I stitched the first stitch....' I like Antoinette's paper because of the voice. It showed more than just pain, it also reflected a dream" — an ironic dream of a sweatshop worker who wants to flee her country for the "freedom" of the United States.

Dirk had written a harshly worded piece from the point of view of a worker for a transnational company; it drew comments from just about everyone. Elizabeth appreciated it because "he used real language to express the feelings of the workers. As he put it, I doubt that the only thing going through their minds is 'I hate this job.'"

As a whole the writings were a lot angrier than they were hopeful; if I'd missed it in their pieces, this came across loud and clear in stu-dents' "common themes" remarks. As Jessica wrote: "One of the things I noticed was that none of the [papers] had a solution to the situation they were writing about." Maisha agreed: "Each paper only showed animosity...."

I expected the unit to generate anger, but I hoped to push beyond it. From the very beginning, I told students that it was not my intention merely to expose the world's abuse and exploitation. A broader aim was to make a positive difference. For their final project, I wanted students to *do* something with their knowledge — I wanted to give them the opportunity to act on behalf of the invisible others whose lives are intertwined in so many ways with their own. I wasn't trying to push a particular organization, or even a particular form of "action." I wanted them simply to feel some social efficacy, to sense that no matter how overwhelming a global injustice, there's always something to be done.

The assignment sheet (see "Global Sweatshops: Making a Difference Project," p. 139) required students to take their learning "outside the walls of the classroom and into the real world." They could write letters to Phil Knight, Michael Jordan, or then-President Clinton. They could write news articles or design presentations to other classes. I didn't want them to urge a particular position if they didn't feel comfortable with that kind of advocacy; so in a letter they might simply ask questions of an individual.

They responded with an explosion of creativity: Three groups of students designed presentations for elementary school kids or for other classes at the school; one student wrote an article on child labor to submit to the Franklin *Post*, the school newspaper; four students wrote Phil Knight, two wrote Michael Jordan, and one each wrote the Disney Co., President Clinton, and local activist Max White.

Jonathan Parker borrowed an idea from an editorial cartoon included in the "Justice. Do It NIKE!" reader. He found an old Nike shoe and painstakingly constructed a wooden house snuggled inside, complete with painted shingles and stairway. He accompanied it with a poem that reads in part:

There is a young girl
who lives in a shoe.
Phil Knight makes six million
she makes just two.

When Nike says "just do it"
she springs to her feet,

stringing her needle
and stitching their sneaks.
With Nike on the tongue,
The swoosh on the side,
the sole to the bottom,
she's done for the night....

When will it stop?
When will it end?
Must I, she says,
toil for Nike again?

The "sculpture" and poem have been displayed in my classroom, and have sparked curiosity and discussion in other classes, but Jonathan hopes also to have it featured in the display case outside the school library.

Cameron, a multi-sport athlete, was inspired by a *Los Angeles Times* article by Lucille Renwick, "Teens' Efforts Give Soccer Balls the Boot," about Monroe High School students in L.A. who became incensed that all of their school's soccer balls came from Pakistan, a child labor haven. The Monroe kids got the L.A. school board to agree to a policy to purchase soccer balls only from countries that enforce a prohibition on child labor.

Cameron decided to do a little detective work of his own, and discovered that at the five Portland schools he checked, 60% of the soccer balls were made in Pakistan. He wrote a letter to the school district's athletic director alerting him to his findings, describing conditions under which the balls are made, and asking him what he intended to do about it. Cameron enclosed copies of Sydney Schanberg's "Six Cents an Hour" article, as well as the one describing the students' organizing in Los Angeles — hinting further action if school officials didn't rethink their purchasing policies.

One student, Daneeka, bristled at the assignment, and felt that regardless of what the project sheet said, I was actually forcing them to take a position. She boycotted the assignment and enlisted her mother to come in during parent conferences to support her complaint. Her mother talked with me, read the assignment sheet, and — to her daughter's chagrin — told her to do the project. Daneeka and I held further negotiations and agreed that she could take her learning "outside the walls of the classroom" by "visiting" online chat rooms where she could discuss global sweatshop issues, and describe these conversations in a paper. But after letting the assignment steep a bit longer, she found a more per-

sonal connection to the issues. Daneeka decided to write Nike about their use of child labor in Pakistan as described in the Schanberg article. "When I was first confronted with this assignment," she wrote in her letter, "it really didn't disturb me. But as I have thought about it for several weeks, child labor is a form of slavery. As a young Black person, slavery is a disturbing issue, and to know that Nike could participate in slavery is even more disturbing." Later in her letter, Daneeka acknowledges that she is a "kid" and wants to stay in fashion. "Even I will continue to wear your shoes, but will you gain a conscience?"

"JUST GO WITH THE FLOW"

At the end of the global sweatshop unit, I added a brief curricular parenthesis on the role of advertising in U.S. society. Throughout the unit, I returned again and again to Cameron Robinson's "masks" metaphor:

The world is full of many masks,
the hard part
is seeing beneath them.

I'd received a wonderful video earlier in the year, *The Ad and the Ego*, that, among other things, examines the "masking" role of advertising — how ads hide the reality of where a product comes from and the environmental consequences of mass consumption (see article, p. 300). The video's narrative is dense, but because of its subject matter, humor, and MTV-like format, students were able to follow its argument as long as I frequently stopped the VCR. At the end of part one, I asked students to comment on any of the quotes from the video and to write other thoughts they felt were relevant. One young woman I'll call Marie wrote in part: "I am actually tired of analyzing everything that goes on around me. I am tired of looking at things at a deeper level. I want to just go with the flow and relax."

I'd like to think that Marie's frustration grew from intellectual exhaustion, from my continually exhorting students to "think deep," to look beneath the surface — in other words, from my academic rigor. But from speaking with her outside of class, my sense is that the truer cause of her weariness came from constantly seeing people around the world as victims, from Haiti to Pakistan to Nepal to China. By and large, the materials I was able to locate (and chose to use)

Nike workers in Bangkok, Thailand take part in a demonstration over working conditions in 2000.

too frequently presented people as stick figures, mere symbols of a relationship of domination and subordination between rich and poor countries. I couldn't locate resources — letters, diary entries, short stories, etc. — that presented people's work lives in the context of their families and societies. And I wasn't able to show consistently how people in those societies struggle in big and little ways for better lives. The overall impression my students may have been left with was that the unit was an invitation to pity and help unfortunate others, rather than as an invitation to join with diverse groups and individuals in a global movement for social justice — a movement already underway.

Another wish-I'd-done-better, that may also be linked to Marie's comment, is the tendency for a unit like this to drift toward good guys and bad guys. In my view, Nike *is* a "bad guy," insofar as it reaps enormous profits as it pays workers wages that it knows full-well cannot provide a decent stan-

> **Teaching about injustice and poverty "over there" in Third World countries may implicitly establish U.S. society as the standard of justice and affluence. There is poverty and exploitation of workers "over here" too.**

dard of living. They're shameless and they're arrogant. As one top Nike executive in Vietnam told Portland's *Business Journal*: "Sure we're chasing cheap labor, but that's business and that's the way it's going to be" — a comment that lends sinister meaning to the Nike slogan, "There is no finish line." My students' writing often angrily targeted billionaire Nike CEO Phil Knight and paired corporate luxury with Third World poverty. But corporations are players in an economic "game" with rules to maximize profits, and rewards and punishments for how well those rules are obeyed. I hoped that students would come to see the "bad guys" less as the individual players in the game than as the structure, profit imperatives, and ideological justifications of the game itself. Opening with the Transnational Capital Auction was a good start, but the unit didn't consistently build on this essential systemic framework.

Finally, there is a current of self-righteousness in U.S. social discourse that insists that "we" have it good and "they" have it bad. A unit like this can settle too comfortably into that wrong-headed dichotomy and even reinforce it. Teaching about injustice and poverty "over there" in Third World countries may implicitly establish U.S. society as the standard of justice and affluence. There is poverty and exploitation of workers here, too. And both "we" and "they" are stratified based especially on race, class, and gender. "We" here benefit very unequally from today's frantic pace of globalization. As well, there are elites in the Third World with lots more wealth and power than most people in this soci-ety. Over the year, my global studies curriculum attempted to confront these complexities of inequality. But it's a crucial postscript that I want to emphasize as I edit my "race to the bottom" curriculum for future classes.

Enough doubt and self-criticism. By and large, students worked hard, wrote with insight and empathy, and took action for justice — however small. They were poets, artists, essayists, political analysts, and teachers. And next time around, we'll all do better. ■

Bill Bigelow (bbpdx@aol.com) teaches at Franklin High School in Portland, Oregon and is a Rethinking Schools editor. Some of the students' names in this article have been changed.

Global Sweatshops:
"Making a Difference" Project

The project you choose is up to you. The major requirement is that you take your learning about Nike; the "global sweatshop"; child labor; conditions for workers in Indonesia, China, Vietnam, Haiti, etc.; outside the walls of the classroom and into the real world. Some examples:

- Write a detailed letter of opinion or inquiry to someone connected with these issues — for example, Phil Knight; Michael Jordan; the President; U.S. labor unions; the Disney Co.; the governments of China, Vietnam, or Indonesia, etc. In this letter, you can either make a strong point and back it up with evidence from class and your own research, or you can raise important questions. However, if you choose to raise questions, you still need to indicate lots of information that you know about the issue.

- Write an article for the Franklin *Post*, *The Oregonian*, or some other journal or newsletter.

- Prepare testimony for the Portland School Board, or some other agency or office.

- Design a presentation for classes at Franklin or a feeder school (Kellogg, Mt. Tabor, et al.) to teach others about these issues.

- Become involved with a group that is trying to make a difference around these issues. Write up your reasons for choosing this group and what you hope to accomplish.

- Produce a rap, audio tape, video, or visual display. (You would also need to accompany this with an essay explaining and defending your point of view.) Write a skit to perform or a story to share.

- An original idea that my teacher-brain was too dull to come up with.

Other Considerations:

- You may work in a group if required by the nature of your project — for example, presenting to other classes or giving testimony before the school board. But I will need to see evidence that each member of the group has participated.

- You must use at least five different sources in your project. At least two of these must be sources you found on your own.

- The final draft of your project must demonstrate clear ideas and support, and it needs to be "correct." No spelling, grammatical, or other errors on the final draft. (People outside of schools are often looking for ways to make students look ignorant; let's not give them any ammunition.)

- Remember to go deep with this. Point out specific conditions that need changing, but also remember to talk about the deeper causes of these problems.

If you'd like to download a copy of this handout to adapt for use with your class, visit www.rethinkingschools.org/rg.

TEACHING ACTIVITY

CLOTHES, TOYS, AND THE WORLD: WHERE ARE THINGS MADE?

BY BOB PETERSON AND BILL BIGELOW

1. After doing the "soccer ball" activity (described on pp. 128-130), ask students if they know where the clothes they are wearing come from. Have each of them check the labels on at least one item of clothing. List the item, brand name, and country of origin on the board. Ask if students can make any generalizations about the places where their clothes are produced. What percentage of their clothing is made in the United States or Canada? Why are so many items of clothing made in other countries? Is it because people in these other countries are more skilled at making clothing? Return to these and other questions after they've completed their homework.

2. Distribute the homework assignment sheet "Researching Our Stuff." Read the instructions aloud so students are clear about what is expected.

3. There are a variety of ways to process the homework information they collect:

- Make a master chart on big poster paper.

- Distribute a blank world map and an atlas. Ask students to label and color in the countries where their items are made.

- Have students write the brand name, country, and item on small stickie notes. They can place the stickies on a world wall-map.

- Post students' labeled maps around the room. Have students circulate throughout the classroom listing several countries that appear frequently on the maps, along with the product and brand name of various items produced in these locations.

- Have students work in pairs and use the scale on the map to calculate the distance that each item traveled to get to your town.

4. Using the information students have assembled, discuss their observations. For example, they will likely notice that items from a particular company — say, Old Navy — are produced in several different countries. This is true sometimes for even the exact same item. Ask students why they think this might be. (If they have done the Transnational Capital Auction, p. 108, they may understand that Capital searches the world for the cheapest labor. Another explanation is that if one plant should go on strike or experience labor organizing, then production can be easily shifted to another location.) Are the producing countries former colonies? Do they tend to be coun-

tries that are predominately white or are they populated by people of color? What are the ecological consequences of constantly transporting so much merchandise from one corner of the earth to another? (Point out that not only is every mile of transit fueled with polluting fossil fuels, but the more miles traveled, the greater the risk of accidents, oil spills, and the like.) Ask about the effect of all this transport on global warming.

5. Using information from the Internet and other sources (see Resources, p. 351), have students find specific information about the companies involved. What wages do they pay? Who works in their factories? What are the conditions of work? What are the environmental consequences of their production?

See www.rethinkingschools.org/rg for an assignment sheet, "The Journey of the _____," that gives students instructions and resources on researching an item that appeared on their lists. You might encourage students to write about the journey of an item from a Third World country to here from the standpoint of the item itself. The following is an excerpt from "The Journey of the Pooh Shirt," written by one high school junior, Sarah Garnes:

> I started out as a little piece of fabric no bigger than a child's fist. This comparison is easy for me to make, because I saw many children on my journey to your closet.
>
> My first view of any place but an enclosed plastic bag was not any better than the place I had started from. This place was dirty and hot and there was a lot of noise. At least it was quiet in my small bag. However, in this place one thing seemed very strange to me: The people here all had dark hair and dark skin as well as dark eyes. All these people seemed very tired. There was no talk, just the loud repetitive sound of the machines grinding and stopping; there was no clean air for these sad women to breathe, and worst of all, no joy in their faces. I was told that Disney products brought joy to all the faces of all the people on earth. This definitely was not happening here.
>
> What I want to know is who are these women working for? Where do they come from?

Sarah uses this opening to begin her exploration of Disney's production in Haiti.

6. Encourage students to write to the companies that produce their clothes or toys, expressing their opinions about conditions under which the clothing is made, or simply asking for more information. ■

RESEARCHING OUR STUFF

Name: _____

HOMEWORK: Find at least ten items of clothing or toys at home. These can be anything: T-shirts, pants, skirts, shoes, Barbie dolls, baseballs, toys, etc. Look at the label on each item to find out where these were made. If the label lists two places, include both below. (For example, the label on a sweatshirt might say that the material was made in the U.S., but the shirt was sewn in Jamaica.) Also write down the brand name of the item. Be accurate in your spelling.

TYPE OF CLOTHING OR TOY	BRAND	COUNTRY
1.		
2.		
3.		
4.		
5.		
6.		
7.		
8.		
9.		
10		
11.		
12.		
13.		
14.		
15.		

Marchers call for an end to sweatshop abuses during a rally in New York City in 1997.

"A Trade Unionist Must Leave Her Fear Behind."

On the surface, Yesenia Bonilla's story is familiar: The oldest of seven, she was forced to quit school at age 16 to contribute to the family income. But rather than be intimidated into silence by abusive supervisors, Yesenia decided to join SITRAKIMIH, the struggling union in the Korean-owned KIMI maquiladora in San Pedro Sula, Honduras, where she worked making clothes for J. C. Penney and other U.S. retailers. "Maquilas," short for maquiladoras — literally translated, places where things are put together — are factories that assemble everything from sweatshirts to electronic components.

In a noisy restaurant across the street from the union's office, this sharp-witted and sharp-tongued young woman described her coming of age in the maquila. We spoke in December 1998, three weeks after Hurricane Mitch had devastated the region. Despite having suffered from a serious illness as a result of the flooding caused by Mitch, Yesenia seemed energized by the new challenge. She was determined that the company was not going to use

the hurricane as an excuse to bust the union.

In July 1999, the union was successful in negotiating a contract. However, the campaign against the union intensified and in May 2000, KIMI owners closed the factory. They continue to fill orders from other non-union factories, including one in Guatemala.

Yesenia worked at KIMI until it closed. She continues to serve on the union's executive committee. At the time of the interview she was 24 years old.

She was interviewed by Marion Traub-Werner.

Marion: How old were you when you started working at KIMI?

Yesenia: I started working at KIMI when I was 16. I live with six brothers and sisters, as well as my father and mother, and my sister's daughter. When you're the oldest in a large family there's not much choice but to work to support the family. So I left school to help out. Besides my father, three of us kids work.

It wasn't easy to get the job at KIMI. The woman in charge of hiring said, "No *chiquita*, you are too young," and escorted me right out of the industrial park. She said the boss didn't want to hire minors because he didn't want to give them all the legal benefits.[1] He wanted them to work the same hours as everyone else.

It was three months before I managed to get them to hire me. I got to know one of the guards at the park, and he snuck me in one day. I went back to KIMI because that's where my mother was working. By that time there was a new director of personnel. He took one look at me and said, "You're very young, but I'll see what I can do." He gave me some tests and when he saw that I could do the work he gave me my needle.[2] That's how I got into the *maquila* at 16.

I was happy to get the job, but it was also bad luck in a way because of the abuse we've had to endure at KIMI.

Marion: What work do you do?

Yesenia: My first job was cutting cloth. I only did that for two days. On the third day, a Korean supervisor who was very tough put me on a machine attaching sleeves. She wanted to take advantage of me because I was so young. She insulted me, made me cry, and hit me. She threw pieces of cloth in my face and demanded that I attach sleeves as fast as the more experienced workers. That's how I learned my first operation. By now I can do many different operations, and I do them well. But mostly I attach sleeves.

Marion: Do your parents work?

Yesenia: Before Mitch, my father worked on a plantation of plantains and cocoa. That's all been lost now. My mother is also at home. She used to work at KIMI, but because of her age they told her she couldn't work there anymore. They don't let a person of 40 or 45 work in the *maquila*.

Actually, the real reason my mother was fired was because she stood up for me when I was unjustly treated. My mother saw how the Korean supervisor mistreated me just because I was the newest and youngest in the line. She challenged her, right there in front of everyone. For that, they fired my mother. And when she went to look for work at other *maquilas*, they wouldn't hire her. They said she was too old.

Marion: Why did you decide to get involved in the union?

Yesenia: I saw so much abuse. We started work at seven in the morning and wouldn't finish until late at night. There was not a scheduled time when our shift ended. That made it very difficult for the people who lived far away.

Another problem was that the company didn't provide purified water. The water was really dirty.

But the worst problem was how they treated us. Like I told you, supervisors would hit us with the fabric pieces. They'd throw them in our faces and swear at us.

So in 1994, we decided to organize a union. We organized almost the whole industrial park, but unfortunately in Honduras the laws favor the bosses and not the workers. The company fired our first executive committee and that really weakened our union.

But we did make some gains. We got purified water. The company started to pay for transportation and they also fixed the road to the factory, which used to be horrible. They put in lights so it wasn't so dark for the workers who had to walk home late at night.

But it didn't take long before they forgot all that and started treating us badly again. They took away our transportation and the other things we had gained.

In 1996, we started to organize again. We organized a work stoppage involving workers from all the factories in the park. In response, KIMI fired the executive committee and 16 other workers, including myself. We had been out of work for a month and a half when the company decided to fire 48 more workers who had continued to organize inside the plant.

That's when we called a strike. It started on October 7 and finished October 12. Through the strike we won recognition of our union. Without the strike, we couldn't have done it. The company was also forced to reinstate all of us with full back pay.

Marion: People often say that it's impossible to organize a factory with lots of young people because they don't think of the future. What do you think?

Yesenia: Well, even though I was very young, I saw the problems from the first days I was at KIMI. I was 17 when I first joined the union, and had only been working with the company for five months.

I didn't really know what a union was, so I asked my father. He had worked in Tela.[3] He told me that a union was a good thing, and that I should go and see what I could do.

The executive committee held meetings in a room three or four blocks away from my house, so I went. They talked with us about what the union could do to help the workers. They also taught us about the labor laws. Once I understood what unions could mean for workers, I was able to recruit a lot of *compañeras*.

But here in Honduras, trade unionists are treated like criminals. If you try to organize a union, they take pictures of you and send them to the other companies. That makes it very difficult for a worker to get a job once she's known as a unionist.

At first, I was afraid, but later I thought, why should I be afraid? Legal is legal, and I'm really only defending the laws of our country.

To this day, I am happy that I made the decision to be a trade unionist. I'm not embarrassed by it, although the bosses always try to make you feel ashamed. At KIMI, we have been able to help workers understand that they shouldn't let the *maquila* bosses take away their rights.

Marion: How much do you earn at KIMI?

Yesenia: That's a complicated question. Our base rate is about 350 lempiras [$25.35] a week. In addition, we get a daily attendance bonus and a weekly production bonus for meeting the production quotas.[4] If the garment style is simple, it's easy to make the quota, and you can earn as much as 400 or 420 lempiras [$29 or $30] for a six-day week.

But it gets even more complicated. If you miss a day, they take away your seventh-day bonus,[5] the day you missed, and usually all or part of your production bonus. So, for missing one day, you lose about half your salary. It's not unusual to earn as little as 200 lempiras [$14.50].

The company uses a lot of tricks to cheat the workers. For example, if a person goes to the doctor, they take away your attendance bonus of 30 lempiras [$2.15]. And at KIMI, we don't get sick pay. They deduct it from our wages, as if it is an absence.

Marion: When you get your salary, what part do you keep for yourself and what part do you give to your family?

Yesenia: I give most of my salary to my mother so she can buy uniforms and notebooks for my younger brothers and sisters. My pay is also used for food, electricity, and water — the necessities.

Marion: Have you ever had health problems at KIMI?

Yesenia: During the seven years, I have been sick with bronchitis a number of times. My lungs have been very affected by the dust, and by all the pressure from the bosses.

If you don't make the production quota, they punish you. So in order to meet the quota, you have to run out and eat real quick at mid-day and return right away to get back to work. All that pressure gives you gastritis, which I've had quite a few times.

The fact is that the quota is too high, although management keeps saying it is too low. But as we have said to the bosses, it's the woman sitting at the machine who knows whether the quota is realistic or not, who knows whether it's humanly possible to meet the quota or not.

A boss may know how to calculate how much time it takes, but it's the workers who know what's possible and what the health problems are. All the bosses know is what quota and quality they want.

That's why we say that yes, the *maquila* has brought work, but it has also brought sickness. When you start working in a *maquila* you're young, healthy, and filled with life. But workers leave the *maquilas* sick.

And what does the boss do when the worker starts to get sick? They ask her or him to quit and refuse to give her severance pay. That's why we decided to organize and why we keep struggling. We want something different. We want to have a future, maybe not for ourselves, but for our children, so that they can have the rights that our parents and their parents couldn't have.

Marion: Have you been threatened or seen people threatened for union activity?

Yesenia: We have been threatened physically. Once the director of personnel grabbed one *compañera* just because she had touched one of the stereo speakers on the shop floor. He had no right to do that, but if you go to the Ministry of Labor and complain, all they do is come and talk with the director, and then they leave. It's unjust not to talk with the worker or the union to find out what happened.

At KIMI, the managers try to scare you. The Korean supervisors especially insult union members on the factory floor in front of everyone. And what does the director of personnel do? He just laughs. It's all to discredit the union. The result is that the workers start to think the union isn't good for anything, that it's more trouble than it's worth.

They harass us in other ways as well. For several years, I was able to work overtime, but that stopped as soon as I became a member of the union executive committee. For the past two years, management has denied union leaders overtime.

Being a trade unionist is seen as a betrayal by the boss. Why? Because as trade unionists we insist that the company apply the laws, and we struggle for all the workers whether they are union members or not. That's not good for the bosses.

Marion: How have you changed personally through being involved in the union?

Yesenia: I was so shy when I started. Almost everything that the boss did to me made me cry.

How do you live on 31 cents an hour?

You are a worker at a garment factory in the Las Mercedes Free Trade Zone in Managua, Nicaragua, sewing clothing for major U.S. labels. Your wages, including overtime, incentives, and bonuses are about 31 cents an hour, or $14.88 per week.

Your weekly expenses are:		
	Round trip bus fare to work	$2.45
	Breakfast (coffee or juice only)	$1.92
	Lunch (rice, beans, some cheese, soft drink)	$6.73
	Rent (cost for sharing a one-room hut with another family)	$3.53
	Water (from one faucet that doesn't always work)	$1.41
	Subtotal (exceeds your $14.88 in weekly wages)	$15.04
Now add:	Electricity	$1.77
	Wood (for cooking on outdoor stove)	$1.88
	Powdered milk (enough for two infants)	$4.08
	Childcare	$6.12
	School (textbooks and supplies)	$0.47
	Total	$29.34

Now the total is $29.34, without even including clothing, medical care, or food for dinner. The minimum wage in Nicaragua is about 25 cents an hour. How will you survive?

Source: National Labor Committee

"It is a lie that our wages are adequate," one garment worker said. "Our children don't even have toys. We make baseballs out of old socks. We cannot feed our children right."

But I learned that you have to defend your rights, not with obscene words but in a dignified way. To me a trade unionist is a person who is very responsible, who has to leave her fear behind and speak frankly with the boss. What we ask is that the bosses respect the rights of the other workers. That is what unionism has taught me. ∎

Excerpted from Women Behind the Labels: Worker Testimonies from Central America, *published by STITCH. See "Organizations and Websites for Global Justice," p. 387.*

1. *Under Honduran labor law, minors between the ages of 16 and 18 can work if they have their parents' permission. They are entitled to special benefits including limits on overtime, a shorter workday, and a guarantee of time off to attend school.*

2. *Tests are usually done on machines without needles. Those that are hired are "given their needle."*

3. *The Tela Railroad Company is the name given to the Honduran subsidiary of Chiquita Banana. The banana workers of Tela/Chiquita are part of one of the oldest and strongest unions in Central America. Why is a banana company called a railroad company? The name dates back to when Chiquita owned the railroad in addition to the banana plantations. Honduras is known as the original "Banana Republic" due to United Fruit's huge influence on its economic development.*

4. *The quota refers to the production goal.*

5. *Workers are paid one day's minimum wage extra a week as a bonus, called the seventh-day bonus.*

Workers operate sewing machines in a *maquiladora* in Ciudad Juarez, Mexico.

The Story of a *Maquiladora* Worker

The following interview was conducted with Omar Gil by David Bacon, Nuevo Laredo, Tamaulipas on September 5, 2000.

I come from Mexico City. My father had a business there, a small bookstore, until I was 11 years old. Then, because of the devaluation of the peso, his store went broke. My parents looked for work in Mexico City, but they couldn't find any, so they decided to come here to the border, to Nuevo Laredo [opposite Laredo, Texas].

We came here looking for a way to subsist.

So I went to school on the border. When I finished preparatory school, my plan was to go back to Mexico City to the university, to study physics and mathematics or law. But I couldn't continue my studies because we didn't have the money. I had to go to work.

At first I began taking classes in air conditioning, so that I could get some training for a better job. It wasn't my intention to work full time, but to study and work at the same time.

But working in the *maquiladoras*, it's not really possible to go to school, mainly because of time. Also, the pay is low, and my job is very insecure. Despite all this, I haven't lost hope yet that I'll be able to go back. It's just that I'm not 100% sure anymore. Now there are other factors as well. I don't have any time to rest, and I'm getting physically exhausted. It's very hard.

I've been in these factories since I was 19 years old, and now I'm 26. I've gotten more and more worried, because I don't have time for any kind of personal life. I leave work so tired that on the weekends I don't want to even leave the house to go anywhere. I just want to rest. All my personal development has been put on hold so that I can just rest, just so I'll be able to work. I feel like my youth has passed me by.

Back in 1993 I got my first job in a *maquiladora*, at Delphi Auto Parts. They paid 360 pesos a week [about $40]. There was a lot of pressure from the foremen on the assembly lines to work hard and produce, and a lot of accidents because of the bad design of the lines. The company didn't give us adequate protective equipment to deal with the chemicals — we didn't really have any idea of the dangers, or how we should protect ourselves.

The union there did nothing to protect us.

From Delphi I went to another company, National Auto Parts. In that plant we made car radiators for Cadillacs and Camaros, and there was a lot of sickness and accidents there too. I worked in the area with the metal presses. There were no ventilators to take the fumes out of the plant, and they didn't give us any gloves. We had to handle the parts with our bare hands, and people got cut up a lot.

I worked in an area with a lot of lead. If you work with lead, you're supposed to have special clothing and your clothes should be washed separately. But the company didn't give us any of that. We had to work in our street clothes.

For all that they paid 400 pesos a week [about $43]. We had no union, and there was the same pressure for production from the foremen and the group leaders as I saw at Delphi.

Now I work at TRW, where I've been for about a month and a half. There's really no difference in the conditions in any of these plants — if anything, my situation now is even worse. You could say it's forced labor, considering how the foremen talk to the workers, and how much psychological pressure they put on people.

We work an average of 14 to 15 hours a day. There's no transport service to and from work, and we get off shift at 4:00 in the morning. Usually we have to wait until 7:00 before we can catch a public bus. And when a bus does come,

getting home costs 20 pesos. That makes a very big dent in your take-home pay — 380 to 400 pesos a week [$40 to $43].

My job is bending steel cables for seatbelts for GM, Ford, and some European car models. The cable is about a centimeter thick, and I have to bend about 3,500 a day. Because of what's passing through my hands every day, I can hardly sleep at night — the pain is so bad. Then I have to get up in the morning to do it again. In the future, I know that I can get carpal tunnel problems, which is a very scary idea. I've asked to change to another position, but no one wants to change because whoever works in this job gets a lot of pain in their wrists.

I feel that in three or four years my hands are going to be useless. I've been thinking that I'll have to get another job. What else can I do?

They say work in the *maquiladoras* is the best paid work here in the city. But there's not much difference from one factory to another. This is all just normal — the standard. Really, I'm leaving my whole life in the factory. Because of the time and money pressure, I have no ability to develop myself even as a worker, much less as a human being.

After I had been working in Delphi for a year, I was invited to join a group that was trying to learn about workers' rights. People in this group said that things needed to be changed and better protections given to us, but that the companies didn't want to do it. At first I was undecided, because I thought that I could get into a lot of trouble if I got involved. I thought I would get fired, or other bad things would happen to me.

I heard about the movement in 1994, when Martha Ojeda [later director of the Coalition for Justice in the Maquiladoras] and others tried to democratize the union at Sony, to make it one which represented the workers and fought for their rights. For many years, Martha was a union leader in Nuevo Laredo, and during that time, she tried to democratize the unions here. But the union leaders in Mexico City refused to recognize her.

> I leave work so tired that on the weekends I don't want to even leave the house to go anywhere. I just want to rest. All my personal development has been put on hold so that I can just rest, just so I'll be able to work. I feel like my youth has passed me by.

In 1994 the union general secretary here called her an agitator and a communist, and she was forced to leave. But she became well-known among the workers because she tried to help them at other plants too. Then it seemed the whole world painted Martha Ojeda as a ghost to scare people, and used her as an example of what could happen if you got into these problems.

But a couple of years later, when I was invited to join one of the groups again, I went.

They invited me to a workshop about health and safety — the problems you could suffer because of repetitive motion. I realized that it was ridiculous to believe that it was bad to show workers the dangers in their jobs. The companies and the newspapers say we're putting the *maquiladoras* in danger, but we're just showing workers what's wrong with the way the work is organized.

When I understood that, I decided to become a volunteer organizer, and we've been working together ever since. Everything I learn I try to pass on, so that it will help everyone else.

Every movement starts with just a small group, but they evolve and get bigger and bigger. Lots of people say you're just wasting your time because you'll never be able to change anything. But I say no. Nothing will ever change if we just sit on our hands. You have to keep trying and trying. And the little that we're able to achieve will grow, step by step. ∎

Maquiladora workers in Ciudad Juarez, Mexico.

David Bacon (dbacon@igc.org) is a widely published journalist and photographer.

They say work in the *maquiladoras* is the best paid work here in the city. But there's not much difference from one factory to another. This is all just normal — the standard. Really, I'm leaving my whole life in the factory. Because of the time and money pressure, I have no ability to develop myself even as a worker, much less as a human being. I feel like my youth has passed me by.

So Mexicans Are Taking Jobs from Americans

BY JIMMY SANTIAGO BACA

O Yes? Do they come on horses

with rifles, and say,

    Ese gringo, gimmee your job?

And do you, gringo, take off your ring,

drop your wallet into a blanket

spread over the ground, and walk away?

I hear Mexicans are taking your jobs away.

Do they sneak into town at night,

and as you're walking home with a whore,

do they mug you, a knife at your throat,

saying, I want your job?

Even on TV, an asthmatic leader

crawls turtle heavy, leaning on an assistant,

and from a nest of wrinkles on his face,

a tongue paddles through flashing waves

of lightbulbs, of cameramen, rasping

"They're taking our jobs away."

Well, I've gone about trying to find them,

asking just where the hell are these fighters.

The rifles I hear sound in the night

are white farmers shooting blacks and browns

whose ribs I see jutting out

and starving children,

I see the poor marching for a little work,

I see small white farmers selling out

to clean-suited farmers living in New York,

who've never been on a farm,

don't know the look of a hoof or the smell

of a woman's body bending all day long in fields.

I see this, and I hear only a few people

got all the money in this world, the rest

count their pennies to buy bread and butter.

Below the cool green sea of money,

millions and millions of people fight to live,

search for pearls in the darkest depths

of their dreams, hold their breath for years

trying to cross poverty to just having something.

The children are dead already. We are killing them,

that is what America should be saying;

on TV, in streets, in offices, should be saying,

    "We aren't giving the children a chance to live."

    Mexicans are taking our jobs, they say instead.

    What they really say is, let them die,

    and the children too.

Jimmy Santiago Baca is the author of Immigrants in Our Own Land & Selected Early Poems,
Martin & Meditations on the South Valley, *and* Black Mesa.
This poem appears in Letters to America: Contemporary American Poetry on Race, *edited by Jim Daniels,*
Detroit: Wayne State University Press, 1995, pp. 29-30.

What Happened to Carmelita

BY NAOMI KLEIN

This reading is excerpted from No Logo: Taking Aim at the Brand Bullies, *by Naomi Klein, a Canadian journalist (New York: Picador USA, 2001). Klein investigated conditions in a Filipino Export Processing Zone (EPZ) in Cavite, 90 miles south of Manila in the town of Rosario. EPZs, located in impoverished countries throughout the world, are concentrations of factories, where corporations take advantage of cheap wages and few, if any, taxes. Cavite is a 682-acre walled-in industrial area with 207 factories producing goods solely for export.*

In Cavite, you can't talk about overtime without the conversation turning to Carmelita Alonzo, who died, according to her co-workers, "of overwork." Alonzo, I was told again and again — by groups of workers gathered at the Workers' Assistance Center and by individual workers in one-on-one interviews — was a seamstress at the V.T. Fashions factory, stitching clothes for the Gap and Liz Claiborne, among many other labels. All of the workers I spoke with urgently wanted me to know how this tragedy happened so that I could explain it to "the people in Canada who buy these products." Carmelita Alonzo's death occurred following a long stretch of overnight shifts during a particularly heavy peak season. "There were a lot of products for ship-out and no one was allowed to go home," recalls Josie, whose denim factory is owned by the same firm as Carmelita's, and who also faced large orders at that time. "In February, the line leader had overnights almost every night for one week." Not only had Alonzo been working those shifts, but she had a two-hour commute to get back to her family. Suffering from pneumonia — a common illness in factories that are suffocatingly hot during the day but fill with condensation at night — she asked her manager for time off to recover. She was denied. Alonzo was eventually admitted to hospital, where she died on March 8, 1997 — International Women's Day.

I asked a group of workers gathered late one evening around the long table at the center how they felt about what happened to Carmelita. The answers were confused at first. "Feel? But Carmelita is us." But then Salvador, a sweet-faced twenty-two-year-old from a toy factory, said something that made all of his co-workers nod in vigorous agreement. "Carmelita died because of working overtime. It is possible to happen to any one of us," he explained, the words oddly incongruous with his pale blue *Beverly Hills 90210* T-shirt. ■

Assembly line workers at the Anlac Footwear Company factory in Ho Chi Minh City, Vietnam.

Just Do What? — Facts About Nike

Number of workers making Nike products worldwide on a given day: 500,000

Number of people employed at the PT Nikomas Gemilang factory in Indonesia which makes Nike runners: 23,000

Average daily wage for Indonesian workers making Nike products: $1.10

Average daily wage for Chinese workers making Nike products: $2

Average daily wage for Vietnamese workers making Nike products: $1.60

Amount Nike CEO Phil Knight's stock in the company is reportedly worth: $4.5 billion

Nike's 1999 revenues: $9 billion

Name of Oregon university student who designed the swoosh: Carolyn Davidson

Amount she charged for the design: $35

Number of Downsview, Ontario workers who lost their jobs in 1994 when Nike shifted production of athletic clothing to cheaper undisclosed locations: more than 100

Estimated cost of doubling the 10¢-an-hour wages of Nike's 80,000 Indonesian factory workers: $22 million a year

Percentage of Nike's annual advertising budget this would represent: 2.8%

Annual amount Nike paid Michael Jordan for promoting Nike products: $20 million

What Nike paid to sponsor the Brazilian soccer team: $200 million

Retail cost of one pair of Nike's Air Tuned Sirocco runners: $120

Approximate cost of making one pair of Nike running shoes: $5

Associated Press/Christof Stache

Nike has paid Tiger Woods millions of dollars in endorsement fees.

From: Behind the Swoosh: Facts About Nike, *by the Victoria International Development Education Association (VIDEA). For more information go to http://videa.ca.)*

Two Young Women

BY DEIDRE BARRY

I'm 18, and years older than that.
I'm 18, and I can't believe I'm that old.

I get up before sunrise, because I have to be at work.
I get up at 6, because I need time to do my hair and makeup before school.

I walk two miles to work, the blisters on my feet open from wear.
I drive to school, and walk carefully, because I need to keep my shoes clean.

I spend my day inside a factory, with hundreds of other girls, unable to take breaks, and unable to leave.
I spend my day in classes, wanting only to get out.

I would give anything to go to school, to learn, to be able to get somewhere in life.
I would give anything to be done with school. Who cares anyway?

I would quit, but I can't. I have parents, brothers and sisters to support, and jobs are hard to find.
I'd drop out, but then my parents would be pissed.

At 4:00, we get a five minute break for water, and then it's back for more work.
At 3:30, we get out, and I head for basketball practice.

I sew the Swoosh on, time after time, hour after hour, until my fingers bleed, and my knuckles ache.
I lace up my Nikes, my new ones.

**I earn barely enough to live, and not even near enough to help my family.
I get paid per pair, and I can only make so many.**
These cost me $130, and everyone has a pair.

My lungs burn with every breath, and I cough up dust every night when I get home.
My lungs sear as I run up and down the court, but I know it only makes me stronger.

I sew pair after pair, trying to earn enough to buy food and clothes.
These shoes hurt my feet. I think I'll buy a new pair.

I go home, and cry. I want out, but it's such a vicious cycle. I work to get out, but I always need to work a little more before I have enough.
I go home, and lie on my water bed. I can't wait till college. I can get out.

Deidre Barry was an 11th grade student at Franklin High School in Portland, Oregon when she wrote this.
See p. 186 for teaching ideas.

In response to growing criticism of working conditions in their overseas factories, many corporations have adopted codes of conduct. There is controversy about how adequate these codes of conduct are. Below is the code of conduct of Nike, a corporation that has been a regular target of human rights activists. Judge for yourself. See the questions on p. 154.

Nike's Code of Conduct*

NIKE Inc. was founded on a handshake.

Implicit in that act was the determination that we would build our business with all of our partners based on trust, teamwork, honesty and mutual respect. We expect all of our business partners to operate on the same principles.

At the core of the Nike corporate ethic is the belief that we are a company comprised of many different kinds of people, appreciating individual diversity, and dedicated to equal opportunity for each individual.

Nike designs, manufactures and markets products for sports and fitness consumers. At every step in that process, we are driven to achieve not only what is required, but also what is expected of a leader. We expect our business partners to do the same. Specifically, Nike seeks partners that share our commitment to the promotion of best practices and continuous improvement in:

1. Occupational safety and health, compensation, hours of work, and benefits standards
2. Minimizing our impact on the environment.
3. Management practices that recognize the dignity of the individual, the rights of free association and collective bargaining, and the right to a workplace free of harassment, abuse, or corporal punishment.
4. The principle that decisions on hiring, salary, benefits, advancement, termination, or retirement are based solely on the ability of an individual to do the job. There shall be no discrimination based on race, creed, gender, marital or maternity status, religious or political beliefs, age, or sexual orientation.

Wherever Nike operates around the globe, we are guided by this Code of Conduct. We bind our manufacturing partners to these principles. Our manufacturing partners must post this Code in all major workspaces, translated into the language of the worker, and must endeavor to train workers on their rights and obligations as defined by this Code and applicable labor laws.

While these principles establish the spirit of our partnerships, we also bind these partners to specific standards of conduct. These standards are set forth below.

1. **Forced Labor:**
   The manufacturer does not use forced labor in any form — prison, indentured, bonded or otherwise.
2. **Child labor:**
   The manufacturer does not employ any person below the age of 18 to produce footwear. The manufacturer does not employ any person below the age of 16 to produce apparel, accessories or equipment. Where local standards are higher, no person under the legal minimum age will be employed.
3. **Compensation:**
   The manufacturer provides each employee at least the minimum wage, or the prevailing industry wage, whichever is higher; provides each employee a clear, written accounting for every pay period; and does not deduct from worker pay for disciplinary infractions, in accordance with the Nike Manufacturing Leadership Standard on financial penalties.
4. **Benefits:**
   The manufacturer provides each employee all legally mandated benefits. Benefits vary by country, but may include meals or meal subsidies; transportation or transportation subsidies; other cash allowances; health care; child care; emergency, pregnancy or sick leave; vacation, religious, bereavement or holiday leave; and contributions for social security and other insurance, including life, health, and worker's compensation.
5. **Hours of Work/Overtime:**
   The manufacturer complies with legally mandated work hours; uses overtime only when each employee is fully com-

*Code of Conduct from the Nike website, nikebiz.com, Oct. 2001.
See Global Sweatshop Teaching Ideas, p. 187 for additional discussion questions.*

pensated according to local law; informs each employee at the time of hiring if mandatory overtime is a condition of employment; and, on a regularly scheduled basis, provides one day off in seven, and requires no more than 60 hours of work per week, or complies with local limits if they are lower.

6. **Management of Environment, Safety and Health (MESH):**
The manufacturer has written health and safety guidelines, including those applying to employee residential facilities, where applicable; has a factory safety committee; complies with Nike's environmental, safety and health standards; limits organic vapor concentrations at or below the Permissible Exposure Limits mandated by the U.S. Occupational Safety and Health Administration (OSHA); provides Personal Protective Equipment (PPE) free of charge, and mandates its use; and complies with all applicable local environmental, safety and health regulations.

7. **Documentation and Inspection:**
The manufacturer maintains on file all documentation needed to demonstrate compliance with this Code of Conduct; agrees to make these documents available for Nike or its designated auditor to inspect upon request; and agrees to submit to labor practices audits or inspections with or without prior notice.

CRITICAL READING QUESTIONS

1. What parts of Nike's Code of Conduct do you think are the most important in protecting workers' rights and the environment?

2. What important rights are missing from this Code that you think should be included in an adequate Code of Conduct?

3. What vague or possibly misleading language, if any, can you notice in the Code of Conduct?

Workers arrive at the Nike shoe factory in Bien Hoa, in the Vietnamese province of Dong Nai.

Stepping Out

Sneakers, "Cool Capitalism," and Black America

BY BILL FLETCHER, JR.

In October 1968 I bought a pair of Pro-Keds at a store in the Bronx for $8.30. Growing up in New York City, there were only two brands of sneakers to wear to be "cool": Converse and Pro-Keds. No other brand was acceptable.

But we did not kill for them.

In the last 25 years, the entire sneaker industry has changed dramatically. Converse and Pro-Keds were displaced as the dominant sneakers of choice, and a ferocious battle ensued — to capture the hearts and minds of youths first and then of other age groups.

Recently, when reading *The Sneaker Book*, by Tom Vanderbilt (New Press), I thought about how urban youths, particularly Blacks and Latinos, have been so successfully manipulated by the sneaker industry and advertising firms. And I started thinking about the issue of conscience and the Black athlete.

It was also in 1968 that several Black athletes made profound political statements. Two brothers, John Carlos and Tommie Smith, whose postures would be forever captured on film, raised clenched fists at the 1968 Olympics. They did this as a statement against the oppressive conditions faced by Black America — and at great personal risk and sacrifice.

Reading *The Sneaker Book* evoked these memo-

Tommie Smith (center of podium) and John Carlos (right of podium) of the U.S. Olympic team raise gloved clenched-fist salutes during an Olympic medal ceremony in Mexico City in 1968. Smith won the gold medal and Carlos won the bronze in the 200-meter run. Both were ordered to leave the Olympics immediately.

Associated Press

ries because in 1968, Black athletes were not advertising much of anything. Today, they are often the poster children for personal advancement, finesse, and "cool." They are also the poster children for sneaker companies.

So what's wrong with advertising for sneaker companies?

First, classy "athletic shoes" (as the companies would prefer we call them) start at $70 and go up from there. Sneaker companies spend nearly $800 million a year on advertising, aiming to convince consumers they need these shoes. Black youths are a major market because, simply put, Black youths define "cool." While Nike claims that 87% of its domestic sales are to whites, this market is very influenced by the trends among Black and Latino urban youths.

But Black youths are sold not only a pair of shoes, which many of them cannot afford. They are also sold an illusion, reinforced by creative marketing, that sneakers make the person.

Second, the sneaker industry made a concerted decision to leave the United States — and the possibility of a unionized workforce — and move offshore. For example, in Indonesia, one of the hotbeds of sneaker production, workers are paid roughly $1.03 a day. Working conditions are horrendous, and workers historically have been denied the right to organize unions to assert their own interests.

This brings us back to the issue of conscience and the Black athlete. The performance of too many of today's Black athletes contrasts dramatically with the actions of Carlos and Smith at the 1968 Olympics. Major figures such as Michael Jordan and Tiger Woods feel no pressure to take a stand against sneaker companies.

The problem is not just that the sneaker companies are not producing shoes in the United States. The problem is that they have chosen to manipulate our youths and exploit Asian workers with not a shred of concern for either population.

The solution: Sneaker companies must be required to sign a covenant that accepts the right of workers to form independent trade unions which are permitted to bargain for the rights and benefits of the workers they represent. There also must be a social clause that sets an international standard for basic wages and benefits.

Sneaker companies must return more of their profits to the communities they so actively target and from which they gain so much revenue.

Contributions from sneaker companies also could be directed toward community economic development programs. Given the economic devastation of so many inner cities, funds from sneaker companies could assist with alternative economic strategies that aim to rebuild our communities.

In this drama, Black athletes play a key role. Their statement or silence on these profoundly moral questions influences millions of youths who look to them as role models. No type of smile makes up for the $1.03 a day, or for the broken dreams of young, Black urban America. ∎

Psalm for Distribution

BY JACK AGÜEROS

Lord,

On 8th Street

Between 6th Avenue and Broadway

In Greenwich Village

There are enough shoe stores

With enough shoes

To make me wonder

Why there are shoeless people

On the Earth

Lord,

You have to fire the Angel

In charge of distribution.

Jack Agüeros is the author of Dominoes and Other Stories from the Puerto Rican, *Curbstone Press, 1993. For nearly ten years he was director of El Museo del Barrio in East Harlem, the premiere Puerto Rican museum in the United States.*

Bill Fletcher, Jr. (bfletcher@transafricaforum.org) is president of TransAfrica Forum and a co-founder of the Black Radical Congress. This article was excerpted from an article that originally appeared in the online publication The Black World Today *(www.tbwt.org).*

Sweatshop Math

BY BOB PETERSON

The issue of sweatshops enlivens my math class and shows students the power of numbers. Many possibilities exist for interjecting global concerns into math — wage inequalities, differentials between wages and cost of living, percentages of people who have access to basic needs, issues of debt, etc. This mini-project is used in an intermediate classroom for review of basic multiplication skills, and also integrates geography and writing skills.

This mini-project is part of a larger unit on sweatshops and global economic inequality (see p. 18). It assumes that students have some background knowledge of sweatshops and child labor.

Materials:

Rulers, glue sticks,
black pens, colored pencils,
large construction paper (12" x 18" or
24" x 36"), atlases, and handouts.

Handouts:

Outline world maps,
"Sweatshop Fact Sheet" (p. 158),
"Sweatshop Multiplication Mini-Project Guide,"
and six copies for each student of
"Country/Sweatshop Math Box."

Procedure:

Tell students: "Today we are going to use our knowledge of geography, writing, and math to make a poster that shows inequality of wages in the world." Connect this mini-project to previous study.

Distribute the "Sweatshop Multiplication Mini-Project Guide" and go over each of the 10 steps. Model how a student would take the information from the sweatshop fact sheet and complete a country/sweatshop math box. Then model how a student would glue the sheet onto the map and label it accordingly.

Have students work individually or in pairs. Depending on the nature of your math program, you might want to allow students to use calculators. The last two steps in the project guide require students to write. One is a short essay and the other is a self-reflection. After most students have completed a project, discuss what they learned and what the graphic representations show.

The Magic Kingdom and its dungeon

Kirk

Sweatshop Fact Sheet

1. INDONESIA

Workers in Indonesia have been organizing for their rights. The minimum wage was raised, but according to human rights observers the average Nike shoe worker in Indonesia still makes only $1.25 per day, working sometimes as long as 10 or 12 hours per shift. According to the Clean Clothes Campaign, this wage is still only about two-thirds of what is necessary to cover basic needs for a single person. In 1997 Nike spent $978 million on advertising, including big contracts with the national Brazilian soccer team and U.S. basketball stars like Michael Jordan. Nike currently pays Tiger Woods $55,555 per day to be their spokesman.

Sources: Clean Clothes Campaign www.cleanclothes.org; and http://nikewages.org/index2.html.

2. HAITI

A garment worker in Port-au-Prince, Haiti, paid the legal minimum wage and working 50 hours a week, would need to work 8.8 hours in order to purchase 5 pounds of beans; 4 hours to purchase 5 pounds of rice; 6.7 hours for 1 pound of yams and 5.6 hours to purchase 1 pound of charcoal for cooking. In Haiti, half a week's pay is required to purchase just these four essential items! Most factories pay their workers on a piece basis, though they are required by law to pay at least the minimum wage of 36 gourdes per day — about $2.17. In violation of the law, workers in some factories do not earn the minimum wage if they do not reach their production quota.

Factory workers told Christian Peacemaker Team delegation members from Italy that $2.17 is not enough money to live on. When asked what would be a fair wage, workers generally replied that $4.50 would be acceptable.

Source: Go to www.citinv.it/associazioni/CNMS/ve/welcome_sp.html.

3. UNITED STATES

Instead of going to school, hundreds of thousands of children work in the fields of California and other agricultural states picking fruits and vegetables. They get paid more than kids around the world, but things cost a lot more in the United States. Sometimes they work in the fields 12 hours a day, six days a week. They get paid by the amount of baskets they fill with strawberries or other fruits and vegetables. For example, in 1998, Sani H., then sixteen, picked chile peppers at the rate of 50¢ per bag (about the size of a bushel). He worked from 7:00 a.m. until 3:00 p.m. and earned about $20 a day, for an average hourly wage of $2.50.

Source: www.hrw.org/reports/2000/frmwrkr

4. VIETNAM

Seventeen-year-old women work 9 to 10 hours a day, seven days a week, earning as little as 6¢ an hour in the Keyhinge factory in Vietnam making giveaway promotional toys — especially Disney characters for McDonald's. At the end of February 1997, 200 workers fell ill, 25 collapsed, and three were hospitalized as a result of acute exposure to acetone. The wages earned by the women don't even cover 20% of a worker's daily food and transportation costs.

Source: National Labor Committee, www.nlcnet.org/DISNEY/mcdisalt.htm.

5. EL SALVADOR

At the Hermosa factory in El Salvador, workers are paid about 60¢ per hour working up to 70 hours per week. At peak times they have worked a 19.5 hour shift (6:30 a.m. to 2:00 a.m.) with workers forced to sleep on the factory floor. They get paid 29¢ for each $140 Nike NBA shirt they sew; 30¢ for each $100 pair of NBA Nike shorts they sew. The drinking water at the factory is contaminated — bacteria levels are 429 times greater than internationally permitted norms. Women raise their babies on coffee and lemonade because they can't afford milk.

Source: National Labor Committee www.nlcnet.org /elsalvador/0401/hermosa.htm.

6. EGYPT

Ten- and eleven-year-old girls work at looms making carpets. They work from 8 a.m. to 6 p.m. in violation of Egypt's labor laws. They work six days a week and make $5 per week. (Hint: figure out their hourly wage by doing something other than multiplication.)

Source: U.S. Department of Labor.

7. BANGLADESH

At the Beximco factory in the Export Processing Zone of Dhaka, Bangladesh, young women sew shirts and pants for Wal-Mart and other retailers. The workshift is from 7:30 a.m. to 8 p.m. seven days a week. The one-hour lunch break is not paid. Sewing operators make 20¢ an hour and helpers make 9¢ an hour. Even though the law requires it, Wal-Mart and its contractor do not pay overtime premiums (extra money after 48 hours). There is no maternity leave and no health care provided workers. In Bangladesh's Export Processing Zone unions are outlawed.

Source: Wal-Mart's Shirts of Misery, July 1999, by the National Labor Committee.

8. GUANGDONG, CHINA

At the Ming Cycle factory in Guangdong, China, workers aged 17 to 25 work in four factories making Wal-Mart Mongoose bicycles. The base wage is 20¢ an hour, but with overtime pay it increases. One pay record shows a skilled assembly line worker in April 2000 working 84 hours a week, and earning 30¢ each hour. At the factory, if a worker is caught dozing off, exhausted by the long hours, he or she is fined a half day's wages and can be fired.

Source: National Labor Committee, www.nlcnet/org/golden_grinch/walmart_mongoose_bikes.htm.

9. QINGDAO, CHINA

At the Daesun Electronic Corp. in Qingdao, China, workers make top-of-the-line Alpine car stereos, some costing up to $1,300 each. They are made by young women who are paid an average (according to the company) of 27¢ to 31¢ an hour. (Starting pay is 20¢ to 22¢ an hour.) They sit hunched over, staring into microscopes nine-plus hours a day, six days a week, soldering parts of the stereos. Above the women is an electronic scoreboard that monitors their progress toward the daily production quota of 720 units.

Source: Made in China, a report by the National Labor Committee, www.nlc.net, May 2000.

10. HONDURAS

At the Evergreen Factory in the Rio Blanco Industrial Park, 630 workers sew McKids Wal-Mart's children's clothing and Arizona clothing for J. C. Penney. The majority of workers are young women of 14, 15, and 16. They are forced to work overtime: Fourteen-hour shifts Monday through Friday, as well as nine-hour shifts on Saturdays and Sundays. In one four-month period in 1998, there were constant, mandatory seven-day work weeks. The workers earn approximately 43¢ per hour.

In some Honduran factories, workers do up to 14-hour daily shifts and occasional mandatory 24-hour shifts, working right through the night. If a worker cannot stay for the overtime, she is suspended without pay or fired.

The 43¢-an-hour base wage meets only 54% of the cost of survival. Workers sewing Wal-Mart clothing cannot afford to purchase milk, juice, meat, fish, fruit, cereals, or vitamins for their children. Nor can they afford to buy new clothes.

Source: www.nlcnet.org/walmart/honwal.htm

11. AMERICAN SAMOA

Clothing is produced for J.C. Penney and other retailers at factories where workers are beaten. Food was so inadequate that workers were "walking skeletons," according to a U.S. Department of Labor report. The factory belonged to Daewoosa, a small Korean-owned clothing manufacturer.

Three hundred workers, brought from Vietnam, were fed watery broth of rice and cabbage, and kept 36 to a room, with two workers to a 36-inch-wide bed. Workers earned about $400 a month, but were forced to pay $150 to $200 a month for food and rent. Workers were sometimes beaten with pipes. Workers' net pay was approximately $1.22 an hour. Samoa has a minimum wage of $2.60 an hour.

Source: "Beatings and Other Abuses Cited at Samoan Apparel Plant That Supplied U.S. Retailers," by Steven Greenhouse, The New York Times, Feb. 6, 2001; and www.sweatshopwatch.org/swatch/newsletters/7_1.html# samoa.

12. MEXICO

In January 2001, workers in the Kukdong factory in Atlixco, Mexico were making $30 for a 45-hour week. They make Nike sportswear (sweatshirts, T-shirts, etc.) for University of Oregon, University of North Carolina, University of Michigan, Michigan State, Georgetown, Penn State, and others.

Source: Campaign for Labor Rights

— *compiled by Bob Peterson*

Sweatshop Multiplication Mini-Project Guide

Name _____Date _____

Follow these directions in order. Check off each one when you are done.

1. Glue a world map onto the center of a large piece of construction paper.

2. Neatly print your first and last name and the date in the lower right hand corner.

3. Using the "Sweatshop Fact Sheet" (or other resources), figure out the wages paid to children and adults for as many countries as you can find. The "Fact Sheet" also includes important information that you can include in the "Comments" section. Write up your work on the Country/Sweatshop Math Box. Print neatly.

4. After you have at least seven Country/Sweatshop Math Boxes filled out, use an atlas to find each country on the world map. Write the name of the country neatly on the map in black ink and color it in with a colored pencil. Use different colors for each country.

5. Lay out your math boxes around the world map in a logical placement — but don't glue them yet! Leave space for a title.

6. Choose a title for your map and write it neatly. Make sure you spell it correctly.

7. Glue down the Country/Sweatshop Math Boxes. Use a ruler to draw a straight line from each Math Box to the country it describes.

8. Draw a colored box around the Math Boxes to match the color of the country.

9. In a short essay, do an analysis of the data and map that you have displayed. Include: In general, what did you notice about wages for "sweatshop" workers in the world? In your opinion, what is important about what you discovered about sweatshops. Be sure to use the math in your arguments. Provide evidence for any statements you make. You may use other materials on sweatshops that we have studied.

10. On a separate sheet of paper, do a self-evaluation that includes answers to these questions: Do you have all parts of the project completed? What is the quality of your work? What did you use as evidence in your analysis? What did you learn from doing this project? How could you improve on projects like this in the future?

Country/Sweatshop Math Box

Country _____

Continent _____

Product _____

Company/Brand _____

Age of workers _____

Hourly pay _____

Daily wage _____

Weekly wage _____

Annual wage _____

Comments: _____

_____

_____

Country/Sweatshop Math Box

Country _____

Continent _____

Product _____

Company/Brand _____

Age of workers _____

Hourly pay _____

Daily wage _____

Weekly wage _____

Annual wage _____

Comments: _____

_____

_____

Country/Sweatshop Math Box

Country _____

Continent _____

Product _____

Company/Brand _____

Age of workers _____

Hourly pay _____

Daily wage _____

Weekly wage _____

Annual wage _____

Comments: _____

_____

_____

Country/Sweatshop Math Box

Country _____

Continent _____

Product _____

Company/Brand _____

Age of workers _____

Hourly pay _____

Daily wage _____

Weekly wage _____

Annual wage _____

Comments: _____

_____

_____

A 15-year-old factory worker in New York's Chinatown (left) talks to a state labor standards investigator (standing right) about working conditions at the factory.

Associated Press/Kathy Willens

Sweatshops Are Us

BY JOANN LUM

It has become fashionable to talk about sweatshops these days. Unfortunately, the public discussion is dominated by a removed, self-righteous, and paternalistic stance. It's those poor women and children in Third World countries being exploited by Nike and Disney. Meanwhile, we turn a blind eye to the sweatshops flourishing right here in the United States. And when those outside of poor communities do notice the sweatshops, too often they think they have nothing to do with them.

But the rising number of sweatshops in Los Angeles or North Carolina or New York is part of an intensification of work and underemployment that affects almost everyone, regardless of their race, ethnicity, geographic location, trade,

or class. Those who want to support workers stuck in sweatshops might start by considering that the conditions these workers face — longer hours, lower wages, and job insecurity — are problems they may be experiencing themselves.

It is true that the Chinese community, along with many other immigrant groups and communities of color in this country, has suffered the brunt of the expansion of what appears to be a global sweatshop. In Chinatown, New York, Chinese immigrant women are toiling in garment factories under illegal, inhuman conditions, even though most shops are unionized. Hours are rising, workers are continually threatened with replacement by cheaper labor, and work is increasingly contracted out to middlemen for whom labor law does not exist. In garment factories and restaurants in New York, Chinese workers — documented and undocumented — are forced to work 70 to 100 hours a week without receiving benefits, overtime pay, or even minimum wage.

The impact of such harsh working conditions is brutal. Garment workers, for example, report a mounting number of job-related injuries. They cannot sleep, they have no time for their children or spouses, and they have no energy for community or civic activities. Children as young as eight work in factories to supplement their families' income.

But what is happening to working conditions beyond these sweatshops? Violations of basic labor laws — governing minimum wage, child labor, overtime, safety, and health — are spreading, even as the inspectors who are supposed to enforce them are downsized. And work days are growing longer and longer as people try to make up for their declining wages.

Sweatshop conditions are most obvious in domestic work, agriculture, hotel cleaning, and meat processing. But firms in all types of industries increasingly rely on subcontracting networks similar to those used by garment makers to evade responsibility for poor conditions. Workers in full-time positions with benefits and pensions are being laid off and replaced with contract labor. Recently, the nation's largest job-finding company for laid-off white-collar workers made an agreement with Manpower, Inc., the nation's largest temp company and the nation's largest employer, to place such workers — managers, engineers, accountants, lawyers and bankers —

> **Firms in all types of industries increasingly rely on subcontracting networks similar to those used by garment makers to evade responsibility for poor conditions.**

when it can't place them in permanent, well-paying jobs. One estimate puts the total number of contingent workers (including part-time, temporary, and contract workers) at 35 million, 28% of the civilian labor force.

These related national trends of overwork and underemployment are creating a desperate climate in our communities, where workers must compete relentlessly for jobs, and we are constantly compromising our basic needs. Yes, we need to challenge the global sweatshop and the multinationals mining the globe for cheap labor. But not without starting with ourselves, right here in this country. We need to address the conditions here, rather than frame it as a Third World problem or marginalize it as an immigrant or low-wage workers' problem.

We need to talk about how much work — or the lack of work — is taking over our lives, controlling our time, reducing us to machines, depriving us of time with our families, friends, communities. How many of us are working 50, 60, 70, and more hours a week to keep our jobs? How many of us are working two or even three jobs? How many of us are suffering from aches and pains and stress related to work? How many of us have looked for a job for ages? If we embrace the idea that control over our time is a human right, then conversations about organizing to end the sweatshop system will be about us too and we will construct the alternative. ∎

JoAnn Lum formerly worked for the Chinese Staff and Workers Association, an independent workers center in New York City active in national mobilization efforts against sweatshop practices. She now works with the National Mobilization Against Sweatshops (NMASS), on the web at at www.nmass.org. This article was first published in Dollars and Sense *magazine.*

INVISIBLE HANDS OF THE MARKET

Kirk

Made in the U.S.A.

BY HELEN ZIA

This is not the usual shopping tour of fashionable San Francisco. The small band of women dodge cable cars in the city's tiny Union Square district, home to chic designer boutiques. They proceed along the bustling sidewalks with their hand-held bullhorn, exhorting shoppers to boycott the high-end, high-frill dresses made by Jessica McClintock, a designer who, until recently, maintained her flagship store in the area.

"Jessica McClintock says 'Let them eat lace,'" proclaim their flyers, which move like hot sale items. Near Macy's, a crowd of high school students gathers around. "I just bought one of her dresses," laments a teenager. "You'll just have to return it," says her friend.

The demonstrators are activists from Asian Immigrant Women's Advocates (AIWA). McClintock first came to AIWA's attention when

a manufacturer of her clothing closed shop, owing more than $15,000 in back wages to 12 seamstresses. The workers turned to AIWA, which came up with something unusual in the garment industry: a highly visible consumer campaign directed not at the contracted manufacturer, but at a company that had hired it to make the clothes. Of all the companies AIWA looked into, Jessica McClintock had the best-known label.

As a point of fact, McClintock had paid for the dresses and had no legal responsibility for a contractor's failing — a point that AIWA readily concedes. But in an industry rife with labor abuses, AIWA reasoned, the responsibility for violations against garment workers goes beyond that of the direct employer. "Jessica McClintock is one of many clothing manufacturers who abdicate responsibility for their workers' health, safety, and just compensation," says Young Shin, executive director of AIWA. "Their sweat and blood made her $145 million in gross sales. She must be accountable to the women who make her clothes."

It's hard to imagine that a parent wants the cute outfits she buys for her child to be made by exhausted women with children of their own whom they rarely see because they're putting in 16-hour days. Despite a campaign to "Buy American," most consumers don't realize that much of the clothing bearing the proud label "Made in the U.S.A." has been produced by women who work for pennies a garment in conditions that rival turn-of-the-century sweatshops. The U.S. General Accounting Office (GAO) defines a sweatshop as a business that regularly violates wage, child labor, health and/or safety laws. The clothing brands found in sweatshops include some of the United States' best known labels: Esprit, The Gap, The Limited, Liz Claiborne, Patagonia, and Ralph Lauren.

The garment industry is like a pyramid, with retailers — department stores like Bloomingdale's, Macy's, Sears, and others — at the top. They buy their fashions from companies like Liz Claiborne and Guess?, who are known as manufacturers although they rarely make their own clothes. The majority farm out their work to thousands of factory owners — the contractors whose factories are often sweatshops. Contractors are the small fry in the pyramid: They are often former garment workers themselves, who can't afford to spend much on equipment or rent, taking in a small profit per garment.

At the bottom of the pyramid is the worker, generally a woman (and sometimes her child) who is paid 50¢ or $1 for a dress that costs $120 at retail. As a general rule, prices within the pyramid follow a doubling effect at each tier. The contractors double their labor costs and overhead when quoting a price to the garment companies, which, in turn, calculate their overhead and double that to arrive at a price to charge the retailer. The retailer then doubles this price, and sometimes adds still more, to assure a profit even after two or three markdowns.

According to a 1994 GAO report, the number of U.S. sweatshops is increasing. Los Angeles and New York City are the largest apparel centers and home to the most sweatshops. San Francisco, Miami, New Jersey, and Texas are not far behind. Most sweatshops are hidden away where inspectors never find them, but about 22,000 contract shops around the country do business openly, sewing clothing for approximately 1,000 manufacturers. Even among these seemingly legal shops, many operate in near-sweatshop conditions.

Working in these contract shops are some 800,000 employees; about 650,000 are women. Latina and Asian immigrants, both documented and undocumented, are thought to be the most heavily represented in the shops.

THE SWEATSHOP

The sweatshop is just off one of the busiest streets in New York City's borough of Queens, near Shea Stadium and the tennis courts of the U.S. Open. To enter, you walk up a trash-strewn parking lot into a gray building, up two flights of cement stairs, down a cold, dimly lit hall to a double set of heavy steel doors and chain-link gates.

Beyond piles of pastel clothes in various stages of completion are two long rows of women, each hunched over a droning sewing machine. They have the dazed look of people who have been performing the same task far too long. It's Saturday night, and most of them have been working since morning.

Rising above the piles of clothes are tangled wires that power the sewing machines and steam presses. A single spark could turn the whole place, crammed with flammable fabric and lint, into a blazing inferno. No one seems concerned; in one section of the crowded room a few workers sit under the "No Smoking" sign, cutting loose threads and puffing away on cigarettes. The only open window in the hot, stuffy room is by the huge steam press that fuses interfacings to fabric.

From out of the stacks of clothes, a smiling,

> It's hard to imagine that a parent wants the cute outfits she buys for her child to be made by exhausted women with children of their own whom they rarely see because they're putting in 16-hour days.

gap-toothed woman appears. Bibi (these are not real names), perspiring and disheveled, steps gingerly over the ladies' blouses she has neatly folded and stuffed into plastic bags, now strewn in slippery piles on the floor. She is 56, but looks much older. Her husband, 65-year-old Kailung, works nearby, putting tags on the blouses. They greet me and introduce me to a few of the other workers, none of whom seem the least surprised to see me — an obviously Chinese woman — show up, ostensibly to help Bibi and Kailung, and perhaps fall into a job for myself. The two are among the shop's few older employees — the sewing jobs are filled by young women, some in their teens. All of them have been working 14 to 16 hours a day, seven days a week, for the last three months. They put in the time because there is no guarantee of more work once the current job is done. And because, with their limited English, they have few choices. "I'm so tired," says Bibi to no one in particular, "This job is going to kill me."

Overtime pay is unheard of. Everyone is paid a piece rate, determined by the garment and the task. A collar is worth more than a straight seam, for instance. In theory, piece rates are not meant to circumvent minimum wage and overtime laws, but to provide an incentive for more productive workers. In practice, however, low piece rates force everyone to work as hard, fast, and as long as they can to make the pennies add up. But no matter how hard they work, the pay almost never reaches minimum wage — a direct violation of federal labor laws.

For her 16 hours on this day, Bibi will take home about $50. In a good year, she may earn $13,000 — about the norm among sweatshop workers. Some like Kailung, who brings home about $8,000 a year, earn much less because they can't work very fast. Good years have been few and far between for Bibi and Kailung — who often end up out of work for long stretches. Since they never know if they will have work — and money for the rent — from month to month, they live in substandard housing, putting dollars aside for the lean times. Bibi's only consolation is that she gets to keep everything she earns — no deduction for Social Security, unemployment insurance, or taxes. Bibi shrugs at the suggestion that the deductions could benefit her. "I need the money more," she says simply.

The total labor cost for assembling the Sunday suit: under $3. Each will retail for about $60.

When they finally leave the factory after midnight, Bibi and Kailung are so tired that they take a bus home. More often, they walk two miles in order to save the $2.50 fare. Home is in the basement of a three-story house. The crudely furnished space has been subdivided into a maze of three bedrooms, a kitchen, and a bathroom. Each of the rooms rents for $250 a month. Bibi and Kailung's home, a 12-by-12-foot cubicle with dark wood paneling that makes it seem even smaller, is filled with broken-down furniture. The old bureau has several missing drawers; no matter, the couple use the space as shelves to store plastic bags, screwdrivers, and an ancient radio. Bibi hurriedly heats up a dinner of Chinese dumplings and soup while Kailung washes their clothes in the bathtub and hangs them by the water heater. After they gulp down their soup, the first meal they've had since lunch, they collapse on the tattered sofa bed.

At 7:30 on Sunday morning, Bibi and Kailung get ready to go back to work. Their bodies stiff with fatigue, they move slowly about the kitchen area. Kailung's face is swollen from a toothache that is so painful he can't eat. Instead, he prepares an herbal concoction in a glass jar to take to work. As Bibi packs a lunch of leftover rice, vegetables, and hard-boiled eggs, she complains about her living quarters. "This place is very dirty. My home in China was much nicer," she says. "In winter there's no heat. But it's all we can pay."

A permanent resident, Bibi emigrated from Shanghai in 1992; Kailung came in 1995. In China, Bibi would soon be retiring from her office job, while Kailung had already retired. They came to the United States in hopes of saving enough money to bring their grandchildren over. Despite their own working conditions, they believe the children will have a better life here. But if the job runs out, they'll soon be on the street. Bibi doesn't speak English well enough to find work as a cleaning woman or in a fast-food restaurant. Even with her green card, she can't quit.

By 9 a.m. they're at the shop. As the workers filter in, Bibi and Kailung sweep up piles of trash and debris from around the work stations. The floor looks as if an explosion dumped pink, yellow, green, and blue fabric everywhere. Most of the seamstresses are from a rural area of China's

Guangdong province. Since Bibi and Kailung's Shanghai dialect is quite different from theirs, they can't talk with their co-workers. The shop owner, a fortyish man also from Guangdong, speaks some Mandarin, as do Bibi and Kailung. In any case, language ability is not critical to the functioning of a garment shop, where tasks can be readily taught nonverbally.

Conversation lulls as the cadence picks up. The pressers start feeding hundreds of skirts to Bibi, who dispatches them to hangers and the proper rack, sized from 8 to 14. Kailung is supposed to be hanging skirts too, but his tooth hurts so much that he is sitting at an unoccupied sewing machine with his head down while Bibi tries — with my inexperienced help — to keep up with his work as well as hers. While the pressers steam their way through bundles of skirts, the seamstresses work on the matching jackets. Because fabrics are pliant and are stitched into curved shapes, the work must be done by hand, ensuring that the sewing process remains labor-intensive.

At the sweatshop, everyone is busy except the boss, who is eating a bowl of noodles. At 11:30, a small entourage arrives: the owner's wife, son, daughter-in-law, and infant grandson. The son, a cheerful-looking twentysomething, with gold chains on his neck and wrists, starts working a steam press. His wife sits at a sewing machine and also begins working. Holding the baby, the boss's wife strolls into a side room where the time clock sits unused, surrounded by posters on state and federal labor laws — all printed in English. She turns on a radio that's piped into the shop: music with a loud disco beat that gets the machines humming faster than ever.

As the jackets are pressed, Bibi and Kailung pair them with skirts, then button on a satiny front panel. They attach tags, then bag the complete ensemble. They'll be paid 15¢ for each outfit. In 12 hours, and with my help, they'll do 400 sets — for a total of $60 between the two of them.

Li Sung Feng, 70, takes part in an anti-sweatshop rally with other garment workers in New York's Chinatown in 1998.

The pressers and the seamstresses get about 25¢ for each outfit they work on. The total labor cost for assembling the Sunday suit: under $3. Each will retail for about $60.

The aroma of rice and Chinese turnips in oyster sauce begins to waft through the shop — the boss has been cooking at a hot-plate in the back. At noon he clears off one of the worktables. "Eat, eat!" he says. The workers walk over, then return quickly to their workstations to eat in silence. "The boss is cooking lunch for us because it's a Sunday," says Bibi. Nevertheless, it's not a regular Sunday event. Within 15 minutes everyone is finished eating, except the boss and his family, who hover like hosts proud to have treated their guests to a fine meal.

The temperature in the shop is rising as the afternoon sun hits the windows. Bibi takes

Beattie

advantage of a break in the pressers' work to rush to the bathroom. First she reaches into the cardboard box near her work area, where she hides her lunch and the house slippers she wears at work. She pulls out a roll of toilet paper. "You have to bring your own," she whispers. We go through the steel doors that are the shop's sole entrance and exit, back into the dark hallway strewn with refuse. To get to the women's room, we walk down several corridors, past other garment shops. "That one is owned by Americans," she says, meaning Caucasians. "Americans work for them," by which she means non-Asians. All the factories in the building share the women's room. The doors on the two grimy wooden stalls don't shut. There is neither toilet paper nor paper towels, not even a trash can, so used paper products, including sanitary napkins, line the floor. The sinks are encrusted with food waste, dirt, and grease. Bibi just shakes her head and leaves as fast as she can.

Back in the shop, the boss's son is picking up the bagged blouses that Bibi folded yesterday, and packing them in boxes. He looks furtively at boxes near Bibi that hold neatly stacked plastic hangers. When he thinks she isn't looking, he dumps out her hangers and takes the box. Bibi

starts yelling at him. The son ignores her, until his father makes him put the hangers back.

Late in the evening, Bibi goes to an area piled high with linen vests. Each one has six tiny buttons. Her job is to button and sort them, for which she gets 3¢ per vest. The buttons are so small that it's hard to work them through the button-holes. After doing several hundred buttons, Bibi's fingers are stiff and sore. Bibi and Kailung are expected to stay until all the vests are buttoned, pressed, hung, tagged, and bagged. But Bibi is so tired she's thinking of quitting. "I don't want to die in this job," she says. Kailung, whose jaw has been aching all day, is also eager to leave. The boss talks them into staying by offering to drive them home when they're done. Reluctantly, they agree. Bibi returns to the vests that bear two labels — one, the name of a popular mall retailer; the other, "Made in the U.S.A."

WHO HAS THE POWER?

Growing consumer concern over the social cost of clothing has spurred a number of recent developments. A women's group called Common Threads, based in Los Angeles, is linking middle-class and working-class women through consumer campaigns to support workplace organizing. "Two-thirds of the clothing purchases are made by women, who are manipulated a million ways as fashion consumers," says sociologist Edna Bonacich of University of California at Riverside, one of the organizers of Common Threads.

Another group, Sweatshop Watch, a coalition of workers' and immigrants' advocates, women's organizations, and legal and civil rights groups across California, is starting a newsletter to inform consumers about the clothes they purchase, providing "Buy" and "Don't Buy" lists. "Our approach is three-pronged," says attorney Lora Jo Foo, an organizer of Sweatshop Watch: "making manufacturers liable through legislative change and legal action, empowering workers through workplace organizing, and enlisting consumer support."

Around the country, workers' centers like Fuerza Unida, La Mujer Obrera, and AIWA joined recently in a national consortium to build a community-based workers' movement.

Consumer consciousness has caused some manufacturers and retailers to develop guidelines, which often set forth high-sounding principles that support fair wages and environmentally sound practices. Yet even these companies continue to get caught in sweatshop violations. And ethics codes rarely cover the new and creative ways that employers come up with to transfer costs to workers. Recently a California contractor was found to be charging seamstresses $126.75 plus tax, each month, for the needles and bobbins they used at work.

According to AIWA's Young Shin, "U.S. consumers have the bargaining power to tell the multinationals what their concerns are, to rid the garment industry of inhuman practices, and make it a humane place to work." ∎

Helen Zia is a contributing editor to Ms. magazine. This excerpt is condensed from an article published in the Jan/Feb 1996 issue of Ms.

My Mother, Who Came from China, Where She Never Saw Snow

LAUREEN MAR

In the huge, rectangular room, the ceiling
a machinery of pipes and fluorescent lights,
ten rows of women hunch over machines,
their knees pressing against pedals
and hands pushing the shiny fabric thick as tongues
through metal and thread.
My mother bends her head to one of these machines.
Her hair is coarse and wiry, black as burnt scrub.
She wears glasses to shield her intense eyes.
A cone of orange thread spins. Around her,
talk flutters harshly in Toisan wah.*
Chemical stings. She pushes cloth
through a pounding needle, under, around, and out,
breaks thread with a snap against fingerbone, tooth.
Sleeve after sleeve, sleeve.
It is easy. The same piece.
For eight or nine hours, sixteen bundles maybe,
250 sleeves to ski coats, all the same.
It is easy, only once she's run the needle
through her hand. She earns money
by each piece, on a good day,
thirty dollars. Twenty-four years.
It is frightening how fast she works.
She and the women who were taught sewing
terms in English as Second Language.
Dull thunder passes through their fingers.

* Chinese dialect.

Laureen Mar's poetry has appeared in Breaking Silence: An Anthology of Contemporary Asian American Poets *and other works.*
This poem is reprinted from The Third Woman, *edited by Dexter Fisher.*

T-Shirts for Justice

BY ARLEN BENJAMIN-GOMEZ

In July 1998, I went to my orientation at UCLA and bought a T-shirt in the campus store for my younger sister. The shirt was made by Fruit of the Loom and assembled in Honduras. The same kind of shirt has subsequently been spotted in campus stores at UC-Berkeley and Georgetown.

Fruit of the Loom is the nation's largest manufacturer of screen print T-shirts, with 30% of the domestic market. From 1995 to 1997, Fruit of the Loom closed down virtually all its U.S. operations and moved overseas. By 1998, over 95% of its goods were being sewn in Central America, Mexico, or the Caribbean.

Together with my mother, Medea Benjamin, who is a human rights activist, I decided to trace the origin of the T-shirt. We called the headquarters of Fruit of the Loom in Chicago, but they wouldn't tell us which factory it was made in. So we called the research department of the garment workers union UNITE, which was able to give us the names and addresses of several factories in San Pedro Sula, Honduras that produce for Fruit of the Loom.

We then traveled to San Pedro Sula, Honduras, to try to visit the factories. By talking to the local Honduras-U.S. Chamber of Commerce, we learned that there were five factories producing for Fruit of the Loom, and we called the local Fruit of the Loom office to see if we could visit any one of them. The local representatives refused to let us in, so instead we met with representatives of a union called the FITH that organizes workers in the garment factories, and with many women workers.

They told us that the conditions in the Fruit of the Loom subcontractor factories were dismal. They said the pay is miserable: Workers earn $3.50 a day when the cost of the basic market basket is $8 a day. Workers are often forced to work long hours of overtime without being adequately compensated. The quotas they have to fulfill every day are so high that the women suffer from tremendous stress and many become sick from the dust in the factories.

San Pedro Sula is an extremely hot town, and the workers said that ventilation in the factories is poor. They complained that managers treated them with disrespect, limiting their use of the bathrooms, yelling at them, frisking them to make sure they were not stealing anything. "They don't treat us like human beings," said one woman.

When workers try to organize and form unions, they are harassed and often blacklisted. In one of the Fruit of the Loom factories called Triple A, the workers tried four times to form a union, but each time the activists were fired.

After my experience in Honduras, I realize that we have no idea where the clothes we buy in our campus stores are coming from. Companies refuse to provide us with the list of factories they use, which is why it is so important to get a provision in our college Codes of Conduct that says the companies must publicly disclose the names and addresses of these factories. Without this information, there is no way that local groups can help us monitor work conditions.

I also realize that the only way workers can ensure that their rights are respected is by organizing unions. While none of the Fruit of the Loom factories had a union, several other factories in San Pedro Sula did have unions. This meant that the workers in these factories could ask for better conditions and better pay, and had a way to channel their grievances. As one of the lawyers we met with said, "The owners are always organized into business associations to pressure for policies that benefit business. So workers must be organized as well in order to gain more power." This is why our campus Codes of Conduct must have a strong provision about the right of workers to form unions or associations of their choice, and their right to bargain collectively.

Finally, it was clear during my visit that the biggest problem the workers faced was low pay. Their low salaries meant that they lived in crowded shacks, did not have good diets, had difficulty providing for their children, and had to work overtime to make ends meet. This is why the issue of a living wage is so critical. Without living wage provisions in college codes, we will not be able to call our school clothing "sweatshop free."

We must continue to work for stronger Codes of Conduct that open the factories to public scrutiny, allow workers to organize unions, and guarantee them fair compensation. Only then can we wear our university clothing with pride. ∎

Arlen Benjamin-Gomez is a student at UCLA. She is a member of UCLA Students Against Sweatshops and has worked at the Coalition for Humane Immigrant Rights in Los Angeles (CHIRLA), the UCLA Labor Center, and Global Exchange. See the review of Medea Benjamin's video, Sweating for a T-Shirt *in "Videos With a Global Conscience," p. 361.*

The cast of "Justice, Do It" takes a bow.

Sweating the Small Stuff
Elementary Students Dramatize Sweatshop Realities

BY MARIA SWEENEY

Sometimes the simplest things in the classroom make the biggest impression. Not too long ago, a two-page article in the newsweekly *Time For Kids* started my students on a journey that took them through a storm of protest over censorship, all the way to the lights of Broadway.

I teach in a predominantly white, upper-middle-class elementary public school in New Jersey. My kids have a lot more privileges than most. But when it comes to magical consumer images from corporations like Nike and Disney, I suspect that my students are as influenced as most other youngsters. Brand-name mania operates strongly in directing my students' materialistic desires and spending choices. And before our study of the global sweatshop, I'm certain they never thought twice about the hands that stitched their soccer balls or glued the soles of their sneakers. This veil of ignorance began to unravel after reading the *Time for Kids* article about children as young as six sewing Nike soccer balls in Pakistan. My students, initially incredulous and then furious, decided to write to Michael Jordan, who was mentioned in the article, and ask him to either stop endorsing Nike or to use his influence to get the company

to improve labor practices. Their letters went unanswered, and probably unread.

During subsequent months, the issue dominated our current events discussions. Many of the children discussed the topic at home and several brought related news articles to class. At the time, press coverage of labor conditions in Third World sweatshops was fairly frequent, including articles describing the hard-hitting Vietnam Labor Watch report on the abysmal treatment of Nike workers. The children, deeply concerned about the terrible conditions for workers, felt betrayed, even lied to, by companies such as Nike.

Their sincere interest prompted me to seek additional related materials. We viewed a *Dateline NBC* segment, "Toy Story," which exposed child labor in Indonesia and China. [See "Videos With a Global Conscience" for suggested videos on child labor.] My students were angry and saddened to see children close to their age assembling Barbie Dolls and other toys in dangerous conditions for pitiful wages. Initially, the topic was brought up only during current events discussions and wasn't a full-fledged unit of study. However, given the students' passion about the issue, I thought they might

choose it for our final class project and thus began gathering more resources.

Each year at the beginning of May, I ask students to choose a topic for an end-of-the-year play to be performed for our school, kindergarten through fifth grade. The topic we choose is often something studied earlier in the year that they want to examine more closely. I require that it be something they care deeply about and that they want to teach to other students. Invariably it is a social justice issue related to a topic that we've studied during the year — one that grows out of students' sense of fairness, of right and wrong. In the past my class has researched and written plays on the Montgomery Bus Boycott, the truth about Columbus, the Paterson Silk Strike of 1913, and the South African elections. Most of this class had seen several of these plays while in earlier grades. When the time came for kids to commit to a project, I was not surprised that they chose global sweatshops as the topic.

We discussed possible companies to focus on. Nike was the clear top choice because of its widespread media coverage and because the Nike brand has such a powerful hold on young people. "Most kids think they can't live without

Nike," one student proclaimed. The others agreed. In fact, several wondered if we could ever convince any students at our school, Hawes, to boycott Nike or write letters of protest to the company. "The whole point of the play would be to get them to join the boycott, but most kids would never stop wearing Nike stuff. It wouldn't be cool at all to be against Nike," cautioned Jessica.

Despite misgivings, the children concluded Nike would have to be one of the companies, because "kids should know all the horrible things they're doing." Because Nike has been a leader in exploitation of Third World low-wage labor, and also because a wealth of information was available on their labor practices, I strongly endorsed their choice.

Choosing a second company was equally straightforward. During an earlier current events discussion, I had shared materials prepared by the National Labor Committee on the inhumane treatment of workers in plants producing Disney products in Haiti. One child suggested we focus on Disney for the younger kids because Nike was more for the older ones. Another called our attention to a statement from a recent Disney annual report I had posted on our current events board: "Today, children around the world go to bed holding Mickey Mouse dolls, and Mickey's likeness appears on clothing, books, and products in lands around the globe. Disney lives in the hearts, memories, and minds of people everywhere." She said: "That's why we have to tell them about Disney, too."

FOURTH GRADERS EXAMINE GLOBAL ECONOMICS

We began the project with four weeks of study on the issue of multinational corporations' exploitation of Third World labor, focusing especially on economic globalization and capitalism's drive for cheap labor and lax environmental regulations in order to drive up profits.

I know what you're thinking: These are awfully complex concepts for nine- and ten-year-olds. But ultimately they are accessible if students experience the dynamics firsthand in simulation and role play, witness people's conditions in videos, and hear their stories in first-person testimonies and from guest speakers.

From an earlier labor history unit, students had already gained a framework for considering workers' struggles. I launched that unit with a version of the "Organic Goodie Simulation" from the labor curriculum, *The Power in Our Hands* (see Resources, p. 375), which put students in the position of needing to band together to protect themselves from a factory owner who relentlessly drives down wages. They also examined the Paterson Silk Strike of 1913, which confronted them with many of the themes they would study in the global sweatshop unit. For example, the Paterson silk mill owners moved most of their operations to the anthracite region in Pennsylvania, where they found cheaper, isolated, and unorganized labor: the wives of coal miners. They did exactly what most corporations are doing today, only now corporations turn to the Third World. Later, during the global sweatshop unit, the children often drew analogies to the Paterson Silk Strike.

Working with partners, students read materials from the Nike Boycott home page and the National Labor Committee's report on Disney; they drafted charts in their notebooks listing key components of the problem. We then synthesized their notes into a class chart which included the following points:

- Pay is not enough to live on.
- Workers are forced to work like crazy to meet quotas.
- They are harassed by bosses.
- They lack health insurance and other benefits.
- They're punished if they try to form unions.

I also defined basic vocabulary such as: subcontractors, minimum wage versus livable wage, benefits, exploitation, quotas, and independent monitoring.

Following this general introduction, students did scavenger hunts at home: They were to bring in all the Nike and Disney products they owned in order to see the way the global sweatshop operated in their own lives. A few children, who didn't have Nike or Disney items, asked if they could just gather things made in Third World countries. This turned out to be an enlightening revision of the activity. The children returned with bags of athletic clothes, pajamas, sneakers, and toys. We again made a class chart, categorizing the various types of items, companies, and countries of origin. The students were amazed to discover that almost nothing was made in the United States.

I then shared the story of H.H. Cutler, the garment company that closed shop in 1994 in Michigan where seamstresses earned $7 to $8 an hour, and moved to Haiti where workers earn 30¢ an hour. One child, who served as devil's advocate with lots of verbal ammunition brought from home, proclaimed that companies have a right to move if they can "make their stuff cheaper someplace else." Another student reminded him of the information recorded on our original chart, which contrasted the earnings of Nike's and Disney's chiefs (Phil Knight and Michael Eisner respectively) with workers' meager wages. I also reminded children that besides the incredible earnings of the CEOs, shareholders reaped great profits. And I referred them to a statistic we had read earlier: Michael Jordan's earnings for one year of Nike endorsements ($20 million) is equal to the combined pay of 12,000 Indonesians working in Nike plants. "Michael Eisner is like a vacuum cleaner," one student said. "He sucks everything out of the workers and gives them just barely enough to survive."

Since all of our materials, both video and print, were designed for adult audiences and consequently were quite dense, I frequently needed to explain their content. Each child had a folder and a learning log for organizing materials, taking notes, and writing reflections. I scheduled several long blocks of time for research, viewing videos, discussion, and writing. Typically, at the beginning of each research period, I introduced a new resource, defined vocabulary, and outlined the major points in the material. I wrote this up on chart paper for the children's reference. I opened the study of each company with a video: *Mickey Mouse Goes to Haiti* on Disney and the CBS *48 Hours* segment on Nike in Vietnam. (While both videos proved excellent introductions to the conditions of workers' lives, I frequently had to pause the tapes in order to answer questions and clarify situations.) After viewing the videos, the children wrote notes as well as quite moving personal responses.

The students reviewed the print materials with partners or in small groups. Finally, together we wrote the fact sheets detailing key problems (such as wage disparities), important statistics (such as the workers' mortality rates), and anecdotes (such as the prohibition on workers'

> The children, deeply concerned about the terrible conditions for workers, felt betrayed, even lied to, by companies such as Nike.

talking, for example) about each company. We kept adding to these sheets as we obtained significant information.

It was at this point, however, that I realized the children had gained a wealth of knowledge without sensing the humanity of the workers whose cause they supported, and whom they would later represent in the play. To stimulate an emotional connection, I assigned the class to do presentations that were to be both written and visual portraits of workers. We read passages describing the lives of several workers in Haiti and Indonesia. I read aloud and had the students close their eyes and "become" the person whose life I read about. We viewed the videos again, this time trying to see and "know" each individual caught in the camera's frame. Then we examined photos of workers and their surroundings.

Each child then wrote a poem, letter, or story from the point of view of a worker or worker's child. I asked students to write something that captured a person's life, thoughts, hopes, and feelings, using clear, strong images and details. They also drew the person, and their impressions of his or her home, community, and workplace. Most of the portraits created were quite detailed and moving.

> I don't believe that simply because most of my students ended up critical of sweatshops and corporate exploitation, this automatically condemns my efforts as "biased."

This activity shifted the tone in the classroom, as it engaged students' sense of the needless human misery caused by global sweatshops. But though they spoke of the workers with greater compassion, they presented portraits of workers both hopeless and helpless, aware of inequity but unable to address it. Fortunately, a former Indonesian Nike worker, Cicih Sukaesih, was touring Canada and the United States. This young woman's story offered my students a heartening example of one worker among many fighting for justice. After she and 23 co-workers were fired for organizing a walkout of 6,200 employees, she was now here to try to meet with Phil Knight and demand back wages and the rehiring of the fired workers. On the web page of Global Exchange (www.globalexchange.org), we read Sukaesih's speeches, which told of the intolerable, abusive conditions in Nike plants and urged independent monitoring of factories. The students now saw that many Third World workers were seriously involved in a movement against sweatshop conditions.

When a parent complained that I was offering only "one side of the story," it made me realize that my unit had some holes in it. I had been presenting speeches, stories, videos, and articles as if all simply represented Truth. Thus I decided to create a short unit, "Perspectives and Interests," to help students think critically about the motivations behind each resource we used, including new materials I obtained from the public relations departments of Nike and Disney. Integrating these documents into our unit marked my attempt to incorporate the companies' side — but critically, not in the traditional, and potentially amoral, "every story has two sides" manner.

Inquiring into the motivations behind each source, we soon decided that those who lobbied for the rights of Nike and Disney workers, such as the National Labor Committee and the organization Press for Change, were not driven by selfish interests and were not getting rich from their work. The corporations' public-relations documents, however, drew harsh criticism from the students. One denial of abusive practices in overseas plants was accompanied by claims that workers enjoyed gardens and basketball courts, to which one student replied: "If there really is a basketball court, big deal. They're cheap to build and the workers probably never have time to play anyway, since they have to work so many hours." Citing the interviews and writings as evidence, the children also insisted that the companies had lied when refuting reports of abusive working conditions and starvation wages.

We discussed the goal of any company's public relations department: to promote a positive public image and thereby enhance earnings. In contrast to the human rights groups, motivated by morality or justice, the corporate motive was profits. During this exercise we also analyzed the perspectives of opinion and editorial pieces, letters to the editor, "objective" news articles, and Internet items. Who were the authors of each piece, and what might they gain by convincing us that their point is the right one? Asking such questions was only a modest introduction to critical reading of resources, but it

High school students march to the Christmas tree in New York's Rockefeller Center in 1998.

helped to demystify the slick documents produced by public relations departments. The exercise also assured students, and students' parents, that we had considered a range of views.

YOUNG PLAYWRIGHTS AT WORK

Finally, after four weeks of research on global sweatshops, students began the playwriting process. For a few nights, their homework was to write up ideas for the play on their own. In class they reviewed our fact sheets, worked in groups brainstorming about possible scenes, and drew ideas from every member of the class. Together we decided on the play's framework and a list of eight scenes. The students signed up for the scene in which they wanted to act, thereby committing themselves to write their own lines. Each scene's writing group received documents relevant to their subject. Every afternoon for a week the groups wrote, acted, and revised their scenes. The entire class viewed each group's scenes and provided feedback.

By the end, we had gone over every aspect of the script several times. While the process proved tedious at times, it was worth the effort to have the entire class agree on what we would present. I took the drafts and typed up the play, making minor revisions for clarity such as providing definitions of "boycott" or "exploitation." I shared my changes with students for their approval.

After grappling with this complex and disturbing information during those first four weeks, the students crafted a cohesive, inspiring, and intelligent piece of writing. The script was impressive and also hard-hitting (visit www.rethinkingschools.org/rg for a copy of the script). The students began with the familiar, scenes taking place on our school playground at recess and at a local McDonald's, then had the audience travel to Nike and Disney factories, then Michael Jordan's mansion and the corporate offices of the two companies. Throughout, they represented their own political education: They showed other kids learning the meaning of the word "exploit" and connecting it to their own purchases; they offered a window through which to view a struggling, hungry family in Haiti; they demonstrated the apathy of Jordan and Eisner (Eisner is counting his millions when first encountered in the play). The play ends on a hopeful note, as two students discuss the growing union movements in the Third World and then present themselves as agents of change in the same movement: "If we can get tons of people to join in this movement," one actor says, "I think we can make a difference." The play concludes with the other actor's response: "So what are we waiting for? Let's get started." It was clear to me that the students truly believed in the message they wanted to communicate.

"INAPPROPRIATE" MATERIAL

That message, however, was stopped before it could be received by anyone. Three days before the performance for the entire school, my principal entered the classroom and told me that the material was inappropriate for the intended audience: The children wouldn't understand the play and the younger students might be upset by it. She also asserted that my students could not have possibly understood an issue as complex as the global sweatshop, as evidenced by the one-sided nature of the script. The performance would be only for parents.

When I announced this decision, one student cried out, "That's censorship!" Others agreed. Students were angry, incredulous, and a few even cried. They insisted on writing letters to the administration to plead their case. Students wrote brilliant and persuasive letters. One wrote that "we know more than you think;" another accused the administration of ageism. But these letters, like those they wrote to Michael Jordan, went unanswered.

What happened next was pure luck. The day of the play, Jeff Ballinger, the founder of Press for Change, learned that students had been forbidden to perform the play for other students. He contacted *The New York Times*, and the article the newspaper ran attracted national attention. Letters of protest poured into the school. Scott Ellis, the resident director of a Broadway theater, The Roundabout, offered the theater for a performance. The kids' play was heading to Broadway.

While I continued to field interview requests from national media throughout the summer, most of the coverage focused narrowly on the kids' Broadway performance rather than on the play's central issues concerning social justice. School officials, meanwhile, reiterated their objections to the play being seen by younger students, but praised the opportunity for students to work with theater professionals.

In closing, I need to ask: Was this project an example of critical teaching for social justice or of indoctrination? I don't believe that simply because most of my students ended up critical of sweatshops and corporate exploitation, this automatically condemns my efforts as "biased." Asking the big "Why?" questions about the vast inequalities embedded in today's global economy should lead students to critical conclusions. At the same time, students must be exposed to multiple perspectives on key issues. Indeed, examining corporate justifications for paying below poverty-level wages in countries that outlaw free trade unions can actually deepen students' critique and awareness of how the powerful insulate themselves from real life.

But this kind of teaching often steps on toes. I try to be brave. Working in the classroom from the standpoint of social justice and critical literacy necessitates that I locate a balance between risk-taking and caution in order to retain my job for future years of transformative teaching.

The story of this particular event in my teaching career became extraordinary only after the decision to ban it from our school audience; until that point, it was an ordinary year, when students once again created a play that took my breath away. Children have tremendous ethical and intellectual capabilities, usually left untapped and undeveloped. As a social justice teacher, I have been unpopular with authorities more than once. Still, I cannot overstate the immense satisfaction I gain from watching students come to social awareness. ∎

Maria Sweeney teaches at Hawes Elementary School in Ridgewood, New Jersey.

ON THE WEB

In "Taking Action Against Disney: A Teacher Struggles with Encouraging Direct Student Action," Steven Friedman describes what happens when his students want to join a demonstration against Disney's sale of sweatshop-produced products.
The complete article is on the web at www.rethinkingschools.org/rg.

The People v. Global Sweatshops

A Role Play Developed by the Portland Area Rethinking Schools Globalization Workgroup

BY RENÉE BALD AND AMANDA WEBER-WELCH

It is a worrisome phenomenon, when people who have not been elected except by their capacity in the marketplace, become sort of a shadow government of the world.

—Ariel Dorfman, Chilean author and activist

In 1997, a group of educators and activists from the Portland, Oregon metropolitan area began to discuss the impact of globalization and ways we might approach this issue in our classrooms. Since then we've amassed background articles and student-friendly readings and developed pieces of curriculum to help students better understand the many elements that form and result from the global economy.

As we learned more about sweatshops and globalization, members of our group began to use aspects of this curriculum in courses on economics, global studies, media, and U.S. history. In each of these instances, teachers used a variety of background materials and activities before beginning the *People v. Global Sweatshops* trial. An understanding of work conditions and company practices is important, but so is an exploration of the urgency of the global environmental crisis, the power of "consumption" in our culture, the changes that occur when Western culture comes into contact with others, the historical basis of class distinctions, and the origin of debt that shapes poorer nations' participation in the global economy. Allowing more time for students to gain an understanding of the roots and consequences of globalization will result in deeper discussions during the actual trial. [See for example, the "Transnational Capital Auction," p. 108, the "Oil, Rainforests, and Indigenous Cultures" role play, p. 268, and videos such as *The Ad and the Ego*, described in "Videos With a Global Conscience," p. 367.]

The trial role play itself is straightforward: Five groups — Multinational Corporations, U.S. Consumers, Poor Country Workers, Poor Country Ruling Elites, and the System of Profit — stand accused of creating social and ecological havoc as a result of their role in initiating and/or perpetuating global sweatshops. The teacher plays the prosecutor and the students in each group defend themselves by accusing the other groups and by explaining the pressures that they are under that they claim make them behave the way they do.

Members of our Portland workgroup have conducted the trial at or near the end of units on globalization, as a way to help students connect many of the issues they have explored. The discussions it generates are lively and raise provocative issues about the roots of global injustice. However, we recognize that it is insufficient to engage students in simply assigning blame for world problems. Insofar as the role play offers students an opportunity to probe for deep causes of injustice, it also invites them to consider the power they hold in their hands to make a difference. For better or for worse, we are all participants at many points in the global economy, and this participation gives us and our students leverage — as workers, as consumers, and as active citizens. Because the problems created by "globalization" are enormous and can feel overwhelming, it's vital that we engage students in discussions about how we can try to make things better.

MATERIALS NEEDED:

1. Copies of "The People v. Global Sweatshops" indictment, included on p. 180 — enough for every student.

2. Copies of the role sheets — enough for one per student in each of the five groups. It may help each group make stronger arguments if all students have all roles, and thus can see the charges against the other groups.

3. Construction or other stiff paper for placards for group names; 5 colored markers.

TIME:

Several class periods. Because length of class sessions varies from school to school, we haven't indicated "Day one," Day two," etc. It's important not to rush preparation, as the better prepared students are, the richer the trial and follow-up discussion will be.

SUGGESTED PROCEDURE:

Trial Preparation

1. Explain that this trial will be a little different from other trials they may be familiar with. In this trial role play there are five groups who have been indicted for their roles in creating the unjust social and ecological conditions of "global sweatshops." Each of these groups will need to defend itself as well as explain to the jury the ways in which other groups are guilty. The jury will be free to decide that more than one group is guilty and can assign different percentages of blame.

2. Read the indictment aloud, listing the poor conditions each group is being accused of creating and/or supporting. Elicit from students examples from their study of globalization that illustrate aspects of the indictment. Before reading the list of accused parties, have students brainstorm who might be among those accused. As they generate the list, have them explain their suggestions. Likely, they will not suggest the system of profit; this is your opportunity to help the class begin to understand the nature of this "defendant". Encourage them to listen closely to your description of each group because it will aid in their group's defense. This pre-discussion will help the class as a whole begin thinking about all of the roles and how they fit together before they focus on their own individual roles.

3. Divide the class into five groups of roughly the same size. Tell students they will be working in these groups and that their job, in preparation for the trial, is to read the charges against their group and to prepare a defense against the accusations. They should also come up with at least two questions to be directed toward one or more of the other groups.

4. Have students gather in their groups around the classroom. Distribute different role sheets to the groups — students in each group receive the same role. Tell them to read their role and discuss their strategy to defend themselves against the accusations in the indictment. (Note: You'll likely need to make extra copies of the roles, because some groups will want the indictments of the other groups in order to better prepare.)

5. Circulate from group to group to make sure that students understand their roles and are developing plausible defenses. Play devil's advocate, reiterating the ways in which they can be blamed for global sweatshops and prompting them to defend themselves on the spot. This may be a good time to talk more with the various groups about the "System of Profit" role, as students often tend to overlook the "intangible" in their deliberations. Encourage students to write out their presentations and to decide in advance who will present which part.

6. Ask for volunteers to serve on an "impartial" jury (one student juror from each group, although if it is a small class, a total of three jurors would be sufficient.) Try to avoid choosing only quiet students or students who were absent and missed early trial preparation. It's important that jurors' questions be knowledgeable and pointed.

The Trial

1. Seat students in a circle. Each group should sit together, with placard visible. Separate out five desks next to each other and seat the jurors in these.

2. Begin by getting the jury to pledge to be fair and impartial despite their preparation with their group. Emphasize that they no longer are members of the defendant groups.

3. Start the trial. Introduce the indictment, briefly explain the format and goals of the trial, and announce the first group to be charged. There is no "correct" order of presentation, but the order that seems to build most effectively in our experience has been: Multinational Corporations, Poor Country Ruling Elites, Poor Country Workers, U.S. Consumers, and the System of Profit.

The teacher plays the prosecutor and either reads or dramatically presents the charges against the "defendant." Members of the accused group will be familiar with this information. Encourage members of other groups to listen carefully to the indictment for ideas about how they might defend themselves and expose others' guilt.

4. After you have read aloud or argued dramatically, members of the accused group will have the chance to defend themselves. Preparation is key to this because this is each group's primary opportunity to present its side of the issues. As part of its presentation, each group may raise questions of other groups if they like — for example, workers might ask ruling elites: "How can you accuse us of having any responsibility for the terrible conditions of global sweatshops when you make it a crime for us to join unions?"

   Once a group has completed its defense against the indictment, members of the jury may raise questions. Afterward, members of other groups may question or criticize points in the group's presentation. This is a time period that can easily balloon — and it is the heart of the trial — so be sure to leave time for this. Generally, plan to allow at least 20 minutes per group. As interesting as the questioning of a particular group may get, try to ensure that time is generally consistent between groups.

5. At the conclusion of group questioning, jury members should deliberate privately. They may assign percentages of guilt — e.g., Multinational Corporations, 35% guilty; U.S. Consumers, 10% guilty, etc. Obviously these should add up to 100%. While jurors discuss their decision, other students in the class should step out of their roles to write their opinions about which group(s) are guilty and why they believe this. Ask students to write at least one paragraph per group and assign a percentage of blame. Even if they think a group is totally innocent, they should explain why in writing.

6. Ask jurors to present their findings and to explain their rationale behind the verdicts.

Debriefing the Trial

1. Begin the debriefing by encouraging other students to share their decisions about who holds guilt for the "crimes" of global sweatshops and why. Some of the questions and issues you might raise in debriefing include:

   - Was anyone entirely not guilty? Were you convinced that the poor country workers were not responsible for the conditions they worked under — why or why not?

   - What stops workers from simply demanding better conditions and pay? How might they go about organizing for change? Which other groups' support would they need?

   - How do you weigh responsibility between the actions of multinational companies and the ruling elites who "invite" these business ventures into the country?

   - What were the findings of the class on the question of U.S. consumers' guilt? In what way does this connect to our own lives? Why was discussing the guilt of this group more difficult for us as a class?

   - What powers for change do each of these groups hold? What might stop each of these groups from putting this power to use for good?

   - What more would you need to know about the System of Profit in order to sort out the guilt that it holds versus the guilt that human groups hold? If the System of Profit is guilty, what should be the "sentence" or remedy? You can't put a system in prison. What needs to happen in order for a system to change?

   - What should be the "sentences" for each of the guilty parties? Is it enough to improve pay and working conditions, or is the destruction of environments and cultures the more central element of this crime? If so, what is the remedy?

Renée Bald teaches at Lincoln High School in Portland, Oregon. Amanda Weber-Welch teaches at Gresham High School in Gresham, Oregon. At the time it developed this role play, the Globalization Workgroup consisted of John Ambrosio, Renée Bald, Bill Bigelow, George Bishop, Tamar Ehrlich, Amy Fulwyler, John Grueschow, Shawn Jarvey, Sylvia McGauley, Hyung Nam, Greg Smith, Julie Treick, and Amanda Weber-Welch.

Indictment

You are responsible for the dehumanizing working conditions and the environmental and cultural destruction caused by the growth of the global economy. You stand accused of the following crimes:

- Paying workers in poor countries less than a living wage.

- Forcing workers to labor long hours with insufficient or no breaks.

- Allowing child labor.

- Intimidating workers with physical and emotional abuse.

- Subjecting workers to hazardous work environments with inadequate lighting and ventilation, exposure to chemicals and pesticides, unbearable temperatures, and other substandard working conditions.

- Destroying rivers and other bodies of water with toxic waste.

- Polluting the land with pesticides and herbicides.

- Polluting the air with poisonous gases.

- Deforesting the land.

- Harming the cultures and values of non-Western peoples.

Multinational Corporations

You are responsible for the dehumanizing working conditions and the environmental and cultural destruction caused by the growth of the global economy.

You represent just one of the many multinational corporations that have relocated overseas in order to raise profits. You once did the majority of your factory work in the United States, but as other corporations sought out countries where they could pay lower wages and not worry so much about environmental regulations, you decided to move most of your production overseas. You may care about the ruined lives you leave behind as you lay off thousands of Americans, but to make a profit you do it anyway.

You should be ashamed of yourself. The people who used to work for you made wages that could support families. Now you pay your workers pennies an hour in places like Haiti, Honduras, Indonesia, and China. You know that the wages you pay cannot support families. Couldn't you at least give your workers a living wage?

In addition to paying miserable wages, you subject your workers to dangerous conditions. Your factories have poor lighting, choking ventilation, and toxic chemicals. Yes, technically you don't own these factories; they are owned by your subcontractors who make your products. But that's just an excuse to have someone else take the blame for your dirty work.

What's really sad is that while workers labor 12 hours a day and barely make a living, your profits have never been higher. It's not fair that the workers produce all the wealth, but you get all the benefits. In fact, the combined sales of a single multinational corporation are often higher than the entire gross national product of many of the countries you operate in.

You make no commitments to the nations in which you have factories. You have little understanding of the cultures there or of the impact your presence has on the people. Your imperial attitude makes you believe that you are doing these nations a favor by providing jobs — that you are helping them "develop." But the fact is, you are *destroying* cultures. Communities are torn apart when you flood markets with cheap manufactured goods and foods that undersell local producers, and when you bombard people with advertising and images of Western lifestyles. Additionally, the environment has been devastated by your factories. Corporations like yours are directly responsible for deforesting the land, ruining the rivers with pesticides, and dumping toxic waste. The poisoned ecosystems can no longer provide the local people with food, water, and resources that have maintained their cultures for hundreds, even thousands, of years.

Another example of your indifferent attitude toward these nations is that you *intentionally* locate in countries that are run by un-democratic and repressive governments. As soon as workers organize unions to demand that you raise wages and improve working conditions, you count on the government to crush them. And if the ruling class can't control the people, you simply move to another country. While your careless attitude says "easy come, easy go," you leave people in economic, political, and emotional turmoil.

Your atrocious record is not limited to your work overseas. You manipulate and use the public in the Western world too, by creating phony "needs" for products. You run sophisticated advertising campaigns that focus on ruining the self image of American consumers. You play on every insecurity imaginable. Without your product, you say, people are ugly, smelly, undesirable, unsuccessful, uncool — in essence, unlovable.

Defense Strategies:

How do workers in poor countries benefit from your relocation? Why do they come work for you?

What are the pressures you are under that lead you to pay low wages, and treat the environment carelessly?

If the foreign governments welcome you into their countries, who are you to tell them how they are to treat their own citizens?

What role did U.S. consumers play in your decision to locate overseas?

Poor Country Ruling Elite

You are responsible for the dehumanizing working conditions and the environmental and cultural destruction caused by the growth of the global economy.

You, the ruling elites of poor countries, are responsible for encouraging global sweatshops to locate in your countries. As economic and political leaders, it is your job to represent the people of your country, not to line your own pockets and help the multinational businesses make money. Because of you, citizens in your country face dehumanizing labor conditions and continue to live in extreme poverty. Because of you, the environment in your country is being attacked in numerous ways. You allow corporations to build factories that pollute, to despoil rainforests with oil wells, to log your forests, to dump toxic wastes in your rivers, etc.

Blame the corporations if you want to, but they didn't put you in power. You represent the aristocracy of your society. Apparently, instead of recognizing your connection to fellow citizens, you see yourselves as superior, and therefore unconcerned with the average citizen of your countries. In fact, you rarely see these people in your daily lives. Instead, you spend your days with a small circle of other members of the elite. You belong to the same exclusive clubs, send your children to private schools, circulate in the same vacation spots, and attend the same parties. Your lives are connected and, because you represent the power in your country, your network of friends is able to make rules and laws that protect and ensure the continuance of your positions of status and wealth.

In your pursuit of further wealth, you allow child labor, close your eyes to violations of minimum wage standards, ignore environmental problems caused by companies and often use support from the military to stamp out worker protests and organizing. Rather than showing compassion for people in your own countries, you idolize the West and the lifestyle it offers. In pursuit of this lifestyle you "sell off" the people and cultures. Yes, multinational companies hire the elites, but the blood and blame of being the middleman is directly on your hands. You are the subcontractors who actually take charge of running these inhumane factories. You are the people who turn your eyes away from the suffering. The profit you make from these actions does not even stay in your own countries. Instead you take the money you make from this venture and invest it elsewhere.

You may argue that in order for companies to locate in your countries, you must make compromises on wages, working conditions and environmental laws. You may argue that these types of industry will lead to "development." What you are really doing is selling the environment, the cultures, and the people for your own benefit.

Defense Strategies:

How does your country benefit from multinational companies choosing to locate here?

If it weren't for these companies and the jobs you help to provide, how would the lower classes of your country survive?

What would happen if you demanded better working conditions for the people of your country?

What has caused you to desire the Western values of profit and accumulation?

Poor Country Workers

You are responsible for the dehumanizing working conditions and the environmental and cultural destruction caused by the growth of the global economy.

You work for a multinational corporation in a poor country. You are on the bottom of this economic pyramid, but your participation is essential. Without workers who are willing to take these jobs, companies would not leave rich countries to relocate in poor countries. You may complain that you are forced into these jobs by the need to survive, but unless you stand up for your rights, how can you expect the situation to change? If you didn't accept low wages and wretched conditions, companies would not be able to exploit you and pollute your country.

Lured by the promise of better lives, you move away from families and communities to take jobs that require long hours in dangerous conditions. The long hours you work lead to less time for your families and communities. Your children, in order to help the family financially, also take jobs at these factories. Rather than enjoying the freedoms of childhood, they are stuck in stifling, cramped areas working 10 to 12 hour workdays. What kind of parent are you to allow your children to work in such poor environments? Isn't there another way for you to survive without asking them to do this? Even with everyone in the family working, however, the wages you all earn are still not enough to maintain an adequate standard of living. You and your family are required to work long hours with little or no extra pay and few breaks. Standard factory conditions include dangerous machinery, inadequate lighting and ventilation, and toxic fumes.

In addition to the impact of these factories on family life, the work that you choose to do contributes to the destruction of your community's environment and culture. You have been pushed off the more fertile land by your country's elite and multinational growers. This move leaves you and your family with little land to use in producing food for your family. Faced with the poor soil and farming conditions, you and other families decided it was not possible to survive in your traditional communities. Despite the fact that your community had close ties, you separated in favor of the economic opportunities in the city. But it didn't offer you all you had heard

it would. Work is difficult. Women and children are the most "sought after" workers because they are more willing to work in poor conditions for less money. The supervising bosses patrol the factories to be sure that everyone is being productive. There is virtually no opportunity to talk with others and if you are suspected of organizing to demand better working conditions, you can expect to be fired, jailed, or even physically attacked. You miss the closeness of your community and you worry that your children will forget their cultural roots. Even though life was never "easy" for you, you used to be able to survive as both a family and a community. Now, you see many things changing — mostly for the worse.

But here's the point that needs to be emphasized: You chose these lives for yourselves. There is no slavery in your country. No one held a gun to your head and said, "Move to the city to work in a factory owned by a multinational corporation." Ultimately, you have to take responsibility for these conditions.

You do not have the financial security, health insurance, or legal options that the middle- and upper-class employers have. But there are things you could do. You could organize and protest. Sure, companies have been known to relocate when workers demand higher wages or better working conditions, but it's always risky to work for change. You could make the effort to educate yourselves and your children. You could draw international attention to your plight in hopes of forming alliances with workers in Western nations and other workers in poor countries. You, however, have chosen to continue to work for a company that exploits its workers and the local environment. And that's why you are on trial here.

Defense Strategies:

How has the ruling elite "sold out" the people of your country?

What motivates multinational corporations to locate in your country?

How can anyone blame you for simply doing what you needed to do to support your family?

How might the conditions of your work improve if U.S. consumers demanded changes from the corporations they support?

U.S. Consumers

You are responsible for the dehumanizing working conditions and the environmental and cultural destruction caused by the growth of the global economy.

You, the buyers of goods and services, are the driving force that keeps multinational corporations in business, and leads to such misery around the world. If it wasn't for *your* demand for goods, there would be no need to supply them.

Just look at your home right now. Your kitchen is full of gadgets and expensive toys — all purchased in the name of "making life easier." Do you really *need* all of those items? Your home is loaded with high-tech goods like stereos, cell phones, TVs, and VCRs — all purchased with little thought of the impact on workers around the world or the environment. Would you feel deprived without them? And check out your closet. It's filled with clothes and accessories — mostly made in Asian countries, by the hands of poor women — all purchased in the name of "looking good." Do you *have* to have a new outfit for every day of the week? Many people in the world live simply. You could too. It's not uncommon for you to spend over $100 dollars on a pair of sneakers. And when you shop for clothes, you check out the brand name — after all, you deserve only the best.

You may not consider yourself "wealthy" compared to the upper class in the United States. True, there is enormous inequality here in the USA. But that doesn't change the fact that you, the average American consumer, spend 20 times more on products than the average person living in South America, Asia, or Africa. Poverty in the United States and poverty in Third World nations are just not the same.

You've heard about global sweatshops. You know that people overseas have it rough — they barely make enough money for their families to survive, they have to work long hours, and the working conditions are often hazardous to their health. But *still* you buy goods from the companies that employ them. It seems that you don't care about the working conditions of these fellow humans — that's their problem. Your greed and desire to keep up with the Joneses make you responsible for the plight of workers around the world.

Additionally, your spending habits are killing our environment. You habitually use materials that can't be recycled, polluting cars, and scarce resources. As 5% of the world's population, U.S. citizens consume almost 40% of the world's resources. At this rate, the earth cannot sustain itself.

Go ahead and blame the corporations, or even the system of profit, if you like. But your dollars are the oil that keeps this hurtful, wasteful economy running.

Defense Strategies:

Where does your "need" for items come from?

What kinds of pressures exist in our consumer society to have the "latest and the best"?

You are so busy trying to make ends meet yourself. How can you be expected to change the entire global economy?

How can it be *your* fault that Third World nations pollute their environment and treat their people poorly?

Aren't you justified in seeking a better life for yourself and your family? Isn't this exactly what everyone in the world is trying to do?

System of Profit

You are responsible for the dehumanizing working conditions and the environmental and cultural destruction caused by the growth of the global economy.

This gets complicated. You are not a person or even a group of people, but a system. We like to blame crimes on people. But in this case, the real criminal is not human. The fact that you are invisible is part of your strength; many people consider you a part of "human nature" and, therefore, unable to change. You force corporations to obey your laws. If corporations don't care more about making a profit than protecting the environment or treating workers and consumers decently, then they go out of business. *You are the rules of the game.*

Participating in this "game" of the profit system also affects people's minds and emotions. You create a feeling that people need to have material wealth in order to be happy. The system of profit has been successful in telling people that money, wealth, and possessions are what make them valuable, a fact that is reinforced by advertising.

The Rules of the Game are simple, but disastrous:

1) Capital must expand; it must make a profit or it "dies." In search of profit, Capital travels the world like a heat-seeking missile, looking for the best situation for itself.

2) The only goal of the system of profit is to make more profit, at whatever cost to the environment and human beings. You — the system — are not concerned with the long-term effects of your actions.

3) To make a profit, Capital must compete with others engaged in this same pursuit.

4) You must get the cooperation of workers and consumers in order to succeed. Without them you cannot survive. The system promises these people that wealth and comfort — rather than human relationships — will make them happy. And besides, so long as the system of profit is the only "game" being played, people have no choice but to play by your rules. To make money and survive, they must serve your system.

5) You have pushed the idea that anyone can share in the benefits of the system of profit, if only they work hard enough. This has been especially powerful in the United States with the idea of the "American Dream." But in practice, this game of profit is controlled by — and mostly benefits — the owners of Capital.

The system of profit pushes people to make decisions based on financial gain rather than what might benefit the community. You rip apart people's communities and ways of life by placing the concern for money above people's right to maintain traditional culture. You may pay money to workers in poor countries (not a livable wage), but at the same time you destroy their society and ways of taking care of each other and their land.

Competition and the quest for riches and financial security lead people to sacrifice other people's welfare for their own immediate gain. It's a lesson that the system of profit teaches so well: Look out for yourself because if you don't, no one else will. This individualism encourages people to purchase products from companies that mistreat workers and the environment. It's an attitude developed by living life in the system of profit.

Some of you may try to blame multinational corporations for the crimes you commit. But they behave the way they do because in order to survive they must obey the laws of the system of profit.

The global system of profit and the impact of multinational companies is far-reaching. How are citizens in poor countries able to make a living when they have been pushed off their land by multinational agribusiness? When consumers demand cheaper products, without raising concerns about the environmental and the human costs of their purchases, how can workers be expected to resist the policies of the companies they work for? Although you are the invisible player in this trial, it is your structure that has created this situation of injustice and inequality in the first place. Therefore, you, the system of profit, must shoulder the blame.

Defense Strategies:

In what ways do the corporations drive the system of profit?

How do consumers help to sustain the system of profit?

What would make poor country ruling elites "sell out" their own people?

If this system is so repressive to workers, why do they agree to participate?

Global Sweatshops

"'A TRADE UNIONIST MUST LEAVE HER FEAR BEHIND'"
Interview with Yesenia Bonilla (p. 142)

Some discussion or writing questions for this reading include:

- Yesenia's mother was told that she was fired from the KIMI factory because she was past the age, 40 or 45, when a woman is considered too old to work in the *maquila*. How would you explain this company policy?
- [As students read, have them mark conditions that need changing.] If you were organizing a union at KIMI, what issues would you propose the union deal with? Make a list, putting the most important first.
- Should Yesenia be hopeful about her future?
- Do you have any advice for Yesenia?
- How could people in the United States help workers like Yesenia?

Imagine and write a dialogue between Yesenia and another worker she's trying to recruit to the union.

Write a dialogue poem between Yesenia and a 16-year-old young woman living in the United States. This could highlight similarities between their lives as well as differences.

"THE STORY OF A *MAQUILADORA* WORKER"
Interview with Omar Gil by David Bacon (p. 146)

Some discussion or writing questions:

- Should Omar Gil be hopeful about his future? Why or why not?
- What similarities and differences do you see in Omar's and Yesenia's (from the previous reading) situations?
- What keeps conditions from changing for the better in the factories where Omar Gil has worked?
- What changes in Omar Gil's work life

might allow him to develop "as a worker" and "as a human being"?

- The companies that Omar and Yesenia worked for tried to stop workers from joining unions. What tactics did they use?
- Draw up a list of demands that you think Omar Gil and other workers might make that, if enacted, would improve conditions at the *maquila* where they work.

"TWO YOUNG WOMEN"
Dialogue poem by Deidre Barry, 11th grade (p. 152)

Deidre Barry's dialogue poem, "Two Young Women," is patterned after the dialogue poem, "Two Women" in *Rethinking Our Classrooms, Volume 1*, pp. 112-113. The dialogue poem is a format that allows students to explore varieties of inequality — how people who are connected to the same events, processes, or products experience those connections very differently. Dialogue poems could be assigned after students watch any of the videos described in the "Global Sweatshop" section of "Videos With a Global Conscience," p. 361, and/or after reading any of the sweatshop (or other) testimonies included in this book, or after completing research on the "journey" of a particular product from the Third World (or domestic sweatshop location) to North America.

Distribute "Two Young Women" to students. Ask for two volunteers, preferably female, to read the poem aloud — one student reading the Nike worker's lines and the other reading the U.S. teenager parts. Ask for students' reactions. You might also read aloud the "Two Women" poem, which is the prompt that generated Deidre Barry's poem; or for younger students, "Honeybees," by Paul Fleischman, in *Rethinking Our Classrooms, Volume 1*, pp. 42-43. Afterward, brainstorm paired writing possibilities with students. Encourage them to be as specific as possible and to use very concrete details in their poems. When they read aloud, be sure that each student enlists a partner to read with him or her. The paired voices make the reading much more powerful.

"NIKE'S CODE OF CONDUCT"
Critical reading activity (p. 153)

Corporations' pledges to respect labor and environmental rights in their operations around the world offer students an excellent opportunity to hone their critical reading skills. Distribute Nike's Code of Conduct to students. Explain that the code is what Nike has promised to require its suppliers to abide by. Remind students that Nike owns no factories itself. Draw students' attention to the "Critical Reading Questions" box on the page. Encourage them to work in pairs or in small groups. They should carefully read the Code of Conduct and respond to the questions. If students did the Transnational Capital Auction (p. 108), or have watched videos on sweatshop conditions in Third World countries, or have read worker testimonies, ask them to keep these in mind as they think about the promises made in Nike's code.

Afterward, discuss these as a class. It's likely that your students will notice a lot of limitations about the code. There is not a single mention of political rights. Nike, of course, would point out that the laws of a country are beyond its control. However, Nike chooses to find contractors located in countries that often suppress workers' rights to organize unions and to speak out for social change. Its plants are in China, for example, but not France or Italy, where workers have long trade union traditions. The code uses the word "applicable" three times and "local" four times — the significance, of course, is that Nike promises to abide by a country's environmental or labor laws, but agrees to be bound by no international standards, except with regard to forced labor, worker ages, and vapor concentrations. The local minimum wage may or may not be a living wage. Local environmental regulations may be vague or even nonexistent. What is legal is often not just.

It's important that students recognize the Grand Canyon-sized loopholes in Nike's Code of Conduct, and those of other transnationals. But at the same time it's important that students appreciate some of the progress that has been made as a result of activism — much of it by students. When we first began teaching about these issues several years ago, Nike had nothing in its code that mentioned abiding by OSHA standards, and Phil Knight even tells Michael Moore

in his film *The Big One* that he's unconcerned that 14-year-old children work in his Indonesian factories. Nike executives didn't suddenly wake up one day and decide to improve conditions. Organizing did that.

"MADE IN THE USA"
Article by Helen Zia (p. 164)

Discuss or ask students to write about:
- What conditions do Bibi and Kailung face that are unfair, oppressive, or dangerous and should be changed?
- What could workers like Bibi and Kailung do to change these conditions?
- Are there lessons from the resistance of other sweatshop workers around the world that might be helpful to Bibi and Kailung?
- Why do they put up with their working and living conditions?
- In the final section of the article, the author, Helen Zia, mentions a number of strategies to change sweatshop conditions in the United States. Which of these do you think would be most effective?
- Why do sweatshop conditions persist in the United States?
- At the close of the article, one anti-sweatshop organizer, Young Shin, says that U.S. consumers have enormous power to change working conditions. Who has more power to change conditions, workers or consumers? What kind of leverage does each group have?

"T-SHIRTS FOR JUSTICE"
Article by Arlen Benjamin-Gomez (p. 170)

Accompany this reading by watching the video *Sweating for a T-Shirt*, which recounts Benjamin-Gomez's trip to Honduras with her mother, long-time social justice activist Medea Benjamin. In the article, Benjamin-Gomez writes that "we have no idea where the clothes we buy in our campus stores are coming from." In the video, she conducts interviews with students on campus to see if they know where their own clothes come from, and if they know anything about the conditions under which they were produced. Students can brainstorm similar questions to ask in interviews of their peers. They might construct other questions to ask of the principal, vice-principal, or student store clerk about purchasing decisions for sweatshirts, T-shirts, baseball hats, and the like. They could videotape or audiotape the interviews and bring them back to class to show and discuss. Ask: What patterns do we notice about people's knowledge and attitudes about where their clothes come from?

USING CARTOONS AND QUOTATIONS AS TRIGGERS
(See pages, 127, 138, 144, 157, 164, 168)

Reproduce the cartoons and quotations in this book to use with students. Reproducing cartoons, quotations, and photos on overheads for large visual displays is particularly effective. Such displays, or "triggers," are useful in helping students to have disciplined conversations, in which they listen and then focus their remarks. Triggers are useful for full-classroom or small-group discussions.

The acronym SHOWED, first used by Nina Wallerstein and Edward Bernstein in a 1988 article about health education and Paulo Freire, is a useful way to help students systematically respond to such a trigger:

S: what do you See?
H: what's Happening to your feelings?
O: relate it to your Own lives.
W: Why do we face these problems?
E
D: what can we Do about it?

This format can help to direct students away from spontaneous conversation and toward a progression that moves from personal reactions to social analysis to consideration of action. It can also be used with articles and other parts of this book.

Make a poster of the SHOWED acronym and keep it up in class.

Use the triggers as examples to have students create their own editorial cartoons drawing attention to sweatshops or other global justice issues.

CHAPTER FIVE

Kids for Sale:
Child Labor in the Global Economy

God to Hungry Child

BY LANGSTON HUGHES

Hungry child,

I didn't make this world for you.

You didn't buy any stock in my railroad.

You didn't invest in my corporation.

Where are your shares in Standard Oil?

I made the world for the rich

And the will-be-rich

And the have-always-been-rich.

Not for you.

Hungry child.

From The Collected Poems of Langston Hughes, *edited by Arnold Rampersad, New York: Vintage Classics, 1994; p. 48. The poem was originally published in 1925.*

Page 189 image: Children carry lime to a kiln in Dronachellan, Andra Pradesh, India. Photo by Heldur Netocny.

Children protesting child labor march through the streets of Brasilia, Brazil in 1997.

Associated Press/Eraldo Peres

INTRODUCTION

Kids for Sale:
Child Labor in the Global Economy

We've seen articles and curricula that lament the horrific conditions for child laborers throughout the world, but express little sympathy for the adult workers who toil in similarly ill-paid and dangerous circumstances. And yet as selections in this chapter and the previous chapter show, children's work and life conditions can't be separated from those of the adults around them. Children are drawn into exploitative work when adult caregivers don't have sufficient means to provide for their children. Thus, ending "child labor" requires an end to poorly paid adult labor, and the deeper economic forces that produce it. "Only a total destruction of the monstrous economic system that dominates the earth today will help us put an end to child labor and starvation," insists the Indian newsletter, *Vigil*, quoted in Beatrice Newbery's article "Rethinking Child Labor."

Newbery also urges us to consider whether all child labor is bad, and whether Western-style childhood and schooling are appropriate in all cultural contexts. She asks if our blanket demand that child labor be stopped could itself be a manifestation of colonial privilege and arrogance.

And yet few doubt that there is something peculiarly — and obviously — evil about appropriating someone's childhood for private profit. Even as we guard against applying Western cultural norms to the issue of "child labor," we can engage students in considering whether there are universal principles of human conduct that we can apply to this issue.

Although we intentionally preceded this chapter with a broader examination of global sweatshops, it may be that *child* labor is what pricks our students' consciences most acutely. Because of this, especially for younger students, you may want to enter issues of globalization by looking first at the lives of children.

Here as elsewhere in the book, there are abundant opportunities to highlight efforts to oppose the exploitation of children. No historical or contemporary data exist to support today's oft-repeated claim that "development" itself will end child labor. Certainly, to the extent that child labor has been greatly reduced in the United States, it is organized opposition, not market forces, that produced change. The famous photos of Lewis Hine, some of which we include here, are products of struggle against child exploitation, not of mere journalistic curiosity.

We hope that material in the chapter fosters empathy and activism. ■

— *The editors*

David L. Parker

Young sex workers in Bangkok, Thailand.

Everywhere on Earth

BY EDUARDO GALEANO

Everywhere on earth, these kids, the children of people who work hard or who have neither work nor home, must from an early age spend their waking hours at whatever bread-winning activity they can find, breaking their backs in return for food and little else. Once they can walk, they learn the rewards of behaving themselves — boys and girls who are free labor in workshops, stores, and makeshift bars, or cheap labor in export industries, stitching sports clothes for multinational corporations. They are manual labor on farms and in cities or domestic labor at home, serving whoever gives the orders. They are little slaves in the family economy or in the informal sector of the global economy, where they occupy the lowest rung of the world labor market:

- In the garbage dumps of Mexico City, Manila, or Lagos they hunt glass, cans, and paper and fight the vultures for scraps.
- In the Java Sea they dive for pearls.
- They hunt diamonds in the mines of Congo.
- They work as moles in the mine shafts of Peru, where their size makes them indispensable, and when their lungs give out they end up in unmarked graves.
- In Colombia and Tanzania they harvest coffee and get poisoned by pesticides.
- In Guatemala they harvest cotton and get poisoned by pesticides.
- In Honduras they harvest bananas and get poisoned by pesticides.
- They collect sap from rubber trees in Malaysia, working days that last from dark to dark.

A construction worker in Kathmandu, Nepal (left), and a tire recycling plant worker in Bogota, Colombia.

David L. Parer

Joe Fish

- They work the railroads in Burma.
- In India they melt in glass ovens in the north and brick ovens in the south.
- In Bangladesh they work at over 300 occupations, earning salaries that range from nothing to nearly nothing for each endless day.
- They ride in camel races for Arab sheiks and round up sheep and cattle on the ranches of the Rio de la Plata.
- They serve the master's table in Port-au-Prince, Colombo, Jakarta, or Recife in return for the right to eat whatever falls from it.
- They sell fruit in the markets of Bogotá and gum on the buses of São Paulo.
- They wash windshields on corners in Lima, Quito, or San Salvador.

- They shine shoes on the streets of Caracas or Guanajuato.
- They stitch clothes in Thailand and soccer shoes in Vietnam.
- They stitch soccer balls in Pakistan and baseballs in Honduras and Haiti.
- To pay their parents' debts they pick tea or tobacco on the plantations of Sri Lanka and harvest jasmine in Egypt for French perfume.
- Rented out by their parents in Iran, Nepal, and India they weave rugs from before dawn until past midnight, and when someone tries to rescue them they ask, "Are you my new master?"
- Sold by their parents for $100 in Sudan, they are put to work in the sex trade or at any other labor.

Reprinted from Upside Down: A Primer for the Looking-Glass World, *New York, Metropolitan Books, 2000.*

A street performer juggles for spare change in Mexico City, Mexico.

David L. Parker

Rethinking Child Labor

BY BEATRICE NEWBERY

Fifteen-year-old Khalid Hussein is one of hundreds of children in his Pakistani village who stitch footballs for a living for a Western corporation. Nobody should have to be in Khalid's position. And, as we all know by now, child labor is A Bad Thing. In order to help Khalid and his kind, it must be stopped. Now. This has been the message coming from Western campaigners for years. The Ethical Trading Initiative speaks for the vast majority of aid agencies and Western NGOs (nongovernmental organizations) in its base code, which begins with the announcement that "Child Labor Shall Not be Used." The International Labor Organization, meanwhile, aims to "work towards the progressive elimination of child labor by strengthening national capacities to address child labor, and by creating a worldwide movement to combat it." Good news for children everywhere, then.

The trouble is that Khalid doesn't agree.

SAVING THE CHILDREN?

Confusingly, the United Kingdom's Save The Children Fund (SCF) has taken up Khalid's case. Take a look at their website (www.one world.org/scf) and you'll find Khalid's story. "I stitch one football [soccer ball] per day after school.... Most of the people in my village stitch footballs. If there was a ban on child labor, most of the people in my village would go hungry."

SCF has decided that the issue of child labor is more complex than it first seems. Prompted by campaigns against child labor that backfired badly, they went back to the drawing board. They remembered when in 1994 the United States threatened to boycott garments made by children in Bangladeshi factories. Scared of losing business, the factories fired nearly 50,000 Bangladeshi children, mainly girls. Most ended up breaking bricks for a living, or turned to begging, even prostitution. Rachel Marcus, research and policy adviser at SCF, says "those who initiated the boycott believed they were combating an abuse of human rights. In Bangladesh it was seen as a case of Westerners selectively applying universal principles to a situation they did not understand."

THE REAL EXPLOITATION

One might reasonably ask what an organization called "Save The Children" is doing apparently supporting the rights of multinational corporations to exploit the children of the poor rather than pay adult workers decent wages to do a decent job. But it is not alone in its rethink of what "child labor" is. For in the Third World, attitudes on this subject are often very different — and Westerners parachuting in with their distinctly Euro-American views of the role of children in society are often seen to be doing more harm than good.

Take these words from an editorial published in *Vigil*, the newsletter of a grassroots Indian NGO:

> No parent will willingly let their children toil for a pittance if they had the means to give them a good life. [But] how many campaigners stop to ask who deprived these parents of their means of livelihood and thus forced them to make their children toil?... Only a total destruction of the monstrous economic system that dominates the earth today will help us put an end to child labor and starvation. This is what all well-wishers and friends of children in India and the world should strive for.

In other words, the type of child labor exploited by multinationals is merely a symptom of an unjust economic system that continues to exploit the poor. Banning that form of child labor will not tackle the root causes that brought it about in the first place — and it might even make the poor poorer. This is a message that many NGOs, who fail to look at the economic big picture, do not want to hear.

WHAT IS CHILD LABOR?

The issue of child labor goes much deeper than the high-profile exploitation of the young in the sweatshops of multinationals. In fact, a closer look at available statistics shows that just 5% of all the world's child workers are involved in the production of internationally traded goods, such as the footballs and athletic shoes that have caused such a furor in recent years. Many of the

A candy hawker on the streets of Baghdad, Iraq.

Associated Press/Peter DeJong

rest are working for their families, on the land, in small artisan shops, or as apprentices in trades that their families have carried out for generations. And some people now argue that attempting to ban such work is not only a supreme example of Western cultural arrogance, but will also facilitate the destruction of small and local economies and aid the march of the global market.

In Ladakh, a small Buddhist kingdom in the Indian Himalayas [see article, p. 308], one mother, or "AmaLe," voices the concerns of many of the local people:

> Education is important, but we should not lose our agricultural way of life which has been practiced for centuries. It is also an education to have knowl-

Children are often among the workers at this emerald mine in Muzo, Colombia.

edge about farming, cooking, and gardening. Here, for instance, a man has to know a lot to run a home and farm, and women also have a lot of skills like spinning, weaving, cooking, and maintaining relationships with the community.

What, in other words, is "labor" and what is "education"? What is the proper role of a child in a community? What is educational and what is damaging? Who decides? These complex questions go to the heart of the child labor debate.

Helena Norberg-Hodge, director of the International Society for Ecology and Culture (ISEC), which has studied the subject of children and work in Ladakh for many years, says the issue cannot be simply defined. "There is a blanket assumption that wherever children work, it is an abuse," she says. "But working with the family and community helps to shape their iden-

tity, gives them a vital role in life and a feeling of responsibility and belonging."

LEARNING BY EXAMPLE

She is backed up by what has happened to Ladakh since its children were taken from the fields and lined up on school benches in the name of progress. High attendance at school and a low incidence of traditional children's work has had ruinous effects on both children and the community at large.

In Ladakhi culture, children used to play a valuable part working in the fields, and grew up learning skills such as threshing, planting, and storing crops. They could milk and herd the dzo, the cross between a yak and a cow that meets most of Ladakh's dairy needs. Today, few children can boast of any agricultural knowledge. Their time is spent learning geography, math, Urdu, and English instead. As Becky

Tarbotton, also from ISEC, explains: "Children go to school in summer and miss out on the harvest. They are losing touch with their roots, the skills of farming and looking after the land."

Meanwhile, the "education" is doing its pupils few favors. "It is Victorian," says Norberg-Hodge. "Children are beaten into learning by rote. It is very crude." The failure rate is 95%. Even pupils who leave school with qualifications have no use for their knowledge at home. A few run businesses or become tour guides in the capital, Leh, but most are unemployed. "School gives them the skills to go to Delhi and be unemployed," says Norberg-Hodge. "It is not giving them the skills to live in their locality, and live healthy, fulfilled lives."

The results are twofold. The impact on the community is vast — there is nobody left to look after agriculture in Ladakh, which until recently was a self-reliant agricultural economy. The removal of young people from the fields is shaking Ladakhi culture and sense of identity. But the impact on the personal development of children is also significant. What they learn in school only serves to make them dissatisfied with the lives of their parents, and the traditional Ladakhi lifestyle. Tarbotton says: "Their textbooks say that roads and dams are progress, so the children go home and think they live in complete squalor. Education has created a generation of young people who are dissatisfied with what they have but can't become stockbrokers in New York either."

EDUCATION FOR POVERTY

While Ladakh serves to illustrate the point, rural communities all over the "developing" world are undergoing these changes. Poor schooling is ruining the lifestyles of small-scale fishermen and farmers in China, Africa, and Mongolia as children "unlearn" traditional trades and join the rest of the class on the road to Western-style unemployment.

It's hardly surprising that many parents fail to see the purpose of such a schooling. "Why should kids read Neruda or go to the theatre if they're just going to end up picking oranges?" asks one exhausted Chilean mother. In the words of Mohamed Idris, coordinator of the Third World Network, a Malaysia-based non-

> **What is the proper role of a child in a community? What is educational and what is damaging?**

profit network of organizations working on development issues: "The school education system as practiced in most countries today is totally devoid of relevance to day-to-day life in rural areas, de-skills children and interferes with the agricultural system that is vital in rural communities."

ASK THE CHILDREN

Duncan Green is author of *Hidden Lives*, a book that gives a voice to the children of Latin America and the Caribbean. In his research, he found that child workers are often enthused about their jobs. Thirteen-year old Marina, from Honduras, for example, makes dough in a tortilla market stall where her father is a porter. "I like working," she says. "We were always bored at home. Here in the market, I see a lot of people, not just my mother and brothers. At home there was nothing much to eat — here I eat all the time!"

This is a million miles away from working long hours in sweatshop conditions for the benefit of a foreign corporation. The blanket Western horror of "child labor," in Green's view, is Eurocentrism. In the West, we believe in happy, carefree young years, where children are left the space to play and learn, without work. But the vast majority of Third World child workers are involved in the "informal sector," a catch-all category that includes those working on their own, rather than for a wage. Much of this is family work, on small-scale farms, or in the urban informal sector like Marina. Green says that this can — under the right circumstances — be a good thing. "The hours are flexible and can be fitted around school or other commitments," he explains, "and often it can take place under the supervision of a parent, relative, or friend, which in Latin America's perilous streets is a reassurance to both family and the child." He quotes a woman living in Lima, Peru who announced: "I don't want my daughter to go out to work. The temptation of the devil is on all sides. I prefer her to sell potatoes here where I can keep an eye on her."

CHILDHOOD ECONOMICS

Just as the informal sector contains positive examples of working children like Marina, it also contains horror stories. But, though multi-

A garbage picker on the streets of Bombay, India.

country had been flooded with nearly $5 billion — but it came with strings attached, and the government was forced to sign a series of agreements with the IMF, World Bank, and others, promising to implement painful structural adjustment "reforms" in exchange for aid.

The main aims of the reforms were to end hyperinflation and to turn Nicaragua from a state-led economy, dominated by government owned farms, state regulation, and nationalized industries, into a system where "market forces" decide the fate of the country. Under pressure, the government raised interest rates and cut public spending to the bone, duly reducing inflation from 13,000% to just 19% by 1993. It privatized companies, removed trade and banking regulations, and pushed up interest rates to squeeze inflation out of the system.

The result was disastrous for Nicaragua. Interest rates rocketed. Layoffs among thousands of state employees pushed unemployment up to 52%. By 1994, three out of four Nicaraguans were living below the poverty line. The state, on the orders of the cash providers, ended all food subsidies and cut most school feeding programs, so children ate less. Green says the results today are clearly visible. "The social impact of such measures is felt throughout the country, not least in shanty towns like Acagualinca, next to the main garbage dump in the capital, Managua. Here, most breadwinners have lost their jobs in recent years, turning whole families into rubbish-pickers, scavenging the dump for recyclable materials." That, unfortunately, includes children.

HYPOCRISY

Across the region, and indeed in the poor countries throughout the world, governments have followed Nicaragua's example, enlisting aid by embracing the global market, to the delight of Western corporations and their governments. "Growing poverty and inequality, combined with the rising cost of schooling as governments cut back on education spending and introduce user fees to parents, have driven families to pull their children out of school and put them to work," says Green. This, then, is the face of genuinely exploitative child labor. And it is the result not of "backward" lifestyles or a lack of "good" (i.e., Western-modeled) education, but of exploitative global economics.

nationals may employ only a small proportion of all the world's "working" children, the global economy, skewed as it is in favor of big business, is still the main reason for genuine child exploitation. Every day, globalization swells the ranks of exploited child workers. The International Labor Organization's Child Labor Programme admits that "specific evaluations of the precise impact of globalization on child labor have yet to be made." However, as Green explains: "Most observers agree that the number of child workers is increasing and the reasons for the increase are not hard to find."

Green takes Nicaragua as an extreme but illustrative example. After the election of the anti-Sandinista candidate, Violeta Chamorro, to the presidency in 1990, the country was rewarded with a rush of U.S. and other aid. By 1997, the

A boy carries a basket of coal for a kiln at Dronachellan, Andra Pradesh, India.

Some see a clear element of hypocrisy when Western governments, even aid agencies and NGOs, offer solutions to the problem of child labor that ignore its economic root causes. As Jeremy Seabrook, an author and journalist specializing in development issues, puts it: "No one —not UNICEF, not the ILO, not national governments, not NGOs — offers any alternative to these structures of injustice, other than platitudes about education and humanitarian pieties." He adds that the rich world is doubly hypocritical in offering solutions based on our own past, while forgetting the distinct advantages that we had when child labor was abolished in the United Kingdom in the nineteenth century. "We put our own child chimney sweeps in school by growing wealthy. And we grew wealthy in part from colonial extraction. That dishonesty lies behind all our recommendations and concerns on the issue of child labor."

MAKING A START

For all the theories, the arguments and the complexities, there are at least some temporary solutions making a difference to children's lives. In Ferozabad, India, CREATE, a Save The Children Fund partner, is helping glass-bangle producers to form co-operatives and deal directly with company owners, rather than middle-men. Through a combination of measures including skills-training for older children and schooling for younger children, CREATE aims to end child labor in harmful operations such as welding, and is working with company owners to reduce the health hazards suffered by children working in the industry.

But ultimately, the issue of child labor cannot be addressed without fundamentally re-examining the deeper currents and problems that contribute to its existence.

This means not only addressing the increasingly obvious inequalities of the global economy, but also questioning Western assumptions about the value systems and lifestyles of other societies, along with the homogenous view of "education" which increasingly dominates around the world.

The real tragedy for the world's child workers is that, until such undercurrents are seriously addressed, positive steps to alleviate the misery of genuinely exploitative child labor — as opposed to valued and valuable child work — are likely to be drops in a bigger, darker and ever-expanding ocean. ■

Beatrice Newbery is a freelance journalist specializing in development and gender issues. A version of this article originally appeared in The Ecologist *magazine, July/August 2000.*

A young carpet weaver in Karachi, Pakistan.

Associated Press/B.K. Bangash

Child Labor: Pain and Resistance

BY BOB PETERSON

When Nirmala was eight her father took her to work as a weaver in a carpet factory near Kathmandu, the capital of Nepal. The family needed money, she said.

Nepali children like Nirmala start work at 6:00 in the morning and work late into the night, sometimes 16 hours a day. They work in "factories" the size of a classroom: A typical factory holds 18 huge weaving looms. Five children work at each loom, tying knots in carpets. The lighting is poor and with no windows, ventilation is bad. There are no bathrooms. Most of the children eat only twice a day and are almost always hungry. Many of them sleep in the factory, crowded into small rooms. This "room and board" is all the "payment" many of the child workers get.

The work is painful: The children's hands often get numb after hours of moving their fingers between the stiff threads. The cramped spaces, long hours, poor nutrition, lack of air, and wool dust cause sore backs and illness. Under these conditions, diseases like tuberculosis can spread quickly from worker to worker.

Carpets are key to Nepal's economy. In 1993 carpets made up more than half — 60% — of all the money the country made through trading products with other countries.

A year later, however, things changed. Some Europeans organizing against child labor convinced a German TV program to do an exposé on the bad conditions of Nepal's child weavers. Many people in Europe were shocked at what they saw, and stopped buying Nepali carpets.

In response to the drop in carpet sales, the Nepali government and carpet factory owners kicked many of the child workers out of the factories. Some children were able to attend special schools set up for former child workers. Nirmala was one of these lucky ones: She delighted in the chance to spend her days learning, playing soccer, and eating nutritious meals instead of working hard at a loom in the semi-darkness.

But other children were much less fortunate. Their families still needed money to survive. Many continued sneaking into their old factories at night, or found other jobs making bricks or serving food.

According to the International Labor Organization (ILO), throughout the world 120 million children between the ages of five and fourteen work full-time. If children who work part-time are included, the number more than doubles to 250 million. This does not include children working as servants in people's homes. Getting exact figures is difficult in some countries. Some people say that the ILO estimate is too high because it includes some children who voluntarily work on their parents' farms or at home. But regardless of the exact number, it is clear that tens of millions of children often work 12 hours a day without a break, sometimes even longer.

DEFINING CHILD LABOR

People who work with the United Nations and the ILO call it "child labor" when one of three things happens:

- Work is done full-time by children under the age of fifteen.
- Work prevents children from attending school.
- Children work at jobs that are dangerous or hazardous to their physical, mental, or emotional health.

This means that if a child does light work or chores after school, it's not child labor. Likewise, helping out with the family farm or business isn't really child labor either, unless it means the child does not get the chance to have a formal education.

Child laborers stitch soccer balls in Pakistan,

Children laid off from factories study in a school in Dhaka, Bangladesh.

Associated Press/Pavel Rahman

sew shirts in Guatemala, pick flowers in Colombia, make carpets in Nepal, polish gem stones in Thailand, assemble toys in China, and sew shoes in Indonesia. Often these children work for pennies a day. Large numbers of them never learn to read and write. Many are often exposed to dangers such as harsh temperatures, sharp tools, heavy loads, and poisonous chemicals. Many child workers are robbed of any real chance to play, have fun, and just be around other family members.

One of the main reasons child labor exists is poverty. Many families are so poor that they must have their children work so that the family does not starve. (Child labor actually causes more poverty: When a child gets a job, it takes that same job away from an adult. Any adults who still want to do that work will have to compete with children, who work for much less money.)

But poor families are not to blame for child labor, any more than they are to blame for poverty. For example, if there are not jobs that pay enough money to support a family, it's not the fault of poor people who do not have jobs. The way the world of business is set up pushes companies to be almost only concerned with making money, increasing their "profits." These companies want to pay workers as little as possible. And of all workers, children are often the very cheapest, the easiest to scare, and the least likely to organize or fight back. In many nations, laws against child labor are often ignored, or simply do not exist. Many nations try to get businesses to move to their country by bragging about how low wages are.

CHILD LABOR
IN THE UNITED STATES

Some people think that child labor is a problem only in the countries of Asia, Africa, and Latin America — and that in the United States it only happened long ago. It's true that in the 1800s and early 1900s, millions of U.S. children worked in mines, textile mills, and other factories, and in homes making things to sell. These children often suffered from accidents and diseases and were not able to go to school.

Many people worked to end child labor in the United States. For example, Lewis Hine took photographs of children working. His photos gave many people their first look at child work-

Former child laborers take part in a protest against child labor in New Delhi, India in 1996.

ers' (see p. 212.) Also labor organizer Mother Jones, and social activist Helen Keller, protested against child labor. Demonstrations against child labor often drew thousands of protesters. By 1914, almost every state had a law saying that no child under 12 could go to work.

In 1916, Congress finally passed a law saying that no product made by children under 14 in factories or under 16 in mines could travel from one state to another. But owners complained, and the U.S. Supreme Court threw out the law. It wasn't until 1938 that Congress passed the Fair Labor Standards Act. One thing this law did was allow children of 14 or 15 to work only outside of school hours, and only in certain jobs. But this law didn't apply to children doing farm work.

Decades later there is still child labor in the United States. In 1988, researchers at one university found that more than 290,000 children were working in the United States — many illegally. Most of them worked in clothing factories or picking fruits and vegetables in farm fields. People continue to organize more protests to get new laws passed and to make sure that existing laws are enforced. Many people want changes so that children are not mistreated in fields, factories, or fast food restaurants. Organizers also work to form unions and to demand rights and better pay for adult workers, so parents don't need to send their children to work.

MOVEMENTS TO
END CHILD LABOR

People are organizing to abolish child labor around the world, too. Some child workers themselves are organizing to get out of slave-like conditions. Perhaps the most famous was Iqbal Masih, the Pakistani child who escaped from where he was forced to work and became an organizer and speaker against child labor. Tragically, he was murdered (see p. 206).

In Brazil some of the 9 million street children have organized the "National Movement of Street Children" and have demanded an end to sexual abuse, police brutality, and economic exploitation. In one of their newsletters they asked, "Who stole my right to live a child's life?"

In India, a group started the RUG-

MARK campaign to ensure that carpets and rugs from South Asia are made without child labor. (See Resources, p. 387, for more information.) RUGMARK representatives check carpet manufacturers to make sure they are not using child labor. If they aren't, then the RUGMARK people put a special RUGMARK label on the carpets, letting buyers know.

In Canada a middle school student, Craig Kielburger, became angry at how children were forced to work in Pakistan and started the "Free The Children" organization to help organize children to demand an end to child labor. Children around the world have set up Free The Children chapters (see p. 325 for more information).

In the United States, a number of organizations — including the National Labor Committee, Campaign for Labor Rights, Sweatshop Watch, and Global Exchange — have demanded an end to sweatshops and to the exploitation of children. In Los Angeles, high school students organized against child-made soccer balls and lobbied the school board to adopt a policy against buying them. At universities across the country, students have demanded that their schools sign agreements that would stop the buying of products made by child labor or by adults who work in sweatshops.

South African Children's Rights Organization

PROBLEMS TO THINK ABOUT

Sometimes when people try to make things better, they actually make them worse. One concern is that, as in Nepal, stopping child labor in one industry can mean that some families will become even poorer. For families barely surviving even with their children working, this could be a disaster. Children might keep working in secret or find other types of jobs even more dangerous than factory or farm work, like prostitution.

The problem of child labor will not end completely through consumer boycotts or passing laws. Those are important steps, but ultimately child labor will end only when world poverty ends. The main reason children work is that their families are in desperate need of money, just to survive. Unless and until adults earn enough money at their jobs (and even have jobs!) to support an entire family, families will be pressured

to send their children off to work.

It's for that reason people opposed to child labor need to learn about the roots of world poverty and inequality and help work to end those problems as well. ∎

Bob Peterson (repmilw@aol.com) teaches fifth grade at La Escuela Fratney in Milwaukee, Wisconsin and is a Rethinking Schools editor.

The above example of Nirmala was excerpted from the excellent book Listen to Us: The World's Working Children *by Jane Springer (Toronto: Groundwood, 1997.) Other information is taken from* Child Labor in the Global Economy, *published by Australian People for Health, Education and Development Abroad, Inc. (APHEDA) of Australia.*
For more information on child labor see the Resource listings, p. 351.

An 11-year-old boy carries empty chile pepper bags across a field in Plainview, Texas.

Child Labor Is Cheap — and Deadly

THE TESTIMONY OF AUGUSTINO NIEVES

Child labor does not happen only in the Third World. It also happens in the United States. The following is recorded in Milton Meltzer's book, Cheap Raw Material. *It's the story of Augustino Nieves, a 14-year-old boy born in Mexico. When Augustino was 13, he began working with his parents as a farm worker. He testified in 1990 before the Employment and Housing Subcommittee of Congress, chaired by Rep. Tom Lantos of California. Through a translator, he told the Lantos Subcommittee about his life as a migrant farm worker:*

I have been working in the fields of California for the past two years. We began by picking grapes in Madera and then moved to Orland where we pick olives. I was unable to begin school in September 1989 because we were still working in the fields. I was not able to enroll in school until January 1990. I missed three months of school.

Augustino wanted to work in the same crew with his father, but the company didn't want to hire him. They said he needed a permit to work. So he went to the company where his uncle worked and they hired him. They knew he did not have an official permit or even a Social Security card, but they hired him.

My job consists of moving up and down long rows of strawberry plants, bent over looking for strawberries. I pick only the good strawberries and place them in a packing box. I move my push cart up and down the field. I may spend the whole day working in a stooped position.

When there are a lot of ripe strawberries in the field our crew begins working at 6:30 a.m. and continues working till 8 p.m. We work 6 days a week. The boss does not pay us by the hour.

On a good day, I can pick about 30 boxes of strawberries. If the strawberries are for the market, they pay us $1.25 a box. If I work really hard, I can make about $36.50 for a 13-hour day. That comes out to about $2.80 an hour.

The conditions in the field are oftentimes very difficult. Since we are working on a piece-rate basis, the boss does not allow us to take 15-minute breaks in the morning or afternoon. We have to work through our breaks. We take only 20 minutes for lunch. By the end of the day, our backs hurt and we are very tired.

The boss is supposed to have clean bathrooms and water for us out in the field. However, there are many days when there are no bathrooms in the field. When there are bathrooms, they are usually several hundred meters away from us, and oftentimes they are very dirty. The boss puts the bathrooms so far away because he wants to discourage us from taking breaks.

The boss often didn't provide them with drinking water. When they were lucky enough to have water, instead of having disposable drinking cups, they all used the same cup.

One of the worst things about working in the strawberry fields is that every eight days, the ranchers apply sulfur to the fields as a pesticide. When we bend over to pick the strawberries, the sulfur gets into our eyes. The sulfur stings our eyes and burns our throats. We have been working — we have to keep working even though we are in great pain.

The foreman always puts great pressure on us to work as fast as we can. The foreman comes up behind us and yells at us to work faster and faster. Oftentimes, he insults me because I am a Mixtec Indian. They scream, "Hurry up, work faster, you *pinche Oaxaqueño*." The foreman especially puts a lot of pressure on me because I still cannot work as fast as an adult man.

We face many indignities in the field. We know that the boss exploits us. However, we cannot complain or the foreman will fire us. There are plenty of people who want our jobs, and we have to put up with these abuses or we will not be able to work.

I wish I did not have to work in the fields but my family needs all the money that I can earn. When my whole family is working in the fields, we can eat meat and drink sodas. When there is no work, we only eat tortillas and beans.

My father has many responsibilities. I have three younger siblings who are still in Mexico, and we need to send them money so they can eat and go to school. My father also has to pay a lot of money for rent. The rent of our apartment is $750 a month. About 25 people live in our three-bedroom apartment.

Associated Press/Amy Sancetta

A 6-year old girl picking cucumbers in Helena, Ohio.

My parents, my sister and myself all sleep on the floor in one of the bedrooms. Next fall, I will begin my first year of high school. Hopefully, my family will be able to stay in Santa Maria for the whole school year.

My dream is to graduate from high school. However, if my family ever needs me to go out to work in the fields, that is where I will be. ■

Milton Meltzer is the author of dozens of books, including Bread and Roses, *a history of the U.S. labor movement and* Bound for the Rio Grande, *about the U.S. war with Mexico. This testimony is found in* Cheap Raw Material: How Our Youngest Workers are Exploited and Abused, *New York: Viking, 1994, pp. 101-104.*

Iqbal Masih, a former child laborer who became a celebrated activist, gives a double thumbs-up salute to the crowd at an awards ceremony in December 1994. At right is actor Blair Underwood.

Fight for Child Workers!
The Story of Iqbal Masih

BY PEADAR CREMIN

Iqbal Masih lived in the village of Muridke in Pakistan. His family was extremely poor and lived in a two-roomed house. When Iqbal was four years old, his family was given a loan of 800 rupees (about $25) in return for putting Iqbal to work in the village carpet factory. About 500,000 children aged between 4 and 14 work in carpet factories in Pakistan. They are considered good workers. Many work for 14 hours a day.

These child workers receive no formal education. They are not allowed to speak during working time, in case they make mistakes in the patterns. They have one 30-minute lunch break per day and often are forced to work overtime without extra pay. Complaints result in beatings, having their fingers plunged into boiling water, or other punishments.

Iqbal was extremely unhappy at the carpet factory but his parents could not afford to have him set free. One day, in 1992, Iqbal heard the

founder of the Bonded Labor Liberation Front (BLLF) speak about their work in freeing bonded laborers, and about new laws which forbade child labor. Iqbal asked how he could be set free. He knew that the factory owner claimed that his parents now owed 16,000 rupees. He was afraid that his entire life would be spent repaying the debt. He wanted to have a childhood like other children.

When Iqbal returned to the factory, he told the owner of his rights under the law and stated that he would no longer work as a slave. The carpet-master was furious and punished him severely, but still the child refused to work. Iqbal said, "I am not afraid of the carpet-master. He should be afraid of me." The factory owner demanded his worker or his money. The family could not convince Iqbal to work and so the factory owner threatened them. The family had to flee from their village.

Iqbal was taken by the BLLF to a school they had in Lahore. He was ten years of age and he worked very hard, quickly learning to read and write. He hoped that one day he could become a lawyer helping to free child laborers.

In 1993, when he was eleven, Iqbal began to work with the BLLF. He sneaked into factories to see where the child laborers were kept. He began to make speeches at the factory gates telling the workers of their rights. As a result, 3,000 child laborers broke away from their masters, and thousands of adults began to demand improved working conditions. In 1993 and 1994, people in the West learned about Iqbal's work. They began to ask questions about carpet production in Pakistan.

Carpet exports fell for the first time in three decades. The manufacturers and exporters blamed Iqbal Masih for the problems in their industry. In 1994, Iqbal was given a number of human rights awards and invitations to visit a number of Western countries. Doctors in Sweden found that he was the size of a child half his age. He suffered from tuberculosis and various vascular and pulmonary problems. His spine was curved, his fingers bent by arthritis. Malnutrition and abuse had left him physically maimed.

On his return from his triumphant visit to the West, Iqbal found that the BLLF was in trouble. Threats of violence had been made against the BLLF's workers and teachers. The government was involved in investigating BLLF's staff. The carpet factory owners were planning to challenge the work of the organization.

In April 1995, Iqbal went on a visit to Muridke to see some members of his family. As he traveled with a cousin through fields near the village, a shot rang out and Iqbal Masih fell dead. A poor laborer called Muhammad Ashraf at first confessed to the killing but later withdrew his confession. International pressure has failed to get any satisfactory answer as to why Iqbal Masih, aged 13, died. ∎

Relatives of Iqbal Masih view his body just before his burial on April 17, 1995.

Peadar Cremin is President of Mary Immaculate College in Limerick, Ireland. Excerpted from 75/25: Development in an Increasingly Unequal World by Colm Regan, Development and Education Center, 1996.

Declaration of the Rights of the Child

By the General Assembly of the United Nations as Unanimously Adopted on November 20, 1959

1. All children, without regard to race, color, sex, language, religion, political or other opinion, national or social origin, property, birth or other status, are entitled to the rights set out in this Declaration of the Rights of the Child.

2. The child shall enjoy special protection and be given opportunities and facilities to develop physically, mentally, morally, spiritually, and socially.

3. The child shall be entitled to a name and nationality.

4. The child should have the right to adequate nutrition, housing, recreational, and medical services.

5. The child who is physically, mentally, or socially handicapped shall be given special treatment, education and care.

6. All children need love and understanding. Whenever possible, the child should grow up with his or her parents. Society and public authorities have the duty to extend special care to children without a family and means of support.

7. The child is entitled to free and compulsory education. Education should promote the child's culture, and help the child become a useful member of society. The child shall have the opportunity for play and recreation.

8. The child shall always be among the first to receive protection and relief.

9. The child shall be protected against all forms of neglect, cruelty, and exploitation. Children should not be allowed to work until an appropriate minimum age. In no case, should the employment of children put them in danger, or harm their health or education.

10. The child shall be protected from practices that discriminate against people — especially against people's race or religion. The child shall be brought up in a spirit of understanding, tolerance, friendship among peoples, peace and universal brotherhood.

Adapted from Human Rights for Children: A Curriculum for Teaching Human Rights to Children Ages 3-12, *developed by the Human Rights for Children Committee, Alameda, CA: Hunter House, 1992. A Children's* Chorus *by UNICEF (see Resources, p. 378) is an excellent picture book that describes these principles. For the complete text of the United Nations Declaration of the Rights of the Child and the U.N. Convention on the Rights of the Child, see www.rethinkingschools.org/rg.*

The Rights of the Child: From Declaration to Convention

The Convention on the Rights of the Child provides an example of the evolution of a United Nations Convention. In 1959 a working group drafted the Declaration on the Rights of the Child, which consisted of ten principles setting forth basic rights to which all children should be entitled.

These principles then needed to be codified in a convention. The formal drafting process lasted nine years, during which representatives of governments, intergovernmental agencies, like UNICEF and UNESCO, and non-governmental organizations like Save The Children and the International Red Cross, worked together to create consensus on the language of the convention.

The resulting Convention on the Rights of the Child (Children's Convention) contains over 54 articles that can be divided into three general categories: 1) protection, covering specific issues such as abuse, neglect, and exploitation; 2) provision, addressing a child's particular needs such as education and health care; and 3) partic-ipation, acknowledging a child's growing capacity to make decisions and play a part in society.

The Children's Convention was adopted by the United Nations General Assembly in 1989 and was immediately signed and ratified by more nations in a shorter period of time than any other U.N. convention. As a result the Children's Convention entered into force shortly thereafter, in 1990. Furthermore, the total number of U.N. member states which ratified the Children's Convention has surpassed that of all other conventions. As of early 2002, the governments of only two countries had not ratified it: Somalia and the United States. ■

Adapted from Human Rights Here and Now, *edited by Nancy Flowers, Minneapolis, MN: Human Rights USA Resource Center, 1987.*
For Every Child: The UN Convention on Rights of the Child in Words and Pictures *by Caroline Castle (see resources, p. 378) is an excellent picture book that describes the U.N. Convention on the Rights of the Child.*

Young workers in Mumbai, India

Teit Hornbak

A young boy works a sewing machine in Hong Kong. Child labor is common in garment factories across Asia.

Sawai's Story
A Garment Worker of Thailand

Sawai Langlah, of Srisaket Province in northeast Thailand, had to find work at the age of 13 when her father, a construction worker, suddenly became paralyzed. There was no work locally so she had to leave school and get a job far from home in the capital, Bangkok, through a cousin who was already working in a small garment factory.

We think my father's paralysis was to do with overworking. One day he came home exhausted and fainted. When he woke up again he was paralyzed. I was very miserable at leaving home and

> I worked from 8 in the morning to midnight. My cousin often worked until 2 in the morning.

frightened of going to the city but I also knew it was my only hope to continue with my schooling. Because I knew nothing about sewing I had to learn everything from scratch. My employer said I would have to do domestic work to repay him for the training I would receive.

It was a very small family business — a three-story house which was also the owner's home. I was paid very little — 500 baht ($25) a month. Out of that I had to pay back 100 baht for my housing and my food; though they gave us only cooked rice and if we wanted anything with it, we had to buy it.

There were six people working in the factory and we all shared one room. The room we worked in was very narrow with about five machines in it and the lighting was very poor. I worked from 8 in the morning to midnight. This was a privilege. My cousin often stayed up sewing until 2 in the morning.

I was supposed to be an apprentice but I wasn't really given any training. I had to do a lot of housework. I washed clothes and cleaned the house and kitchen. I could be called to do it at any time. I was lucky to have my cousin there: When my employer was out she would teach me and I would also watch how the others worked. That's how I got trained. I learned quickly. Usually it takes eight months. Within a couple of months my sewing was in demand.

I don't think the owner was a bad man. He did not abuse me. He shouted at me only if I yelled at his child. Sometimes he let us watch TV. He was just stingy.

After I was there two and a half months he took a big order from a factory making clothes for little children and needed more labor. He said I was ready to take on bulk work. If I agreed I would make a little more money. But my cousin was worried: I would have to work seven days a week and stay up late, sometimes working right through the night, going without sleep for 48 hours. My cousin feared that the pressure of bulk work would be too great for a child of 13. She advised me to take a job in a bigger factory, where I might also have an opportunity for education on Sundays.

It was a medium-sized factory with 20 machines. From outside you could hardly tell it was a factory — the windows were high up and barred and we were not allowed to open them. It was very closed; no one could see inside. There were 20 workers. Most of the others were between 15 and 17. We worked six days a week. It was a registered factory and so had to meet government regulations. However, the owners had no kindness. They were very stingy, too; the pay was very low and they never raised our salary. They didn't care.

There were several organizations in Bangkok providing activities for working children but most operated during the day when I couldn't attend. Then I heard of the Child Labor Club, whose activities are on the weekend. So I started attending nonformal education on Sundays. They also provide shelter and health care for children with problems. I'm 16 now and in

January I quit my job to work for the Club part-time, reaching out to other working children. The Club pays me 3,000 baht (about $150) a month and they give me a room without rent, which I share with two other girls. ∎

Sawai was interviewed by Anthony Swift. This interview was first published in "Child Labor, Children Organizing," a special issue of the New Internationalist, *July 1997. See www.newint.org.*

Paul Duquesnoy

The Boy with One Shoe

A person overseas reported seeing a boy with one shoe. When asked how he lost his other shoe the boy responded: "I didn't. I found this one."

El niño con un zapato

Una persona nos contó que un día vio a un niño que sólo tenía un zapato. Cuando le preguntó cómo fue que perdió uno de sus zapatos, el niño respondió: "No lo perdí, encontré este que tengo puesto."

"Little girl spinner in Mollahan Cotton Mills, Newberry, South Carolina." (1908)

Lewis Hine's Photographs

Proponents of corporate-driven globalization argue that adhering to principles of "free trade" will solve the world's economic ills. As U.S. Trade Representative Robert Zoellick claims: "The global trading system has demonstrated, from Seoul to Santiago, that it is a pathway out of poverty and despair."

However, history shows that what actually makes people's lives better is people themselves working to *make* them better. Thus it was not the magic of the marketplace that greatly reduced the incidence of child labor in the United States, but organized efforts to stop it.

Lewis Hine, a few of whose photos are reproduced here (with his original captions), was one such social justice activist. Hine's startling photographs of children at work were not the product of mere curiosity, but were part of an anti-

child labor campaign. In 1908, Hine left a teaching position to work full-time as an investigative photographer for the National Child Labor Committee, which was fighting against the exploitation of children at work. His first photo essay of child laborers was published in 1909. It would be many years before legislation would be passed eliminating some of the most egregious types of workplace exploitation of children. But what is certain is that change occurred because people worked for it.

(For a link to a story on coal and child labor, illustrated with Hine's photos, that could be used with elementary-aged children, visit our website at www.rethinkingschools.org/rg.)

Hine's photos can be viewed today as artifacts of one important struggle for social justice. ■

—The editors

Top: "Boys going home from W.B. Conkey Co., Hammond, Indiana." (1908)

Left: "Manuel the young shrimp picker, age 5, and a mountain of child labor oyster shells behind him. He worked last year. Understands not a word of English. Biloxi, Mississippi." (1911)

"**Woman and girl kneeling while preparing embroidery thread as two children and another woman watch.**" (1912)

The Night Before Christmas

AUTHOR UNKNOWN

In this poem, written by a social worker in 1911 in New York City, a privileged child talks with her doll — a doll that was made in sweatshop conditions in a tenement where the family who made the doll lived.

Lewis Hine, the American photographer who took thousands of pictures of children at work, printed this poem along with a photo of the Catena family of 71 Sullivan Street in New York City. The family was making dolls' legs. One of the children, Rosalie, is disabled; one is named Nettie. They all work after school and often until 10:00 p.m. — and not only during the Christmas rush.

Dolly dear, dolly dear, where have you been?

"I've been in a world you have never seen."

Dolly dear, dolly dear, how came you there?

"I was born in a tenement, up a back stair."

Dolly, my dolly dear, what did you see?

"I saw little children make dollies like me."

How old were these motherkins, when did they play?

"They don't play in that world, they work every day."

Dolly, but dolly, how long does it take?

"They nodded, we nodded, that night half awake."

Why didn't they feed you and take you to bed?

"The children who made me were often unfed."

Dolly, but dolly, what were they named?

"There was Nettie with measles, and Rosalie lamed."

These sick little children, what could they sew?

"They stitched on my dresses, an arm then a toe."

Left: A fishing platform worker in Indonesia. Right: A cotton picker in Turkey.

A Child's View of Exploitation

BY AUGUSTO BOAL

People in Lima, Peru, were asked to take photographs of exploitation. Some adults thought of pictures of slaves or of poor people being badly treated by rich tourists.... One child took a photograph of a nail on a wall. Few adults understood it, but all the other people were in complete agreement that the picture expressed their feelings in relation to exploitation. The discussion explained why. The simplest work boys engage in at the age of five or six is shining shoes. Obviously, in the *barrios* [districts] where they live there are no shoes to shine and, for this reason, they must go to downtown Lima in order to find work. Their shine-boxes and other tools of the trade are of course an absolute necessity, and yet these boys cannot be carrying their equipment back and forth every day between work and home. So they must rent a nail on the wall of some place of business, whose owner charges them two or three *soles* [Peruvian units of money] per night and per nail. Looking at a nail, those children are reminded of oppression and their hatred of it. ■

Excerpted from The Theater of the Oppressed, *Pluto Press, 1985.*

Fitting It All In —
Student Clubs as an Option

BY BOB PETERSON

As a classroom teacher it's hard to fit in all the curriculum we are supposed to "cover," to say nothing about topics such as child labor and global sweatshops that aren't included in district or state guidelines.

There are multiple connections between global sweatshops and all aspects of curriculum — from writing, geography, and social studies to current events and even math. In my fifth-grade classroom I've incorporated the topic into a literature unit on homelessness and creative writing, a math unit on multiplication skills (see activity, p. 157), world geography study, and current events.

Nonetheless, once when we finished our unit on sweatshops (see "Planting Seeds of Solidarity," p. 18) I wasn't satisfied. Some students wanted to continue to study and take action on the issue, while others had had enough. I realized that given all the things we needed to cover, I couldn't justify spending more time on this single issue, no matter how much I integrated it into other aspects of the curriculum.

I discussed this time dilemma with students, and one came up with the idea of forming a club. We decided that it should include all interested third, fourth, and fifth graders, and would meet once a week during lunch-time recess. I volunteered to be the advisor and the librarian agreed to let us meet in the school library.

The club's activities so far have included: presentations by fifth graders to the third and fourth graders on what they've learned; watching and discussing videos on child labor; read-ing and reflecting on articles on the subject; inviting in a group of high school students to explain their campaign to get the City Council to pass an ordinance against buying sweatshop-produced goods; exploring sites on the Internet; a petition campaign among students and parents; letter writing to the President and other elected officials; discussion with a local union activist; participation in an anti-NAFTA rally; designing a bulletin board; writing poetry and skits; and making a video on child labor for use by club members.

I gave each student a pocket folder to keep handouts and their work, and each member designed a special "No Child Labor Club" lapel button, which serves as a pass from the cafeteria to the library. We meet weekly (except when rain forces me to have indoor recess duty in my own classroom).

The club allows some children — and me — to explore child labor in depth. It provides an opportunity for kids to act on their concerns. I'm able to encourage students to take social action without imposing it on students who may not have that interest. Finally, I get to meet and work with some of the most socially conscious third and fourth graders before they are in my class. This will provide a jump start for following years — both in terms of my ability to identify student leaders and in the depth of understanding that they will bring into the class. ■

Bob Peterson (repmilw@aol.com) teaches fifth grade at La Escuela Fratney in Milwaukee, Wisconsin and is a Rethinking Schools editor.

Kids for Sale

"GOD TO HUNGRY CHILD"
Poem by Langston Hughes (p. 190)

Teach the following terms before you share the poem: stock, invest, corporations, share, and Standard Oil. Then read the poem with students a couple of times. Ask:

- What is Hughes' message?
- What technique does he use?

Ask students to imagine similar techniques of someone talking to another (parent to child, boss to worker, ancestor to family member, etc.) Have students decide on a message they would like to convey in a poem about hunger or other related issues and then write a poem using Hughes' poem as a model.

"EVERYWHERE ON EARTH"
Excerpt from a book by Eduardo Galeano (p. 192)

Ask students what kinds of jobs or chores they have to do and how much time those jobs take. Tell them you'll be reading together a list from a famous Uruguayan writer who is concerned that in many parts of the world children work for little money in unsafe situations, instead of doing educational things such as going to school or learning from elders. This short piece can be used to show students how geographically widespread child labor is, and the diversity of jobs it encompasses.

Distribute copies of the list to each student and read it together. Help students find some of the locations on a wall map. After going through the list, have students number each item. Working in pairs and using an atlas, have students mark the numbers on a world map indicating where child labor exists.

Another approach is to give each student a small stickie note and have them draw a symbol representing the type of work and the name of the place. Then have students place the stickie notes on a large wall map.

Ask students what they notice about the distribution of child labor. Ask them why they think child labor is so widespread. Have students generate more questions as a basis for future study of child labor issues.

Another useful activity with this list is for stu-dents to match Galeano's written descriptions with photos of child labor from around the world. Collect several books and photocopies depicting child labor. Have students in groups try to match photos with the written descriptions. This encourages observation and discussion skills. After groups have worked on making comparisons, have each group report back to the whole class on what they found, noting similarities and differences. As a follow-up, students could draw their own pictures based on Galeano's description and display them on a bulletin board entitled "Everywhere on Earth." They also could add to Galeano's list, based on their own study.

After students examine child labor more thoroughly, Galeano's list could be used to generate ideas for poetry, interior monologue assignments, or short improvisations.

For a comprehensive list of the kinds of jobs that child workers have in different countries, check out the U.S. Department of Labor's report, *By the Sweat and Toil of Children, Volume Five,* 1989, at www.dol.gov/dol/ilab/public/media /report/iclp/sweat5/appendixc.htm.

"CHILD LABOR: PAIN AND RESISTANCE"
Article by Bob Peterson (p. 200)

Use this introductory essay with students after viewing a video or looking at photos that spark students' interest. (See video suggestions in "Seeds of Solidarity," p. 18, and in the Child Labor section of "Videos With a Global Conscience," p. 365.) Depending on the reading level of your students, have them read the essay individually, in groups, or as a whole class. Have students identify difficult words or concepts as they read. Use some of these questions for discussion:

- What was life like for Nirmala?
- Why did she go to work?
- What do you think happened to her after the Europeans stopped buying so many carpets?
- What exactly is "child labor"? Give examples of children working that we would

not consider "child labor." (For an interesting interactive exercise on the web have your students check out www.us.ilo.org/ilokidsnew/day.html.)

- Why would some people think that there is no child labor in the United States?
- Why do you think a nation as rich as the United States allows child labor to continue?
- What have some young people done to fight child labor?
- What are some of the problems mentioned at the end of the article about the efforts to stop child labor?

Using the Sweatshop Fact Sheet on p.158 and other sources your students can uncover on the Internet and through other means, have students in groups of five or six develop skits that reveal aspects of child labor. Videos such as *When Children Do the Work, Zoned for Slavery, Tomorrow We Will Finish,* or *Sweating for a T-Shirt* might help inspire ideas. For example, a skit might feature two reporters (one with a video camera) sneaking into a sweatshop where they talk with two or three workers. Perhaps one worker is hesitant and fearful of losing his or her job, while another is more bold. Then have the manager or owner enter and find the reporter in the factory.

Another kind of role play that requires more preparation is a mock student rally against child labor. Students prepare short speeches and design picket signs and then hold a mock rally. This is a good activity to gauge how much students know about child labor and sweatshops, and gives them practice making persuasive speeches. If it seems that the class expresses sufficient interest, students may want to rally other students in school against child labor.

"DECLARATION OF THE RIGHTS OF THE CHILD"
A children's bill of rights, adopted by the U.N. General Assembly, 1959 (p. 208)

"ALL CHILDREN HAVE A RIGHT TO...."
Graphic from South Africa (p. 203)

Ask students what they think a "right" is. Ask them also to discuss a "need" versus a desire. Before reading the Declaration, ask students if they agree that children deserve special rights, separate from the rights of adults. Why?

Tell students that years ago people came together to make a public declaration about the rights of children. In small groups or as a whole class, ask students to brainstorm a big list of rights. These should be written out so that they are visible to the entire class. Discuss whether the items on students' lists are "rights" — real needs all children should have met — or merely "desires" that would be nice to have but are not essential for a decent life.

Distribute the handout, "Declaration of the Rights of the Child" and read it together. Also share the graphic from South Africa and one or both UNICEF books *For Every Child* and *Children's Chorus* (see p. 378). Discuss the differences in students' lists with the Declaration. Ask students questions such as:

- Why do some children have these rights and not others?
- Which of these rights do you think you have or don't have?
- Whose responsibility should it be to make sure all kids have those rights?
- What could kids do to make sure they themselves, and others, have these rights?
- Do you disagree with any of the rights listed in the Declaration?

Divide students into small groups. Assign each of them a different principle (there are ten of these in the Declaration). Their job is to design posters illustrating the principle assigned to their group. Encourage them to summarize the principle in a sentence or short title. Again, see the South African poster on p. 203 as an example. These could be displayed around the school. Alternatively, students might be encouraged to perform skits dramatizing each principle.

"CHILD LABOR IS CHEAP — AND DEADLY"
The testimony of Augustino Nieves (p. 204)

Bring enough strawberries to school so each student can have one. Give each student a strawberry and ask them to write down observations and thoughts about it. Have them briefly share their observations. Let them eat their strawberries and then pass out the article. Read and discuss the article together. Tell students to add some more thoughts to the lists they made before reading. Ask students to recount some difficulties that many farm workers face. Encourage students to check out the United

Farm Workers website at www.ufw.org to learn about some current struggles of farm workers who pick strawberries and other fruits and vegetables.

Ask students to draw up a list of demands that would substantially improve conditions for Augustino Nieves and his co-workers. What needs to change beyond the workplace that would make a positive difference in Augustino's life? Think globally. How might things need to change in other countries?

Discuss:
- Should Augustino's parents allow him to work in the fields?
- What advice would you give Augustino?

Ask students to identify which rights, as defined in the "Declaration of the Rights of the Child," are violated in the situations described in the reading.

Have students write an ode to a piece of fruit. Use odes from Pablo Neruda as an example. (For more information on teaching students to write odes, see *Rethinking Our Classrooms, Volume 1*, pp. 17-18 and the teaching ideas described in Linda Christensen's article, "Celebrating the Joy in Daily Events," p. 16.)

Math connection: Ask students to assume that Augustino was paid the federal minimum wage. What would his income be? How much more is this than what he makes now? Most states require time-and-a-half overtime after eight hours of work. If this were the case, what would he earn? What could students or other workers do in order to increase the wages of workers like Augustino?

Read "Federico's Ghost" by Martín Espada (p. 222) and compare the story in that poem to this article.

"FIGHT FOR CHILD WORKERS!"

A story about Iqbal Masih
by Peadar Cremin (p. 206)

Show the video *When Children Do the Work* (see p. 365 which has a section on Iqbal Masih. Read this summary of Iqbal's life as a follow-up. Have students also look at the web page dedicated to Iqbal Masih (www.childrensworld.org/engiqbal/intro.asp) and the school for former child workers (www.mirrorimage.com/iqbal/) They can read parts of his biography. The story is a gripping one for students and helped launch the international organization, Free The Children. See p. 325 for a speech by Craig Kielburger, its founder.

Questions for discussion:
- Why do children like Iqbal become child laborers?
- What difficulties do you think Iqbal had when he decided to escape and start organizing for justice?
- What would you have done in a similar situation?
- What could students in other countries do to support children like Iqbal?

Have students write a news story about Iqbal, pretending it is the anniversary of his death. As a class, they might write a play or children's books about him and the conditions that he tried to change.

Improvisation possibilities: Have students imagine an argument between Iqbal and his boss; Iqbal and another child worker who is hesitant to escape; between the head of the Bonded Labor Liberation Front and Iqbal when he first arrived.

See the video *Tomorrow We Will Finish*, an evocative dramatization of the lives of several girls who toil in a carpet-making factory (reviewed in "Videos With a Global Conscience," p. 365.)

"SAWAI'S STORY"

Interview with a Thai garment worker (p. 210)

Read the story together. Make a chart comparing what students do during their day and what Sawai did while she was working. Have students use the interactive website www.us.ilo.org/ilokidsnew/day.html to compare a day in their lives to typical days in the lives of other children working around the world.

Math connection: Using the figure Sawai gives for numbers of hours worked and her monthly wage, figure out her hourly wage. How many hours does she need to work simply to pay back her employer for food and housing?

Brainstorm how students who don't have to work all day can help child workers around the world.

To supplement this reading, you might use the video *Made in Thailand*, which reveals the conditions of Thai sweatshop workers, as described by the workers themselves.

"LEWIS HINE'S PHOTOGRAPHS"

"THE NIGHT BEFORE CHRISTMAS"
Lewis Hine photographs, and poem, author unknown; (pp. 212-214)

This poem can be used as a model for a dialogue poem. (See *Rethinking Our Classrooms, Volume 1*, p. 42, and see p. 152 in this book for other examples.) In a dialogue poem, two characters talk to each other or about the same events or issues from different perspectives. Photos of child workers or sweatshop laborers can be used to inspire poetry writing. In pairs, students examine the pictures and then write a dialogue poem — between a boss and a worker, between a child worker and child student, between a poor child and a rich child, etc.

Students might pattern a poem after "The Night Before Christmas" and have a more privileged child talk to an object and wonder about the child behind the product.

Have students choose one of the Lewis Hine photos and write an interior monologue from the child's point of view. (More photos can be found in Russell Freedman's *Kids at Work: Lewis Hine and the Crusade Against Child Labor*, see Resources, p. 373; they can also be found online: see www.rethinkingschools.org/rg for an up-to-date link.) Ask students to imagine: What is s/he thinking and feeling? Why is s/he at work? What hopes does s/he have?

Another alternative: Copy the Hine photos for use on an overhead projector. Using the trigger format (p. 188) discuss the photos. Suggest that students read about Mother Jones and the struggle against child labor in the United States (see p. 373 for listing of possible books).

"THE BOY WITH ONE SHOE"
Picture and quote (p. 211)

Show an overhead of the picture and ask what the students see. Have students imagine what happened to the other shoe. Then show the students the quote. Ask:

- Why did we assume that the child lost one of his shoes?
- Why do you think the boy doesn't have shoes?
- Where do shoes come from? Who makes them?

Read the poem, "Psalm for Distribution," by Jack Agüeros (p. 156) to the students.

Using the data given in the "Sweatshop Fact Sheet," (p. 158), have students calculate how much time a sweatshop worker would have to work to buy a pair of Nikes or other comparable shoes.

CHILD ASLEEP SEWING SOFTBALL
Photo (p. 1)

Using the "trigger" questions (p. 188) discuss this photo with the children. Have the students imagine what the ball means to different children — the one who makes it and the one who plays with it. Students could do a dialogue poem starting off "I sew softballs." and "I play with softballs."

CHAPTER SIX
Just Food?

Federico's Ghost

BY MARTÍN ESPADA

The story is
that whole families of fruitpickers
still crept between the furrows
of the field at dusk,
when for reasons of whiskey or whatever
the cropduster plane sprayed anyway,
floating a pesticide drizzle
over the pickers
who thrashed like dark birds
in a glistening white net,
except for Federico,
a skinny boy who stood apart
in his own green row,
and, knowing the pilot
would not understand in Spanish
that he was a son of a whore,
instead jerked his arm
and thrust an obscene finger.
The pilot understood.
He circled the plane and sprayed again,
watching a fine gauze of poison
drift over the brown bodies
that cowered and scurried on the ground,
and aiming for Federico,
leaving the skin beneath his shirt
wet and blistered,
but still pumping his finger at the sky.

After Federico died,
rumors at the labor camp
told of tomatoes picked and smashed
at night,
growers muttering of vandal children
or communists in camp,
first threatening to call Immigration,
then promising every Sunday off
if only the smashing of tomatoes would
stop.
Still tomatoes were picked and
squashed
in the dark,
and the old women in camp
said it was Federico,
laboring after sundown
to cool the burns on his arms,
flinging tomatoes
at the cropduster
that hummed like a mosquito
lost in his ear,
and kept his soul awake.

Martín Espada is the author of numerous books of poetry, including Rebellion Is the Circle of a Lover's Hand, *Willimantic, CT: Curbstone Press, 1990, from which this poem is excerpted. Espada is professor of English at University of Massachusetts-Amherst.*

Page 221 image: Juan Talavar carries bananas on a plantation near Rio Frio, Costa Rica. Photo by Kent Gilbert for Associated Press.

A McDonald's restaurant in Tokyo advertises a sale on hamburgers.

INTRODUCTION

Just Food?

The globalization of agriculture is not new. It began in earnest when Columbus planted sugar cane in the Indies in 1493, and with the European appropriation of previously unknown (to them) foods like corn, potatoes, and tomatoes. Traditional scholarship calls this first major globalization of agriculture the Columbian Exchange — but it was never an exchange between equals. It was an exchange between master and servants, enforced by swords, cannon, armor, mounted soldiers, and enormous attack dogs.

As readings in this chapter point out, the globalization of agriculture is still an unequal exchange driven by greed.

Capitalist globalization treats land and food simply as commodities. The free trade regime enforced by the World Trade Organization insists that corn grown and marketed by agribusiness giants should be treated no differently than corn grown by subsistence farmers in Mexico or Zimbabwe. Globalization's "collateral damage" — displaced farmers, destroyed communities, swollen urban ghettos — is regarded simply as unfortunate but inevitable byproducts of free enterprise. Imported food is cheaper food, argue the proponents of food globalization. "Eating more cheaply on imports is not eating at all for the poor in Mexico," counters one critic. Global warming — greatly exacerbated by today's version of globalization — will have an enormous impact on food security around the world. We will touch some on this issue in Chapter 7.

Corporations are also commodifying traditional food knowledge, acquired over millennia, as they secure patents on nature. A Texas-based corporation, Rice Tec, cross-bred two varieties of basmati rice — eaten in India for centuries — and was granted patent #5,663,484, for their "novel invention." Corporations are also commodifying new food varieties through genetic engineering — for example, constructing corn with its own built-in pesticides, with unknown consequences on biodiversity, human health, and cultures.

Articles, stories, poems, and activities in this chapter propose alternative perspectives on food and agriculture. Food is inextricably linked to culture, as scholar-activist Vandana Shiva suggests in her fine book, *Stolen Harvest*. "We will give up our lives, but we will not give up our rice," declared village after village in one peasant movement in India. Embedded in food are the lives and labor of the people who produced it, insists Benjamin Saenz in his story, *"Cebolleros."* Food is not just a thing to be bought and sold; it is a series of relationships.

As with the chapter on global sweatshops, this chapter asks students to think about those relationships. At every meal, whose lives do we touch? And how does the globalization of food touch us? ■

— *The editors*

Indian farmers in New Delhi protest new laws in 2001. The laws, changed to reflect a World Trade Organization agreement, allowed other countries to export hundreds of new products to India.

Stealing Nature's Harvest

BY VANDANA SHIVA

Food is our most basic need, the very stuff of life. According to an ancient Indian Upanishad, "All that is born is born of anna [food]. Whatever exists on Earth is born of anna, lives on anna, and in the end merges into anna. Anna indeed is the first born amongst all beings."

More than 3.5 million people starved to death in the Bengal famine of 1943. Twenty million more were directly affected. Export of food grains continued in spite of the fact that people were going hungry. At the time, India was being used as a supply base for the British military. More that one-fifth of India's national output was appropriated for war supplies. The starving Bengal peasants gave up over two-thirds of the food they produced. Dispossessed peasants moved to Calcutta. Thousands of female destitutes were turned into prostitutes. Parents started to sell their children.

As the crisis began, thousands of women organized in Bengal in defense of their food rights. "Open more ration shops" and "Bring down the price of food" were the calls of women's groups throughout Bengal.

After the famine, the peasants also started to organize. At its peak the Tebhaga movement, as it was called, covered 19 districts and involved 6 million people. Everywhere, peasants declared, "We will give up our lives, but we will not give up our rice." In the village of Thumniya, police arrested some peasants who resisted the theft of their harvest, charging them with "stealing paddy."

A half-century after the Bengal famine, a new and clever system has been put in place that is once again making the theft of the harvest a right and the keeping of the harvest a crime. Hidden behind complex free-trade treaties are innovative ways to steal nature's harvests of seed and nutrition.

I focus on India both because I am an Indian and because Indian agriculture is being especially targeted by global corporations. However, this phenomenon of the stolen harvest is not unique to India. It is being experienced in every society, as small farms and small farmers are pushed to extinction, as monocultures replace biodiverse crops, and as farming is transformed from the production of nourishing and diverse foods into the creation of markets for genetically engineered seeds, herbicides, and pesticides.

SEED

For centuries, Third World farmers have evolved crops and given us the diversity of plants that provide us nutrition. Indian farmers evolved 200,000 varieties of rice. They bred rice varieties such as Basmati. They bred red rice and brown rice and black rice. They bred rice that grew 18 feet tall in the Gangetic floodwaters and saline-resistant rice that could thrive in coastal water.

The seed, for the farmer is not merely the source of future plants and food; it is the storage place of culture and history. Free exchange of seed among farmers has been the basis of maintaining biodiversity as well as food security; it involves exchanges of ideas and knowledge, of culture and heritage. It is an accumulation of tradition and of knowledge of how to work the seed. Farmers learn about the plants they want to grow in the future by watching them grow in other farmers' fields.

Paddy, or rice, has religious significance in most parts of India and is an essential component of most religious festivals. The Akti Festival in Chattisgarh, where a diversity of indica rices are grown, reinforces the many principles of biodiversity conservation. In Southern India, rice grain is considered auspicious; it is mixed with *kumkum* and turmeric and given as a blessing. New seeds are first worshipped, and only then are they planted. Festivals held before sowing seeds, as well as harvest festivals celebrated in the fields, symbolize people's intimacy with nature.

For the farmer, the field is the mother; worshipping the field is a sign of gratitude toward the Earth, which, as mother, feeds the millions of life forms that are her children.

CLAIMING SEED AS PROPERTY

The new intellectual-property-rights regimes, which are being universalized through the Trade Related Intellectual Property Rights Agreement of the World Trade Organization (WTO) [see Chapter 3], allow corporations to usurp the knowledge of the seed and monopolize it by claiming it as their private property. Over time, this results in corporate monopolies over the seed itself. Corporations like RiceTec of the United States are claiming patents on Basmati rice. The soybean, which evolved in East Asia, has been patented by Calgene, which is now owned by Monsanto. Calgene also owns patents on mustard, a crop of Indian origin. Centuries of collective innovation by farmers and peasants are being hijacked by corporations claiming intellectual property rights over plants.

Today, 10 corporations control 32% of the commercial seed market, valued at $23 billion, and 100% of the market for genetically engineered, or transgenic, seeds. These corporations also control the global agrochemical and pesticide market. Just five corporations control the global trade in grain. In late 1998, Cargill, the largest of these five companies, bought Continental, the second largest, making it the single biggest factor in the grain trade. Monoliths such as Cargill and Monsanto were both actively involved in shaping international trade agreements, in par-

ticular the Uruguay Round of the General Agreement on Tariffs and Trade, which led to the establishment of the WTO.

This monopolistic control over agricultural production, along with structural adjustment policies that favor exports [see Chapter 3], results in floods of exports of foods from the United States and Europe to the Third World. As a result of the North American Free Trade Agreement (NAFTA), the proportion of Mexico's food supply that is imported increased from 20% in 1992 to 43% in 1996. After 18 months of NAFTA, 2.2 million Mexicans lost their jobs, and 40 million fell into extreme poverty. One out of two peasants is not getting enough to eat. As Victor Suares has stated, "Eating more cheaply on imports is not eating at all for the poor in Mexico."

ENGINEERING LIFE

Global corporations are not just stealing the harvest of farmers. They are stealing nature's harvest through genetic engineering and patents on life forms. Crops such as Monsanto's Roundup Ready soybeans, designed to be resistant to herbicides, lead to the destruction of biodiversity and increased use of agrochemicals. They can also create highly invasive "super weeds" by transferring the genes for herbicide resistance to weeds.

Crops designed to be pesticide factories, genetically engineered to produce toxins and venom with genes from bacteria, scorpions, snakes, and wasps, can threaten non-pest species and can contribute to the emergence of resistance in pests and hence the creation of "superpests."

To secure patents on life forms and living resources, corporations must claim seeds and plants to be their "inventions" and hence their property. Corporations like Cargill and Monsanto see nature's web of life and cycles of renewal as "theft" of their property. During the debate about the entry of Cargill into India in 1992, the Cargill chief executive stated, "We bring Indian farmers smart technologies, which prevent bees from usurping the pollen." During the United Nations Biosafety Negotiations, Monsanto circulated literature that claimed that "weeds steal the sunshine."

A worldview that defines pollination as "theft by bees" and claims that diverse plants "steal" sunshine is one aimed at stealing nature's harvest. This is a worldview based on scarcity. A worldview of abundance is the worldview

Ravi Jaggu (background) gets ready to cycle to work as his grandfather and young neighbors sit outside their thatched hut in the Indian village of Bhimnagar Tanda in 1998. Ravi's father, a farmer, borrowed money to buy pesticides that were supposed to kill caterpillars that were infesting the cotton crop. When the caterpillars didn't die, the moneylenders encouraged the farmers to commit suicide, so that the debts could be repaid out of their liquidated assets. Ravi's father and more than 150 others succeeded in killing themselves — by swallowing the pesticide.

of women in India who leave food for ants on their doorsteps, even as they create the most beautiful art in kolams, mandalas, and rangoli with rice flour. Abundance is the worldview of peasant women who weave beautiful designs of paddy to hang up for birds when the birds do not find grain in the fields. This view of abundance recognizes that, in giving food to other beings and species, we maintain conditions for our own food security. It is the recognition in the Isho Upanishad that the universe is the creation of the Supreme Power meant for the benefits of (all) creation. Each individual life form must learn to enjoy its benefits by forming a part of the system in close relation with other species.

In the ecological worldview, when we consume more than we need or exploit nature on principles of greed, we are engaging in theft. In the anti-life view of agribusiness corporations, nature, renewing and maintaining herself, is a thief. Such a worldview replaces abundance with scarcity, fertility with sterility.

What we are seeing is the emergence of food totalitarianism, in which a handful of corporations control the entire food chain and destroy alternatives. The notion of rights has been turned on its head under globalization and free trade. The right to food, the right to safety, the right to culture are all being treated as trade barriers that need to be dismantled.

SAVE THE SEED

In 1987, the Dag Hammarskjold Foundation organized a meeting on biotechnology called "Laws of Life." This watershed event made it clear that the giant chemical companies were repositioning themselves as "life sciences" companies, whose goal was to control agriculture through patents, genetic engineering, and mergers. At that meeting I decided I would dedicate the next decade of my life to finding ways to prevent monopolies on life and living resources, both through resistance and through building creative alternatives.

The first step I took was to start *Navdanya*, a movement for saving seed, protecting biodiversity, and keeping seed and agriculture free of monopoly control. The Navdanya today has thousands of members who conserve biodiversity, practice chemical-free agriculture, and have taken a pledge to continue to save and share the seeds and biodiversity they have received as gifts from nature and their ancestors.

On March 5, 1998, on the anniversary of Mohandas Gandhi's call for the salt *satyagraha*,* a coalition of more that 2,000 groups started the *bija satyagraha*, a non-cooperation movement opposing patents on seeds and plants. Literally, *satyagraha* means the struggle for truth. Gandhi said, "As long as the superstition that people should obey unjust laws exists, so long will slavery exist. And a nonviolent resister alone can remove such a superstition."

In 1999, news of Monsanto's genetic-engineering trials in India leaked to the press. These trials were being carried out in 40 locations in nine states. State agricultural ministers objected that they had not been consulted on the trials, and they released the locations of the trial sites. Immediately, farmers in Karnataka and Andhra Pradesh uprooted and burned the genetically engineered crops. In Andhra Pradesh, the farmers also got a resolution passed through the regional parliament and put pressure on the government to ban the trials. After the first uprooting by farmers, the government itself uprooted the crops in other locations.

Gandhi defied the British colonialists' monopoly on salt by leading a 24-day march to the sea to collect salt illegally.

FOOD DEMOCRACY

In India, the poorest peasants have been organic farmers because they could never afford chemicals. Today, they are joined by a growing international organic movement that consciously avoids chemicals and genetic engineering.

- In Britain, the Genetix Snowball movement, was launched in 1998 when five women uprooted Monsanto's crops in Oxfordshire.

- In February 1999, an alliance of U.K. farm, consumer, development, and environmental groups launched a campaign for a "Five-Year Freeze" on genetic engineering.

- In 1993 in Switzerland, a grassroots group, the Swiss Working Group on Genetic Engineering, collected 111,000 names favoring a referendum to ban genetic engineering. The biotech industry hired a public relations company for $24 million to defeat the referendum in 1998. But the debate is far from over. A similar referendum was organized by Greenpeace and Global 2000 in Austria.

- In Ireland, the Gaelic Earth Liberation Front dug up a field of Roundup Ready sugar beet at Ireland's Teagase Research Centre at Oakport.

- In France, farmers of *Confederation Paysanne* destroyed Novarti's genetically engineered seeds. France later imposed a moratorium on transgenic crops.

Throughout Europe, bans and moratoriums on genetic engineering, in response to growing citizen pressure, are increasing.

A survey released in November 1998 by the agribusiness-affiliated International Food Safety Council found that 89% of U.S. consumers think food safety is a "very important" issue — more important than crime prevention. Seventy-seven percent were changing their eating habits due to food-safety concerns. A *Time* magazine poll published in its January 13, 1999, issue found that 81% of U.S. consumers believe genetically engineered food should be labeled; 58% said they would not eat genetically engineered foods if they were labeled.

A DEMOCRACY OF LIFE

Ecological and organic agriculture is referred to in India as ahimsic krishi, or "nonviolent agriculture," because it is based on compassion for all species and hence the protection of biodiversity in agriculture.

Our movements advocate the recovery of the biodiversity and intellectual commons. By refusing to recognize life's diversity as a corporate invention and hence as corporate property, we are acknowledging the intrinsic value of all species and their self-organizing capacity. By refusing to allow privatization of living resources, we are defending the right to survival of the two-thirds majority that depends on nature's capital and is excluded from markets because of its poverty. The movement is also a defense of cultural diversity, since the majority of diverse cultures do not see other species and plants as "property" but as kin.

This larger democracy of life is the real force of resistance against the brute power of the "life sciences industry," which is pushing millions of species and millions of people to the edge of survival.

These are exciting times. It is not inevitable that corporations will control our lives and rule the world. We have a real possibility to shape our own future. We have an ecological and social duty to ensure that the food that nourishes us is not a stolen harvest. In this duty, we each have the opportunity to work for the freedom and liberation of all species and all people no matter who we are, no matter where we are. ■

Vandana Shiva, director of the Research Foundation for Science, Technology and Ecology, is a physicist and one of India's leading social and ecological justice activists. This article is adapted from her book Stolen Harvest: The Hijacking of the Global Food Supply, *Cambridge, MA: South End Press. 2000.*

Dozens of farmers ransack a Kentucky Fried Chicken restaurant in the southern India city of Bangalore in 1996.

Associated Press

Farmers in Karnataka, India set fire to cotton plants at a Monsanto test field in 1998.

"We Will Reduce Your Fields to Ashes"

An Open Letter from Indian Farmers

The following letter was issued in late 1998 by the Karnataka State Farmers Association (KRRS) in India as a response to the Monsanto Corporation's agricultural practices in their country. Among other activities, Monsanto has introduced "Bt" cotton in India, going so far as to offer free samples to farmers without informing them of the risks. Bt cotton is genetically engineered with DNA from the soil microbe Bacillus thuringiensis in order to produce proteins poisonous to the bollworm, a cotton pest. While some proponents claim that this will cut down on the need for chemical pesticides, opponents argue that pests will develop greater resistance to toxins, and organic pest control strategies will be made ineffective. They also point out that once genetically engineered crops are introduced, these will pollute other crops, as has happened, for

example, with genetically engineered corn in the United States. Monsanto, activists say, is concerned with the welfare of its stockholders, not of Indian farmers. The actions described in the letter below have received wide publicity in India.

Dear Friends,

Monsanto's field trials in Karnataka will be reduced to ashes, starting on Saturday. Two days ago, the Minister of Agriculture of Karnataka gave a press conference where he was forced by the journalists to disclose the sites where field trials with Bt cotton are being conducted. KRRS activists have already contacted the owners of these fields to explain to them which action will be taken, and for what reasons, and to let them know that the KRRS will cover any losses they will suffer. On Saturday the 28th of November, at midday, thousands of farmers will occupy and burn down the three fields in front of cameras, in an open, announced action of civil disobedience.

These actions will start a campaign of direct action by farmers against biotechnology, called Operation Cremation Monsanto, which will not stop until all the corporate killers like Monsanto, Novartis, Pioneer, etc. leave the country. Farmers' leaders from the states of Maharastra, Gujarat, and Madhya Pradesh (states where Monsanto is also conducting field trials) were yesterday in Bangalore to prepare the campaign.

The campaign will run under the following slogans:

- Stop Genetic Engineering
- No Patents on Life
- Cremate Monsanto
- Bury the WTO

along with a more specific message for all those who have invested in Monsanto:

- You should rather take your money out before we reduce it to ashes.

We know that stopping biotechnology in India will not be of much help to us if it continues in other countries, since the threats that it poses do not stop at the borders.

We also think that the kind of actions that will be going on in India have the potential not only to kick those corporate killers out of our country; if we play our cards right at the global level and coordinate our work, these actions can also pose a major challenge to the survival of these corporations in the stock market. Who wants to invest in a mountain of ashes, in offices that are constantly being squatted (and if necessary even destroyed) by activists?

For these reasons, we are making an international call for direct action against Monsanto and the rest of the biotech gang. This call for action will hopefully inspire all the people who are already doing... brilliant work against biotech, and many others who so far have not been very active on the issue, to join hands in a quick, effective worldwide effort.

This is a very good moment to target Monsanto, since it has run out of cash in its megalomaniacal attempt to monopolize the life industry in record time. It is going now through a hard time of layoffs and restructuring in a desperate effort to survive, since it cannot pay its bills. It is also a good time because several recent scandals ... have contributed to its profile as corporate killer, which, being the creators of the Vietnam War's Agent Orange and rBGH [bovine growth hormone], was already good enough anyhow.

We are hence making a call to:

- Take direct actions against biotech TNCs (transnational corporations), particularly Monsanto (be it squatting or burning their fields, squatting or destroying their offices, etc.).

> **On Saturday the 28th of November, at midday, thousands of farmers will occupy and burn down the three fields in front of cameras, in an open, announced action of civil disobedience.**

- [Keep] the local or/and national press informed about all the actions going on around the world.

- Take direct actions at stock exchanges, targeting Monsanto to draw attention to its state of bankruptcy.

We are making this call for action on the line of Peoples' Global Action (PGA), a worldwide network of peoples' movements in order to emphasize the political analysis beyond our opposition to biotechnology.

This analysis does not only take environmental concerns into account and is not limited to the defense of food security — it attacks neoliberal globalization as a whole, the WTO regime as its most important tool, and the global power structures (G8, NATO, etc.) as the roots of all these problems.

We are calling ONLY for nonviolent direct actions. Nonviolence in this context means that we should respect all (nongenetically modified) living beings, including policemen and the people who work for these TNCs.

The campaign will take place in a decentralized manner, and nobody should speak on behalf of other people involved in the campaign without their consent (also not on behalf of PGA, of course); however, people are welcome to report about the actions of others without pretending to represent them.

—Karnataka (India)
State Farmers Association

A farmer uses traditional equipment to level a rice paddy near Makari City in the Philippines.

The Parable of the Golden Snail

Third World Farmers See Biotech Crops as a First World Disaster in the Making

BY PETER ROSSET

When a group of Filipino farmers were asked recently for their thoughts on genetically engineered rice seeds, a peasant leader responded with what might be called the Parable of the Golden Snail.

It seems that rice farmers had long supplemented the protein in their diet with local snails that live in rice paddies. At the time of the Marcos dictatorship, Imelda Marcos had the idea of introducing a snail from South America that was said to be more productive and, as such, a means to help end hunger and protein malnutrition. But no one liked the taste, and the project was abandoned.

The snails, however, escaped, driving the local snail species to the brink of extinction — thus eliminating a key protein source — and forcing peasants to apply toxic pesticides to keep them from eating the young rice plants.

"So when you ask what we think of the new GE [genetically engineered] rice seeds, we say, that's easy," the leader said. "They are another Golden Snail."

Third World governments and farmers are being told over and over again that genetically engineered seeds are being created to end hunger and that they should brush aside other concerns in the name of ending it quickly. Yet the reality is that far more than enough food exists today to provide an adequate diet for every human being on the planet. In fact, overproduction is a leading problem. The truth is that many people are too poor to have access to the abundance around them. Furthermore, the diverse, integrated farming systems found on smaller farms can be far more productive than the uniform monocultures that genetically engineered seeds are designed for. Meanwhile, patents on life allow biotech companies to privatize the genomes of crop varieties bred by farmers, without compensation, while the escape of novel genes through pollen threatens local crop varieties and food security.

Five hundred angry South Asian farmers recently took a bus caravan across Europe to dramatize their opposition to genetically engineered crops and the free-trade measures embodied in the World Trade Organization. They say that WTO regulations allowing transnational corporations to patent germ plasm from seeds their ancestors have bred over millennia amounts to "biopiracy." Indian peasant leader Lal Shankar called their struggle "a fight of indigenous agriculture and traditional systems against the North-dominated gene technology and free market." He added: "They are stealing and creating hybrid seeds and then selling them back to us." Indian farmers have singled out biotech giant Monsanto for its heavily hyped public relations claims and full page ads about ending hunger. Last year the Karnataka State Farmers Association, which claims 10 million Indian peasants as members, announced its "Cremate Monsanto" campaign (see p. 228). Since then they have been publicly burning Monsanto's experimental plots in India. In London, on the caravan, farmer Kumud Chowdury said, "My husband is taking care of our farm, while I am here to kill Monsanto before it kills families like mine."

In Brazil, the powerful Landless Workers' Movement (MTS) has made stopping Monsanto soybeans a top priority, vowing to destroy any genetically engineered crops planted in Rio Grande do Sul state, where the sympathetic governor has banned them. Meanwhile, a Brazilian federal court judge has suspended commercial release of Monsanto's soy pending further testing.

In Mexico, where the maize plant originated when it was bred in pre-Columbian times from wild relatives, Mexican farmers still maintain 25,000 native varieties. Fears that pollen from imported genetically engineered corn could contaminate and irreversibly damage this invaluable genetic heritage recently led the Mexican government to announce a ban on its import from the United States. Meanwhile Mexico's largest corn-flour company moved to calm consumer fears by eliminating genetically engineered corn from its products.

In Thailand, the government, consumers, environmentalists, and even exporters are concerned about genetically engineered crops. In late 1999, the Thai government slapped a temporary ban on genetically engineered seeds, just as a controversy exploded over genetically engineered cotton plants being grown illegally by farmers near a Monsanto experimental plot. Thai environmental and consumer organizations immediately voiced their opposition to such crops because of their impact on native biodiversity and food safety. With the new ban in place, the commerce minister suggested that Thailand capitalize on the concerns of European consumers by promoting Thai food exports internationally as free from genetic engineering. Thai cooking oil and seasoning exporters rushed to jump on the bandwagon.

It seems that Filipino peasants are not the only ones concerned about a repeat of the Golden Snail. Growing legions through the Third World are asking if they really need these so-called miracle seeds. Certainly the sordid history of technology "altruistically" sent by the North to solve the problems of the South — like large dams that displace thousands, only to silt up rapidly, and pesticides that poison millions, only to become ineffective as pests develop resistance — is enough to make anyone think twice about Golden Snails and magic bullets. ∎

Peter Rosset is executive director of Food First/The Institute for Food and Development Policy, and is a co-author of World Hunger: Twelve Myths, *Grove Press, 1998. More information on these issues can be found at www.foodfirst.org.*

> "We abuse land because we regard it as a commodity belonging to us. When we see land as a community to which we belong, we may begin to use it with love and respect."
>
> —Aldo Leopold, from *A Sand County Almanac*, 1949

French anti-globalization activist José Bové takes part in a protest against genetically modified foods during the G-8 Summit meeting in Genoa, Italy in 2001.

Genetically Engineered Foods

Changing the Nature of Nature

BY MARTIN TEITEL AND KIMBERLY WILSON

Imagine yourself one morning on a modern jet-liner, settling into your seat as the plane taxis toward the active runway. To pass the time you unfold your morning newspaper, and just as the plane's rapidly building acceleration begins to lift the wheels from the ground, your eye catches a front page article mentioning that engineers are beginning a series of tests to determine whether or not the new model airplane that you are in is safe.

That situation would never happen, you say to yourself. People have more foresight than that. Yet something we entrust our lives to far more often than airplanes — our food supply — is being redesigned faster than any of us realize, and scientists have hardly begun to test the long-term safety of these new foods.

For thousands of years, people have used the naturally occurring processes of genetics to gradually shape wild plants into tastier, more nutritious, and more attractive food for all of humanity. At the beginning of the 21st century enough genetically engineered crops are being grown to cover all of Great Britain plus all of Taiwan, with enough left over to carpet Central Park in New York. With this abrupt agricultural transformation, humanity's food supply is being placed in the hands of a few corporations who practice an unpredictable and dangerous science.

As we eat genetically altered food and read about new safety tests, we may start to realize that we are the unwitting and unwilling guinea pigs in the largest experiment in human history, involving our entire planet's ecosystem, food supply, and the health and very genetic makeup of its inhabitants. Worse yet, results coming in from the first objective tests are not encouraging.

Scientists regularly issue cautionary statements, ranging from problems with monarch butterflies dying from genetically modified corn pollen to the danger of violent allergic reactions to genes introduced into soy products, as well as experiments showing a variety of actual and suspected health problems for cows fed genetically engineered hormones and the humans who drink their milk.

Three features distinguish this new kind of food:

- First and most important, the food is altered at the genetic level in ways that could never occur naturally. As genes from plants, animals, viruses, and bacteria are merged in novel ways, the normal checks and balances that nature provides to keep biology from running amok are nullified.

- The second novel feature of the revolution in our food is that the food is owned. Not individual sacks of wheat or bushels of potatoes, but entire varieties of plants are now corporate products. The term "monopoly" takes on new power when one imagines a company owning major portions of our food supply, the one thing that every single person now and into the future will always be dependent on.

- Finally this new technology is "globalized." This means that local agriculture, carefully adapted to local ecology and tastes over hundreds and thousands of

> **We may start to realize that we are the unwitting and unwilling guinea pigs in the largest experiment in human history, one involving our entire planet's ecosystem, food supply, and the health and very genetic makeup of its inhabitants.**

years, must yield to a planetary monoculture enforced by intricate trade agreements and laws.

Biotech's commandeering of our food is widespread, but hardly inevitable. Tens of thousands of natural seeds still exist to form the basis of a diverse, healthy, and locally controlled food supply that will be put into the hands of farmers and food suppliers and all the rest of us, for the sake of our health and our environment, and for the future that we leave to our children's children. ∎

Martin Teitel is President of the Council for Responsible Genetics and edits GeneWatch *magazine. Kimberly Wilson works on the GE-Free Food campaign for Greenpeace. Excerpted from* Genetically Engineered Foods: Changing the Nature of Nature, *by Martin Teitel and Kimberly Wilson, Park Street Press, 2001.*

The Hidden Grain in Meat

BY STEPHANIE KEMPF

One billion of the world's people do not get enough to eat and half the grain grown in the world is fed to livestock. Why? To fatten the cattle up for sale to people who can afford to buy expensive meat. (Chronically hungry people rarely have the money to buy beef.)

Most cattle today do not graze freely on pasture grasses — if they did, their meat would be leaner and healthier. Instead, they are penned up in crowded "feed-lots" and given large quantities of grain. The meat from grain-fed cattle is higher in fat.

For every 16 pounds of grain fed to a steer we get only one pound back in meat on our plates. Producing that pound of meat requires 2,500 gallons of water. (In many areas of the world people do not have access to even a small amount of clean drinking water and must walk miles a day to get it.)

Math: If your entire class went to McDonald's and each student ate one quarter-pounder, how much grain was used to produce the class's lunch? How much water was used?

Explain why you think this is or is not a problem. If it is a problem, what are possible solutions?

From Finding Solutions to Hunger: Kids Can Make a Difference, *New York: World Hunger Year, 1997.*

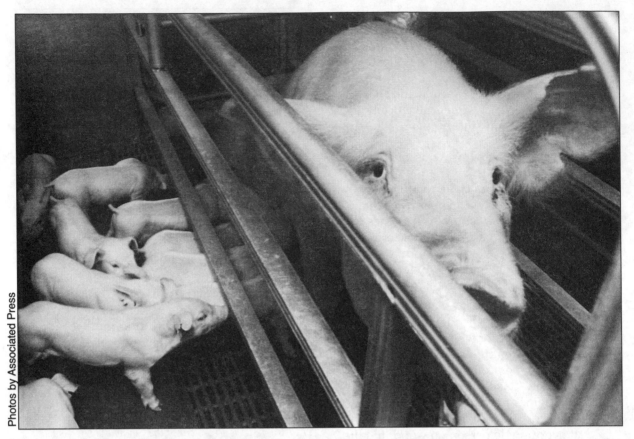

Photos by Associated Press

Top: A sow nurses her pigs at a University of Nebraska research center. After scientists at the school claimed to have developed a new breed of pig that delivers larger litters, the biotechnology giant Monsanto bought exclusive rights to the breed for 10 years. Bottom: An ear grown from human cells on the back of a mouse in Shanghai, China. The ear is meant for reconstructive surgery.

No Patents on Life!

The plants, animals, and microorganisms comprising life on earth are part of the natural world into which we are all born. The conversion of these species, their molecules or parts into corporate property through patent monopolies is counter to the interests of the peoples of this country and the world.

No individual, institution, or corporation should be able to claim ownership over species or varieties of living organisms. Nor should they be able to hold patents on organs, cells, genes, or proteins, whether naturally occurring, genetically altered or otherwise modified. ■

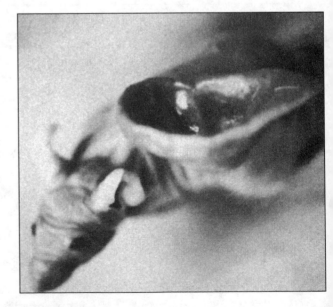

Excerpted from a petition of the No Patents on Life! campaign organized by the Council for Responsible Genetics. Thousands of people in more than 50 countries have signed it. For more information contact CRG at www.genewatch.org.

234 **RETHINKING GLOBALIZATION** ▪ TEACHING FOR JUSTICE IN AN UNJUST WORLD

Nature Is Not for Sale

We, indigenous peoples from around the world, believe that nobody can own what exists in nature except nature herself. A human being cannot own its own mother. Humankind is part of Mother Nature, we have created nothing and so we can in no way claim to be owners of what does not belong to us. But time and again, western legal property regimes have been imposed on us, contradicting our own cosmologies and values.

We view with regret and anxiety how Article 27.3b of the Trade-Related Aspects of Intellectual Property Rights (TRIPS) of the World Trade Organization (WTO) Agreements* will further denigrate and undermine our rights to our cultural and intellectual heritage, our plant, animal, and even human genetic resources, and discriminate against our indigenous ways of thinking and behaving. This Article makes an artificial distinction between plants, animals, and microorganisms and between "essentially biological" and "microbiological processes" for making plants and animals. As far as we are concerned, all these are life forms and life-creating processes which are sacred and which should not become the subject of proprietary ownership.

We know that intellectual property rights as defined in the TRIPS Agreement are monopoly rights given to individual or legal persons (e.g., transnational corporations) who can prove that the inventions or innovations they made are novel, involve an innovative step, and are capable of industrial application. The application of this form of property rights over living things as if they are mechanical or industrial inventions is inappropriate. Indigenous knowledge and cultural heritage are collectively and accretionally evolved through generations. Thus, no single person can claim invention or discovery of medicinal plants, seeds, or other living things.

The inherent conflict between these two knowledge systems and the manner in which they are protected and used will cause further disintegration of our communal values and practices. It can also lead to infighting between indigenous communities over who has owner-ship over a particular knowledge or innovation. Furthermore, it goes against the very essence of indigenous spirituality, which regards all creation as sacred.

[The TRIPS Agreement] will lead to the appropriation of our traditional medicinal plants and seeds and our indigenous knowledge on health, agriculture, and biodiversity conservation. It will undermine food security, since the diversity and agricultural production on which our communities depend would be eroded and would be controlled by individual, private, and foreign interests.

Our proposals:

Article 27.3b should be amended to disallow the patenting of plants and animals including all their parts, meaning genes, gene sequences, cells, proteins, seeds, etc.

The provision for the protection of plant varieties... should:

- Disallow the use of patents to protect plant varieties.

- Build upon the indigenous methods and customary laws protecting knowledge and heritage and biological resources.

- Allow for the right of indigenous peoples and farmers to continue their traditional practices of saving, sharing, and exchanging seeds; and harvesting, cultivating, and using medicinal plants.

- Prevent the appropriation, theft, and piracy of indigenous seeds, medicinal plants, and the knowledge around the use of these by researchers, academic institutions, and corporations, etc.

- Prevent the destruction and conversion of indigenous peoples' lands which are rich in biodiversity through projects like mines, monocrop commercial plantations, dams, etc. and recognize the rights of indigenous peoples to these lands and territories....

From a statement signed by indigenous peoples organizations, non-governmental organizations, and networks in more than 30 countries — United Nations, Geneva, Switzerland, July 1999.

Article 27 of the TRIPS (Trade Related Aspects of Intellectual Property Rights) Agreement of the WTO concerns patents. Section 3b requires that all WTO member governments protect patents on all kinds of life, including plant varieties, micro-organisms, and "biological processes" — such as genetic engineering — to produce plants and animals.

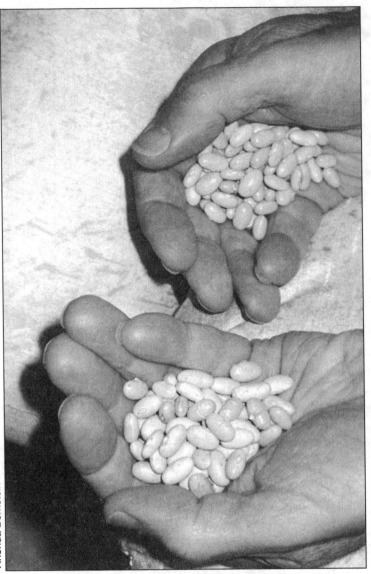

The enola beans patented by Colorado farmer Larry Proctor (top), and the mayacoba beans grown for generations in Mexico (bottom).

The Mystery of the Yellow Bean
The Politics of Patenting Foods

BY SANDY TOLAN

Meet bean person No. 1: Larry Proctor, in jeans, western shirt, and red beard, nodding to a sign by his scalehouse — "Red Beard Beans." We're on the Western Slope of the Colorado Rockies, in a stunning valley framed by the San Juans, the Raggeds, and Needle Rock. "The house due to the east of us here is the house that I was raised at and the farm that I grew up on," says Proctor. The mountains to the northeast of us hide the town of Aspen.

From the southeast, the Gunnison River runs down Black Canyon and into irrigation canals to water this hard, rocky valley, and its rows of corn and peas, onions, and beans. It is in this place, a few miles away, that Larry Proctor began work on what he calls a new invention.

In Mexico a while back, Larry Proctor bought a bag of beans at a local market. Some of them were beans he'd never seen before: creamy color, with a yellowish tint. He was curious. So he brought them over to his friend Harold, a retired dairyman whose home sat on a piece of land far from other bean fields — so that the two men could try out an idea, without fear of cross-pollination from other plants.

Proctor points to where they planted the yellow beans and says, "We planted them here because, at that time, none of the farm ground in this area here grew beans." They laid the seeds in the earth, and began to watch, generation after generation, selecting each time for ever-yellower colors. With each generation, Proctor says, the roots ran deeper than other bean plants; the pods were more hardy, more resistant to moisture.

"Every day [Harold would] call up and say, 'Well this one's flowering, that one's flowering. Man, those are mondo leaves!' Every day. And he'd say, 'Come over!'" Proctor explains. "I started getting the idea that there was something going on, and that there might be something worthwhile out of our basically playing. And eventually, kind of like a light, it just kind of dawned."

This was special, Proctor thought, and he wanted to protect it. So he applied for and got a plant variety protection certificate from the U.S. Department of Agriculture, which gave his family-run company exclusive rights to multiply the new creation: the enola bean, after his wife's middle name. Then he went a step further, to the U.S. Patent and Trademark Office, to apply for a patent for his new invention. This would prevent others from developing any new beans based on the enola. And, he thought, it would give hurting farmers in this valley a chance to grow beans that could fetch a better price. In 1999, the government awarded the patent to Proctor's company. The basis of the patent? Its color.

MARTÍN ROBLES AND THE MAYACOBA

Twelve hundred miles to the south, meet bean person No. 2.

Martín Robles is an agronomist who works with a bean cooperative in Los Mochis, Mexico, near Tobolabampo and the Sea of Cortez. We stand on the soil of the Rio Fuerte valley, good land for beans, watered by the rivers of the Sierra Madre. Martín explains his surroundings: "Right now we are seeing here a lot of different kinds of beans. Some alluvial beans, some canario beans, some asufrado beans, grown for tests...."

All around us are men with clipboards and baseball caps, fingering leaves, crouching in front of seed pods. "This is *campo experimental*, experimental field. There are some agronomists working here all the time, doing research and trying to improve the characteristics of the crop," says Robles. It is here, Robles says, that Mexican breeders came up with their own new life form. He says the beans have been around. Years ago, archaeologists discovered yellow beans in a cave in the Peruvian Andes and dated them back at least four millennia, to before the Incas. Thousands of years later, Mexican agronomists crossed two yellow-tinted varieties and came up with the modern version of the yellow bean. This was back in 1978. They called it mayacoba, after a nearby village in Sinaloa state. Mayacobas have been coming out of this valley, thousands of tons worth, ever since.

Robles says, "It's ironic that people here developed that variety of beans, that they actually have a name, mayacoba beans, for the community that first grew them. Some researchers here devoted many years to do research and experiments. And in two or three years, someone [Larry Proctor] claimed them as their own invention."

REBECCA GILLILAND: A BEAN EXPORTER SHUT DOWN

All this brings us to bean person No. 3 and her Nogales, Mexico warehouse, buzzing with forklifts carting not beans but fresh produce, from semi-trailer to drive-in cooler. If Rebecca Gilliland had her way, the coolers wouldn't even be running. This warehouse would be choked with bags of yellow beans. Instead?

Gilliland says, "We have eggplants, we have roma tomatoes, we have cucumbers, we have pickles...." But not a hill of beans in sight. In the early '90s, Gilliland retired as a small oil producer in California and came to Arizona, wanting to do something at the onset of the North American Free Trade Agreement. She traded produce for a couple of years, but all the time kept thinking of the yellow beans she ate as a child, two hundred miles to the south, in Obregon, Mexico.

"In 1994 I was missing, here in the United States, the beans they've been eating in Mexico," says Gilliland, "the one I grew up with, the peruano mayacoba. It's very, very delicious. Once you eat this bean, you never eat the pinto again. The taste is so unique."

"Besides the taste, it doesn't give you gas," she laughs.

Mexicans love these beans, Rebecca Gilliland thought, and more and more Mexicans are living in the United States. So she started talking to Martín Robles' colleagues down in Los Mochis about exporting the Mexican yellows. Soon she was doing it, building up the business slowly, working on the distributors and grocery chains.

"They don't want to buy in the beginning," Gilliland says. "I say, 'Fine, don't buy it. Just let me put it there. If you sell it, good, you pay for it. If you don't we come and pick it up.' So they did. And they sell it. As soon as the consumers know that they're bringing that kind of bean into the United States, they started requesting it. And the demand started getting bigger and bigger, you know."

The first year, Gilliland says, she imported half a million pounds of yellow beans; then a million. And by 1999, she says, she was up to 6 million pounds, or about a semi-truck load every couple of days. The next year, she says, business was to triple. The market was ready.

"In '99, the whole dream collapsed," says Gilliland.

> "They actually have a name, mayacoba beans, for the community that first grew them. And in two or three years, someone claimed them as their own invention."

That's when a letter arrived from Larry Proctor's company in Colorado, saying they invented the yellow bean. "And it was against the law," says Gilliland, "illegal for me to continue bringing that bean from Mexico. So they say they're very proud to notify me that they own the patent, they invent it. In the beginning I thought it was a joke." She laughs.

In fact, Proctor's company now owned the U.S. patent for any beans falling within a range of yellow on the color spectrum. And so Larry Proctor, with associates and a legal team, flew down for a meeting with Becky Gilliland on the border.

"They asked me when I started selling the beans. And I told the guy, 'Way before you invented it. These beans are from Mexico, and these beans are being legally declared through customs. We're not smuggling anything.' And I say it's very surprising that you just invent it when I've been eating it for 30 years, you know?" Gilliland says.

Proctor suggested they could work it out if she paid a licensing fee — up to 6¢ per pound. For bringing in the very beans she grew up eating? Gilliland didn't think so. So Proctor's lawyers slapped a patent complaint on her desk, saying, "You are legally served."

WHO OWNS THE BEANS?

Now suddenly this was no ordinary hill of beans, and a lot more than three people were fighting over it. Some were lawyers, some were farmers, and some represented an astonished Mexican government. Ricardo Hernandez Muñoz, a commerce specialist in the international affairs division of Mexico's Department of Agriculture, says, "We got to the point where we said, 'Well, I don't know where they got the idea that they can register something that's used all the way back to the Aztecs!'"

"I thought, well, let's register hamburgers then. And let's charge a penny for every hamburger that an American eats. It's the same way. It's something that's part of the country. You cannot take it out just and say, 'Hey, I discovered a yellow bean.' Sorry, my friend. That has existed for more than nations," Muñoz says.

Bean breeders in the United States and Latin America tend to agree. The Center for International Tropical Agriculture, in Cali, Colombia, is challenging Proctor's patent. The action is pending before the U.S. Patent and Trademark Office. CIAT holds 260 kinds of yellow beans in its public seed collection. It has done DNA analysis comparing six of those yellow varieties to Proctor's beans.

The findings, according to center director Joachim Voss: "We're comparing the genetic fingerprint of the enola beans with the most likely candidates in our gene bank, and what we've found preliminarily is that we have an identical print with a number of other varieties that we have in our gene bank."

Plant geneticists say there wasn't enough time between when Proctor first bought the beans in Mexico — 1994, according to his patent application — and when he first applied for the patent, to make a real invention. Proctor now says he went to Mexico in 1990 — hasn't been back since, he says again and again — a timeline which could give more credibility to his claim of having had sufficient breeding time to invent a new bean.

THESE BEANS LOOK YELLOW, YOUR BEANS LOOK YELLOW

Back on the Western Slope, Jason Proctor, Larry's son, is flanked by rows of one-ton bags of yellow beans; before him is a quivering, bubbling, dry, yellow river — beans on the march down the sorter. "As they come across the conveyer up atop of the roof," Jason explains, "you can see where they're dropping into this bin. This is a series of four screens here that take out sticks, dirt clods, rocks, and splits."

I pick up a handful. They look to me a lot like the mayacobas from Mexico. I'd like to look at the two kinds side by side, but Larry Proctor says no. On the advice of counsel, he says I can't take them with me.

Later, by the patch of land where the enola was born, Larry Proctor insists: The enola is not the same as the mayacoba. "It's not. It's not of the same color. It's not the same as what I started with here," Proctor reiterates.

This seems as good a time as any to pull some beans, yellow and from Mexico, from my pocket. "Well you know what, I brought a few beans. Do these look familiar? They're yellow."

Proctor replies, "Notice the darkness of the bean and how round it is here. In my warehouse you saw beans that were more oblong."

"So these are different to you. These beans look yellow; your beans look yellow. But you see a difference?" I ask.

"I can see a difference."

So, I ask Proctor, if they are so different, then how could the beans from Mexico be infringing on your patent? He suggests that some of the beans Becky Gilliland was importing could actually have been enolas. He tells the story of some enolas he shipped down to a trade show in Mexico City a few years ago. They never arrived; perhaps, he suggests, they were intercepted. Or there's the possibility that Mexican migrants, who work the fields nearby, could be responsible.

"And a lot of those people, they stock up on yellow beans for their trip home," Proctor adds. "And where they take it, and what they do with that, is not always known to us."

It's not clear why anyone would want to take Larry Proctor's enolas to Mexico, and re-export them to the United States, when Mexico has had the mayacoba for decades.

A WISE USE OF
THE PATENT SYSTEM?

Whatever differences may exist between the enola and the mayacoba, when it comes to getting them to the marketplace, they seem to be treated pretty much the same. A bean trader in Denver says every time he gets a bag of enolas from Larry Proctor, he slaps a mayacoba label on it so consumers know what they're getting. Warehouses in Los Angeles and Chicago say as far as they're concerned, the beans are interchangeable. Most seem to agree that this niche Latino market in the United States, dominated now by Proctor's enola beans, was created with the initiative of Rebecca Gilliland, the would-be bean trader in Nogales.

Gilliland says after Proctor demanded that U.S. Customs agents begin inspecting her yellow bean shipments at the border, and with Proctor's lawsuit and demands of up to 6¢ a pound for a licensing fee, her Mexican growers had had enough.

In Mexico, not even a trickle of beans heads north to the border. Anticipating NAFTA, the bean co-op in the Rio Fuerte Valley made a big investment in the sorters and stoners that made for an export quality yellow bean — equipment that now lies idle, except when curious visitors pass.

Bean breeders all over the United States wonder: If you can patent a yellow bean, why not a black bean? Or a red bean, or a navy bean? Is this the proper way, they ask, to use the patent sys-

tem? Another U.S. patent has been granted to a popping bean, whose origin lies in Peru. And to a variety of American basmati rice, with genetic heritage in the Indian subcontinent. And there are patents for corn and soybean, genetically engineered to resist herbicides, and rice infused with Vitamin A. And for pesticides based on the genetic properties of the Neem tree in India.

> "The problem arises in an increasingly competitive global climate that corporations and individuals seek any means available to gain competitive advantage."

CLAIMING GENETIC WEALTH

Back in Colombia, CIAT director Joachim Voss says: "The problem arises in an increasingly competitive global climate that corporations and individuals seek any means available to gain competitive advantage." In the current climate, public seed banks like CIAT are now demanding that researchers in the United States and elsewhere sign agreements not to use the seed for commercial purposes, lest this public knowledge get locked up by private interests. Now Voss's colleagues at CIAT find themselves urging Third World countries to lay claim to their genetic heritage before someone else claims it. Voss also suggests protecting a name, like France did for champagne or the Scots did for Scotch whiskey, but India has not done for basmati.

As crop varieties come increasingly under the patent system, he says, farmers in the Third World will now have to get their minds around an utterly foreign concept. "I've worked with farmers in Asia, Africa, Latin America," says Voss. "Universally those farmers freely exchange varieties between themselves as a form of reciprocal seed exchange. And they're delighted when someone else recognizes the value of the varieties that they are using. For them the idea that you might put proprietary claim on a variety is coming from the moon, if I can use that expression. It's just totally outside the realm of their social values." ∎

Sandy Tolan is co-founder of Homelands Productions, which specializes in stories about the intersection of the global economy and local communities. A similar version of this story was broadcast in 2001 on American Radio Works, a documentary collaboration between Minnesota Public Radio and National Public Radio News.

TOMASITO'S TOUR
A Guide to America's Food

STOP ONE

Tomasito's tour begins on land in the state of Jalisco, Mexico. The land was acquired by the U.S.-based Jolly Green Giant Company in partnership with a Mexican development corporation. Mexican farmers used to work this land together on communally owned cooperative farms called *ejidos*. Reforms in the 1980s opened up Mexican agriculture to large-scale private investment and pushed small landholders off the land.

STOP TWO

The next stop on Tomasito's tour is Davis, California, headquarters of Calgene Inc. where the tomato seed that produced Tomasito was developed. The seed is a hybrid, patented and owned by this transnational company. The seed was originally developed from a Mexican strain. With a research grant paid for by U.S. taxpayers, transnational companies are fighting for longer and stronger protection of their seed patents.

STOP THREE

Now Tomasito stops in St. Louis, Missouri, headquarters of Monsanto Corporation, a large transnational chemical manufacturer. To prepare the land for the mass cultivation and export of tomatoes, the land is first fumigated with chemicals. After the crops are planted, they are sprayed with more chemicals to kill insects and weeds. Monsanto produces these chemicals, and is one of the largest polluters in America.

STOP FOUR

Our tour now takes us to Emelle, Alabama, a poor, predominantly African-American community. Monsanto ships production waste from its manufacturing plant here to the world's largest hazardous waste landfill. Birth defects have increased in the community, as well as other unusual illnesses.

STOP FIVE

Tomasito takes us back to Mexico, where we meet local farm workers who make approximately U.S. $2.50 per day cultivating the land and harvesting the food which is exported. Growers give these workers no protection from the pesticides. They have no gloves, masks, or safety instructions, and no access to health care. The farm workers no longer have land on which to produce their own food, and cannot afford to buy the tomatoes they grow on the wages they earn.

STOP SIX

To take Tomasito and his friends to their final destiny, truckers drive across Mexico, through the U.S., and to Canada. Tomasito begins the trip with a poorly paid non-union Mexican driver who can take the produce only as far north as the border. There, the tomatoes are transferred to a warehouse while they wait for a new driver. The U.S. driver earns significantly more money for the same work as the Mexican. (Note: As of early 2002, it was still illegal for Mexican truckers to travel more than a few miles into the United States. The Mexican government was protesting, saying this was a violation of the North American Free Trade Agreement.)

STOP SEVEN

Our final stop is a fine Canadian restaurant where a customer orders a salad. The waitress, a Canadian woman, is serving up Tomasito. She was formerly employed in a food processing plant that closed down and moved production to Mexico. Workers in Canada and the United States are losing their jobs because they cannot afford to compete with low Mexican wages, which are kept far below their actual level of productivity [because it is difficult for workers there to organize unions]. The waitress now works part-time for minimum wage with no benefits. Like her Mexican friends in Canada, she cannot afford to order food in this restaurant.

adapted from *Many Faces of Mexico,* by Octavio Madigan Ruiz, Amy Sanders, and Meredith Sommers, Minneapolis, MN: Resource Center of the Americas, 1995.

Hunger Myths

BY FOOD FIRST/THE INSTITUTE FOR FOOD AND DEVELOPMENT POLICY

Hunger is not a myth, but myths keep us from ending hunger. At least 700 million people do not have enough to eat. Every year hunger kills 12 million children worldwide.

Why is there so much hunger? What can we do about it?

To answer these questions, we must unlearn much of what we have been taught. Only by freeing ourselves from the grip of widely held myths can we grasp the roots of hunger and see what we can do to end it. (See Teaching Ideas, p. 257, for ways to engage your students with this material.)

MYTH #1: THERE IS NOT ENOUGH FOOD TO GO AROUND.

Reality: Abundance, not scarcity, best describes the world's food supply. Enough wheat, rice, and other grains are produced to provide every human being with 3,500 calories a day. That doesn't even count many other commonly eaten foods — vegetables, beans, nuts, root crops, fruits, grass-fed meats, and fish. Enough food is available to provide at least 4.3 pounds of food per person a day worldwide: two and a half pounds of grain, beans and nuts, about a pound of fruits and vegetables, and nearly another pound of meat, milk, and eggs — enough to make most people fat! The problem is that many people are too poor to buy readily available food. Even most "hungry countries" have enough food for all their people right now. Many are net exporters of food and other types of agricultural products.

> Human institutions and policies determine who eats and who starves during hard times.

MYTH #2: NATURE IS TO BLAME FOR FAMINE.

Reality: It's too easy to blame nature. Human-made forces are making people increasingly vulnerable to natural events, like hurricanes or drought. Food is always available for those who can afford it — starvation during hard times hits only the poorest. Millions live on the brink of disaster in south Asia, Africa, and elsewhere, because they are deprived of land by a powerful few, trapped in the grip of debt, or miserably paid. Natural events rarely explain deaths; they are simply the final push over the brink. Human institutions and policies determine who eats and who starves during hard times. Likewise, in the United States many homeless die from the cold every winter, yet ultimate responsibility does not lie with the weather. The real culprits are an economy that fails to offer everyone opportunities, and a society that values economic efficiency over compassion.

MYTH #3: THERE ARE TOO MANY PEOPLE IN THE WORLD.

Reality: Although rapid population growth remains a serious concern in many countries, nowhere does population density explain hunger. For every Bangladesh, a densely populated and hungry country, we find a Nigeria, Brazil, or Bolivia, where abundant food resources coexist with hunger. Costa Rica, with only half of Honduras' cultivated acres per person, has a life expectancy — one indicator of nutrition — 11 years longer than that of Honduras and close to that of wealthier countries. Rapid population growth is not the root cause of hunger. Like hunger itself, it results from underlying inequities that deprive people, especially poor women, of economic opportunity and security. Rapid population growth and hunger are found especially in societies where land ownership, jobs, education, health care, and old age security are beyond the reach of most people.

MYTH #4: MORE TECHNOLOGY AND THE "GREEN REVOLUTION" WILL END HUNGER.

Reality: It's true that under the "Green Revolution" — which introduced new seeds and agricultural technology — food production increased. That's no myth. Thanks to the new seeds, millions of tons more grain a year are harvested. But focusing only on increasing production cannot stop hunger because it fails to change the unequal distribution of economic power that determines who can buy additional food. That's why in countries that were home to several of the biggest Green Revolution success-es — India, Mexico, and the Philippines — grain production, and in some cases exports, have climbed, while hunger has persisted and the long-term productive capacity of the soil is degraded.

MYTH #5: MORE LARGE FARMS ARE NEEDED TO FIGHT HUNGER.

Reality: Large landowners who control most of the best land often leave much of it idle. Unjust farming systems leave farmland in the hands of the most inefficient producers. By contrast, small-scale farmers typically achieve at least four to five times greater output per acre than large-scale farmers, in part because they work their land more intensively and use integrated, and often more sustainable, production systems. Without secure tenure, the many millions of tenant farmers in the Third World — farmers who rent their land from large landowners — have little incentive to invest in land improvements, to rotate crops, or to leave land fallow for the sake of long-term soil fertility. Future food production is undermined. On the other hand, redistribution of land can favor production. Comprehensive land reform has markedly increased production in countries as diverse as Japan, Zimbabwe, and Taiwan. A World Bank study of northeast Brazil estimates that redistributing farmland into smaller holdings would raise output an astonishing 80%.

> A World Bank study of northeast Brazil estimates that redistributing farmland into smaller holdings would raise output by an astonishing 80%.

MYTH #6: MORE FREE TRADE WILL HELP FEED THE PEOPLE OF EVERY COUNTRY.

Reality: Increasing trade between countries has failed to decrease hunger. In most Third World countries, exports have boomed while hunger has continued or actually worsened. While soybean exports boomed in Brazil — to feed Japanese and European livestock — hunger spread from one-third to two-thirds of the population. Where the majority of people have been made too poor to buy the food grown on their own country's soil, those who control productive resources will, not surprisingly, orient their production to more profitable markets abroad. Export crop production squeezes out basic food production. Pro-trade policies like the North American Free Trade Agreement (NAFTA) and the General Agreement on Tariffs and Trade (GATT) pit working people in different countries against each other in a "race to the bottom," where they compete to see who will work for less, without adequate health coverage or minimum environmental standards. The relationship between Mexico and the United States is a case in point: Since NAFTA took effect in 1994, the United States has had a net loss of 250,000 jobs, while Mexico has lost 2 million, and hunger is on the rise in both countries.

MYTH #7: MORE U.S. AID WILL HELP THE HUNGRY.

Reality: More U.S. government aid works directly against the hungry. Foreign aid can only reinforce, not change, the status quo. Where governments answer only to elites, foreign aid not only fails to reach hungry people, it strengthens the very people working against them. U.S. aid is used to impose free trade and free market policies, to promote exports at the expense of food production, and to provide the arms that repressive governments use to stay in power. Even emergency or humanitarian aid, which makes up only 5% of the total, often ends up enriching U.S. grain companies while failing to reach the hungry, and it can dangerously undercut local food production in the recipient country. It would be better to use the foreign aid budget for unconditional debt relief, as it is the foreign debt burden that forces most Third World countries to cut back on basic health, education, and anti-poverty programs. ∎

This article is adapted from the book World Hunger: Twelve Myths *(2nd edition), by Frances Moore Lappé, Joseph Collins and Peter Rosset, with Luis Esparza, New York: Grove, 1998. More information is available at the Food First website, www.foodfirst.org.*

A 4-year-old boy picks coffee beans in Palmira, Panama.

Associated Press/Julie Plasencia

Just a Cup of Coffee?

As consumers, we're taught to evaluate commodities based on price and quality. In this reading, Alan Durning suggests that we should also consider the environmental impact of commodity production: It's not "just a cup of coffee" — or anything else we eat or drink. See Teaching Ideas on p. 257 for activities related to this reading.

BY ALAN THEIN DURNING

BEANS

I brewed a cup of coffee.

It took 100 beans — about one-fortieth of the beans that grew on the bush that year. The bush was on a small mountain farm in the region of Colombia called Antioquia. The region was cleared of its native forest in the first coffee boom three generations ago. These "cloud forests" are among the world's most endangered ecosystems.

The beans ripened in the shade of taller trees. Growing them did not require plowing the soil, but it did take several doses of insecticides, which were synthesized in factories in the Rhine River Valley of Europe. Some of the chemicals entered the respiratory systems of farm workers.

Others washed downstream and were absorbed by plants and animals.

The beans were picked by hand. In a diesel-powered crusher they were removed from the fruit that encased them. They were dried under the sun and shipped to New Orleans in a 132 pound bag. The freighter was fueled by Venezuelan oil and made in Japan. The shipyard built the freighter out of Korean steel. The Korean steel mill used iron mined on tribal lands in Papua New Guinea.

At New Orleans the beans were roasted for 13 minutes at temperatures above 400 degrees F. The roaster burned natural gas pumped from the ground in Oklahoma. The beans were packaged in four-layer bags constructed of polyethylene, nylon, aluminum foil, and polyester. They were trucked to a Seattle warehouse and later to a retail store.

BAG

I carried the beans out of the grocery store in a brown paper bag made at an unbleached kraft paper mill in Oregon. I transported them home in an automobile that burned one-sixth of a gallon of gasoline during the five-mile round trip to the market.

GRINDER

In the kitchen, I measured the beans in a disposable plastic scoop molded in New Jersey and spooned them into the grinder. The grinder was assembled in China from imported steel, aluminum, copper, and plastic parts. It was powered by electricity generated at the Ross Dam on the Skagit River in Washington state.

I dumped the coffee in a gold-plated mesh filter made in Switzerland of Russian ore. I put the filter into a plastic-and-steel drip coffee maker.

I poured eight ounces of tap water into the appliance. The water came by pipe from the Cedar River on the west slope of the Cascade Mountains. An element heated the water to more than 200 degrees Fahrenheit. The hot water seeped through the ground coffee, dissolved some of its oils and solids, and trickled into a carafe.

PAPER CUP

The coffee mugs were all dirty so I poured the coffee into a paper cup. The cup was from wood pulp bleached in Arkansas. A fraction of the chlorine from the bleach was discharged from the pulp mill into the Arkansas River. In the river, the chlorine ended up as TCDD, which is often simply called dioxin. It is the most carcinogenic substance known.

CREAM

I stirred in one ounce of cream. The cream came from a grain-fed dairy cow in the lowlands north of Seattle. The cow liked to graze on a stream bank and walk in the stream. This muddied the water and made life difficult for native trout.

The cow's manure was rich in nitrogen and phosphorus. The soils of the pasture where the cow grazed were unable to absorb these quickly enough, so they washed into the stream when it rained. The infusion of nutrients fertilized algae, which absorbed a larger share of the oxygen dissolved in the water. The shortage of water made life more difficult for native trout.

SUGAR

I measured out two teaspoons of sugar. It came from the cane fields south of Lake Okeechobee in Florida. These plantations have deprived the Everglades of water, endangering waterfowl and reptile populations. ■

Alan Thein Durning is president of Northwest Environmental Watch. Previously he was a senior researcher at Worldwatch Institute, where he specialized in ecologically sound development. Durning is author of the prize-winning book, How Much is Enough? The Consumer Society and the Future of the Earth, *W.W. Norton, 1992. This article first appeared in* Adbusters *Magazine — www.adbusters.com.*

Emetario Pantaleón — *Campesino*

The old man works the earth most days before the sun pulls itself over the eastern ridges. With his horse grazing on the grassy borders of his field, he stoops over the black dirt, tilling the soil, removing weeds, and harvesting fresh vegetables and herbs. Those, in addition to dried beans and corn made into tortillas, provide breakfast, lunch, and supper for him and the other families who share this land, 365 days of the year.

He has spent most of his 97 years here, his world defined by the dry hills that ring this little valley, his soul anchored to this piece of ground.

His name is Emetario Pantaleón, and he is one of the few remaining members of the guerrilla army led by Emiliano Zapata during the Mexican Revolution. It was a war for the land, fought by the many who had nothing against the few who held almost all of it. It was a peasant's struggle, as bloody as any in the world.

"The days I come here I am content," Emetario says, his voice rising and his body shimmering with enthusiasm. "I need to feel the earth in my hands."

But now, just three generations after the revolt that won them their land, many of Mexico's *ejido** farmers face losing it once again. Emetario Pantaleón pulls off his sandals and lifts his face to the sun, "It is sad that the people leave the farms. It is the earth that sustains us," the old rebel says. "It is the earth that sets the mind free and cures the body of life's indignities. It is the earth that endures. This land. This very dirt. This life. This is what matters. These lands are not for sale."■

* Ejidos *are small farms in Mexico that have been owned by communities "in trust." They could not be sold, so people could not be forced to sell land if they fell into debt. Mexico changed its constitution in the early '90s, allowing for sale of* ejidos, *in order to ensure passage of the North American Free Trade Agreement, or NAFTA.*

Excerpted from an article by Oakley Biesanz, Octavio Madigan Ruiz, Amy Sanders, and Meredith Sommers, which is posted on our website, www.rethinkingschools.org/rg.

Facing the Farm Crisis

How Globalization Hurts Farmers and Destroys Farm Communities

BY STEVEN GORELICK

In country after country, farmers are said to be in "crisis," a word that only hints at the devastation of rural communities. In Europe, 200,000 farmers and 600,000 beef producers gave up agriculture in 1999. United Kingdom farm income, according to the *Farmer's Guardian*, has dropped by as much as 75% between 1998 and 2000, driving more than 20,000 farmers from the land. The price that British farmers actually receive for a commodity, called farm-gate prices, are so low that farmers are getting less for them than they cost to produce. This is true for virtually every commodity — including beef, lamb, milk, pork, chicken, eggs, rapeseed oil, fruits, and vegetables.

American farmers are doing no better. Farm income in the United States declined by nearly half between 1996 and 1999, with farm-gate prices so low at the end of 1998 that pork was selling for barely one-quarter of the farmer's break-even price. The U.S. Department of Agriculture estimated that the price for major commodities like cotton and soybeans in 2000 would be the lowest in more than 25 years. This economic disaster is translating directly into human suffering: Suicide is now the leading cause of death among American farmers, occurring at a rate three times higher than in the general population.

Since farmers and farm workers are the economic linchpins of their communities, entire rural economies are in decline. In the United Kingdom, for instance, 90% of rural businesses were forced to lay off staff in 1999. Rural economies also depend heavily on farmers: When 235,000 farms failed during the mid-1980s farm crisis in the United States, 60,000 other rural businesses went down with them.

If rural communities in the industrialized world are under siege, their counterparts elsewhere are even worse off. In China, for example, the modernization of agriculture has already led to the uprooting of more than half the rural population during the last two decades. Pastoralists in West Africa have been displaced by cheap meat imports from Europe, while Indian farmers — who grow traditional oilseeds like sesame, linseed, and mustard — are being driven under by soya imported from the United States. Mexican beef producers are losing ground to U.S. producers, whose inroads into Mexico's markets have tripled since NAFTA took effect in 1994.

EXPORT-LED DESTRUCTION

It is not surprising that farmers, connected as they are to an immobile landscape, suffer in a globalized economy that subsidizes mobility and rewards those with no allegiance to place. Today's economic "winners" include investors who scour the planet for the highest return, moving capital from country to country at electronic speeds. Farmers, however, can't simply pull up stakes and move their farm. Once they are hooked into the global economy, they are easily victimized by an economic and technological juggernaut that destroys the smallest and most localized enterprises. Nonetheless, the precise aim of agricultural policy almost everywhere is to pull farmers into an export-led global economy that is likely to be their undoing.

Meanwhile, most policymakers are so wedded to their economic assumptions that they are unable to acknowledge how disastrous the globalization of food has been for rural communities. Even when the negative impact of the global economy is acknowledged, governments usually prescribe more of the same as a remedy: They call for expanded export markets, lower trade barriers (particularly in other countries), improved "productivity"

> Today's economic "winners" include investors who scour the planet for the highest return, moving capital from country to country at electronic speeds. Farmers, however, can't simply pull up stakes and move their farm.

through higher technology and — in rare moments of honesty — fewer farmers.

What the framers of farm policy must be aware of, however, is that the very structure of today's global economy is fatal for the small farmer. Not so long ago, each region offered numerous economic niches for small, diversified farms, which provided the wide range of products nearby consumers needed.

The globalization of food, on the other hand, forces every region to specialize in whichever commodity its farmers can produce most cheaply, and to offer those products on global markets. Almost all foods consumed locally, meanwhile, must be brought in from elsewhere.

The highly specialized farms this system favors are most "efficient" when they are large, monocultural, and employ heavy machinery. Attaining the scale needed and the equipment required can drain capital reserves of all but the biggest farmers, saddling the rest with a debt burden few can escape. Eventually, small farms are driven under, their lands consolidated into those of the largest and wealthiest farmers.

> Large corporations now monopolize almost every aspect of farm production and distribution from seeds, fertilizers, and equipment to processing, transporting, and marketing.

THE TECHNOLOGICAL TREADMILL

The continual need to purchase the latest equipment, the most potent chemical inputs, and the highest-yielding seeds places farmers firmly on the "technological treadmill." Advances in technology may raise single-crop yields, but they also often lower the farmer's net income: Capital expenses, debt service, and production costs eat up a higher proportion of the farmer's proceeds, while overall increases in output merely cause the price of global commodities to drop. In the United States, for example, factory farming techniques — including carefully controlled heating and lighting, specially formulated feed, and heavy doses of antibiotics — enable the average poultry producer to raise 240,000 birds each year. But after expenses this prodigious (and inhumane) production earns the farmer only $12,000, or a mere 5¢ per bird.

Meanwhile, the global economy's emphasis on free trade often forces farmers into competition with producers in countries where costs are lower due to more favorable climate and geography, lower labor costs, or less stringent environmental standards. Farmers are pressured to become still more "efficient" by increasing the size of their farms, becoming more narrowly specialized, and adopting newer technologies. The treadmill speeds up, and farmers inevitably fall further behind.

Farmers in the global South face similar problems. Those still embedded in a local economy can feed their families with their diversified production, selling the remainder in local markets. But those who have been drawn into the global food system must specialize their production for export, using the income to buy food. A farmer in South America or Africa can easily be destroyed by a recession in Europe or a bigger-than-expected harvest in Asia. Meanwhile, an increasing proportion of the newly "modernized" farmers' proceeds must be used to pay for equipment and inputs, placing them, as well, on the technological treadmill. The smallest farmers cannot afford those inputs, and are eventually pushed out of agriculture altogether.

CORPORATIZING AGRICULTURE

Another detrimental effect of the globalization of food is the immense power global corporations have accumulated. The selling of food to consumers, for example, has increasingly shifted from independent shopkeepers to huge supermarket chains whose virtually identical outlets colonize rural economies. In the United Kingdom, each out-of-town retail development built by 1992 corresponded with the closing of roughly 10 independent shops. During the 1990s, some 1,000 locally owned groceries, bakeries, butchers, and fish markets closed each year.

Overall, food corporations take an ever-increasing share of the price people pay for food, while the farmers' share keeps shrinking. In the United States, only 21¢ of every dollar spent on domestically produced food goes to farmers, while the remaining 79¢ goes to corporate middlemen and marketers.

Large corporations now monopolize almost every aspect of farm production and distribution from seeds, fertilizers, and equipment to processing, transporting, and marketing. Through its ownership of grain elevators, rail links, terminals, and the barges and ships needed to move grain around the world, one company, Cargill, controls 80% of global grain distribution. Four other companies control 87% of U.S. beef, and another four control 84% of American cereal. Five agribusinesses (AstraZeneca, DuPont, Monsanto, Novartis, and Aventis) account for nearly two-thirds of the global pesticide market, almost one-quarter of the global seed market, and virtually 100% of the genetically engineered seed market. Control over food has become so concentrated that in the United States, 10¢ out of every food dollar now goes to Philip Morris; 6¢ goes to Cargill.

ENDING CORPORATE FEUDALISM

With corporations firmly in control, farmers hooked to the global economy have been reduced to little more than serfs in a corporate feudal system. This metaphor is nowhere more appropriate than in the U.S. hog and poultry industries, where Continental, ConAgra, and Tyson effectively dictate the prices farmers will receive.

Many dispossessed rural people are coming to understand the broad systemic forces that are undermining economies and cultures the world over. But the mix of hopelessness and anger, particularly in America's economically broken heartland, has made others receptive to right-wing conspiracy theories that blame rural woes on racial minorities, Catholics, immigrants, a "Jewish banking conspiracy," or a world government run by the United Nations and policed by swarms of black helicopters.

The message, surely, must be a clear one: We need a new way of farming. We need new approaches to agriculture by governments, policymakers and farmers themselves. This is not some pipe dream: It can be done. These problems can be tackled at both policy level and on the ground, in the farmyard itself. ∎

Steven Gorelick coordinates U.S. programs for the International Society for Ecology and Culture. A version of this article first appeared in The Ecologist magazine, Vol. 30, No. 4, June 2000.

Campaign for Labor Rights

Farmers shovel wheat at the grain market of Amritsar, India.

Relocalization, Not Globalization

BY VANDANA SHIVA

We are often told that when farmers, NGOs (non-governmental organizations) or campaigners in the global North oppose the current system of trade in agriculture they are being "protectionist." This is used as a derogatory term, implying backwardness, selfishness, and a desire to cling to privilege. The supporters of open trade in agricultural produce can often be heard saying that the poor of the global South "need" — indeed are desperate for — access to the markets of the West. To deny them this "market access" is to deny them the chance to "develop" as the West has done. And what, after all, could be worse than that?

In fact, the term "market access" like the term "development" is actually a weapon used by the rich against the poor. It has become a catch-all phrase that facilitates the process of robbing the poor of the South of their last resources and their

meager means of survival for the benefit of northern market hegemony. "Market access" has become the new code word for giving priority to exports above local needs, and putting the resources of the South in the service of luxuries of the North and the profits of the big corporations.

In fact, what would be best for farmers everywhere — in Europe, Africa, Asia, and in my country, India — is a focus on relocalizing production and consumption, and on meeting the needs of everyone, rather than corporations, rich consumers and amorphous "global markets."

Currently, crops grown in Thailand, Brazil, and India provide cattle feed for Europe's intensive livestock industry. Scarce land in Colombia and India is diverted to produce flowers for Europe. African countries produce green beans for American markets while African children are denied access to basic food and nutrition.

This, at root, is what the market is about.

Each kilogram of food traveling across the world, from poor producer to rich consumer, produces 10 kilograms of CO_2, the leading contributor to global warming. And it is the poor of the global South who bear the costs of this, too. The drought in Gujarat and Rajasthan, India, the worst in living memory, has left millions without food and water. These are the costs of globalization and export-driven economies. Who do they benefit?

Not us.

The alternative is relocalization — and it is a realistic alternative. It does not imply "going backwards," it implies living within the limits set by nature and ourselves. Relocalization in the global North would mean that the poor in the South, who depend on scarce land, water, and biodiversity, have access to livelihoods and resources for meeting their own needs and, importantly, have the possibility of conserving their resources for themselves.

They would not be forced to grow export crops for the rich, from which they see little benefit.

The language of "market access" through globalization and free trade is often linked to "special and differential" treatment for the South. But the banana dispute decided by the WTO, for example, robbed Caribbean banana growers of their markets in Europe. [The WTO ruled that it was an unfair trade practice for European nations to buy a certain amount of bananas from small growers from Caribbean countries, many of them former colonies. The U.S. government made the WTO complaint on behalf of large corporations, especially Chiquita, which grow bananas on huge plantations in Central and South America with poorly paid workers.]

The "market access" rules of the WTO work for the Chiquita banana corporation, not the small holder. They work for Cargill, not the Punjab farmer. Special and differential treatment is excluded by the rules of "free trade," and market access is embedded in such rules. But it is market access based on relocalization, not market access based on globalization which will provide fair, just, and sustainable markets to the poor people of the Third World. Relocalization combined with fair trade would recover the banana markets for the Caribbean peasant.

Relocalization implies, very simply, that what can be grown and produced locally should be used locally, so that resources and livelihoods can be protected. Since the West will never be able to grow tea, coffee and bananas, the South will have its markets for these unique tropical products. There will be trade, but it will be fair, and on the South's terms.

Relocalization everywhere — in the South and in the North — would conserve resources, generate meaningful work, fulfill basic needs and strengthen economic and political democracy. I hope that people of the North will bring about movements for self-rule and localization, so that the environmental and economic burden is lifted from the South, and we can all shape our economies, political systems, and resource-use patterns to provide for our own needs, together. ∎

> "Market access" has become the new code word for giving priority to exports above local needs, and putting the resources of the South in the service of luxuries of the North and the profits of the big corporations.

Vandana Shiva, director of the Research Foundation for Science, Technology and Ecology, is a physicist and one of India's leading social and ecological justice activists. This article is excerpted from The Ecologist, *Vol. 30 #4, June 2000.*

Associated Press/Marta Lavandier

An 8-year-old boy picks green beans in Homestead, Florida.

Cebolleros

BY BENJAMIN ALIRE SÁENZ

Cebolla *is Spanish for onion* — cebolleros: *those who work in the onion fields.*

1967

My father lost his job that spring. That was the way of the construction business. That spring, no one was building. I heard my parents talking in the kitchen. I could hear them always — I could hear everything from everywhere. No one had any secrets. I was sitting in our room trying to read a book. I used to get lost in books, but that evening I wasn't lost. My parents were talking about what had to be done. The money my mother was making at the factory where she inspected pantyhose wasn't enough. It wouldn't be much of a summer without money. No swimming, no movies. No money, no summer. "I'll have to keep looking," my father said, "*tiene que haber trabajo*" [one has to have work]. And then he said that my older brother had to find a job to help out. I tried to imagine my brother working,

the brother I always fought with, the brother who slept in the same bed I did, my brother who was only one year older than me. Fifteen wasn't old enough to get a job. "He's too young," I heard my mother say, "*no quiero que se salga a trabajar tan joven*" [I don't want him to go to work so young].

"He can lie about his age," my father said. But I knew no one would believe he was old enough to work. He couldn't even grow a mustache. After a long silence my father said there might not be a job for him anyway, maybe a job for no one.

I heard my two younger brothers arguing over what they should watch on television. They were always fighting, but they were always happy. School would be out in another week. They would laugh and fight all summer. I walked out of our room and told them both to stop arguing or I'd turn off the television. They made faces at me — then laughed. Julian, the youngest, told me he wanted a television that showed things in color. "Just pretend," I told him, "it's more fun that way." I walked into the kitchen where my parents were drinking coffee. My father kept combing his hair with his fingers, always working. He had big hands, rough, strong like his voice. I stared at his mustache that covered his whole face. I wanted to say something but didn't know what, so I said nothing. I looked at my mother and smiled. She smiled back — we had secrets. I remember that spring.

There wasn't much to do after school let out. My father was home all the time, so we had to ask him for permission to do everything. It was better when he was working — when he was working, we could go anywhere we wanted. We couldn't even have a good fight because it made my father nervous. My brother and I kept wishing Dad would find a job before everyone exploded.

I was always reading books. Library books; long books about English people, novels about men and women falling in love in London or in the country. I remember thinking that where they lived was not like New Mexico. It was green, not like the desert. I imagined their rivers were blue, and they probably had boats, and the people in all those books didn't need to work. But I knew they were just books, and people didn't want to read books about people's work — so they kept the work out of it. I kept an eye on my younger brothers as I read, and every day it was my job to make lunch. Mostly I warmed up the food my mother left for us. My father was very quiet when we ate.

After two weeks, I heard my father tell my mother that we were going to pick onions. "Not much pay," he said, "*pero siquiera no me vuelvo loco*" [but it will keep me from going crazy]. That Sunday, my father told us that the onions were ready. He had spoken to a man he knew, and the man told him to come to the fields. "We're all going," he said. My brother and I looked at each other, but said nothing. "The kids too?" my older brother asked. "They can't stay here," my father said, "there's no one to take care of them. They can help us out."

Monday morning, when it was still dark, my mother woke us up with her whispers. She sounded like the rain. Everyone was too sleepy to say anything at breakfast, so we sat and heard each other eat. I watched my mother make the burritos, watched her hands move quietly. I watched her wide-awake face and the lines around her eyes. I wondered what she was thinking.

My father came into the kitchen and said it was time to go to the fields. I thought of the fields in the book I was reading, green and full of trees, English trees. My father reminded me and my brother that this was serious business. "We're here to work — not play. *No anden jugando*" [Don't go around playing]. We nodded and looked at each other. As we walked outside, the sky was already turning blue. The morning, cool and soft, reminded me of my grandfather. In the morning, his chocolate eyes had been almost blue, showing me everything I ever wanted to see.

My father had collected plastic buckets for the onions — empty five-gallon paint buckets that had been washed out. I looked at the scissors and turned them over in my hands. "I don't know how to use them," I told my brother. "Dad will show us," he said, "it'll be easy." He thought everything was easy. To me everything seemed hard like the cement driveway my father had poured last year.

We reached the fields as the sun lifted itself into the sky, turning the sky dusty blue. The people in the fields, wearing reds and pinks and blues, began claiming their rows. My father claimed some rows, and we followed him. My younger brothers were excited, and they kept running up and down the rows like it was a playground. The onions had been turned up by a machine and were lying on the ground waiting to be picked up. The smell of earth and onions dug into my skin, and I wanted to be an onion. I wanted to be the earth.

Everyone was talking. No one spoke English. I liked the sound of Spanish — it made me happy like the songs of my grandfather. My father went to talk to some of the men and then returned to the rows we had claimed and said we had to get to work. He looked at my brother and me and showed us how to clip the roots and

> "We're all going," he said. My brother and I looked at each other, but said nothing. "The kids too?" my older brother asked. "They can't stay here," my father said, "there's no one to take care of them. They can help us out."

the wilting tops. "We should have bought some gloves," he said, "but we can't be spending money on them right now. Maybe next week. You'll get blisters." He laughed. "It's all right, men's hands should have blisters."

I thought of the English novels where the men had no blisters on their hands, smooth, white hands — not like my father's. Dad rubbed my hair, and that made me smile. We got to work. I bent down and scooped up a smooth onion and cut it with my scissors, just the way my father had taught me. The snip sounded tinny as I cut the roots and the stems. Cutting. One onion, then another, then another. I was careful not to cut too close, because if I cut too close to the onion I'd ruin it, and we didn't get paid for ruining good onions. I watched myself cut the onions, cut them, and toss them carefully into my bucket until it was full. I pretended I was filling a basket with Easter eggs, yellow eggs, but it was hard to pretend because my hands were already getting blisters. The eggs were growing on my hands. "My hands are too soft," I mumbled, "they're not a man's hands." I stood straight, unbent my back, and showed my hands to my brother. He grinned and showed me his.

> We worked, we ate, we slept. I was getting used to the work, and we were up to 70 sacks of onions a day.

Onions, yellow onions the color of my grandfather's teeth.

In the next row two women were talking as they worked. They were fast, much better than me and my brother. I thought of a man I had once seen drawing a church — he did it fast, perfect — perfect like the women in the next row. I heard them talking, voices like guitars singing serious songs: "*Bueno, mi esposo es muy bueno pero toma mucho. Y mis hijos salieron peor. Dios mio, no se que voy hacer con esos hijos que tengo — pero son muy trabajadores*" [Good, my husband is a good man but he drinks too much. And my children are doing poorly. My god, I don't know what I am going to do with the kids that I have — but they are very hard workers].

My youngest brother came to take the bucket to empty it into a gunny sack. It was too heavy for him. I picked him up and threw him in the air — he was so small and happy. "Do it again," he yelled, "do it again." My other brother showed up, and together they carried the bucket of onions away. "This is fun," they yelled. But it wasn't. My back was beginning to feel bent and crooked. I arched myself as far back as I could — my neck stretching away from the ground. The woman in the next row smiled at me: "*Que muchachito tan bonito*" [What a handsome young boy]. I bowed my head, bent my back toward the earth again — toward the earth and the onions.

By the end of the day I did not know how many sacks of onions we had picked. My brother asked my father. "Thirty," he said. Thirty, I thought, maybe a world record. My brother and I looked at each other and smiled. "Your nose is sunburned," my brother said. "So is yours." We fell to the ground wrestling and

Associated Press/Eric Draper

A mother and her 6-year-old son pick chiles in Berino, New Mexico.

laughing. I heard my father talking to the men. They were laughing about something, too.

We walked back to my father's Studebaker, and my brother kept saying it was a dumb truck and that we needed a new one. He kept talking all the way home, but I wasn't listening. My nose was hurting; my back felt as if I had been carrying someone all day; my blisters were stinging. I wanted to go home and sleep. I didn't care how bad I smelled; I wanted to sleep or die or wake up in the fields of my novels. When we got home, my mother had dinner ready. She took my youngest brother in her arms and laughed. She looked so clean. She kissed me on the cheek and told me to take a shower.

I felt the hot water hit my body — I was a candle. I was melting into nothing. I ate the warm dinner but couldn't taste it. I was too tired to talk. My father told my mother we were going to have to work harder: "Only 30 sacks. *A viente y cinco centavos el costal nunca la vamos hacer* [At twenty five cents a bag we are never going to make it]. Tomorrow we'll work harder."

I went to bed and did not read my English novel. My brother told me he was glad I wasn't going to read because he hated for the light to be on while he was trying to sleep. "You read too damn much anyway." I looked at him and wanted to stick my fist through his face. I threw my book across the room and turned off the light. I dreamed I had a horse and lived in a house where they played only Mexican music, a house where I could dance in every room.

The second day was the same as the first, only we worked harder, and wore hats. By the end of the day, we had picked 55 sacks. It was better, but it still wasn't enough. I dreamed I was standing on a hill made of onions. There was a huge crowd of English people yelling at me: "*¡Cebollero! ¡Cebollero!*" I woke up and smelled the onions and the dry earth. I walked into the bathroom and threw up. I didn't read any more books that summer.

The whole week was the same. We worked, we ate, we slept. The second week was better. I was getting used to the work, and we were up to 70 sacks of onions a day. I started hating the sun and the earth and the onions, but the voices of the people played over and over in my mind, the music. The music kept me working.

We moved to another field in the middle of the

An 11-year-old boy picks chiles in Berino, New Mexico at sunrise.

second week. When we left the old field I felt I was leaving something behind, but when I searched with my eyes, I saw nothing but graying earth and sacks of onions waiting to be picked up by other workers who would sort them. I half-thought that if I looked in each sack, I would find people hiding.

The first day of the third week was the same — until the afternoon. The sun was hotter than usual — white, blinding, everything feeling as if it were touched by flames. My father made sure we were drinking plenty of water. The afternoon was too hot for talking, and everyone worked quietly. In the silence all I could hear was the onions being dumped into gunny sacks and scissors snipping at roots and stems, but the sounds were distant — almost as if the sun were swallowing all the sounds we made with our work. The fields were strange. We were in another country, a country I didn't know.

"I'm an onion," I said out loud, "but I don't want to be one." My brother looked at me and told me I was saying dumb things. "If you say something like that one more time, I'm going to tell Dad you've had too much sun." "I am an onion," I said, "and so are you." He shook his head and kept working.

In the heat I heard a voice yelling, and some of the people working in the fields ran and hid in a nearby ditch. Other people just kept working. I didn't know why people were hiding, and the woman in the next row told me not to say anything to the *Migra* [immigration officials]. "*Nomas no digas nada, mijo*" [Just don't say anything, my son]. I nodded, but I wasn't sure what she was talking about. I was keeping a secret but

I didn't know the secret. I looked at my brother and again I knew I was an onion.

The Border Patrol van stopped at the side of the road, and some men dressed in green uniforms got out and walked into the fields. They looked like soldiers. The men stopped and asked people questions. Some of the workers showed them pieces of paper and others showed them their wallets. One of the men in green came closer to our row. He asked the women in the row next to ours a strange question: "*¿Tienen papeles? ¿Permisos?*" [Do you have papers? Documents?] I smiled at his Spanish, not like music, not even like a language. The women spoke to him in fragmented English. "I don't need paper," one woman told one of the men in green. Her voice was angry like a knife. She showed him a driver's license and what I thought was a birth certificate. The officer reached for the document. She pulled it away. "I'll hold," she said, "don't touch." He nodded, and walked away. "*Muchachos*," he said to my brother and me, "*¿tienen papeles?*" Neither one of us said anything. I moved closer to my brother. He asked his question again. "I don't know what that is," I said. He smiled. "You're a U.S. citizen, are you?" "Yes, sir," we both said. "Who was the first president?" he asked. "That's easy," I said, "George Washington." He winked at us and kept walking down the row. I didn't go back to work until I knew my father was safe.

1985

The young man in his early 30s drove into the parking lot of the grocery store. Lines were forming around his eyes, and his hair was prematurely graying. He checked his coat pocket for the list his wife had made for him that morning. The afternoon sun was so hot it seemed to be melting everything, but the man did not seem to be bothered by the heat. He had a sort of lazy walk, and he was singing to himself in Spanish, a song, a Mexican song that was always sticking in his mind, and he swayed his body to the internal rhythm.

Inside the grocery store, he grabbed a cart and pretended he was driving a car in a race. He laughed to himself. He had given up trying to change — now he just enjoyed the games he played. He looked over the list and headed for the fresh vegetables. He felt the heads of lettuce and talked to them. He found just the right one and tossed it in his basket as though it were a ball going through a hoop. He smiled. He picked out fresh cilantro, tomatoes, jalapeños. He tore a plastic bag from the roll hanging above the vegetables and waited behind two women who were standing above the onion bin.

"God," one of them said, "these onions are absolutely beautiful. What would we do without onions?"

"Eat boring food, I suppose," the other answered. "Who invented them anyway?"

The other lady laughed. "No one invented them — the farmers grow them. It's amazing how farmers can grow things, isn't it?"

"And the nice thing about onions is that they're so cheap."

The man with the mustache nodded to himself. For a moment he did not seem like the happy young man who had skipped into the grocery store. He looked like a lost child, fenced in, a little boy who was lost in the fields of a summer in a country he had left but still dreamed of — a country that had claimed him forever, a country he would never understand. "Onions are cheap," he said aloud, "dirt cheap." ∎

Benjamin Alire Sáenz teaches at the University of Texas at El Paso. Excerpted from Flowers for the Broken, *Seattle: Broken Moon Press, 1992.*

Associated Press/Eric Draper

An 8-year-old girl carries a chile bucket in Berino, New Mexico.

The United Fruit Co.

BY PABLO NERUDA

When the trumpet sounded, it was
all prepared on the earth,
and Jehovah parceled out the earth
to Coca-Cola, Inc., Anaconda,
Ford Motors, and other entities:
The Fruit Company, Inc.
reserved for itself the most succulent,
the central coast of my own land,
the delicate waist of America.
It rechristened its territories
as the "Banana Republics"
and over the sleeping dead,
over the restless heroes
who brought about the greatness,
the liberty and the flags,
it established the comic opera:
abolished the independencies,
presented crowns of Caesar,
unsheathed envy, attracted
the dictatorship of the flies*,
Trujillo flies, Tacho flies,

Carias flies, Martinez flies,
Ubico flies, damp flies
of modest blood and marmalade,
drunken flies who zoom
over the ordinary graves,
circus flies, wise flies
well trained in tyranny.
Among the bloodthirsty flies
the Fruit Company lands its ships,
taking off the coffee and the fruit;
the treasure of our submerged
territories flows as though
on plates into the ships.
Meanwhile Indians are falling
into the sugared chasms
of the harbors, wrapped
for burial in the mist of the dawn:
a body rolls, a thing
that has no name, a fallen cipher,
a cluster of dead fruit
thrown down on the dump.

*Dictators of the Dominican Republic, Nicaragua ("Tacho" was Anastacio Somoza's nickname),
Honduras, El Salvador, and Guatemala, respectively.

Considered one of the finest poets of the 20th century, Pablo Neruda was born in Chile in 1904, the son of a railroad worker. This translation by American poet Robert Bly is from the book, Neruda and Vallejo: Selected Poems, *edited by Robert Bly, Boston: Beacon Press, 1971.*

Just Food?

"STEALING NATURE'S HARVEST"
Reading by Vandana Shiva (p. 224)

Some discussion questions:

- What is meant by the peasants' declaration, "We will give up our lives, but we will not give up our rice"?

- According to Shiva, what are the new "innovative ways" that the rich countries "steal nature's harvest"? What are all the different kinds of theft that Shiva describes in the article?

- What is meant by Shiva's statement that "The seed, for the farmer, is not merely the source of future plants and food; it is the storage place of culture and history"?

- Why would corporations believe that they can patent seeds developed over millennia by Third World farmers?

- Which, if any, of the resistance efforts described in the "food democracy" section do you think are effective?

Shiva's descriptions are often metaphorical: "for the farmer, the field is the mother;" the collective innovation of farmers and peasants has been "hijacked" by corporations; crops are described as "pesticide factories." As a way of literally picturing the concepts that Shiva introduces, students could do metaphorical drawings. Or wait until the end of the unit and do drawings on the theme of food and globalization.

"WE WILL REDUCE YOUR FIELDS TO ASHES"
Open letter from Indian farmers, (p. 228)

After reading the article, have students perform an improvisation involving farmers from the Karnataka State Farmers Association (KRRS) and farmers who have accepted Monsanto's offer of genetically modified seeds. KRRS activists have come to burn down the fields of the farmers who have accepted seeds from Monsanto. They worry that possible genetic pollution threatens food security in India, and their livelihoods.

Discuss with students the efficacy of the KRRS "Operation Cremation Monsanto" strategy. What effects do the farmers anticipate their actions will have? Encourage students to list and evaluate these.

Students could do a web-search to chart other global protests against unwanted genetic invasions. (We've found the simple "genetic engineering protest" effective as a web-search title in locating numerous sites and articles.)

How do Monsanto and other corporations listed here, e.g., Novartis, defend themselves? Have students also visit these websites to evaluate the pro-biotechnology arguments. Locate most corporate websites simply with the company name followed by ".com".

"THE PARABLE OF THE GOLDEN SNAIL"
(Reading by Peter Rosset, p. 230)

Before reading the article, tell the class to imagine that they are a group of Filipino farmers. Tell them that they are being offered genetically engineered seeds that will result in rice with increased amounts of Vitamin A and other vital nutrients. Many people in their families suffer ailments made worse by a lack of needed vitamins. Ask them to talk among themselves to decide what questions they have before deciding whether or not to accept the seeds.

Afterwards, read the article with students and compare Third World farmers' experiences with novel species to what students concluded.

"THE MYSTERY OF THE YELLOW BEAN"
(Reading by Sandy Tolan, p. 236)

Discuss:

- On what basis did Larry Proctor claim the right to patent the yellow bean, which he called the enola?

- Should Proctor have been given a patent?

- Should people be able to patent a type of food as their "innovation"? What are arguments in favor and opposed?

- When he learns of Proctor's patent, an official with the Mexican Department of Agriculture says, "Well, let's register hamburgers then. And let's charge a penny for every hamburger that an American eats. It's the same way." Do you agree? Is it the same?

- How does the enola/mayacoba story show how people in rich countries might benefit from the patent system at the expense of people in poor countries?

- Should countries start patenting their "genetic heritage" as Colombian Joachim Voss, director of the Center for International Tropical Agriculture, suggests, or should countries fight to change the entire patent system? If so, how?

"RICH LAND, POOR PEOPLE"
Reading by Oakley Biesanz, Octavio Madigan Ruiz, Amy Sanders, and Meredith Sommers (on the web, www.rethinkingschools.org/rg)

Before class, tape off the room into two sections — one totaling 12% of the "land" in the classroom, the other making up the remaining 88%. This represents the division of Mexico's arable land: 88% for the cultivation of export crops, and the grazing of cattle; 12% for small-scale farms that produce for local markets. Use this division as a visual emphasis of the amount of Mexican agricultural land that largely serves foreign export markets compared to the land used to grow food for Mexicans. This division of the classroom raises other simulation possibilities.

"TOMASITO'S TOUR"
Illustrated reading (p. 240)

Before students read "Tomasito's Tour," ask them to make two columns on a piece of paper and to label one "Who Benefits" and the other, "Who is Harmed." These can be completed individually, in small groups, or as a whole class. As they read, encourage students to consider groups not listed on the "tour." For example, the longer the distance that food is shipped, the more oil that is consumed — oil which increasingly is found on the land of indigenous groups in South America. Thus, indirectly these groups are harmed by Tomasito's long tour.

Afterwards, review students' lists with them

and ask: Where did you put yourself on that list? Are you personally a winner or loser from the globalization of food? Discuss the different groups who are harmed by this system. (Some of these might include U.S. workers who lose jobs to Mexican workers desperate for work, Mexican farmers on collectively owned *ejidos*; the Black community of Emelle, Alabama; U.S. taxpayers who subsidize Calgene; and U.S and Canadian tomato eaters who ingest increasing amounts of possibly hazardous chemicals from pesticide residues.) Who benefits? (Calgene; Monsanto; perhaps companies or individuals involved directly in long-distance shipping; in a narrow sense, people in the North who are able to eat fruits and vegetables out of season.) Brainstorm strategies to "help the harmed." What social changes need to occur? Who would need to stick together to work for these? Are there laws that would make a positive difference? (See lesson for "Just a Cup of Coffee?" for additional ideas.)

"HUNGER MYTHS"
Article based on a book by Frances Moore Lappé, Joseph Collins, and Peter Rosset (p. 241)

Divide students into seven groups. Assign each of the myths to a different group. Students need to research their "myths and realities" to find information that supplements what is included here. Afterwards, they are responsible for teaching their myth and reality to the rest of the class. They should use specific examples from different countries and draw on insights gleaned in their study of colonialism. They might also design posters to illustrate various themes.

"JUST A CUP OF COFFEE?"
Reading by Alan Thein Durning (p. 243)

In "Clothes, Toys, and the World" (p. 140), we suggested that students could research the origin of their clothes or toys. They can do a similar activity with food. Have students list all the food they ate the previous day — this may take several sheets of paper! Ask them to choose one of the items on their lists and research this food thoroughly enough to be able to write an ecological diary, as Durning did. Alternatively, they might illustrate this like "Tomasito's Tour."

Note that Durning is not especially alert to the human involvement in his coffee. The tip-off to this neglect is how much passive voice he uses, which hides the human subject: beans "were dried under the sun," and "shipped to New Orleans." By whom? "The shipyard built the freighter...." "Shipyards" don't build freighters, people do. The beans "were trucked to Seattle." Again, by whom? Discuss these omissions with students and encourage them to be alert in their research to both human and ecological factors.

Give students a world map and have them find all the locations involved in Durning's cup of coffee. They might illustrate their maps.

"CEBOLLEROS"
Story by Benjamin Alire Sáenz, (p. 250)

Ask students: How does the work described in "1967" affect the narrator and his family? This was "child labor." Was it wrong? How does this compare to work experiences students themselves have had?

Assume that the man in his early 30s walking into the grocery store in 1985 is the boy who narrates the first section (1967) of the reading. Have students write his interior monologue (his inner thoughts) as he hears the Anglo women talking about the beautiful and cheap onions. Students might write a poem or interior monologue from the standpoint of an onion, or another vegetable or fruit. Focus on the human labor embedded in "cheap" food.

Read with students Martín Espada's "Federico's Ghost." Students might use parts of the story, "Cebolleros" or what they learn from a video on farm workers' struggles like ¡Aumento Ya! to write a similar poem (see "Videos With a Global Conscience," p. 365). They could begin, "The story is..." as Espada does in "Federico's Ghost."

"THE BEEF HORMONE CONTROVERSY"

On the Web:
www.rethinkingschools.org/rg

In "The Beef Hormone Controversy: Whose Free Trade?" Renée Bald and Bill Bigelow describe a lesson that engages students in debating whether nations may exclude products that they believe may be hazardous to public health. Students consider the implementation of World Trade Organization rules that regulate global trade in everything from clothes to meat. Complete roles and instructions are on the web at www.rethinkingschools.org/rg.

CHAPTER SEVEN
Culture, Consumption and the Environment

"It is important to realize that the new free trade agreements were designed and promoted by associations of businesses for whom environmental regulations are no more than costs that interfere with profits, and therefore must be minimized."

— Edward Goldsmith,
environmentalist

"Much of the glorious rise in productivity is fueled by a gigantic through-put of fossil energy, which requires mining the earth on the one side and covering it with waste on the other."

— Wolfgang Sachs,
author of *The Development Dictionary*

"The great, centralized economic entities of our time do not come into rural places in order to improve them by 'creating jobs.' They come to take as much of value as they can take, as cheaply and as quickly as they can take it. They are interested in 'job creation' only so long as the jobs can be done more cheaply by humans than machines. They are not interested in the good health — economic, natural, or human — of any place on this earth. If you should undertake to appeal or complain to one of these great corporations on behalf of your community, you would discover something most remarkable: These organizations are organized expressly for the evasion of responsibility. They are structures in which, as my brother says, 'the buck never stops.' The buck is processed up the hierarchy until finally it is passed to 'the shareholders,' who characteristically are too widely dispersed, too poorly informed, and too unconcerned to be responsible for anything. The ideal of the modern corporation is to be anywhere (in terms of its own advantage) and nowhere (in terms of local accountability). The message to country people, in other words, is: Don't expect favors from your enemies."

— Wendell Berry,
poet, teacher, ecologist

Page 259 image: Cartoon by Ewk, courtesy of Cartoonists and Writers Syndicate.

"Peasant ecologists" stand in an old-growth forest in Guerrero, Mexico, where residents have waged a David-and-Goliath battle with the U.S. lumber company Boise Cascade to preserve the trees.

INTRODUCTION

Culture, Consumption, and the Environment

Corporate globalization is *inherently* hostile to the ecological health of the planet, whether it's the polluting of the natural environment or the spectre of global warming that threatens the earth's delicate biosphere.

What are globalization's premises that contribute to such dire consequences?

Expansion of international trade. U.S. consumers' shirts and pants and radios and VCRs are not produced in the next town, the next state, or often even in the next country, but on the next continent — shipped to us by fossil-fuel-guzzling ships and trucks. Of course, the profit-driven economic system has always sought to expand markets everywhere regardless of the social or ecological consequences. But the current free trade orthodoxy, enforced by institutions such as the World Trade Organization and the International Monetary Fund, pushes every economy in the world to become an export machine. The better this system "works," the more it harms the earth — manufacturing, as it does, increasing amounts of greenhouse gases. Each report from the Intergovernmental Panel on Climate Change has offered increasingly frightening predictions about the effect of these emissions on the earth's climate.

Endless growth. Globalization's aim of economic growth is rarely questioned, even by many critics of aspects of globalization. But infinite economic expansion must inevitably collide with the imperatives of a finite planet. Imagine the ecological consequences if every country on earth "succeeded" in becoming a consumer culture like that of the United States. The United States by itself, with only 5% of the world's population, consumes about one third of the world's resources, produces half of the world's non-organic waste, and generates nearly 30% of the world's carbon dioxide emissions.

Market supremacy. Naturally, as people around the world see the rapacious nature of this system, their inclination is to organize to protect the environment from further damage. Transnational corporations, however, exert such power that governments often succumb to their demands — whether for permission to drill for oil in pristine wildlife areas or to forgo even minimal environmental standards, permitting factories to pollute the land. And globalization's

Supreme Court, the WTO, greatly restricts the power of communities or nations to introduce what it considers "non-trade-related barriers," such as prohibitions on the importation of wood from ancient forests, or of tuna caught in ways that endanger dolphins or sea turtles.

Monoculturalism. Globalization's aim is to open up every nook and cranny of the earth to investment — to McDonald's, to global media conglomerates, to golf courses, to automobile factories. Cultural diversity is the loser. As activities in this chapter show, especially regrettable is the loss of viable, ecologically responsible cultures.

"MOUNTAINS OF THINGS"

One of the key aims of this book is to help students become aware of the social and ecological costs of the things we buy — the "mountains of things," as described in the Tracy Chapman song. Articles and activities in this chapter focus on the role advertising plays in doing precisely the opposite. Advertising seeks to produce consumers who inquire no further than two questions about any commodity — "Do I want it?" and "Can I afford it?" — and, of course, urges them to answer always in the affirmative. Advertising thrives on and reinforces selfishness.

So what's the problem with a little selfishness? As Stuart Ewen points out in the video *The Ad and The Ego*, "The problem, of course, is that the ads are encouraging people to participate in cycles of disposal which represent, on an ecological level, some of the most fundamental crises of contemporary life." Overconsumption might be a recipe for ecological disaster, but until it shows up as red ink on corporations' balance sheets, it's full steam ahead.

Ultimately, advertising is education. It teaches people to find meaning in consumption — to conclude: I am what I buy. And it discourages us from thinking about other social arrangements that might lead to more genuine satisfaction and that might preserve the environment.

The articles and activities described in this chapter explore ways students might begin to employ an *eco*-logic to think critically about a system that is more and more represented as an inevitable and natural result of human development. As Sut Jhally, another critic of global consumer culture says, "We need to get the fish to think about the water." ∎

—The editors

> Overconsumption might be a recipe for ecological disaster, but until it shows up as red ink on corporations' balance sheets, it's full steam ahead.

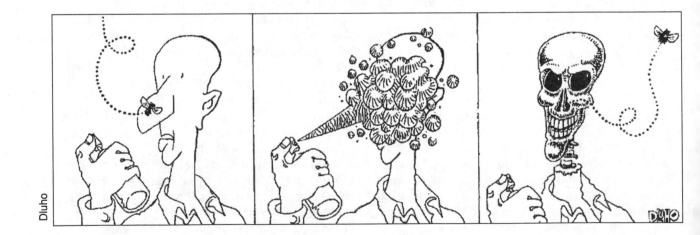

Dluho

A billboard in Grand Rapids, Michigan draws attention to the dangers of global warming.

Global Warming:
The Environmental Issue from Hell

BY BILL MCKIBBEN

When global warming first emerged as a potential crisis in the late '80s, one academic analyst called it "the public policy problem from hell." The years since have only proven him more astute.

How well we handle global warming will determine what kind of century we inhabit — and indeed what kind of planet we leave behind to everyone and everything that follows us down into geologic time. It is the environmental question, the one that cuts closest to home and also floats off most easily into the abstract. So far it has been the ultimate "can't get there from here" problem, but the time has come to draw a roadmap — one that may help us deal with the handful of other issues on the list of real, world-shattering problems.

The first thing to know about global warming is this: The science is sound. In 1988, when scientists first testified before Congress about the potential for rapid and destabilizing climate change, they were still describing a hypothesis. It went like this: Every time human beings burn coal, gas, oil, wood, or any other carbon-based fuel, they emit large quantities of carbon dioxide. (A car emits its own weight in carbon annually if you drive it the average American dis-

tance.) This carbon dioxide accumulates in the atmosphere. It's not a normal pollutant — it doesn't poison you, or change the color of the sunset. But it does have one interesting property: Its molecular structure traps heat near the surface of the planet that would otherwise radiate back out to space. It acts like the panes of glass on a greenhouse.

The hypothesis was that we were putting enough carbon dioxide into the atmosphere to make a difference. The doubters said no — that the earth would compensate for any extra carbon by forming extra clouds and cooling the planet, or through some other feedback mechanism. And so, as scientists will, they went at it. For five years — lavishly funded by governments that wanted to fund research instead of making politically unpopular changes — scientists produced paper after paper. They studied glacial cores and tree rings and old pollen sediments in lake beds to understand past cli-

> How well we handle global warming will determine what kind of century we inhabit — and what kind of planet we leave behind.

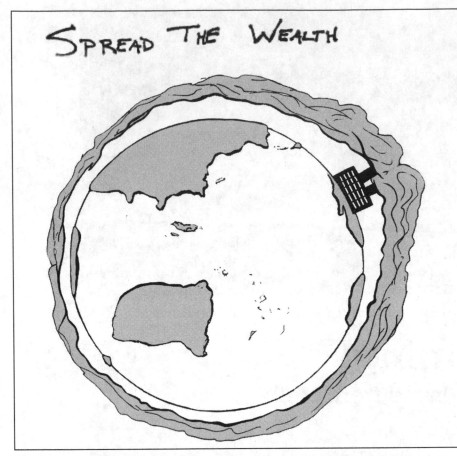

SPREAD THE WEALTH

Angela Bolster was an eleventh grade student at Franklin High School in Portland, Oregon when she drew this cartoon.

mates; they took temperature measurements on the surface and from space; they refined their computer models and ran them backward in time to see if they worked. By 1995 they had reached a conclusion. That year the Intergovernmental Panel on Climate Change (IPCC), a group of all the world's climatologists assembled under the auspices of the United Nations, announced that human beings were indeed heating up the planet.

The scientists kept up the pace of their research for the next five years, and in 2001 published a series of massive updates to their findings. These results are uniformly grimmer than even five years before. They include:

- The prediction that humans will likely heat the planet 4 to 6 degrees Fahrenheit in this century, twice as much as earlier forecast, taking global temperatures to a level not seen in millions of years, and never before in human history.

- The worst-case possibility that we will raise the temperature by as much as 11 degrees Fahrenheit, a true science-fiction scenario that no one had seriously envisaged before.

- The near certainty that these temperature increases will lead to rises in sea level of at least a couple of feet.

- The well-documented fear that disease will spread quickly as vectors like mosquitoes expand their range to places that used to be too cool for their survival.

But it isn't just the scientists who are hard at work on this issue. In the first years after the first IPCC report, it's almost as if the planet itself was peer-reviewing their work. We've had the warmest years on record — including 1998, which was warmer than any year for which records exist. And those hot years have shown what even small changes in temperature — barely a degree Fahrenheit averaged globally — can do to the earth's systems.

Consider hydrology, for instance. Warm air holds more water vapor than cold air, so there is an increase in evaporation in dry areas, and hence more drought — something documented on every continent. Once that water is in the atmosphere, it's going to come down somewhere — and indeed we have seen the most dramatic flooding ever recorded in recent years. In 1998, 300 million humans, one in 20 of us, had to leave their homes for a week, a month, a year, forever, because of rising waters.

Or look at the planet's cryosphere, its frozen places. Every alpine glacier is in retreat; the snows of Kilimanjaro will have vanished by 2015; and the Arctic ice cap is thinning fast — data collected by U.S. and Russian nuclear submarines show that it is almost half gone compared with just four decades ago.

In other words, human beings are changing the planet more fundamentally in the course of a couple of decades than in all the time since we climbed down from the trees and began making clever use of our opposable thumbs. There's never been anything like this.

Yet to judge from the political response, this issue ranks well below, say, the estate tax as a cause for alarm and worry. In 1988, there was enough public outcry that George Bush the

Elder promised to combat "the greenhouse effect with the White House effect." In 1992, Bill Clinton promised that Americans would emit no more carbon dioxide by 2000 than they had in 1990 — and that his administration would do the work of starting to turn around our ocean liner of an economy, laying the foundation for the transition to a world of renewable energy.

That didn't happen, of course. Fixated on the economy, Clinton and Gore presided over a decade when Americans, who already emitted a quarter of the world's carbon dioxide, actually managed to increase their total output by 12%.

In November of 2000, the hope of global controls on carbon dioxide production essentially collapsed at an international conference in the Hague, when the United States refused to make even modest concessions on its use of fossil fuels, and the rest of the world finally walked away from the table in disgust.

In the face of all this, what are those of us who care about the environment to do? The normal answer, when you're mounting a campaign, is to look for self-interest, to scare people by saying what will happen to us if we don't do something: All the birds will die, the canyon will disappear beneath a reservoir, we will choke to death on smog.

But in the case of global warming, those kinds of answers don't exactly do the trick, at least in the timeframe we're discussing. At this latitude, climate change will creep up on us. Severe storms have already grown more frequent and more damaging. The seasons are less steady in their progression. Some agriculture is less reliable. But face it: The U.S. economy is so enormous that it handles those kinds of changes in stride. Economists who work on this stuff talk about how it will shave a percentage or two off GNP over the next few decades — not enough to notice in the kind of generalized economic boom they describe. And most of us live lives so divorced from the natural world that we hardly notice the changes anyway. Hotter? Turn up the air conditioning. Stormier? Well, an enormous percentage of Americans commute from remote-controlled garage to office parking garage — they may have gone the last year without getting good and wet in a rainstorm. By the time

the magnitude of the change is truly in our faces, it will be too late to do much about it: There's such a lag time with carbon dioxide in the atmosphere that we need to be making the switch to solar and wind and hydrogen right about now. Yesterday, in fact.

So maybe we should think of global warming in a different way — as the great moral crisis of our moment, the equivalent in our time of the Civil Rights Movement of the '60s.

Why a moral question? In the first place, because we've never figured out a more effective way to harm the marginalized and poor of this planet. Having taken their dignity, their resources and their freedom under a variety of other schemes, we now are taking the very physical stability on which they depend for the most bottom-line of existences.

The U.S. economy can absorb these changes for a while, but for a moment consider Bangladesh. A river delta that houses 130 million souls in an area the size of Wisconsin, Bangladesh actually manages food self-sufficiency most years. But in 1998, the sea level in the Bay of Bengal was higher than normal, just the sort of thing we can expect to become more frequent and severe. The waters sweeping down the Ganges and the Brahmaputra from the Himalayas could not drain easily into the ocean — they backed up across the country, forcing most of its inhabitants to spend three months in thigh-deep water. The fall rice crop didn't get planted. We've seen this same kind of disaster in the last few years in Mozambique or Honduras or Venezuela or any of a dozen other wretched spots.

And a moral crisis, too, if you place any value on the rest of creation. Coral reef researchers indicate that these spectacularly intricate ecosystems are also spectacularly vulnerable — rising water temperatures will likely bleach them to extinction by mid-century. In the Arctic, polar bears are 20% scrawnier than they were a decade ago: As pack ice melts, so does the opportunity for hunting seals. All in all, this century seems poised to see extinctions at a rate not observed since the last big asteroid slammed into the planet. But this time the asteroid is us.

A moral question, finally, if you think we owe any debt to the future. No one ever has figured

> So maybe we should think of global warming in a different way — as the great moral crisis of our moment, the equivalent in our time of the Civil Rights Movement of the '60s.

out a more thorough-going way to strip-mine the present and degrade what comes after. Forget the seventh generation — we're talking 70th generation, and 700th. All the people who will ever be related to you. Ever. No generation yet to come will ever forget us — we are the ones present at the moment when the temperature starts to spike, and so far we have not reacted. If it had been done to us, we would loathe the generation that did it, precisely as we will one day be loathed.

But trying to make a moral campaign is no easy task. In most moral crises, there is a villain — some person or class or institution that must be overcome. Once they're identified, the battle can commence. But you can't really get angry at carbon dioxide, and the people responsible for its production are, well, us. So perhaps we need some symbols to get us started, some places to

sharpen the debate and rally ourselves to action. There are plenty to choose from: our taste for ever bigger houses and the heating and cooling bills that come with them; our penchant for jumping on airplanes at the drop of a hat; and so on. But if you wanted one glaring example of our lack of balance, you could do worse than point the finger at sport utility vehicles.

SUVs are more than mere symbol. They are a major part of the problem — one reason we emit so much more carbon dioxide now than we did a decade ago is because our fleet of cars and trucks actually has gotten steadily less fuel efficient for the past 10 years. If you switched today from the average American car to a big SUV, and drove it for just one year, the difference in carbon dioxide that you produced would be the equivalent of opening your refrigerator door and then forgetting to close it for six years. SUVs essentially are machines for burning fossil fuel that just happen to also move you and your stuff around.

But what makes SUVs such a perfect symbol is the brute fact that they are simply unnecessary. Go to the parking lot of the nearest suburban supermarket and look around: the only conclusion you can draw is that to reach the grocery, people must drive through three or four raging rivers and up the side of a trackless canyon. These are semi-military machines (some, like the Hummer, are not semi at all), Brinks trucks on a slight diet. They don't keep their occupants safer, they do wreck whatever they plow into — they are the perfect metaphor for a heedless, supersized society. And a gullible one, which has been sold on these vast vehicles partly by the promise that they somehow allow us to commune with nature.

That's why we need a much broader politics than White House-lobbying or mass-market mailing. We need to take all the brilliant and energetic strategies of local grassroots groups fighting dumps and cleaning up rivers, and we need to make those tactics national and international. So that's why some pastors are starting to talk with their congregations about what car they're going to buy, and why some college seniors are passing around petitions pledging to stay away from the Ford Explorers and Excursions and Extraneouses, and why some few auto dealers have begun to notice informational picketers outside on Saturday mornings urging their customers to think about gas mileage when they go inside.

The point is not that by themselves such actions — any individual actions — will make any real dent in the production of carbon dioxide pouring into our atmosphere. Even if you got 10% of Americans really committed to changing energy use, their solar homes wouldn't make much of a dent in our national totals. But 10% would be enough to change the politics of the issue, to insure the passage of the laws that would cause us all to shift our habits. And so we need to begin to take an issue that is now the province of technicians and turn it into a political issue — just as bus boycotts began to take the issue of race and make it public, forcing the system to respond. That response is likely to be ugly — there are huge companies with a lot to lose, and many people so tied in to their current ways of life that advocating change smacks of subversion. But this has to become a political issue — and fast. The only way that may happen, short of a hideous drought or monster flood, is if it becomes a personal issue first. ∎

Bill McKibben is the author of The End of Nature *and* Long Distance. *A version of this article first appeared in* In These Times.

> All in all, this century seems poised to see extinctions at a rate not observed since the last big asteroid slammed into the planet. But this time the asteroid is us.

> We need to take all the brilliant and energetic strategies of local grassroots groups fighting dumps and cleaning up rivers, and we need to make those tactics national and international. That's why some pastors are starting to talk with their congregations about what car they're going to buy, and why some college seniors are passing around petitions pledging to stay away from the Ford Explorers and Excursions and Extraneouses, and why some few auto dealers have begun to notice informational picketers outside on Saturday mornings urging their customers to think about gas mileage when they go inside.

Oil, Rainforests, and Indigenous Cultures

A Role Play on Oil and the Huaorani Indians in the Ecuadorian Rainforest

BY BILL BIGELOW

The idea for this role play came to me while reading Joe Kane's book *Savages*. The book's title is intentionally ironic, and Kane makes no secret whom he sees as the real savages in his story — hint: not the Huaorani Indians portrayed on the book's cover. No, the savagery described in Kane's narrative is a complex tapestry that includes oil-thirsty "developed" economies, transnational oil companies, arrogant missionaries, a debt-strapped Ecuadorian government, and (although also victims) impoverished, land-starved "settlers" who eagerly follow the oil companies into the rainforest wreaking further environmental havoc.

In the role play, students portray five groups: Huaorani Indians, U.S.-based Maxus Oil Company representatives, Ecuadorian environmentalists, evangelical missionaries, and poor settlers or "colonists." The teacher plays the Ecuadorian president, who presents a plan for "development" of the Oriente — eastern Ecuador, home to the Huaorani and numerous other indigenous groups, with more biodiversi-

ty than just about any other place on earth. It's this plan that is the focus of student debate and alliance-building, as different groups defend their interests and discover where those interests either intersect or clash with those of other social groups.

I follow the role play with Christopher Walker's haunting video *Trinkets and Beads* (see "Videos With a Global Conscience," p. 367). Writer Wendell Berry once noted that social elites "cannot take any place seriously because they must be ready at any moment, by the terms of power and wealth in the modern world, to destroy any place." Berry could have made this observation after watching Walker's video. *Trinkets and Beads* patches together indelible images of the ecological and social devastation of oil "development" with quotes of great insight as well as great idiocy. The Huaorani leader Moi pleads for solidarity with the rainforest: "We must all be concerned because this is the heart of the world and here we can breathe." An oil company consultant meanwhile insists that the rainforest is a myth, a *National Geographic* fiction: "The jungle is the jungle is the jungle sort of thing."

The Huaorani role play, followed by *Trinkets and Beads*, can offer students an intimate glimpse at how globalization plays out in one corner of the world. I've found that by looking hard with students at a very small piece of the international puzzle, they can begin to understand some of its most basic features. They can begin to bring into focus the human lives and ecological complexity obscured by metaphors of progress, development, and economic growth. And they can begin to recognize their own role in a system that is hard at work turning every aspect of life into marketable commodities. But these activities can also alert students to individuals and organizations trying to craft alternatives. It's a unit about the devastation wrought by development, but it's also about pockets of resistance that continue to inspire hope.

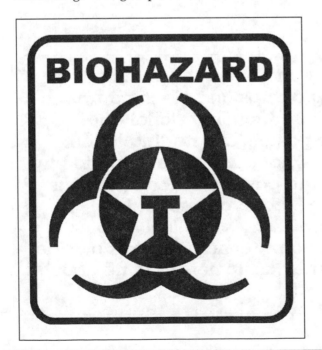

1. THE ROLE PLAY

Materials Needed:

1. Construction or other stiff paper for placards; crayons or markers.

2. Copies of roles —
   one per student in each of the five groups.

3. Copies of the "President's Statement on Development of the Oriente" —
   one for every student in the class.

4. Optional: Copies of the map of Ecuador and the Oriente — one for every student. (Can be reproduced from Joe Kane's *Savages*.)

3. Optional: Copies for all students of the excerpts from the prologue of *Savages*, described below.

Suggested Procedure:

1. Before beginning the activities with students, write the following on the board or overhead:

Time: Now
Place: The Oriente
   (the rainforests of eastern Ecuador)
Roles:
   Huaorani Indians
   Maxus Oil Company
   "Colonists"/Workers
   Evangelical Missionaries
   Ecuadorian Environmentalists

Questions for the national debate on development:

1. Should the Maxus Oil Co. be allowed to explore for oil, build roads, oil wells and pipelines on Huaorani land in the Oriente? Why or why not?

2. If not, what alternative do you have to develop Ecuador and the Oriente?

3. Should the government and missionaries build schools to civilize the Huaorani? Why or why not?

2. Distribute the map of Ecuador and the Oriente to students. Tell them that the Huaorani Indians live in the eastern part of Ecuador, called the Oriente, in the rainforests around the headwaters of the Amazon River. Draw students' attention to the inset in the upper right of the map: Notice how the tributaries of the Amazon finger up into Huaorani land. (The ecological implications are clear: Pollution from oil exploration will affect not only the environment and everyone in the immediate vicinity, but will ultimately drain into the Amazon itself.)

To introduce students to the Huaorani, I read excerpts from the prologue to *Savages*: pages 3 and 4, up to the top of page 5, at the break; and from the break at the top of page 7 through the break at the bottom of page 8. I use these sections to pique their curiosity about the Huaorani leader Moi and the culture he comes from: "[Moi] dressed himself completely and had me tie his tie. Then, fully clothed, he got into bed. As he does at home, he would wake several times during the night — to eat, to pace our suite, to analyze the new sounds he was hearing." This is someone students want to learn more about. However, the role play will stand on its own without this introduction.

3. Tell students that each of them will portray one of the five groups listed on the board or overhead. They have been invited by the president of Ecuador to a national debate on the development of the Oriente. You might tell something about each of the groups, not to give away where they will likely stand on all the questions, but to preview some of the tensions students will encounter in the role play. Draw their attention to the questions for the national debate. (You might copy these on the back of the map. They are also included here as a student handout.) Tell students that each group must arrive at answers to all of the questions, but that they will also have a chance to meet and negotiate with the other groups.

4. Divide the class into five groups of roughly the same size. Have students form small circles around the classroom and distribute roles to each group. All students in a group receive the same role.

5. Ask students to read their roles carefully. They should consider how they might answer the questions for the national debate. Encourage them to underline important information. With some students, it helps if the group reads the role aloud; offer this as an option for the class.

Circulate among the different groups to distribute the placards and markers so students in each group can create a sign indicating who they are.

6. After students have finished reading, ask them to write an interior monologue — the inner thoughts — from the standpoint of the role they are representing. Suggest that students invent a persona: Who you are, what you fear, what you hope for, what experiences made you who you are, etc. They might invent a family. For example, the oil company executive may have a huge mortgage and a daughter starting college next year. The "colonist" may have been living in Quito, Ecuador's capital city, unable to find jobs that pay a living wage but not wanting to be forced to send the children to work; living in the Oriente seems like the last available option.

In their small groups, ask students to read their interior monologues to each other when they finish. If you like, encourage each group to select one of these to be shared with the entire class. This allows the groups to "meet" each other prior to the negotiating/alliance-building session.

7. Get students' attention to begin the opening round of the National Debate on Development of the Oriente. Introduce the process from here on out:

- The president of Ecuador — played by the teacher — will read the "President's Statement on Development of the Oriente."

- Members of the different groups will have a chance to briefly question and comment on the president's statement.

- Afterward, in their small groups, students will discuss the President's statement and arrive at tentative answers to the three questions on development.

- Representatives of the groups will have a chance to meet with one another to negotiate and build alliances on their positions on the questions.

- Everyone will re-assemble and groups will present their stands on "development" for the Oriente.

8. Introduce yourself as President of Ecuador. With appropriate pomp, read your statement on development of the Oriente. After reading, encourage members from the different groups to ask questions, but tell them not to make speeches. This will come later. During this question-and-answer session your aim is to encourage students to begin to respond to the issues from their group's standpoint, but to cut off discussion at a point that leaves them hungry for more.

9. Afterward, in their small groups, students should discuss the president's statement and decide where they stand on the three national debate questions — at least at this point. Go from group to group — in your role either as teacher or president of Ecuador, depending on which feels more productive in provoking dis-

cussion — to make sure that the positions they arrive at are generally consistent with those that their group would likely adopt in real life. Make sure that — especially in the case of the Huaorani and the environmentalists — they know that they can challenge the terms "develop" and "civilize" in the questions.

10. Ask each group to choose half its members to be "traveling negotiators." Negotiators need not travel together. Their job is to move from group to group discussing the issues, testing out their positions, seeing if alliances can be built, "deals" made, etc. Urge them to be as creative as possible. Emphasize that the information in their role is very likely not included in the other roles, so they will need to teach the other groups about their group's situation. Obviously, there is power in numbers, so the more groups they can enlist behind a single "program," the more likely they will be to carry the day. (You might have the negotiators from each group wear badges indicating their group and that they are "travelers.")

Note that it is essential that travelers not meet with other travelers during this session; travelers are to meet with the remaining "non-travelers" in each group. It's important that you enforce this rule because there is sometimes a tendency for kids to stand around in little clumps making deals with each other.

11. You want to cut off this negotiation session before students feel talked out — generally, after about 15 or 20 minutes. Send the travelers back to their home groups. Here, they should prepare their presentations for the national debate. Depending on time, you can require that these be very formal, written speeches, or simply make sure that each group is clear on its positions, but allow them to speak from notes at the national debate. Whichever you choose, encourage students to figure out a way to involve everyone in their group in the presentations. Also remind them that they must have positions on all three questions.

12. Seat students in a circle, everyone in their respective groups, with placards visible. It's important to remind students that a role play is not real life, that role plays can teach us a lot if we get into them and attempt to portray our characters with accuracy and passion. However, we should remember that people in class will be saying things that they don't really believe in real life, so "don't make it personal and don't take it personal." Encourage them to argue and criticize in the role play, but with part of their heads they should remember that we're just playing. One of my favorite quotes from the great Brazilian educator Paulo Freire is that "conflict is the midwife of consciousness." But conflict can also be the midwife of hurt feelings, so it's up to the teacher to monitor the mood of the class.

Reintroduce yourself as the president, and tell the "assembly" that whatever plan we decide on for development of the Oriente, you expect 100% agreement. Of course that's nonsense, but it lets students know that you want them to argue for their positions and not just to sit back and ultimately cast a "no" vote.

I generally run these meetings by allowing a given group to make its complete presentation and then, immediately following, other groups may question or challenge. This seems to work better than hearing from all the groups prior to discussion, which would require that people only listen for long periods of time. At the end, take a vote on the questions if you like. But you can simply say "Thank you for your opinions," and emphasize that you are president, and you'll be making the decisions yourself.

13. Follow the National Debate meeting by asking students to step out of their roles to write. Ask them to write on the same three questions that they responded to from the perspective of their social group. Perhaps ask them to write on what they think is happening right now in the Oriente in Ecuador. Ask them whether any of the alliances they made in the role play were realistic.

14. Discussion of the role play needn't be exhaustive, because the issues will return with even greater intimacy and force after students see *Trinkets and Beads.* In addition to the questions above, some other possible discussion questions:

• Why would the government of Ecuador even consider opening up such an ecologically fragile region to oil development?

• There are not that many indigenous people living in the Oriente. In his statement, the president said that it was selfish for them to deny the rest of the country access to oil and the development that it could bring. Do you agree?

• Why do indigenous groups like the Huaorani need so much land? Couldn't they do fine on a little less? Play devil's advocate: "Folks, it's just a jungle. What's the big deal?"

• Are the Huaorani holding up progress? Isn't it in their own interests to become "civi-lized"? Explain.

• What are your thoughts about the work that the missionaries are doing with the Huaorani?

• The Maxus Oil Company is just trying to make a profit supplying the oil that you use every day. Couldn't it be argued that Maxus isn't the problem, but you are?

• Isn't it true that without the capital that oil companies like Maxus bring into Ecuador, the country will never be developed? What's your alternative?

• What kind of changes are needed here in North America and in other "developed" countries in order for the Huaorani people (and other peoples in similar positions) to live more secure lives?

2. TRINKETS AND BEADS

Materials Needed:

1. A copy of the video *Trinkets and Beads,* which is available online from www.teachingforchange.org.

2. Copies of "*Trinkets and Beads*: Selected Quotes" for each student (available on the web at www.rethinkingschools.org/rg.)

Suggested Procedure:

1. Naturally, you should preview the video before showing it to students. There is some brief nudity, and in some school contexts you may need to consider how to deal with that. When I show *Trinkets and Beads,* I skip the very first scene of two Huaorani men hunting. I worry that it could feed students' stereotypes about, well, "savages in the jungle." But it's a judgment call.

2. Show the video. Ask students to take notes on quotes or images that they find especially moving or shocking. You may need to stop the video from time to time to clarify what's going on, but it's a compelling story and my high school juniors are always thoroughly engaged.

3. Afterward, distribute the handout "*Trinkets and Beads*: Selected Quotes." Ask students to complete a "talk-back journal" on scenes or quotes from the video. They can use the quotes to question, argue with, criticize, comment on, express agreement with, etc. They should choose 5 to 10 quotes or images and write a minimum of a paragraph on each of them.

4. Use these as the basis of a class discussion. You might go quote by quote encouraging students to read or summarize their reactions to each of them.

Other possible discussion questions:

- If we were to consider the pollution of the Oriente to be a crime, who or what would we say is guilty?

- Oil company consultant Alan Hatly dismisses people who suggest that oil companies intentionally try to destroy the environment or corrupt people. If he's right, that they don't try to behave maliciously, then how can we explain all the harm done by oil exploration?

- How would you respond to Moi when toward the end of the video he asks, "Why do rich countries come here?... Why do you want oil?"

- What responsibility do we have for what is happening to indigenous groups and the rainforests in places like Ecuador?

- What can we do as individuals? What *can't* we do as individuals?

5. Follow-up assignments:

- Students can use their talk-back journals as the basis of essays on the Huaorani, the culture of oil, "development," "progress," "civilization," and/or missionaries.

- Students can do "metaphorical drawings" or editorial cartoons on the issues raised in the role play and video.

- Students can write and illustrate children's books about these issues, and take them to elementary schools to teach younger children. Several of my students have written delightful books with titles like "Where Does Your Oil Come From?" "The Little Forest Book," and the unambiguous "What the Bad Oil Did to the Good Huaorani."

- Encourage students to read Joe Kane's *Savages* to learn more about the Huaorani people's struggle to preserve their way of life. Several of my students read *Savages* in preparation to lead a workshop they titled "Mi casa es su casa," about oil in the Oriente, for a student-run conference on globalization, social justice, and the environment. Several excerpts from *Savages* are included on our website. Students who are confident readers could take a look at Barbara Kingsolver's wonderful novel *The Poisonwood Bible*, about U.S. missionaries in the then-Belgian Congo.

- Students might visit the website of the Rainforest Action Network (www.ran.org) — searches for "Huaorani" will yield a number of updates about the situation in the Oriente — and Cultural Survival (www.cs.org.) Other resources and organizations are listed in *Savages*. Another video that students might view is *Amazonia: Voices from the Rainforest*, distributed by The Video Project, which comes with a helpful 92 page "resource and action guide." Contact The Video Project online at www.videoproject.org.

Bill Bigelow (bbpdx@aol.com) teaches at Franklin High School in Portland, Oregon and is a Rethinking Schools editor.

Trinkets and Beads *is available from the Teaching for Change catalog, www.teachingforchange.org or at 800-763-9131. See "Videos with a Global Conscience, p. 367, for a more detailed description of* Trinkets and Beads.

Huaorani People

No one ever conquered the Huaorani people. The government of Ecuador may say that they own oil rights under your land, but you never signed away or gave away any rights to your land. Your people lived and hunted on this land long before there even was a government of Ecuador.

Your culture values independence. And the only way you can be independent is if you rely on the abundance of the forest. The forest provides all. Your people hunt turkey, monkey, caiman (reptiles similar to alligators), and other game. From the materials of the forest you make spears and blowguns and hammocks. You use the forest to make treatments for illnesses. Your elders know every inch of this forest. They have detailed knowledge about hundreds of plants and animals. But take you and your people out of this particular forest, and you wouldn't know how to live. This is the only place you know how to survive. *Without the forest you are nothing.*

It is true that you are few people, probably fewer than 2,000, in a large territory. But you need that territory to live. For example, only one species of tree provides the covering for the darts used in your blowguns. Only one species of palm tree among 150 different palm tree varieties provides just the right wood for the darts. The old people take the young into the forest to teach them all that they know. Huaorani culture is directly connected to the entire forest where they live.

You have no need to become like the "civilized" people.

You've seen what happens when the roads and the oil people come in. The colonists who follow the company into the forest cut down trees and scare off animals. They make loud explosions which also scare off animals. Roads mean bad hunting. And when they build roads on other forest people's land, the other people invade your land to hunt and you must fight them to drive them off. When the oil company builds pipelines, there are oil spills and when these get in your water they cause terrible sickness. Sometimes you think they spill oil on purpose so that your people will leave and they can be left alone with no more Huaorani.

Above all else you value peace and harmony in your community. The only way to ensure peace is if there is an abundance of the food and water and medicine that the forest provides for you. Roads, wells, and pipelines threaten the abundance. And thus they threaten the very existence of you as a people. Although you value peace in your community, you are warriors who deal harshly with outsiders who threaten your way of life.

You've heard the Maxus Oil Company say that it is the "environmental" oil company. Maybe so. But if not, your entire culture could be destroyed. ■

"Colonists"/Workers

You are some of the poorest people of Ecuador. Some of you are Shuar or Quichua Indians who have been forced off your land when "development" arrived: roads, oil exploration, tourism, and towns. Others of you migrated into the Oriente from other parts of Ecuador because you and your families were almost starving where you were living.

When you heard that the oil companies were beginning to build roads in the Oriente, you saw this as a real opportunity. Some of you went to find jobs building roads, cutting down the jungle, building the pipelines, working on the oil wells, cleaning up the frequent spills, or cooking food for other workers. Others of you went because you knew that when they built the road you could find a little patch of land to hack out a small farm from the jungle. The soil is bad for growing coffee or raising cattle but there are game nearby to kill, and with luck you can scrape by.

You don't like or trust either the oil company or the Huaorani Indians. The Huaorani see you as invading their land. Well, you are invaders, but there are so few of them and they have so much land — and you have none. Share and share alike, right? But sometimes the Huaorani attack you, burn your crops, or kill your animals.

The oil company, however, is not your friend either. Sure, it will hire you to do all the dirty work they don't want to do themselves, but they pay you almost nothing and don't care at all about your health or safety. When you work on the road-cutting crews they pay you a dollar a day and then charge you half of that for room and board. It's typical to have more than 20 people living in three rooms. And the company provides no school for your kids. When there is an oil spill — and there are lots of oil spills — the company blames the workers instead of taking responsibility themselves. They try to save money by not making frequent enough repairs to the oil pipeline and it rusts out and bursts, or trees fall on it.

But the worst thing about working around oil is that it is poisoning you and your families. Your skin is always swollen and itchy. Your kids frequently have diarrhea and lumps on their chests. The "funny" thing about it is that where you live and work is supposed to be a wildlife preserve and a national park. Go a few hundred yards outside the house you stay in, take your machete and slice into the hillside. Black gunk bleeds through the soil as if you'd cut into a piece of chocolate cake. The nearby well bursts all the time, spilling oil right onto the land around you. This is where some of you had once hoped to farm. This is where your kids play. ∎

Evangelical Missionaries

You are evangelical missionaries from the United States. This is dangerous work that you do. But it is God's work. You live on the edge of the jungle in the Oriente region of Ecuador where you bring the word of the Lord to the savages. The Huaorani Indians, whom you are working to convert and teach, are known for being a ferocious people. In the past they have attacked and viciously killed your fellow missionaries with spears. But you stay because this is important work.

The savages are an uncivilized people who are still in the Stone Age. Until you came, they all went naked as the day they were born. They had never heard of God, and instead worshipped the spirit world, especially the jaguar. They were nomads, who wandered from place to place hunting game. They often would kill other Indians who came onto "their" land, even though there were no property markers indicating who owned what. Truly, these were an immoral people, who were even known to bury small children alive with their parents, if their parents died before the young were old enough to take care of themselves.

You built a chapel and a school to teach the children how to speak Spanish, how to salute the flag, how to read the Bible, how to wear clothes. They were especially impressed by the "magic" that you brought with you: the small airplanes you arrived in, mirrors, and salt. Of course, civilized people take these things for granted, but they are strange and wonderful to the natives. You taught the Huaorani to stop stealing from you. You've been trying to teach them the concepts they need to live in the modern world: to settle down and farm, to raise barnyard animals, to put away their spears, to be industrious. In the Huaorani language, there is no word for "lazy," so you even had to teach them that when they were not producing they were *wasting* time.

It's not that you love everything about "progress" and the arrival of the oil company. The oil boom has brought alcohol, gambling, and prostitution to this part of the world. There are people here who are very far from God. And this disturbs you greatly. But it is not your place to question whether the oil company is good or bad. It just *is*. And so your job is to prepare the Huaorani for the arrival of civilization. Your hope is that through the church and school, you can bring them into the modern world, so that they can lead productive, Christian lives.

Ironically, although much of what the company brings is very un-Godly, the company has helped you by providing money and material for your school. Clearly, they share your concern about the need to civilize the savages. ■

Maxus Oil Company

You are executives with the Maxus Oil Co. You live in Texas. You are not a huge company like Texaco or Exxon, but the government has invited you in to explore parts of the Oriente. Frankly, this is your big chance, because it's estimated that there is $2 billion worth of oil to be found, and this would keep your company alive and healthy. Let's be blunt: If this doesn't work out, your company may go bankrupt and you'll be out of a well-paying job.

People complain that oil is dirty, that it pollutes the environment, that it poisons people. You've heard it all before. Well, everyone should realize that to get something of so much value to the world, there are trade-offs. You have to break an egg to make an omelet. But the dangers are vastly overstated. You use the most modern safety procedures wherever you explore. In fact you pride yourself on being the "environmental oil company." But certain things can't be helped. There will inevitably be some spills, some pollution. You use dynamite for your seismic tests, and this scares off some game that may or may not return. The worst environmental problems, however, are caused by the "colonists." When you begin to build a road, these poor people from all over Ecuador flock in to cut out a little piece of the jungle next to the road. The trees they cut down fall on the pipeline, or sometimes colonists even punch holes in the pipeline. Worried about the environment? Blame the colonists, not Maxus, The Environmental Oil Company.

The government of Ecuador needs you badly. They are heavily in debt to international banks, and oil provides half of all government revenue. And the price of oil has dropped on the world market, so they need to pump more and more just to stay even. If it was up to the government, they'd let you in to explore, drill, and pipe the oil in a second.

However, there are a lot of well-meaning but naïve environmentalists in Ecuador and around the world who hate development and are trying to prevent progress. And there are a handful of Huaorani Indians who live in the Oriente who believe that their old ways of hunting with spears are better than joining the modern world. If at all possible, you need to convince the Huaorani, or at least some portion of them, that oil development is OK. You're willing to offer them jobs, money for schools, clothes, food, motorboats, tools, whatever they want to join the modern world. And, frankly, if it takes offering some incentives (bribes) to their leaders, you'll do that too.

Whoever is telling the Huaorani that they can stop development is lying to them. Oil fuels the global economy. The world wants it and needs it, and a handful of Indians with spears cannot stand in the way of progress. Ultimately, you believe that when the Huaorani have been introduced to television, the consumer world, and all the comforts of settling down, they'll be glad to give up their wandering ways for something better. ■

Ecuadorian Environmentalists

You are environmentalists, based in Ecuador's capital city, Quito. You don't live in the rainforests of the Oriente, but you care deeply about what happens there.

The government and the oil company talk about the Oriente region of Ecuador as if it were just a piece of real estate. In fact, it is perhaps the most biologically diverse forest in the world. The Oriente is home to an estimated 8,000 to 12,000 species of plants — as much as 5% of what is found in the entire world. At one single station near the Napo River, observers recorded 491 species of bird. In the Cuyabeno Wildlife Reserve researchers have found 473 species of tree in one square kilometer, more than are native to all of western Europe. There are parrots, turtles, caimans, monkeys, herons, harpy eagles, and even jaguar. So, let's be honest: We're not talking about a patch of dirt that just happens to have oil under it.

Other parts of the Oriente opened up for oil drilling have been devastated environmentally. For example, one Texaco pipeline ruptured 27 times, spilling almost 17 million gallons of oil. (By contrast, the terrible Exxon Valdez disaster in Alaska spilled about 11 million gallons.) In 20 years, Texaco opened 339 wells, cut 18,000 miles of trail and 300 miles of road, and built 600 toxic waste pits. People in the areas where Texaco "developed" have high rates of birth defects, spontaneous abortions, nerve disorders, and higher rates of cancer are beginning to show up. So don't let the government and oil companies say, "Oh, there won't be much environmental impact if we continue to develop oil in the Oriente." They're lying.

Here's what one journalist wrote about a typical oil company drill-site in another part of the Oriente: "Inside the barbed-wire fence surrounding the compound for oil company managers is a satellite dish, neatly trimmed lawns, and a volleyball court. Outside the fence: an oil-blackened pond. On the bank three workers in yellow rain slickers stare into the muck. At the far end of the pond: black muck overflowing into a creek. Farther on: two bulldozers driving trees and mud down into a pit of oil."

The government talks about how it needs money from oil "development" to turn Ecuador into a modern, industrialized nation. That's just not true. Most of the money goes right back to the United States to purchase oil equipment and supplies, or it goes to U.S. banks to pay interest on loans the government took out years ago, or it goes into the secret Swiss bank accounts of Ecuadorian government officials and oil company executives. Oil money most definitely does not go to help the poor of Ecuador. According to the government's own figures, there is more poverty and hunger in Ecuador than before the era of oil began — and greater inequality between rich and poor.

You support the Huaorani Indians because they are the caretakers of the earth. They've lived in harmony with the forest for hundreds, perhaps thousands, of years. They know it, they love it, they protect it. All the oil companies care about is sucking the land of its riches and then finding someplace else to destroy. They must be stopped. ∎

President's Statement on Development of the Oriente

My fellow countrymen, we have a wonderful opportunity that awaits us. An opportunity that — should we move forward and seize it — will benefit everyone in Ecuador. Indeed it will indirectly benefit everyone in the world.

As many of you know, we are a poor country. Like the rest of the Third World, living standards have been declining. Partly this is due to how much money we owe to international banks — a total of more than $15 billion. That is 15 thousand million dollars. Just to pay the interest on this debt is terribly difficult. Yes, we are a poor country, but we have rich resources. God saw fit to give our nation an abundance of oil. And it is with that oil that we will progress as a nation, that we will develop ourselves into a modern country, like those in North America and Europe. Half of the entire revenue of our nation comes from oil.

It would be nice if the oil were simply in ponds and we could go and scoop it up and sell it. But it's not that simple. The richest oil reserves are in the most difficult-to-reach parts of our country. They are in the jungles east of the Andes Mountains. It has been learned that reserves in Block 16 of the Oriente region contain oil worth as much as $2 billion.

These particular jungles are inhabited by a few hundred Huaorani Indians. I want to emphasize that the government is not trying to push the Huaorani out of their land. But, as you probably know, according to Ecuadorian law, the government owns all the mineral rights in this territory — and that includes the rights to the oil. But I want to say right here, that we want to cooperate with the Huaorani in the development of these resources so that everyone benefits.

There are some who may suggest that we just leave the oil right where it is. That would be selfish, and I cannot agree to that. There are hungry people in my country, people who need jobs, who need schools for their children, who need hospitals and roads. This oil belongs to ALL the people of Ecuador, not just to the people who by chance happen to live on top of it.

My offer to the Huaorani in the name of the Ecuadorian people is this:

From you, we need to build roads onto your territory, we need to explore so we will know where to locate the wells, we need to build the wells, and we need to construct a pipeline to bring the oil to the coast to ship it around the world. Perhaps 90 miles of roads, 120 wells.

In exchange for these simple things:

1. We will get agreement from the American oil companies who will be building the roads, wells, and pipelines that they will not harm the environment that we all so greatly cherish.

2. With some of the oil money, we will build schools for your children, buy you some motorboats with gasoline included, provide a medical clinic, and offer other benefits of civilization.

Refusal by the Huaorani is not an option. We need to work this out as a people. ∎

Questions for the national debate on development of the Oriente

1. Should the Maxus Oil Co. be allowed to explore for oil and build roads, oil wells, and pipelines on Huaorani land in the Oriente? Why or why not?

2. If not, what alternative do you have to develop Ecuador and the Oriente?

3. Should the government and missionaries build schools to civilize the Huaorani? Why or why not?

Jailed environmentalist Rodolfo Montiel Flores displays the Sierra Club's "Chico Mendes Award" from behind prison bars in Guerrero, Mexico in 2000. President Vicente Fox ordered his release in late 2001.

Mexican Peasant-Ecologists Fight to Preserve Forests

On Sunday morning, May 2, 1999, anti-logging environmentalist Rodolfo Montiel Flores stood with his wife and daughter on the main street of the tiny town of Pizotla in the state of Guerrero, Mexico, talking to neighbors and friends. Their conversation was suddenly interrupted by gunshots. "We didn't understand what was going on," said Montiel during a court hearing. "We just ran, we didn't know if they were the military or someone else. They were shooting to kill." One local farmer was shot in the head and killed immediately.

Rodolfo Montiel and his colleague Teodoro Cabrera Garcia were detained and taken to a military camp. For the next several days they were both tortured, threatened at gunpoint, and forced to confess to charges that they were guilty of possession of illegal weapons and cultivation of marijuana. However, a report by Mexico's National Human Rights Commission found that Montiel and Cabrera were not in possession of weapons at the time of their arrest, and that no evidence existed linking them to the cultivation of marijuana. International observers have condemned the convictions, believing that the charges were politically motivated.

Since the spring of 1995 when Boise Cascade Corp., the Idaho-based multinational logging company, signed a milti-year deal with the Mexican state of Guerrero to buy from local forestry *ejidos* (villages organized as communal production units), Mexican farmers or *campesinos* have watched as entire forests have been logged and hauled away by the truckload. According to Montiel: "We didn't know the name of the company back then, but whoever was behind it, [they] were taking everything: old trees, new trees, dead trees, live trees. If they had a permit for six thousand cubic meters, they'd take ten thousand and no one would say anything."

The deal between Guerrero and Boise Cascade, made possible by terms of the North American Free Trade Agreement (NAFTA), caused a dramatic surge in the rate of destruction of one of North America's last old-growth pine and fir forests.

As the logging continued, the healthy mountain forests — which are an essential component of the water cycle — began to show signs of strain as streams and springs began drying up. As loggers cut down more of the towering pines in the hills above Montiel's village, the mountainsides could no longer soak up and store rainwater. Instead, water cascaded off the land during the rainy season, dragging topsoil with it, and the terrain stayed scorched through the six-month dry season.

The *campesinos* grew concerned about the area's capacity to produce basic food staples like corn and beans. "We used to harvest up to three tons [of corn] per hectare, without fertilizer, and now we don't even get half a ton," said a *campesino* in an interview. "Now I can't even harvest enough for my own kids."

"When I arrived here 38 years ago, this place was full of marshes. It was wet even in the dry season," said Perfecto Bautista Martinez, of Banco Nuevo, a hamlet of 20 families.

"But then they started to cut down the forests and clear fields, and now it's just dust," he said. "We are ecologists now because we have seen the symptoms of the destruction all these years. We had to think of our children: Do we want them to receive a desert from us? That's why we organized."

Rodolfo Montiel and Teodoro Cabrera were among many *campesinos* of the Sierra who decid-

> **"We just ran, we didn't know if they were the military or someone else. They were shooting to kill."**

ed something had to be done to protect the massive destruction of their forests. In the summer of 1995, a group of farmers belonging to the *Campesino* Organization of the Southern Sierra (OCSS by its name in Spanish) was on its a way to stage a demonstration in the capital of the state when they were stopped by hundreds of federal police officers. Without warning, the police began shooting, killing 17 *campesinos* and injuring 20 more.

Frightened but not defeated, other villages began organizing. In late 1997, Montiel and other *campesino* leaders began forming the Organization of Ecologists of the Sierra de Petatlán. Their tactics were simple and peaceful. They wrote letters to government officials asking that the Mexican forestry agency evaluate the ecological effects of logging on the Sierra and distributed information sheets, educating other *campesinos* of the consequences of indiscriminate logging.

On a few occasions their protests actually stopped the logging, forcing subsidiaries of Boise Cascade like Costa Grande Forest Products to sit at the table with the *campesinos* and listen to their grievances. Eventually, Boise Cascade left the area, claiming that the inconsistency of wood supply had forced them to close shop. But many others were convinced it was

Women pass through a field of pine logs cut for timber in Tlaxiaco, Mexico.

Associated Press/Gregory Bull

> "They were taking everything: old trees, new trees, dead trees, live trees. If they had a permit for six thousand cubic meters, they'd take ten thousand and no one would say anything."

directly related to the activities of Montiel's organization.

Among the people most angered by the work of the *campesino* activists and community leaders were the *caciques*, or land owners, who profited from selling the hardwoods to Boise Cascade. Many *caciques* have close ties to the military and to corrupt government officials. They blacklisted several community organizers, including Montiel, and accused them of planting marijuana and belonging to leftist guerrilla movements.

The Mexican army began looking for Montiel and the other *campesino* leaders who were hiding in the Sierra. The army used intimidation to track down the leaders, threatening townspeople that they would be killed or tortured if they didn't give them information on the whereabouts of Montiel and the others.

After months of hiding in the mountains, Montiel and Cabrera were illegally arrested on May 2, 1999. Hardwood logging resumed almost immediately after their arrests.

The two were tortured and forced to confess to crimes they say they did not commit. Over 100 Mexican environmental and human rights organizations were convinced that they had not broken any Mexican laws. Their lawyers demanded that the charges against them be dropped immediately and unconditionally.

Meanwhile, the forests continue to disappear. In order to compete with Boise Cascade, several Mexican logging companies have increased their production more than ten-fold. Without people to protect them, the last old-growth forests in the continent are rapidly disappearing.

According to environmental and human rights organizations, the Mexican army has created a state of terror and intimidation among the small,

Associated Press

A protester calls for the release of Rodolfo Montiel Flores and Teodoro Cabrera Garcia during a rally in Los Angeles in 2001.

isolated communities of the southern mountains of Guerrero. Montiel and Cabrera's case is not an isolated situation, as environmental activists in the area as well as all over Mexico and the Third World face a dangerous future defending the environment, their land, and their rights. ■

This article is based on reports from the Sierra Club, the Rainforest Action Network, and the Los Angeles Times. *See the searchable website of the Rainforest Action Network, www.ran.org, for more information.*

In November 2001, Mexican President Vicente Fox ordered the release of Rodolfo Montiel Flores and Teodoro Cabrera Garcia from prison.

Ecological Footprints

BY DAVID HOLTZMAN

What is to blame for global warming, depleting fossil fuels, and other environmental problems? Overpopulated Third World countries with lax environmental standards, as the Heritage Foundation and other conservative think tanks assert, or overconsuming First World economies, as most environmentalists maintain?

Mathis Wackernagel and William Rees, two community planners at the University of British Columbia in Canada, developed an innovative way to answer this question in their book *Our Ecological Footprint*. Their statistical measure — what they call an ecological footprint — reveals the impact each country has on the world's resources.

Not surprisingly, "modern" economies, such as the United States, have the largest ecological footprints. These economies require far more land, energy, and water, and emit much more of the carbon dioxide that is so harmful to human health and the atmosphere, than do the poorer nations, even though poor nations are home to most of the world's population.

The ecological footprint measures the resources consumed by a community or a nation, whether they come from the community's backyard or from around the globe. Earlier studies had determined a community or nation's "carrying capacity" — the number of people a society can support before it loses its ability to support itself. Wackernagel and Rees' innovation adds in richer countries' use of trade and technology to import resources they don't possess.

Wackernagel and Rees ask how many hectares or acres are needed per person to support a nation's consumption of food, housing, transportation, consumer goods, and services. They calculate how much fossil energy use, land degradation, and garden, crop, pasture, and forest space it takes to produce all that consumers buy.

For example, Wackernagel and Rees determined that Vancouver, British Columbia — their home — runs a large "ecological deficit" with the rest of the world. As they calculate it, Vancouver needs an area 19 times larger than its 4,000 square kilometers to support the food production, forestry products, and energy consumption of the region.

Based on figures published in the 2000 Living Planet Report, the U.S. ecological footprint was 12.22 hectares per person, or more than 30 acres. In contrast, each resident of India requires 1.06 hectares or just over two and a half acres to maintain his or her livelihood per year (see table). To sustain these inequitable ecological footprints, most rich countries run large ecological deficits with the rest of the world.

The implications for world development are profoundly disturbing. For instance, for everyone on earth to enjoy the ecological standards of average residents in Canada and the United States, an additional planet or two would be necessary. If the ecological marks left by all the world's people are to be distributed more equitably, then U.S. citizens, Canadians and other residents of wealthy countries are going to have to make radical changes. ■

Excerpted from Dollars & Sense *magazine, July/Aug. 1999. p. 42. David Holtzman was an intern at* Dollars & Sense *when he wrote this article. For more information see* Our Ecological Footprint: Reducing Human Impact on the Earth, *by Mathis Wackernagel and William Rees, New Society Publishers, 1996). To determine an individual's footprint, visit www.myfootprint.org. For the full* Living Planet Report, *go to www.rprogress. org/ef/LPR2000.*

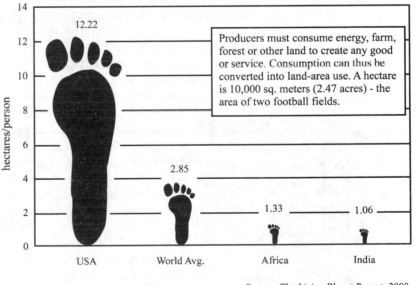

CONSUMPTION PER PERSON BY HECTARES, 2000

Producers must consume energy, farm, forest or other land to create any good or service. Consumption can thus be converted into land-area use. A hectare is 10,000 sq. meters (2.47 acres) - the area of two football fields.

USA — 12.22
World Avg. — 2.85
Africa — 1.33
India — 1.06

Source: *The Living Planet Report, 2000*

Water, Water Everywhere?

BY THE TURNING POINT PROJECT, ET AL.

The planet is running out of fresh water, but not because of thirsty people. Ninety percent goes to global industry: mostly high tech manufacturing and industrial agriculture. Now corporations want to ship river and lake water across the ocean to Asia, in giant "bladders." It's for thirsty computer companies. We'd like to believe there's an infinite supply of water on the planet. But the assumption is false. Available fresh water equals less than one-half of one percent of all the water on earth. The rest is sea water, or polar ice. Fresh water is renewable only by rainfall, at the rate of 40-50,000 cubic kilometers per year. The supply is finite. That's all there is.

Global consumption of fresh water is doubling every 20 years. That's more than twice the rate of human population growth. But human beings actually use only 10% of the planet's fresh water.

About 65% of the world's fresh water goes to industrial agriculture, which uses water at a much higher rate than the small self-sufficient family farmers who are being replaced. The rest goes to other industrial uses, like high-tech and computer manufacturing. (Silicon chips require massive supplies of pure water.)

According to the United Nations, more than one billion people on earth already lack access to clean fresh drinking water. Still, industrial water users expect to double their consumption within the next 25 years. By then, two-thirds of the world population may be suffering from severe water shortage.

• • •

As the water crisis becomes worse, one would hope that governments and global bureaucracies, conscious of the planet's limits, would advocate conservation. Instead, some propose a new solution: Privatize and globalize the remaining fresh water. Sell it to corporations, and let the global market decide who gets to drink it, or use it. New trade agreements like the North American Free Trade Agreement (NAFTA) and the World Trade Organization already define water as a "commodity" and have rules that require governments to permit water exports under certain conditions.

Corporations are excited. Water could become more valuable than oil, so there are billions to be made. Among their schemes is to ship North American lake water across the Pacific. Picture a gigantic supertanker crossing the ocean while towing a humongous floating balloon carrying part of Lake Superior. The water will be sold to Asia's high-tech industries (and U.S. companies in Asia). Very few thirsty people can afford to buy the water for drinking.

STATE OF THE WORLD'S WATER

This new form of fresh water diversion is only the latest in a century of water projects — dams, aquifer pumping, canals, and other diversions — that have left the world's water resource in a desperate state. Here's a quick summary:

- In the United States, only 2% of rivers have not been dammed. The Colorado and the Rio Grande rivers are so over-tapped that little of their waters reach the sea. The High Plains Ogallala aquifer, stretching 1,300 miles from Texas to South Dakota, is being depleted eight times faster than nature can replenish it.

- In Mexico City, pumping exceeds natural recharge by 50-80% per year. Arabian Peninsula groundwater use is three times greater than recharge. Saudi Arabia may be completely depleted in 50 years. Israel's extraction exceeded replacement by 2.5 billion meters in the last 25 years; 13% of its coastal aquifer is contaminated by agricultural chemicals or sea water.

- In Africa, the aquifers barely recharge at all. Water is being depleted by some 10 billion cubic meters a year. Northern China has eight regions of aquifer overdraft, while the water table under Beijing dropped 37 meters over the last 40 years. The land under Bangkok has actually sunk due to overpumping. And the Nile River, the Ganges, and the Yellow River in China, like the Colorado in the United States, are so dammed and diverted that the waters do not reach the sea.

> Available fresh water equals less than one half of one percent of all the water on Earth. The rest is sea water, or polar ice.

- Cities and industrial zones are now in direct competition for water with industrial agriculture. In "free trade zones," like the *maquiladoras* of Mexico, nearly all water goes to manufacturing. (During one drought, Mexican authorities cut off water supplies to everyone but industrial users.)

- Some countries are near war over water. Namibia and Botswana are arguing about diversions of the Okavango River. Malaysia has threatened to cut off Singapore's water supply (which flows from the north).

- In India, families pay 25% of their income for drinking water. Poor residents of Lima, Peru, pay $3 for a cubic meter of often contaminated water. More than 5 million people, mostly children, die every year from bad drinking water.

- The effects on wildlife and biodiversity are beyond tragic. The United States has lost 50% of its wetlands. So has Canada. California has lost 95% of its wetlands, and populations of migratory birds and waterfowl have dropped from 60 million in 1950, to 3 million now. About 37% of America's freshwater fish are at risk of extinction; 51% of crayfish; 40% of amphibians; and 67% of freshwater mussels, mostly from poisoned waters that run off from the agriculture industry. About 40% of U.S. rivers and streams are too dangerous for fishing, swimming, or drinking.

- In England, 30% of the rivers are down to one-third their average depth. Seventy-five percent of Poland's rivers are so contaminated that their water is unfit even for industrial use. There is simply no way to overstate the water crisis of the planet today.

A man draws water from a well north of Agadez, Niger.

Associated Press/David Guttenfelder

CLEAR CHOICES

What now? There are few rivers left to dam. Aquifers are in crisis. So then, is the best solution to let global corporations export lake and river

Water could become more valuable than oil, so there are billions to be made.

water by towing it in balloons across the oceans, for profit? Does anyone really believe that will solve more problems than it causes?

There's only so much water. Once we accept that, we can make some logical moves:

1) Recognize that water is life to all species. Water should not become a commodity; it is part of the commons, owned by all of us forever. It should not be privatized or traded or globalized.

2) Leave water where nature put it, in its own watershed, as part of larger ecological systems. Decisions about its use should be localized.

3) Full conservation and reclamation programs should begin now. Industrial users should pay.

4) Industrial agriculture should be phased out. It's too toxic, and energy and water intensive. A return to small-scale local farming will save water and energy, and it will keep our rivers clean. Strict controls are needed on water use by high-tech manufacturing.

5) International agreements should determine where emergency fresh drinking water is needed. Nonprofit organizations, like the Red Cross, should supply such regions, as needed. Free. ∎

Some of the organizations contributing to this article, and listed in "Organizations and Websites for Global Justice" p. 382, include:

The Council of Canadians

Friends of the Earth

International Forum on Globalization

David Suzuki Foundation

Global Exchange

Rainforest Action Network

Research Foundation for Science, Technology and Ecology

Institute for Agriculture and Trade Policy

50 Years is Enough: U.S. Network for Global Economic Justice

Michael Trokan

Children wash clothes at a community water faucet, one of three in all of Rio Blanca, Nicaragua.

Capitalism and the Environment:
The Thingamabob Game

BILL BIGELOW

Compare the six days of the Book of Genesis to the 4 billion years of geologic time. On that scale, one day equals about 666 million years. All day Monday until Tuesday noon Creation was busy getting the earth going. Life began on Tuesday noon and the beautiful organic wholeness developed over the next four days. At 4 pm Sunday, the big reptiles; 5 hours later when the redwoods appeared there were no more big reptiles. At three minutes before midnight man appeared. One quarter of a second before midnight Christ arrived. At 1/40 of a second before midnight the Industrial Revolution began. We are surrounded by people who think that what we have been doing for 1/40 of a second can go on indefinitely. They are considered normal. But they are stark raving mad.

These words are from the late renowned environmentalist David Brower, spoken toward the end of the video *Earth and the American Dream* (see "Videos With a Global Conscience," p. 366.) Loaded with contrasting quotes about humanity's relationship to nature, *Earth and the American Dream* convinces most students that since the arrival of the first European settlers — whose leaders spoke of the new land as "a hideous and desolate wilderness, full of wild beasts and wild men" — American culture has celebrated ideas and dreams that are fundamentally hostile to the environment. As the video sweeps through the decades, pairing quotes about nature with images of ecological degradation, students can't help but be overwhelmed by the language of conquest and consumption woven into the fabric of American life. Perhaps too overwhelmed.

The video quotes are so effective in portraying a culture consumed with consuming that students may conclude that if only we "rethought" our attitudes toward the earth, we could chart a course to a more environmentally friendly future. What this notion fails to address is the way that the imperatives of a global capitalist economic system propel us toward ecological ruin. Growth, competition, and consumption are not just ideological constructs, they are systemic requirements. Ideas matter, but so do the economic structures that animate and in turn are nurtured by ideas. I wanted to create an activity

in which students could experience classroom doses of the economic pressures felt by competing producers. Then when my students considered solutions to the environmental crisis, I hoped such reflection would be grounded in a fuller appreciation of the roots of that crisis.

In the Thingamabob Game, small groups of students represent competing manufacturers of "thingamabobs" — consumer goods that, as in the real world, require natural resources to produce. And, as in the real world, at some point in the future, the cycles of production and consumption will exhaust the earth's resources and capacity to contain the pollution generated by these cycles. Endless growth is a physical impossibility. Armed with knowledge of the earth's limits, the competing groups of students/manufacturers see if they can be environmentally responsible, given the rewards offered by — and punishments exacted from — a profit-based economy. The game can be fun, frenetic, and frustrating. But from this activity students can gain more clarity about strategies for saving the planet.

Materials Needed:

1. Copies of "The Thingamabob Game" role sheet; one for each student.
2. Five Thingamabob Production Round slips per group. I generally have seven groups, depending on class size. (Cut these up beforehand.)
3. Several candy bars or other desirable food products. (See the "Thingamabob Game Role Sheet" for the exact number you could end up needing.)

Suggested Procedure:

1. Before beginning the game, put the chart on page 288 on the board or overhead.

2. I show the video *Earth and The American Dream* immediately before the class does The Thingamabob Game. But the game could be incorporated into any unit that deals with environmental issues. See *Rethinking Columbus*, which includes two pages of quotes from the video as well as discussion/writing questions.

Distribute copies of "The Thingamabob Game

Role Sheet" to students. Read it aloud. You'll notice that for simplicity's sake, each "company" doesn't have to worry about developing markets for its goods. The game assumes that whatever is produced can be sold. Thus with each round, every company increases its capital and can produce even more thingamabobs, if the student "managers" of that company so choose. (See #10, below for caveats on the game's limitations.)

The math is simple: Each company starts out with $1,000. Thingamabobs sell for $2 a piece and cost $1 to produce. So a company makes a dollar for every thingamabob produced. Companies can't spend any more money than they have. So for the first round, their maximum production is 1,000 thingamabobs, that would leave them with a total of $2,000 after the round, if they decided to produce as much as possible.

Note that the role sheet promises candy for all the winners. It's important that you have desirable candy awards ready, and that you show these to students to motivate them to try to win. However, every class I have ever done this with has produced so many thingamabobs that it triggered environmental ruin, so the reward you select will likely be moot.

The concluding paragraph of the instructions warns students that at the end of the five rounds if the *total* number of thingamabobs produced (i.e., by all seven groups in all five rounds) exceeds the trigger figure, every company loses the game. Students don't know the precise trigger point of environmental destruction. *I set the figure at 35,000 thingamabobs,* and have that written on the board but covered up. Students know only that the figure is somewhere between 20,000 and 40,000 thingamabobs. Emphasize the tension in the game — as in real life: *They will be rewarded based on how much profit they produce for their company; but the more thingamabobs they produce, the closer they bring the planet to environmental devastation.*

3. Divide the class into seven groups. It's fine if there are only a couple of students in a group, or five or six (if you're in a school district like mine whose class sizes are ballooning due to big budget cuts). Tell each group to come up with a thingamabob company name.

4. Distribute five Thingamabob Production Round Slips to each group. Ask them to make their first production decisions. They should discuss these among themselves, complete the

COMPANY NAME		ROUND 1		ROUND 2		ROUND 3		ROUND 4		ROUND 5	
		AVAIL. CAPITAL	"THINGS" PRODUCED	AVAIL. CAPITAL	"THINGS" PRODUCED	AVAIL. CAPITAL	"THINGS" PRODUCED	AVAIL. CAPITAL	"THINGS" PRODUCED	AVAIL. CAPITAL	"THINGS" PRODUCED
1.		1000									
2.		1000									
3.		1000									
4.		1000									
5.		1000									
6.		1000									
7.		1000									
	TOTAL THINGAMABOBS PRODUCED (running total)										

information on the slip, and hand them to you without revealing their numbers to their competitors.

5. Begin by writing all the company names on the board or overhead. Then post the first round production figures. Be sure to add up the number of thingamabobs produced in each round and to keep a running total of all the thingamabobs produced in the game. Point out the "loser" companies whose profits don't match those of their competitors. Tell these companies that their stockholders are getting restless because their competitors are so much more successful, even though they began with the same amount of capital. If one company decides that it wants to carry the banner for the earth and produce no or few thingamabobs, I may declare that company bankrupt and distribute those students to other groups so that they get the message that failing to compete has consequences.

6. Continue round by round, indicating the most and least profitable companies. Also emphasize how the total thingamabob production count is getting dangerously high. (Remember, you know that the trigger figure of environmental no-return is 35,000 thingamabobs; they know only that it is between 20,000 and 40,000.) Finish all five rounds, even if they exceed the 40,000 figure. Or you may do as I did one year and tell them that new "scientific discoveries" found that the trigger point is higher, between 40,000 and 50,000. My students in that class still went over, topping out at somewhere around 60,000.

7. If by some miracle at the end of round five, thingamabob production of all companies has not exceeded the 35,000 trigger number, award the prizes to the groups as indicated on their role sheet.

8. Afterwards, before discussing, ask students to write about the activity. Keep it simple, something like: Why did you destroy the earth? You saw it coming, but you did it anyway. Perhaps ask students to comment on the observation by ex-financier James Goldsmith that "winning" in a game like this is like "winning at poker on the Titanic." You might also ask them at this point to reflect on what, if anything, they could have done that would have led to a more positive outcome.

9. Begin the discussion by getting students to talk about what they wrote. Some further discussion questions include:

• Describe what went on in your group. What pressures did you feel?

• What prevented you from being more ecologically oriented?

• In what ways does the game resemble what happens in real life? What was unrealistic about the game?

• Is the game "rigged"? Could the rules be changed in ways that would not lead to environmental destruction?

• Invent a new set of rules for the "game" that would not lead to environmental destruction. What different behaviors could be rewarded?

10. Now for the fine print. Simulations are metaphors. They're useful in illuminating aspects of reality, but they can obscure or miss other important aspects. The Thingamabob game effectively highlights how the capitalist market has no built-in alarm system to protect the earth. As social critic David Korten writes, "There are no price signals indicating that the poor are going hungry because they have been forced off their lands; nor is there any price signal to tell polluters that too much CO_2 is being released into the air, or that toxins should not be dumped into soils or waters." But the simulation may imply that we all suffer equally as the earth deteriorates. Nothing in the activity suggests that environmental impacts reverberate unevenly through the global landscape, affecting the Third World, the poor, and people of color differently than the upper classes. And the game's cataclysmic end may distort the way things are likely to play out in real life, as pockets of the world become unlivable but the privileged exist relatively comfortably in gated communities, on bottled water and perhaps even "bottled" air.

As mentioned earlier, to underscore the pressure on corporations to maintain high production, even at great ecological peril, vagaries of the market do not factor into the Thingamabob game. Obviously, in real life everything that is produced is not necessarily purchased. This is one of the central contradictions of market economies: They tend toward overproduction and boom-and-bust cycles. And the production of every "thingamabob" will not be equally unfriendly to the environment. Indeed, some production — for example, solar panels — may soften humans' effect on nature. These and other limitations can and should be discussed with students. Still, the game's essential caution — that a profit-oriented economic system is incompatible with environmental responsibility — is one that is hard to deny. ∎

The Thingamabob Game

Role Sheet

You are managers of a company that produces thingamabobs. You are in competition with other thingamabob companies. In the new "global economy" there is especially fierce competition as you fight to get new markets around the world for your products. Even though you have important and highly paid managerial jobs, these jobs are not necessarily secure. As with any capitalist company, you need to continually grow and make a profit. Your stockholders expect a high rate of return on their investments. Should you not deliver, stockholders will be unhappy, you may have difficulty attracting new investors, and banks may be unwilling to lend you money. Fail to return a sufficient profit and you'll lose your job.

And like all companies that make things, you must use up some of the earth's resources in the production process. The more you produce, the more of the earth you use up, the more pollution that results, and the more greenhouse gases that are generated. Ultimately, if the earth dies, it doesn't make any difference how much profit you've made because, guess what? You're dead.

RULES OF THE GAME

Each company will begin the game with $1,000 in capital. Each thingamabob costs $1 to produce. You will make $2 off of every thingamabob you produce and sell. (So, for example, if you produce 100 thingamabobs in round one, you will spend $100, but you'll get $200 back, and end up with a total of $1,100.) Of course, with every thingamabob produced, the earth comes one step closer to its death.

To simulate the real-life consequences, here's how scoring will work. There will be five "production" rounds. At the end of the fifth round, you will be rewarded based not on how nice you are to each other, or to the earth, but on how much profit you've made for the company.

REWARDS:

Top two groups: ....Candy for every group member

Group 3 ....Two candy bars to split between group members

Group 4 ....One candy bar to split between group members

Group 5 ....Nothing

Group 6 ....Nothing

Group 7 ....Nothing

Should all groups tie, each group will receive one candy bar to share.

Here's the catch: If the total production for all groups goes over the trigger number — somewhere between 20,000 and 40,000 thingamabobs — the earth's environment is damaged beyond repair, and no one will receive any candy.

THINGAMABOB PRODUCTION

Round # _____

Company name: _____Available capital ($): _____

Number of thingamabobs produced this round:_____

Total available capital after production: _____

- -

THINGAMABOB PRODUCTION

Round # _____

Company name: _____Available capital ($): _____

Number of thingamabobs produced this round:_____

Total available capital after production: _____

- -

THINGAMABOB PRODUCTION

Round # _____

Company name: _____Available capital ($): _____

Number of thingamabobs produced this round:_____

Total available capital after production: _____

- -

THINGAMABOB PRODUCTION

Round # _____

Company name: _____Available capital ($): _____

Number of thingamabobs produced this round:_____

Total available capital after production: _____

- -

THINGAMABOB PRODUCTION

Round # _____

Company name: _____Available capital ($): _____

Number of thingamabobs produced this round:_____

Total available capital after production: _____

TV and the Cloning of Culture

In this interview, environmentalist Charlene Spretnak interviewed Jerry Mander about TV and its impact on indigenous peoples.

CS: You have witnessed firsthand the effects of television being brought into the culture of traditional peoples. What happens?

Mander: In 1984, I was invited by the Native Women's Association of the Northwest Territories of Canada to participate in some workshops they were conducting. The women are Dene Indian and Inuit people of the Mackenzie River Valley, which extends from the Great Slave Lake on the south to the area beyond Great Bear Lake on the north, about 1,500 miles, including about one-third of the territories above the Arctic Circle.

Twenty-six communities of Native people live in that region in pretty much the same fashion as they always have, communally, with several generations together in log houses on the ice. Twenty-two Native languages are still spoken there, and the culture is still very much intact. The men take their dog teams out to go ice fishing and check the trap lines; the women repair the nets or work in the smokehouses. This is a part of the world where even the Canadian government barely had a presence until the 1960s.

About 10 years ago, however, television arrived in the region. It began in Yellowknife, the largest city in the Northwest Territories, with a population of about 9,000. (Every other community has only a few hundred people in it.) Television has now been accepted into about 19 of the 26 communities. The process by which it's accepted involves a great deal of pressure by the Canadian government. Representatives from the government repeatedly come around and ask these communities, "Do you want television?" Over the years, the communities have voted no again and again, but finally, one of the meetings would be attended by only a small number of people and the government would be able to push it through.

The women invited me because they're very, very worried about what the arrival of television has meant in their cultures.... In the few short years television has been in place, they have already seen tremendous changes, mainly among the young people, but also among the whole fabric of the communities. I was told up there that community life has been very much shattered and it happened quickly, within the space of a couple of years. The main activity of social life used to be people visiting each other in the evening, but now people stay in their own houses and watch television.

What they're watching on television is programming that comes to them from the United States (more than 50%) and from Toronto or Ottawa. There's only one program, one-half hour a month, of locally produced television. Even that is not necessarily Indian- or Eskimo-related material. So they're sitting in their log houses now watching programs like *Dallas*, *The Edge of Night*, and American situation comedies — the throwaway American reruns — or by satellites, current broadcasts of the evening soaps.

What the women told me is that they're watching *values*: the people in *Dallas* standing around swimming pools drinking cocktails, competing with each other for economic gain, sleeping with each other's spouses. They're portraying values that are antithetical to survival in the North, where people have to work together in cooperation with each other and maintain a strong respect for family values. These materialistic, individualistic images are almost like science-fiction stories coming into their log houses as weird stuff from Texas.

> The main activity of social life used to be people visiting each other in the evening, but now people stay in their own houses and watch television.

CS: And lots of commercials.

Mander: Oh, lots of commercials, right. The effect is that there is no longer any interest among the children in the Native language, which was always the first language. English is not spoken by a lot of people in that region, or it might be a third or fourth language. Even in the schools, English is the second language. But the young people are now beginning to be ashamed

A worker in traditional Lao dress builds a stack of television sets in a store in Vientiane, Laos.

to speak the Native tongues and are extremely interested in the commodities being advertised and the lifestyle being portrayed on television. They're using the lingo and the American slang. They're talking about cars — and there aren't even any roads in that region!

Also, junk food is appearing in the trading posts that was never there before, and the young people are much more interested in alcohol than they used to be. They're wearing American T-shirts, and they're becoming much more aggressive and much more speedy. They're no longer out on the ice, not interested in learning how to fish or how to trap. Instead, they're lured by the oil projects that are also coming into that region.

In fact, that's a major reason the government wants television to be in there: It helps inculturate people in ways that serve commercial development of the sort that industrialized societies desire to achieve. Those forces want to eradicate the traditional forms and replace them.

CS: The culture clash must be intense between the youth culture on television and the traditional people's culture of respect for the elders.

Mander: That's what the women said is the most important change as far as they were concerned — the tremendous loss of respect taking place among the young for the old. The relationship between the old and the young was absolutely critical for the survival of the people in the North. Among traditional peoples that's always the case. The old people are a kind of window into the past, a way for the people to see their roots.

In that role, old people relate primarily to the young. While the middle generation is out on the ice, is out working and doing business, taking care of things, the old and the young hang out together for the most part in traditional cultures. Now the young people are becoming increasingly disrespectful of the old. In fact, there have even been cases of elder-beating, as well as suicide among the young people — both of which I think are extreme expressions of cultural self-hatred. Elder-beating is one of the most shocking phenomena because loss of the elders means loss of the culture, since they're the repository of culture.

The kids don't want to listen to them anymore. And here's a concrete example: The women agreed emphatically that probably the single most important effect of the arrival of television was the wiping out of the storytelling process among the people. The traditional stories told among the Dene and Inuit people are teaching systems. They're also filled with incredible characters that are manifest powers of those cultures. The powers of the animals in the region and their interactions with each other and with humans really explain the relationships of things in that kind of harsh environment.

The women told me that when they were kids, this was the thing they looked forward to all day — getting together to hear the elders tell these stories and using their own imaginations to visualize the characters. This process was the concrete way in which the mutual awe and the love relationship between the old and the young took place. All of this has been wiped out. The women told me that no storytelling is taking place in communities that have television. I think it's a keen perception on their part — that they don't see how their culture can survive if this continues. They now have to use much more artificial means to try to convey the cultural transmission, and that's a very serious problem.

> ## The government wants television to be in there: It helps inculturate people in ways that serve commercial development of the sort that industrialized societies desire to achieve.

CS: Why do you suppose it was the women who took action to address the problem, and to what extent did the men participate in these workshops?

Mander: The workshops I went to had very few men in them. Why that would be the case, I don't know. The women in those cultures are in charge of the internal family situation to a much greater extent than the men. The men are out more of the time.

CS: Do the men find the lure of technological society more seductive than the women do?

Mander: Well, they're the ones who are impacted by it the most because it's the men who go away when Canada comes around wanting workers. They usually come back very frustrated because they get the worst jobs and can't really deal with the kind of life in those oil-rigging communities that are beginning to spring up... in that region. There's a lot of racism, drinking, prostitution, and fighting.

The Canadian government puts a lot of direct pressure on traditional peoples to get them to move from the bush into the cities and towns. They want people to come in and organize themselves into ethnic communities with centralized governmental systems that can negotiate on their behalf — and can make deals with the government and can provide labor for projects and so on. The government, partly through television, simultaneously convinces people that the dominant culture is desirable, and that they provide the means by which the people can have more of the dominant culture through labor in the oil fields.

CS: Why is it that what you call "mega-tech culture" cannot tolerate thriving indigenous cultures? The materialist response, of course, is that those cultures are often sitting on rich mineral deposits and that the industrialized, dominant culture wants Native peoples' labor. But isn't there something else? Is there something deeper about an earth-based, thriving traditional culture that contains what the industrialized culture needs to negate and forget?

Mander: Yes. The main reason why the West — as well as the [former] USSR and China — is spreading itself over indigenous peoples everywhere in the world, and has always done so, is to get those people off the land, to get at the stuff that's in the ground, to chop down the trees, to control the land, to spread a certain culture, and so on. The indigenous peoples are just physically in the way.

The more subtle reason is what you've just said. If those people are right about how they live, about their attitudes toward nature and the balance of things, about the multi-dimensionality of life and the ways of viewing reality and relationships and culture and so on — if they're right about all that, then we're wrong about what we're doing, and we're operating on a series of misconceptions. I think that we've had to drive out of ourselves a whole construct of feelings, perceptions and sensitivities that have made it possible for us to live in the manner in which we now live.

If we believed that the earth were alive, or that trees were creatures, or that there really was a balance that you couldn't violate or you'd go over the edge, or that nature was our spiritual equal and that there was spirituality in all of nature, then we really couldn't go on living our lives the way we do because we are constantly chewing up and killing nature. We repackage it into some artificial form that's useful to us, killing off whatever spiritual dimension it formerly had and making that aspect invisible to ourselves so that we cannot even have access to it in our minds and feelings.

Any time we have contact with traditional people, they remind us about the lost dimensions and it's difficult to take. There is the desire to step on it. So the "traditionals" (as opposed to the "progressives") within the indigenous cultures are treated by the dominant culture as subversives, as radicals and outlaws, who are basically paid no attention.

CS: It seems that the success of the political resistance by the "traditionals" would depend on their linking forces with those of us in the dominant culture who are groping our way back to an earth-based politics and spirituality.

Mander: Movements like bioregionalism, Green politics, and appropriate technology are good models, but for the dominant culture at-large to even consider the viable alternative presented in the living philosophy of the traditional peoples, we first have to let go of the assumption that evolution has brought us to the point where technology is the answer. Faith in technology was sold to us as being beneficial to human health and welfare, to democracy and peace and freedom, to expansion of the mind and the spirit.

But the great experiment has turned out to be unsuccessful. Meanwhile, the primary victims of the aggressive experiment, which is one of tremendous scale and power, are the millions of indigenous people who still live in land-based cultures.

We have to give up our assumption that we are the royalty here, and we need to listen to what other people have been saying all along about our set of assumptions and then make some hard choices for ourselves. My own argument is that if we want to continue on the mega-tech course we're following and go over the cliff, that's up to us, perhaps, but we have no right to take everyone else with us. ■

Jerry Mander is author of In the Absence of the Sacred *and co-editor of* The Case Against the Global Economy. *Charlene Spretnak writes and speaks on issues of peace, culture, and the environment. Her published work includes* Green Politics, *written with Fritjof Capra. This interview was first published in* Creation *magazine, Nov/Dec 1988, and was reprinted in* Adbusters, *Vol. 1, No. 3.*

No TV Week — Critical Media Literacy

BY BOB PETERSON

"**O**ne thousand and ninety-five hours!" Elizabeth shook her head in disbelief as she announced to the class the amount of time she would "have for herself" each year if she reduced her TV watching from five to two hours a day.

"That's over 45 days of time!" added Dennis, as he quickly figured it out on the calculator.

The class brainstormed what a kid could do with that much time — learn to juggle or to play a musical instrument, read scores of books, write their own book, get good at a sport. Of course, several in the class proudly proclaimed that if they had that much extra time, they'd do what they liked to do best — watch TV.

I think of my own classroom as I read Mander and Spretnak's depiction (p. 292) of the devastating effect that the introduction of TV culture has had on certain Native communities. While the impact on my students has not been as sudden, it has been nearly as dramatic. Most of the ten- and eleven-year-olds that I teach are addicted to TV. And with that addiction comes a growing obsession with things — oftentimes at the expense of positive human relationships and a nurturing attitude toward our planet.

In my two decades of teaching, technological "advances" in video, hand-held gameboys, cable TV, and video and computer games have enveloped my students' lives with such an intensity that I have no alternative but to incorporate critiquing the media within my curricu-

> **Most of the ten- and eleven-year-olds that I teach are addicted to TV.**

lum. While the notable increase in the media's sexual explicitness and violence is a concern, equally worrisome is the equating of happiness to hyper-consumerism, devoid of any concern for ecological or social consequences.

At La Escuela Fratney, the kindergarten-through-fifth-grade school where I teach, the staff decided to tackle the problems head-on and sponsor an annual No-TV Week. Our goal was not only to decrease the amount of television students watch but to increase students' skills in critically analyzing television and other media.

LIMITING THE HABIT

Students need to recognize that TV watching can develop into an addiction. Students are familiar with the word "addiction" and link it to drugs. The anti-TV-addiction commercials available on video from the Media Foundation can spark discussion of TV addiction (see "Videos With a Global Conscience," p. 368). The commercials show entranced children watching television, and explain how children are addicted. Students can explore the meaning of addiction and how people overcome addictions.

Statistics can help. According to A.C. Nielsen, Inc., children watch an average of 24 to 28 hours of television per week. The average five-year-old will have spent 5,000 hours in front of the TV

> The average five-year-old will have spent 5,000 hours in front of the TV before entering kindergarten — more time than he or she will spend in conversation with his or her parents for the rest of their lives, and longer than it takes to get a college degree.

before entering kindergarten — more time than he or she will spend in conversation with his or her parents for the rest of their lives, and longer than it takes to get a college degree.

The success of reducing kids' TV watching is related directly to educators' capacity to work closely with students' families. No-TV Week is not aimed just at students and staff, but also at family members. During the week, we ask everyone — staff, students, and family members — to voluntarily pledge not to watch TV for a week.

To prepare students for the week, teachers raise students' awareness of how much time they spend watching television. Students keep a week-long log of the TV they watch, including names and times of programs. Students tabulate the hours they watched TV, making comparisons and reflecting on the differences. Some classes rank their favorite shows and discuss why they are popular. Sometimes students figure out the average hours of TV watched daily, weekly, annually, or project how many hours they will have watched from the time they were five years old to when they turn eighteen.

Some classes prepare "No-TV Week Survival Kits" with alternative, non-consumer oriented home activities such as playing games, going on a bicycle ride, making cookies, or reading a book. One year my class coordinated a school-wide campaign to come up with 500 things to do instead of watching TV. Usually my fifth-graders go to each class and survey students about the types of communication devices in their homes — from TVs to computers, from phones to video players. They tally the data, figure out the percentages, and make bar graphs to display the survey's results. In one recent year,

tv turn off week

www.adbusters.org www.tvturnoff.org

Finally, a hemorrhoid medication for children

TV-CIDE

MOVIE OF THE WEAK
STARE TREK

Youth-anasia

Kids 24hr
Shopping
Channel

Video
Parenting

After
School
Sit-Calm
Special

87602 12901

Doug Minkler

While she didn't like the habit, she wasn't sure how to change it. After No-TV Week, she said she felt confident enough to ban television during dinner and call for family conversation instead. Another parent said that after the week, she started telling her kids at breakfast several times a week that it would be a No-TV Day. A third parent said her children even ask for No-TV evenings because they like to play games with Mom and Dad.

CRITIQUE

After the first No-TV Week, parents suggested we put more emphasis on helping children critique and analyze television. They were concerned not only about the shows but about the commercials.

Teachers started by focusing on commercials. On average, children see 20,000 commercials a year, according to Action on Children's Television. One of my homework assignments asks students to "add up the ads" and to keep track of the TV ads they see in one night — both the number and the minutes. This shows children how commercials saturate our lives, and gets them to begin thinking how the television industry depends on advertising dollars.

Teachers videotape certain commercials and later watch them with students. We explain the difference between implicit and explicit messages. Students ponder many questions such as: "What messages do commercials send and why?" "Who benefits from the commercials?" "What would happen to our air if everyone bought a car like those advertised on TV?" "What other environmental effects would there be if everyone bought all the things advertised?" After watching and discussing various commercials, students write about the ads. Maria noted: "You seem to be always happy if you eat that cereal." John concluded: "There always are pretty ladies next to new cars. It must be so men come in to look at them."

One year I had my students just count the number of car commercials they saw in one evening. The results ranged from a couple to several dozen. During the discussion the next day I showed the students a news article about how cars are a major contributor to air pollution. I also explained how the auto corporations

they found that 65% of third, fourth and fifth graders had TVs in their bedrooms and half of those had cable TV — this in a school where over 70% of the students receive free or reduced-price lunch.

Because many children have difficulty conceptualizing "life before TV," I have children interview a family member or friend who grew up without television. Questions include: What did you do instead of watching TV? How did your life change after you got a television set?

Parent response to No-TV Week has ranged from wildly enthusiastic to highly supportive to nonchalant. Although most families fall in the middle, a number tell wonderful stories about how the week forced them to reconsider their television habits. One parent explained how her family had always watched TV during dinner.

helped to stop the expansion of other modes of transportation like buses and trains. I asked, "Why do you think people are so attracted to owning newer and bigger things like cars, even when it might cause lots of pollution?"

TV shows can be critiqued in the same way. I've taped segments of cartoons, sit-coms, and the World Wrestling Federation and viewed them with students. I ask: How are problems solved? Who does most of the talking? What race, gender, and age are the characters in the shows — or commercials? How many instances of violence does one observe? How many put-downs are there? What is the attitude of the show towards the earth and the environment?

My fifth-graders seem thrilled to learn we were going to watch a segment from the WWF. They claimed they were not affected by the violence and gender stereotyping. However, when asked what effect such shows had on their younger siblings, fifth graders were much more willing to be critical, and admitted that their younger brothers mimicked the wrestlers' words and actions.

In one follow-up homework assignment, students interviewed a family member about the positive and negative messages of TV shows. One parent answered, "Children tend to believe that violence is the way to solve problems like in violent TV shows." Another responded, "TV has a bad effect because it absorbs much of the brain."

How much of our kids' brains TV will "absorb" is an open question. But media literacy projects like our No-TV Week present the question for discussion and allow collective reflection on one of the most powerful influences in our children's lives. From an environmental standpoint, TV is the most important mechanism that keeps consumer demand at a high level. Thus, critical media literacy is a vital skill for the longterm health of the earth. ■

WATCH MORE TELEVISION

My God... I never realized how unattractive, unsuccessful, and unappealing I was... Those people look better than I do... I need to look more like that... Mine isn't as good as theirs... I need a better one... If only I had one more of those, then I'd be happy... I don't have enough of that name brand in my wardrobe... Who cares how much it costs: it will make me more popular...

Thanks to commercials, I have seen my flaws and shortcomings... but most importantly, they have shown me the solutions and answers to these problems. Thank you television... for opening up my eyes.

YOU NEED TO KNOW YOUR INADEQUACIES

Aaron Shogren created this "anti-ad" taking aim at TV commercials when he was a senior at Franklin High School in Portland, Oregon.

Bob Peterson (repmilw@aol.com) teaches fifth grade at La Escuela Fratney in Milwaukee, Wisconsin. A version of this article first appeared in Rethinking Our Classrooms, Volume 1 Milwaukee, WI: Rethinking Schools, 1994. For related websites on the impact of TV on kids, see www.adbusters.org, www.aap.org/advocacy/mediamatters.htm, www.turnoffyourtv.com, www.whitedot.org.

$$\frac{(24)^3}{\sqrt{ab}} = \frac{\$5.50}{hr.}$$

CIVICS 101

The Masks of Global Exploitation

Teaching About Advertising and the Real World

BY BILL BIGELOW

One aspect of learning to critically read the world entails asking questions about our "stuff": Where does it come from? Who makes it? Under what conditions and with what ecological consequences? What resources are consumed to get it from where it's made to here? The more students pursue these questions — and discover answers — the more they are able to recognize most advertising as disinformation, a seductive *masking* of social reality. I want my students to pry behind ads for what they say and *don't* say: "Think about this shiny, powerful car; forget the fact that if we continue to produce

shiny, powerful cars like this, the planet won't survive."

I taught a short unit on advertising and globalization as part of my eleventh grade Global Studies class, with the unit culminating in two assignments: essays analyzing the world of advertising, and a project designed to "advertise the truth."

A key resource for the unit was the extraordinary video *The Ad and the Ego* (available from the Teaching for Change catalog, which is online at www.teachingforchange.org.) Although its narration is dense and at times academic, it is fast-moving, funny, and most importantly is about a topic with which students are intimately familiar. I stopped the video every few minutes to raise questions, ask for examples, or emphasize a point from the narration that may have been a bit obscure.

One of the video's strengths is its breadth of vision, covering the rise of advertising as an industry; its production of personal discontent and insecurity; its power to shape our sense of "the good life" and human happiness; the objectification of women; advertising's devastating environmental effects (making the using up of resources beautiful and desirable, and "translating the process of consumption into an erotic spectacle"); and its monopolization of public space, squeezing out alternative social and ecological visions.

The distributor, California Newsreel, has helpfully provided a transcript of the video on its website*, and I made copies of selected portions of this for my class. After we watched the video, I cut out about 50 ads from magazines ranging from *Cosmopolitan* and *Seventeen* to *Newsweek* and *People*, and posted these around the classroom. I asked students to find a specific ad that seemed to illustrate one of the video quotes and to write about that, or to treat the ads as a group and write about how they related to one or more of the quotes. I encouraged students to wander around the room and look over the ads before deciding what to write. (I left the ads posted on the bulletin boards for several weeks, and we frequently referred to them in class discussions. However, the spectacle of Marlboro men and Wonder Bra women tacked up around the room did generate some raised eyebrows when colleagues dropped by to talk.)

In previous years I've asked students to find their own ads and to write critiques of these. This has the advantage of encouraging students to re-see the commercial messages of the magazines that they read themselves, and I hope the activity allows them to gain a certain critical distance from messages that they may have previously simply absorbed as "natural." As Bernard McGrane suggests in *The Ad and the Ego*, "It's like breathing the air. You don't notice the pollution." In past years, I've used an opaque projector to display each of the ads students bring in. Students share their insights with the class and I require them to raise at least two discussion questions about their ads.

This particular year, I wanted them to expend their creative energy writing essays on advertis-

ing, and afterward constructing projects to "advertise the truth." (See box on p. 302.) I began by putting students in small groups and asking them to use the *Ad and the Ego* transcripts to brainstorm at least ten possible thesis statements that could power their essays. Later I asked students to choose one of these, and as a class we reviewed possible types of essay introductions: a question, a personal anecdote, a quote from the video, a story, an amazing fact, a hard-hitting thesis statement, the description of a particular magazine ad or TV commercial, etc. (Generally, before I let students begin an essay, I require that they write at least two different introductions, so they don't just pick the first thing that comes to mind.) I had other essay requirements as well. See the "Producing Consumers Essay" box on p. 304.

As students considered their topics, I supplemented *The Ad and the Ego* with parts of the PBS

> "The function of advertising became the production of discontent in human beings. One of the sub-texts in all advertising is you're not OK, you're not OK the way you are, things are bad, you need salvation. And in that sense advertising is designed to generate endless self criticism, to generate all sorts of anxieties, all sorts of doubts, and then to offer the entire world of consumer goods as salvation. That's where salvation rests, anything and everything that you can buy."
>
> —Bernard McGrane
> Chapman University

ADVERTISING THE TRUTH

In a poem for my Global Studies class one year, Cameron Robinson wrote:

> The world is full of many masks,
> the hard part is seeing beneath them.

As we've seen in *The Ad and The Ego*, the ads posted around the room, and in the video, *Affluenza*, advertising creates masks about society. It teaches us that buying products can fulfill our deepest needs, at the same time that it *hides* the conditions under which those products are made as well as the environmental consequences of endless consumption. For example, in a Nike ad, we never see the working or living conditions of Nike workers in Indonesia or China. In a Texaco ad we never see the effects of twenty years of oil drilling and dumping in the Ecuadorian rainforests. Of course, ads don't encourage us to think critically about the ads themselves, and how they can affect us psychologically.

Assignment choices:

1. Choose a product (possibly the one you did in your "Journey of the _____" research*) and make an ad (either magazine or TV). Tell a deeper truth about the product than would be told in an actual ad. For example, you might have the ad narrated by one of the workers who make this product — perhaps in Honduras or Saipan. Have him or her tell about what *really* goes into the product that the advertiser is selling. They could talk about wages, working conditions, or living conditions.

Or: Write about this product from the standpoint of the environment. Perhaps have "Mother Earth" be the narrator. How does Mother Earth view all the chemicals, packaging, waste, etc. created by mass consumption? Or, for example, have the Huaorani leader, Moi, narrate a car ad and describe the effects of the global automobile culture on the Huaorani people and the rainforest.‡

2. Another way to get at this: Choose one of the ads posted on the wall or another one you find from a magazine (or TV). Write about that product in the way you think it should be written about. "The people who make this product want you to think.... but really....." Make an "ad" to teach people how to read the deeper meaning of an ad.

3. Model an ad after the Adbusters "Uncommercials" that try to raise awareness about over-consumption. Choose an idea that you've had this year about the world that you think is important. Find a creative way to "advertise" that idea. You could do it as a short play, like the girls in the *Affluenza* video.

4. Write and illustrate a children's book about advertising, or about some aspect of the "global sweatshop" and consumerism.

Students chose one of their possessions (a shirt, a teddy bear, sneakers) made in a poor country and researched the company that produced it and the country where it was produced.

‡ *See the excellent video* Trinkets and Beads, *described in "Videos With a Global Conscience" p. 367.*

Note: This box is on the Rethinking Schools website at www.rethinkingschools.org/rg should you want to adapt it for your classes.

documentary *Affluenza*. Although *Affluenza* covers some of the same territory as *The Ad and the Ego*, — and much of it not as well — it focuses more broadly on the politics of *stuff*, and our responsibility to deal with the social and ecological implications of consumption as a way of life. Some teachers have told me that younger students have an easier time with *Affluenza* than with *Ad and the Ego*, and that they appreciate *Affluenza*'s greater emphasis on ways that young people can respond to the disease of consumerism.

Students wrote fine essays, although these tended to focus more on how ads affected them individually than on the broader role that advertising plays in the global economy or global environmental problems. Consequently, their writing also tended to propose individual solutions to social problems — many of which boiled down to "Be yourself; don't be influenced by the harmful messages of ads." That said, many of the papers were passionate and insightful. Sarah Garnes wrote an essay titled, "After All, You're Ugly. Right?" which reads in part:

> Have you ever looked in the mirror and it seemed to look back at you as it ridiculed your every flaw?
>
> Where's your cleavage, girl? Your butt is just way too big! And those thighs, what is there to do about those big mama thighs? You're staying in this house, I don't want you to humiliate both of us. Try a plastic surgeon, girl, 'cause you need a miracle....
>
> Advertising tries to make women increasingly uncomfortable in their lives. When a woman sees another woman on television or on the street, usually the first thing that comes to her mind is, "She's so beautiful, if only I could look like that." Then automatically that woman looks for methods to increase her beauty....

The market of products out there never lets you know you're OK or that you too are a beautiful person. Rather, they try to show you how you need to increase your beauty. Get a tan, get luscious lashes, fuller lips, and shiny nails.

After all, you're ugly. Right?

A number of my students were also enrolled in my colleague Bill McClendon's social psychology class, and this overlap was especially valuable in deepening the feminist critique of advertising. To look at the social construction of gender roles, Bill shows Jean Kilbourne's video *Still Killing Us Softly*, as well as Sut Jhally's disturbing *Dreamworlds*, about the image of women and sexuality in music videos. These were somewhat beyond the scope of my advertising unit, but they should definitely be considered for broader units on critical media literacy.

As part of offering students prompts for their "Advertising the Truth" projects, following their essays, I showed them the *Culture Jammer's Video* including six "uncommercials" produced by the Media Foundation (see "Videos With a Global Conscience," p. 368). I wanted to offer video as a possible medium for students to use with their projects, but I also hoped that the strong environmental orientation of the uncommercials — as well as their quirky irreverence — would nudge students to consider approaches they may not have considered when choosing essay topics.

I also shared with my classes several playful and astute projects completed by students of fellow Franklin High School global studies teacher Sandra Childs (including a full-color travel brochure to "Disney Haiti"), as well as projects completed the previous year by two of my U.S. history students, Angela Bolster ("The Little Book on Ads," a simple but not simplistic story about the effects of advertising, written for her little sister) and Aaron Shogren ("Watch More Television," a sardonic poster advertising TV to teenagers). Experience has taught me that the more varied examples of excellent student work that I can share as I give an assignment, the more diverse and imaginative the results will be.

One of my favorite projects completed by a student was Erin Olinghouse's "Sweatshop Barbie." Earlier in the term we'd watched a *Dateline* hidden-camera exposé called "Toy Story" that showed young girls in Indonesia and China making toys, including Barbie dolls, destined for the U.S. market. A number of the factories were dank and crowded, with electric cords

> "The problem, of course, is that the ads are encouraging people to participate in cycles of disposal which represent, on an ecological level, some of the most fundamental crises of contemporary life."
>
> —Stuart Ewen
> Hunter College,
> author, *Captains of Consciousness*

hanging dangerously above the machines. Erin had also researched sweatshop conditions in Nike's Vietnamese factories (see for example, www.globalexchange.org). For her "truth ad," Erin not only designed an alternative Barbie "ad," she assembled the entire Sweatshop Barbie doll and packaging. "Pay her just 20¢ an hour, like in a real Nike Factory!!" screams the outside of the box. "'I work cheap!' She says: 'I love my job.... I love my job.... I love my job....' 'I haven't met my quota yet!'" "Have her work in your make-believe Nike factory!" The doll itself is barefoot, holding a miniature Nike shoe. The "promo" material on Erin's package reads:

> This SweatShop Barbie came straight from a Vietnam Nike shoe factory. She works along with many other women and young girls until her quota for the day is met. This could be for up to 26 to 27 days out of the month and 40-45 hours of overtime. This SweatShop Barbie isn't done working yet! After work she has a family to take care of. She has to give up meals so that she can feed, clothe and pay rent on a daily wage of $1.60.... Don't worry about the conditions you put this worker in, if she can survive a Nike factory, she can survive anything! Buy your Barbie today.

Amanda Muldoon's project was a book of "un-ads," and included one for Target stores, showing a woman lost in her Target-purchased sheets and pillows. The text: "Is it possible to get lost in your own home?" With Amanda's reply just below:

> How much stuff will it take to make you this happy? How many hours will you have to work, to earn enough money to buy the stuff

PRODUCING CONSUMERS ESSAY

The video *The Ad and the Ego* uses advertising to ask important questions about our society. Write an essay on an aspect covered in the video. Some questions you might address, but are not limited to:

- What kind of people do ads try to "produce"?
  How do advertisers try to produce men and women differently?

- What is the relationship between consumption and some of the problems we've looked at in the rest of the world? Sweatshop workers, the Huaorani, the Ladakhis, the Inuit, etc.?

- How are you personally affected by ads?

- What do ads teach us about the meaning of life? What is the story of happiness and fulfillment that ads tell?

- What can be done to "make a difference" in transforming consumer culture?

- Is the culture of consumption environmentally sustainable? Can we continue endlessly "producing" consumers here and in other countries? And, if not, what social changes need to occur?

BASIC ESSAY CHECKLIST

(Attach this sheet to your essay when you turn it in.)

_____ Clever, inviting title.

_____ Engaging, imaginative introduction.

_____ Important, clear thesis. *Write thesis statement here:*

_____ *Different* kinds of evidence (e.g., quotes from the films, quotes from articles, examples from your own life, examples from history, examples from contemporary society, etc.)

_____ At least two quotes used as evidence.

_____ Thesis is convincingly "proved"/demonstrated.

_____ Strong conclusion (summarizes, ties back to your introduction, raises further questions, etc.)

_____ Typed or in ink, legibly written or printed.

_____ No major errors of punctuation, grammar, spelling, paragraphing.

Note: This box is on the Rethinking Schools website at www.rethinkingschools.org/rg should you want to adapt it for your classes.

---

that makes you this happy? How do you feel doing your part to end life on this planet?

Jeny Hetum and Catherine Aiken produced a video spoofing the "Got Milk?" ad campaign. The video scans the dozens of milk-mustachioed celebrity magazine ads they've collected and segues into an "ad" for milk that features, among other skits, talking cows warning viewers of the health dangers posed by bovine growth hormones and antibiotics in our milk. They both scolded me on the last day of school, when I brought the class doughnuts and regular, non-organic milk. Kids these days.

* * *

Underpinning this short unit were assumptions about advertising's role in the global economy. At its most immediate level, advertising is designed to sell specific products. But the more important *social* function of advertising is to sell the entire system of commodity production. Advertising is the smiling face of global capitalism, telling us and our students that everything is fine and getting better. More things will secure happiness and fulfillment for all.

The process of production doesn't exist in Ad-World. Who makes products, and under what conditions, is invisible, irrelevant. What matters are all the new toys that will make our lives richer. Vast global inequalities or the consequences of Third World debt don't make it onto the map of Ad-world. Neither does the frightening global environmental crisis.

To the extent that ads feature nature, it represents merely the out-of-doors site of our commodity-filled playpen — a place to drive our new Jeep Cherokee. In essence, ads strive to make us stupid; they make us *not-think, not-question, not-critique*.

Former British Prime Minister Margaret Thatcher once said that society doesn't exist; there are only individuals and families. This is the advertising message as well: Think for yourself; be an individual; satisfying your wants and needs is all that matters. Ads invite us to meet the world of commodities as individual consumers. Indeed this is the advertising definition of freedom: personal choice. Ads tell you to think for yourself, not to think for humanity, not to think for the earth, not to think for the oppressed. But there is a different world that we never hear about in ads: a world of collective action, of people organized in unions, environmental organizations, women's organizations, cross-border alliances for social justice, etc.

Advertising is so pervasive, its message so consistent, so monolithic, that it may be wishful thinking to expect a brief critical examination of its worldview to make much of a difference in kids' thinking. Or maybe not. Perhaps a unit like this one has even more power, because of the silence of critical voices in the commerce-controlled media, Perhaps its critique is amplified because of its absence in the rest of students' lives.

And perhaps a critical unit on advertising can affect students' thinking because it gives them a new conceptual vocabulary to describe things that have been bothering them all along. The world that advertising portrays may be seductive, but in countless ways it's a lie. Prospects for the success of critical teaching rest in part on the hope that students would prefer fuller, more accurate knowledge with which to guide their lives. ∎

Bill Bigelow (bbpdx@aol.com) teaches at Franklin High School in Portland, Oregon and is a Rethinking Schools editor.

A teaching guide for The Ad and the Ego *is available at www.robwilliamsmedia.com/downloads/ robwilliams_adego.pdf. Selected quotes can be found on the Rethinking Schools website, www.rethinkingschools. org/rg. For ordering information for* Affluenza, *see the PBS website, www.pbs.org.*

"That's one of advertisement's most brilliant accomplishments, to get us to believe that we're not affected by advertising."

—Bernard McGrane

"The very processes which may endanger human survival are often portrayed as, you know, intense sensual experiences, and there's a whole industry which is involved, in fact, in translating the process of consumption into an erotic spectacle.... Part of what advertising does, I mean, if you want to talk about what are the messages embedded within advertising as a whole, I would say the number one thing is the very principle of consumption, that is to say, making beautiful and desirable the using up of resources.... Consumer culture is predicated on premeditated waste, that is to say, the health of the consumer economy is intimately connected to the sickness of the environmental structure."

—Stuart Ewen

Critical Global Math Literacy

BY BOB PETERSON

"I didn't know fractions could make such a powerful point about the world," one of my fifth graders reflected after finishing her math assignment. The assignment was an outgrowth of the class watching an anti-consumerism Adbusters commercial (see "Videos With a Global Conscience," p. 368). In the 30-second video spot, an "American Excess" pig emerges out of a map of North America, burps, and announces: "A tiny 5% of the people of the world consumes one-third of its resources and produces almost one-half of the non-organic waste. Those people are us."

The assignment had been to change the percentages to fractions, to draw a graph contrasting the data, and to write about the significance of the information. The mini-project took only one class period and was integrated into our study of percent, fractions, and decimals. It allowed me to observe students' understanding of one aspect of percent and fractions, as well as their graphing and thinking skills. It also allowed students to begin to see the power of math and express their concerns about world problems. During one such lesson we had a lengthy debate about responsibility that wealthy countries have towards the earth's environment and people. After the discussion one of my students wrote, "When I think about the poverty I feel sad. I think the problem is 'countryism' as we are supposed to be at the same level. It's like sexism when men and women aren't at the same level."

Mathematics, like language, is both a discipline unto itself and a tool to understand and interact with the world and other academic disciplines. Just as written and oral language help a student understand one's surroundings, so too can written and oral mathematics.

Most of my students learn that mathematics is a powerful and useful tool because I flood my classroom with examples of how math is central to many "hot topics" that kids like to discuss and study. I regularly clip news articles and file them for future use — articles such as "25% of the Mammals Species Now Extinct," "Women Government Leaders Underrepresented," "10 Million Land Mines Threaten Afghanistan." Through lessons that integrate math and social studies and science, students see how math is central to understanding issues of social and ecological justice (and injustice) in our world.

For example, after my students participated in the International Beach Sweep (sponsored by The Ocean Conservancy) one September we tallied up all the types of debris that we had found on the shores of Lake Michigan. Of all the items found, 51% were cigarette butts. As students made graphs of their data we spoke of both individual and corporate responsibility towards the earth. We practiced understanding big numbers and place value by looking at the profits that tobacco companies made in one year and the number of deaths caused by tobacco each year in the United States (more than 400,000) and around the world (6,000,000). Using data that the tobacco industry spent over $65 million dollars lobbying Congress in 1998, students calculated the average amount of money spent per U.S. Representative. We examined why Congress has failed to put limits on the U.S. tobacco industry as it expands its global reach —

"I didn't know fractions could make such a powerful point about the world," one of my fifth graders reflected after finishing her math assignment.

two-thirds of U.S. tobacco company sales and nearly half of their profits come from overseas.

The Adbusters video has other "un-ads" alerting students to the influence of advertising and consumerism on the earth. Every day, students are targeted by corporate advertising to consume. When they see anti-consumerism ads, students stop and take stock. I explain that studies show that kids are three times as sensitive to tobacco advertising than adults and are more likely to be influenced to smoke by cigarette marketing than by peer pressure. We use statistics from UNICEF to show how small amounts of money can buy life-saving medicines and then contrast the cost of those items with advertisement-related tobacco costs. We figure out how much medicine could be bought with the money spent by just one individual who smokes a pack a day and by the tobacco industry that annually spends $8.4 billion dollars on advertising and promotion in the United States.

Throughout the year, students examine different social and ecological problems using math. I encourage students to bring in math-related items they see in the news. I regularly search the Internet for background statistics on topics like global warming, deforestation, water depletion, land mines, tobacco, and child labor to bring my math lessons alive. For math "class," I pose problems that have social significance that help students practice whatever particular skill we are focusing on. All together, by the time students leave my fifth grade classroom their skill and understanding of math is improved, and their understanding of the world is sharpened. ■

Bob Peterson (repmilw@aol.com) teaches fifth grade at La Escuela Fratney in Milwaukee, Wisconsin and is a Rethinking Schools editor.

Rethinking "Primitive" Cultures:

Ancient Futures and Learning from Ladakh

A video on a little-known culture prompts students to consider the meaning of "development."

BY BILL BIGELOW

I'm old enough to be part of the generation — and perhaps the social class — whose mothers told us: "Eat everything on your plate. There are people starving in India." The impression I got from such exhortations, as well as from the school curriculum, was that we in the United States were healthy, economically comfortable, and happy. People in "underdeveloped" countries were hungry, poor, and miserable.

The story of Ladakh calls these stereotypes into question, and also makes us rethink the idea that "development" is a good thing — or perhaps that there even is such a category as "development."

I begin my eleventh grade Global Studies curriculum by examining the contact between some indigenous cultures and the modern world. I want students to question the "primitive-to-advanced" continuum that has long been a fundamental myth of Western cultures. Of course, I'm not anxious for them to imagine indigenous cultures as conflict-free Edens or to conclude that everything "modern" is corrupt. Nonetheless, I do want students to appreciate key aspects of many traditional societies — ecological sustainability, cooperation, interdependence, considering "us" instead of only "me" — that may be crucial as we confront the future of the earth and humanity. I also want my classes to "visit" societies that prompt them to reconsider basic features of our own society. Words and concepts like economic growth, progress, development, and individual freedom are often presented to students (and all the rest of us, for that matter) as synonyms for "good." But these

> Words and concepts like economic growth, progress, development, and individual freedom are often presented to students (and all the rest of us, for that matter) as synonyms for "good".

metaphors are not unproblematic. They are ideological building blocks for practices that are inherently unsustainable — for example, proposing that an automobile-based consumer society like ours is the model of "development" for countries around the globe. They celebrate the production of a cornucopia of *things*, while turning our attention away from a social and ecological emergency — an emergency that includes the frightening pace of global warming, rainforest destruction, species extinction, pesticide proliferation, and the like. Finally, growth and development metaphors also discourage us from considering fundamental alternatives to the current damaging socio-cultural arrangements.

Central to this curricular rethinking in my classes is an extraordinary video, *Ancient Futures: Learning from Ladakh*, which is based on a book of the same name by Helena Norberg-Hodge. (See "Videos With a Global Conscience," p. 366.)

Ladakh is located in the northern Indian state of Jammu and Kashmir, and is so high in the Himalayas that it is snowed under for eight months of the year. In fact, it's the highest place in the world where people live year-round. It's the size of England, but is home to only 130,000 people.

When I first watched *Ancient Futures* I was fascinated by its portrayal of traditional Ladakh, a place where people appear to be deeply content yet lacking the material possessions valued in industrial societies. In this harsh land, with only 4 inches of rainfall a year and very short growing seasons, Ladakhis had worked out an elaborate system of cooperation, environmental care, and economic self-sufficiency. The video details the effects of the area's rapid incorporation into the global economy: In about two decades, cheap grain undermined traditional agriculture, new roads brought buses and trucks that filled the thin air with choking exhaust, and Ladakhis were bombarded with the values and temptations of consumer culture. As the video's narrator points out, "In the short term, cheap imported food might be a real benefit, but the result is that increasingly Ladakhis are being tied to a global economy, putting them at the mercy of market forces far beyond their control." The video's critique is not that new material goods in and of themselves are bad, but that their arrival is on the terms of a profit-oriented global economy and not of the Ladakhi people. Ladakhi poet and Buddhist scholar Tashi Rapkis, concludes in the video that Ladakhis are "getting more money, they're having more technology, they are getting very comfortable. But comfort and luxuries don't bring happiness." The video vividly brings this observation to life.

As I said, I was fascinated by the video, but how would students respond? Would *Ancient Futures* feel like just another *National Geographic* portrayal of exotic people in a pretty place? I was gratified that my students (and the students of teacher after teacher affiliated with the Rethinking Schools globalization workgroup in Portland) responded to the video with both wonder and alarm.

USING *ANCIENT FUTURES*

I tell students that we're going to watch a video about a place that most of them have likely never heard of before. On a world map, I point out the state of Jammu and Kashmir in far northern India, squeezed between Pakistan and Tibet (a country controlled by China). I tell them that as they watch the video, they should note as many aspects of Ladakhi culture as they can, and ask students for the meaning of "culture." We needn't settle on any particular dictionary-like definition, but I want them to begin with the understanding that culture is a totality, it's everything human that is not strictly biological: habits, patterns and ways of thinking and behaving. It's what we can see, like clothing; what we can hear, like language and music; what we can

A small boy with a sickle helps harvest barley in Ladakh.

taste, like food; but it's also the values and attitudes that give meaning to any particular cultural artifact. On the board I make three columns:

1. Ideas/attitudes/beliefs
2. Behaviors/relationships
3. "Artifacts"/elements of culture: animals used/tools/clothes/homes, etc.

Students copy these down and take notes in the columns as they watch the video. I urge them to write about what they see, not merely what they learn from the narrator.

The beginning of the video alerts viewers that Ladakh has been dramatically transformed by "development." I don't want students to learn about Ladakh's transformation until they've been exposed to traditional Ladakh and until we do an activity predicting how Ladakhi culture might be affected by Westernization. So we begin the video about five minutes into it, with a

Associated Press/Arthur Max

A woman wearing goggles — a gift from tourists — fingers her prayer beads in Ladakh.

ness, and violence. Of course, the filmmakers may have played up the culture's positive aspects, including its egalitarianism, and down-played less admirable qualities of traditional Ladakh. For example, the video ignores the reportedly poor treatment of some tribal people, and generally fails to deal forthrightly with questions of social class. But throughout the school year, the video lingers as a kind of touch-stone, reminding us that human nature may be less rapacious than we have come to accept as a result of living in a society that so lavishly rewards greed.

The following excerpt from a student paper is typical of the seeds of doubt planted by the video about the universality of aggressive self-ishness:

> Ladakh seems like a fantasy, something most people couldn't imagine. From my experiences, this would lead me to believe it's too good to be true. But then I would have to ask myself, "Is it too good to be true? Or could it just be that the society I live in has led me to be this untrusting?"

I stop the video before the arrival of modern-ization, right after several still shots of smiling Ladakhi men and women. (This first part is 21 minutes long, not including the piece I skip at the very beginning.) I ask students to look back over their notes and to talk about what they see as the key cultural elements that have sustained Ladakh for over 1,000 years. Are there particular pieces of the culture that, if taken away, would make Ladakh stop being Ladakh, that would begin to erode the culture? I want students to begin to feel some discomfort with the glib terms that textbooks and commentators use to describe today's countries and cultures. I ask: Would you call Ladakh a developed society, an underdevel-oped society, a developing society? Is it primi-tive, backward, advanced?

Students readily see the difficulty in applying these conventional terms to a society that had none of the comforts of their homes, and yet had worked out such an elaborate system of cooper-ation to take care of each other and the land. "People don't waste anything in Ladakh," says Ladakhi elder Tashi Rapkis:

> It may be wood, it may be stones, it may be grass, it may be water. They don't waste it, they take care of it. In that way we could say that the Ladakhis are the real economists. Not like the modern economists, increasing production,

scene of Ladakhi men blowing long horns, immediately following Helena Norberg Hodge saying that traditional Ladakh "shows how we might get out of this mess that we've created."

I'm generally good at predicting whether a reading, activity, or video will captivate stu-dents, but as I mentioned, I wasn't confident that students would respond positively to the video, or to the traditional culture it portrayed. To my delight, most seem enchanted by the ecological sophistication, the cooperation, the playful inter-actions between young and old, the relative eco-nomic equality, and the joy people appeared to take in their work. Many students seem gen-uinely relieved to discover a place that appears not to be consumed with materialism, selfish-

---

destroying all the natural resources. Not like that. Rather, taking care of natural resources, and how to develop them.

As one of my students summed up nicely: "The people knew their earth and used it well."

For homework I sometimes give students Chapter 4, "We Have to Live Together," from Helena Norberg-Hodge's book, so they have more information for discussions and later essay writing. The chapter explores the tension between individual rights and the culture's need to maintain solidarity. For older students, Norberg-Hodge's entire book might be assigned.

CULTURAL INVASION

I tell students that several years ago, Ladakh began experiencing a kind of cultural invasion, what some people call Westernization, modernization or development. "Based on what you've learned about Ladakh," I say, "I want us to see if we can predict some of the consequences of these changes on traditional Ladakhi culture." On the board, I list six different features of the Western cultural invasion: tourism; compulsory schooling; highway development; foreign movies; imports of inexpensive barley and wheat; and the arrival of new retail stores. I divide the class into six groups and assign each of them one of these features. Each group's task is to brainstorm as many consequences for Ladakhi culture as they possibly can, and to do these as a "spillover chart," sometimes called a concept map. I like the term spillover chart because it's a metaphor that captures the idea that the effects from one social change keep spilling over into further effects. It helps us imagine society as a network of interconnections, rather than as discrete institutions.

I do an example with them. On the board I write "Unemployment doubles" and I circle it. Then I ask them to brainstorm as many consequences as they possibly can for how a doubling of unemployment could affect life in Portland. I emphasize that this is speculative; there aren't any correct answers, but their projections should be reasonable. I ask about the effects on young people, on mental health, on family life, on government programs, and encourage them to draw on their own experiences. For each student comment — for example: "People wouldn't be able to buy as much" — I ask about additional consequences, and connect each consequence by drawing a line to the previous consequence.

I assemble students in their six groups and distribute large pieces of blank easel paper, roughly

Spanning the generations in Ladakh.

two feet by three feet, along with magic markers and a card with a brief description of the aspect of Westernization that they'll be working on (see "Ladakh Situations," p. 315).

When they finish, I ask students in their small groups to discuss among themselves which three of the spillover effects they think would most deeply affect life in Ladakh, and to somehow highlight these on their charts. The first year I did this, each group reported on its entire spillover chart and this quickly became tedious. Asking them to indicate and then to elaborate on their top three consequences speeds up presentations and doesn't sacrifice anything major. Students' predictions are uncannily, and depressingly, accurate. Sometimes they veer off into the silly or tangential, but the top three predictions will almost always be verified by what they learn from watching the second part of the video.

We post their spillover charts around the classroom. As we begin the second part of the video,

I ask them to take notes on which of their predictions came true, and to list any additional consequences of Westernization that they notice.

If the first part of the video has left students enchanted with and intrigued by Ladakh, the second part will leave them angry. In this 33-minute segment, students see each of the dire predictions for Ladakh from their spillover charts come true. A man interviewed on the street in Ladakh's capital, Leh, summarizes the changes wrought by development: "People used to have peace of mind. They were happy and they used to help one another. These days there are motorbikes and things, there have been all sorts of improvements, but on the inside I don't see the same kind of happiness."

Tsering Dolkar, a Ladakhi farmer, laments the loss of shared work on each other's farms that characterized traditional Ladakh: "Now everyone's going off looking for paid jobs, you can't get any help with plowing or harvesting without paying for it."

Sonam Wangchuk is a brilliant, articulate Ladakhi student leader interviewed in the video. He talks about how "development" has affected young people, as they've been compelled to attend school to learn in Urdu and then in English, both foreign languages to Ladakhis. He says that 90 to 95% of Ladakhi students fail their final school exams, and emphasizes what a tragedy this is for them and for the entire culture:

> When students fail their school exams they are really in trouble. They cannot go back to the traditional life and start doing farming and other things because they are so confused because they have been kept away. And they are rejected by the modern sectors. So they belong to none of these. They are rejected by the modern, they are cut off from the traditional.

Following the video, I give students a writing assignment: "Who or what is to blame for the decline of Ladakhi culture? Write this as an essay answer, with a clear thesis (implied or stated), introduction, several pieces of evidence, and a conclusion. And, if you like: What could be done to stop the destruction of Ladakhi culture?"

Where students are uniformly dismayed by the erosion of traditional Ladakhi culture, there is no such uniformity in their essays. Some attack U.S. and European tourists for their insensitivity and for introducing the virus of materialism to Ladakh. Others go after the Indian government for building roads that allow tourists and Western culture free access to Ladakh. Others see the "enemy" more systemically, as global capitalism or Western Civilization in general. A student in one recent class provocatively blamed people in the United States for exporting a vision of the "good life" throughout the world that was both undesirable and unattainable for those living in other cultures. Still others blamed the Ladakhis themselves; no one had forced these changes on them — ultimately the defense and preservation of their culture was no one's responsibility but theirs.

I first read Helena Norberg-Hodge's book *Ancient Futures* several years ago and though I found it enormously insightful, I was struck by its lack of clarity in specifying the cause of the cultural calamity that she details so passionately. At various times the culprit is "modern technologies," "industrial culture," "industrialized

Associated Press/Arthur Max

The Drung Durung glacier at the foot of Z-3, one of the highest mountains in Ladakh.

society," "the scientific perspective," or "the development process." To these, the video adds "Western notions of progress" and "the new economy." Thinking clearly about underlying causes is not simply an academic nicety. The effectiveness of strategies to build societies of social and ecological justice depends on the accuracy of our diagnoses of the roots of global ills. As Norberg-Hodge argues herself in *Ancient Futures*, the central moral imperative of our time is to "tackle the underlying causes behind social and ecological destruction."

THE TRIAL OF LADAKH

Students' wildly varied responses to the question about the roots of the problem in Ladakh gave me the idea of structuring our discussion about this issue as a trial. The crime would be the harm done to traditional Ladakhi culture. I used students' diverse essay responses to decide on "defendants," and even borrowed language from students' papers to craft the indictments. (See www.rethinkingschools.org/rg for the text of these.) I played prosecutor, and students were divided into groups, each representing one of the accused.

The description of "The Case of Cultural Destruction" that I gave students began:

> This is a complicated crime: A culture that existed in relative peace and harmony for generations is in the process of being destroyed. Greed has replaced cooperation; pollution has replaced care for the earth; insecurity has replaced security; "look out for number one" has replaced family and community. If this process continues it will destroy a viable, ecologically responsible culture. The people there will be the big losers, but everyone in the world is harmed at least indirectly when we lose a culture like this.

That's the crime. But who or what is to blame? Defendants included:

- U.S. and European Tourists (for thoughtlessly introducing Ladakh to Western materialism);
- The Indian Government (for promoting Ladakhi "development");
- The Ladakhis themselves (for their failure to resist cultural invasion);
- The Global Capitalist System (for being the economic motor that powers development and cultural invasion);

- "Modern" ideas (for teaching Ladakhis that their culture was inferior to so-called developed cultures); and
- People in the United States (for unwittingly creating a model of development that spreads and negatively impacts other cultures around the globe.)

Each student received all indictments, so groups could use arguments from an indictment against another group in their own defense. (See p. 177, "The Global Sweatshop Trial" for a model of this teaching strategy.)

In their post-trial write-ups distributing responsibility, I asked students to assign percentages of blame to each group. Students spared none of the defendants, including the Ladakhis. Noah gave 8% of the blame to Ladakhis: "They really didn't do much to stop the development of their country, but what can you expect? Their culture is based around non-aggression."

Lauren gave 25% of the blame to People in the United States: "The ones who walk with their eyes closed and their fingers in their ears. 'La, la, la, we are the only country in the world, la, la, la.' Being absolutely oblivious does not mean you're not guilty." Colleen gave 20% of the blame to the Indian government, who "literally paved the road for capitalism, modern ideas, U.S. and European tourists" to "open the can of worms."

In an exceptionally lucid paper, Andrea fingered the economic system:

> The Global Capitalist Economy bears the greatest blame for what has happened in Ladakh. This mysterious and intangible entity exists behind the action of all others. It is global capitalism that seeks to turn every corner of the globe into a marketplace to be exploited, and every man, woman, and child into a lifetime consumer of useless products.

My aim with this activity was not to reach consensus about a single cause for the decline of indigenous cultures like Ladakh. Just the opposite. Yes, some factors play a greater role in the trend toward a monocultural world dominated by commercial values, but I'd hoped that students would see how these factors interrelate, and how any strategy for change needs to address a very large picture indeed.

But Leela criticized my requirement to assign percentages of guilt and pointed out how this requirement didn't facilitate students' exploration of interrelationships:

A monastery near Mulbeckh in Ladakh, sitting at the foot of a 30-foot Buddhist figure carved into the rock face during the 8th century.

Leela closed her paper with an additional criticism of the Ladakh unit: "We covered who was to blame quite thoroughly, but just pointing a finger is not enough. We need to work towards solutions." She was right again: Analysis of wrongdoing does not automatically suggest possible alternatives. Thus I concluded the unit by asking students to imagine that they were activists with the International Society for Ecology and Culture (ISEC) (see Organizations and Websites for Global Justice, p. 186): "You are committed to helping to preserve indigenous cultures around the world — not because you think they are 'quaint,' but because you believe that indigenous cultures hold great wisdom about how all human beings should relate to each other and to the earth." In a whole-class discussion as ISEC activists, they brainstormed three projects — either in cooperation with groups in Ladakh, or in this country — that could "reverse the trend of globalization and cultural destruction." We followed this discussion by watching an ISEC-produced video, *Local Futures*, about the group's work in Ladakh and Great Britain (available from ISEC, www.isec.org.uk). The video drifts a bit toward self-promotion, but it's valuable for students to see that organizers around the world are creatively addressing the problems they witnessed in *Ancient Futures*.

* * *

As an early warning system, miners used to take canaries with them into the mines. The birds were affected by the presence of dangerous gases before the miners would be. When the canaries' songs fell silent, disaster was close at hand. Ladakhis are not canaries; they are human beings. But the arrival of "development" and the decline of traditional cultures as depicted in *Ancient Futures* ought to be a warning to us all. Throughout the world, canaries have stopped singing. *Ancient Futures* helps students notice the silence. ∎

Creating easily definable groups made it easy for students to understand who was involved in the situation in Ladakh and what their role was.... However, assigning blame seems to over-simplify the situation.... Each group is to blame, but in different ways. I find it impossible to compare them directly in terms of percentages.

Hers was a valid point, and I've since dropped the percentage requirement. Nonetheless, the trial does allow students to glimpse myriad ways in which all of us are implicated — albeit differently. Ironically, this offers some hope: If responsibility for the destruction of cooperative, ecologically sensitive cultures like Ladakh is so dispersed, it means that we don't need to travel half way around the world to make a global difference; we can be effective change-makers by engaging in projects close to home. But these implications need to be explicitly drawn out.

Bill Bigelow (bbpdx@aol.com) teaches at Franklin High School in Portland, Oregon and is a Rethinking Schools editor.

Ladakh Situations

Tourism

Lots of wealthy tourists from India, Europe, and the United States are beginning to arrive in Ladakh.

Compulsory Schooling

The government of India requires all children — including Ladakhi children — to attend public school. School will promote "progressive" ideas about the need for India and Ladakh to become more developed, like the United States and Great Britain. Primary school will be conducted in Urdu (a language not traditionally spoken in Ladakh) and secondary school will be conducted in English. These languages are considered more "modern."

Highway Development

The government has constructed new highways connecting Ladakh with the large cities of India. This will allow more travel to and from Ladakh. The government hopes that increased transportation will help Ladakh to "develop."

Foreign Movies

New theatres have opened in Ladakh. They show movies from all over the world. "Bollywood" movies — those made in Bombay, India, patterned after Hollywood movies — are the most common. They are Indian versions of U.S. films like the James Bond or *Lethal Weapon* series and *Independence Day*, etc.

Inexpensive Imported Barley and Wheat

"Free trade" means that goods from all over the world are being sold in India and in Ladakh. Merchants are importing large quantities of wheat and barley grown on huge mechanized farms owned by multinational corporations. Even after being transported long distances, the barley and wheat is sold for much less money than that grown in Ladakh.

New Stores in Ladakh

Merchants have moved into Ladakhi towns to open new stores. The stores sell goods from all over the world: TVs, VCRs, radios, refrigerators, posters of U.S. movie stars and sports heroes, etc. Many of the things for sale have never been seen before in Ladakh.

TEACHING IDEAS

"SPREAD THE WEALTH"
Cartoon by Angela Bolster (11th grade), (p. 264)

As we've indicated throughout this book, it's helpful to get students to literally *picture* what is going on in the world. In her cartoon, drawn as part of a project to create visual representations of globalization, eleventh grader Angela Bolster shows her perspective on the "wealth" that is being spread around the globe.

Ask students to create cartoons or metaphorical drawings that depict the impact of globalization on the environment.

"GLOBAL WARMING: THE ENVIRONMENTAL ISSUE FROM HELL"
Article by Bill McKibben (p. 263)

Divide students into small groups and have them do "spillover charts" anticipating diverse consequences of global warming. The idea is simply to imagine the "spillover" or ripple effects of various aspects of global warming — listing effects of the effects of the effects, etc. For example, students could speculate about what would happen if the oceans rose significantly. How would that spill-over through the world? Have them locate other details from McKibben's article. Students will need large sheets of display paper to list or draw all the consequences that they will brainstorm. (See p. 311, in the article on teaching the video *Ancient Futures*, for a more thorough description of spillover charts.)

- McKibben writes, "The normal answer, when you're mounting a campaign, is to look for self-interest, to scare people by saying what will happen to us if we don't do something: All the birds will die, the canyon will disappear beneath a reservoir, we will choke to death on smog." He says that won't work. Why not?

- McKibben believes that one reason this must be a moral crusade is because it is the wealthy countries attacking the poorer countries — "we've never figured out a more effective way to harm the marginalized and poor of this planet." How does global warming disproportionately affect the world's poor?

- McKibben states that the villain of global warming is us. Who exactly is "us"? Do you think that all people and social classes are equally to blame for the causes of global warming? Do we all benefit equally from, say, the decision to produce SUVs? Do we all suffer equally from their effects?

- McKibben writes that SUVs are a real cause of global warming, but also a perfect symbol of what's wrong with our society. Identify other cultural symbols that have negative ecological impacts. Do we have any symbols that exemplify ecological responsibility?

Global warming is also a moral issue for McKibben because it will affect people and other species for generations to come. Ask students to assume the personas of individuals in the next century or after, and write a letter to people in the early 21st century, saying what they could and should have done to address global warming before its effects became so devastating. McKibben writes that, "If it had been done to us, we would loathe the generation that did it, precisely as we will one day be loathed."

Ask students to list all the solutions or activist ideas that McKibben proposes. Have students work in small groups to map out campaigns to fight global warming. Urge students to be visionary, and to think of the deep economic and cultural changes that will need to occur to deal fundamentally with the causes of global warming. Encourage them to think about steps that individuals can take but also to imagine the changes that will require organizational and collective action. (Too often, students are encouraged to think about change-making from only an individual standpoint.)

"MEXICAN PEASANT-ECOLOGISTS FIGHT TO PRESERVE FORESTS"
Article (p. 280)

Mexican farmer Rodolfo Montiel, whose activities are chronicled in this article, won the $125,000 Goldman Environmental Prize for "courageous activism." Have students work in small groups to research other activists who might deserve such an award. Create a class award, and have a ceremony to present it. Use this to talk about the kind of activism that will be required to deal *fundamentally* with the environmental challenges that your classes have encountered in their studies.

"ECOLOGICAL FOOTPRINTS"
Article and graphic,
by David Holtzman (p. 283)

Discussion and activities:

- Holtzman says: "If the ecological marks left by all the world's people are to be distributed more equitably, then U.S. citizens, Canadians and other residents of wealthy countries are going to have to make radical changes." What might some of these "radical changes" be?

- How could the United States reduce its "ecological footprint"? Think in terms of laws, policies, tax incentives, dramatic social changes.

- How could you and your family reduce your ecological footprint?

Download the Living Planet Report (www.rprogress.org/ef/LPR2000). Divide students into five groups corresponding to the "footprint" categories in the report: cropland, grazing land, forest, fishing ground, and carbon dioxide. Have each group report to the class on the footprint inequalities for their respective categories and propose strategies to address the inequality and overconsumption described in the report.

Note: In this activity, make sure to alert students to the problem of using averages. For example, the ecological footprint of Indonesia will be a good deal smaller than the United States. But there is an upper class in Indonesia whose consumption is a great deal more than the vast majority of U.S. families.

"WATER, WATER EVERYWHERE"
Article by The Turning Point Project and numerous environmental organizations (p. 284)

Have students use an atlas and a world map to find and mark all the places mentioned in this article. They can make symbols or drawings to illustrate the problems described.

Ask students:
- What's wrong with simply allowing the global market — supply and demand — to determine who in the world gets fresh water?

- If the global market is not used to allocate fresh water, then what should be used to allocate it?

- The writers indicate: "As the water crisis becomes worse, one would hope that the governments and global bureaucracies, conscious of the planet's limits, would advocate conservation." Why don't governments and bureaucracies currently advocate conservation?

Have students design a survey about global water usage. The object is twofold: 1. to determine survey participants' level of knowledge about water issues; and 2. to teach participants important information that they may not know. Students can use "Water, Water Everywhere?" to develop questions. For example, they might ask: What percentage of the world's fresh water goes to industrial agriculture? How much goes directly to human beings? How many people on earth lack access to clean, fresh drinking water? Students can chart their findings and decide on ways to report their results to the school or larger community.

Assign students to write science fiction stories about "When Everything is Privatized...." Students might simply use the example of water, as outlined here, and imagine a future if these trends continue. Allow them to also imagine circumstances, such as organized resistance, that could interrupt these trends.

The last section in the article is headed "Clear Choices." Instead of reading this with students, when you copy the article, block this section out. Tell students that the authors of this article proposed five needed changes in the way that water is used globally. Ask students to work in small groups to develop their own five proposals. After they've finished, discuss these and then share with them The Turning Point Project's five proposals.

"TV AND THE CLONING OF CULTURE"
Interview with Jerry Mander by Charlene Spretnak (p. 292)

For many students, this will be a difficult reading. Encourage students to read the interview in small groups and to complete the following questions as they read. Use these as the basis of discussion:

- In what ways did the arrival of television erode (hurt) the culture of the Inuit?

- Why was the Canadian government so anxious for Inuit people to be exposed to television?

- How do men and women appear to be affected differently by the arrival of television and other aspects of "modernization"?

- Mander says, "We've had to drive out of ourselves a whole construct of feelings, perceptions, and sensitivities that have made it possible for us to live in the manner in which we now live." What does he mean by that? Do you agree?

- What does Jerry Mander think should be done about the destruction of indigenous culture?

- What do *you* think should be done?

- Mander attributes the decline of traditional culture to the arrival of television. What other factors could be at work?

In the interview, Mander discusses the *values* that people learn from TV. Ask students to watch an hour of TV, and to write about what it is that people on TV appear to value. Be sure to have them include the ads, as well. Ask them to pay special attention to attitudes about the earth and the environment. (See Bob Peterson's article, p. 296, for further ideas.)

"MOUNTAINS O' THINGS"
Song by Tracy Chapman

The lyrics to "Mountains o' Things" can be found at many websites. For an up-to-date link visit www.rethinkingschools.org/rg.

Play the song, which comes from Tracy Chapman's outstanding first album. The song describes the dreams that our culture leads people to have. Ask students:

- Where do we get these dreams that Chapman describes?

- What other dreams are possible?

So many of our dreams depend on the consumption of things. Ask students to draw or write about an alternative "dream." Have people list all the activities that bring them joy that don't require the consumption of "mountains of things" or "exploiting other human beings." What do these have in common? What would it be like to organize a society around these kinds of activities instead of around the production and consumption of "mountains of things"?

CHAPTER EIGHT
Final Words

The Low Road

BY MARGE PIERCY

What can they do
to you? Whatever they want.
They can set you up, they can
bust you, they can break
your fingers, they can
burn your brain with electricity,
blur you with drugs till you
can't walk, can't remember, they can
take your child, wall up
your lover. They can do anything
you can't stop them
from doing. How can you stop
them? Alone, you can fight,
you can refuse, you can
take what revenge you can
but they roll over you.

But two people fighting
back to back can cut through
a mob, a snake-dancing file
can break a cordon, an army
can meet an army.

Two people can keep each other
sane, can give support, conviction,
love, massage, hope, sex.
Three people are a delegation,
a committee, a wedge. With four
you can play bridge and start
an organization. With six
you can rent a whole house,
eat pie for dinner with no
seconds, and hold a fund raising party.
A dozen make a demonstration.
A hundred fill a hall.
A thousand have solidarity and your
own newsletter;
ten thousand, power and your own
paper;
a hundred thousand, your own media;
ten million, your own country.

It goes on one at a time,
it starts when you care
to act, it starts when you do
it again after they said no,
it starts when you say *We*
and know who you mean, and each
day you mean one more.

Reprinted from The Moon is Always Female, *New York: Alfred A. Knopf, 1981.*

Page 319 image: Members of the Indigenous People's Group in Brazil protest the decision by Israel and the United States to pull out of a world conference on racism in 2001. Photo by Obed Zilwa for Associated Press.

Subcomandante Marcos stands amid Zapatista women and their children in Chiapas, Mexico.

Prayers for a Dignified Life
A Letter to Schoolchildren
About the Zapatista Uprising

BY SUBCOMANDANTE MARCOS

The Zapatista uprising in Mexico began on New Year's Day 1994, the day that NAFTA — the North American Free Trade Agreement — took effect. The rebels of the Zapatista National Liberation Army (EZLN) came out of the Lacandón Forest in the southeastern state of Chiapas, demanding an end to the exploitation and repression of the largely indigenous peasantry of the region.

Chiapas is home to almost a million Indians — Ch'ol, Lacandón, Tzeltal, Tzotzil, Tojolabal, and Zoque. At the time the rebellion began, according to government statistics, 35% of the dwellings of the region had no electricity, and 51% had dirt floors. Four out of every 10 workers made less than the official minimum wage of about $3 a day. But conditions for most indigenous peo-

ple of Chiapas and Mexico were much worse.

The region itself is not poor. For example, more than half of all of Mexico's hydroelectricity comes from dams in Chiapas. But, as Zapatista leader Subcomandante Marcos wrote in 1992, before the rebellion began: "Chiapas is bled through thousands of veins: through oil ducts and gas ducts, over electric wires, by railroad cars, through bank accounts, by trucks and vans, by ships and planes, over clandestine paths, third-rate roads, and mountain passes."

Soon after the rebellion began, Marcos wrote the following letter to schoolchildren in Guadalajara, in response to a letter they had written.

—The editors

To the Solidarity Committee of Elementary Boarding School #4, "Beatriz Hernández," Guadalajara, Jalisco, Mexico.

Boys and girls,

We received your letter of February 19, 1994, and the poem "Prayer for Peace" that came with it. It makes us very happy to know that boys and girls who live so far away from our mountains and our misery are concerned that peace should come to Chiapan lands. We thank you very much for your brief letter.

We would like you (and your noble teachers) to know that we did not take up arms for the pleasure of fighting and dying; it is not because we don't want peace that we look for war. We were living without peace already. Our boys and girls are like you, but infinitely poorer. For our children there are no schools or medicines, no clothes or food, not even a dignified roof under which we can store our poverty. For our boys and girls there is only work, ignorance, and death. The land that we have is worthless, and in order to get something for our children we have to leave home and look for work on land that belongs to others, powerful people, who pay us very little for our labor. Our children have to begin working at a very young age in order to be able to get food, clothing, and medicine. Our children's toys are the machete, the ax, and the hoe; from the time they are barely able to walk, playing and suffering they go out looking for wood, cleaning brush, and planting. They eat the same as we do: corn, beans, and chile. They cannot go to school to learn Spanish because work kills the days and sickness kills the nights. This is how our children have lived and died for 501 years.

We, their fathers, mothers, sisters, and brothers, no longer want to carry the guilt of not doing anything to help our children. We look for peaceful roads to justice and we find only mockery, imprisonment, blows, and death; we always find pain and sorrow. We couldn't take it anymore, boys and girls of Jalisco, it was too much

> **For our children there are no schools or medicines, no clothes or food, not even a dignified roof under which we can store our poverty.**

pain and sorrow. And then we were forced to take the road to war, because our voices had not been heard.

Boys and girls of Jalisco, we do not ask for handouts or charity, we ask for justice: a fair wage, a piece of good land, a decent house, an honest school, medicine that cures, bread on our tables, respect for what is ours, the liberty to say what is on our minds and to open our mouths so that our words can unite with others in peace and without death. This is what we have always asked for, boys and girls of Jalisco, and they didn't listen. And it was then that we took a weapon in our hands, it was then that we made our work tools into tools of struggle. We then turned the war that they had made on us, the war that was killing us — without you, boys and girls of Jalisco, knowing anything about it — we turned that war against them, the rich and the powerful, those who have everything and deserve nothing.

That is why, boys and girls of Jalisco, we began our war. That is why the peace that we want is not the peace that we had before, because that wasn't peace, it was death and contempt, it was pain and suffering, it was disgrace. That is why we are telling you, with respect and love, boys and girls of Jalisco, to raise high the dignified flag of peace, to write poems that are "Prayers for a Dignified Life," and to search, above all, for equal justice for everyone.

Salud, boys and girls of Jalisco.

From the mountains of the Mexican Southeast
CCRI-CG of the EZLN
Mexico, February 1994
Subcomandante Insurgente Marcos

Excerpted from Shadows of Tender Fury: The Letters and Communiqués of Subcomandante Marcos and the Zapatista Army of National Liberation, *translated by Frank Bardacke, Leslie López, and the Watsonville, California Human Rights Committee, New York: Monthly Review Press, 1995.*

Human Rights for a New Millennium

BY EDUARDO GALEANO

In 1948 and again in 1976, the United Nations proclaimed long lists of human rights, but the immense majority of humanity enjoys only the rights to see, hear, and remain silent. Suppose we start by exercising the never-proclaimed right to dream? Suppose we rave a bit? Let's set our sights beyond the abominations of today to divine another possible world:

- The air shall be cleansed of all poisons except those born of human fears and human passions.
- In the streets, cars shall be run over by dogs.
- People shall not be driven by cars, or programmed by computers, or bought by supermarkets, or watched by televisions.
- The TV set shall no longer be the most important member of the family and shall be treated like an iron or a washing machine.
- People shall work for a living instead of living for work.
- Written into law shall be the crime of stupidity, committed by those who live to have or to win, instead of living just to live like the bird that sings without knowing it and the child who plays unaware that he or she is playing.
- In no country shall young men who refuse to go to war go to jail, rather only those who want to make war.
- Economists shall not measure living standards by consumption levels or the quality of life by the quantity of things.
- Cooks shall not believe that lobsters love to be boiled alive.
- Historians shall not believe that countries love to be invaded.
- Politicians shall not believe that the poor love to eat promises.

Fishing for food in the polluted waters of Rio de Janeiro, Brazil.

- Earnestness shall no longer be a virtue, and no one shall be taken seriously who can't make fun of himself.
- Death and money shall lose their magical powers, and neither demise nor fortune shall make a virtuous gentleman of a rat.
- No one shall be considered a hero or a fool for doing what he believes is right instead of what serves him best.
- The world shall wage war not on the poor but rather on poverty, and the arms industry shall have no alternative but to declare bankruptcy.
- Food shall not be a commodity nor shall communications be a business, because food and communication are human rights.
- No one shall die of hunger, because no one shall die from overeating.

- Street children shall not be treated like garbage, because there shall be no street children.

- Rich kids shall not be treated like gold, because there shall be no rich kids.

- Education shall not be the privilege of those who can pay.

- The police shall not be the curse of those who cannot pay.

- Justice and liberty, Siamese twins condemned to live apart, shall meet again and be reunited, back to back.

- A woman, a Black woman, shall be president of Brazil, and another Black woman shall be president of the United States. And an Indian woman shall govern Guatemala and another Peru.

- In Argentina, the crazy women of the Plaza de Mayo shall be held up as examples of mental health because they refused to forget in a time of obligatory amnesia.

- The Church, holy mother, shall correct the typos on the tablets of Moses and the Sixth Commandment shall dictate the celebration of the body.

- The Church shall also proclaim another commandment, the one God forgot: You shall love nature, to which you belong.

- Clothed with forests shall be the deserts of the world and of the soul.

- The despairing shall be paired and the lost shall be found, for they are the ones who despaired and lost their way from so much lonely seeking.

- We shall be compatriots and contemporaries of all who have a yearning for justice and beauty, no matter where they were born or when they lived because the borders of geography and time shall cease to exist.

- Perfection shall remain the boring privilege of the gods, while in our bungling, messy world every night shall be lived as if it were the last and every day as if it were the first.

Excerpted from Upside Down: A Primer for the Looking-Glass World, *New York: Metropolitan Books, 2000, pp. 334-336.*

Kids Can Be Activists or Bystanders

BY CRAIG KIELBURGER

The following is adapted from a speech by Craig Kielburger, a student from Canada who has been active in building a campaign against the use of child labor to produce products such as sports equipment, clothing, and handmade rugs. The speech was delivered before the American Federation of Teachers at its 1996 convention.

We have started a movement called Free The Children, a youth group made up of young people mainly between 10 and 16 years of age. Our purpose is not only to help those children who are being abused and exploited, but to also empower young people to believe in themselves and to believe that they can play an active role as citizens of this world.

People sometimes look at me and say, "Well, you're only 13 years old, and 13-year-olds don't do these types of things, and is it normal?" And I ask you, why are people so surprised when young people get involved in social issues?

In other countries, children our ages and younger are working up to 16 hours a day in factories and fields. They are fighting in wars and supporting entire families. Drug dealers don't underestimate the ability of children. So often I find myself believing that the schools and that the adults in our lives underestimate who we are or what we can do, the good that we can do in making this world a better place.

We have been receiving hundreds of copies of letters written by children all over the United States, and I would like to read one of them to you now. This letter is to the president of the Nike Corporation.

"Dear Mr. Nike President: My name is Jamie, and I am eight and three-quarters years old. My Nike shoes are all worn out, but I will buy no more Nike running shoes if you don't tell me that you have no child labor in all of your factories" — and "all" is underlined. "Yours truly, Jamie."

Jamie may only be eight and three-quarters years old, but he's already learning that he does have a voice, that he is important. Jamie is learning to be an active citizen of this world.

It is not often that a young person my age has the opportunity to give his teacher advice — let alone nearly 3,000 teachers. But I believe that in this information age, with its global economy and global human rights, one of the greatest challenges that you as teachers and educators will face is to prepare your students to live in the new global village and to become active citizens of this world. As young people, we are capable of doing so much more than simply watching TV, playing video games, hanging around malls, or simply regurgitating information that is fed to us through schools or the media.

Now, don't get me wrong. I personally love hanging out with my friends and playing video

Child labor activist Craig Kielburger, then 13, in 1996.

> **We can either grow up as bystanders simply closing our eyes and becoming immune to what is happening to the people in the world around us, or we can be taught that we can participate, that we do have a voice, that we are important, and that we can bring about a change.**

games. But there is much more on top of that that young people can do. Today, young people in North America are more aware, more informed, and perhaps more frustrated than any other generation of youth, for we see all the poverty and injustices in the world. Yet, what role do we play in today's society? Where are the infrastructures, the opportunities which allow us to participate, to give, and to help?

We can either grow up as bystanders simply closing our eyes and becoming immune to what is happening to the people in the world around us, or we can be taught that we can participate, that we do have a voice, that we are important, and that we can bring about a change. And this is why I believe so strongly that service to others, whether at a local — for we have many problems in our own neighborhoods — at a national, or even an international level should be an integral part of our school, of our education.

I say education because when young people are challenged to look at others and to help others, we realize how lucky we truly are. We learn leadership skills and self-respect. We are able to put our energy and enthusiasm to a worthwhile cause. We learn that we can make this world a better place. Some people say that I am exceptional. But to me, the true heroes are the boys and the girls who work in near slave-like conditions to make the soccer balls which your children play with, to make the clothes which your children wear, and who even make the surgical equipment which saves lives in American hospitals.

As educators, you are such a powerful group. You have the power to motivate people, to stand up, and to bring about a change. What will you do to help these children? People, especially young people, live up to those expectations which others draw for them.

Today, if I leave behind one message with you, it will be to believe in us, the young people of today. Don't be afraid to challenge us to play a greater role in society, and please, don't underestimate who we are or what we can do. Our generation may just surprise you. ∎

Craig Kielburger continues to work with Free The Children (see "Organizations and Websites for Global Justice," p. 384). Free The Children describes itself as the "largest network of children helping children with over 100,000 active youth in 35 countries around the world."

A Revolution of Values

BY DR. MARTIN LUTHER KING, JR.

On April 4, 1967, exactly one year before his assassination, Martin Luther King, Jr. delivered a speech in New York City on the occasion of his becoming Co-Chairman of Clergy and Laymen Concerned About Vietnam (subsequently re-named Clergy and Laity Concerned.) Titled "Beyond Vietnam," it was his first major speech on the war in Vietnam — what the Vietnamese aptly call the American War. In these excerpts, King links the escalating U.S. commitment to that war with its abandonment of the commitment to social justice at home. His call for a "shift from a 'thing-oriented' society to a 'person-oriented' society" and for us to "struggle for a new world" has acquired even greater urgency than when he issued it decades ago.

Speaking in New Jersey a week before his murder, Dr. Martin Luther King, Jr. criticizes U.S. policy in Vietnam.

Now, it should be incandescently clear that no one who has any concern for the integrity and life of America today can ignore the present war. If America's soul becomes totally poisoned, part of the autopsy must read Vietnam. It can never be saved so long as it destroys the deepest hopes of men the world over. So it is that those of us who are yet determined that "America will be" are led down the path of protest and dissent, working for the health of our land....

The war in Vietnam is but a symptom of a far deeper malady within the American spirit, and if we ignore this sobering reality we will find ourselves organizing Clergy and Laymen Concerned committees for the next generation. They will be concerned about Guatemala and Peru. They will be concerned about Thailand and Cambodia. They will be concerned about Mozambique and South Africa.

We will be marching for these and a dozen other names and attending rallies without end unless there is a significant and profound change in American life and policy....

In 1957 a sensitive American official overseas said that it seemed to him that our nation was on the wrong side of a world revolution. During the past 10 years we have seen emerge a pattern of suppression which now has justified the presence of U.S. military "advisors" in Venezuela. This need to maintain social stability for our investments accounts for the counter-revolutionary action of American forces in Guatemala. It tells why American helicopters are being used against guerrillas in Colombia and why American napalm and Green Beret forces have already been active against rebels in Peru....

I am convinced that if we are to get on the right side of the world revolution, we as a nation must undergo a radical revolution of values. We must rapidly begin the shift from a "thing-oriented" society to a "person-oriented" society. When machines and computers, profit motives, and property rights are considered more important than people, the giant triplets of racism, materialism, and militarism are incapable of being conquered....

True compassion is more than flinging a coin to a beggar; it is not haphazard and superficial. It comes to see that an edifice which produces beggars needs re-structuring. A true revolution of values will soon look uneasily on the glaring contrast of poverty and wealth.

With righteous indignation, it will look across the seas and see individual capitalists of the West investing huge sums of money in Asia, Africa, and South America, only to take the profits out with no concern for the social betterment of the countries, and say: "This is not just." It will look at our alliance with the landed gentry

> **When machines and computers, profit motives and property rights are considered more important than people, the giant triplets of racism, materialism, and militarism are incapable of being conquered.**

of Latin America and say: "This is not just." The Western arrogance of feeling that it has everything to teach others and nothing to learn from them is not just.

A true revolution of values will lay hands on the world order and say of war: "This way of settling differences is not just." This business of burning human beings with napalm, of filling our nation's homes with orphans and widows, of injecting poisonous drugs of hate into the veins of peoples normally humane, of sending men home from dark and bloody battlefields physically handicapped and psychologically deranged, cannot be reconciled with wisdom, justice, and love. A nation that continues year after year to spend more money on military defense than on programs of social uplift is approaching spiritual death....

These are revolutionary times. All over the globe men are revolting against old systems of exploitation and oppression and out of the wombs of a frail world new systems of justice and equality are being born. The shirtless and barefoot people of the land are rising up as never before. "The people who sat in darkness have seen a great light." We in the West must support these revolutions....

Our only hope today lies in our ability to recapture the revolutionary spirit and go out into a sometimes hostile world declaring eternal hostility to poverty, racism, and militarism. With this powerful commitment we shall boldly challenge the status quo and unjust mores and thereby speed the day when "every valley shall be exalted, and every mountain and hill shall be made low, and the crooked shall be made straight and the rough places plain...."

Now let us begin. Now let us re-dedicate ourselves to the long and bitter — but beautiful — struggle for a new world. ■

Young protesters in Boston in 2000 accuse Gap stores and Nike of unfair labor practices.

Defeating Despair

BILL BIGELOW

How can we teach about the enormity of injustice in the world and the threats to humanity and the earth without leaving our students in despair? In discussions with teachers over the years, that's the question that comes up repeatedly. If we've reached any consensus, it's that no matter what curricular steps we take to address students' hopelessness, we can never do too much.

An interesting irony is that the more clearly students come to see the interconnected nature of global problems, the greater the danger that they will be overwhelmed by this awareness. As the student we quote in the Introduction laments: "If everything is connected, then you can't change anything without changing everything. But you can't change everything, so that means that you can't change anything."

But there is a hopeful dimension to the world's growing interconnectedness: We have more opportunities to recognize the far-flung social and ecological webs that we are a part of, and simultaneously more points of leverage to make a global difference. For example, in her article for

> **There is a hopeful dimension to the world's growing interconnectedness: We have more opportunities to recognize the far-flung social and ecological webs that we are a part of, and simultaneously more points of leverage to make a global difference.**

Rethinking Schools (available on the website at www.rethinkingschools.org/rg), "The Student Union vs. Jostens Inc.," high school senior Andrea Townsend and other student union members discovered that their graduation gowns were sewn by underpaid workers in Mexico, using oil-based materials, shipped great distances consuming fossil fuels, and sold at exorbitant prices to students in the United States. It did not take much digging to discover connections to people around the world, and because of the corporate concentration in the market for graduation goods, Andrea's discoveries were immediately relevant to teenagers across the country, whose schools also contracted with the Jostens giant. The ubiquitous reach of globalization offers the potential for new allies, as well as increasing vulnerabilities for those who profit from the system.

As many Portland students sensed through their confrontation with the transnational corporation that produced their graduation gowns, hope can emerge in the process of trying to make change. Townsend writes at the conclusion of her article, "[N]o one who has tasted the thrill of solidarity can go back to fighting alone."

THE QUESTION OF ALTERNATIVES

In *Rethinking Globalization*, we don't feature classroom activities that present worked-out alternatives to corporate-driven globalization. Frankly, when I've tried to design lessons to get students to imagine full-blown social alternatives, they haven't been pedagogically compelling. The distant and utopian feel to imagining the Good Society can unwittingly make fundamental change seem less attainable, more dream-like.

Which is not to say that imagining alternatives is unimportant. On the contrary: If we don't find

ways to emphasize possible alternatives to today's increasingly privatized, ecologically ruinous version of globalization, then we run the risk of losing students to cynicism. Writing about how McCarthyism crippled U.S. political discourse long after Joseph McCarthy was gone, *Salt of the Earth* director Herbert Biberman said, "One was free to attack our mores, institutions, personages without limit or fear, so long as one also despaired and offered no alternative." Critique without alternative equals despair.

To provide a sense of alternatives, we have focused more on highlighting past and present resistance to the dire threats posed by profit-driven globalization. *Rethinking Globalization* is filled with instances from which students can find hope and vision for the future. But unless these are made explicit, students may continue to lock in on, "This is sooooo depressing," and fail to recognize the glimpses of hope along the way. Thus it's important to draw students' attention to how moments in the past and present can prefigure aspects of a world we'd like to live in. Over the course of a school year, we can also help students recognize how much their own global awareness has grown, and perhaps their commitment to act for justice. This too can be a source of hope.

Arguments against radical change are almost always premised on gloomy portraits of human nature: People are *naturally* selfish and materially acquisitive. Hope for a more cooperative, egalitarian and peaceful future must be grounded in a contrasting set of interlocking beliefs about human beings, abundant evidence of which can be found in this volume. These include:

- **People can recognize and act on their connections to others around the world.**
  Countless individuals highlighted in this book see and act on a "self" interest that includes others. Langston Hughes (p. 55) addresses himself to the British empire in the poem "Gandhi is Fasting," as he applauds Mahatma Gandhi's fast against colonialism, "For I am also jim crowed — as India is jim crowed by you." Craig Kielburger, at 13 years old, organized Free The Children to fight child exploitation around the world, but also to empower young people in North America (p. 325.)

- **People can develop great courage as they struggle for better lives for themselves and others.**
  Honduran unionist Yesenia Bonilla daily

"has to leave her fear behind" as she risks her livelihood to struggle for workers' rights (p. 142). Leticia Bula-at describes the courage and collective determination of the Kalinga women to oppose the Chico Dam project in the Philippines: "For us, land is life, it is sacred.... This land is what kept generations of our people alive and this is where we are going to die...." (p. 89). In "Stories of Debt and Hope" (p. 83.), Einar, in Barquisimeto, Venezuela, continues to speak out even though it creates havoc in his family. "It is hard for me to keep quiet when I see something wrong, and this has often gotten me in trouble."

- **People have a tremendous capacity to change and grow.**
Students in New Jersey teacher Maria Sweeney's fourth grade class went from zero to expert as they learned about sweatshop conditions around the world. And when their principal banned the play that they had produced as "inappropriate," the kids ended up performing it on Broadway (p. 171). Bob Peterson reminisces about his transformation from privileged middle-schooler to social justice activist as he relentlessly pursued "Why?" questions when confronted with poverty in Egypt (p. 18). Rodolfo Montiel went from Mexican peasant/farmer to prominent environmental activist, winning the prestigious Goldman Environmental Prize, as he came to see the destructive relationship between logging and topsoil-stripping floods. The roadblocks he built to halt logging trucks landed him in prison, but his actions initiated an international solidarity network (p. 280).

- **Ordinary people can confront injustice and make change.**
Certainly, the above individuals reveal this. And there are many more stories in this book: The Huaorani Indian Moi and fellow tribespeople who have resisted the encroachment of their lands by oil companies and "settlers" in the rainforests of eastern Ecuador (p. 268). *Maquiladora* worker Omar Gil, who bounced from one low-paid, dangerous job to another, but never lost his hope for a better life, and became a union activist: "Nothing will ever change if we just sit on our hands. You have to keep trying and trying" (p. 146). The low income multinational, multiracial, multilingual coalition in Los Angeles who with humor

Skjold Photographs

and intelligence effectively challenged the city's biased transportation priorities — and offered object lessons in the importance of race and class analysis (as described in the video *Bus Riders Union*, p. 361).

You get the point. Belief in the possibility of a very different, very much better world must be grounded in the confidence that ordinary people are capable of creating such a world — that human nature is not narrowly self-centered. There are countless examples in this book that offer students supporting evidence.

Another related argument against fundamental change — one that has gained new momentum in the era of globalization — is that people really don't need to work for a radical redistribution of wealth and power, because prosperity is the product of open markets and free trade. Indeed, taken to its logical conclusion, people don't need to work for justice and equity at all — the free market will take care of that. As *The New York Times* columnist Thomas Friedman argues, global trade expansion is "the only route out of poverty for the world's poor." The *only* route. Not unions, not women's organizations, not solidarity movements, not alliances of farmers and workers — just more global trade, more

about. The people mentioned above — Craig Kielburger, Yesenia Bonilla, et al. — are not simply Lone Rangers for justice; they are embedded in social movements that inform and amplify their efforts. For our students, hope needs to be grounded in that knowledge. We need to familiarize them with an array of social movements for global justice past and present — not uncritically, but to alert students to the role that these movements have played, and could play, in global transformation.

It's especially vital that students come to recognize the importance of organization and collective action because so much of young people's education emphasizes the opposite. For example, they learn about Rosa Parks, the tired but heroic lone seamstress who challenged segregation and launched the modern Civil Rights Movement; instead of learning about Rosa Parks, long active in a movement that consciously sought to overthrow segregation and white supremacy. Textbooks and teaching materials often allow Great Individuals their moments in the curricular sun — e.g., Mahatma Gandhi, Nelson Mandela — but rarely the social movements that nurtured and ultimately were responsible for whatever accomplishments they are credited with.

ORGANIZATIONS FOR GLOBAL JUSTICE

Students may find persuasive evidence that change is possible by "meeting" the myriad organizations that comprise today's global justice movements. Encountering these groups allows students to recognize concretely the outlines of a more hopeful future that is immanent in the present. And because, increasingly, social justice groups offer rich websites linked to other similarly oriented organizations, activities that put students in touch with these groups have the potential to both inform and inspire.

I designed a two-part lesson (see handouts, pp. 335-338) to introduce students to the scope of the organizations listed in our Resources section (online and hot-linked for students' ease of use at www.rethinkingschools.org/rg). The first part is a self-guided tour, a kind of scavenger hunt with a conscience, that poses students several

foreign investment, he says.

Put another way, here's the argument: Corporations' and individuals' zeal for private gain will lead to social betterment; the pursuit of one's own riches will diminish the poverty of others. This self-serving formula corresponds precisely to my dictionary's definition of "superstition": an irrational belief that an action not related to a course of events influences its outcome — that somehow, free market alchemy turns greed into good.

I remember confronting this same superstition when I was active in the anti-apartheid movement in the 1980s. The Reagan administration and corporate America argued that what would end apartheid was not organized resistance — demonstrations, boycotts, and sanctions in solidarity with the democratic movements within South Africa. Instead, if we let the magic of the marketplace work through "constructive engagement" with the apartheid regime, freedom would come. As with the latest incarnation of market fundamentalism, evidence for this claim was lacking. Between 1960 and the mid-1980s, a period of ferocious repression in South Africa, U.S. direct investment there had increased from $150 million to $2.5 billion. Free markets did not lead to free people.

No, meaningful social change must be made by human beings, *organized to bring that change*

questions and tasks using the "Organizations and Websites for Global Justice" list in the Resources. For example, one question asks students to: "Find a group that works on environmental issues. What is the group? What is one important environmental issue this group is concerned with? What is it doing to deal with this issue?"

Students can return from their "tour" to share their discoveries with other class members. This is also an opportunity to talk about the global justice movement as a whole — what commonalities do we find in these groups, what differences? It's hard not to be impressed by the diversity and determination manifested by the global justice activist organizations. Similar activities could be designed to introduce students to the excellent "journals for global justice" available in the Resources section and also hotlinked on our website, which can be found at www.rethinkingschools.org/rg. Too often, teachers — this one included — fail to alert students to the alternative media oases that provide welcome relief from the corporate-owned McMedia fare that offers little critical perspective on the issues addressed in this book.

Part two of the assignment asks students to choose one of the organizations or websites that they or one of their classmates visited and reflect more on the group's mission and projects. The activity has several aims. One is to invite students to "try on" the worldview of a group of people who have chosen to confront injustice with activism — and to meet this group in its own language and with images that it has chosen to represent itself. I want students to encounter people — virtually, as well as in real life — who understand important aspects of global injustice, but who refuse to be defeated by that knowledge. I want students to "enter" these organizations, but not without a critical eye. One question on the "Profile" asks students: "How deep is this group going? In your opinion, is it addressing the *roots* of the problem(s)?" Ultimately I want students to recognize that they needn't be mere *consumers* of global justice organizations' tactics and strategies, but they

can think critically about them and propose others that seem more effective or more profound.

This kind of student research is genuine discovery. I may have found the initial collection of global justice organizations and websites, but there are hundreds of links that students can follow. As they explore, they will find sites that are revelations — to them and to me. In fact, some of the sites on our list of "Organizations and Websites for Global Justice" are ones that students have run across in previous years. This kind of discovery can transform student into teacher in delightful ways.

HORROR INTO HOPE

Earlier on, I noted the irony that the more firmly students grasp how global problems are linked to one another, the greater the danger that they might be overwhelmed by this consciousness. But there is another irony, one that is more hopeful, and that I know from personal experience. I began my activism as a teenager protesting the war in Vietnam. The more I read, the more horrified I became at the atrocities committed by the U.S. government, and by the government's consistent lying about Vietnam, going back to the end of World War II. My first emotions were ones of bitterness and anger — emotions that found expression in Bob Dylan's unforgiving song, "Masters of War," which I listened to over and over. But activism against the war led me to communities of other like-minded people. The people I came to know and work with — many of whom were members of Vietnam Veterans Against the War — were well aware of the horrors committed against the Vietnamese by the U.S. government. Some had witnessed these first-hand, and even participated in them. And yet, in the process of joining together in opposition to the war, and to seek its root causes, something else began to happen: We developed an affirmative vision of a cooperative, non-militaristic society — a vision nurtured by the way we worked and treated one another in anti-war communities. The irony is simply this: Horror and disgust at injustice can turn to hope when individuals of conscience find one another and

> Belief in the possibility of a very different, very much better world must be grounded in the confidence that ordinary people are capable of creating such a world — that human nature is not narrowly self-centered.

Skjold Photographs

begin to act on their common commitments.

The great Brazilian educator Paulo Freire once said that pedagogy needs to become more political and politics needs to become more pedagogical. Speaking as a teacher and as an activist, I can say that this has never been more true.

When we teach honestly about the frightening constellation of global forces that threatens the survival of whole cultures, of ecosystems, and of the very planet itself, we can't ignore the potential impact that this may have on our students. Our pedagogy has to be more political: We need to invite students to consider alternatives — we need to invite them to become a part of *making* alternatives. How do students come to a deep awareness of global injustice without losing hope? Perhaps like Andrea Townsend, they need to experience the "thrill of solidarity." They need to recognize that they can make a difference, with others — and that engagement in the world can defeat cynicism. ∎

Bill Bigelow (bbpdx@aol.com) teaches at Franklin High School in Portland, Oregon and is a Rethinking Schools editor.

When we teach honestly about the frightening constellation of global forces that threatens the survival of whole cultures, of ecosystems, and of the very planet itself, we can't ignore the potential impact that this may have on our students. Our pedagogy has to be more political: We need to invite students to consider alternatives — we need to invite them to become a part of making alternatives.

Exploring Organizations
for Global Justice

Answer the questions below as fully as possible by visiting some of the websites listed in "Organizations and Websites for Global Justice," (p. 382) or at the Rethinking Schools website, www.rethinkingschools.org/rg). Find different groups to answer each question.

1. Find an organization not based in the United States.
   Give at least three examples of issues that are important to this group.

2. Find a group that works around the issue of sweatshops. From its website, list some of the ways that this group is working to oppose sweatshop abuses.

3. Find an organization concerned about food and agriculture issues. What is one problem this group identifies? What is it doing to deal with this problem?

4. Find a group that works on environmental issues. What is the group? What is one important environmental issue this group is concerned with? What is it doing to deal with this issue?

5. Go to the website of any one of the groups listed in "Organizations and Websites for Global Justice." Find the links that this group includes in its website. Choose one of the links and click on it. What is the group you chose? What are the aims of this group?

6. Visit at least three more websites. These can be ones listed in "Organizations and Websites for Global Justice" or others that are included as links. List these groups. What do you find interesting or attractive about these groups? What do they have in common? How do they differ?

Organizations and Websites for Global Justice: Profile

Your Name: _____

Name of Organization: _____

Website/Address: _____

1. Write a brief summary, in your own words, of this group's "mission" — what it is trying to accomplish in the world.

2. What are some serious problems, according to this group?

3. What actions is this group taking — and/or urging others to take — to address these problems?

4. How deep is this group going? In your opinion, is it addressing the *roots* of the problem(s)? Explain.

5. What questions, concerns, or disagreements do you have with this group's activities?

6. What do you like about the analysis or activities of this group? Explain.

7. Based on the activities or recommendations of this group, find at least one thing that you might do to make a positive difference in the world. Tell what this is and what difference it could make.

8. What new information did you learn from this site?

9. What did you learn from this site that reminds you of something you've studied this year?

Sheltering Hope

BY EDUARDO GALEANO

For much of the 20th century, the existence of the Eastern bloc, so-called real socialism, encouraged the independent forays of countries that wished to escape the trap of the international division of labor. But the socialist states of Eastern Europe had a lot of state and little or nothing of socialist. When they fell, we were all invited to the funeral of socialism, but the undertakers were mistaken about who had died.

In the name of justice, so-called socialism had sacrificed freedom. The symmetry is revealing: In the name of freedom, capitalism sacrifices justice day in, day out. Are we obliged to kneel before one of these two altars? Those of us who believe that injustice is not our immutable fate have no reason to identify with the despotism of a minority that denied freedom, was accountable to no one, treated people as children, and saw unity as unanimity and diversity as treason. Such petrified power was divorced from the people it ruled. Perhaps that explains the ease with which it fell, without pity or glory, and the rapidity with which a new power emerged featuring the same personalities. Bureaucrats turned a quick somersault and in a flash reappeared as successful businessmen and mafia capos. Moscow now has twice as many casinos as Las Vegas, while wages have fallen by half and in the streets crime grows like a mushroom after a rain.

We are in the midst of a tragic but perhaps healthy crisis of convictions — a crisis for those who believed in states that claimed to belong to everyone but were really of the few and ended up being no one's; a crisis for those who believed in the magic formulas of the armed struggle; and a crisis for those who believed in political parties that went from withering denunciations to bland platitudes, that began by swearing to bring down the system and ended up administering it. Many party activists now beg forgiveness for having believed that heaven could be built. They work feverishly to erase their own footprints and climb down from hope as if hope were a tired horse.

End of the century, end of the millennium, end of the world? How much unpoisoned air do we

Supporters of the Zapatistas cheer as a caravan carrying Subcomandante Marcos and other leaders of the rebel group passes through Mexico City in March 2001.

have left? How much unscorched earth? How much water not yet befouled? How many souls not yet sick? The Hebrew word for "sick" originally meant "with no prospect," and that condition is indeed the gravest illness among today's many plagues. But someone — who knows who it was? — stopped beside a wall in the city of Bogotá to write, "Let's save pessimism for better times."

In the language of Castile, when we want to say we have hope, we say we shelter hope. A lovely expression, a challenge: to shelter her so she won't die of the cold in the bitter climate of these times. According to a recent poll conducted in 17 Latin American countries, three out of every four people say their situation is unchanged or getting worse. Must we accept misfortune the way we accept winter or death? It's high time we in Latin America asked ourselves if we are to be nothing more than a caricature of the North. Are we to be only a warped mirror that magnifies the deformities of the original image: "Get out if you can" downgraded to "Die if you can't"? Crowds of losers in a race where most people get pushed off the track? Crime turned into slaughter, urban hysteria elevated to utter insanity? Don't we have something else to say and to live?

At least now we hardly ever hear the old refrain about history being infallible. After all we've seen, we know for sure that history makes mistakes: She gets distracted, she falls asleep, she gets lost. We make her and she looks like us. But she's also, like us, unpredictable. Human history is like soccer: Her finest trait is her capacity for surprise. Against all predictions, against all evidence, the little guys can sometimes knock the invincible giants for a loop.

> **Against all predictions, against all evidence, the little guys can sometimes knock the invincible giants for a loop.**

On the woof and warp of reality, tangled though it be, new cloth is being woven from threads of many radically different colors. Alternative social movements don't just express themselves through parties and unions. They do that, but not only that. The process is anything but spectacular and it mostly happens at the local level, where across the world a thousand and one new forces are emerging. They emerge from the bottom up and the inside out. Without making a fuss, they shoulder the task of reconceiving democracy, nourishing it with popular participation and reviving the battered traditions of tolerance, mutual assistance, and communions with nature. One of their spokesmen, ecologist Manfred Max-Neef, describes these movements as mosquitoes on the attack, stinging a system that repels the hug and compels the shrug. "More powerful than a rhinoceros," he says, "is a cloud of mosquitoes. It grows and grows, buzzes and buzzes."

In Latin America, they are a species at risk of expansion: organizations of the landless, the homeless, the jobless, the whateverless; groups that work for human rights; mothers and grandmothers who defy the impunity of power; community organizations in poor neighborhoods; citizens' coalitions that fight for fair prices and healthful produce; those that struggle against racial and sexual discrimination, against machismo, and against the exploitation of children; ecologists, pacifists, health promoters, and popular educators; those who unleash collective creativity and those who rescue collective memory; organic agriculture cooperatives, community radio and television stations, and myriad other voices of popular participation that are neither auxiliary wings of political parties nor priests taking orders from any Vatican. These unarmed forces of civil society face frequent harassment from the powerful, at times with bullets. Some activists get shot dead. May the gods and the devils hold them in glory: Only trees that bear fruit suffer stonings.

With the odd exception, like the Zapatistas in Chiapas or the landless in Brazil, these movements rarely garner much public attention — not because they don't deserve it. To name just one, Mexico's El Barzón emerged spontaneously in recent years when debtors sought to defend themselves from the usury of the banks. At first it attracted only a few, a contagious few; now they are a multitude. Latin America's presidents would do well to learn from that experience, so that our countries could come together, the way in Mexico people came together to form a united front against a financial despotism that gets its way by negotiating with countries one at a time. But the ears of those presidents are filled with the sonorous clichés exchanged every time they meet and pose with the president of the mother country, the United States, always front and center in the family photos.

It's happening all across the map of Latin America: Against the paralyzing nerve gas of fear, people reach out to one another, and together they learn to not bow down. As Old Antonio, Subcomandante Marcos' alter ego, says, "We are as small as the fear we feel, and as big as the enemy we choose." Such people, unbowed, are having their say. There is no greater authority than one who rules by obeying. Marcos represents the sub, the under — the underdeveloped, the underfed, the underrated, the underheard. The indigenous communities of Chiapas discuss and decide, and he is but the mouth that speaks with their voices. The voice of those who have no voice? People obliged to remain silent do have a voice, a voice that deserves to be heard. They speak by their words but also by their silence.

Official history, mutilated memory, is a long, self-serving ceremony for those who give the orders in this world. Their spotlights illuminate the heights and leave the grass forts in darkness. The always invisible are at best props on the stage of history, like Hollywood extras. But they are the ones — the actors of real history, the denied, lied about, hidden protagonists of past and present — who incarnate the splendid spectrum of another possible reality. Blinded by elitism, racism, sexism, and militarism, the Americas continue to ignore their own plenitude. And that's twice as true for the South: Latin America has the most fabulous human and vegetal diversity on the planet. Therein lies its fecundity and its promise. As anthropologist Rodolfo Stavenhagen puts it, "Cultural diversity is to the human species what biological diversity is to the genetic wealth of the world." If Latin America is to realize the marvels promised by our people and our land, we'll have to stop confusing identity with archeology and nature with scenery. Identity isn't frozen in museums and ecology can't be reduced to gardening.

Five centuries ago, the people and the land of the Americas were incorporated into the world market as things. A few of the *conquistadores*, those who were themselves conquered, managed to see America's splendor and to revel in it. But the powers behind the Conquest, a blind and blinding enterprise like every other imperial invasion, could see Indians and nature only as objects of exploitation or as obstacles. In the name of the one and only God, the one and only language, and the one and only truth, cultural diversity was written off as ignorance and criminalized as heresy, while nature, that ferocious beast, was tamed and obliged to turn itself into money. The communion of indigenous peoples with the earth was the essential truth of American cultures, a sin of idolatry that merited punishment by lash, gallows, and the pyre.

We no longer speak of "taming" nature; now its executioners like to say it must be "protected." Either way, nature was and still is viewed as *outside* us: Civilization, which confuses clocks with time, also confuses postcards with nature. But the vitality of the world, which wriggles out of all classifications and is beyond explanation, never sits still. Nature realizes itself in movement and we, too, children of nature, exist in motion. We are who we are and at the same time are what we do to change who we are. As Paulo Freire, the educator who died learning, liked to say, "We become by walking."

Truth lies in the voyage, not the port. There is no greater truth than the search for truth. Are we condemned to crime? We all know that we human creatures are busy devouring our neighbors and devastating the planet, but we also know that we would not be here if our distant Paleolithic grandparents hadn't learned to adapt to the natural world to which they belonged and hadn't been capable of sharing what they hunted and gathered. Living wherever, living however, living whenever, each person contains many possible persons. Every day, the ruling system places our worst characteristics at center stage, condemning our best to languish behind the backdrop. The system of power is not in the least eternal. We may be badly made, but we're not finished, and it's the adventure of changing reality and changing ourselves that makes our blip in the history of the universe worthwhile, this fleeting warmth between two glaciers that is us. ■

Eduardo Galeano is one of Latin America's most distinguished writers. He is author of the Memory of Fire *trilogy and* Open Veins of Latin America, *among many other works. He lives in Uruguay. This article is excerpted from* Upside Down: A Primer for the Looking-Glass World, *New York: Metropolitan Books, 2000; pp. 318-329.*

Protesters fill the streets of Quito, Ecuador in 2001 in response to economic austerity measures.

To Open a Crack in History
Movements for Global Justice in the 21st Century

BY KATHARINE AINGER

When Macbeth saw what seemed like a grey mist pouring over the horizon, fear rose in his throat. As it came closer he could make out the branches of the trees which the forces of opposition carried aloft. The forest was coming to the centre of power to confront the tyrant.

In March 2001 the forest marched on Mexico City.

The Zapatistas, the indigenous rebels hiding deep in the Lacandon jungle, had done the unthinkable. The most wanted men and women in Mexico had emerged to travel from Chiapas through 13 states, arriving at the Zocalo — the central square of the capital — to demand a place in the constitution. Their voices echoed round the Zocalo: "It is the hour of the Indian peoples, we who are the colour of the earth. We are rebels because the land rebels when someone sells and buys it, as if the land did not exist, as if we who are the colour of the earth did not exist.

"Mexico City: We are here. We are here as the rebellious colour of the earth which shouts: Democracy! Liberty! Justice!"

"*Y la selva se movió*," declared the poster advertising the march. And the forest walked.

In Mexico a jungle came to the city; in Thailand a village came to the capital, Bangkok.

On January 25, 1997, some 20,000 rural poor gathered at the gates of Government House. They were villagers affected by big dam projects, small farmers, fisherfolk who had come together to create a rural coalition — the Assembly of the Poor — of those left out of Thailand's tiger economy. The people erected a makeshift "Village of the Poor" of plastic shacks which stretched back down the Nakhon Pathom Road for more than a kilometre. Amidst the cacophony of economic growth, they camped here in the stink of the smog and the traffic for 99 days, surviving by growing vegetables illegally along the banks of the city's river.

They declared: "Rivers and forests on which the survival of rural families depend have been plundered from the people. The collapse of agricultural society forces people out of their communities to cheaply sell their labour in the city.

The people must set up the country's development direction. The people must be the real beneficiaries of development." In 1998 the village came again, this time to join the coalition of protest movements against the International Monetary Fund's (IMF) bailout programme in the wake of the Asian financial crisis; and again when thousands converged on the Asian Development Bank meetings in Chiang Mai in May 2000. On their backs the protesters carried a tombstone on which were inscribed the words: "There is a price on the water, a meter in the rice paddies, dollars in the soil, resorts in the forests."

For the indigenous people of Ecuador, the IMF-imposed "dollarization" of the beleaguered Ecuadorian economy might as well have come from outer space.

In response, the Confederation of Indigenous Nations of Ecuador (CONAIE) turned into a storm that broke over the city of Quito in February 2000: "The indigenous and popular insurrection has advanced from the field to the city. The buses travelling between towns have received orders to transfer 'any thing, person, even animals, except Indians.' Buses in the military zones are stopped and all those who are dressed in Indian clothes or appear Indian are forced off. But the insurrection grows like a swelling waterfall.

"[The President] has decreed the dollarization of the Ecuadorian economy. This means that while the pay is 40 dollars, the shopping basket for a family of five is 250 dollars. In the agricultural field, inputs are no longer within reach of indigenous people and farmers. Will we have to leave the fields?

"We cannot walk about on our own earth. They prohibit us from meeting. But we have defied with what little power we have left, with civil disobedience.

"For that reason we have advanced to the taking of Quito. The [indigenous people] have passed like rain, like fog, like the wind, deceiving the military controls. Now we are more than ten thousand indigenous people in Quito."

A forest, a village, a rainstorm. The most marginal people on earth gather their forces and enter the cities to march on the centers of power. These are the excluded, the expendable, the invisible people whom globalization ignores or eradicates. As the cycle of destruction spins ever faster — a forest felled, a people uprooted, a village displaced by a dam — new coalitions of the dispossessed are uniting not just within their countries, but internationally. These are the

> **As the cycle of destruction spins ever faster — a forest felled, a people uprooted, a village displaced by a dam — new coalitions of the dispossessed are uniting, not just within their countries, but internationally.**

social movements of the South which form the invisible mass of resistance to economic globalization. They want land, constitutional recognition, meaningful participation in development planning.

A GLOBAL FABRIC OF STRUGGLE

Seattle, Melbourne, Prague, Quebec, Genoa, Washington. The cities of the North, where thousands of the uninvited have turned up to blockade international summits, have taken on iconic status. No institution of global governance — the World Trade Organization, the World Bank, the International Monetary Fund — has been able to meet in recent years without being accompanied by protest.

Filipino activist Walden Bello says that, despite the material differences between North and South, people in industrialized nations are being "structurally adjusted" too. In Europe we are in danger of losing our free healthcare systems, victims of an identical ideology that imposes "proper systems of charging" on the poor of Zimbabwe or Ghana. Our resistances arise separately, but we are beginning to recognize one another — and the protests on the streets of London, Seattle, and Genoa have not been on behalf of, but in solidarity with, the poor.

Medha Patkar of the Narmada Bachao Andolan (Save Narmada Struggle) in India was with us on the streets of Prague in September 2000, protesting against the World Bank and the IMF. She told me: "It's not about the First and Third World, North and South. There is a section of the population that is just as present in the U.S. and in Britain — the homeless, unemployed people, on the streets of London — which is also there in the indigenous communities, villages and farms of India, Indonesia, the Philippines, Mexico, Brazil. And all those who face the backlash of this kind of economics are coming together — to create a new, people-centred world order."

Activists in San Francisco in 1995 protest Nigeria's execution of Ken Saro Wiwa with a mock hanging.

Owens Wiwa, brother of murdered Nigerian activist Ken Saro Wiwa, describes the civil disobedience of the Ogoni people of Nigeria, who formed human shields to prevent Shell from drilling for oil on their lands. He told me: "I was in Seattle. It was incredibly gratifying to see the disruption of these meetings. But one thing the protesters in this movement need to know: If we want to stop the big transnational corporations, we have got to stop them at the point of production too."

And dozens of "Seattles" have occurred across the South. In 1998, 200,000 Indian farmers erupted onto the streets of Hyderabad to protest the WTO; when WTO head Mike Moore visited India in 2000, he joked rather uncomfortably that in no other place on earth had so many effigies of him been burned.

These disparate threads are the early stages of a movement that is reconstituting the global landscape, reshaping the way politics is played out in the new century.

Antonio Negri and Michael Hardt, in their work *Empire*, call this grassroots network "the multitude." The multitude embodies the real world below, the sphere of all that is not reducible to a commodity to be bought and sold on a global marketplace: human beings, nature, culture, diversity. In each locality, the moment when the people cry *"Ya Basta!"* — "Enough!" — is different, but it is usually when something regarded as sacred, central to the culture, comes under assault.

For the Zapatistas it was the signing of the NAFTA agreement which outlawed the common ownership of land. For much of Southeast Asia it was the IMF austerity measures imposed on their shattered economies after the financial crisis of 1997. For France it was the WTO's attack on their food culture. In Britain it may be the slow sell-off of the National Health Service to private healthcare multinationals.

Against the single economic blueprint where the market rules, the multitude represents diverse, people-centred alternatives. In the Zapatistas' words: "One no, many yeses." Against the monoculture of economic globalization it demands a world where many worlds fit.

DOLLARS IN THE SOIL

Over the past decade a transformation has been taking place as the threads of local movements are woven into a new global fabric of struggle. They are beginning to understand that unless they can organize transnationally, they're dead.

Via Campesina, the international peasant union uniting farmers, rural women, indigenous groups and the landless is one of the most extraordinary examples of this form of international networking. Its members include the Landless of Brazil (MST) and the radical Karnataka State Farmers' Association, who burned Monsanto's genetically modified cotton crops (see p. 228).

With a combined membership of millions, it represents probably the largest single mass of people opposed to the World Trade Organization. Not just the farmers of Thailand, of India, of Bangladesh, but the indigenous of Ecuador, Aotearoa/New Zealand, Mexico. The U'wa of Colombia, the Ogoni of Nigeria, the dam protesters of the Narmada Valley in India.

Corporate globalization requires the eradication of the peasantry, small farmers, indigenous people the world over. Food is to be produced in large industrial monocultures; the rural poor must migrate to the cities to be cheap labourers or sleep under the flyovers of Manila and New Delhi. In the eyes of the World Bank, forest-dwelling peoples are the ones destroying their natural resources — as opposed to the large logging companies — and must be removed.

In response, movements of natural-resource-based communities are creating coalitions of the dispossessed.

For example, members of a network of Indian adivasi (tribal) activists invaded World Bank offices in New Delhi and plastered its walls with cow dung. They declared: "For the World Bank and the WTO, our forests are a marketable commodity. But for us, the forests are a home, our source of livelihood, the dwelling of our gods, the burial ground of our ancestors, the inspiration of our culture. We do not need you to save our forests. We will not let you sell our forests. So go back from our forests and our country."

The National Alliance of Peoples' Movements, galvanized by the incredible energy of the Narmada Bachao Andolan (NBA), unites over 100 mass organizations — from fisherfolk to farmers — in India. Common to all their struggles is the fight for peoples' control over their own lives and resources. Sanjay Sangavi of the NBA describes this as "the emergence of a new politics of environmental socialism in India." As NAPM leader Thomas Kocherry explains: "Two-thirds of our population depends directly on the water, the forests, and the land." For them, questions of ecology and social justice are one and the same.

The potential political force as grassroots groups like these begin to link up internationally can't be overstated.

THIS IS WHAT DEMOCRACY LOOKS LIKE

Each resistance movement, in its own way — usually operating outside the structures of state power — has attempted to recreate models of direct democracy. The dispersal of power back to the people themselves is at the heart of this emerging movement. Perhaps it is best framed as a "pro-democracy movement." Rather than conduct a guerrilla war that might destroy as many communities as it saved, in July 1995 the Zapatistas called for a consulta to determine conditions for an autonomous peace. This was an attempt to replicate their village-level democracy on a wider stage. Thousands of activists across Mexico mobilized a million people to vote, radicalizing communities as they went. An old man from Morelos told them: "You came and found us sleeping, but now we are awake."

In a similar way, for the Ecuadorian indigenous people, power is a collective concept. Their word for it, *ushay*, means the capacity to develop collectively. They echo the Zapatistas in their claim: "Our struggle is not for power itself. There are many more important things than power for its own sake, such as society changing from within." In India the idea of decentralized democracy is evident in the way rural people have demanded control over their rivers and forests. One adivasi village — Mendha in Maharastra — has adopted the slogan *"hamare gaon mein hamara sarkar"*: "in our village, we are the government." They formed their own forest-protection committee which has kept at bay the incursions of paper mills and dam projects. This is so effective that, in an unprecedented development, government forest officials have agreed to abide by their rules.

> But the biggest lesson Northern protesters can learn from Southern movements is that we must move into our communities and build broad-based social movements at home.

But the biggest lesson Northern protesters can learn from Southern movements is that we must move into our communities and build broad-based social movements at home. This will take time and patience. While we must continue to delegitimize the institutions of global governance, and develop our alternative economic models, we must also begin the slow work of rebuilding democracy from the ground up. Above all, we need to become the change we wish to see enacted.

On the outskirts of Mexico City we are breakfasting, under a large canopy, on tortillas, beans, and coffee before the big entrance into the Zocalo. Everybody is busy getting things ready. I walk out into the hot sun. A man with a pony-tail is holding a brush dripping with bright-blue paint. He walks over to me and takes one of my hands. Then he grins and paints the entire surface of my palm a thick blue colour. He gestures over to a banner spread out on the dry earth, where his friend is mapping out some large lettering. I lean over and press my palm hard against the sheet. My palm-print joins hundreds of others in different shapes, sizes and colours. The banner says: *"La historia se construye con éstas."* "History is made with these." ∎

Katharine Ainger is a co-editor of the New Internationalist *magazine, www.newint.org.*

Terrorism and Globalization

BY BILL BIGELOW AND BOB PETERSON

As we moved into the final stages of editing this book, the horrific events of September 11, 2001 exploded into our lives. Teachers frantically tried to figure out how to equip students to reflect on the enormity of the attacks, and what caused them. For our part, Rethinking Schools responded to the crisis with a special issue, "War, Terrorism, and America's Classrooms," and with a new section of our website, www.rethinkingschools.org/sept11.

The United States immediately declared war, not on a particular nation, but on "terrorism." President Bush announced to the world: "Either you are with us, or you are with the terrorists." Government officials, however, endeavored not only to prepare for war against the Taliban and al-Qaeda, but also sought to link the terrorist attacks with the movement against corporate-driven globalization. As Canadian journalist, Naomi Klein, wrote: "After September 11, politicians and pundits around the world instantly began spinning the terrorist attacks as part of a continuum of anti-American and anticorporate violence: first the Starbucks window, then, presumably, the World Trade Center."

To oppose "free trade" was to oppose freedom itself. As U.S. Trade Representative Robert Zoellick wrote: "On September 11, America, its open society and its ideas came under attack by a malevolence that craves our panic, retreat and abdication of global leadership.... This President and this administration will fight for open markets. We will not be intimidated by those who have taken to the streets to blame trade — and America — for the world's ills."

Not only were those who dissent from the free trade/free market orthodoxy painted as terrorist fellow travelers, but free trade was presented as the antidote for repressive fundamentalism. Writing in *The New York Times Magazine*, Michael Lewis argued that those killed in the World Trade Center were targeted as "not merely symbols but also practitioners of liberty.... They work hard, if unintentionally, to free others from constraints. This makes them, almost by default, the

September 11, 2001 in New York City.

spiritual antithesis of the religious fundamentalist, whose business depends on a denial of personal liberty in the name of some putatively higher power."

Both government and press demonstrated disappointingly little curiosity about the circumstances that prompted the September 11 attacks, or about the roots of Islamic fundamentalism more broadly. The position seemed to be that terrorism requires no explanation, it is simply an evil that needs to be crushed. True, major media printed occasional "Why do they hate us?" pieces — but these were few and far between. Moreover, even the best of these focused almost solely on specific U.S. policies in the region: U.S. troops in Saudi Arabia, the human toll resulting from sanctions against Iraq, and U.S. aid to Israel in its conflict with the Palestinians. These accounts were valuable but neglected the profound social changes wrought by the global economy in virtually every corner of the world — including the Islamic world.

Nor did government or press seek to establish a fuller definition of "terrorism" — one that might question whether government-promoted violence like U.S. sponsorship of the Nicaraguan Contras or support of the Chilean dictatorship of Augusto Pinochet, might not count as "terrorism." Also ignored was what might be considered corporate terrorism — for example, Texaco's 20-year poisoning of Ecuador's rainforests, or Union Carbide's callous disregard for safety at its factory in Bhopal, India — site of the worst industrial accident in history.

The Indian environmentalist and scholar Vandana Shiva, whose articles we feature in this volume (p. 224 and p. 248) urges us to embrace a still more expansive notion of terrorism. She asks us to consider "economic policies which push people into poverty and starvation as a form of terrorism," such as International Monetary Fund/World Bank-mandated structural adjustment programs that force governments to cut food and medical programs, with the full knowledge of the misery this will engender. In India, Shiva writes:

> Fifty million tribals who have been flooded out of their homes by dams over the past four decades were also victims of terrorism — they have faced the terror of technology and destructive development.... The whole world repeatedly watched the destruction of the World Trade Center towers, but the destruction of millions of sacred shrines and homes and farms by forces of injustice, greed, and globalization go unnoticed.

"FREE MARKET" FUNDAMENTALISM

We believe that the violence of September 11 and the continuing threats from fundamentalist-inspired terrorists are inexplicable without considering how profit-driven globalization is impacting cultures around the world. Indeed, the writer Wendell Berry suggests that the global "free market" has become its own fundamentalism:

> The "developed" nations [have] given to the "free market" the status of a god, and [are] sacrificing to it their farmers, farmlands, and communities, their forests, wetlands, and prairies, their ecosystems and watersheds. They [have] accepted universal pollution and global warming as normal costs of doing business.

But what is the relationship between free market fundamentalism and Islamic fundamentalism?

> Both the government and the press demonstrated disappointingly little curiosity about the circumstances that prompted the September 11 attacks, or about the roots of Islamic fundamentalism more broadly.

While scholarship linking globalization and terrorism is only beginning, it's not too soon to suggest that economic upheavals created by globalization might lead to an unforeseen, but ferocious backlash.

For example, in a provocative *Progressive* magazine article called "The Mystery of Mysogyny," author Barbara Ehrenreich asks about the roots of Islamic fundamentalism's deep hostility to women. She wonders if the answer might not lie in part in how globalization has posed peculiar threats to men:

> Western industry has displaced traditional crafts — female as well as male — and large-scale, multinational-controlled agriculture has downgraded the independent farmer to the status of hired hand. From West Africa to Southeast Asia, these trends have resulted in massive male displacement and, frequently, unemployment. At the same time, globalization has offered new opportunities for Third World women — in export-oriented manufacturing, where women are favored for their presumed "nimble fingers," and, more recently, as migrant domestics working in wealthy countries.

As Ehrenreich proposes:

> While males have lost their traditional status as farmers and breadwinners, women have been entering the market economy and gaining the marginal independence conferred even by a paltry wage. Add to the economic dislocations engendered by globalization the onslaught of Western cultural imagery, and you have the makings of what sociologist Arlie Hochschild has called a "global masculinity crisis."

George Caffentzis links the rise of Islamic fundamentalism as a political force in Egypt to "the impoverishment of urban workers and agricul-

> **We're not suggesting some mechanistic theory whereby an Egyptian fisherman loses his livelihood, moves to the city, and joins al-Qaeda to strike a blow at global capitalism. What we propose is that the global economy is so disrupting the world, that many people's allegiances and identities are dramatically shifting.**

turists... caused by Structural Adjustment Programs and import liberalization." He points out that "Islamic fundamentalism has distinguished itself, in addition to its unmitigated bolstering of patriarchal rule, for its attempt to win over the urban populations through the provision of some basic necessities such as schooling, healthcare, and a minimum of social assistance."

Research reported by the Middle East Research and Information Project (www.merip.org) also chronicles the huge social dislocations occurring in Egypt, where free market reforms encouraged "the most exuberant dreams of private accumulation — and a chaotic reallocation of collective resources."

One poignant example of the attack on the "commons" is what's happening to small fishermen and their families who depend on Egypt's lakes in the Nile delta. Historically, communities of fishermen were able to catch enough fish for their families and to sell a small surplus. According to researchers Ray Bush and Amal Sabri, a complex set of customs and rights governed fishing practices to insure sufficient time for fish to grow and breed before harvesting. But the government has supported privatization schemes, leasing lake front property to large-scale fish farms, whose guards drive small fishermen off with guns and vicious dogs. Meanwhile, women in the traditional fisher communities are forced by economic necessity to seek work in the fish processing plants. Fish production has increased enormously — as have exports, a sacred component of globalization theology — but so has the misery of fish-dependent families. The current fishing practices are enormously profitable, but also unsustainable, and are wreaking ecological havoc in Egyptian lakes.

As one 45-year-old father of six lamented: "In 1993, Lake Manzala was a source of income for all fishermen of 'Izbat al-Burg. Now [5 years later] the farms have destroyed everything."

Similar "free market" reforms have been introduced in Egyptian agricultural and labor relations. In 1992, Law 96/92 was passed, overturning long-standing traditional relationships between landlords and tenants. All old contracts were abolished. Now owners are free to dispose of their property however they like. Rents tripled in the first five years, with many tenants facing eviction. In Upper Egypt landlords tend to be Coptic Christians, and most tenants are Muslims. Class tensions can turn religious, as they did in the village of Kafr Demian, where "[a] crowd of several hundred Muslims raided Coptic houses, killed their animals and burned down their stables."

Other Egyptian laws wiped out rent controls in the cities and made it easier for employers to lay off workers. Meanwhile, the slums of Alexandria and Cairo continue to swell.

What does all this have to do with the growth of Islamic fundamentalism in Egypt and in other countries undergoing similar "free market" reforms? As writer Norm Diamond suggests:

> [T]hose who have been uprooted from their communities and gone off hoping to find work in the cities, as well as those who have stayed behind attempting to fight back, are vulnerable to recruiting by Islamic fundamentalism. Their new life, their new encounters with unemployment and the merciless market, requires a new self-understanding, a new identity, a new doctrine to make sense of their new activities and surroundings. This is precisely the social grouping, peasants torn from the land and drifted into the city, that has been the basis of fundamentalist Christian growth in Latin America in recent decades.

Lest we be misunderstood: We're not suggesting some mechanistic theory whereby an Egyptian fisherman loses his livelihood, moves to the city, and joins al-Qaeda to strike a blow at global capitalism. What we propose is that the global economy is so disrupting the world, that many people's allegiances and identities are dramatically shifting — and this is true not only for peasant and working classes, but for other social strata as well.

Members of Pakistan's militant religious parties at a rally in Islamabad, Pakistan on Sept. 15, 2001.

Vandana Shiva summarizes how she sees this process working:

Economic globalization is fueling economic insecurity, eroding cultural diversity and identity, and assaulting political freedoms of citizens. It is therefore providing fertile ground for the growth of fundamentalism and terrorism. Globalization fuels fundamentalism at multiple levels:

1. Fundamentalism is a cultural backlash to globalization as alienated and angry young men of colonized societies and cultures react to the erosion of identity and security.

2. Dispossessed people robbed of economic security by globalization cling to politicized religious identities and narrow nationalisms for security.

3. Politicians robbed of economic decision making as national economic sovereignty is eroded by globalization organize their vote banks along lines of religious and cultural difference on the basis of fear and hatred....

We agree with Shiva: "The 'war against terrorism' will not contain terrorism because it does not address the roots of terrorism." Tragically, the strategy of U.S. government and business leaders is more free market reform, more global trade, more privatization — this, of course, in addition to increased military and "security"

spending, and an erosion of civil liberties. We are more than skeptical about this alleged route to peace and security.

We hope that the materials in this book and the supplemental materials found at our website will help educators enlist students in a deep inquiry about the causes of terrorism, but more importantly, about building the kind of democratic society that can address those causes.* Given the "you're either with us or against us" ethos, asking our students to think critically about these issues and to consider alternatives, can appear "unpatriotic." In the post-September 11 world, the pressures to conform to official stories have been intense. This simply makes it all the more important to urge students to search for the roots of global conflicts. Our teaching and our activism must insist, in Naomi Klein's words, "that justice and equality are the most sustainable strategies against violence and fundamentalism."■

Bill Bigelow (bbpdx@aol.com) teaches at Franklin High School in Portland, Oregon and is a Rethinking Schools editor. Bob Peterson (repmilw@aol.com) teaches fifth grade at La Escuela Fratney in Milwaukee, Wisconsin and is a Rethinking Schools editor.

* Links to all the articles referred to here can be found at our website, www.rethinkingschools.org/rg.

TEACHING IDEAS

"PRAYERS FOR A DIGNIFIED LIFE"
A letter to schoolchildren about the Zapatista uprising from Subcomandante Marcos (p. 321)

Ask students to collect as much information as they can about what has happened in Chiapas following Marcos' letter in February of 1994. (See the Zapatista website, www.ezln.org.) How many of the Zapatista aspirations have been realized? What plans does the Mexican government have for the region of Chiapas? How have the Zapatistas responded to government proposals?

"HUMAN RIGHTS FOR A NEW MILLENNIUM"
Article by Eduardo Galeano (p. 323)

In "Human Rights for a New Millennium," Eduardo Galeano writes that "the immense majority of humanity enjoys only the rights to see, hear, and remain silent. Suppose we start by exercising the never-proclaimed right to dream?" Galeano makes a playful yet pointed list as he endeavors to "divine another possible world."

Have students write their own "human rights for a new millennium." Encourage them to be both playful and serious, as Galeano is. Or encourage students to choose an individual or organization they've encountered while studying the issues in this book — Moi in Ecuador's Oriente region; Leticia Bula-at, an anti-dam activist with the Cordillera Women's Education and Resource Centre in the Philippines (p. 89); individuals in "Stories of Debt and Hope" (p. 83), etc. Students could write from any of these people's perspectives.

"A REVOLUTION OF VALUES"
Speech by Dr. Martin Luther King, Jr. (p. 327)

Write the speech that Dr. King might deliver today if he were alive. Perhaps it could cover issues addressed in this book, such as sweatshops, child labor, "free trade," as well as the "war on terrorism." Do you think Dr. King would support U.S. global policies today? What evidence from his 1967 speech supports your conclusion? What policies would he urge?

Dr. King talks about the giant triplets of racism, materialism, and militarism. In what ways are these giant triplets at work in the world today? Ask students to make charts headed with these categories and to list all the ways they see these forces at work in current circumstances. Ask them to choose one of the triplets and to design a poster illustrating it.

Write a dialogue between Dr. King and another individual: you, the President of the United States, someone you learned about from studying the issues covered in this book, etc.

Note: See additional teaching ideas in "Defeating Despair," p. 329.

CHAPTER NINE
Resources

Resources

Songs with a Global Conscience:
Using Songs to Build International Understanding and Solidarity

BY BOB PETERSON

Songs, like poetry, are powerful tools to build consciousness and solidarity on global issues. We begin everyday in my classroom with our "song of the week." Students receive the song lyrics and keep them in their three-ring binders. The songs generally relate to topics of study. I allow students to bring in songs as well, although they must know the lyrics and have a reason for sharing the song with classmates. By the end of the week, students may not have memorized the words to the "song of the week," but they are familiar enough with the lyrics and music so that the song becomes "theirs." Even with some of the songs that I would imagine the children think poorly of — say, some of the slower folk songs — by the end of the week the children demand to hear them a second or third time each morning.

When I introduce a song, I go over the geographical connections using a classroom map. I also explain any vocabulary words that might be difficult. Finally, and most importantly, I give the social context. Depending on whether I use the song at the beginning of a unit of study, or in the middle, the amount of "context setting" varies greatly. For example, I use Nancy Schimmel's "1492" as a way to introduce the Columbus controversy. We ultimately locate the geographical origin and learn something about the Native nations she mentions. The following is a listing of songs that teachers and activists might find useful as they teach for justice in an unjust world. This list is in no way comprehensive, and I would appreciate receiving any additional suggestions. (Visit www.rethinkingschools.org/rg for an updated list.)

Page 351 image: Skjold Photographs

THE COLONIAL PAST

Ballad of the Soldier's Wife
lyrics by Bertolt Brecht, music by Kurt Weill, sung P.J. Harvey. (September Songs: The Music of Kurt Weill CD, Sony Music, 1997.)
A telling tale of the human toll of foreign wars.

Bury My Heart at Wounded Knee
written by Buffy Sainte-Marie, sung by the Indigo Girls. (1200 Curfews CD, Epic Records Group, 1995.)
A folk/rock song that critiques U.S. policy towards Native Americans.

Colonial Man
Hugh Masekela. (Colonial Man and Boy's Doin' It CDs, Verve, 1998.)
A lively anti-colonial song that includes the understatement "Vasco Da Gama, he was no friend of mine."

Famine
Sinead O'Connor (Universal Mother CD, Chrysalis Records, 1994.)
An angry song that describes how the Irish potato famine was actually a result of British colonialism.

1492
Nancy Schimmel. (Rainbow Sign CD, Rounder, 1992.)
A lively, pro-Native American song that asks the question, "Could anyone discover the place when someone was already here?" (Classroom use is described in *Rethinking Columbus*, 1998.)

The Great Nations of Europe
Randy Newman. (Badlove CD, Dream Works SKG, 1999.)
A satirical look at the devastating impact of colonialism on the rest of the world.

My Country, 'Tis of Thy People You're Dying
Buffy Sainte-Marie. (The Best of Buffy Sainte-Marie CD, Vanguard, 1987.)
An angry, powerful song which describes the colonization of Native Americans and the hypocrisy of the U.S. commitment to freedom.

CURRENT NORTH/SOUTH GLOBAL REALITIES

Beds Are Burning
Midnight Oil.
(Diesel and Dust CD, Columbia, 1988.)
A powerful rocker, from the savvy political Australian band led by Peter Garret, about the theft of land from the aborigines.

Biko
Peter Gabriel. (Shaking the Tree: Sixteen Golden Greats CD, Geffen Records, 1990.)
A stunning, mournful tribute to Steve Biko, leader of the Black Consciousness movement in South Africa, and to the power of struggle against police brutality. "You can blow out a candle/But you can't blow out a fire. Once the flames begin to catch/The wind will blow it higher."

Bombs over Baghdad
John Trudell. (AKA Graffiti Man CD, Rykodisc, 1992.)
An angry anti-war poem/song, from a long-time Native American activist.

Bullet the Blue Sky
U2. (The Joshua Tree CD, Islands Records, Ltd., 1987.)
A poetic indictment of bombing "mud huts as the children sleep," written during the U.S.-supported war against the people of El Salvador.

Call It Democracy
Bruce Cockburn.
(World of Wonders CD, Columbia, 1986.)
A powerful song that targets the International Monetary Fund, which Cockburn accuses of fostering "insupportable debts." He sings of "hungry military profiteers" who turn "countries into labor camps." Teachers should be aware that there is one swear word in the song.

Equal Rights
Peter Tosh. (Equal Rights; and Scrolls of the Prophet: The Best of Peter Tosh CD, Sterling Sound, 1999.)
A reggae song that says "everybody wants peace, but nobody wants justice."

If I Had a Rocket Launcher
Bruce Cockburn. (Stealing Fire CD, Columbia, 1984.)
A personalized critique of Central American secret wars of the 1980s in which U.S.-made helicopters were used to massacre villagers in Guatemala. Includes some strong language.

Johannesburg
Gil Scott-Heron.
(The Best of Gil Scott-Heron CD, Arista Records, 1991).
A lively song that describes the struggle against apartheid in South Africa.

Masters of War
Bob Dylan. (Freewheelin' Bob Dylan CD, Columbia, 1963.)
This song was written at the beginning of U.S. involvement in Vietnam but speaks to the broad issue of investment in instruments of death and destruction versus human needs.

Mothers of the Disappeared
U2. (The Joshua Tree CD, Islands Records, Ltd., 1987.)
A sorrowful ballad about the sons and daughters "taken from us...." "In the wind we hear their laughter, in the rain we see their tears."

Redemption Song
Bob Marley. (Uprising CD, Tuff Gong, 1980.)
An upbeat reggae song that references trans-Atlantic slavery and calls on listeners to "emancipate yourselves from mental slavery."

Santo Domingo
Phil Ochs. (There But For Fortune CD, Elektra Asylum Records, 1989.)
A song protesting the 1965 U.S. military intervention of 23,000 Marines against a popular revolt which sought to restore democratically elected Juan Bosch to power after a U.S.-supported military coup a year and half earlier.

They Dance Alone (*Cueca Solo*)
Sting. (Fields of Gold: Best of Sting CD, Gateway Mastering Studios, 1994.)
A moving song about the Mothers of the Disappeared in Argentina. Available in Spanish (Sting and Ruben Blades) on *Nada Como el Sol* CD, Gateway, 1988.

200 Years
G. Love and Special Sauce.
(Yeah, It's That Easy CD, Sony Music, 1997.)
A jazzy rap song that suggests "look how you're living First World, look what you did to Third World."

Universal Soldier
Buffy Sainte-Marie.
(The Best of Buffy Sainte-Marie CD, Vanguard, 1987.)
A classic anti-war song that raises the question of individual responsibility in times of war and social crisis.

War/No More Trouble
Bob Marley and the Wailers.
(Rebel Music CD, Tuff Gong, 1986.)
An anti-racist anthem that calls for a guarantee of human rights without regard to race.

We're the Cops of the World
Phil Ochs. (There But For Fortune CD, Elektra Asylum Records, 1989.)
A Vietnam-war era song that criticizes how the U.S. military has secured the world for U.S. business — "the name for our profits is democracy."

GLOBAL SWEATSHOPS

Bread and Roses
written by James Oppenheim, sung by Judy Collins.
(Forever: The Judy Collins Anthology CD, Elektra Entertainment, 1997.)
Inspired by the 1912 strike of mostly women textile mill workers in Lawrence, Massachusetts. It links issues of economic security and quality of life, and addresses the role of women in the struggle for justice.

Ode to the International Debt
Sweet Honey in the Rock. (Live at Carnegie Hall with Sweet Honey in the Rock CD, Flying Fish, 1987.)
A short, pithy song that suggests much of the money going overseas from the United States was used to buy guns and death, and should not have to be repaid by the people of the world.

Why?
Tracy Chapman. (Tracy Chapman CD, Elektra Entertainment, 1988.)
I use this song to begin the school year. It helps set a problem-posing atmosphere in my classroom for the entire school year. It raises issues of poverty and military spending, and alludes to the doublespeak of powerful groups who use words like peace and justice when the opposite is true.

FOOD AND AGRICULTURE

Deportee (Plane Wreck at Los Gatos)
written by Woody Guthrie, sung by Judy Collins. (Tribute to Woody Guthrie CD, Warner Brother Records, 1968.)
A moving song about the treatment of "illegal" workers in the fields of California.

Something in the Rain
Tish Hinojosa. (Culture Swing CD, Rounder Records, 1992.)
A moving song about a boy's little sister, poisoned by the pesticides that farm workers are exposed to in the United States.

GLOBALIZATION ON THE HOMEFRONT

Alien (Hold on to Your Dreams)
Gil Scott-Heron. (1980 CD, Arista, 1980.)
A plaintive song about crossing the border, facing danger, and retaining hope. "Midnight near the border trying to cross the Rio Grande/Running with coyotes where the streets are paved with gold/You're diving underwater when you hear the helicopter/Knowing it's all been less than worthless if you run into patrols."

Career Opportunities
The Clash. (Sandinista CD, Epic, 1980.)
A sharp, funny song about finding a job/career.

The Ghost of Tom Joad
Bruce Springsteen. (The Ghost of Tom Joad CD, Columbia, 1995.)
A mournful ballad: "Welcome to the new world order/ Families sleepin' in their cars in the Southwest/No home no job no peace no rest."

Help Save the Youth of America
Billy Bragg. (Talking to the Taxman about Poetry CD, Elektra Entertainment, 1986.)
A catchy plea to open the eyes of American youth to the problems of the world: "You can fight for democracy at home/And not in some foreign land."

Lives in the Balance
Jackson Browne. (Lives in the Balance CD, Asylum, 1986.)
A powerful ballad about poverty in a Los Angeles barrio and sending young men to Vietnam.

My Hometown
Bruce Springsteen. (Born in the USA CD, Columbia, 1984.)
A working-class ballad about the effects of globalization on an American city.

Mr. Wendell
Arrested Development. (Eyes As Hard as a Million Tombstones CD, Chrysalis Records, 1993.)
A moving rap song that describes the life of a homeless person.

Wasteland of the Free
Iris DeMent. (The Way I Should CD, Warner Brothers Records, 1996.)
A country and western song that cuts to the heart of the economic troubles facing North Americans: "We've got CEOs makin' 200 times the workers' pay/ But they'll fight like hell against raisin' the minimum wage/ And if you don't like it mister/ They'll ship your job to some Third World country 'cross the sea."

CULTURE, POWER AND ENVIRONMENT

Garbage!
written by Bill Steele, sung by Pete Seeger. (Pete CD, Living Music, 1996.)
A wonderfully spirited song that looks at all aspects of the environmental crisis from an anti-corporate

perspective. He sings about how the sea, the air and our minds are being filled with garbage. Kids love it.

It Is One
Jackson Browne. (Looking East, Elektra Entertainment, 1996.)
From space, the earth has no borders. It is one and should be protected by all.

The World Turned Upside Down
Leon Rosselson, sung by Billy Bragg.
(Back to the Basics CD, Elektra, 1987.)
The story of the 1649 revolt of the dispossessed in England who fought against the vested interest of the propertied. A vision of society that is cooperative and in harmony with the earth.

Lost in the Supermarket
The Clash. (The Story of the Clash CD, Epic, 1988.)
A bouncy punk song takes on the false promises of consumer culture ("I'm all lost in the supermarket/I can no longer shop happily/I came in here for that special offer/A guaranteed personality").

Mountains o' Things
Tracy Chapman.
(Tracy Chapman CD, Elektra Entertainment, 1988.)
The song questions our need to consume so many things, and to find meaning in consumption.

TEACHING AND ORGANIZING FOR JUSTICE

If I Had a Hammer
words by Lee Hays, music by Pete Seeger, sung by Peter, Paul, and Mary. (Peter, Paul, and Mary, Too CD, Warner Reprise Video, 1993.)
Written in 1949 and recorded originally by the Weavers, this song responded to the Cold War and the McCarthyism that swept the United States during this time. It is hopeful and calls on people to spread justice throughout the world.

Imagine
John Lennon.
(Shaved Fish CD, Parlophone, 1975.)
A beautiful song that pushes the envelope: "Imagine there's no countries." "Imagine no possessions." "Imagine no need for greed or hunger."

The Internationale
Billy Bragg.
(The Internationale CD, Elektra, no date.)
A good update of the classic workers' anthem. All Bragg lyrics are at www.billybragg.co.uk.

It Could Have Been Me
Holly Near. (Journey CD, Redwood, 1983.)
This inspirational song suggests that people must continue the struggle for social justice, referring to the student anti-war protesters who were killed at Kent State University by the Ohio National Guard in May of 1970, and also to the murder of Victor Jara during the 1973 CIA-supported coup in Chile.

Paz y Libertad
José-Luis Orozco. (Rainbow Sign CD, Rounder, 1992.)
An easy bilingual ballad that calls for peace and freedom in the world. Great for young children as well as upper elementary.

Unite Children
The Children of Selma.
(Rainbow Sign CD, Rounder, 1992.)
A spirited song that calls on children to unite against poverty, racism, sexism, and violence. Each year it is the favorite song of my fifth grade class.

United Minds
Arrested Development.
(Zingalamaduni CD, Chrysalis, 1994.)
An upbeat, hip-hop anthem about people coming together for justice. The playful, catchy lyrics touch on everything from drug dealing to foreign policy to diet.

Ella's Story
Bernice Reagon. (Breaths CD, Flying Fish, 1983.)
Written by Reagon as a tribute to civil rights leader Ella Baker, this inspiring gospel song says that "We Who Believe in Freedom Cannot Rest."

You've Got the Power
Third World
(You've Got the Power CD, Columbia, 1982.)
A pretty, hopeful song with the lyric "people everywhere just want to be free."

Videos with a Global Conscience

BY BILL BIGELOW

Videos can help "story" the world visually for students. They can bring global realities into a classroom in a way that the printed word cannot. Through follow-up discussion, role play, improvisation, interior monologue, and poetry, students can drive deeper into the realities of a particular society, social issue, or into their relationships with distant — and sometimes not so distant — others. But like any "text," video needs to be read critically. Educators need to encourage students not to be mere spectators, but to raise critical questions about how a video frames social reality: Whose story is featured, who speaks and who does not, what factors are highlighted to explain a given problem, what alternatives are explored or ignored?

The videos listed below are ones that can help students rethink globalization. There are many more that are not included here. One criterion for selection was that the resources be relatively easily accessed by U.S. teachers. However, teachers should be aware that this requirement biases these "Videos With a Global Conscience" in favor of filmmakers and videographers from so-called developed countries, who have more access to distribution channels here. I'm sure that I've missed countless other worthy videos, and I hope that readers bring these to my attention. All starred videos are available from the important catalog Teaching for Change, www.teachingforchange.org; 800-763-9131.

LEGACY OF INEQUALITY: COLONIAL ROOTS

This Magnificent African Cake (Part 6 of "Africa")
Basil Davidson. 1984. 57 min.
Available from multiple sources, including Blockbuster.com.

The title of Basil Davidson's sixth episode from his "Africa" series comes from Belgium's King Leopold, speaking at the 1884 Berlin conference to carve up Africa: "I am determined to get my share of this magnificent African Cake." Tragically, as this video later reveals, Leopold did get a share, which he exploited with unimaginable brutality.

Davidson's video is a good overview of the origins of European colonialism in Africa and some of its effects. He surveys various colonial modes from British settlers in Kenya, to "indirect rule" in Nigeria, to the French attempts at assimilation, to Leopold's "reign of terror" in the Congo, to the forced labor in the mines of Southern Rhodesia — which, Davidson tells us, killed an astonishing 20 people a week for 30 years. But the video's breadth is also its weakness, as we don't really get to know one situation well enough to understand its nuances, or to truly appreciate the effects of colonialism on people's lives.

The material here is presented conventionally as a kind of illustrated lecture that does not engage most students. Still, there are surprisingly few videos that deal with European colonialism, and the information that the eminent historian Davidson presents is solid and can be effectively shown and discussed with students in short segments.

Taxi to Timbuktu
Christopher Walker. First Run/Icarus. 1994.
50 min. Taxi to Timbuktu *was produced by Christopher Walker, who also made the excellent* Trinkets and Beads.

This is a somewhat slow-moving film about Alpha, who emigrates from Mali in Africa to New York, Paris, and Tokyo. It offers an intimate portrait of his life at home and abroad, and the communities he is a part of. Unlike many films professing sympathy for the wretched of the earth, *Taxi to Timbuktu* offers a glimpse of African poverty that emphasizes people's enormous resourcefulness and creativity. Although some students may find the video hard to follow or even tedious, its slow pace is also its strength, as the complexity of people's lives comes into focus.

There is no narration to the film, so little context is offered to explain the roots of poverty in Mali, but in his commentary, Alpha suggests some of the colonial roots to the desertification of his country. The video would be a valuable follow-up to *This Magnificent African Cake*, about the consequences of European colonialism. Or it could be an excellent addition to a unit on immigration.

Other films that teachers have used in examining the consequences of colonialism include *Gandhi* — which deals with anti-colonial struggles in South Africa and in India — and *Earth*, about the partition of India and Pakistan.

THE GLOBAL ECONOMY: COLONIALISM WITHOUT COLONIES

Life and Debt

Stephanie Black.
New Yorker Films. 2001. Approx. 90 min.

This may be the best video overview of the effects of globalization on one society — in this instance, Jamaica. *Life and Debt* focuses on the role of the International Monetary Fund (IMF) in Jamaica, but it's much more than that. It weaves together interviews with the IMF deputy director, farmers, workers, scholars, a former Prime Minister (Michael Manley); a narration based on Jamaica Kincaid's *A Small Place* (see p. 54); Jamaican music; life in a tourist hotel; and a kind of Greek chorus of Rastafarian men who comment on Jamaica's neo-colonial plight. The conclusion: Jamaican society has been devastated by high interest payments on its external debt (52% of the entire national budget), cheap imports (potatoes, peanuts, carrots, milk powder, chicken), the WTO ruling forcing Jamaica's bananas into direct competition with much cheaper bananas from Central and South America, and exploitative practices in Jamaica's World Bank-pushed "free zone." (Of course, there are some economic winners: Because of high crime, one security firm featured has gone from 120 guards employed to between 1800 and 1900 guards and over 300 dogs.) It's this relatively comprehensive video walk through Jamaica's economy that can help students see the relationship between farm conditions and sweatshops, and provides a partial answer to the sweatshop defense: "Well, no one is forcing people to go to work in these places."

The video returns periodically to the tourist delights of Montego Bay, with Kincaid's incisive and sardonic narrative:

> Every native of every place is a potential tourist. And every tourist is a native of somewhere. Every native would like to find a way out. Every native would like a rest. Every native would like a tour. But some natives — most natives in the world — cannot go anywhere. They're too poor to escape the realities of their lives. And they're too poor to live properly in the place where they live. Which is the very place that you the tourist want to go. So when the natives see you, the tourist, they envy you. They envy your own ability to leave your own banality and boredom. They envy your ability to turn their banality and boredom into a source of pleasure for yourself.

Life and Debt is so issue-rich that it could be the centerpiece of a unit that looked at the transition from colonialism to "freedom," and the character of that freedom.

As with many examinations of globalization, *Life and Debt* is stronger on critique than it is on alternatives. Former Prime Minister Michael Manley describes Jamaica's helplessness in the face of the IMF/World Bank juggernaut, but was the Jamaican state entirely without recourse? The video explores no possibilities. And is Jamaica without recourse now? Toward the video's conclusion, one member of the Rastafarian chorus proclaims that "Our salvation rests in the hands of the Almighty." Unspecified is the nature of that salvation and what responsibilities rest in the hands of Jamaicans, other Third World people, and we in the "developed" countries. This speaks to an important weakness of the video: We don't hear from Jamaicans who are organizing for change. What strategies are being pursued, and who is pursuing them? Indeed, the many interviews with small producers who lament their decline lend the video a nostalgia that may be unwarranted.

Nonetheless, this is a clever, patient examination of what the global economy has visited on one corner of the world.

Two videos that look specifically at resistance to the World Trade Organization, highlighting the dramatic 1999 demonstrations in Seattle, are *Showdown in Seattle* (www.indymedia.org), and *This is What Democracy Looks Like* (www.thisisdemocracy.org.)

*Global Village or Global Pillage

Jeremy Brecher. 1999. 28 min.

Global Village or Global Pillage makes two arguments: People around the world are being pitted against each other in a "race to the bottom," where "all are being driven down to the level of the poorest and most desperate;" and this process can only be reversed through global solidarity.

The video opens with Westinghouse worker, Janet Pratt, who lost her job when the company decided to move production from the United States to Juarez, Mexico. To add insult to injury, Westinghouse invited Pratt to travel south to train the workers who would now being doing her job. Despite misgivings, she accepted and found Juarez workers living in miserable conditions and earning 85¢ an hour for what she had been making $13.65 an hour to do. It's the video's initial illustration of a process that is going on throughout the world as capital rushes to find the cheapest labor it can, as well as the least restrictive environmental regulations.

Part two of *Global Village or Global Pillage* argues for what the producers call the "Lilliput Strategy" — named for the Lilliputians tying up of Gulliver with hundreds of pieces of thread. Students might be encouraged to think about the strengths and weaknesses of this metaphor in considering the potential nature of movements for global justice. Examples in the video of this strategy include a consumer campaign to support GAP workers in El Salvador, a global campaign to aid Indian villagers combating a World Bank-supported dam, and worker solidarity struggles to force Bridgestone-Firestone to rehire U.S. workers it had fired and replaced with 2300 strike-breakers. In this campaign, Brazilian workers held one-hour stoppages and then "worked like turtles," the Brazilian expression for a slowdown.

These are inspiring examples that point toward a world where people support each other not simply for moral or humane reasons, but also out of self-interest, to create decent living and working conditions in their own societies. In a 28-minute video, the producers can be forgiven for sidestepping more detailed questions of strategy. Does the Lilliput strategy imagine a world of regulated global capitalism, with a social and environmental "floor," or are humane and environmental objectives fundamentally incompatible with a system based on private profit, and thus require a non-capitalist global order? They don't say.

This is a worthwhile overview to many of the issues covered in *Rethinking Globalization*.

*Banking on Life and Debt
Robert Richter. Maryknoll. 1995. 30 min.

"It's easier to get a camel through the eye of a needle than for a banker to feel sorry for a child who is starving, dying of starvation," claims the Brazilian radical politician "Lula" in *Banking on Life and Debt*. The video is an overview of World Bank and International Monetary Fund policies that promote poverty, starvation, and ecological ruin. Measured by its ability to engage most high school students, *Banking on Life and Debt* is spread too thin, covers too much history and too much political economy, and is narrated by too many talking heads. Nonetheless, through examining World Bank and IMF policies in Ghana, Brazil, and the Philippines, the video offers a convincing portrait of an international economic order that drains resources from poor countries in the name of development. And if used with other readings and activities that explore the global debt crisis, this can be an important resource.

The snapshot of Brazil helps clarify the relationship between debt crisis and environmental crisis. Brazil has been ordered to turn more of its land to production for export. Increasing amounts of land are planted in soybeans. As Brazil's Cardinal Arns points out, "The food that we were supposed to eat [is] being sent to cows and pigs in other countries." Other poor countries receive the same prescription, and flooded commodity markets pull down prices of Third World raw materials. Meanwhile, poor Brazilian farmers lose their land to huge corporations and become squatters, every year hacking down more and more Amazon rainforest.

The video doesn't bubble over with hope, but we do meet activists in every country visited who describe efforts to organize for alternatives to debt slavery.

The Debt Crisis: An Unnatural Disaster
Social Action Centre, Jamaica/Friendship Press, (includes a short teaching guide). 1990. 28 min.

Using delightful skits, songs, and expert testimony, this video is a primer on the history and social consequences of the Third World debt crisis and structural adjustment programs, especially focusing on the Caribbean. It has something of a homemade feel to it and lacks the polish that students are used to, but it is a clear and hard-hitting overview of the severe difficulties the debt crisis creates in poor countries. One of the video's strengths is that it is entirely narrated, and the skits acted, by Caribbean people themselves. *The Debt Crisis* covers much the same ground as *Banking on Life and Debt*, although its Caribbean focus is narrower. However, the playfulness (some might argue, silliness) of its skits and its concentration on a smaller geographic area probably make this more accessible for many students.

Deadly Embrace: Nicaragua, the World Bank, and the International Monetary Fund
Elizabeth Conner and Ashley Eames. Global Exchange. 1996. 30 min.

A poor Nicaraguan woman points out that, "Before, during the Sandinista times, there was war but there was never hunger. Now there is no war but there is hunger." The "deadly embrace" of the video's title refers to the post-Sandinista government's acceptance of the structural adjustment policies of the World Bank and IMF, which have devastated Nicaragua's economy — at least from the standpoint of the vast majority of the people. According to the video, unemployment has rocketed to 60%, credit to small farmers has been slashed, public school teachers work in deteriorating conditions for $60 to $70 a month, and public programs of all kinds have been eliminated. Meanwhile, free trade zones welcome transnational corporations who pay pennies an hour to desperate workers.

In its ability to hold most students' attention, the video is somewhat less effective than *Banking on Life and Debt* or *The Debt Crisis*, but its strength is its focus on one country. This could be a helpful resource in an area study of Central America or in a broader look at the forces that compel people to seek work in global sweatshops.

Cancel the Debt, Now!
The Jubilee 2000 Campaign. 2000. Approx. 20 min.

Cancel the Debt, Now! outlines the immorality of the global debt crisis. Activists from numerous countries tell about the impact of debt on the poorest people in their societies, as well as the effects on the environment. The video emphasizes the global Jubilee 2000 Campaign to cancel the debt for the poorest countries and explains why this is not "charity." Although the campaign is Biblically-grounded (in the Book of Leviticus) — and thus the video has religious overtones — this should not prevent its use in public schools. Its strength is in its advocacy for activism in solidarity with the world's poor, and in its scope. However, other than their dire poverty, we learn little about the lives of people affected by the debt crisis.

*Where Are the Beans?
Mennonite Central Committee. 1994. 13 min.

Where Are the Beans? is a kind of detective story — and an excellent classroom resource. Linda Shelly, of the Mennonite Central Committee, lived in La Esperanza, Honduras for several years. While there, she loved to eat red beans, a staple of the Honduran diet. But when she returned in 1993, she found that no one ate beans any longer. Where are the beans? is the question that Shelly pursues as she visits old friends to learn about how their lives have changed.

Shelly discovers the answer in the structural adjustment policies that the International Monetary Fund pressed the Honduran government to adopt: fewer subsidies to the poor, currency devaluation, no more government loans to small farmers, and increased exports of ... you guessed it: red beans. "The small Honduran farmers have been pulled into the global economy — pulled in at the bottom," says Shelly. "Their new position in this system demands more and more from them and offers them less and less." The video closes with Shelly's thoughts on how people in this country can respond to the increased inequities between rich and poor countries, although she overstates the extent to which all Americans benefit from this system.

Where Are the Beans? makes a nice complement to *Sweating for a T-Shirt*, reviewed below, because it helps explain the forces pushing people off the land and into sweatshops. A 19-page study guide supplements the video and includes a classroom-friendly bean bag simulation.

Universal Declaration of Human Rights
Stephen R. Johnson/Reebok Foundation. 1988. 22 min.

One could say that this is the music video for the U.N. Declaration of Human Rights. Short psychedelic cartoons illustrate each of the Declaration's 30 articles. They are mostly clever and amusing. For example, the segment for Article 12, which includes guarantees against arbitrary interference with correspondence, features a letter ripped out of an envelope and attacked by an army of needles poking and shredding. The entire series of short cartoons — almost all of which are 30 seconds or less — would make an excellent prompt for students to complete their own illustrations of these and any other rights they believe should be universal. Students could also be divided into small groups to perform improvisations based on the Universal Declaration or to create pantomimes and perform them as in a game of charades, with other students guessing which article is being acted out.

Roger and Me
Michael Moore.
Widely available at video stores. 1989. 91 min. (Awarded an absurd 'R' rating, apparently for a bit of foul language and the on-camera butchering of a rabbit.)

"First, close eleven plants in the U.S., then open eleven in Mexico where you pay the workers 70¢ an hour. Then use the money you've saved building cars in Mexico to take over other companies — preferably high tech firms and weapons manufacturers. Next, tell the union you're broke and they happily agree to give back a couple billion dollars in wage cuts. You then take that money from the workers and eliminate their jobs by building more foreign factories. Roger Smith was a true genius." This is filmmaker Michael Moore describing the business strategy of General Motors' then-chairman, Roger Smith.

Roger and Me chronicles Michael Moore's long quest to confront Smith with the human consequences of his business decisions on Moore's hometown of Flint, Michigan, where GM eliminated 30,000 jobs. You can find the film in the comedy section at your local video store. And it is a comedy, with a Detective Columbo-like Moore relentlessly pursuing Smith and encountering one ludicrous GM evasion after another. But the film's laughs are squeezed from the sorrow and outrage we also experience as Moore juxtaposes the deterioration of workers' lives with the empty-headed patter of Flint's elite, and the Pat Boones, Anita Bryants, and assorted hucksters who troop through town. Moore interviews a GM spokesman who is indignant that Moore would dare suggest that GM owes anything to the workers who built the company. General Motors is in business solely to make a profit, he insists, plain and simple. Capitalism 101. (In the credits we learn that the PR man also loses his job.)

The film ends with Moore cutting back and forth between Roger Smith offering pious-sounding platitudes at a GM Christmas party and the wrenching eviction of a Flint family on Christmas eve.

To the extent that a key goal of teaching about globalization is to lay bare its human dimensions, this is a valuable classroom resource. However, an equally important goal is to encourage students to reflect on alternatives. The film's nostalgia for an American society based on the mass production of automobiles reveals a key limitation of *Roger and Me*.

A British film that complements *Roger and Me* is *Brassed Off*, starring the brilliant Pete Postlethwaite. It may be a bit too slow or simply odd for most high school students, but at least rent it sometime for yourself. Like *Roger and Me* it's a humorous, if heartbreaking, look at the consequences of "downsizing" — in this case, Margaret Thatcher's Tory government closing profitable, and heavily unionized, coal pits in Yorkshire. The film explores the miners' travails through the fortunes of the town's brass band.

The Ties That Bind
Maryknoll, 1996. 56 min.

Divided into three sections, the first of these is too narrator- and interview-dense for most students. But part two, "Just Between Us," and part three, "The Common Bond" are more accessible. Through the story of two women who emigrated from Mexico to the United States, "Just Between Us" humanizes the issue of "illegal" immigration. It points out the contradiction between the rhetoric of openness and "free" trade on the one hand and the militarization of the border on the other. But it does this concretely, through story.

The final part, "The Common Bond," is largely the inspiring story of Carmen Anaya, a feisty former teacher from Monterrey, Mexico who immigrated to the United States and worked in the fields. Anaya became a community organizer and leader of Valley Interfaith, a multi-ethnic, church/community alliance that boasts membership of 60,000 families in the Rio Grande Valley. Through a translator, Anaya narrates a story that recalls the "conductors" on the Underground Railroad of an earlier era:

> It was 2 in the morning. How can I forget it? The doorbell rang and I saw all these men. "What's the matter?" I asked. They were with Immigration. "Open the door," they said. "Are you Carmen Anaya?" "Sure. How can I help you?" I said. "We want you to go open the church." I asked them "Why? Do you want to pray?" They said, "We're not joking around. We've been told that you're hiding many undocumented persons in there." I said to them, "I will never open that door if you're going there with any other intention than to pray. So you do whatever you want with me. But I'm not opening that door." And I didn't. — We suffered a lot. Because not everyone agreed with us, but we knew that God agreed with us.

Although it includes the use of Mexican story-songs to effectively illustrate points, the video also features an unfortunate soundtrack with soap opera-like music that will annoy some viewers, matched by a narration that occasionally dips into the well of God-family-country boilerplate. *The Ties That Bind* is big-hearted but lacks a sustained analysis about why people are emigrating from Mexico and what economic and political changes would address the Mexican economic crisis — a crisis that the video largely takes for granted.

*Fear and Learning at Hoover Elementary
Laura Angelica Simón. Transit Media, 1996. 53 min.

On the day that California voters approved Proposition 187 — denying "illegal" immigrants public education and access to health care — one of Laura Angelica Simón's students asked her if she was now a "cop" and was going to kick them out of school. *Fear and Learning at Hoover Elementary* is Simón's intimate look at the emotional pain caused by Prop. 187 in one California school: hers. Hoover is the largest elementary school in Los Angeles, enrolling 2,700 kids, 90% of them from Mexico, Guatemala, and El Salvador. The video "stars" Mayra, a precocious Salvadoran fifth grader who takes us on a tour of the school and invites us into her home — a one-room apartment across from crime-plagued McArthur Park that she shares with her mother, uncle and sister. Mayra and other students we meet represent living criticisms of the dehumanizing term "illegal alien," and their humor and intelligence offer viewers an opportunity to rethink lingering stereotypes. But the video is not content to confront anti-immigrant attitudes simply by introducing us to sweet kids. We also meet Dianne Lee, a seven-year teaching veteran whose grandparents immigrated from Russia; Carmen Arcote, a conservative Mexican-American parent who voted for 187; and Mr. Peakmeyer, the Anglo librarian who engages Hoover students in an impromptu debate about the causes of the neighborhood's decline, and with help from these astute youngsters trips over his own contradictions.

My students enjoyed this personal video essay about immigration issues, and found lots to talk and write about. However, the video can't stand on its own. Although early on, Simón, the narrator, labels the students "economic and political refugees," that's the only hint of the forces that propel so many Latin Americans to move north. It was beyond the video's scope, but unless students explore the broader economic factors hurting poor countries — in large measure Made in the USA and other industrialized nations — they won't be able to think deeply about the wrongheadedness of anti-immigrant crusades. Without this broader context, students may be left sympathetic to immigrants' plights but unaware of how economic and political choices made here create social dislocations throughout Latin America. Limitations notwithstanding, the video is provocative and useful.

To engage students in the ordeal of immigrating to the United States from Central America or Mexico, many teachers use *El Norte* (available at many video

---

rental outlets). Although it focuses on immigrants fleeing military repression in 1980s Guatemala, aspects of this film are timely, and it's been a favorite with students.

*Bus Riders Union
Haskell Wexler/The Strategy Center. 2000. 86 min.

In this extraordinary video, Academy Award-winning cinematographer Haskell Wexler records the several-year-long struggle of the Los Angeles Bus Riders Union (BRU) to win better service and to challenge the race and class bias in city spending priorities. Sure, at 86 minutes, it's long for classroom use and drags in a few places for many high school students, but what a rich documentary this is. At the outset, Kikanza Ramsey, a young BRU organizer, explains that the union is "a political, social experiment to see if we can build a multiracial, bilingual, gender-balanced mass movement of working class people that is willing to fight for a set of demands that challenges corporate capital." And this is not mere rhetoric. The remainder of the video brings her words to life, revealing the twists and turns, highs and lows of this struggle, as seen through the eyes of participants. We desperately need more classroom resources like this one. First, because in many respects the union is victorious; in the end they win lots more buses — and less polluting ones, at that — to ease overcrowding for their mostly immigrant, poor, people of color, working class constituency. And students need to learn that struggle matters. But it's how the BRU organizes — especially across lines of race, nationality, and language; with humor; with song; with determination; with an eye on the bigger systemic picture — that will leave a lasting impression. Hope is scarce in many of these "videos with a global conscience;" in *Bus Riders Union* it plays a starring role.

*Arms for the Poor
Maryknoll. 1998. 25 min.

Arms for the Poor almost suffocates students with statistics, but it offers a convincing portrait of the U.S. government in cahoots with arms exporters spreading destruction and wasting the precious resources of poor countries: Since the end of the Cold War, the U.S. has doubled its arms sales; the U.S. sells more weaponry abroad than all other 52 arms exporters combined; 80% of U.S. arms sales go to repressive, non-democratic governments; land mines — 95% of which are U.S. made — kill or injure 500 people per week. Activists and experts interviewed consistently link U.S. arms sales to the maintenance of global inequality; although this is asserted more than demonstrated in the video.

Well, at least "we" benefit from this arrangement, right? Not according to a *Boston Globe* investigation described in the video that found that over a four-year period, six of the largest U.S. arms exporters laid off 178,000 workers but at the same time tripled executives' salaries. This was a point that stuck with my predominantly white, working class students, some of whom occasionally express a tolerance for global inequities because this arrangement benefits "us."

As with other Maryknoll videos like *The Business of Hunger* and *Banking on Life and Debt*, *Arms for the Poor* hops around the globe, featuring example after example, offering one eloquent testimony after another. It's a technique that is information-rich, and effectively presents broad global patterns, but also holds students at a distance from the victims of U.S. economic and military policies; we never linger in a place long enough to really get to know anyone. Nonetheless, it's an important resource, one that generated a good discussion when I used it with my students.

GLOBAL SWEATSHOPS

*Sweating for a T-Shirt
Medea Benjamin, Global Exchange. 1999. 24 min.

Narrated by first year college student Arlen Benjamin-Gomez, *Sweating for a T-Shirt* is a fine video introduction to the issue of global sweatshops. It opens with Benjamin-Gomez buying her sister a UCLA T-shirt made in Honduras, and then wandering the campus asking students where their clothes were made. It's an engaging lead-in to her visit to Honduras with mother, Medea Benjamin, a long-time social justice activist and co-founder of Global Exchange.

In Honduras, the video contrasts comments by industry PR representatives with interviews of sweatshop workers and union organizers, and visits to workers' homes. No problems here, say the industry folks. "I hate that word, 'sweatshops,'" complains an Apparel Manufacturers spokesman.

But the video demonstrates convincingly that there are problems here, and that the word "sweatshop" is well-deserved when applied to Honduran *maquiladoras* — labor-intensive factories owned or contracted with by transnational corporations — producing for global giants like Fruit of the Loom, Dockers, and Nike: Workers make around $3 a day, but the cost of living is $8; hours are long; air in the factories is poor, and health problems like severe bronchitis and skin allergies are common; no talking is allowed and bathroom breaks are few; workers are fired for illness and especially for organizing unions; pregnant workers are fired and denied maternity benefits; youngsters regularly begin factory work around the age of 12, and are unable to pursue further schooling.

Meanwhile, the Honduras-U.S. Chamber of

Commerce representative tells Benjamin: "I don't think they even have the need to have a union, because they are considered to be privileged workers. They work in a very nice environment."

Significantly, the video doesn't encourage us to pity the workers as powerless victims. It emphasizes people's own efforts to organize to fight for better conditions. As the narration and Hondurans themselves stress, they need our solidarity, not charity.

At the beginning of Benjamin's time in Honduras, the Apparel Manufacturers spokesman promises to get them in to see first-hand the excellent working conditions. He smiles and tells them, "I'll arrange that you leave impressed." But in the end, despite repeated telephone calls, the factories refuse to allow Benjamin and her daughter in the door. As Benjamin says, putting down the phone for the last time, "Well, I guess they've got something to hide."

Maquila: A Tale of Two Mexicos
Saul Landau and Sonia Angulo.
Cinema Guild. 2000. 55 min.

The "two Mexicos" referred to in the title of this video are the countryside and the industrial border zones, home to numerous *maquiladoras*. Although the video's portrait of *maquiladora*-centered urban life is much fuller than its depiction of rural life, this is an important resource.

As one observer points out, the *maquila* boom may represent economic growth, but it is certainly not genuine development. Using Ciudad Juarez — just across the Rio Grande from El Paso, Texas — as a case study, the video demonstrates how *maquilas* cheat workers out of wages, undermine unions, pollute surrounding neighborhoods, offer miserable health and safety conditions, and abuse the largely female labor force. Interviews with workers offer glimpses into the intimate humiliations they confront. One woman *maquila* worker says that factory managers will fire any worker who becomes pregnant; they require women to take pregnancy tests and go so far as to demand to see their sanitary napkins to make sure they are menstruating.

Another startling feature of the video is its investigation into the huge number of disappearances and murders of poor women in Juarez. A crime wave that might be portrayed as horrifying but inexplicable by the mainstream media is here given economic and social context. Be aware that there is an especially gruesome scene of a murdered young woman that could upset some students. But this segment is not unrelievedly grim. The video features a large and inspiring demonstration of hundreds of women waving white handkerchiefs, chanting *"Ni una mas!"* (Not one more!)

Although we don't learn about conditions in the countryside in as much depth as we learn about urban life, there are effective scenes of peasants in Chiapas resisting the militarization of their lands, and interview segments with the Zapatista leader Subcomandante Marcos.

Maquiladoras depend on a ready supply of desperate people willing to trade their freedom and sometimes their health for a regular, if inadequate, wage. This video begins to ask, "Why?" and to locate sweatshops in a broader process of globalization.

Something to Hide
The National Labor Committee. 1999. 25 min.

"If you think of the worst nightmare of the major corporations, it's that young people will start to ask serious questions about where their stuff is produced," says the National Labor Committee's Charles Kernaghan at the close of *Something to Hide*. This video demonstrates that some students are most definitely posing those questions and seeking answers. *Something to Hide* follows Kernaghan and a delegation of U.S. college students to El Salvador to learn about *maquiladora* conditions. As Medea Benjamin and her daughter Arlen discover in *Sweating for a T-Shirt*, about their similar quest in Honduras, factories are closed to observers. Not only are they closed, they are often barricaded behind enormous concrete walls or fences topped by razor wire. In interviews with workers outside the factories we hear a litany of abuses, which include the harassment of women who "get pregnant too often," low pay, long hours, attacks on union organizers, and humiliation by the Korean managers — whose motives and positions are, regrettably, not scrutinized, as is true in the NLC's earlier video, *Zoned for Slavery* (see below). The U.S. students also meet a worker who was fired for daring to speak with a solidarity delegation from the United States.

Something to Hide serves as a worthwhile introduction to the issue of global sweatshops, and also as an invitation to join with other students to "put a human face on the global economy."

"Free Trade in Mexico"
segment from TV Nation, Vol. One, Michael Moore.
(Available in some video stores and from amazon.com.)
1994. Approx. 15 min.

Michael Moore spoofs the era of free trade in this amusing segment of his now-defunct NBC show *TV Nation*. He travels to Reynoso, Mexico to pretend to explore the economic benefits of relocating TV production there. In Reynoso, he visits a Whirlpool factory that produces washing machine parts formerly made in Indiana, Arkansas, and Tennessee. The workers there make 75 ¢ an hour, and don't have Whirlpool machines of their own, because, as the manager tells Moore, "One of the problems is that a lot of the folks don't have plumbed-in water." Moore's Reynoso tour guide shows off life across the border in McAllen, Texas — home to mansions and 20 golf courses — where U.S. managers of Mexican factories can enjoy the quality of life they are accustomed to. The episode is a lighthearted vehicle for Moore to drive home his point that in practice, free trade means freedom for corporations to export jobs to low-wage havens with lax enforcement of environmental protections.

*Zoned for Slavery:
The Child Behind the Label
National Labor Committee. 1995. 23 min.

United States corporations operating in Central American free trade zones "pay no corporate taxes, no income taxes, no social security or health benefits, and they treat their workers like slaves. There are no inspections, no regulations, and when workers try to organize, they are fired." As *Zoned for Slavery* emphasizes, these miserable conditions are subsidized by U.S. taxpayers, with over $1 billion funneled to free trade zones by the U.S. Agency for International Development. Most of the workers are young women — teenagers — who work for wages that are 5 to 10% of the wages earned by U.S. apparel workers. Children are the losers, forced to choose between work and school, as employers insist on mandatory overtime. In his commentary in the video, the National Labor Committee's Charles Kernaghan insists that with their forced overtime policies, companies "are telling these young women: 'It's school or it's work — you decide. If you're going to go to school tonight, don't bother coming back tomorrow, 'cause you're fired.'"

Kernaghan's indignation at the youngsters' exploitation courses through the video. A Gap shirt made in El Salvador sells in the United States for $20, but the workers receive just 12 ¢. Who gets the other $19.88? he demands. The video is relentlessly polemical, but why shouldn't it be? Kernaghan's outrage is an appropriate response to the degradation he witnesses.

With Kernaghan, we sneak into a Honduran *maquiladora* and hear from the teenage workers about their conditions. In open garbage pits outside the factories we see discarded packets of the birth control pills that factory managers force on young women workers. Not explained, unfortunately, is the role of the Korean subcontractors who appear as the video's only on-camera bad guys.

As with the NLC video *Mickey Mouse Goes to Haiti* (reviewed here), *Zoned for Slavery* is marred by its failure to highlight the ongoing organizing efforts of Central Americans themselves. By almost entirely ignoring labor and human rights activities there, the producers implicitly suggest that people in the United States must shoulder sole responsibility to confront sweatshop abuse. Still, *Zoned for Slavery* is an excellent — some teachers think the best — intro-

duction to issues of child labor and global sweatshops. It's an important resource, one I've found especially valuable as a follow-up to the Transnational Capital Auction (see p. 108).

Mickey Mouse Goes to Haiti:
Walt Disney and the Science of
Exploitation
Crowing Rooster Arts/National Labor Committee. 1996. 17 min.

This is an angry video that returns again and again to the wretched wages and living conditions of Disney's Haitian workers. We travel to Haiti with Charles Kernaghan, the intense and indefatigable director of the National Labor Committee, as he interviews Haitians about their work lives and standards of living. The video is especially effective when Kernaghan holds up a Disney T-shirt and reveals to workers how much it sells for in the United States. Their collective gasps and shouts of disbelief offer indisputable testimony about Disney's exploitative practices.

Now that sweatshops have been in the news for awhile, many of my students have heard from parents or teachers that yes, wages are low in Third World countries, but living expenses are so low that it all equals out. To test such claims, *Mickey Mouse Goes to Haiti* shows viewers exactly what a worker can buy for her family's dinner with 20 gourdes — $1.20 — if she were so lucky as to end her day with that much left over: a bit of spaghetti, an onion, a small amount of oil and tomato sauce, garlic, a bullion cube and two small pieces of salt fish. The harsh details of Disney workers' lives, such as these, make this an effective video to use with students. What it lacks in the polish of a network news magazine segment, it more than makes up for with its sense of justice and outrage.

One drawback of the video, and it's an important one, is its failure to portray Haitians — and by extension, people in poor countries in general — as agents of change. We never get any sense that Haitians themselves are resisting Disney's "science of exploitation." In an interview, one worker says, "We are like the living dead. The boss has benefits and we have nothing. The boss can say anything to us and we can say nothing." Surely there is truth to this, but the video's underlying message is that we in the United States need to act for Haitians, because they cannot act for themselves. It's a plea for charity rather than for solidarity.

Guess Who Pockets the Difference?
UNITE! 1995. 8 min.

Think that sweatshops are only in other countries? Think again, argues this short video about Guess workers' drive for a union contract. Brief interviews with Guess' mostly Latin American immigrant workers tell of forced overtime, low wages, and humiliating conditions of work. Through a translator, one woman explains the contract system: "We've tried to talk to our boss, but he tells us that Guess is pressuring them — that they lowered their prices. It isn't fair that they are the ones in competition for the prices and we are the ones who pay the consequences."

The video's brevity is an obvious limitation — we learn very little about workers' lives or their struggle to improve conditions — but it could be a useful resource, especially if students were researching the labor practices of particular corporations, or sweatshop practices in the United States.

*Salt of the Earth
Herbert Biberman. 1954. 94 min.

Set in "Zinctown, New Mexico," *Salt of the Earth* uses a combination of actors and non-professional community people to tell its story. And a great story it is. Sparked by a mine accident, the workers, mostly Mexican Americans, go on strike. Safety is the issue, but is inextricably linked with racial discrimination as Anglo miners work in pairs, while Mexican-Americans are forced to work alone. The film consistently highlights the racial dimension to the class struggle. As one of the white managers says about the workers: "They're like children in many ways. Sometimes you have to humor them. Sometimes you have to spank them. And sometimes you have to take their food away." And the film also addresses racism within the union. The white organizer from the international union is committed to the workers' cause and to union democracy, but his paternalism still creeps in. He is criticized by one of the workers, Ramón Quintero: "When you figure everything the rank and file's to do down to the last detail, you don't give us anything to think about. Are you afraid we're too lazy to take initiative?"

But this is especially a feminist story, as women insist that their issues for indoor plumbing and hot water in the company-owned housing also be included as a demand of the all-male union. This is the women's story at least as much as the men's, and they continue to push for equality the more they participate in strike activities. This struggle comes to a head as Esperanza confronts her husband, Ramon, about his determination to keep her in her place: "Have you learned nothing from this strike? Why are you afraid to have me at your side? Do you still think you can have dignity only if I have none?... Do you feel better having someone lower than you? Whose neck shall I stand on to make me feel superior?... I want to rise and push everything up as I go."

Comforting Esperanza a bit later, one of the women says, "Anything worth learning is a hurt. These changes come with pain." As effectively as any other

film in my curriculum, *Salt of the Earth* celebrates the possibility of people being able to create a very different, very much better society through solidarity and collective action.

When I first showed *Salt of the Earth* a number of years ago, I worried that students would be put-off by a black and white film that had quite a bit of amateurish acting and melodramatic music. I was wrong. What the film lacks in polish it more than makes up for in substance. And most students recognize that.

Bread and Roses
Ken Loach. [Available at video stores.] Lions Gate Films. 2001. 106 min. [Rated 'R' for some sexual references, and lots of harsh language.]

This is the fictionalized account of episodes in the Justice for Janitors campaign in Los Angeles. The film opens with Maya's harrowing illegal entrance into the United States from Mexico and follows her travails as she secures a cleaning job in a large downtown office building. Perez, the on-site manager for the cleaning contractor, keeps workers in line through incessant badgering. Maya bristles at this treatment, and is receptive to overtures from the cocky white union organizer Sam, but her sister Rosa has learned hard lessons in self-preservation, and wants no part of a risky union struggle, especially one led by this guy. "'We, we,' when was the last time you got a cleaning job?" she demands of Sam early in the film.

The best scenes in *Bread and Roses* are the tense conversations between workers about whether or not organizing is worth the risk. Maya's would-be boyfriend, Ruben, has a law school scholarship waiting, if only he plays it safe and keeps his job. Why would Maya want to endanger her job, Ruben wants to know. She snaps back:

> What was it that you said when they fired Teresa [an older woman who worked with them cleaning the office building]? "She looks like my mother." That's why I'm doing it. I'm doing it because my sister has been working 16 hours a day since she got here. Because her husband can't pay for the hospital bills. He doesn't have medical insurance.... I'm doing it because I have to give Perez two months of my salary and I have to beg him for a job. I'm doing it because we feed those bastards, we wipe their asses, we do everything for them. We raise their children, and they still look right through us.

Bread and Roses is engaging start to finish and can generate lots of excellent writing and discussion — about treatment of immigrant workers, tensions between immigrant and non-immigrant workers, risks and benefits of organizing, and many others. But it's not without its flaws. This is supposed to be a struggle to reclaim workers' lost dignity, but every union tactic is decided upon by the organizer, not by the workers. They may be in meetings together, but Sam does virtually all the talking — deciding every move, making pronouncements about how he is going to "personally embarrass" the new part-owners of the office building. (Someone in *Bread and Roses* should have criticized him the way the Ramón criticized the organizer in *Salt of the Earth* — above.) And the romance between Sam and Maya was a needless and inappropriate — if predictable — insertion by writer/director Ken Loach. But these are not fatal flaws, and this is a valuable film.

By the way, Loach is a prolific filmmaker, underappreciated in the United States. Two of his films that would make excellent additions to a global studies curriculum are *Hidden Agenda,* about British repression in Northern Ireland; and *Land and Freedom,* about the Spanish Civil War.

CHILD LABOR

When Children Do the Work
The Working Group, 1996. 27 min.

When Children Do the Work borrows key segments from the National Labor Committee's video *Zoned for Slavery* (see review in this article) and an episode of the PBS series *Rights and Wrongs* to alert viewers to the use of child labor around the world. The narration opens with the claim that as a society "we" did away with child labor at the turn of the century, suggesting that child labor is a problem only in other countries, and closes glibly with a list of U.S. firms that have pledged not to use child labor — neglecting to mention that, to date, none of them has promised to pay a living wage to its workers. Nonetheless, the segments are short and hard-hitting, and offer a dramatic introduction to the global workplace exploitation of children.

The *Rights and Wrongs* segment features an interview with a Pakistani carpet factory manager who matter-of-factly reports that he has 40 looms worked by 100 children. "We chain them three or four hours a day to teach it (sic) not to run away," and adds that the children also sleep chained to their looms. But scenes of abuse are also paired with stories of resistance, and the video highlights the story of Iqbal Masih, a former child worker who became an activist with the Bonded Labor Liberation Front.

A final segment features the work of the Women's Network of the United Food and Commercial Workers union which targets Wal-Mart's sale of products made by eight- to twelve-year-olds in Bangladesh.

Despite its overly rosy assessment of the progress that has been made in eliminating child labor, the video's broader message is clear: There are serious problems in the world, and we can work to make things better.

Tomorrow We'll Finish
UNICEF (distributed by Maryknoll). 1994. 26 min.

Tomorrow We'll Finish dramatizes the lives of three Nepalese girls in a rug factory in Katmandu. Although it may feel a bit melodramatic or contrived to some students, the video is an effective introduction to child labor in the rug industry. Its attention to details — the rigors of the girls' working conditions, their sexual harassment by their "middleman" overseer, the pressure to produce in order to pay back loans to their families — lends the video a feeling of authenticity and invites students to look at life from the girls' points of view. Especially touching is the tenderness in the three girls' relationships and how they look out for one another. I've used the video only once, but my students — mostly high school sophomores at the time — enjoyed it and found it more affecting than reporter-narrated TV newsmagazine segments.

Viewers get only a glimpse of how the girls' labor relates to the global economy when a European-looking rug buyer enters the factory to bargain for the finished product. The failure to examine the broader global context of child labor could be considered a weakness of the video. On the other hand, it demonstrates effectively how both consumers and producers are often invisible to each other.

See also *Zoned for Slavery.*

FOOD AND AGRICULTURE

¡Aumento Ya! (A Raise Now!)
[In English, some subtitles.]
Tom Chamberlin/PCUN (Pineros y Campesinos Unidos del Noroeste). 1996. 50 min.

"They look at us as if we're their tractor," says one farm worker organizer, describing the white growers' attitudes about their largely Mexican workforce. *¡Aumento Ya!* is the dramatic story of Oregon farm workers' confrontation with those discriminatory attitudes, and the miserable working and living conditions that accompany them.

The video, presented as the personal narrative of a woman who came to volunteer with the farm workers union, can be roughly divided into two parts: the first, a short overview of farm worker conditions in Oregon and the farm workers' union, Pineros y Campesinos Unidos del Noroeste (PCUN); the second, the story of the strikes held over the summer of 1995 by workers in the strawberry fields. This is not a highly polished video, but its story is compelling, and my students have found *¡Aumento Ya!* engaging and moving. It's one of those "small" videos that allow students to encounter social forces as they manifest themselves in real people's lives.

Workers begin with the simple demand to be paid 17¢ a pound for strawberries rather than the 10 to 12¢ the growers are paying. Beginning with the first walkout from the fields, the video takes us day by day through the strike. A few days into the strike, as workers gain confidence, they add demands about their housing — shacks of blue plastic walls that sleep six or more. Workers call for separate showers for men and women, heat in the cabins, leaking roofs to be fixed, cleaning equipment made available, locks on doors, one telephone for the camp. For my students, the modesty of these demands underscored the wretchedness of farm workers' living conditions.

It's not easy to find teaching materials that show ordinary people taking action to better their lives. *¡Aumento Ya!* is inspiring without being romantic or overstating workers' accomplishments.

Bring some strawberries to class, ask students to write whatever comes to mind about the berries, and then show *¡Aumento Ya!* for a different point of view [see p. 128.]

The Fight in the Fields: César Chávez and the Farm Worker Struggle
Ray Telles and Rick Tejada-Flores/Paradigm Productions. 1997. 116 min.

This is an excellent film about the life of César Chávez and the history of Mexican-American farm workers — the best I've seen. *The Fight in the Fields* begins in the California fields in the 1860s and closes with the death of Chávez in 1993. In between is a solid history of the heroic farm worker movement, with a keen eye for the multiracial solidarity that weaves through the long struggle: Mexicans and Okies join forces in the 1930s, Filipinos and Mexicans later; an Arab-American striker was the first person killed in the grape strikes of the late 1960s.

Yes, it's largely a talking head documentary — at times, narrator-heavy. Yes, it's long. And, yes, some students may find it boring. But it's a wonderful film, rich in details, told mostly from the point of view of the organizers and farm workers who made the history.

Although later sections on the grape and lettuce boycotts could be excerpted for use in class, the film draws its power from the panoramic view it offers of the farm worker struggle.

*The Global Banquet
Two parts: "Who's Invited?" and "What's On the Menu?"
Maryknoll. 2001. 50 min.

The Global Banquet is a good introduction to the themes explored in our chapter "Just Food?" The video asks who benefits from the global market in agriculture and concludes: only large corporations. In the United States and Canada, small farmers can't compete with the corporate food behemoths, and often receive less for their food commodities than these take to produce. In the Third World, small farmers are crushed in the marketplace by subsidized food from the "developed" countries. Defeated by the global market, small farmers in poor countries migrate to the cities, to other countries, or become migrant workers: "The fresh fruit and vegetables that most of us eat are picked by the hands of farmers who have been displaced on their own land, and are now very low wage farm workers." As one Central American farmer, Jorge Mejia says in the video: "You feel very sad, like you've been abandoned."

The video argues that free trade in agricultural goods means that countries are "free" to have their food self-sufficiency destroyed. And for those who don't have the cash to participate in the global food market? They're free to starve. As critic David Korten points out in the video, the market responds only to those who have the cash to make it respond.

The video briefly covers other aspects of food-for-profit, including one section on genetically modified produce. And alternatives are also touched on, but without the kind of rich detail that would have been valuable. Still, mentions of CSAs (Community-Supported Agriculture), farmers' markets, and small diversified farms hint at viable alternatives to the corporate globalization of food.

See also *Where Are the Beans?* in "The Global Economy: Colonialism without Colonies". Another video that teachers might find useful is *The Greening of Cuba* (Jamie Kibben. Food First. 38 min. 1996) about the revolution in small-scale organic agriculture in Cuba.

CULTURE, CONSUMPTION, AND THE ENVIRONMENT

*Earth and the American Dream
Bill Couterie. Direct Cinema Ltd. 1993. 77 min.

See "Capitalism and the Environment: The Thingamabob Game," p. 287, for a description of this fine and useful video.

*Ancient Futures: Learning from Ladakh
John Page/International Society for Ecology and Culture. 1993. 60 min.

See the article "Rethinking 'Primitive' Cultures: *Ancient Futures* and Learning from Ladakh," p. 308, on ways to work with this video. It's a must-use resource.

Local Futures
International Society for Ecology and Culture. 1998.

See the article "Rethinking 'Primitive' Cultures: *Ancient Futures* and Learning from Ladakh," p. 308. Although not as strong as *Ancient Futures*, *Local Futures* concentrates on local alternatives to globalization, and features activities from a Ladakhi women's organization not included in *Ancient Futures*.

*Trinkets and Beads
Christopher Walker. 1996. 52 min.

Trinkets and Beads is a haunting video about international oil companies versus the indigenous people of the rainforests of eastern Ecuador (see "Oil, Rainforests, and Indigenous Cultures," p. 268). There's a billion and a half dollars worth of oil in Ecuador's Oriente, enough to power U.S. cars for 13 days, and in order to get it oil companies are willing to destroy indigenous cultures and the land they live on. One oil company consultant in the video expresses contempt for the very idea of a rainforest: "The jungle is the jungle is the jungle kind of thing." It's a small film about big issues, and my students were fascinated and outraged.

A major theme of *Trinkets and Beads* is the role of evangelical missionaries who, in the words of one of them, view the Bible as a tool to "cut though a culture where they never had it." In the video we see missionaries attempt to groom the indigenous Huaorani people for "civilization" and the arrival of oil companies.

But we also meet Moi, a Huaorani leader whose eloquence will stay with students long after the VCR is turned off: "We must all be concerned because this is the heart of the world and here we can breathe." *Trinkets and Beads* features Moi's stories of Huaorani resistance and includes scenes of indigenous people's raucous demonstrations in Quito. Its images of environmental violence are indelible, and will infuriate students, but images of defiance should also inspire them. My students watch the video early in the school year, but by the end of the year it is still vivid for them, and they use it as a conceptual touchstone in ongoing conversations about "development" and "progress."

Amazonia: Voices from the Rainforest.
Rosainés Aguirre and Glenn Switkes.
The Video Project. 1991. 69 min.

This is an ambitious and somewhat meandering video about the wonders of the Brazilian Amazon rainforests and the struggle over their future. It lacks the focused storytelling approach of *Trinkets and Beads*, but its more comprehensive emphasis is also a strength. By the conclusion, we've met indigenous people, rubber tappers, and poor farmers who,

according to the video's narration, have begun to see the need to build alliances against the forces of "development," which include cattle ranchers, loggers, gold miners, power companies, and the Brazilian military. As the rubber workers union leader, Chico Mendes (since murdered) says: "Today we have become aware. It's been so important that Indians and rubber tappers have discovered they are not enemies. Our biggest enemies were those who caused this conflict between us. And our true enemies are those who are devouring us and devastating our forests and who want to do away with Amazonia." Despite the environmental and human ravages described in some detail, this is a hopeful video that emphasizes the enormous resourcefulness of Amazonia's people and their growing resistance.

Stepan Chemical:
The Poisoning of a Mexican Community
Mark R. Day. Coalition for Justice in the Maquiladoras. 1992. 18 min.

The same economic priorities that produce global sweatshops also produce global cesspools. *Stepan Chemical* begins as the story of a U.S. chemical corporation taking advantage of lax environmental regulations and enforcement in Mexico to pollute the air, soil, and groundwater of a Matamoros, Mexico neighborhood — just across the border from Brownsville, Texas. We learn, for example, that xylene levels in water around the plant are 53,000 times greater than allowable levels in the United States and that babies in Matamoros have been born with severe birth defects, a possible result of xylene poisoning. Every time it rains, the water runs out of the factory into the yards of neighborhood homes where kids play.

Instead of being just another muckraking tale of corporate abuse, the video highlights the growing resistance in Matamoros in alliance with the Texas-based Coalition for Justice in the Maquiladoras. The short video ends with the defiant words of neighborhood resident, Erna Mendez: "We'd die first before leaving. They're not going to force us out. We were born here, we grew up here, and we're not leaving." But as she speaks these words, it appears that the struggle is heating up, so students will want to learn more about the current situation.

The Ad and the Ego
Harold Boihem. California Newsreel, 1996. 60 min.

See the article "Masks of Global Exploitation" (p. 300) for ways of working with this essential resource — the best video I've seen on the nature of advertising. Also included on our website (www.rethinkingschools.org/rg) are quotes from the video that can be used with students.

6 TV Uncommercials and the Culture Jammer's Video
Kalle Lasn. Adbusters Media Foundation. 15 min.

This valuable resource is a collection of alternative "uncommercials" that prompt us to reflect on fundamental aspects of North American life. They are pointed, playful, and profound. One uncommercial for "American Excess" features an oinking pig protruding from a map of North America: "A tiny 5% of the people in the world consume one-third of its resources, and produce almost one-half the non-organic waste. Those people are us. Nothing is destroying this planet faster than the way we North Americans live."

Another uncommercial features a bull marauding through a china shop. The voice-over: "For years, people have defined the economic health of a country by its gross national product. The trouble is that every time a forest falls, the GNP goes up. With every oil spill the GNP goes up. Every time a new cancer patient is diagnosed, the GNP goes up. If we're to save ourselves, economists must learn to subtract." This segment carries the unfortunate title, "Voodoo Economics," borrowing George Bush's racist put-down of Ronald Reagan's economic policies in the 1980 Republican primary campaign. (Why is Voodoo the only belief system considered a synonym for "loony"?)

Thirty- and sixty-second uncommercials are bound to be limited, but these will encourage students to think critically about the typical TV fare and will suggest possible uncommercials they themselves might want to produce.

Advertising and the End of the World
Sut Jhally. The Media Education Foundation. 1998. 47 min.

Sut Jhally is a brilliant analyst of advertising's deep cultural messages, and the dire ecological effects of a society whose raison d'être is the production of commodities for profit. *Advertising & the End of the World* has the feel of an illustrated lecture; it is rich in ideas. But it is dense and academic, and would be difficult to follow for most high school students — and impossible to absorb in one sitting. Nonetheless, it could be used effectively in short segments. Indeed, Jhally's analysis of advertising is so careful and systematic that the video could serve as a unit outline for the cultural impact of advertising. His discussion of the environmental consequences of advertising, toward the end of the video, is especially enlightening — and frightening.

*Making a Killing: Philip Morris, Kraft, and Global Tobacco Addiction
Kelly Anderson and Tami Gold. INFACT. 2000. 29 min.

Making a Killing highlights the tobacco industry's despicable practice of marketing to young people — concentrating on Philip Morris as one of the most egregious offenders. What sets this video apart from other network media fare covering similar ground is that it focuses especially on tobacco marketing around the world. Despite attempts by impoverished countries like Vietnam to ban cigarette advertising, Philip Morris dances around restrictions by paying attractive young women to dress in short skirts and distribute cigarettes to young men: The first one is free — no joke. With the arrival of capitalism and "free trade," countries like the Czech Republic have experienced a 40% rise in the number of 15- and 16-year-old smokers.

As a number of people in the video point out, tobacco addiction around the world is not only a health problem, it's also an economic issue: The profits of tobacco sales are private but the costs of caring for the afflicted are socialized. In poor countries, this gives anti-tobacco organizing special urgency.

Making a Killing is one of those videos that should be seen by every student.

VIDEO DISTRIBUTORS

Note: All starred videos above are available from the Teaching for Change catalog: www.teachingforchange.org or 800-763-9131.

Cinema Guild
130 Madison Ave., 2nd Floor
New York, NY 10016-7038
Tel: 800-723-5522; Fax: 212-685-4717
www.cinemaguild.com

Coalition for Justice in the Maquiladoras
530 Bandera
San Antonio, TX 78228
Tel: 210-732-8957
e-mail: cjm@ipc.apc.org.

First Run/Icarus Films
32 Court Street, 21st Floor
Brooklyn, NY 11201
Tel: 718-488-8900; Fax: 718-488-8642
e-mail: info@frif.com
www.frif.com

Friendship Press Videos
Tel: 800-889-5733;
www.ncccusa.org (click on Friendship Press)

Global Exchange
Global Exchange Online Fair Trade Store
2017 Mission St. #303
San Francisco CA 94110
Tel: 800-497-1994 x237
www.globalexchange.org

**The International Society
for Ecology and Culture**
e-mail: isecuk@gn.apc.org
www.isec.org.uk

Maryknoll Sisters
P. O. Box 311
Maryknoll, NY 10545-0311
Tel: 914-941-7575; Fax: 914-923-0733
www.maryknoll.org

Media Education Foundation
26 Center St.
Northampton, Massachusetts 01060
Tel: 800-897-0089 or 413-584-8500
Fax: 800-659-6882 or 413-586-8398
e-mail: mediaed@mediaed.org
www.mediaed.org

National Labor Committee
275 Seventh Ave., 15th Floor
New York, NY 10001
Tel: 212-242-3002; fax: 212-242-3821;
e-mail: nlc@nlcnet.org
www.nlcnet.org.

New Yorker Films
Tel: 212-247-6110; Fax: (212) 307-7855
e-mail: info@newyorkerfilms.com
www.newyorkerfilms.com

Paradigm Productions
www.paradigmproductions.org

PCUN
300 Young St.
Woodburn, OR 97071
Tel: 503-982-0243; fax: 503-982-1031
www.pcun.org

Strategy Center Publications
Tel: 213-387-2800;
www.busridersunion.org;
www.thestrategycenter.org.

Transit Media
22D Hollywood Ave.
Hohokus, NJ 07423
Tel: 800-343-5540

UNITE!
1710 Broadway
New York, NY 10019
Tel: 212-265-7000
www.uniteunion.org

The Video Project
Tel: 800-475-2638
www.videoproject.org

The Working Group
1611 Telegraph Ave. # 1550
Oakland, CA 94612
Tel: 510-268-9675
www.theworkinggroup.org

Books and Curricula for Global Justice

Note: All books and curricula that are starred are available from the Teaching for Change catalog, www.teachingforchange.org, or 800-763-9131.

THE GLOBAL ECONOMY: FRAMING THE ISSUES

Against Empire
Michael Parenti.
San Francisco: City Lights Books, 1995.
Critical essays on U.S. foreign policy.

The Case Against The Global Economy
edited by Jerry Mander and Edward Goldsmith.
San Francisco: Sierra Club Books, 1996.
An impressive collection of essays on all aspects of globalization from some of the most distinguished activists and scholars around.

A Citizen's Guide to the World Trade Organization
Steven Shrybman.
Toronto: James Lorimer and Co. and Canadian Centre for Policy Alternatives (www.policyalternatives.ca), 1999.
A valuable overview of the effects of the World Trade Organization and the regime of free trade.

Corporations Are Gonna Get Your Mama: Globalization and the Downsizing of the American Dream
Kevin Danaher, ed.
Monroe, ME: Common Courage Press, 1996.
A collection of short critical essays on globalization and resistance.

Democratizing the Global Economy
Kevin Danaher, ed.
Monroe, ME: Common Courage Press, 2001.
Short articles describe popular challenges to the policies of the International Monetary Fund and the World Bank. Many of these could be used with students.

*Eyes of the Heart: Seeking a Path for the Poor in the Age of Globalization
Jean-Bertrand Aristide.
Monroe: ME: Common Courage Press, 2000.
A short but moving book about the plight of the poor in a time of market domination. Clear and brief chapters could be used with students.

*The Field Guide to the Global Economy
Sarah Anderson and John Cavanagh, with Thea Lee.
New York: The New Press, 1999.
Illustrated with charts, graphs, and political cartoons, this accessible and engaging guide reveals the harmful effects of corporate-driven globalization. It explains current trends in the global economy, the driving forces behind globalization, and the organizations and individuals working to reverse these destructive forces.

50 Years Is Enough: The Case Against the World Bank and the International Monetary Fund
edited by Kevin Danaher.
Cambridge, MA: South End Press, 1994.
A short but important book that offers a devastating overview of the negative impact of the debt crisis and "structural adjustment programs." Lots of case studies that could be drawn on for classroom activities.

Global Ethnography: Forces, Connections, and Imaginations in a Postmodern World
Michael Burawoy, et al.,
Berkeley: University of California Press, 2000.
A collection of provocative ethnographies which look at the interaction between local struggles and global forces.

Global Village or Global Pillage: Economic Reconstruction from the Bottom Up
Jeremy Brecher and Tim Costello.
Cambridge, MA: South End Press, 1994.
Provides a helpful wider framework to consider the "race to the bottom," but also focuses on grassroots responses worldwide. Good source of examples and quotes to share with students. [See also the video of the same title.]

Globalization from Below
Jeremy Brecher, Tim Costello, and Brendan Smith.
Cambridge, MA: South End Press, 2000.
A useful book to reflect on organizing choices to confront globalization from above.

Globalize This! The Battle Against the World Trade Organization and Corporate Rule
edited by Kevin Danaher and Roger Burbach,
Common Courage Press, 2000.
A valuable collection of short readings that capture the breadth of the anti-globalization movement that coalesced in Seattle in late 1999.

*Invisible Government: The World Trade Organization — Global Government for the New Millennium?
Debi Barker and Jerry Mander. San Francisco: International Forum on Globalization, 1999.
The best short introduction to the rationale behind and the workings of the World Trade Organization. The authors provide several case studies to highlight their points.

*No Logo: Taking Aim at the Brand Bullies

Naomi Klein
New York: Picador, 1999.
A lively and wide-ranging book that takes a critical look at corporate marketing and production strategies. Klein also documents the contradictions of many of these corporate policies and how they contribute to the growth of opposition movements.

*A People's History of the United States

Howard Zinn.
New York: HarperCollins, 1995.
The best single-volume U.S. history. Lays the groundwork for understanding the role of the United States in world affairs.

Shifting Fortunes: The Perils of the Growing American Wealth Gap

Chuck Collins, Betsy Leondar-Wright, and Holly Sklar.
Boston: United For a Fair Economy, 1999.
Very readable handbook with many charts and graphs showing the increasing wealth divide in the United States.

***Upside Down:
A Primer for the Looking-Glass World**

Eduardo Galeano.
New York: Henry Holt, 2000.
A funny, brilliant, wide-ranging look at the latest incarnation of globalization. Much of this book could be excerpted for classroom use.

**Views from the South:
The Effects of Globalization and
the WTO on Third World Countries**

edited by Sarah Anderson.
San Francisco: International Forum on Globalization, 1999.
Defenders of corporate globalization are fond of criticizing opponents as ex-hippies and "paid union activists," and claim that people in the Third World are hungry for more not less globalization. Here is a book that presents essays by such prominent Third World scholar-activists as Vandana Shiva, Walden Bello, Martin Khor and Oronto Douglas that reveal the concrete effects of capitalist globalization.

*The War on the Poor

Randy Albelda, Nancy Folbre, and the Center for Popular Economics.
New York: New Press, 1996.
A readable description of how current U.S. welfare policy harms the poor and doesn't eliminate domestic poverty. Great graphics, classroom-friendly.

COLONIAL ROOTS
OF GLOBAL INEQUALITY

Capitalism and Slavery

Eric Williams.
University of North Carolina Press, 1994.
A look at the relationship between the rise of capitalism and the transatlantic slave trade.

The Colonizer and the Colonized

Albert Memmi.
Boston: Beacon, 1967.
A classic critical treatise on colonialism.

Discourse on Colonialism

Aimé Césaire.
New York: Monthly Review, 1972.
A succinct, angry, poetic indictment of colonialism by the Martinique scholar-activist, Césaire. Parts could be used with students.

How Europe Underdeveloped Africa

*Walter Rodney. Washington, DC:
Howard University Press, 1981.*
A detailed and well-documented analysis of the impact of European colonialism on Africa.

**King Leopold's Ghost: A Story of Greed,
Terror, and Heroism in Colonial Africa**

Adam Hochschild.
New York: Mariner Books, 1998.
An in-depth look at the history of colonialism and resistance in central Africa. An excellent book to complement Barbara Kingsolver's *The Poisonwood Bible*.

**No Trespassing: Squatting, Rent Strikes,
and Land Struggles Worldwide**

Anders Corr.
Cambridge, MA: South End Press, 1999.
A fine account of struggles throughout the world, from the homeless of New York City's Tompkin Square to the agricultural workers on Chiquita banana plantations in Honduras. Several uplifting stories worth sharing with students. Excellent bibliography.

***Open Veins of Latin America: Five
Centuries of the Pillage of a Continent**

Eduardo Galeano.
New York: Monthly Review Press, 1998.
The classic indictment of imperialism in the Americas.

School of Assassins

Jack Nelson-Pallmeyer.
Maryknoll, NY: Orbis Books, 1997.
Presents the case for closing the School of the Americas, which trains military officers from countries of Latin America, some of whom have been implicated in torture and suppression of people's movements in their country.

Stolen Continents: The "New World" Through Indian Eyes Since 1492

Ronald Wright.
New York: Viking, 1992.
An examination of the "discovery," resistance, and rebirth of five major Native nations: Aztec, Maya, Inca, Cherokee, and Iroquois.

What Do You Know About Racism?

Pete Sanders and Steve Meyers.
Copper Beach Books, 1995.
A children's book from England that directly addresses racism with clear definitions and realistic comic strips. Gr. 4/up.

GLOBAL SWEATSHOPS

Behind the Swoosh: The Struggle of Indonesians Making Nike Shoes

edited by Jeff Ballinger and Claes Olsson.
Upsalla, Sweden: Global Publications Foundation, 1997.
A collection of articles and documents about Nike.

The Global Factory: Analysis and Action for a New Economic Era

Rachael Kamel.
Philadelphia: American Friends Service Committee, 1990.
A bit dated, but offers still-useful short examples about the effects of globe-trotting factories and the variety of ways people resist.

The *Maquiladora* Reader: Cross-Border Organizing Since NAFTA

Rachael Kamel and Anya Hoffman, eds.
Philadelphia: American Friends Service Committee, 1999.
A collection of articles and resources describing the heroic story of how *maquiladora* workers have organized.

No Sweat: Fashion, Free Trade and the Rights of Garment Workers

Andrew Ross, ed.
New York: Verso, 1997.
A creative collection of photos, writings, and statistics on the status of garment workers in the United States and abroad.

Reclaiming America: Nike, Clean Air, and the New National Activism

Randy Shaw.
Berkeley, CA: University of California Press, 1999.
Recounts how popular activism has played a crucial role in raising awareness about sweatshop abuses around the world.

Runaway America: U.S. Jobs and Factories on the Move

Harry Browne and Beth Sims.
Albuquerque, NM: Resource Center Press, 1993.
Provides an overview of the history and economics of the phenomenon of corporations moving operations outside of the U.S. Also provides case studies of how activists, workers, and community leaders have fought against runaway shops.

The Sneaker Book: Anatomy of an Industry and an Icon

Tom Vanderbilt.
New York: New Press, 1998.
Loads of information on one of the most important clothing items for kids.

Sweatshop Warriors: Immigrant Women Workers Take on the Global Factory

Mirriam Ching Yoon Louie.
Cambridge, MA: South End Press, 2001.
A richly detailed book describing the strategies of sweatshop workers to challenge oppressive conditions. Many of these stories could be used with students or drawn upon to create engaging lessons.

With These Hands: The Hidden World of Migrant Farm Workers Today

Daniel Rothenberg.
New York: Harcourt Brace, 1998.
A readable documentation of the U.S. farm labor system through the voices of workers, growers, union organizers, farm worker families and others.

CHILD LABOR

Cheap Raw Materials: How the Youngest Workers are Exploited and Abused

Milton Meltzer.
New York: Viking, 1994.
A fine history of child labor in the United States and how the problem persists today. Gr. 5/up.

Child Labor: A Selection of Materials on Children in the Workplace

compiled by the American Federation of Teachers, International Affairs Dept., 555 New Jersey Ave. NW, Washington, DC 20001-2079 (iadaft@aol.com) (single copy, $1).
Includes a number of articles that could be useful with students, e.g., "Child Labor in Pakistan," by Jonathan Silvers; and "Six Cents an Hour," by Sydney Schanberg.

Child Labor: A World History Companion

Sandy Hobbs, Jim McKechnie, and Michael Lavalette.
Santa Barbara, CA: ABC-CLIO, 1999.
A one-volume encyclopedia on child labor organized alphabetically. Good library resource.

Child Labor in America

Juliet Mofford, ed.
Carlisle, MA: Discovery Enterprises, Ltd. 1997.
A short collection of first person and primary source material on child labor. 4th grade and up.

A Children's Chorus: Celebrating the 30th anniversary of the Universal Declaration of the Rights of the Child

by UNICEF. [See "Picture Books."]

Exploitation of Children

Judith Ennew.
Austin, TX: Raintree Steck-Vaughn, 1997.
An internationalist perspective that describes both the conditions and types of child exploitation along with efforts by people organizing against it.

Iqbal Masih and the Crusaders Against Child Slavery

Susan Kuklin.
New York: Henry Holt and Company, 1998.
An excellent biography that sets the short life of Iqbal Masih in the context of the historic struggle against child labor. Gr. 5/up.

Kids at Work: Lewis Hine and the Crusade Against Child Labor

Russell Freedman.
New York: Clarion Books, 1994.
An impressive collection of Hine's photos and an accessible description of his life work. Students will be amazed by his photographs.

Listen to Us: The World's Working Children

Jane Springer.
Toronto: Groundwood Books, 1997.
A beautifully done book with impressive photos that clearly lays out the story of child labor in the world and how people are fighting against it.

Mother Jones and the March of the Mill Children

Penny Colman.
Brookfield, CN: Millbrook Press, 1994.
A story book with quality photos that tells of the historic march against child labor in 1903.

One Day We Had to Run

Sybella Wilkes.
Brookfield, CN: Millbrook Press, 1994.
Child refugees from Sudan, Somalia, and Ethiopia tell their stories in words and paintings.

Stolen Dreams: Portraits of Working Children

David Parker.
Minneapolis, MN: Learner Publications Co., 1998.
Striking black and white photos of children working throughout the world. Accompanying text includes many primary sources with children describing their working conditions, struggles and dreams.

Voices from the Fields: Children of Migrant Farm Workers Tell Their Stories

S. Beth Atkin.
Boston: Little, Brown, and Co., 1993.
Interviews and photographs that describe the reality of child labor in American fields.

We Have Marched Together: The Working Children's Crusade

Stephen Currie.
Minneapolis, MN: Learner Publications, 1997.
A description of the 1903 march against child labor led by Mother Jones in which children marched from from Kensington, PA to Oyster Bay, New York. Quality photos and inspirational quotes from Mother Jones. Gr. 5/up.

We the Children

UNICEF.
New York: W.W. Norton & Co., 1990.
Photographs by the world's leading photojournalists show diverse children at play, school, work, and rest.

JUST FOOD?/CULTURE, POWER AND THE ENVIRONMENT

Against the Grain: Biotechnology and the Corporate Takeover of Your Food

Marc Lappé and Britt Bailey.
Monroe, ME: Common Courage Press, 1998.
This book focuses especially on Monsanto to evaluate the corporate claims for the benefits of genetically engineered food.

Ancient Futures: Learning from Ladakh

Helena Norberg-Hodge.
San Francisco: Sierra Club Books, 1991.
Tells the story of Ladakh in northern India to highlight the way in which development is destroying ecologically viable indigenous cultures. See also the video *Ancient Futures,* an important classroom resource.

Biopiracy: The Plunder of Nature and Knowledge

Vandana Shiva.
Cambridge, MA: South End Press, 1997.
A passionate but scholarly denunciation of the West's plunder of Third World biodiversity.

The Fate of the Forest: Developers, Destroyers and Defenders of the Amazon

Susanna Hecht and Alexander Cockburn.
New York: Harper Perennial, 1994.
An important overview of the social and ecological dynamics of rainforest destruction and resistance. Helpful appendices — interviews, manifestos, truths and myths, etc. — that could be excerpted for students.

A Green History of the World: The Environment and the Collapse of Great Civilizations

Clive Ponting.
New York: Penguin, 1991.
A history book that pays especially close attention to the effects of colonialism and neo-colonialism on the earth and the indigenous people who depend on it.

In the Absence of the Sacred: The Failure of Technology and the Survival of the Indian Nations

Jerry Mander.
San Francisco: Sierra Club Books, 1991.
Mander is director of the International Forum on Globalization. In this book, he offers a powerful critique of cultures based on modern technologies, and argues that these technologies are not politically neutral. Mander explores the negative consequences when these imperialistic cultures collide with indigenous cultures.

The No-Nonsense Guide to Climate Change

Dinyar Godrej, ed.
Toronto: New Internationalist, 2001.
A short, readable summary of the causes and consequences of global warming, focusing on human health, farming, and wildlife.

Power Politics

Arundhati Roy.
Cambridge, MA: South End Press, 2001.
Arundhati Roy writes passionately about a range of issues in this book of essays, but especially about the politics of dams in India — which Roy sees as metaphor for the consequences of "development" worldwide.

Redesigning Life? The Worldwide Challenge to Genetic Engineering

Brian Tokar, ed.
New York: Zed, 2001.
Perhaps the best critical overview to the genetic engineering debates, featuring the most prominent scholar-activists.

Resource Rebels: Native Challenges to Mining and Oil Corporations

Al Gedicks.
Cambridge, MA: South End Press, 2001.
Gedicks chronicles transnational indigenous movements that oppose mining and oil company exploitation. These are some of the most important struggles on the planet.

*Savages

Joe Kane.
New York: Vintage Books, 1996.
A fast-paced account of the invasion of the Oriente rainforest in eastern Ecuador by U.S.-based oil companies and the resistance of Huaorani Indians. Much of it is suitable for high school use.

Save My Rainforest

Monica Zak. Wonderful illustrations by
Bengt-Arne Runnerström.
(Available also in Spanish and Swedish). 1992.
True story of a young boy who leads a mass march to save the rainforest of his country.

*Stolen Harvest: The Hijacking of the Global Food Supply

Vandana Shiva.
Cambridge, MA: South End Press, 1999.
Details the impact of the increasing corporate control over the world's food supply. An important and devastating critique.

World Hunger: Twelve Myths

Francis Moore Lappé, Joseph Collins
and Peter Rosset.
New York: Food First/Grove, 1998.
This book marches through the most widely held myths about why people are hungry around the world, and punctures them one by one. The authors argue that overpopulation, lack of technology, or failure to apply modern farming techniques, are not to blame for hunger. The issue is how land is owned and controlled — too much marketplace, not enough democracy.

The World Is Not for Sale: Farmers Against Junk Food

José Bové and François Dufour.
New York: Verso, 2001.
Interviews with French farmer José Bové, a prominent activist against corporate-driven globalization of food, and François Dufour, General Secretary of the French Farmers' Confederation.

CURRICULA/REFERENCE BOOKS

*The A to Z of World Development

edited by Andy Crump and Wayne Ellwood.
The New Internationalist, 1998.
A valuable reference book for student research. It includes over 600 entries on key terms and concepts for understanding global issues.

*Beyond Heroes and Holidays

edited by Deborah Menkart, Enid Lee,
Margo Okazawa-Rey.
Washington DC: NECA, 1998.
A compilation of teaching and staff development activities that emphasize anti-racist, social justice approaches.

*Caribbean Connections

edited by Catherine Sunshine.
Washington, DC: Network of Educators on the Americas/EPICA, 1991.
Stories, interviews, songs, drama, and oral histories, accompanied by lesson plans for secondary language arts and social studies. Separate volumes on Puerto Rico, Jamaica, Regional Overview, and Moving North.

*Child Labor Is Not Cheap

Amy Sanders and Meredith Sommers.
Minneapolis: Resource Center of the Americas, 1997.
A three-lesson unit for grades 8-12 on the 250 million children throughout the world who spend most of their day on the job.

***Colonialism in the Americas:
A Critical Look
and Colonialism in Asia: A Critical Look**

Susan Gage.
Victoria, British Columbia: VIDEA, 1991.
Accurate descriptions of colonialism in an easy to read, comic book format. Through dialogue and cartoons, each booklet traces the development of colonialism and its legacy. Teaching ideas are included in each volume.

***Finding Solutions to Hunger:
Kids Can Make a Difference**

Stephanie Kempf.
New York: World Hunger Year, 1997.
Engaging, interactive and challenging lessons for middle school, high school and adult education on the roots of, and solutions to domestic and global hunger. Examines colonialism, the media, famine vs. chronic hunger, the working poor and more.

Human Rights for Children

The Human Rights for Children Committee
of Amnesty International USA.
Alameda, CA: Hunter House, 1992.
A curriculum for teaching human rights to children ages 3 to 12.

**Human Rights Here and Now:
Celebrating the Universal Declaration
of Human Rights**

a publication of The Human Rights Educators' Network of Amnesty International USA, Human Rights USA, and the Stanley Foundation, 1998.
(To order contact: Human Rights USA Resource Center, 888-HREDUC8 or hrusa@tc.umn.edu;
website: www.hrusa.org.)
A collection of background articles and lesson activities for teaching kindergarten through high school students about human rights. Don't be discouraged by the labored rationale for human rights education; many of the activities and resources are excellent.

***The Line Between Us: Teaching About the
Border and Mexican Immigration**

Bill Bigelow.
Milwaukee, WI: Rethinking Schools, 2006.
Curriculum materials that explore the roots and human consequences of Mexican migration to the United States. Includes simulations, role plays, short stories, poetry, background articles, and extensive resources. The book brings a "rethinking globalization" lens to one important issue.

***Open Minds to Equality: A Sourcebook
of Learning Activities to Affirm Diversity
and Promote Equity (second edition)**

Nancy Schniedewind and Ellen Davidson.
Boston: Allyn and Bacon, 1998.
This resource inspires teachers to teach for justice and provides classroom-ready ideas that work. The lessons integrate various curricular areas and are presented in a sequential fashion. Includes an excellent resource bibliography.

*Peters Projection World Map

New York: Friendship Press.
This is a map, not a curriculum, but it comes with a teaching guide. It presents all countries according to their true size. Traditional Mercator projection maps distort sizes, making Europe appear much larger than it actually is.

***The Power in Our Hands:
A Curriculum on the History of Work
and Workers in the United States**

Bill Bigelow and Norm Diamond.
New York: Monthly Review, 1988.
A widely used curriculum on labor history. Role plays, simulations, first-person readings, and writing activities help students explore issues of work and social change.

***Resistance in Paradise:
Rethinking 100 Years of U.S. Involvement
in the Caribbean and the Pacific**

edited by Deborah Wei and Rachael Kamel.
Philadelphia: American Friends Service Committee, 1998.
In 1898, the United States annexed the Pacific Islands of Guam, Hawai'i, and Samoa, as well as Cuba, Puerto Rico, and the Philippines. These major events in U.S. history are barely mentioned in school textbooks. *Resistance in Paradise* fills the gap with over 50 lesson plans, role plays and readings for grades 9-12.

***Rethinking Columbus:
The Next 500 Years**

edited by Bill Bigelow and Bob Peterson.
Milwaukee, WI: Rethinking Schools, 1998.
A collection of over 80 essays, poems, short stories, interviews and lesson plans that re-evaluate the legacy of Columbus.

***Rethinking Globalization:
Teaching for Justice in an Unjust World**

edited by Bill Bigelow and Bob Peterson.
Milwaukee, WI: Rethinking Schools, 2002.
The most comprehensive volume of background readings, from-the-classroom articles, role plays, lesson plans, poetry, interviews, and resources, on teaching about globalization.

***Rethinking Our Classrooms, Volume 1:
Teaching for Equity and Justice**

edited by Bill Bigelow, Linda Christensen, Stan Karp,
Barbara Miner, and Bob Peterson.
Milwaukee, WI: Rethinking Schools, 1994.
A collection of lessons, reflections, poems, and resources for social justice teaching.

***Rethinking Our Classrooms, Volume 2:
Teaching for Equity and Justice**

edited by Bill Bigelow, Brenda Harvey, Stan Karp,
and Larry Miller.
Milwaukee, WI: Rethinking Schools, 2001.
Extends and deepens many of the themes introduced

in *Rethinking Our Classrooms*, Volume 1, which has sold more than 100,000 copies. Practical from-the-classroom stories from teachers about how they teach for social justice.

*Seeing Through Maps: The Power of Images to Shape Our World View

Ward Kaiser and Denis Wood.
Amherst, MA: ODT, 2001.
A provocative book to get students thinking critically about the politics of how the world is represented in maps.

75/25: Development in an Increasingly Unequal World

edited by Colm Regan
Birmingham, England: The Development Education Centre [Gillett Centre, 998 Bristol Road, Selly Oak, Birmingham, England B29 6LE], 1996.
Contains many lessons that examine inequalities between the global North and the South.

Sweatshop Series

Susan Gage, Richard Morrow and Stacey Toews. Victoria, British Columbia: VIDEA, 2001.
This series includes three short booklets — *Sweatshops: Clothes*; *Barbie's Trip Around the World*; and *Behind the Swoosh: Facts about Nike* — and a 44-page teaching guide for the entire series. This is a valuable resource, with lots of helpful teaching ideas.

*Teaching Economics As If People Mattered: A High School Curriculum Guide to the New Economy

Tamara Sober Giecek.
United for a Fair Economy, 2000.
Field-tested by high school teachers, this innovative economics curriculum looks at the human implications of economic policies.

*That's Not Fair: A Teacher's Guide to Activism with Young Children

Ann Pelo and Fran Davidson.
St. Paul, MN: Redleaf Press, 2000.
Children have a sense of what's fair and what's not. This book helps teachers learn to use this characteristic to develop children's belief that they can change the world for the better. Includes real-life stories of activist children, combined with teachers' experiences and reflections. Original songs for children and a resource list for both adults and children.

*A Very Popular Economic Education Sampler

The Highlander Research and Education Cente,. 1997.
Skits, role plays, group-building activities and methods for identifying and analyzing issues.

The Universal Declaration of Human Rights: An Adaptation for Children

Ruth Rocha and Otavio Roth.
New York: United Nations, 1995.
A concise description of both the origins and content of the Declaration. Simple yet well-illustrated.

*The World Guide: An Alternative Reference to the Countries of Our Planet

compiled by the Third World Institute.
The New Internationalist, 2000.
Profiles the countries of the world, but in addition to including standard information about history and politics, it also addresses the environment, women's roles, human rights, militarism, etc.

FICTION

All Souls Rising

Madison Smartt Bell.
New York: NY Penguin Books, 1995.
A powerful novel of the 1790s Haitian slave rebellion which explores issues of class, color, and freedom.

Buru Quartet

Pramoedya Ananta Toer.
New York: Penguin, 1996.
(A four book set: *This Earth of Mankind*, *Child of All Nations*, *Footsteps*, and *House of Glass*.) Sections of each could be used with high school students. The four books chronicle the effects — economic, cultural, psychological — of Dutch colonial rule in the then-Dutch East Indies (now Indonesia), and the growing anti-colonial movements that grew up in response.

Chain of Fire

Beverley Naidoo.
New York: HarperTrophy. 1993.
Fifteen-year-old Naledi fights against resettlement of her village under the apartheid South African government. (Sequel to *Journey to Jo'Burg*.) Gr. 6/up.

Charlie Pippin

Candy Dawson Boyd.
New York: Puffin, 1988.
Charlie, an African-American 11-year-old girl, gets in trouble for setting up an illegal store in her school. But her real trouble revolves around understanding her Vietnam War veteran father. When she sets up a "war and peace" committee in school she begins to understand a lot. Gr. 5/up.

*Color of My Words

Lynn Joseph.
New York: HarperCollins, 2000.
A beautifully written book from the perspective of Ana Rosa Hernandez, a poor 12-year old girl in the Dominican Republic, who loves to write but must steal paper to be able to do so. When the government threatens to bulldoze her village to expand the tourist trade, Ana's family and her community must come together for a life-threatening struggle. Gr. 5/up.

David Copperfield

Charles Dickens. (various imprints), 1850.
The classic novel on child labor in industrial
England.

Eating Fire, Drinking Water

Arlene Chai.
New York: Ballantine, 1998.
Set in the Philippines at the time of the fall of the
Marcos regime, a reporter investigates a student
demonstration in which the army killed an unarmed
man. She discovers much — not only about the
unfolding revolution, but of her own personal past.
A multi-layered, powerful work.

The Farming of Bones

Edwidge Danticat.
New York: Penguin, 1998.
Haitian writer describes the events in the Dominican
Republic of 1937, when a nationalist uprising on the
part of Haitian workers resulted in a little-known
massacre.

Grab Hands and Run

Frances Temple.
New York: HarperTrophy, 1992.
Set during the civil war in El Salvador, a family flees
north to escape the government soldiers. Gr. 4/up.

A Hand Full of Stars

Rafik Schami.
New York: Puffin, 1990,
A first-person account of a teenage boy who keeps a
journal and becomes increasingly angry with the
repressive Syrian government, which arrests and tor-
tures his father. The boy embarks on a dangerous
mission of publishing an underground newspaper.
Gr. 6/up.

Journey to Jo'Burg

Beverley Naidoo.
New York: HarperTrophy, 1986.
When her sister becomes ill, Naledi and her younger
brother travel to Johannesburg, looking for their
mother. Through people they meet, they discover the
painful reality of apartheid. Gr. 4/up.

Lyddie

Katherine Paterson.
New York: Puffin, 1994.
Set in an east coast mill town in the 1880s. A
Vermont farm girl confronts family problems and
horrible working conditions. Inspiring historical fic-
tion. Gr. 5/up.

Memory of Fire

Eduardo Galeano.
New York: W.W. Norton & Co., 1998.
(A trilogy: *Genesis, Faces and Masks,* and *Century of
the Wind.*)
A brilliant and poignant overview of European colo-
nialism, neo-colonialism, and indigenous resistance.

Because Galeano uses short vignettes to illustrate different episodes, sections of the books are especially
well-suited to classroom use.

My Name Is Maria Isabel

Alma Flor Ada.
New York: Atheneum, 1993.
For Maria Isabel Salazar Lopez, the hardest thing
about being the new girl in school is that the teacher
doesn't call her by her real name. Named for her
Papa's mother and for Chabela, her beloved Puerto
Rican grandmother, Maria Isabel must find a way to
make her teacher understand that if she loses her
name, she's lost an important part of herself. Gr.
3/up.

My Name is Not Angelica

Scott O'Dell.
New York: Dell Publishing, 1989.
A fictionalized account of an enslaved 16-year-old
who risks her life for others. Set in the context of the
1733 slave rebellion on St. John Island in the
Caribbean. Gr. 5/up.

My Year of Meats

Ruth L. Ozeki.
New York: Penguin Books, 1998.
A humorous but biting tale about two women — one
Japanese, one Japanese-American — and the production of a TV series about meat in the United States. In
a cross-cultural way, the novel addresses issues of the
role of media, the impact of a meat culture on health
and environment, and gender bias. Mature high
school students.

Naming the Spirits

Lawrence Thornton.
New York: Doubleday, 1995.
A lyrical story told through the eyes of a survivor of a
massacre of the Argentina military junta. Hgh school.

Nectar in a Sieve

Kamala Markandaya.
New York: New American Library, 1990.
The story of Rukmani, a peasant in an Indian village
who is forced to marry at age 12. Her village suffers
from hunger, pollution, and other ills of industrialization. Though hunger and despair dominate much of
village life, Rukmani's struggle for survival generates
hope. Gr. 9/up.

*The Other Side of Truth

Beverley Naidoo.
New York: HarperCollins, 2001.
Set in Lagos, Nigeria, after the execution of environmental activist Ken Saro-Wiwa. Twelve-year-old Sade
must flee with her younger brother. Her mother is
murdered by the military dicatorship and her journalist father is being persecuted. Sade and her fifth grade
brother arrive in London and face the double difficulties of being refugees and dealing with their father's
imprisonment. Gr. 6/up.

Petals of Blood

Ngugi Wa Thiong'o.
New York: E.P. Dutton, 1978.
An anti neo-colonial novel about the erosion of traditional life in Kenya after "independence." Skilled high school readers.

The Poisonwood Bible

Barbara Kingsolver.
New York: Harper Perennial, 1998.
Set against the arrival of independence in the former Belgian Congo, this novel follows the story of missionary parents and their four daughters who try to "convert the natives" of an African village. An elegantly written critique of colonialism in its many incarnations. High school.

A Small Place

Jamaica Kincaid.
New York: New American Library, 1985.
An angry and beautifully written denunciation of colonialism and its corrupt aftermath in a Caribbean island nation. (See p. 54.) High school.

*Taste of Salt: A Story of Modern Haiti

Frances Temple.
New York: Harper Trophy, 1992.
A gripping novel about politics in contemporary Haiti as told through the voices of an injured member of Jean-Bertrand Aristide's election team and a young man assigned to record his story. Gr. 6/up.

Things Fall Apart

Chinua Achebe.
New York: Prentice-Hall, 1994. The classic tale of Nigerian tribal life before and after European colonialism. A short, powerful tragedy that examines the impact of European economic and cultural domination on traditional life in Nigeria. High school.

Tonight, by Sea

Frances Temple.
New York: HarperTrophy, 1997.
Set in Haiti in 1993 after the military coup that ousted President Aristide. Young Paulie and her uncle and grandmother make preparations to leave their homeland by boat. They must deal with the *macoutes* — government thugs — who come with guns and knives and try to stop them. A stirring account of an escape to freedom. Gr. 4/up.

Widows

Ariel Dorfman.
New York: Penguin, 1983.
A moving tale of how widows, mothers, daughters and lovers mourn the loss of their "disappeared" loved ones. High school.

PICTURE BOOKS FOR ALL GRADES

America Is Her Name

Luis Rodriguez.
San Francisco: Curbstone Press, 1998.
A young Latina immigrant in Chicago searches for a place of belonging. (Available in Spanish, *La Llaman America.*)

A Children's Chorus: Celebrating the 30th anniversary of the Universal Declaration of the Rights of the Child

UNICEF. New York: E.P. Dutton, 1989. Beautifully illustrated picture book summarizes the 1959 Declaration of the Rights of the Child which speaks to issues of nutrition, housing, recreation, and medical services as well as freedom from discrimination, special attention for the handicapped, and the right to be treated equally regardless of income.

The Composition

Antonio Skarmeta. Groundwood Books, 2000.
This picture book views a Latin American dictatorship through the eyes of a nine-year-old boy. He has to confront issues of living in a police state.

A Country Far Away

Nigel Gray and Philippe Dupasquier.
New York: Orchard Books, 1988.
A double set of stylized drawings contrasts the daily life of an agricultural African village and a white suburb in the United States.

For Every Child: The U.N. Convention on Rights of the Child in Words and Pictures

Caroline Castle (text adaptation),
forward by Archbishop Desmond M. Tutu.
New York: Phyllis Fogelman Books, 2001.
A beautifully illustrated description of the key components of the U.N. Convention.

From Slave Ship to Freedom Road

Julius Lester, paintings by Rod Brown.
New York: Puffin Books, 1998.
A beautifully illustrated book that presents the slave experience — from auction block to emancipation.

*The Long March: A Famine Gift for Ireland

Marie-Louise Fitzpatrick and Gary WhiteDeer. Hillsboro, OR: Beyond Words Publishing, 1998.
Based on a true story of solidarity, this picture book for all ages tells of the Choctaws in 1847 who collected $170 from their meager savings for the people of Ireland during the Potato Famine. The story's protagonist, Choona, a young Choctaw, grapples with whether he is willing to extend help to a group of Europeans after the pain his own family has experienced.

The Middle Passage

Tom Feelings.
New York: Dial Books for Young Readers, 1995.
A dramatic set of drawings depicting the horror of the Middle Passage and the resistance of enslaved Africans.

The People Shall Continue

Simon Ortíz, illustrated by Sharol Graves.
Emeryville, CA: Children's Book Press, 1987.
An epic story of Native American peoples extending from the creation to modern times. A "teaching story" of destruction, fightback, and survival.

The People Who Hugged Trees

adapted by Deborah Lee Rose, illustrated by Birgitta Säflund. Niwott, CO: Roberts Rinehart, 1990.
An environmental folk tale based on the legend from India in which Amrita Devi and several hundred villagers gave up their lives while protecting the forest. This struggle continues today in the form of the Chipko "Hug the Tree" Movement whose members support nonviolent resistance to tree cutting.

*The Red Comb

Fernando Pic, illustrated by María Antonia Ordez.
Ri Piedras, Puerto Rico: Ediciones Huracán, 1991.
(Also available in Spanish.)
In a story set in Puerto Rico, two women conspire to save a young woman from a slave catcher. Based on historical documents, this beautifully illustrated book brings to children another aspect of the struggle against slavery in the Americas.

Rose Blanche

Christopher and Roberto Innocenti. Translated from Italian by Martha Coventry and Richard Craglia.
Mankato, MN: Creative Education, 1985.
During World War II a young girl shows courage in the face of injustice when she takes food to the prisoners of a concentration camp.

The Sad Night: The Story of an Aztec Victory and a Spanish Loss

Sally Schofer Mathews.
Boston: Clarion Books, 1994.
A vivid description of "La Noche Triste" — June 30, 1520 — when the Aztecs fought off the invading Spaniards in their great city of Tenochtitlán. An afterword explains how a year later Cortés laid seige to the city and finally defeated the Aztecs.

Save My Rainforest

Monica Zak. Illustrations by Bengt-Arne Runnerström (Also available in Spanish and Swedish.) Volcano, CA: Volcano Press, 1992.
True story of a young boy who leads a mass march to save the rainforest in Chiapas, Mexico. Wonderful illustrations.

Stolen Spirit

Peter Hays and Beti Rozen, illustrated by Graça Lima.
Fort Lee, NJ: Sem Fronteiras Press, 2001.
One interpretation of how a Native boy might have reacted to the first encounter in 1500 with Portuguese explorers who chop down trees that the boys' people think are sacred. Beautifully illustrated.

*The Streets Are Free (*La calle es libre*)

Kurusa.
Scarsborough, Ontario: Firefly Books, 1981.
A delightful story about how a group of children in a Caracas, Venezuela slum struggle to get a park.

*Talking Walls: The Stories Continue

Margy B. Knight and Anne S. O'Brien.
Gardiner, ME: Tilbury House, 1996.
Illustrations and text tell the stories of walls, and the people they divide, throughout the world. Includes the stories of Chinese detainees who wrote poetry on the walls of Angel Island, children who wrote poetry on the fence around the home of Pablo Neruda in Chile, children who created a garden in Philadelphia from an abandoned lot and painted a mural on the surrounding wall, children in Belfast who are divided by a wall constructed by the army in the 1970s, and more.

The Universal Declaration of Human Rights: An Adaptation for Children

Ruth Rochu and Otavio Roth.
New York: United Nations, 1995.
A concise description of both the origins and content of the Declaration. Simple yet well-illustrated.

Journals for Global Justice

Many of the organizations listed earlier have their own newsletters or journals that may not be listed in this section. Unless otherwise indicated, the addresses below are editorial offices.
We have not included subscription prices because these change frequently.
Visit a particular journal's website to learn subscription information and address.

ColorLines Magazine

www.arc.org.
1322 Webster St., Suite 402, Oakland, CA 94612;
tel: 510-465-9577; fax: 510-465-4824. Published quarterly by the Applied Research Center. An award-winning magazine that covers race, culture, and community organizing, with a particular focus on issues that affect communities of color. ARC's website is excellent — well worth a visit.

Dollars and Sense

www.dollarsandsense.org.
740 Cambridge St., Cambridge, MA 02141-1401; tel.: 617-876-2434; fax: 617-876-0008;
e-mail: dollars@dollarsandsense.org.
A vital resource for teachers, *Dollars and Sense* is a clearly written bi-monthly magazine that explains the workings of the U.S. and global economies to non-economists. Short articles are useful for classroom use. The website includes current articles and an archive of past issues. *Dollars and Sense* also publishes anthologies that repackage some of the most useful articles from back issues.

The Ecologist

www.theecologist.org.
Subscriptions and back issues:
P.O. Box 326, Sittingbourne, Kent ME9 8FA, U.K.;
tel.: +44 -0-1795 414963; theecologist@galleon.co.uk.
Published monthly, this is an outstanding journal that challenges basic assumptions about "development," "progress," and "growth." *The Ecologist* features important articles that can help students and teachers consider the environmental consequences of globalization. Many past articles are archived on their website.

Extra!

www.fair.org.
Fairness and Accuracy in Reporting, Fair/Extra!
Subscription Service, P.O. Box 170,
Congers, NY 10920; 800-847-3993.
Editorial office: 130 West 25th Street, New York, NY 10001; tel.: 212-633-6700; fax 212-727-7668;
e-mail: fair@fair.org.
An excellent magazine that "unmasks the lies, distortions, and omissions of the establishment media." Great for teaching ideas. Their website offers additional articles, reports, archives of back issues as well as FAIR's weekly radio show, CounterSpin.

In These Times

www.inthesetimes.com.
2040 N. Milwaukee Ave., Chicago, IL 60647;
tel.: 773-772-0100; fax: 773-772-4180;
e-mail: itt@inthesetimes.com.
A bi-weekly news magazine that promotes an anti-corporate perspective on national and international issues and "opposes the tyranny of marketplace values over human values." An important source for alternative news and analysis on global issues. Its website is searchable.

Labor Notes

www.labornotes.org.
7435 Michigan Ave., Detroit, MI 48210;
tel.: 313-842-6262; fax: 313-842-0227.
A monthly magazine of news and analysis dealing with on-going labor union and rank-and-file activities. It describes itself as "a place to learn about the struggles, strategies, and solutions within the labor movement today." *Labor Notes* also publishes books and sponsors forums. Its website is searchable.

Middle East Report

www.merip.org.
1500 Massachusetts Ave. NW, Suite 119, Washington, DC 20005;
tel: 202-223-3677; fax: 202-223-3604.
MERIP is a venerable organization that has been offering astute analyses of events in the Middle East since 1971. Its value was proved once again in the wake of September 11, 2001, when its journal and website were essential sources for making sense out of the global crisis.

Monthly Review

www.monthlyreview.org.
122 W. 27th St., New York, NY 10001;
tel: 212-691-2555;
e-mail: mrmag@monthlyreview.org.
Thoughtful socialist monthly journal that looks at international issues from a Marxist point of view. *Monthly Review* regularly publishes important analyses of global issues. MR is also one of the most important U.S. publishers of progressive books.

Multinational Monitor

www.essential.org/monitor.
1530 P St. NW, Washington, DC 20005;
tel.: 202-387-8030; fax: 202-234-5176;
e-mail: monitor@essential.org.
Multinational Monitor tracks corporate activity, especially in the Third World, focusing on the export of hazardous substances, worker health and safety,

labor union issues and the environment. The website announces that it is the internet's "most comprehensive database on the activities of multinational corporations."

NACLA Report on the Americas

www.nacla.org.
NACLA (North American Congress on Latin America), 475 Riverside Dr., Suite 454, New York, NY 10115; tel: 212-870-3146; fax: 212-870-3305; e-mail: nacla@nacla.org.
NACLA publishes a bimonthly magazine *Report on the Americas*, which is the most widely read English language publication on Latin America. Excellent, hard-to-find analyses.

The Nation

www.thenation.com.
33 Irving Place, New York, NY 10003; tel.: 212-209-5400; e-mail: info@thenation.com.
An important progressive weekly that covers a host of domestic and international issues. Excellent columnists include Alexander Cockburn, Katha Pollit and Patricia Williams. The website is comprehensive.

The New Internationalist

www.newint.org.
U.S. subscriptions: P.O. Box 1143, Lewiston, NY 14092; tel.: 800-661-8700.
A fine monthly magazine that deals with international issues from the perspective of the poor and oppressed. An essential journal for a classroom or school library. Their website includes a section on teaching global issues, and also includes lessons specifically written for learners of English as a second language.

Our Schools/Our Selves

www.policyalternatives.ca.
Subscription info: Canadian Centre for Policy Alternatives; 410-75 Albert St., Ottawa, ON, Canada, K1P 5E7; tel.: 613-563-1341; fax: 613-233-1458.
Our Schools/Our Selves publishes valuable articles on an array of education issues, including: environmental activism; feminism; commercialism in schools; labor, education and the arts; stratification of schools; schools and social justice; and teaching for democratic citizenship. *OS/OS* is especially alert to the intersection of schools and global economic trends.

The Progressive

www.progressive.org;
409 East Main Street, Madison, WI 53703; tel.: 608-257-4626; fax: 608-257-3373.
The Progressive opposes "militarism, the concentration of power in corporate hands, the disenfranchisement of the citizenry, poverty, and prejudice in all its guises. We champion peace, social and economic justice, civil rights, civil liberties, human rights, a preserved environment, and a reinvigorated democracy." It's a monthly magazine that seems to have gotten better and better over the years — with columns

by Howard Zinn, Barbara Ehrenreich, et al., analytical articles, interviews, reviews, and reports on activism.

Race & Class

www.irr.org.uk.
Subscription info: Sage Publications (www.sagepub.co.uk), 6 Bonhill St., London, EC2A 4PU, UK; tel.: 44-0-20-7374-0645.
Race & Class describes itself as a "journal for black and Third World liberation," and is published quarterly by the Institute of Race Relations in Great Britain. This is a hard-to-find but extraordinary journal that uses race and class as lenses to analyze global issues of all kinds, from immigration to the Third World debt crisis to popular culture. The Institute of Race Relations website (www.irr.org.uk) is searchable and features a number of articles from back issues.

Rethinking Schools

www.rethinkingschools.org.
1001 E. Keefe Ave., Milwaukee, WI 53212; tel.: 800-669-4192; fax: 414-964-7220
Rethinking Schools is a quarterly magazine produced largely by classroom teachers with a focus on social justice and equity. The magazine regularly publishes articles on teaching global issues from a social justice perspective. The website contains this entire resource list with all addresses hot-linked, so all you need to do is click on them and you are taken to each site. The website also features a number of additional articles on teaching about globalization, including further resources and lesson plans that are mentioned in this book.

Third World Resurgence

www.twnside.org.sg.
Third World Network, 228 Macalister Rd., 10400 Penang, Malaysia; tel.: 60-4-226-6728; e-mail: twn@igc.apc.org.
Third World Resurgence is a monthly magazine that features valuable articles on global economic issues from Third World perspectives. Its website is an online center for reports, books, and other resources on North/South issues.

Z Magazine

www.zmag.org.
Subscription info: 18 Millfield St., Woods Hole, MA 02543; tel.: 508-548-9063; fax: 508-457-0626; e-mail: eric.sargent@zmag.org.
Published monthly, Z Magazine is an activist journal that features provocative in-depth articles on global and domestic issues. Z has been especially alert to the kinds of issues that we tackle in *Rethinking Globalization*. As indicated in the Organizations section, the Z-Net website is one of the best around.

Organizations and Websites for Global Justice

Note that in addition to those found below, other valuable websites may be listed with their journals in the category "Journals for Global Justice." It is impossible to list all the organizations working for a more just world. Websites of the organizations listed below include hundreds of links to other worthy groups. See "Defeating Despair," p. 329, for lesson ideas to accompany this listing of organizations and websites.

Adbusters Media Foundation
www.adbusters.org

1243 West 7th Ave.,
Vancouver, BC, V6H 1B7, Canada;
tel.: 604-736-9401; fax: 604-737-6021;
e-mail: adbusters@adbusters.org.

Adbusters describes itself as "a global network of artists, activists, writers, pranksters, students, educators and entrepreneurs who want to advance the new social activist movement of the information age." Adbusters publishes a glossy, provocative magazine of the same name, sponsors Buy Nothing Day and TV Turnoff Week, produces clever "uncommercials" and seeks to agitate so that folks "get mad about corporate disinformation, injustices in the global economy, and any industry that pollutes our physical or mental commons."

AFL-CIO
www.aflcio.org

815 16th Street, NW, Washington, DC 20006;
tel: 202-637-5000; fax: 202-637-5058.

The AFL-CIO is the largest labor organization in the United States. Its website includes abundant information on organizing campaigns, links to member unions, news articles on union drives, updates on student activism, and sections on union culture and history.

Amazon Watch
www.amazonwatch.org

2350 Chumash Road, Malibu, CA 90265;
tel: 310-456-9158; fax: 310-456-9138;
e-mail: amazon@amazonwatch.org.

Amazon Watch works with indigenous and enviromental organizations in the Amazon Basin to defend the enviroment and advance indigenous peoples' rights in the face of large-scale industrial development, oil and gas pipelines, power lines, roads, and other mega-projects. Its website is a good source for up-to-date information and resources, and includes extensive links.

American Friends Service Committee
www.afsc.org

1501 Cherry St., Philadelphia, PA 19102;
tel: 215-241-7132; fax: 215-241-7275;
e-mail: afscinfo@afsc.org.

This venerable social justice organization has a Mexico-U.S. Border Program and publishes an assortment of resources. AFSC also has a Youth and Militarism project that organizes against JROTC and military presence in public schools. The Cambridge, Massachusetts AFSC publishes *Peacework*, a monthly journal serving movements for nonviolent social change. AFSC also maintains a film and video library.

Amnesty International USA
www.amnesty.org

322 8th Ave., New York, NY 10001;
tel: 212-807-8400.

AI seeks to promote the human rights included in the Universal Declaration of Human Rights, focusing especially on prisoners of conscience, ending the death penalty, and combating torture. Amnesty's website includes the complete text of the Universal Declaration of Human Rights as well as numerous links to human rights groups around the world, articles, video clips, reports, and action opportunities.

Campaign for Labor Rights
www.campaignforlaborrights.org

1247 E Street SE, Washington, DC 20003.

Although not the simplest web address to remember, CLR offers an invaluable e-mail listserv of alerts on sweatshop and solidarity issues. Their website includes past updates, links, resources, leaflets, and the like. The site also features a document library on the Nike campaign, Disney in Haiti, Guess jeans, child labor issues, Mexico, Central America, farm worker issues, as well as youth and campus activism. CLR publishes a useful newsletter ($35 a year) filled with audio-visual resources, fact sheets and updates on campaigns to support worker organizing around the world.

Catholic Worker Movement
www.catholicworker.org

36 E. 1st St., New York, NY 10003;
tel: 212-777-9617.

The Catholic Worker Movement is "grounded in a firm belief in the God-given dignity of every human person." Since its founding in 1933 they have protested war, violence and injustice in all forms. Its journal is *The Catholic Worker*.

Clean Clothes Campaign
www.cleanclothes.org

P.O. Box 11584, 1001 GN Amsterdam,
The Netherlands; tel.: 31-20-4122785;
fax: 31-20-4122786;
e-mail: info@cleanclothes.org.
A coalition of European groups aiming to improve working conditions in the global garment industry. Conducts campaigns and provides information on companies such as Adidas, Benneton, C & A, Disney, Phillips-Van Heusen, Gap, H & M, Levi-Strauss, Nike, and Otto.

Coalition for Justice in the Maquiladoras

530 Bandera, San Antonio, TX 78228;
tel.: 210-732-8957; e-mail: cjm@ipc.apc.org.
A tri-national coalition of religious, environmental, labor, Latino and women's organizations working to pressure U.S.-based transnational corporations to adopt socially responsible practices. Publishes a newsletter and various reports.

Co-op America
www.coopamerica.org

1612 K Street NW, Suite 600, Washington, DC 20006;
tel.: 800-58-GREEN;
202-872-5307; fax: 202-331-8166.
Valuable information on sweatshops, consumer boycotts, and strategies to use "consumer and investor power for social change." Co-op America is a national nonprofit organization that helps individuals find businesses that are environmentally responsible and engage in fair trade, and offers technical assistance to companies aiming for social and environmental responsibility.

The Council of Canadians
www.canadians.org

502-151 Slater St., Ottawa, Ontario, K1P 5H3, Canada;
tel.: 613-233-2773 or 800-387-7177;
fax: 613-233-6776.
This independent organization provides analyses on key issues from a critical and progressive standpoint. Its director, Maude Barlow, is perhaps the leading critic of schemes to privatize the world's freshwater supplies.

CorpWatch
www.corpwatch.org

P.O. Box 29344; San Francisco, CA 94129.
tel: 415-561-6568; fax: 415-561-6493;
e-mail: corpwatch@corpwatch.org.
Indispensable resources and news about globalization and justice struggles around the world. An online issue library includes topics such as biotechnology, Globalization 101, grassroots globalization, sweatshops, the WTO and the IMF/World Bank. Very extensive links. A similarly valuable but unrelated site is Corporate Watch, in Great Britain, (www.corporatewatch.org.uk; 16b Cherwell St. Oxford OX4 1BG, United Kingdom.

Cultural Survival
www.cs.org

215 Prospect Street, Cambridge, MA 02139;
tel.: 617-441-5400; fax: 617- 441-5417;
e-mail: csinc@cs.org.
Cultural Survival sponsors basic research on indigenous peoples, particularly examining the effects of "development." The results of this research are published in its *Cultural Survival Quarterly*. The website includes an education archive with curriculum resources offered, including Rainforest Peoples and Places (grades 6-9), The Chiapas Maya (grades 6-12) and the Rights of Indigenous Nations.

The David Suzuki Foundation
www.davidsuzuki.org

Suite 219, 2211 West 4th Avenue, Vancouver, BC V6K 4S2 Canada; tel: 604-732-4228; fax: 604-732-0752;
e-mail: solutions@davidsuzuki.org.
David Suzuki is one of the world's leading geneticists and environmentalists. The foundation is especially active in the area of climate change, focusing on the "urgent need for practical strategies to reduce global warming caused by human activities."

The Edmonds Institute
www.edmonds-institute.org

20319 92nd Avenue West, Edmonds,
Washington 98020; tel: 425-775-5383;
fax: 425-670-8410; e-mail: beb@igc.org.
The Edmonds Institute focuses on biosafety and enacting legally-binding international regulation of modern biotechnologies, as well as on intellectual property rights and just policies for the maintenance and protection of biodiversity, including policies that foster recognition and sustenance of agricultural biodiversity.

ETC Group
www.etcgroup.org

431 Gilmour Street, 2nd Floor, Ottawa, ON K2P 0R5, Canada; tel: 613-241-2267; fax: 613-241-2506.
ETC Group is dedicated to the conservation and sustainable improvement of agricultural biodiversity, and to the socially responsible development of technologies useful to rural societies. ETC Group deals with issues such as the loss of genetic diversity — especially in agriculture — and about the impact of "intellectual property rights" on agriculture and world food security. Their searchable website is very useful, featuring articles, publications, and issue updates.

Fairness & Accuracy In Reporting
www.fair.org

130 W. 25th Street, New York, NY 10001.
tel.: 212-633-6700; fax: 212-727-7668;
e-mail: fair@fair.org.
FAIR is a national media watch group that has offered well-documented criticism of media bias and censorship since 1986. FAIR publishes the excellent, classroom-friendly *Extra!*, an award-winning maga-

zine of media criticism; and distributes regular updates, available via their listserv. FAIR also produces a weekly radio program, *CounterSpin*. A vital source to get students thinking critically about media coverage of world events.

50 Years Is Enough
www.50years.org

1247 E Street SE, Washington, DC 20003.
A coalition of over 200 grassroots, faith-based, policy, women's, social- and economic-justice, youth, solidarity, labor, and development organizations dedicated to the profound transformation of the World Bank and the International Monetary Fund. Its website features excellent, classroom-ready factsheets about globalization issues, especially about the consequences of the Third World debt crisis.

Focus on the Global South
www.focusweb.org

Too often discussions of globalization are dominated by those of us in the North, however well-intended or well-informed we may be. Focus on the Global South's website features wonderful, hard-to-find, in-depth articles from the perspective of activists and scholars in the global South — the so-called Third World. See their "publications" section.

Food First/Institute for
Food and Development Policy
www.foodfirst.org

398 60th Street, Oakland, CA 94618.
tel: 510-654-4400; fax: 510-654-4551;
e-mail: foodfirst@foodfirst.org.
Food First describes itself as "a 'peoples' think tank and education-for-action center." Over the 25-plus years that this pioneering organization has been around, it has published some of the most useful books on food and hunger issues. Through its publications and activism, it continues to offer leadership to the struggle for reforming the global food system from the bottom up. The catalog is online at their website.

Free The Children
www.freethechildren.org

1750 Steeles Avenue West, Suite 218, Concord, Ontario, Canada, L4K 2L7;
tel: 905-760-9382; fax: 905-760-9157;
e-mail: info@freethechildren.com.
Free The Children was started by Canadian young people after hearing the heroic story of Iqbal Masih, the Pakistani child who was sold into slavery and then escaped to fight against it. Its goals are to free children from poverty, exploitation and abuse; and to give children a voice, leadership training, and opportunities to take action on issues which affect them from a local to an international level.

Friends of the Earth
www.foe.org

1025 Vermont Ave. NW, Washington, DC 20005;
tel: 877-843-8687 or 202-783-7400;
fax: 202-783-0444; e-mail: foe@foe.org.

Friends of the Earth is a national environmental organization dedicated to preserving the health and diversity of the planet. FOE distributes valuable publications ranging from books on global warming to the IMF's effects on the environment.

Global Exchange
www.globalexchange.org

2017 Mission Street #303, San Francisco, CA 94110;
tel.: 415- 255-7296; fax 415- 255-7498;
e-mail: info@globalexchange.org.
Founded in 1988, Global Exchange is an organization dedicated to promoting environmental, political, and social justice around the world. In the late '90s, Global Exchange was perhaps the most important organization drawing attention to Nike's sweatshop abuses. Their expansive website gives a flavor for the diversity of activities they have initiated, which include "people to people" projects, such as "reality tours" to Third World countries, managing "fair trade" stores, and publishing resources on global justice issues. Global Exchange is one of the key global justice organizations.

Greenpeace International
www.greenpeace.org

Keizersgracht 176, 1016 DW Amsterdam, The Netherlands; tel: 31-20-523-62-22; fax: 31-20-523-62-00.

Greenpeace USA
www.greenpeaceusa.org

702 H Street NW, Washington, DC 20001; tel: 800-326-0959.
Greenpeace began in 1971 when activists went to "bear witness" to nuclear weapons testing planned for Amchitka island, off Alaska. Today Greenpeace is one of the leading organizations using nonviolent direct action to expose global environmental problems and to promote solutions that are essential to what the organization hopes will be a "green and peaceful future." It sponsors campaigns on global warming, environmental toxics, destructive fishing, genetic engineering, nuclear power and weapons, and saving ancient forests. Both websites feature extensive background materials on these issues, action alerts, ways to get involved, and numerous links to other organizations.

The Independent Media Center
www.indymedia.org

This is the CNN of the global social justice movement and a wonderful resource. The Center acts as a clearinghouse of information and provides up-to-the-minute reports, photos, audio, and video footage of global social justice struggles through its website. Launched during the Seattle WTO protests of late 1999, Indymedia is a fascinating, colorful site. Updated regularly. Great graphics.

The Indigenous Peoples Council on Biocolonialism
www.ipcb.org

P.O. Box 818, Wadsworth, Nevada 89424;
tel: 775-835-6932; fax: 775-835-6934;
e-mail: ipcb@ipcb.org.
The IPCB is organized to assist indigenous peoples in the protection of their genetic resources, indigenous knowledge, and cultural and human rights from the negative effects of biotechnology.

INFACT
www.infact.org

256 Hanover St., Boston, MA 02113;
617-742-4583.
A non-partisan national grassroots organization whose purpose is to stop life-threatening abuses by transnational corporations. Through the Tobacco Industry Campaign, INFACT is pressuring Philip Morris to stop addicting new young customers around the world, and to stop interfering in public policy on issues of tobacco and health. INFACT promotes a boycott of Philip Morris-owned Kraft foods and distributes the important video *Making a Killing*, exposing Philip Morris's brand of tobacco imperialism around the world. Articles posted on their website, like "The Marlboro Man Goes Overseas," could be used with students.

Institute for Agriculture and Trade Policy
www.iatp.org

2105 1st Avenue South, Minneapolis, MN 55404.
tel: 612-870-0453; fax: 612-870-4846.
The Institute for Agriculture and Trade Policy promotes resilient family farms, rural communities and ecosystems around the world through research and education, and advocacy. Their website includes background readings, articles, and forums on vital issues of agriculture and trade.

Institute for Global Communications (IGC)
www.igc.apc.org

Presidio Building 1012, First Floor,
Torney Avenue; Write: P.O. Box 29904,
San Francisco, CA 94129-0904;
tel.: 415-561-6100; fax: 415-561-6101.
"The mission of IGC is to advance the work of progressive organizations and individuals for peace, justice, economic opportunity, human rights, democracy and environmental sustainability through strategic use of online technologies." IGC is an outstanding resource, with a fabulous search engine that is linked to social justice networks of all kinds.

Institute for Policy Studies
www.ips-dc.org

733 15th St. NW, Suite 1020, Washington DC, 20005.
tel.: 202-234-9382; fax: 202-387-7915.
An important think tank on global issues from a social justice perspective. IPS has programs on Peace and Security, the Global Economy, and Paths for the 21st Century, supplemented by several projects that address specific issues.

International Education and Resource Network (iEARN)
www.iearn.org

475 Riverside Drive, Suite 540, New York, NY 10115.
tel.: 212-870-2693;
e-mail: iearn@us.iearn.org.
iEARN is a nonprofit organization made up of almost 4,000 schools in over 90 countries. It aims to empower teachers and young people (K-12) to work together online at low cost through a global telecommunications network.

International Rivers Network
www.irn.org

1847 Berkeley Way, Berkeley, CA 94703.
tel.: 510-848-1155; fax: 510-848-1008;
e-mail: info@irn.org.
IRN is an important network that works to support communities around the world struggling to protect rivers and watersheds. They see this work as part of a movement for "environmental integrity, social justice and human rights." IRN's website is a valuable source of information about global water struggles.

Interfaith Center on Corporate Responsibility
www.iccr.org

475 Riverside Drive, Rm. 566, New York, NY 10115;
212-870-2295.
A coalition of 275 Protestant, Roman Catholic and Jewish institutional investors that organizes corporate campaigns to press companies to be socially and environmentally responsible. Publishes the newsletter, *The Corporate Examiner.*

International Forum on Globalization
www.ifg.org

The Thoreau Center for Sustainability,
1009 General Kennedy Avenue #2,
San Francisco, CA 94129 ;
tel.: 415-561-7650, fax.: 415.561.7651;
e-mail: ifg@ifg.org.
Begun as an alliance of over 60 scholars, activists and writers, the IFG has sponsored important conferences to evaluate the social and environmental impact of globalization. They have published numerous booklets. Their website features worthwhile resources on the World Trade Organization, the World Bank and the International Monetary Fund, among others.

International Labor Organization
www.ilo.org

4 Route des Morillons, CH- 1211 Geneva 22, Switzerland.
The ILO is the UN agency that promotes internationally recognized human and labor rights. The organization maintains a searchable website on labor issues of all kinds, such as child labor, and includes useful articles, links, and reports.

International Labor Rights Fund
www.laborrights.org

733 15th St., NW #920, Washington, DC 20005;
tel.: 202-347-4100; fax: 202-347-4885;
e-mail: laborrights@igc.org.

The ILRF is a nonprofit organization that takes action on behalf of working people, and creates innovative programs and enforcement mechanisms to protect workers' rights. Current campaigns include child labor, monitoring labor rights in China, sweatshops, forced labor in Burma, and examining IMF/World Bank practices. Provides detailed information on the effects of NAFTA.

International Relations Center
www.irc-online.org

P.O. Box 2178, Silver City, NM 88062-2178;
tel.: 505-388-0208; fax: 505-388-0619

A research and policy institute that produces books, reports, and periodicals on U.S. foreign policy. Publishes annual *Cross-Border Links Directories* which lists and annotates fair-trade networks, labor, and environmental groups. Publishes the newsletter, *Borderlines*.

The International Society for Ecology and Culture
www.isec.org.uk

Foxhole, Dartington, Devon TQ9 6EB, UK;
tel: (01803) 868650; fax: (01803) 868651;
e-mail: isecuk@gn.apc.org.

ISEC promotes locally based alternatives to the global consumer culture. ISEC produced the extraordinarily useful video *Ancient Futures*, about the negative effects of the arrival of "development" in the Himalayan region of Ladakh.

Jobs With Justice
www.jwj.org

501 Third Street NW, Washington DC 20001-2797;
tel.: 202-434-1106; fax: 202-434-1477;
e-mail: jobswjustice@jwj.org.

A national campaign, with local affiliates, to organize support for workers' rights struggles. JwJ's Student Labor Action Project is an initiative focused on supporting student activism around issues of workers' rights as well as social and economic justice. Extensive information on current campaigns at their website.

Jubilee USA Network
www.j2000usa.org

222 E. Capitol Street, Washington DC 20003-1036.
tel.: 202-783-3566; fax: 202-546-4468;
e-mail: coord@j2000usa.org.

Jubilee USA Network is a coalition of faith-based and activist organizations who denounce the debt owed by impoverished nations to the IMF and the World Bank as illegitimate and pledge to oppose the "debt domination" by wealthy nations. A fine source for

action ideas, links and additional resources on the effects of the Third World debt crisis and resistance to it. Also valuable is Jubilee 2000 UK, on the web at www.jubilee2000uk.org. Jubilee 2000 UK is the British affiliate of the international movement calling for cancellation of the unpayable debt of the world's poorest countries under a fair and transparent process. Its website includes articles, links and ways for people to get involved in the global movement for economic justice.

Maquiladora Health & Safety Support Network www.igc.org/mhssn

A volunteer network of occupational health and safety professionals providing information, technical assistance and on-site instruction regarding workplace hazards in the over 3,800 *"maquiladora"* (foreign-owned export-oriented assembly plants) along the U.S.-Mexico border. Their website includes excellent resources and links on *maquiladora* health and safety issues.

Maquila Solidarity Network
www.maquilasolidarity.org

606 Shaw Street, Toronto, Ontario M6G 3L6, Canada;
tel: 416-532-8584; fax: 416-532-7688;
e-mail: info@maquilasolidarity.org.

The Maquila Solidarity Network is a Canadian network promoting solidarity with groups in Mexico, Central America, and Asia organizing in *maquiladora* factories and export processing zones to improve conditions and win a living wage. Their website includes hard-to-find resources on *maquilas* by country or company, and many articles on sweatshop issues. Valuable links to other Canadian and international organizations concerned with workers' rights issues.

National Labor Committee
www.nlcnet.org

275 Seventh Avenue, 15th Floor, New York, NY 10001;
tel: 212-242-3002; fax: 212-242-3821;
e-mail: nlc@nlcnet.org.

NLC's goal is to "end labor and human rights violations, ensure a living wage tied to a basket of needs, and help workers and their families live and work with dignity" — through education and activism. The organization, under director Charles Kernaghan, has been one of the most effective groups in raising awareness about super-exploitation and horrific conditions in global sweatshops. The National Labor Committee is the producer of some valuable videos and reports on sweatshop and labor rights issues around the world (see, for example, the videos *Zoned for Slavery* and *Mickey Mouse Goes to Haiti*).

One World International
www.oneworld.net

One World is "a community of organizations working from a range of perspectives and backgrounds to promote sustainable development and human rights." Described as the "global supersite on sustainable development and human rights," this is truly an amazing website, filled with photo galleries, news, special country reports, campaigns, and the like.

Oxfam America
www.oxfamamerica.org
26 West Street, Boston, MA 02111; tel: 800-77-OXFAM and 617-482-1211; fax: 617-728-2594; e-mail: info@oxfamamerica.org.
Oxfam America is dedicated to creating lasting solutions to hunger, poverty, and social injustice through long-term partnerships with poor communities around the world. Their website features lots of educational materials and links to other global education sites.

Rainforest Action Network
www.ran.org
221 Pine Street, Suite 500, San Francisco, CA 94104; tel: 415-398-4404; fax: 415-398-2732.
RAN works to protect the earth's rainforests and support the rights of their inhabitants through education, grassroots organizing, and nonviolent direct action. Theirs is a must-visit, comprehensive website that includes a wealth of information, including ideas for activities and activism with students, classroom-friendly factsheets, and links to indigenous rainforest groups. RAN has a Beyond Oil Campaign that should be of interest to students who are responsive to activities in *Rethinking Globalization*'s chapter on consumption and the environment.

Resource Center of the Americas
www.americas.org
3019 Minnehaha Ave., Minneapolis, MN 55406. tel.: 612-276-0788; fax: 612-276-0898; e-mail: info@americas.org.
The Resource Center provides information and develops programs that demonstrate connections between people of Latin America, the Caribbean, and the United States. Over the years they have published a great deal of curriculum in this area. Their website includes an on-line catalog of these and other classroom materials, along with resources on critical issues about the Americas.

Rethinking Schools
www.rethinkingschools.org
1001 E. Keefe Ave., Milwaukee, WI 53212; tel.: 414-964-9646; fax: 414-964-7220; e-mail: rethink@execpc.com.
Publisher of *Rethinking Globalization: Teaching for Justice in an Unjust World*. Its quarterly journal, *Rethinking Schools*, is produced largely by classroom teachers with a focus on social justice and equity. The website contains this entire resource list with all website addresses hot-linked, so all you need to do is click on them and you are taken to each site. The Rethinking Schools website also features a number of additional articles on teaching about globalization, including further resources and lesson plans that are mentioned in this book. Rethinking Schools publishes *Rethinking Columbus* and *Rethinking Our Classrooms*, volumes 1 and 2.

RUGMARK Foundation
www.rugmark.org
733 15th Street, NW, Suite 920, Washington, DC 20005; tel: 202-347-4205; fax: 202-347-4885; e-mail: info@rugmark.org.
RUGMARK is a global nonprofit organization working to end child labor and offer educational opportunities to children in India, Nepal, and Pakistan. It organizes loom and factory monitoring, sponsors consumer labeling, and runs schools for former child workers. RUGMARK recruits carpet producers and importers to make and sell carpets that are free of child labor.

Schools for Chiapas
www.schoolsforchiapas.org
or www.mexicopeace.org
1717 Kettner Blvd., Suite 110, San Diego, CA 92101; tel: 619-232-2841; fax: 617-232-0500; e-mail: schoolsforchiapas@mexicopeace.org.
An organization working in solidarity with the struggles in Chiapas, Mexico. Mobilizes people and resources to build schools in Chiapas. The organization also sponsors trips to study Spanish and Mayan language and culture in Chiapas. The website features news articles, historical information and other resources.

STITCH
www.stitchonline.org
4933 S. Dorchester, Chicago, IL 60615; tel: 773-924-2738; e-mail: hf52@aol.com.
STITCH is a network of U.S. women working to support women's organizing for a just wage and fair treatment on the job in Central America. STITCH has a project to document women's organizing experiences in export industries in Central America. The interview with Yesenia Bonilla in *Rethinking Globalization* (see p. 142) is excerpted from STITCH's booklet, "Women Behind the Labels: Worker Testimonies from Central America."

Sweatshop Watch
www.sweatshopwatch.org
310 Eighth Street, Suite 309, Oakland, CA 94607; tel.: 510-834-8990.
And: 1250 So. Los Angeles Street, Suite 206 Los Angeles, CA 90015; tel.: 213-748-5945; e-mail: sweatwatch@igc.org.
Sweatshop Watch is a coalition of labor, community, civil rights, immigrant rights, women's, religious, and student organizations committed to eliminating sweatshop conditions in the global garment industry. Their website provides updates on current sweatshop issues, links, and reports. Monthly e-mail action alerts available.

Teaching for Change
www.teachingforchange.org
P.O. Box 73038, Washington, DC 20056-3038. 800-763-9131; fax: 202-238-0109.
Teaching for Change publishes excellent multicultural,

global justice teaching materials, such as the *Caribbean Connection* series and the widely used *Beyond Heroes and Holidays*. The Teaching for Change catalog is the single best source for resources to rethink and teach about globalization.

Third World Network
www.twnside.org.sg

228 Macalister Road, 10400 Penang, Malaysia.
An independent nonprofit international network of organizations and individuals involved in issues relating to development, the Third World, and North-South issues. Publishes the valuable *Third World Resurgence* magazine. The magazine and website is an essential resource to learn more about Third World perspectives on globalization issues.

TransAfrica Forum
www.transafricaforum.org

1744 R St., NW, Washington, DC 20009;
tel: 202-797-2301; fax: 202-797-2382.
TransAfrica Forum provides commentary and scholarship on policy issues related to Africa and the Caribbean. The organization seeks to educate Americans in general, and African Americans in particular, on human rights and global economic policy. Reports on TransAfrica's website deal with issues such as the Sub-Saharan Africa debt burden, the impact of tourism in the Caribbean, and landmines.

UNITE HERE!
www.unitehere.org

1710 Broadway, New York, NY 10019;
tel.: 212-265-7000.
UNITE HERE! was formed by the merger of the Union of Needletrades, Industrial and Textile Employees and Hotel Employees and Restaurant Employees. Its website offers information on campaigns against sweatshops, as well as government and organizational links.

United Farm Workers
www.ufw.org

UFW National Headquarters,
P.O. Box 62, Keene, CA 93531.
Affiliated with the AFL-CIO, the UFW is the oldest and most prominent farm worker union in the United States. Their website includes links, current news articles, updates, and background white papers, such as "Fingers to the Bone: United States Failure to Protect Child Farm Workers," "Fields of Poisons: California Farm Workers and Pesticides," "Five Cents for Fairness: The Case for Change in the Strawberry Fields," "Trouble on the Farm: Growing Up With Pesticides in Agricultural Communities," and "Pesticides in Our Food and Water."

United for a Fair Economy
www.faireconomy.org

37 Temple Place, 2nd Floor, Boston, MA 02111;
tel.: 617-423-2148; fax: 617-423-0191.
UFE provides numerous resources to organizations and individuals working to address the widening income and asset gap in the United States and around the world. They publish graphic-rich training and curriculum materials, and their website is a valuable one, including an economics library, research library, and fact sheets.

UNICEF - United Nations Children's Fund
www.unicef.org

3 UN Plaza, New York, NY 10017;
e-mail: netmaster@unicef.org.
UNICEF produces educational materials and distributes funds to children's programs throughout the world. Their annual *The State of the World's Children* provides useful statistics.

Women of Color Resource Center
www.coloredgirls.org

2288 Fulton Street, Suite 103, Berkeley, CA 94704-1449.
tel.: 510-848-9272; fax: 510-548-3474;
e-mail: chisme@igc.apc.org.
WCRC develops and distributes resources about women of color that advance social justice movements. WCRC published the valuable curriculum guide *Women's Education in the Global Economy*. Their website includes excellent hard-to-find links to projects that organize around issues concentrating on women of color.

Zapatistas
www.ezln.org

The Zapatistas, based in the southern-most Mexican state of Chiapas, have drawn worldwide attention to the plight of indigenous people in the era of free trade. Their website is mostly in Spanish, although it does have some English translations. It's a fascinating site and the links will put students in touch with indigenous movements around the world.

ZNet/Z Magazine
www.zmag.org

Z Net is one of the most amazing websites we've found. Forums, commentaries from around the world, song lyrics for 530 songs-with-a-conscience, courses, analyses on global issues of all kinds. Many pre-college students might find some of the writing a bit hard-going, but there is a tremendous amount here. *Z Magazine* is available the old fashioned way — in print. See "Journals for Global Justice," p. 381.

Index

This index includes comprehensive entries for chapters 1 through 8. See the lists of resources in Chapter 9 for more information about additional organizations, publications, and educational materials.

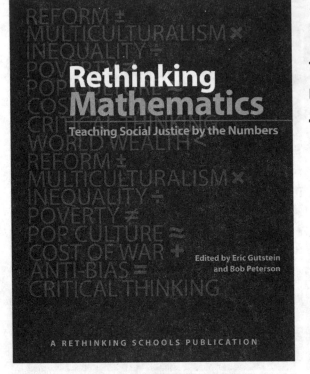

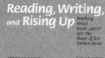